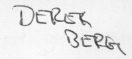

DEREK
BERG

Teaching Mathematics in Elementary and Middle School

Developing Mathematical Thinking

Joseph G. R. Martinez
University of New Mexico

Nancy C. Martinez
University of New Mexico

PEARSON

Merrill
Prentice Hall

Upper Saddle River, New Jersey
Columbus, Ohio

Library of Congress Cataloging in Publication Data

Martinez, Joseph G. R.
      Teaching mathematics in elementary and middle school: developing mathematical
thinking / Joseph G. R. Martinez, Nancy C. Martinez.
            p. cm.
      Includes bibliographical references and index.
      ISBN 0-13-054978-9
      1. Mathematics—Study and teaching (Elementary)—United States. 2.
Mathematics—Study and teaching (Middle school)—United States. 3. Mathematical ability
in children—United States. I. Title: Developing mathematical thinking. II. Martinez, Nancy
C. (Nancy Conrad) III. Title.

QA135.6.M367 2007
372.7—dc22

2005056380

Vice President and Executive Publisher: Jeffery W. Johnston
Senior Editor: Linda Ashe Bishop
Associate Editor: Meredith Sarver
Senior Production Editor: Mary M. Irvin
Design Coordinator: Diane C. Lorenzo
Senior Editorial Assistant: Laura Weaver
Text Designer: Kristi Holmes
Cover Designer: Candace Rowley
Cover Image: Fotosearch
Production Manager: Pamela D. Bennett
Director of Marketing: David Gesell
Marketing Manager: Darcy Betts Prybella
Marketing Coordinator: Brian Mounts

This book was set in Garamond by Carlisle Publishing Services. It was printed and bound by
Courier/Kendallville. The cover was printed by Coral Graphics.

Photo Credits: p. 73 (top), Bob Pennell/Mail Tribune (Medford, OR); p. 73 (bottom),
Jim Craven/Mail Tribune (Medford, OR). All other photos by the authors.

Pearson Education Ltd.
Pearson Education Singapore Pte. Ltd.
Pearson Education Canada, Ltd.
Pearson Education—Japan

Pearson Education Australia Pty. Limited
Pearson Education North Asia Ltd.
Pearson Educación de Mexico, S.A. de C.V.
Pearson Education Malaysia Pte. Ltd.

10 9 8 7 6 5 4 3 2 1
ISBN: 0-13-054978-9

For professor emeritus Dr. Wayne Moellenberg, mentor, model, and friend, whose work in cognition laid the foundation for our research and for our teaching students to love learning and to think mathematically

Preface

Teaching Mathematics in Elementary and Middle School: Developing Mathematical Thinking is a book for classroom teachers (preservice and inservice)—the frontline, in-the-trenches superheroes of education. It is for elementary teachers—those amazingly versatile and creative people who **must** teach mathematics, whatever their personal backgrounds, attitudes, or preferences. And it is for middle-school teachers, who face the demands of a technological and scientific age to teach more mathematics to more students. This book answers the questions both elementary and middle school teachers have about their varying roles in teaching mathematics.

- What are the challenges of teaching mathematics in the 21st century?
- How do students learn mathematics?
- How does diversity affect mathematics learning? Will one-size-fits-all strategies work, or do we need more versatile approaches in today's classrooms?
- What is mathematical thinking and how can teachers help students to think mathematically?
- What roles should national standards play in mathematics education?
- How can we as teachers deal with learning challenges such as math anxiety (our own and our students') and build confidence for teaching and learning mathematics?
- How can we make mathematics real and important to students? How can we make it a subject students want to learn and enjoy learning? How do we engage students and help them stay on task? How do we make mathematical problem solving an adventure and mathematical concepts, tools to help students make sense of their worlds?
- How do we as teachers prepare students to meet the future mathematical challenges of a global society that will require mathematical thinkers and problem solvers?

Answers to these questions are fundamental to mathematics teaching. Equally important is the process of asking and exploring additional questions about effective learning. Mathematics teaching and learning that makes sense to students (and teachers) does not start with answers or a body of facts and procedures to be memorized and applied. Rather, it begins with inquiry and must be discovered and constructed—concept by concept, problem by problem, question by question. Therefore, the processes of learning and teaching mathematics are first and foremost **processes of inquiry**.

In this book and the accompanying CD of activities and lesson plans, we emphasize inquiry as both a learning technique and a teaching method. We pose questions that not only have multiple answers but also generate more questions. For example, there are many answers to the question, "What is the best way to teach mathematics?" and each of those answers leads to more questions: "If one of the best ways to teach mathematics is with manipulatives, which manipulatives work best for which topics? How can students represent their hands-on problem solving? And how might teachers use manipulatives to introduce standard algorithms?"

The result is not a cut-and-dried recipe for teaching mathematics—a list of ingredients and procedures to be mixed together for instant mathematics learning. Rather, the result is an introduction to both **the science and the art of mathematics education**—to the ideas, methods, and strategies needed to discover and construct mathematics as a way of making sense of the world in which we live and to the creativity, aesthetics, and genuine fun of teaching and learning mathematics.

The Focus–Developing Mathematical Thinking

Throughout the text and its accompanying CD, we emphasize **mathematical thinking.** To think or reason mathematically provides the foundation for learning mathematics with understanding. In the preface to the NCTM yearbook *Developing Mathematical Reasoning in Grades K-12*, Lee Stiff writes:

> One important decision that each teacher must make is how best to engage students in thinking and reasoning about mathematics. . . . [Because of] the different types of mathematical reasoning that students may be asked to perform (e.g., algebraic, statistical, geometric, probabilistic, inductive, deductive, and so on), it is clear that the effectiveness of the organization and character of the curriculum, the nature of the classroom environment, and the instructional practices of teachers must be addressed. (1999, vii)

When learning materials and experiences as well as teaching methods and the dynamics of classroom instruction promote mathematical thinking, students begin to develop a "web of mathematical knowledge" and understandings. This web provides the foundation for "mathematical memory" or "mathematical sense" and "the basis for insight into mathematical problems" (Russell 1999, 1). On the one hand, developing mathematical thinking or reasoning leads to a **mathematical world view**—a way of looking at the world and our place in it relative to mathematics. On the other hand, it helps students forge the mathematical mind tools they need to make sense of their own worlds and of mathematics itself.

Because developing students' ability to think mathematically is foundational, we approach the subject from several directions. In the text we **discuss** what it means to think mathematically. In the student examples, features, and CD activities, we **show** what it means. For example, in Chapter 3, Preparing Students to Think Mathematically, we review the importance and the processes of mathematical thinking. We look at the effects of the cognitive and affective domains of learning on mathematical thinking, interactions in math anxiety and math confidence, and applications in problem solving. Student examples show how students represent and talk about math concepts; features and activities revolve around the big ideas of mathematics and the process of mathematical problem solving.

The Method—Active Teaching for Active Learning

A practical and effective approach to learning mathematics is by "doing" mathematics. A similarly practical approach to learning to teach mathematics is by "doing" activities and learning experiences, exploring concepts, and solving problems in an active, laboratory-style setting. In our own math-methods courses, this approach results in class sessions that are lively, noisy, and what one preservice teacher called "productively chaotic."

A class session on teaching geometry might focus on discovering and understanding *pi* by measuring circular objects. Working in small groups and at stations around the math lab, students measure the circumference and diameter of hula hoops, paper plates, baskets, bottles, Frisbees, and dozens of other circular objects. They develop strategies to measure the circumference and diameter of basketballs, footballs, balloons, and even donut holes (a favorite strategy is to eat half and measure what's left). And then for each set of measurements, they divide the circumference by the diameter to find a number that approximates (more or less) pi.

Or the class might begin with a video excerpt of the classic water jar problem from the movie *Die Hard III*. Students see and discuss the problem—how to fill a container with exactly 4 gallons of water when you have a 5-gallon container, a 3-gallon container, and a supply of water but no other tools to work with. Then they experiment with their own containers of water to find not one, but two or three solutions.

A class on teaching place value begins with making a counting board with large sheets of colored paper and red and black "sticks" made from chenille wires for an introduction to Chinese stick math. Field trips to the zoo, the mall, or an amusement park provide data for counting, analyzing, and representing with graphs and charts. Preservice teachers find math in the newspaper; teach each other concepts with math games, math stories, and hand-made manipulatives; and work with containers of pinto beans, M&Ms, and Goldfish crackers to develop estimation strategies.

Our students' responses to the active teaching/active learning approach often begin with surprise that changes quickly to excitement about teaching mathematics. In their reflection papers at the end of the course, students write about what they have learned and its impact on how they will teach mathematics in their own classrooms.

In the preservice teachers' own words—

- I went into this class very disappointed that I had to take another math class before teaching elementary school. . . . Now I have been inspired. . . . Math can be fun, and math is relevant to my life also.
- I need to show my students that math is everywhere. It exists in every subject in school, and in practically every facet of daily life. . . . It is more than just an abstract bunch of number problems. It is in their homes, hobbies, and lives.
- An important lesson I learned in this class is that the teacher doesn't have to have all of the answers. It is important to allow your students to question and wonder. If you don't know the answer, then you can all discover it together. A classroom is a place of discovery, for students and teachers alike.
- I have a great passion for learning and teaching mathematics. My goal is to become a middle-school math teacher. . . . By doing different math activities, I have changed the way that I thought I would teach math. I now realize that teaching math successfully involves more than just writing the problem on the board and explaining it.

The Means—Multiple Strategies, Diversity, Flexibility

Making mathematics accessible to all students is a major tenet of our teaching philosophy. To this end, our math-methods courses and this textbook have two key goals:

1. providing the means for every student to learn mathematics, and

2. providing the means for every teacher to teach mathematics successfully.

Because diversity is the rule rather than the exception in learning as well as in teaching, we emphasize multiplicity. Teachers need multiple methods for teaching concepts—multiple ways to engage students, to present and represent ideas, to assess performance and understanding. Students need multiple perspectives and contexts for concepts as well as a variety of tools for solving problems, expressing solutions, and making sense of mathematics.

Multiple approaches are reflected in the narrative and illustrations, in the chapter Topics, Issues, Exploration (TIE) boxes, in the features, in the CD of activities and lesson plans that accompany this book, in the resources for mathematics literature and for making your own manipulatives (in both the text and CD), and in the ancillaries.

Narrative and Illustrations

In most chapters, a special section on Diversity in Learning and Thinking Mathematically emphasizes the importance of flexibility in teaching mathematics. Different learning styles, different cultures, different learning experiences and backgrounds—all of these factors and more affect the way students learn mathematics. Using a variety of teaching strategies rather than a one-size-fits-all approach not only engages more students in the learning process but also helps individual students to develop the different perspectives that aid mathematical thinking and encourage students to make connections and understand relationships.

Throughout the book, examples of student work show the different ways students approach problem solving and make sense of mathematical concepts and processes. Students demonstrate their mathematical thinking verbally in journal entries and word problems, in drawings that illustrate mathematical situations and problem-solving processes, and in representations of invented as well as standard algorithms.

TIEs: Topics, Issues, Explorations

Each TIE brings together key ideas from the text, encouraging readers to see and respond to relationships and connections. TIEs let students react to what they have read, explore their own experiences, and begin to think about the implications of what they have learned for their own teaching. TIEs also encourage readers to identify, think through, and even adopt positions on various controversies in mathematics education.

Text Features

Text features focus on applications in the classroom, including activities and resources that many teachers have found valuable. Many of the learning experiences described in the features are designed to be adapted for different grade and achievement levels. For example in Chapter 2, the *Mathematics in the Real World* feature asks students to find numbers everywhere. When preservice teachers do the activity themselves, they often find numbers from their adult worlds such as their social security numbers, bank account and credit card numbers, and amounts in paychecks and taxes. When they ask students in their own classes to find the important numbers in their lives, younger children often emphasize small numbers such as their ages and number of

siblings or pets while older children add some larger numbers such as the speed of light or distance to the moon.

- *Mathematics in the Real World.* Making math real and meaningful to students is essential to engaging students in the learning process. This feature helps students discover and make sense of the mathematics that is all around them. It answers questions such as, "When will I ever need to know this?" and "Why should I care about math?"
- *Googol: Big Ideas in Mathematics.* Students need to understand the big ideas of mathematics—the concepts behind the procedures and problem-solving processes. The activities and teaching ideas described in Googol Mathematics emphasize learning with understanding, knowing the *why*'s as well as the *what*'s behind procedures and processes.
- *Mathematical Thinking.* The focus of this feature is the mathematics process—the strategies and methods of problem solving, the habits of thought that lead to mathematical "sense," and the development of a mathematical perspective and the mathematical "mind tools" needed to make sense of mathematical situations.
- *Mathematics Across the Curriculum.* Just as students can find mathematics in the real world, they can find mathematical connections throughout the curriculum. Science, of course, uses mathematics as an important tool to investigate, understand, and explain phenomena. In addition, mathematics plays a key role in art and architecture and in social sciences, and there are important connections in literature and history as well.
- *Mathematics in Literature.* This feature highlights the mathematics in stories. Activities suggest ways to use the imaginative contexts as a basis for exploring and understanding mathematical ideas and applications.
- *Math Manipulatives.* The importance of hands-on learning experiences cannot be overstated. Using manipulatives helps students visualize and understand concepts and makes abstract ideas concrete. The feature introduces different types of manipulatives, including manufactured, hand-made, and virtual manipulatives, and suggests ways to use them effectively in the classroom.
- *Mathematical Games.* Preservice teachers are often surprised to discover that learning mathematics can be fun. The games described in this feature usually include different levels of play and provide opportunities to apply a variety of concepts and problem-solving strategies. For example, two Scrabble-style math games, 'Smath and Equate, let students add, subtract, multiply, and divide; write equations; and (in advanced versions of Equate) work with fractions, exponents, and negative numbers.
- *Math and Technology.* The technological resources for teaching mathematics are rich, numerous, and increasingly

accessible to the classroom teacher. We look at websites, including government sites devoted to the National Assessment of Educational Progress and the No Child Left Behind Act, and resources such as the National Library of Virtual Manipulatives and NCTM's Illuminations E-Resources. We also explore ways to use videos, calculators, and computers effectively in the classroom.

- *Idea Files.*   These collections of teaching strategies, lesson ideas, materials, and resources give readers easy-to-reference summaries and overviews for classroom applications.
- *Teacher and Lesson Pro-Files.*   These "pro" or professional files showcase extraordinary teachers and extraordinarily successful learning experiences. These features provide background and context as well as procedures and outcomes for activities and/or teaching methods. Many include the teacher's comments, including discussions of teaching philosophies and motivations.
- *Windows on Learning.*   Many chapters include classroom scenarios or vignettes that illustrate different teaching methods. For example in Chapter 2, the Learning Windows show us contrasting behaviorist and constructivist classrooms.

Activities for Mathematical Thinking CD-ROM

The CD-ROM of activities that accompanies the text reinforces our approaches to teaching and learning and at the same time builds a bridge from theory to applications. Activities are inquiry-based and describe detailed lesson plans for **exploring** concepts, **inventing** or **constructing** strategies for problem solving, and **discovering** insights, connections, and applications. More than 100 activities and lesson plans—many of them expanded versions of lesson ideas introduced in the text features—cover topics such as understanding numbers and number systems, geometric and algebraic thinking, and bridging the gap from elementary to middle-school mathematics. Marginal notes in the main text refer readers to individual activities. The CD-ROM also features more than 30 reproducible, full-page worksheets.

Appendices

Both the text and the accompanying *Activities for Mathematical Thinking CD-ROM* include valuable resources on manipulatives and mathematics literature. The *Make-Your-Own Manipulatives* resource provides patterns and directions for making fraction circles, squares, and strips; tangrams; multiplication arrays; counters, geoboards; base-10 blocks; pattern blocks; and polygon cutouts as well as various useful forms and handouts, including an inquiry-based lesson plan. The *Mathematics in Literature* resource lists hundreds of stories by NCTM Content Standards as well as subcategories such as number sense, place value, perimeter, patterns and symmetry, geometric shapes, and multicultural topics.

Ancillaries

Text ancillaries offer practical, hands-on help for students and instructors.

Instructor Resource Center

The Instructor Resource Center at **http://www.prenhall.com** has a variety of print and media resources available in downloadable, digital format—all in one location. As a registered faculty or instructor, you can access and download pass-code protected resource files, course management content, and other premium online content directly to your computer.

The Instructor's Manual located at the Instructor Resource Center—complimentary to adopters—presents not only sample syllabi, chapter objectives, test bank and answer key, and discussion points, but also guidelines for teaching math. These include advice for dealing with common issues such as coping with math anxiety, encouraging math confidence, and meeting national expectations for standards and performance. These materials provide suggestions for teaching, additional resources such as handouts and worksheets, and strategies for integrating the CD-ROM, the PBS Mathline videos, and other technologies in the course.

PBS Mathline DVD

Five videos, free to adopting professors, accompany this text. These videos, discussed further in the Instructor's Manual, are part of the PBS/Mathline Video Series. They feature classroom sessions with teacher commentaries from both the Elementary School Math Project (ESMP) and the Middle School Math Project (MSMP). The videos included are:

Elementary School Math Project, Grades K–5
- Video Segment 1
  - Mathline Overview
  - Number sense/Computation lessons for various grade levels
- Video Segment 2
  - Geometry and Spatial Relations lessons for various grade levels
- Video Segment 3
  - Patterns and Relationships lessons for various grade levels

Middle School Math Project, Grades 5–8
- Video Segment 4
  - Mathline Overview
  - Measurement lessons for various grade levels
- Video Segment 5
  - Computation and Estimation (including fractions, decimals, percents, ratio) lessons for various levels

Companion Website

The Companion Website allows students to link directly to urls named in the text and also provides students with self-regulating assessment questions to check their own understanding. NCTM and state standards, research, and topics and issues discussed in the book are further explored.

Thanks and Appreciation

We would like to thank all of those who contributed to this project.

To our editors—thank you for your patience, support, and expertise: Linda Bishop, our one-in-a-googol chief editor and good friend, who shepherded the project through its numerous transformations and revisions; Brad Potthoff, who persuaded us to begin the work; Meredith Sarver, whose help during the final stages has been invaluable; Kathryn Terzano, who read and commented so carefully on the final drafts; Mary Irvin, whose work in production made the book come together as a whole; Laura Larson, whose copyediting ensured accuracy and a smooth style; Ben Prout, who helped us connect text and activities with marginal notes; Carol Sykes, who prepared the photos; Kristi Holmes, who provided the interior design for the book; and Candace Rowley, who designed the cover.

To the many reviewers—thank you for your time, your insights, and your suggestions: Thomasenia Lott Adams, University of Florida; Jane Bonari, California University of Pennsylvania; Sandra L. Canter, Ball State University; Margaret Capraro, Texas A&M University; Yolanda De La Cruz, Arizona State University; Ron Falkenstein, Mott Community College; Gerald R. Fast, University of Wisconsin Oshkosh; David Fuys, Brooklyn College; Lowell Gadberry, Southwestern Oklahoma State University; Bruce Godsave, SUNY, Genesco; Neal Grandgenett, University of Nebraska at Omaha; John Hinton, Hofstra University; William O. Lacefield, Mercer University; Chris Ohana, Western Washington University; Clyde Paul, Southwest Missouri State; Walter Ryan, Indiana University, South East; Michelle Scribner-Maclean, University of Massachusetts Lowell; and Judith A. Wells, University of Southern Indiana.

To the preservice and inservice teachers who classroom-tested materials, provided student examples, appeared in photos, and suggested activities—thank you for all of your contributions, direct and indirect: Adrienne Alinder, Louie Anaya, Shannon Apodaca, Monica Aragon, Thelma Aragon, Rand J. Barker, Allison Bisio, Erica Bowman, Jessica Briggs, Stella Bramleth, Iris Calderon, Timothy Carlyon, Bernadine Chavez, Bernadetta Crawford, Brianna Dinham, Blue Chambers, Erica Daughetee, Jameson Davis, Crista Gallegos, Bernadette Garcia, Bethany Gonzales, Jamie Hetherington, Meisha Johnson, Mark Johnson, Amy Johnston, Deborah Kahler, Rebecca Kennerly, Adrian Koch, Iris Lovato, Amy J. Lowe, Micaela Lund, Carmen Macerine, Nicole Miner, Rachel Montoya, Andrea Moya, Lisa Mueller, Victoria Newcomm, Virginia R. Nighbert, Darice Ortiz, Becca Rainey, Debbie Rider, Yolanda Rodriguez-Medrano, Theresa Sandoval, Richard Shanks, Larry Smith, Chris Speck, Karen Steinman, Lauren Stern, Donna Waid, Doris Ward, Talia Ward, Connie Wattenburger, Larry Smith, Tracy Webb, J. Wiegmann, Nathan Work, and all of the students in our elementary and secondary math-methods courses.

Joseph G. R. Martinez
Nancy C. Martinez

TEACHER PREP

MERRILL
PRENTICE HALL

Teacher Preparation Classroom

Your Class. Their Careers. Our Future. Will your students be prepared?

We invite you to explore our new, innovative and engaging website and all that it has to offer you, your course, and tomorrow's educators! Organized around the major courses pre-service teachers take, the Teacher Preparation site provides media, student/teacher artifacts, strategies, research articles, and other resources to equip your students with the quality tools needed to excel in their courses and prepare them for their first classroom.

This ultimate on-line education resource is available at no cost, when packaged with a Merrill text, and will provide you and your students access to:

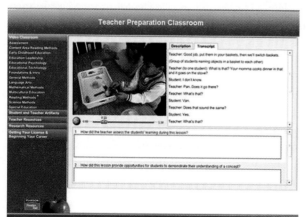

Online Video Library. More than 150 video clips—each tied to a course topic and framed by learning goals and Praxis-type questions—capture real teachers and students working in real classrooms, as well as in-depth interviews with both students and educators.

Student and Teacher Artifacts. More than 200 student and teacher classroom artifacts—each tied to a course topic and framed by learning goals and application questions—provide a wealth of materials and experiences to help make your study to become a professional teacher more concrete and hands-on.

Research Articles. Over 500 articles from ASCD's renowned journal *Educational Leadership*. The site also includes Research Navigator, a searchable database of additional educational journals.

Teaching Strategies. Over 500 strategies and lesson plans for you to use when you become a practicing professional.

Licensure and Career Tools. Resources devoted to helping you pass your licensure exam; learn standards, law, and public policies; plan a teaching portfolio; and succeed in your first year of teaching.

Contents

APPENDIX A

APPENDIX B

Note: Every effort has been made to provide accurate and current Internet information in this book. However, the Internet and information posted on it are constantly changing, so it is inevitable that some of the Internet addresses listed in this textbook will change.

Special Features

CHAPTER 1

Teaching Mathematics in the 21st Century

LOOKING AHEAD >>>>

The first decade of the new millennium is a good time to remember the past, consider the present, and plan for the future. The past century brought changes that transformed education. Some of the most drastic changes have come in mathematics education. At the turn of the last century, children studied arithmetic in the elementary grades. They did sums or long division on slates or, later, in lined paper tablets, and they memorized the times tables. Today, the third- and fourth-generation descendents of those schoolchildren log onto the Internet for information about fractals and Fibonacci numbers. In class they work with manipulatives and study economic concepts such as supply and demand; they even personally interact with astronauts as they conduct experiments on space shuttles.

In this chapter we will look at some of the factors that brought about these changes and how the changes are working together to reconstruct or remake mathematics education for the 21st century. Building a consensus and setting standards for mathematics education have proceeded in the context of national debates over curriculum, evaluation, and professional development—debates sometimes called the "math wars." From these "wars" have emerged goals and documents such as *Principles and Standards for School Mathematics* and Project 2061 as well as standards at the state and local levels. Mathematics educators may hold differing ideas about methods, curriculum, content, and even criteria for excellence. Most, however, share a commitment to increasing the scope, accessibility, and excellence of mathematics education in the 21st century.

Being a Teacher in the 21st Century

Fifty years ago in a small-town classroom, a teacher with a vision for the future told her students, "By the end of this century you may be living in automatic houses where everything from cooking to cleaning is done for you. You might wear disposable clothes. You might vacation on the moon or work on Mars." What she predicted hasn't happened yet, although we have taken the first steps toward interplanetary travel; in Canada there are experimental "smart" towns; and our refrigerators may soon be able to talk to us about souring milk or needed grocery list items. The teacher wasn't totally accurate, but she was clairvoyant—a clear seer. What she saw and what she helped her students see was that the future was filled with wonderful possibilities if only they would "dream big"—set high goals, work to make dreams happen, and believe in themselves.

"Dreaming big" will be a prerequisite for teachers in the 21st century. Never before has so much been expected of us, and never before has so much depended upon us.

A hundred years ago a teacher had succeeded if she taught a few things to the many and many things to the few. Those who fell behind or dropped out could always find jobs on farms and in factories. Their livelihood didn't depend upon "school" learning; learning outside the school provided enough to get by in their agrarian, blue-collar world.

All of that has changed. Few can live on the wages from semi- or unskilled labor. It's brains, not brawn, that are needed to survive in the information age, and brains need more than basic training to function at their best; they need knowledge and understanding.

Activities CD

For an activity that promotes understanding of probability, see Activity 77, Probability: Coin Tossing, on the CD-ROM that accompanies this text.

Activities CD

For an activity in which students collect data from the world around them, see Activity 69, Collecting Data in Our Worlds, on the CD-ROM that accompanies this text.

Beyond Shop-and-Yard Mathematics

The challenge for teachers and students to "dream big" is perhaps greatest in mathematics education. In the first half of the 20th century, curriculum development emphasized shop-and-yard skills. Prompted by the idea of functionalism (education you can use), some educators focused on identifying minimal competencies needed to perform jobs: dollars-and-cents math for clerking, feet-and-inches math for carpentry, measuring-cups-and-spoons math for cooks and homemakers.

The changing needs of a changing world have made this restrictive view not only obsolete but also dangerous. The student who knows only shop-and-yard mathematics risks being left behind in a job market that increasingly emphasizes technology and information systems; risks being left out of the national and international discourses about economics, politics, science, and health care; risks, in short, the handicap of mathematical illiteracy. (Figures 1.1 and 1.2 give examples of important mathematical topics being tackled by fifth and even second graders today).

In Step with the New Mathematical Literacy

The National Council of Teachers of Mathematics (NCTM) has identified five imperatives or needs for all students (NCTM 1998, 45-46):

1. Become mathematical problem solvers.
2. Communicate knowledge.
3. Reason mathematically.
4. Learn to value mathematics.
5. Become confident in one's ability to do mathematics.

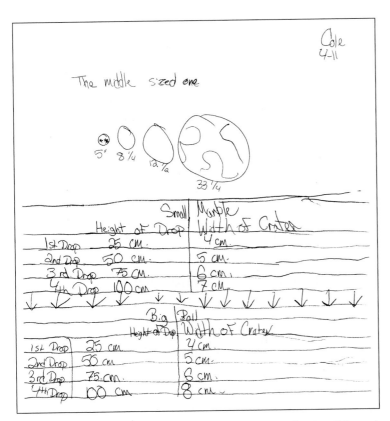

Figure 1.1 Tackling the information age task of data collection, fifth graders collect data on crater sizes made by dropping different objects from different heights.

Figure 1.2 Second graders explore the language of probability.

Teachers' Self-Inventory

1. What can I hope to accomplish as a teacher in the 21st century?

2. Am I ready for the challenge of teaching everything to everyone?

3. Am I ready to dream big—to aim for excellence as a teacher of mathematics?

4. Can I instill the ability to dream big in my students—excellence in learning mathematics?

5. Can I go beyond teaching basic skills and model the joy and beauty of mathematics?

6. Do I appreciate mathematics myself?

7. Do I really believe—not just think, but believe— that everyone can learn to reason mathematically?

8. Do I feel confident in my mathematical ability?

9. Have my own mathematical abilities been developed beyond the level of performing basic procedures?

10. Do I understand and can I interpret for my students the mathematical worlds that surround us?

Figure 1.3   Teachers' self-inventory.

Topics, Issues, and Explorations

As teachers, we model behaviors and attitudes for our students—some consciously, some unconsciously. What kinds of models for teaching mathematics have you had? Which models do you want to be like? Which models do you not want to be like?

These are in effect the cornerstones of the new mathematical literacy—what's needed to survive and thrive in the next century.

Meeting these imperatives calls for more than hard work and good intentions; it calls for belief—belief in our own abilities to teach and belief in our students' abilities to learn. The Teachers' Self-Inventory in Figure 1.3 suggests some things to think and talk about as you set your goals for professional development and growth.

Changing Views About Who Should Learn Mathematics

During much of the 20th century, opportunities to study mathematics were often unequal. All students studied arithmetic, but only the college-bound elite tackled mathematics. The exclusionary process frequently targeted women and minorities, creating a hierarchy of expectations and opportunities that pushed children in one direction or the other from the earliest grades—often without the children or their teachers realizing what was happening.

Research data show that millions of people have been victims of false assumptions about who has the ability to master mathematics.

These assumptions become self-fulfilling expectations, which ultimately undermine the self-concepts of female students, impoverished students and students of color.

The single most important change required involves a national consciousness raising. Teachers, parents, and the students themselves must recognize that virtually every child has the capacity to master mathematics. . . . This is true for females as well as for males, for poverty-stricken students as well as those from more affluent backgrounds, and for persons of every ethnicity.

(Drew 1996, 2–3)

NCTM took a significant step toward "consciousness-raising" by recommending the Standards for all students. Instead of tiering objectives—more mathematics for the college bound, less for prospective trade school students, and almost none for at-risk students—the Council asks for more mathematics—more emphasis, more complexity, more challenging goals and objectives—for *all* students.

Tradition and Myths

But, you might ask, is this wise? Are we ignoring meaningful differences in aptitude in the interest of equity and fair play? Won't expectations be lowered and students who excel in mathematics, shortchanged? Behind these questions lie some of the most damaging of the math education myths:

- Mathematics is a subject so demanding that few can hope to understand it.
- Equal treatment to one group somehow subtracts something from another.
- Mathematics education should be layered—advanced concepts for the few, basic concepts for the many, math facts for the rest.

It is a mark of the power of tradition that myths such as these continue to fuel the national debate over reforming mathematics curricula. Look outside our own country and the arbitrary nature of some of our curriculum "truths" becomes apparent. In China, where far fewer resources can be devoted to education, almost everyone learns advanced mathematics. "It is assumed," writes David Drew (1996), "that everyone can master advanced concepts and everyone is expected to do so" (9). Robert Reich (1991), in *The Work of Nations*, says, "Japan's greatest educational success has been to assure than even its slowest learners achieve a relatively high level of proficiency" (228). In the Trends in International Mathematics and Science Study (TIMSS), the United States has been consistently outperformed by third world countries—countries whose "slowest learners" might have been suspected of "holding back" the majority if they had been studying in American classrooms (Gonzales et al. 2004; USDE 1998).

Equity Reforms

In the United States, recent reforms probably began to affect performance in measurable ways in the 1990s (see Figure 1.4 for an example of one reform, a bilingual math class). However, while test

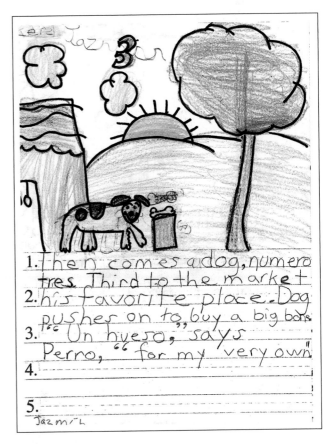

Figure 1.4 Mixing English and Spanish in bilingual math classes.

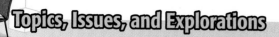

Topics, Issues, and Explorations

How do you see knowledge of mathematics—as an abundant or a scarce resource? If you select the former, what are some of the issues involved in the teaching challenge Drew mentions? If the latter, how would you decide who should be given the opportunities to learn the higher levels of mathematics?

Activities CD

For an activity related to a bilingual lesson in Spanish and English, see Activity 20, Animals, Numbered and On the Town: A Bilingual Lesson in Spanish and English, on the CD-ROM that accompanies this text.

scores for women and minorities have risen significantly, the performance of students who traditionally do well on achievement tests has neither declined nor fallen behind (National Center for Education Statistics 1998, 72–73; Stevens 2003). And study after study shows the benefits of mainstreaming and integrating rather than separating students (see also West 1991).

We have two choices as teachers, Drew (1996) writes: we can assume that

1. virtually everyone can master the material and the challenge is to present it in a manner that allows them to do so, or
2. the material is tough and only a few of the best and brightest will be able to learn it.

(1996, 9)

The assumptions we make will not only affect our classroom behaviors and expectations but also students' perceptions about their own abilities and potential to learn mathematics.

Changing Views About How Students Learn

Perhaps the most dramatic changes in school mathematics during the 20th century were in the way children study mathematics. Consider the classroom scenarios described in the Windows on Learning feature.

The children in the first scenario are learning what one writer calls "muscle" or "muscular" mathematics (Betz 1948, 203). They exercise their mental muscles with repetitions intended to make responses automatic, without thought. The teacher is the center of the class, in control of learning as well as behavior. The environment of the class is disciplined and quiet. The consequences of failure are immediate and devastating—public discussion of errors with a pejorative thrust.

The mathematics activity in the second scenario reflects some changes in our perspective, both about learning and about student–teacher roles in the learning process. Instead of drilling and memorizing facts, these children explore ideas like scientists, with a problem to solve, materials to experiment with, and a spirit of inquiry. This is dynamic instead of passive or static learning, and the children rather than a teacher direct and shape the process. Multiple rather than single outcomes are not only possible but also encouraged. The activity is open ended; the learning, cooperative. The small group is a learning team in which the flow of ideas is unstructured and spontaneous and the possibilities are limitless.

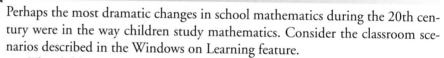

Changing Views About What Should Be Learned

In 1994, NCTM changed the name of its journal for elementary teaching from *The Arithmetic Teacher* to *Teaching Children Mathematics*. The change marked a major transition in the way we think and talk about mathematics learning in the elementary grades as well as changes in the content itself. Today mathematics is

Windows on Learning

"Two Times Two Is Four"

The year was 1954; the place, Mrs. Taylor's third-grade classroom at Briscoe Elementary School.

The students sat quietly, their hands folded in front of them, at desks lined up in five neat rows, with six desks to a row. The desks were all filled. The first group of baby boomers were entering the public schools, and space and teachers were at a premium.

Mrs. Taylor stood before the class at a chalkboard. She had just finished correcting the work of six students who were called to the board to do multiplication problems involving two-digit numbers. The exercise had not gone well, and Mrs. Taylor was frustrated.

"Billy, you multiplied 33 times 33 and got 66. You know that can't be right; 3 plus 3 is 6, so 3 times 3 can't be the same thing.

"Suzanne, you say 15 times 55 is 770. How can that be if 5 times 5 is 25? The number can't end with a 0.

"What's happening, class, is we are forgetting our times tables." She picked up a stick and pointed to a chart above the chalkboard.

"Everybody stand."

The students slipped quickly out of their desks and stood with their hands at their sides and eyes on the chart. Everyone was careful not to look at Billy and Suzanne, who were red faced and embarrassed.

"All right, everyone, together now on the count of three."

Mrs. Taylor tapped the chart three times with her stick, and the children began to chant, "One times 1 is 1, 2 times 2 is 4. . . ."

"Two Times Two Is Square"

The year was 2004 (half a century later). At Lowell Elementary School, in Room 123, fourth graders were experimenting with multiplying numbers by themselves.

Tino, Shelley, Angie, Hussein, and Letitia were working in a small group around a circular table. In front of them were manipulatives, some colored blocks, various tools for measuring, and scratch paper and pencils for sketching and trying out ideas.

"What are we supposed to be doing?" Tino asked.

Letitia consulted a list of objectives in her three-ring journal.

"We've done the map activity and the frequency count. That leaves multiplying and shapes for this week. Which one would you rather do?"

The group decided to work on multiplying and leave shapes for the next day. The assignment was simple: find out what happens when you multiply numbers by themselves.

"That's easy," Angie said. "It's like adding them up over and over."

"Like this," Hussein agreed and began to arrange blocks on the table in front of them, two sets of two blocks, one on top of the other, for 2 times 2; three sets of three blocks for 3 times 3.

Shelley sat watching Hussein line up the blocks. She didn't say anything, but she had a feeling he was missing something by lining the blocks up.

Meanwhile, Tino was verbalizing what Hussein was doing. "You put two sets of two together and get 4, three sets of three and get 9, four sets of four and get 16, five sets of five and get 25."

"Hey, everybody, look at this," Angie said, looking up from the pad where she had been doodling. "If you write all the numbers down, 1's odd, 4's even, 9's odd, 16's even, 25's odd."

Letitia was working with cuisenaire rods, arranging and rearranging them as she looked for patterns.

Then Shelley reached a tentative hand toward the blocks in Hussein's 2 times 2 line. "I think these would look better like this," she said and quickly rearranged the blocks into a square.

Hussein saw what she was doing and joined in.

"Does it do that every time?" Angie stopped doodling to ask.

"I don't know. I think so," Shelley said and kept on moving blocks. Finally, all of Hussein's blocks had been arranged into squares.

"It happens every time. The blocks make a square," Hussein observed.

"So when you multiply a number by itself, you get a square," Letitia summarized.

Later when the group discussed the activity with one of the class's team teachers, Ms. Lee, she suggested they see what the math software the class used had to say about squaring. The computer software reinforced the block arranging Shelley and Hussein had done with graphics of squares being multiplied into larger and larger squares. It also showed them how to represent the squaring process in math language with a superscript ^{2}.

a foundational discipline. It provides tools and ways of thinking that impact learning across the curriculum.

Some factors that influenced the changing mathematics curriculum in the 20th century included changes in our economic and social worlds, historical events and trends, and new developments in technology and science.

Tying the Curriculum to Mental Age and Social Utility

Early attempts to design a mathematics curriculum focused on matching content to students' mental age and, therefore, readiness to learn. For example, in the 1920s, school administrators collected survey data to tie arithmetic topics to children's "mental ages." They used their correlations to sequence the curriculum, "delaying" introduction of many topics such as multiplication and division because of students' supposed "mental" unreadiness (Washburne 1931, 210, 230–31). Readiness, according to these administrators, could be determined by a combination of intelligence and achievement tests, which would allow teachers to "ability-group" students or individualize instruction. They concluded that arithmetic was too hard for most elementary school students and should be taught in junior high or high school instead (see Brownell 1938, 495-508, for a critique).

Just as the Great Depression turned nations inward, the social utilitarians of the mid-20th century advocated a short-range rather than a long-range view for the mathematics curriculum. Guy Wilson, one of the movement's leading proponents, believed the schools should teach the skills required to do adult jobs. In 1948 he wrote:

> The proper basis for functional arithmetic is the social utility theory. This theory posits (1) that the chief purpose of the school is to equip the child for life, life as a child, life as an adult, and (2) that the skills, knowledges, and appreciations should receive attention in school somewhat proportional to usefulness in life.
>
> *(321)*

Wilson (1948) identified basic arithmetic facts needed by the majority of workers and used them to calculate what he called "the drill load of arithmetic"—the facts and skills for a drill mastery program in which "[o]nly success is wanted and only perfect scores" (327, 335). Students, according to Wilson, should memorize 100 primary facts each for addition, subtraction, and multiplication:

(1) *Addition*—100 primary facts, 300 related decade facts to 39 + 9, 80 other facts for carrying in multiplication to 9 × 9. . . . Whole numbers only. . . .

(2) *Subtraction*—100 primary facts, all process difficulties. . .whole numbers only. . . .

(3) *Multiplication*—100 primary facts, all process difficulties, whole numbers only. . . .

(4) *Division*—emphasis on long division. . . .

(5) *Common fractions*—. . .halves and quarters, thirds, possibly attention to eighths and twelfths separately.

(327–28)

Activities CD

For an activity to help discover the meanings and importance of real numbers, see Activity 102, Real Numbers in the Workplace, on the CD-ROM that accompanies this text.

Wilson (1948) recommended little or no work with decimals since "decimals represent specialized figuring learned on the job" (329). Measures, percentages, geometry, and algebra were relegated for the most part to what he called "appreciation" study—studies undertaken for "fun" and used to "lure" the brightest students forward. Wilson also argued that the metric system should not be taught because English measures were more convenient: "The housewife, even in a metric country, wants a pound of butter" (327). Light-years, parsecs, measurements related to the electronic age—should they be taught? "No, of course not," wrote Wilson. "The numbers using [them] are too few" (337).

The social utility argument continues to influence curriculum choices. As recently as the 1980s the National Center for Research in Vocational Education published a series called Math on the Job, with special kinds of numbers for the grain farmer, mechanic, clerk, machinist, cashier, and so forth.

Responding to a Bigger World

Even as the utilitarians were urging a reduced mathematics curriculum, others were calling for expansion. World War II had shown Americans a bigger world—a world where Swiss students studied calculus in high school, where scientific breakthroughs were needed, not just to win but to survive. The Commission on Post War Plans called for more, not less, mathematics in education. In 1947 the President's Commission on Higher Education proposed increasing college enrollments drastically for a minimum of 4.6 million by 1960—a change that would require a college-track mathematics curriculum for millions. By the time the Soviet Union launched *Sputnik* in 1957 and galvanized public opinion for the space race, educators were already experimenting with new mathematics curricula.

The "new math," as it was popularly called, emphasized mathematics structure. Students studied sets, number systems, different number bases, and number sentences. Teachers guided children to discover concepts rather than lecturing about them. While many ideas of the new math had merit, application may have been flawed. Textbooks were often hard to read and overly formal. Many parents complained that they could not understand their children's homework.

In the meantime, the social revolution of the 1960s and 1970s flooded colleges with students—many from backgrounds and groups that traditionally had not attended college. To what extent this new college population affected test scores remains unclear, but between 1963 and 1975 SAT scores declined, leading to several major concerns for the mathematics curriculum in the final decades of the century, including how to:

- upgrade the curriculum to match the demands of an increasingly technological society,
- balance student needs with the needs of society and of mathematics itself, and
- teach the expanded curriculum to all of the students.

There were no easy answers. A back-to-the-basics movement called for a return to traditional mathematics—teacher lectures, drills, and tests. But many argued that traditional approaches had worked for no more than 5% to 15% of the students; what was needed was a challenging mathematics curriculum that prepared every student to think mathematically—to develop the foundations in

Activities CD

For an activity to help find decimals and percents in students' lives, see Activity 96, Finding Decimals and Percents in Your World, on the CD-ROM that accompanies this text.

Activities CD

For an activity about understanding numbers in the bigger world, see Activity 72, Exploring Data in the Bigger World, on the CD-ROM that accompanies this text.

mathematical reasoning, concepts, and tools needed for advanced mathematics education as well as enlightened living in the age of technology.

The National Council of Supervisors of Mathematics (NCSM) responded with a list of basic skills (1977) and later with "Essential Mathematics for the Twenty-first Century" (1989). NCTM did the same, producing an *Agenda for Action* in 1980, the first version of the *Curriculum and Evaluation Standards* in 1989, and now the Standards 2000 document, *Principles and Standards for School Mathematics*, compiled with the input of thousands of mathematics teachers responding over the World Wide Web. Some major points of consensus between the NCSM and the NCTM recommendations include the following:

- that all students benefit from a challenging mathematics curriculum;
- that mathematics reasoning and higher-order thinking skills should be integral to the curriculum;
- that problem solving should be a priority;
- that algebraic thinking, geometry, statistics and probability are essential rather than add-on skills;
- that the emphasis in computation should be on meaning and patterns;
- that communication of mathematical ideas in a variety of ways (oral, written, symbolic language, everyday language) is critical to the learning process;
- that students need opportunities to explore and apply mathematics in hands-on and real-life activities.

Topics, Issues, and Explorations

An effective curriculum is multidimensional. It responds to the needs of society, the needs of the individual, and the needs of the subject. Think about the changes in the mathematics curriculum in the 20th century. Which changes do you think reflected concerns about which needs? Which changes seem most worthwhile or least worthwhile?

Activities CD

For an activity applying mathematics to real-life contexts, see Activity 101, Population Percentages, on the CD-ROM that accompanies this text.

Building Consensus and Setting Standards

Changes in curriculum and pedagogy are not like changes in the seasons, though they may be just as inevitable. Few of the changes described in the previous sections have come smoothly or without controversy. In his 1998 address, "The State of Mathematics Education: Building a Strong Foundation for the 21st Century," then-secretary of education Richard W. Riley called for a "ceasefire" in the "math wars" about "how mathematics is taught and what mathematics should be taught." "We need," he told the meeting of the American Mathematical Society and the Mathematical Association of America,

to bring an end to the shortsighted, politicized, and harmful bickering over the teaching and learning of mathematics. I will tell you that if we continue down this road of infighting, we will only negate the gains we have already made—and the real losers will be the students of America.

I hope each of you will take the responsibility to bring an end to these battles, to begin to break down stereotypes, and make the importance of mathematics for our nation clear so that all teachers teach better mathematics *and* teach mathematics better.

Riley appealed for "civil discourse" and openness to change. The controversy reached mud-slinging levels in the 1990s, with reformers accused of teaching "fuzzy math" or "placebo math" or "dumbing down to promote classroom equality" (Mathematically Correct 1997; Leo 1997, 14). But reforming the mathematics curriculum has always been a stormy process. In 1948 William Betz complained, "For nearly six decades we have had unceasing efforts at reform in mathematics," and, he pointed out, "milestones in this epic struggle" go back to 1892 (197). He wrote, "We have looked at a picture which is no doubt perfectly familiar to every experienced teacher of mathematics. It is that of a battle between two sharply contrasting positions regarding the educational role of mathematics" (205). In the National Society for the Study of Education's 1970 yearbook, *Mathematics Education*, Lee Shulman, citing articles published in 1930, 1935, and 1941, says they "can almost read as a history of controversies, cease-fires, and temporary truces" (23).

Although the tone of the controversies may at times have sunk below the levels of civil discourse urged by Secretary Riley, the controversies themselves may not be unproductive. In fact, even the emotionally charged skirmishes may serve a purpose since they tend to involve the public in the dialogue about reform.

Nonetheless, if consensus among mathematicians is neither clear nor stable, is it worthwhile to set standards, and can the standards set be worthwhile? If we think of standards as commandments engraved in stone, the answer may be no. However, if we accept setting standards as an ongoing and open-ended process, the answer is yes. According to *Webster's New World Dictionary*, the word *standard* originally meant "a standing place." The meaning has grown to include flags or banners that symbolize nations, causes, or movements; levels of attainment set as benchmarks; and even foundation supports. Finding out where we stand and establishing goals, benchmarks, and supporting structures for those ideas have all been part of the standard-setting process—or process*es* since efforts to set standards are ongoing at state and national levels and for a variety of curriculum and development areas.

Although driven by a dialogue that has ranged in tone from the rational to the acrimonious, these standards-setting processes have succeeded at several levels. First, they have generated research and ideas that have disrupted the status quo, jarring entrenched assumptions about mathematics education and opening the way for new concepts and methods. Second, they have focused attention on critical issues, such as equity and technology in teaching mathematics. And third, they have generated public interest and involvement at unprecedented levels. When in our history has mathematics in the schools been discussed and debated with greater intensity and urgency? Making mathematics education a national issue may have been one positive outcome of the math wars. Mathematics, like science, occurs in a social context (see Drew 1996, 17). Engaging society in the debate over what is taught and how it is taught ensures that reform takes place within rather than outside the social context and remains responsive to the needs and demands of those most directly affected by the changes.

Topics, Issues, and Explorations

Identify and explain one concept, content area, or process that you believe should be learned during a specific grade. Share your ideas in a group or class. How much agreement or disagreement do you find?

National Standards for Mathematics Education

In *Goals 2000: Educate America Act*, Congress proposed in 1994 "a national framework for education reform" and called for "the development and adoption of a voluntary national system of skill standards and certification" (see Figure 1.5). The act responded in part to efforts already under way by professional groups

---

**The 1994 *Goals 2000: Educate America Act*
challenged schools both to achieve and to compete.**

(A) By the year 2000, United States students will be first in the world of mathematics and science achievement.

(B) The objectives for this goal are that—

  (i) mathematics and science education, including the metric system of measurement, will be strengthened throughout the system, especially in the early grades;

  (ii) the number of teachers with a substantive background in mathematics and science, including the metric system of measurement, will increase by 50 percent and

  (iii) the number of United States undergraduate and graduate students, especially women and minorities who complete degrees in mathematics, science, and engineering will increase significantly. (*Educate America Act of 1994;* see also National Education Goals Panel 1995)

Figure 1.5 Setting national goals for mathematics education.

such as NCTM and the American Association for the Advancement of Science (AAAS).

Underlying these goals and objectives are several basic assumptions: that having an informed citizenry is essential to national security and productivity; that being informed entails higher levels of achievement in mathematics and science; that "being first" is a desirable and feasible outcome; that a nation that exemplifies diversity can set common standards and achieve common goals in mathematics education.

NCTM's Principles and Standards 2000

Principles and Standards for School Mathematics (2000) integrates areas covered by three earlier Standards publications: *Curriculum and Evaluation Standards for School Mathematics* (1989), *Professional Standards for Teaching Mathematics* (1991), and *Assessment Standards for School Mathematics* (1995). The purpose of the Standards 2000 document is ambitious and broad: "to set forth a comprehensive and coherent set of goals for mathematics for all students from prekindergarten through grade 12 that will orient curricula, teaching, and assessment efforts during the next decades" (NCTM 2000, 6). To this end, the document proposes a vision, principles, and standards to be applied across four grade bands: prekindergarten through grade 2, grades 3–5, grades 6–8, and grades 9–12. The vision is both idealistic and far-reaching:

NCTM Vision for School Mathematics*

Imagine a classroom, a school, or a school district where all students have access to high-quality, engaging mathematics instruction. There are am-

---

*Reprinted with permission from *Principles and Standards for School Mathematics,* copyright © 2000 by the National Council of Teachers of Mathematics. All rights reserved. Standards are listed with the permission of the National Council of Teachers of Mathematics (NCTM). NCTM does not endorse the content or validity of these alignments.

bitious expectations for all, with accommodation for those who need it. Knowledgeable teachers have adequate resources to support their work and are continually growing as professionals. The curriculum is mathematically rich, offering students opportunities to learn important mathematical concepts and procedures with understanding. Technology is an essential component of the environment. Students confidently engage in complex mathematical tasks chosen carefully by teachers. They draw on knowledge from a wide variety of mathematical topics, sometimes approaching the same problem from different mathematical perspectives or representing mathematics in different ways until they find methods that enable them to make progress. Teachers help students make, refine, and explore conjectures on the basis of evidence and use a variety of reasoning and proof techniques to confirm or disprove those conjectures. Students are flexible and resourceful problem solvers. Alone or in groups and with access to technology, they work productively and reflectively, with the skilled guidance of their teachers. Orally and in writing, students communicate their ideas and results effectively. They value mathematics and engage actively in learning it.

(NCTM 2000, 3)

NCTM's Vision for School Mathematics assumes both the importance of knowing mathematics in the 21st century and the need to continually improve mathematics education to meet the challenges of a changing world (see Figure 1.6 for an example of two second graders' use of modern technology in a counting activity). Understanding and using mathematics is described as an essential underpinning of life, a part of our cultural heritage, and a prerequisite for success in the workplace. And providing all students with "the opportunity and the support to learn significant mathematics with depth and understanding"

Activities CD

For an activity using computers and counting, see Activity 69, Collecting Data in Our Worlds, on the CD-ROM that accompanies this text.

Figure 1.6 Counting with computer graphics.

is linked to "the values of a just democratic system" and "its economic needs" (NCTM 2000, 5).

NCTM's Principles for School Mathematics are equally far-reaching:

NCTM Principles for School Mathematics

- **Equity:** Excellence in mathematics education requires equity—high expectations and strong support for all students.
- **Curriculum:** A curriculum is more than a collection of activities: it must be coherent, focused on important mathematics, and well articulated across the grades.
- **Teaching:** Effective mathematics teaching requires understanding what students know and need to learn and then challenging and supporting them to learn it well.
- **Learning:** Students must learn mathematics with understanding, actively building new knowledge from experience and prior knowledge.
- **Assessment:** Assessment should support the learning of important mathematics and furnish useful information to both teachers and students.
- **Technology:** Technology is essential in teaching and learning mathematics; it influences the mathematics that is taught and enhances students' learning.

(NCTM 2000, 11)

Together with the Standards, these Principles comprise key components of NCTM's vision of high-quality mathematics education. The Principles are, in effect, ideals to live by—foundational ideas that influence curriculum and professional development on the larger scale as well as instructional decisions in the classroom on the smaller scale. The Standards are more like building materials. They outline mathematics content and processes for students to learn. Instead of the multiple standards of the 1989 document, *Principles and Standards for School Mathematics* proposes 10 standards that "specify the understanding, knowledge, and skills students should acquire from kindergarten to grade 12."

The Content Standards—Number and Operations, Algebra, Geometry, Measurement, and Data Analysis and Probability—explicitly describe the content that students should learn. The Process Standards—Problem Solving, Reasoning and Proof, Communication, Connections, and Representation—highlight ways of acquiring and using content knowledge.

(NCTM 2000, 29)

Each Standard entails goals that apply across all grades plus differing emphases for the grade bands. For example, number and measurement are emphasized in the early grades, while later grades spend more instructional time on formal algebra and geometry. Arranging the curriculum into 10 standards that span the grades offers a coherent structure for an overall curriculum (see Figure 1.7). Specific details are left to those who will apply and implement the ideas.

Topics, Issues, and Explorations

NCTM gives detailed "Expectations" or specific objectives for each Content Standard by grade group. Study the Expectations in *Principles and Standards for School Mathematics* for the grade you are teaching or plan to teach. Do any surprise you? Discuss your reactions in small groups. Go to http://standards.nctm.org/document/appendix/numb.htm

Process Standards
Instructional programs from prekindergarten through grade 12 should enable all students to—

Problem Solving
• Build new mathematical knowledge through problem solving
• Solve problems that arise in mathematics and in other contexts
• Apply and adapt a variety of appropriate strategies to solve problems
• Monitor and reflect on the process of mathematical problem solving

Reasoning and Proof
• Recognize reasoning and proof as fundamental aspects of mathematics
• Make and investigate mathematical conjectures
• Develop and evaluate mathematical arguments and proofs
• Select and use various types of reasoning and methods of proof

Communication
• Organize and consolidate their mathematical thinking through communication
• Communicate their mathematical thinking coherently and clearly to peers, teachers, and others
• Analyze and evaluate the mathematical thinking and strategies of others
• Use the language of mathematics to express mathematical ideas precisely

Connections
• Recognize and use connections among mathematical ideas
• Understand how mathematical ideas interconnect and build on one another to produce a coherent whole
• Recognize and apply mathematics in contexts outside of mathematics

Representation
• Create and use representations to organize, record, and communicate mathematical ideas
• Select, apply, and translate among mathematical representations to solve problems
• Use representations to model and interpret physical, social, and mathematical phenomena

Content Standards
Instructional programs from prekindergarten through grade 12 should enable all students to—

Number and Operations
• Understand numbers, ways of representing numbers, relationships among numbers, and number systems
• Understand meanings of operations and how they relate to one another
• Compute fluently and make reasonable estimates

Algebra
• Understand patterns, relations, and fractions
• Represent and analyze mathematical situations and structures using algebraic symbols
• Use mathematical models to represent and understand quantitative relationships
• Analyze change in various contexts

Geometry
• Analyze characteristics and properties of two- and three-dimensional geometric shapes and develop mathematical arguments about geometric relationships
• Specify locations and describe spatial relationships using coordinate geometry and other representational systems
• Apply transformations and use symmetry to analyze mathematical situations
• Use visualization, spatial reasoning, and geometric modeling to solve problems

Measurement
• Understand measurable attributes of objects and the units, systems, and processes of measurement
• Apply appropriate techniques, tools, and formulas to determine measurements

Data Analysis and Probability
• Formulate questions that can be addressed with data and collect, organize, and display data to answer them
• Select and use appropriate statistical methods to analyze data
• Develop and evaluate inferences and predictions that are based on data
• Understand and apply basic concepts of probability

Figure 1.7 NCTM Process and Content Standards.
Reprinted with permission from *Principles and Standards for School Mathematics,* copyright© 2000 by the National Council of Teachers of Mathematics. All rights reserved. Standards are listed with the permission of the National Council of Teachers of Mathematics (NCTM). NCTM does not endorse the content or validity of these alignments. (pp. 392–403)

Project 2061, Science for All Americans

A parallel project to NCTM's Principles and Standards began in 1985, the date of the last visit of Halley's comet. Sponsored by AAAS, Project 2061 is named for the date when Halley's comet will return and assumes that children who were beginning school in 1985 will see a lifetime of changes in science and technology before the comet's return in 2061. To prepare them for these changes, Project 2061 proposes educational reforms akin to those promoted by NCTM. Culotta (1990) suggests seven major areas of commonality (see also Drew 1996):

- Less memorization
- Involvement of teachers in the reform process
- Integration of disciplines and study
- Greater emphasis on hands-on activities
- Greater focus on listening to students' questions and ideas
- Connections between discipline and society
- Emphasis on the scientific process and how problems are solved

Activities CD

For an activity that integrates science and math, see Activity 68, Mini Gardens, on the CD-ROM that accompanies this text.

Project 2061 defines mathematics as "the science of patterns and relationships" and describes it as "the chief language of science" (AAAS 1989). In the project's "Design for Scientific Literacy," mathematics is included in most of the building blocks for a Project 2061 curriculum: "For purposes of general scientific literacy, it is important for students (1) to understand in what sense mathematics is the study of patterns and relationships, (2) to become familiar with some of those patterns and relationships, and (3) to learn to use them in daily life" (AAAS 1989).

In Project 2061's "Benchmarks for Scientific Literacy", as shown in Figure 1.8, specific educational objectives are outlined by grade, with an emphasis upon outcomes or "what students should know" and understand. The Benchmarks emphasize the importance of experiencing mathematics, of establishing connections between ideas and areas of inquiry, of "making multiple representations of the same idea and translating from one to another" (AAAS, 2000). Implicit in the various objectives are ties to development; for example, the emphasis in the early grades is on the specific, concrete, and immediate, with the gradual introduction of abstract ideas and "grand categories" in later grades. "Doing mathematics," like "doing science," is encouraged from the earliest grades, and mathematical inquiry leading to the valid development of mathematical ideas also starts in the earliest grades when children explore concrete objects to discover what they tell us and what they can be used to show about the world around them.

Overall, Project 2061 proposes specific educational objectives within a context of scientific values and attitudes, including attitudes about learning:

> Students in elementary school have a spontaneous interest in nature and numbers. Nevertheless, many students emerge from school fearing mathematics and disdaining school as too dull and too hard to learn. . . .
>
> It is within teachers' power to foster positive attitudes among their students. If they choose significant, accessible, and exciting topics in science and mathematics, if they feature teamwork as well as competition among students, if they focus on exploring and understanding more than the rote memorization of terms, and if they make sure all their students know they are expected to explore and learn and have their achievements acknowledged, then nearly all of those students will indeed learn. And in learning successfully students will learn the most important lesson of all—namely that they are able to do so.
>
> *(AAAS, 1989 chap. 12)*

Topics, Issues, and Explorations

Discuss NCTM's Standards and Project 2061's Benchmarks for learning mathematics. How are they alike? How are they different? Which Standards and Benchmarks seem most important to you?

Kindergarten through Grade 2
  By the end of the 2nd grade, students should know that:
  • Circles, squares, triangles, and other shapes can be found in nature and in things that people build.
  • Patterns can be made by putting different shapes together or taking them apart.
  • Things move, or can be made to move, along straight, curved, circular, back-and-forth, and jagged paths.
  • Numbers can be used to count any collection of things.
  • Numbers and shapes can be used to tell about things.

Grades 3 through 5
  By the end of the 5th grade, students should know that:
  • Mathematics is the study of many kinds of patterns, including numbers and shapes and operations on them. Sometimes patterns are studied because they help to explain how the world works or how to solve practical problems, sometimes because they are interesting in themselves.
  • Mathematical ideas can be represented concretely, graphically, and symbolically.
  • Numbers and shapes—and operations on them—help to describe and predict things about the world around us.
  • In using mathematics, choices have to be made about what operations will give the best results. Results should always be judged by whether they make sense and are useful.

Grades 6 through 8
  By the end of the 8th grade, students should know that:
  • Usually there is no one right way to solve a mathematical problem; different methods have different advantages and disadvantages.
  • Logical connections can be found between different parts of mathematics.
  • Mathematics is helpful in almost every kind of human endeavor—from laying bricks to prescribing medicine or drawing a face. In particular, mathematics has contributed to progress in science and technology for thousands of years and still continues to do so.
  • Mathematicians often represent things with abstract ideas, such as numbers or perfectly straight lines, and then work with those ideas alone.

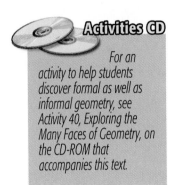

Activities CD

For an activity to help students discover formal as well as informal geometry, see Activity 40, Exploring the Many Faces of Geometry, on the CD-ROM that accompanies this text.

Figure 1.8 Project 2061 Benchmarks in mathematics for the elementary grades through middle school.
Source: AAAS (2000).

State and Local Standards

Efforts to develop national standards have had a significant impact on mathematics education overall. For example, in 1996 the framework for the National Assessment of Educational Progress (NAEP) was revised to reflect NCTM curricular emphases and objectives (USDE 1999, 2–3). National standards have also influenced the development of standards at the state and local levels. Some states have adapted the national standards to fit their own school districts' needs (see, for example, *Colorado Model Content Standards* 2005.) Others have created their own benchmarks and detail what students should know grade by grade. Georgia's

Topics, Issues, and Explorations

What standards has your state or district established for mathematics? The information may be available at your state or county Web site, or you can ask a school librarian for help. How do these standards compare to NCTM's Standards 2000 or to Project 2061?

performance-based standards are actually aligned with Japanese standards as well as the Georgia Criterion-Referenced Competency Tests (www.georgiastandards.org and www.glc.k12.ga.us/).

Meeting the Challenges of the 21st Century

The 20th century began the process of reconstructing mathematics education. In 1900, according to a writer in NCTM's First Yearbook, the purpose of teaching arithmetic had as much to do with discipline as curriculum. "It was felt that the subject should be hard in order to be valuable, and it sometimes looked as if it did not make so much difference to the school as to what a pupil studied so long as he hated it" (Smith 1926, 18–19). Responding to the period's rigid and often lifeless teaching methods and materials, the president of the American Mathematical Society, Eliakim Moore (1903), appealed to teachers:

> Would it not be possible for the children in the grades to be trained in power of observation and experiment and reflection and deduction so that always their mathematics should be directly connected with matters of thoroughly concrete character? . . .
>
> The materials and mathematics should be enriched and vitalized. In particular, the grade teachers must make wiser use of the foundations furnished by the kindergarten. The drawing and paper folding must lead directly to systematic study of intuitional geometry, including the construction of models . . . with simple exercises in geometrical reasoning. . . . The children [should] be taught to represent, according to usual conventions, various familiar and interesting phenomena and study the properties of the phenomena in the pictures to know, for example, what concrete meaning attaches to the fact that a graph curve at a certain point is going down or going up or is horizontal.
>
> (45–46).

For an activity that promotes simple geometric reasoning with manipulatives, see Activity 38, 7 Magic Pieces: Tangrams, on the CD-ROM that accompanies this text.

Activities CD

For a hands-on activity for representing, see Activity 5, Graphing with Candy Hearts, Jellybeans, or Gumdrops, on the CD-ROM that accompanies this text.

Meeting the Challenges as a Nation

A hundred years later we can say that many elements of Moore's vision for learning mathematics are not only possible but also an accomplished fact. Hands-on, dynamic learning is becoming the norm in elementary classrooms (see Figure 1.9 for an example of a kindergartner's graphing of a hands-on counting activity). Technology has helped us enrich and vitalize the learning process with interactive learning experiences such as the National Center for Education Statistics' Students' Classroom (see the Math and Technology feature, "Explore Your Math Knowledge"). Increasingly, lessons emphasize understanding and context and deemphasize rote memorization of isolated facts and procedures. The elementary curriculum is no longer limited to arithmetic but includes geometry, algebraic thinking, and mathematical reasoning that were once considered too abstract for children.

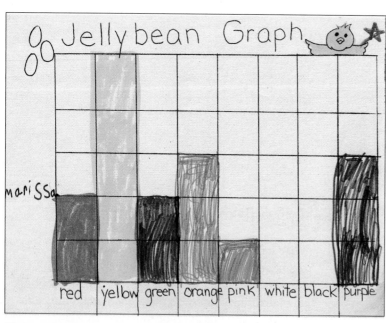

Figure 1.9   Marissa represents counting jelly beans with a bar graph.

Evidence is mounting that these approaches are working and working well. After decades of declining test scores and public alarm about deficiencies, the trends seem to be reversing, as shown in the graph in Figure 1.10. From 1990 to 2005, the National Assessment of Educational Progress (NAEP), the nation's report card, showed steady gains (2003; Perie, Grigg, and Dion 2005). SAT and ACT mathematics scores are up. The 2003 Trends in International Mathematics and Science Study (TIMSS) showed both U. S. fourth and eighth graders scoring above the international average in mathematics and science (Gonzales et al. 2004; NCES 2005; USDE 1997).

Does this mean that the goals and objectives proposed by the *Educate America Act* have been reached? In the first decade of the 21st century, is the United States first in the world in mathematics and science achievement? Perhaps yes, perhaps no. If being first is measured by achievements in the world of science and mathematics, the United States could stand at the top. If we look (as many in the national media do) at test scores, our position is less clear.

Although the results of the 2003 TIMSS placed U.S. fourth and eighth graders above the international averages, U.S. fourth graders were outperformed by students in 11 countries and U.S. eighth graders by students in 9 countries. Students in four Asian countries—Chinese Taipei, Hong Kong SAR, Japan, and Singapore—outperformed both U.S. fourth and eighth graders (Plisko 2004). In addition, the 2003 Program for International Student Assessment (PISA) placed U.S. 15-year-olds below the international average for both mathematical and scientific literacy (Lemke et al. 2004). Data collected for NAEP in the 1990s showed no significant improvement in elementary or middle school teachers' preparation to teach mathematics (Hawkins, Stancavage, and Dossey 1998). The shortage of qualified mathematics teachers continues to grow, and women and minorities continue to be underrepresented in mathematics (Seymour 1995a, 1995b; Chaddock 1998).

Nonetheless, progress is being made. In the 1991 International Assessment of Educational Progress (IAEP), U. S. elementary school students scored below rather than above the international average (USDE 1997). Middle school students' performance improved significantly since the 1999 TIMSS. Moreover, data from NAEP show positive linear trends or overall increases in mathematics performance at all age levels tested from 1990 to 2004,

Math and Technology

Explore Your Math Knowledge

The National Center for Education Statistics (NCES) has developed a Students' Classroom with activities, games, and learning experiences to encourage mathematics learning. The Web site is http://nces.ed.gov/nceskids/eyk/index.asp?flash=false.

The Explore Your Knowledge activity features questions from national tests such as TIMSS. Students respond to the questions and then check their answers. The activity tracks the number of correct answers and prompts students to "Try Again?"

Activity

Visit the NCES Students' Classroom. Explore some of the math questions, responding correctly and incorrectly. Discuss the various resources available at the site, and brainstorm ways to use the activities in the classroom, including the possibilities for using the questions to help students prepare for various national tests.

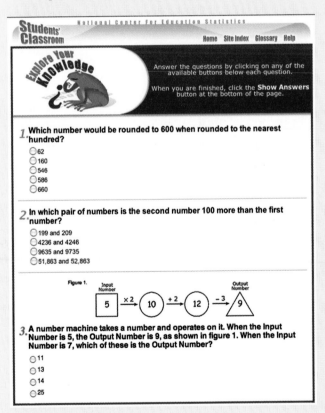

This report presents the national and state results of the NAEP assessment in mathematics and compares them to results from assessments in 2003 and in the first year data were available, usually 1990. In 2005, nationally representative samples of about 172,000 fourth-grade and 162,000 eighth-grade students nationwide participated in that assessment.

*Significantly different from 2005.

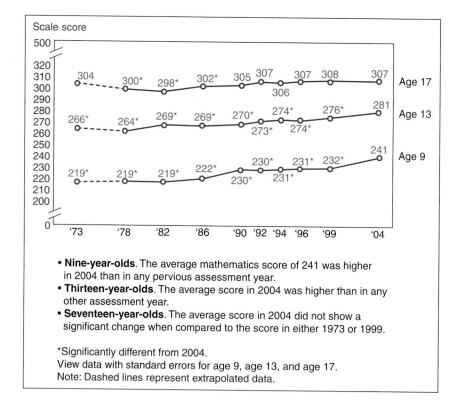

Figure 1.10 NAEP 1990–2005 trends chart.
Source: U.S. Department of Education, Institute of Education Science, National Center for Education Statistics. National Assessment of Educational Progress (NAEP), various years, 1990–2005 Mathematics Assessment.

- **Nine-year-olds**. The average mathematics score of 241 was higher in 2004 than in any pervious assessment year.
- **Thirteen-year-olds**. The average score in 2004 was higher than in any other assessment year.
- **Seventeen-year-olds**. The average score in 2004 did not show a significant change when compared to the score in either 1973 or 1999.

*Significantly different from 2004.
View data with standard errors for age 9, age 13, and age 17.
Note: Dashed lines represent extrapolated data.

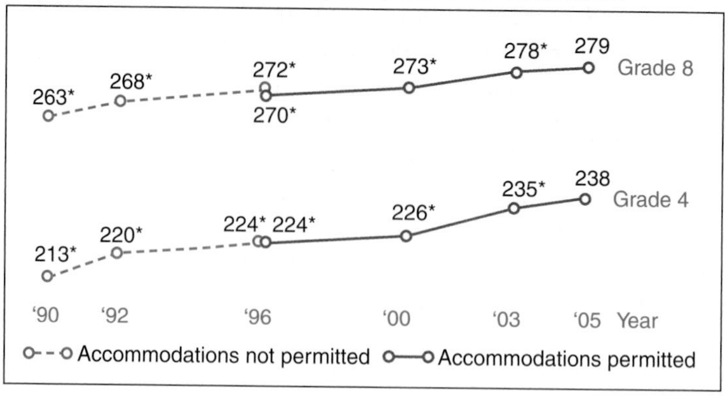

Figure 1.11 NAEP 1973–2004 trends chart: National trends in mathematics by average scale scores.
Source: U.S. Department of Education, Institute of Education Sciences, National Center for Education Statistics, National Assessment of Educational Progress (NAEP), selected years, 1973–2004 Long-Term Trend Mathematics Assessments.

continuing a positive trend begun in 1973 (see Figure 1.11; Perie et al. 2005; Perie and Moran 2005; USDE 2003, 1).

Comparisons of average scores in 1990 and 2005 show that the number of both fourth and eighth graders performing at or above the NAEP mathematics performance levels increased significantly (Perie et al. 2005, 1). The percentage of fourth graders who can perform basic numerical operations (adding, subtraction, multiplying, and dividing with whole numbers) and solve one-step problems more than doubled from the 1970s to 2004 (20% to 42%). The percentage of eighth graders performing at or above this level increased from 65% to 83% (Perie and Moran 2005). NAEP trends since the 1970s suggest a closing of the gender and race gaps at the fourth and eighth grade (USDE 1996, 1997, 1999, 2000; Perie and Moran 2005). Since 1982 the percentage of Hispanics and American Indians/Alaskan Natives taking mathematics courses beyond the basics more than doubled, and proficiency scores on the NAEP show steady improvement for all ethnic and racial groups (National Center for Education Statistics 1997, 1999; USDE 2000; Plisko 2003; Perie et al. 2005; Perie and Moran 2005; see the Math and Technology feature for Web sites devoted to NAEP, TIMSS, and other tests).

Mathematics education continues to face major challenges as we begin the new millennium:

Challenge 1: Building a national consensus about the value and accessibility of a challenging mathematics education for everyone

Challenge 2: Building a professional consensus about teaching and learning mathematics

Challenge 3: Continuing the reconstruction of mathematics education—

- reconstructing our views of mathematics—how we look at and think about mathematics;
- reconstructing our views of education—how we see our roles as educators, our students' roles, our teaching goals and outcomes;
- reconstructing assessment—developing and interpreting new tools that let us look beyond right or wrong answers and evaluate problem-solving strategies and mathematical thinking;
- training teachers who are committed to the ideals and ready to face the challenges of teaching meaningful mathematics to all students.

Meeting the Challenges in the Classroom

What kind of teacher is needed to implement reforms in mathematics education? What kind of teaching is needed to make reformers' vision for learning mathematics in the 21st century a reality? Val Penniman, the teacher profiled in this chapter, discovered that change meant reinventing herself both as a math learner and as a math teacher. Although Val had had negative learning experiences in mathematics, she considered herself to be a good math teacher. She had memorized the scope and plan of her class's textbook and felt confident about her traditional method of teaching. The change for Val

Topics, Issues, and Explorations

According to researchers, a difference between the United States and most competing countries, including those that participated in the TIMSS study, is our lack of a national curriculum. What do you think of the idea of a national curriculum? Do we need a national curriculum in mathematics? How would it differ from current practice? What might we lose and what might we gain?

Math and Technology

You can find reports on TIMSS and NAEP as well as the latest research analyses and commentary on the Web.

http://nces.ed.gov/nationsreportcard/
This site provides updates on the National Assessment of Educational Progress, including study data, sample test items, and information about current tests.

http://nces.ed.gov/programs/coe
The National Center for Education Statistics prepares an annual report entitled *The Condition of Education*. The report includes a section on learner outcomes with specific data about mathematics proficiency and participation.

http://nces.ed.gov/timss/
Reports and analyses from the 2003 TIMSS are available at this site as well as information about earlier studies, including the 1999 TIMSS-Repeat, which focused on the progress of eighth graders in improving performances.

http://www.ed.gov/legislation/GOALS2000/TheAct/index.html
The text of the *Educate America Act* outlines plans for American education in the future. The act's intent is "to improve learning and teaching by providing a national framework for education reform."

http://www.ed.gov/nclb/overview/intro/4pillars.html
The website for the *No Child Left Behind Act* provides not only information about the act itself but also about the conditions it attempts to address and about successful teaching methods.

Preservice teachers develop materials and practice using hands-on methods for teaching math.

Activities CD

For a hands-on activity in which students make their own manipulatives to help understand fractions, see Activity 81, Fraction Kits, on the CD-ROM that accompanies this text.

came with a SummerMath for Teachers program at Mount Holyoke College in Amherst, Massachusetts. She learned a problem-solving approach in workshop classes that modeled effective methods for hands-on, collaborative learning. The result was a new approach to learning and teaching mathematics that has paid off in the classroom with high test scores and excitement about learning.

Penniman's experience underscores the need for change in both the way teachers teach mathematics and the way they themselves are prepared to teach mathematics. NCTM's *Professional Standards for Teaching Mathematics* emphasizes teaching that helps students develop mathematical power. The six standards for teaching and six standards for professional development present a view of teaching and teacher education that focuses on students and is flexible and adaptive rather than formulaic (see Figure 1.12).

While the Standards 2000 document does not spell out new standards for teaching and teacher development, it does illustrate effective practices. Each segment devoted to process standards includes a discussion of the teacher's role in implementing the standard. The standards for teacher education complement the performance-based standards of the National Council of Accreditation of Teacher Education (NCATE), which took effect in 2001.

Figure 1.12 NCTM Standards for mathematics teaching.
Source: From National Council of Teachers of Mathematics, *Professional Standards for Teaching Mathematics* (Reston, VA: Author, 1991), 19–67, 123–73. Reprinted with permission from *Professional Standards for Teaching Mathematics,* copyright© 1991 by the National Council of Teachers of Mathematics. All rights reserved. Standards are listed with the permission of the National Council of Teachers of Mathematics (NCTM). NCTM does not endorse the content or validity of these alignments.

Standards for Teaching Mathematics

Standard 1: The teacher should pose worthwhile mathematical tasks.

Standard 2: The teacher's role in discourse should be responsive—posing questions, listening, asking, monitoring.

Standard 3: Students' role in discourse should be active and interactive—listening and responding but also questioning, exploring, debating.

Standard 4: Students should be encouraged to use tools to enhance discourse, including technology, models, writing, visuals, and oral presentations.

Standard 5: The teacher should create a learning environment that fosters the development of mathematical power.

Standard 6: The teacher should engage in ongoing analysis of teaching and learning.

Standards for the Professional Development of Teachers of Mathematics

Standard 1: Mathematics and mathematics education instructors in preservice and continuing education programs should model good mathematics teaching.

Standard 2: The education of teachers of mathematics should develop their knowledge of the content and discourse of mathematics.

Standard 3: The preservice and continuing education of teachers of mathematics should provide multiple perspectives on students as learners of mathematics.

Standard 4: The preservice and continuing education of teachers of mathematics should develop teachers' knowledge of and ability to use and evaluate instructional materials, methods, strategies, and outcomes.

Standard 5: The preservice and continuing education of teachers of mathematics should provide them with opportunities to develop and grow as a teacher.

Standard 6: Teachers of mathematics should take an active role in their own professional development.

NCATE's standards call for focusing on student learning; developing meaningful learning experiences; using national and state standards to develop, design, and assess programs; using multiple forms of assessment; emphasizing field and clinical practice; working with diverse student populations; and being committed "to a high quality education for all of America's children" (Mathematical Association of America 2000).

The Conference Board of the Mathematical Sciences (CBMS) seems to be heading in the same direction with its *Mathematical Education of Teachers Project*. The board's (2000) recommendations include:

1. ensuring that future teachers "develop an in-depth understanding of the mathematics they will teach" (1),
2. designing mathematics education courses that "develop careful reasoning and mathematical 'common sense' in analyzing conceptual relationships and in applied problem solving" (2),
3. modeling "flexible interactive teaching" (2),
4. showing "multiple ways to engage students in mathematics" (2).

The task ahead of us, both as a nation and as teachers in the classroom, is neither easy nor simple. The 1996 NAEP found that "46 percent of fourth-grade teachers had little or no knowledge of the standards proposed for mathematics education by the National Council of Teachers of Mathematics; another 32 percent said they were only somewhat knowledgeable" (Hawkins et al. 1998, 41–42). That places 78% outside the mainstream of efforts toward reform. At the same time, polls show that 90% of young people expect their children to attend college and 90% of young people plan to attend college, yet half of these youngsters want to study no more than minimal mathematics and drop the subject altogether as soon as they can. "There is a disconnect about mathematics in this country," said Secretary Riley (1998), but "Mathematics Equals Opportunity. There could be no more crucial message to send to parents and students of America as we prepare for the coming century."

Teacher Pro-File

**Val Penniman
Second and Third
Grade**

An Elementary Teacher Transformed

Like many elementary school teachers, Val Penniman's own learning experiences in mathematics were somewhat negative:

"I was never a great math student. At one point in algebra class in high school, I was told to stop raising my hand!"

That she can remember this with a laugh illustrates Penniman's current confidence in her accomplishments as a math educator. At this point in her 20-year teaching career in Amherst, Massachusetts, Penniman has been chair of the district-wide mathematics committee. She recently served as the district's first mentor teacher assigned specifically to assist teachers new to the district, and she has developed and marketed an innovative set of calendar-based mathematics materials.

Perhaps even more significantly, Penniman has several years experience as staff member and Director of the Elementary Institute at SummerMath for Teachers (SMT) at Mount Holyoke College. It is this program that Penniman credits with transforming her from an elementary teacher who clung to skill drills and homogenous grouping to one who creates problem-solving lessons for students with a wide range of abilities. Formerly an advocate of text-based teaching, Penniman is now adept at planning classroom activities based on careful attention to what her students tell her about their mathematics understanding.

Making the change was not a quick or easy process.

Resisting Change

The first steps of Penniman's journey began in 1989, right as the standards of the National Council of Teachers of Mathematics (NCTM) were being published. At that time, Penniman's building was set up as a multiage school organized in teaching teams. She and a partner team-taught 50 to 55 children in a combination second and third grade class. Penniman's first contact with SMT was through her teaching partner.

Penniman remembers, "She said that she was going to be taking this course at Mount Holyoke that was going to help her teach math. At that time, we split the students by ability grouping; I took the 'high' kids, and she took the 'low' kids. I can remember the conversation. She was explaining that this was a program that would help her teach students to really understand the concepts about math more than just the skills, and, for instance, they might spend the entire period working on one problem."

She laughs, "We had a big argument. I said, 'No way are they going to learn math if they only do one problem a day. This is crazy!' In fact, it got to the point that she reminded me that I didn't work with the students who 'don't get it' and that I didn't understand. With that challenge, I started working with some of the lower students, too."

By the next summer, Penniman was ready to try the first two-week course at SMT; her teaching partner was scheduled for the second, advanced SMT institute. Penniman was still skeptical, and she later discovered that her partner "actually warned some of the staff that I was coming and that I was going to be a hard sell since I was a complete non-believer at that point."

By the end of her first two-week session at SMT, Penniman relates, "I was pretty much converted." Now she faced the challenge of applying her new beliefs in her classroom.

Making Change Work

Since both Penniman and her partner had been to SMT, they agreed on the changes they wanted to make in their classroom. Says Penniman, "The support for each other was magnificent. We did not break the students into homogeneous groups; we kept them in heterogeneous groups, and that was a very big change."

The two also decided not to use the textbook, which was a tremendous challenge. "It was very hard work," recalls Penniman. "There were no materials out there at that time, so we would write a couple of problems to try out during the day with the students and then we would get together and ask 'What are the next steps? What should we do? Where should we go?' We were just staying about one step ahead."

She describes an example of the type of problem they tried to find: "We have coat hooks out in the hall, and at the beginning of the year we have something like 60 new students in the quad. That year when we were trying to figure out how many coat hooks each kid could have, we looked at each other and said 'We shouldn't figure that out—that is a problem for the students!' Those second and third graders took about a week and a half to solve that one problem."

In addition to the day-to-day challenges of running the classroom, each teacher had internal issues to work through. Penniman recalls, "I had the textbook scope and sequence memorized. I would be comparing, thinking 'If we were using a book, we would be working on this skill. . . .'"

Garnering Support for Change

Penniman and her partner found that their second and third graders were quick to accept this way of learning math, and even the parents did not question it. This she attributes to preparation, "At the beginning of the year, we had borrowed a tape from SMT to show to parents at parent night to begin to explain to them what we were doing. We didn't say this is earth shattering. We didn't say this is new math. What we did talk about is children getting to a better conceptual understanding of the math that they were learning."

The school administrators were also receptive. Says Penniman, "The principal didn't really quite understand, but he had heard of SummerMath and he was a supporter. There were a few people who had attended SMT before, so this wasn't a brand new idea. And we didn't talk about it a whole lot to other staff members unless they were interested. It wasn't like we were trying to reform anyone or say this is what you should be doing."

"The principal would sometimes send people in to observe what I was doing. Sometimes they would understand and sometimes they didn't. The assistant principal in our school liked what I was doing a lot, and she would often come in. If there were something fun going on in class, I would invite her in to see it. She encouraged me to do mathematical bulletin boards out in the main hall, which was something we had not done much before."

Committing to Change

It is easy to stay committed to a change decision when things are going well. Then there are the difficult days. Penniman admits, "There were a lot of times when we were stuck. We would say 'What are we doing?' I would be thinking that students were way behind where they should be, or we would be worried about some of the kids who didn't seem to be getting it.

"I can remember one time when I was having a very hard time with getting the students to multiply, and I remember what I call sort of 'falling off the wagon' because I just couldn't get [the concept] across with what we were doing." Penniman showed the children the traditional algorithm, and when she turned around, "these kids are staring at me—just these blank faces, like, 'What are you talking about?'

"I realized then that I couldn't go back to the old method of teaching. We had already made such a change in the way students were learning math that just to get up and show them how to do something wasn't going to work anymore. I can remember thinking, 'Well, we have made the change and I can't just switch back to the way we used to teach.'"

And Penniman would not have it any other way. Her students' scores on standardized tests have remained high and are especially strong in mathematical applications. Even more important to Penniman is the attitude her students have toward mathematics. "Students like getting up and telling the class how they see things. It is empowering when you say to a kid: 'How did you solve this problem?' When the child explains, and the other students listen—hopefully attentively—they are exposed to a new way of solving a problem. Then we all clap."

Source: From Eisenhower National Clearinghouse (ENC) for Mathematics and Science Education, *Teacher Change: Improving Mathematics* (Columbus, OH: Author, 1999) Used by permission.

◄◄◄◄ LOOKING BACK

The 20th century was a time of continual upheaval in mathematics education. Efforts early in the century to minimalize the curriculum and delay mathematics study gave way at midcentury to experimental curricula and, at the end of the century, to an emphasis on "active mathematical reasoning in elementary school classrooms" (Russell 1999, 1) and changes in educational policies to support curriculum reform in urban and rural areas (Tate and Johnson 1999, 230).

The 20th century also saw the development of goals and standards that put mathematics education in the public eye. The Nation's Report Card drew attention to achievement levels, and international studies raised concerns and even threatened the public's national pride. The Goals 2000 rallying cry—"be first in the world by 2000"—responded not only to the public's outcry but also to the conviction that a citizenry who understands and can use mathematics is essential to the United States' future. The nation that aspires to lead the world economically, politically, and socially must also lead the world in education, with mathematics and science at the top of the must-know list.

The reform movement gained momentum during the last two decades of the 20th century. Two outstanding projects among many are AAAS's Project 2061 and NCTM's projects to develop standards for curriculum, teaching, and assessment. Outcomes of these projects have posed both a focus and a challenge for individual teachers and for the profession as a whole.

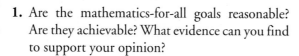

Questions for Further Thought, Discussion, and Research

1. Are the mathematics-for-all goals reasonable? Are they achievable? What evidence can you find to support your opinion?

2. Will it be more important to be mathematics literate in the 21st century than it was in the 20th century? Why or why not?

3. What are your own strengths and weaknesses as a learner of mathematics? How might those strengths and weaknesses impact your effectiveness as a teacher? How can you build on the strengths and remedy the weaknesses?

4. When Halley's Comet returns in 2061, will the reformers' vision for mathematics education have been realized? What do you believe, and why do you believe it?

5. How would you define *mathematical literacy*? Do you consider yourself to be mathematically literate? Why or why not?

6. Several of the organizations proposing standards for teacher education suggest the need for teachers to take more mathematics courses and to study the discipline of mathematics as well as methods to teach it. CBMS would like to see elementary school teachers take at least 9 semester hours of mathematics and middle-school teachers, 21 semester hours. Does the proposal have merit? How does it compare to your own program's requirements?

CHAPTER 2

Empowering Students to Learn Mathematics

LOOKING AHEAD >>>>>

Providing every student with the access and the opportunity to learn and to excel in mathematics has long been a goal of reformers. Legislation supporting this goal includes *Goals 2000: Educate America Act*, the *Individuals with Disabilities Education Improvement Act*, and the *No Child Left Behind Act*. However, to make the goal a reality will require more than laws and high expectations. It will require a better understanding of how students learn mathematics as well as better models for teaching mathematics.

Learning is power, and learning to learn is empowering. But how do students learn? Do they learn by conditioning—repeating behaviors until they have established a habit of responses? Do they learn by memorizing and repeating facts or exploring and using concepts, by drilling and testing or by constructing and validating? Do all children learn the same way and at the same speed or with the same outcomes?

The answers to these questions are neither simple nor final. Learning is a complex, multifaceted process, and practicing teachers as well as researchers are continually developing new insights about how children learn and what it means to learn mathematics. Applying these insights to teaching mathematics calls for teaching methods and materials that are flexible and responsive to students' needs and perspectives. Some effective teaching/learning models include mastery learning, inquiry-based learning, and universal design.

Teaching Important Mathematics to All Students

NCTM's Vision for School Mathematics imagines a classroom in which all students have the opportunity and means to learn important mathematics and to think mathematically, resources and technology are readily available, and teaching methods are flexible and innovative (NCTM 2000). These goals, as the authors of *Principles and Standards for School Mathematics* suggest, are ambitious but within reach, if we are willing to change our models for education. Step 1 in effecting change is a series of legislative acts that emphasize inclusiveness and equity in the classroom. Step 2 involves redefining learning goals within the context of inclusiveness—ensuring a challenging mathematics curriculum and high expectations for every student.

Legislation for Equity and Excellence

The need for change in how we conceptualize educational experiences is highlighted by several important legislative acts: the *Goals 2000: Educate America Act,* the *Individuals with Disabilities Education Improvement Act* (IDEA), and the *No Child Left Behind Act.*

Goals 2000: Educate America Act ties high standards for all students in mathematics to national goals:

- All students will leave grades 4, 8, and 12 having demonstrated competency in challenging subject matter, including . . . mathematics . . . ; and every school in America will ensure that all students learn to use their minds well. . . .
- United States students will be first in the world in mathematics and science achievement.

(Goals 2000)

Activities CD

For an example of an inclusive lesson about fractions, see Activity 88, Finding Fractions in Your Life, on the CD-ROM that accompanies this text.

The 2004 *Individuals with Disabilities Education Improvement Act* calls for instructional designs that both address individual needs and ensure access to the general curriculum. The content, methodology, or delivery of instruction must be specially designed to be inclusive rather than exclusive:

> Almost 30 years of research and experience has demonstrated that the education of children with disabilities can be made more effective by . . . having high expectations for such children and ensuring their access to the general education curriculum in the regular classroom, to the maximum extent possible.

(IDEA Section 1400[c][5])

A Mathematics and Science Initiative is a critical part of the *No Child Left Behind Act* of 2001. The rationale for the initiative echoes *Goals 2000:*

Activities CD

For an activity that connects the Stock Market with data collection and analysis, see Activity 76, $10,000 Stock Market Contest, on the CD-ROM that accompanies this text.

> [T]he public must realize that advances in technology and productivity, necessary for the United States to remain competitive in the global economy, depend on *all* students learning more mathematics and science than is currently required, and also on increasing the number of students who extend their mathematical knowledge beyond algebra so they may proceed to more advanced scientific and technical subjects.

(http://www.ed.gov.nclb, 1)

Key components of NCLB include the following:

- Partnerships between every sector of society and schools to improve achievement in mathematics and science

■ Incentives to attract excellent and experienced mathematics and science teachers,

■ Increased emphasis on research and measurement to find and demonstrate the most effective ways to teach mathematics and science.

("Facts," USDE 2004, 2)

Taken together, these statutes provide a legal mandate as well as a challenge. Traditionally, multitracking or grouping students according to abilities and needs has presented a rainbow of curricula—different methods, different content, different goals. Ensuring access to one general curriculum redefines the problem: Instead of multiple paths to multiple learning goals, we need multiple paths to the same goals; instead of a dichotomy between mainstream and alternative curricula, we need an integrated curriculum that makes learning essential mathematical concepts and important mathematics part of every child's educational experiences.

Important Mathematics

Of course, some type of mathematics instruction has always been part of every curriculum track; however, traditionally the focus of most curricula, especially those designed for students with special needs or learning challenges, has been on mastering facts and basic skills rather than on exploring the important mathematics of concepts, processes, or foundational ideas. Consider the classroom scenarios presented in the Windows on Learning box that begins on this page.

Topics, Issues, and Explorations

Both national statutes and the goals of national organizations, such as NCTM, have mandated mainstreaming students in mathematics instruction. In general terms, this means one curriculum and many paths of access, but what does it mean specifically for teachers and students? Search your own memories and experiences. Did you learn mathematics in a mainstreamed curriculum or a multitrack curriculum? How did the curriculum affect what teachers did in the classroom? How did it affect students? Did some students benefit more than others from the curriculum, or did all benefit equally?

Discuss your ideas and observations in a small group or class. As a group, make a list of challenges involved in mainstreaming mathematics instruction, and do some preliminary thinking about strategies to meet those challenges.

Activities CD

For another example of a money-counting activity, see Activity 10, How Much Money?, on the CD-ROM that accompanies this text.

Windows on Learning

Counting Money

Brian Murray's first-grade class was studying money values. While children in the most advanced group filled out worksheets that had them write and add amounts of money, children in a second group identified and counted coins.

The children sat around a table with paper and pencils in front of them. Mr. Murray stood in front of a chart and highlighted pictures of coins with his laser pointer.

"Today," said Mr. Murray, "we are going to learn about pennies, nickels, and dimes. Who can tell me what this is?" The laser touched a drawing of a penny.

No one answered. The children looked confused.

"That's a penny," Mr. Murray answered his own question. "A penny is one cent." He pointed to the number 1 and then to the symbol for cent.

"Now let's count the pennies in this row. All together: one penny, two pennies, three pennies, four pennies, five pennies."

The children followed along, counting aloud.

"Good! Now can anybody tell me what five pennies add up to?"

Again, no response. Mr. Murray waited a few seconds and then gave the answer.

"A nickel! Five pennies make a nickel, and a nickel is five cents." The laser touched the number 5 and the symbol for cent.

"Now can somebody name the coins in this row?" He pointed to the picture of a nickel followed by three pennies.

"Pennies?" Jamie asked more than said.

"Now they can't all be pennies. Look at how different this first coin is from the others. It's a different color, and it's bigger."

"Nickels?" Jamie tried again.

"Money Counts"

Deborah Friedland's class was a combined first and second grade in the Children's Workshop School.

Ms. Friedland described the objective of her lesson as working with money to develop number sense. To emphasize the connection with real-life experiences, she used actual coins.

The children sat on the carpet around a wooden box filled with coins. To begin the lesson, Ms. Friedland wrote the day's date on an easel set close to the floor at the children's eye level.

Nadia read the date, "June 11." Then Ms. Friedland focused on the number 11 and on translating it into coins.

"Who can show us one way to make 11 cents?"

"One dime and one penny," replied Kelly. She took coins from the box and lined them up on the carpet.

"Henry, come up and show another way to make 11 cents."

Henry put two nickels and a penny below Kelly's coins.

When all of the ways to represent 11 cents had been found, Marshall still thought he could find another way. Below a row with a nickel and six pennies, he put six pennies followed by a nickel.

"That looks different," spoke up a girl, "but it's not. It's still the same."

Ms. Friedland explained that the order was different but the composition of the 11 cents was not; then she praised Marshall for showing it a different way and for challenging himself and the other students to understand both the difference and the similarity.

"We can use the same coins and change the order, but it will still be worth the same amount of money."

Source: Adapted from "Money Counts," *Mathline* Elementary School Math Project video, (Washington, DC: PBS, 1997).

The emphasis in Brian Murray's lesson was upon learning facts—facts about the identity of coins and their value and number facts involved in counting. Because the entire lesson was done with paper illustrations, the information was more abstract than concrete; that is, the images Mr. Murray's pointer highlighted were representations of coins rather than the coins themselves. As a result, students seem unengaged and confused. They have difficulty identifying the pictures and making connections between pictures of pennies and pictures of nickels.

Deborah Friedland's lesson emphasized concepts. She started by asking students to identify the day's date. Then, to develop number sense, she had the children look at the number 11 from different perspectives: 11 as the date, 11 as money, 11 as different combinations of coins. Finding all of the different ways to make 11 cents with dimes, pennies, and nickels introduces students to the important mathematical idea of equivalence, and at the same time they learned that there can be multiple ways to represent a single value. Although Ms. Friedland's lesson focused on number concepts, she grounded students' explorations in the concrete by having students work with real coins. Later in an extension of the activity, she set up a classroom store where the children applied what they had learned. They used coins to buy materials to make puppets. Figure 2.1 shows how students determine how many nickels they would need to buy various treats from the school cafeteria.

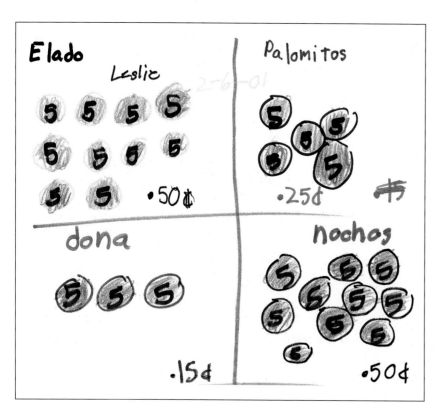

Figure 2.1 Exploring what nickels can buy.

NCTM's Description of Important Mathematics

What do we mean by "important mathematics"? NCTM's (2000) *Principles and Standards* describes it in this way:

> School mathematics curricula should focus on mathematics content that are worth the time and attention of students. Mathematics topics can be considered important for different reasons, such as their utility in developing other mathematical ideas, in linking different areas of mathematics or in deepening students' appreciation of mathematics as a discipline and a human creation. Ideas may also merit curricular focus because they are useful in representing and solving problems within or outside mathematics.

(15)

The authors of *Principles and Standards* list five categories of important mathematics:

1. *foundational ideas*—such as place value, equivalence, proportionality, function, rate of change;
2. *mathematical thinking and reasoning*—including making conjectures, developing sound arguments;
3. *concepts and processes*—such as symmetry and generalization;
4. *mathematics related to real-world phenomena;*
5. *concepts, skills, and processes supporting quantitative literacy*—developing the ability to judge claims, find fallacies, evaluate risks, and weigh evidence.

(NCTM 2000, 15–16; see also Price 1997)

Making the commitment to teach important mathematics to all students means letting go of the idea that learning mathematics is like climbing a pyramid, with a ground level of arithmetic facts accessible to everyone but with the higher levels of algebra, geometry, and advanced mathematics accessible only to those with exceptional abilities. A preservice teacher who described herself as "math anxious" once asked us not to use the word *mathematics*. "Math," she said, "is friendly. I can do math. Mathematics is for people who are smarter than me."

To make the big ideas and important processes of mathematics "friendly" calls for learning experiences that engage students and make concepts accessible. For example, the Googol and Mathematics in the Real World features emphasize big ideas, activities that challenge and stretch thinking, and experiences that make concepts real and alive. The Googol activity on Fibonacci numbers guides children to explore number patterns and series as well as applications of math in science; the Real World activity helps children generalize the number symbols they are learning and make connections with the world around them.

Topics, Issues, and Explorations

Identify some of the important mathematical concepts associated with money. Brainstorm in small groups ways to engage children in the first, second, or other grades to learn these concepts. Then create a two-column table listing concepts and concrete activities.

Activities CD

For an activity related to understanding patterns in number sequences, see Activity 63 on the CD-ROM that accompanies this text.

Topics, Issues, and Explorations

Teaching Children Mathematics and *Mathematics Teaching in the Middle School* are NCTM publications that feature action or classroom research and teaching ideas. Read and review strategies for teaching mathematics described in one or more articles. Discuss how the materials focus on important mathematics.

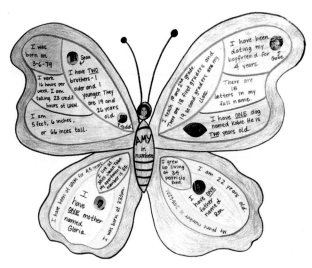

A preservice teacher represents the numbers in her life.

Googol: BIG IDEAS in Mathematics

Fibonacci Numbers

The series of numbers called Fibonacci numbers follow a simple but amazing pattern:

1. Start a number line with the numbers 0 and 1.

   0, 1

2. Add the first two numbers to get the third number in the line.

   0, 1, 1

3. Add the next two numbers to get the fourth number in the line.

   0, 1, 1, 2

4. Continue adding adjacent numbers to generate the Fibonacci series.

   0, 1, 1, 2, 3, 5, 8, 13 . . . .

Activity 1

Create a number line of Fibonacci numbers. Begin with 0 and continue the series for 25 numbers. Or see how many numbers you can calculate in 15 minutes.

Activity 2

Fibonacci, a 13th-century Italian, developed the series that is named for him in response to a problem about multiplying rabbits:

> Begin with a single pair of one-month-old rabbits. The rabbits and their offspring begin reproducing at two months old. Each pair produces a new pair each month. How many pairs of rabbits will there be after one month, two months, three months, four months, a year?

Use counters or other manipulatives to show how the rabbits multiply. Then make a chart such as a branching tree diagram of your findings. Do you find a pattern of Fibonacci numbers?

Activity 3

Look for Fibonacci numbers in nature. For example, count the number of petals in daisies, spirals in seeds of a sunflower, or right and left spirals in pine cones.

Note: For more about Fibonacci numbers and more activities, see "Fibonacci Numbers Introduction" at NetAdventure, http://www.concord.org/resources/netadventure.

Mathematics in the Real World

Numbers Everywhere

We live in a world filled with numbers. Dates, mailing addresses, telephone numbers, time of the day, rooms in our schools and other buildings, highways and street signs—all use numbers to organize and help us find our way through a complex world. Our finances—dollar amounts, credit card and bank account numbers, paychecks, and taxes—use the language of numbers. Even our identities are often tied to numbers, such as our Social Security numbers.

Encouraging students to identify and understand the numbers around them is an important step in helping them appreciate numbers as an important tool for making sense of the world and for daily living.

Activity

Choose a number between 1 and 100. Write the number you choose in words and in numerals. Look for your number in the world around you.

Look for it in your schoolroom. Look in books, on the walls, in the teacher's desk, out the window.

Look for it at home. Look in the kitchen, in the living room, in the garage, in your bedroom.

Look for it on the street. Look at house numbers, street signs, license plates.

Look for it at the store. Look at prices, signs, labels.

Make a list or draw a record in pictures of all the places you found your number. Tell about what you learned.

Understanding How Students Learn Mathematics

The national mandate to teach all students important mathematics raises several foundational questions:

- How do students learn?
- What does it mean to learn mathematics?
- What approaches to learning mathematics work best?
- How do we factor in the diversity of student populations as we set goals and teach mathematics?

A good starting point to answering these questions is the ideas about and approaches to learning that have shaped the way we teach mathematics, both in the past and in the present.

Changing Perspectives of Learning

During the 20th century, mathematics educators saw changes not only in the bottom line—*what* students should learn—but also in our understanding of *how* children learn. No longer do we recommend giving children lists of facts to memorize and conditioning them to manipulate numbers automatically, without thinking. No longer do we assume that children's imitating an electronic calculator equals children's excelling in mathematics.

Today we emphasize mathematical reasoning and understanding (NCTM 2000). We go beyond *how* and *what* to *why* and *how come*. Children learn by exploring, by problem solving, by being young scientists—collecting and interpreting data, posing and testing hypotheses. Instead of hushed depositories of knowledge, classrooms are active and often noisy laboratories. Instead of oracles of knowledge, teachers are facilitators and guides. Instead of passive recipients of knowledge, children act to experience, construct, and represent ideas. Instead of doing pages of drills, students might create images such as those in Figure 2.2 that connect geometric shapes and words about them.

These changes in teaching mathematics reflect dramatic changes in the way we look at learning and learners. In the mid-20th century, behaviorism influenced educators to emphasize observable behaviors; later, cognitive psychology and constructivism shifted the focus to thinking and mental processes. Today's methods are not so much a flat rejection of earlier ideas as they are a blending of approaches based on a variety of learning theories. On the one hand, classroom dynamics and activities show the influence of cognitive psychology and constructivism with learning experiences that emphasize discovery, collaboration, and creativity. On the other hand, some of the best ideas of behaviorism, such as step-by-step instruction, learning for mastery (including repeated testing), the importance of immediate feedback, and recognition that students learn at different rates are reflected in computer-assisted learning programs and performance-based curricula.

Activities CD

For an activity that helps students develop number sense, see Activity 7, Walking on the Googol Side, on the CD-ROM that accompanies this text.

Activities CD

For an activity utilizing student drawings and observations in the study of geometric shapes, see Activity 39, "Buggy" Geometry, on the CD-ROM that accompanies this text.

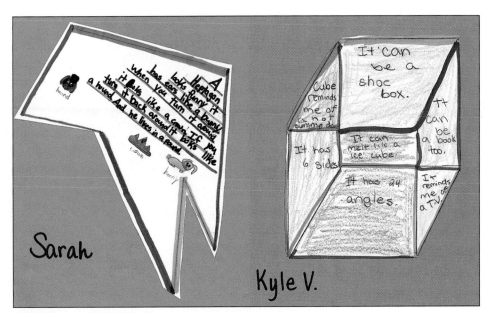

Figure 2.2 Connecting geometric shapes with drawings and words.

For an activity that emphasizes math facts, see Activity 32, Multiplication and Division: Maps of Facts, on the CD-ROM that accompanies this text.

Examining Behaviorist Learning Theory

Reduced to its simplest, observable behaviors, the learning process as envisioned by behaviorists seems relatively simple. Students are trained step-by-step, to repeat behaviors that lead to a desired result. Teachers "shape" the process by constructing "carefully arranged sequences of contingencies leading to the terminal performances which are the object of education" (Skinner 1972, 195). Teachers study only the external actions of their students, behaviors they can observe with the senses and measure or record quantitatively. "The teacher begins with whatever behavior the student brings to the instructional situation, by selective reinforcement, he [sic] changes that behavior so that a given terminal performance is more and more closely approximated" (Skinner 1972, 195)

Learning mathematics in a behaviorist way often begins with a test to discover what the student already knows; it then proceeds through a series of carefully sequenced exercises that lead systematically to the learning objective. The teacher's role consists primarily of finding the beginning point and setting conditions for the learning experience, adapting various programmed materials to match the student's needs, and reinforcing (encouraging, rewarding, providing positive feedback) correct responses. The object here is not trial-and-error learning or learning by mistakes. "At best," according to leading behaviorist B. F. Skinner (1972), the student "learns not to make mistakes again" (202–3).

Predictably, behaviorist learning emphasizes the roles of materials, the learning environment, and learning systems and deemphasizes the role of teachers and the "thinking" activity of learners. "Teaching," says Skinner (1972), "is the expediting of learning. Students learn without teaching, but the teacher arranges conditions under which they learn more rapidly and effectively" (195). To this end, some early behaviorists focused on the development of materials for programmed instruction and teaching machines to deliver that instruction (see Keller 1968 and Martinez and Martinez 1988 for contrasting views of the role of teaching in learning).

Figure 2.3 shows an example of programmed instruction as it might appear in a printed textbook. One side of the page contains the sequenced information; the other side, set off with lines, gives prompts and answers for the preceding frame. Students studying a programmed text usually cover the answers while they work their way down the page, composing their own responses before they look at the printed answers.

Figure 2.4 on page 36 shows an updated and more technically sophisticated example of a programmed instruction sequence from the popular Math Blaster computer program. Computers allow more imaginative presentations and more flexible responses, but the basic approach of programmed instruction remains the same:

- identify specific learning objectives—ideas, facts to be learned, or skill to be developed;
- divide concept or skill into its smallest increments;
- sequence increments;
- shape the learning path with responses that give information as well as reinforcement.

Topics, Issues, and Explorations

Try your hand at writing a step-by-step sequence for a math concept or procedure, such as adding fractions to make a whole. Develop a series of closed-ended tasks—that is, tasks that typically have one correct answer—leading step-by-step to your objective. If you have experience with computer programming, you may want to write responses for some common errors as well as the target answers. Otherwise, you might use the split-page format of programmed texts. Ask a friend or a classmate to review your lesson by working through the sequence. Does it make sense? Are there any gaps in the steps? Is the lesson interesting? Would it be interesting to children as is, or would you need to make changes to engage them?

Pretest	Answers
Try these questions. Check your own answers. Each question is worth 5 points. If your score is 20 or higher, you should not need this program.	Cover the answers until you have responded to each question. Then check the frame below and to the right of the question.
1. Identify the shape. 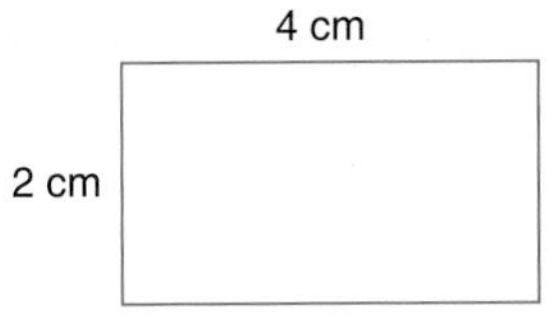 4 cm 2 cm Is this a square? Is this a quadrilateral? Is this a triangle? Is this a circle?	(Answer in frame below.)
2. Half of the shape as dotted would be what shape? 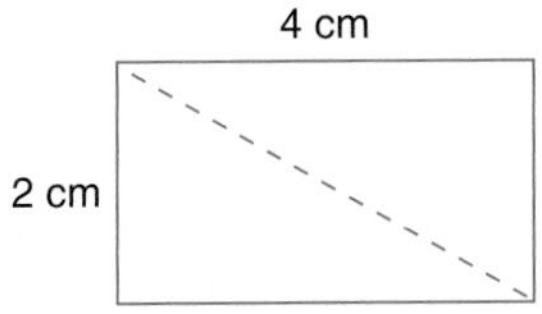 4 cm 2 cm Two rectangles? Two equilateral triangles? Two isoceles triangles? Two right triangles?	A quadrilateral.
3. What is a right angle?	Two right triangles.
4. Can you draw a rectangle 1 cm by 2 cm by 1 cm by 3 cm?	An angle in the corner of a rectangle or square, an "upright' angle of 90°.
5. Identify the circumference, the diameter, and the radius of the circle below. 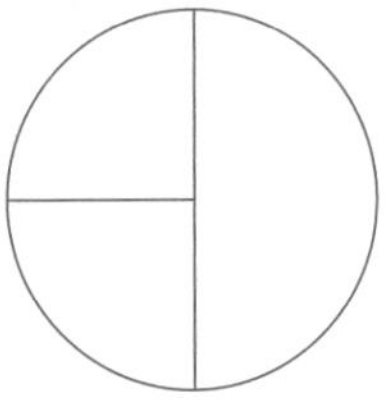	No, opposite sides are equal in a rectangle.
6. What is pi? How can you compute it?	*Diameter* is the line across the center; *radius*, the line from the center to the edge; *circumference*, the distance around.
	Pi is 3.14159. Pi is equal to the circumference of a circle divided by the diameter.

Figure 2.3 Programmed learning text.
Source: Adapted from ideas presented in Leedham and Unwin (1965, 60–61).

Contrasting Views of Children's Learning

One implication of some of the more extreme behaviorist strategies could be that a child is a learning machine. Seeing children's learning as machinelike focuses attention on input and output—the materials put in the machines and the results or answers that come out of them. From this perspective, correct input should lead to correct output and vice versa or, in computer slang, GIGO (garbage in/garbage out). However, approaching learning in terms of mental or thought processes has led to different ways of looking at both the products and the processes of mathematics education. Seeing children as thinkers, problem solvers, or even information processors

Space Zapper 1

Instructions: Help Blasternaut chase Gelator to the planet Moldar! You'll earn energy shots by correctly answering math problems, then use the shots to zap space objects for bonus points.

Math Round: Multiplication, Middle Level.

Math Problem	Player's Answer	Program Response	
		Audio	**Visual**
6 x 6 =	32	bloop	——
6 x 6 =	76	bloop	——
6 x 6 =	35	bloop	——
2 x 6 =	12	zap	red energy charge game points
6 x 6 =	36	zap	red energy charge game points
5 x 5 =	25	zap	red energy charge game points
5 x 1 =	5	zap	red energy charge game points

Reinforcement: Game time to shoot asteroids and satellites. Each shot uses energy charges from math round.

Figure 2.4 Programmed learning computer program.
Source: From Davidson & Associates (1999).

Activities CD

For an activity about multiplicative thinking, see Activity 29, "A Remainder of One," on the CD-ROM that accompanies this text.

shifts the focus to how children's minds work with information and how they arrive at results. From this perspective, the emphasis is not so much upon correctly inputting and outputting math facts, such as $5^2 = 25$, but upon understanding the concepts of squaring and using exponents and developing strategies for working with these ideas.

The following brief dialogues contrast the views of child as learning machine with child as thinker. The first dialogue depicts a learning sequence that is simple and easy to control; the second, a learning experience that is complex, with the potential for chaos as well as creativity.

Child as Learning Machine

Teacher: Watch closely as I hold up the flash cards. As soon as you have the answer, raise your hand. (She holds up a card with 6×6). Jaime, what's the answer?

Jaime: 6 times 6 is 30.

Teacher: No, try again.

Jaime: 32?

Teacher: No. Anyone else? Elena?

Elena: 6 times 6 is 36.

Teacher: Correct. Next card . . . .

Child as Thinker

Teacher: What happens when you multiply something by 2?

Student 1: You double it.

Teacher: What does that mean?

Student 2: You get twice as much.

Teacher: Can you show me?

Student 2: (working with frog-shaped counters) You have two frogs and then add two more.

Teacher: What if you started with four frogs?

Student 3: Here's four frogs and four more, five, six, seven, eight frogs.

Student 2: That's two times as many.

Teacher: How about 2 times a bigger number, like 20 or 40?

Student 1: We can't.

Teacher: Why not?

Student 1: We don't have enough frogs.

Teacher: Could you show the numbers another way?

Student 3: We could draw them.

Student 2: Or just make marks. (Makes and counts slashes on a piece of paper.) Two times 20 is 40. It will take longer to figure out 2 times 40.

Student 3: No, just count the marks over again. (Counts slashes starting with 40.) That makes 80.

Teacher: So what happens when we multiply 40 by 2?

Student 1: You get 80. That's twice what you get when you multiply 2 times 20.

Exploring Cognitive and Early Constructivist Learning Theories

What goes on inside children's heads when they learn mathematics? Gestalt psychologists from the early 20th century might answer, "Insights." An insight occurs when children put together information and arrive at answers that are greater than the sum of the parts—for example, finding the pattern in the series 1, 1, 2, 3, 5, 8 and inferring the basic idea of the Fibonacci sequence. Jerome Bruner—a contemporary derided by behaviorists as a "mentalist"—would add, "Concept learning and discovery learning." Exploring the pattern in the series results in discovering the concept of Fibonacci numbers.

Both Bruner and Jean Piaget tie mental processes to cognitive development. Bruner's (1971) idea of a *spiral curriculum* calls for reteaching basic concepts as minds mature and processes become more complex. Geometric figures, then, would be introduced to preschoolers with attractive shapes to be touched, ordered, and matched and revisited several times in the early grades to examine area, perimeters, and perhaps fractals.

Piaget depicts learning as a natural process in which physical growth and action are linked to mental growth and action (Sund 1976; Mayer 1992). How children learn and what they learn depend, according to Piaget, upon their developmental stage. As they interact physically and mentally with their environment, children develop mental structures or schemes to organize what they have learned. These structures are built by mental action, which follows a process that can be compared to balancing weights on a beam (see Figure 2.5). Initially, there is a state of balance or equilibrium; the learner is comfortable with previously learned concepts. When a new idea or information is introduced, the balance is disturbed, and the learner is in disequilibrium. Dealing with this new material requires two important mental activities: assimilation and accommodation. *Assimilation* fits

Math and Technology

Computers and Programmed Learning

Early attempts at programmed learning often resulted in learning experiences that were thorough but dull; moreover, the careful sequencing of tasks and material tended to eliminate the challenge of learning and promote passive rather than active learning strategies. Modern computer programs counteract these flaws by setting sequenced material in imaginative contexts.

The popular Math Blaster series (Davidson & Associates 1999) engages learners in a series of adventures and games. The emphasis is upon learning various math facts and making quick calculations. Repeatable activities with different levels of difficulty drill children in basic skills. Math-help options give how-to explanations and extend information represented in the games.

Reinforcement, positive and negative, is built into activities. Correct answers and high scores are rewarded with video-arcade-style games. Incorrect answers threaten the mission and may cause the Blasternaut to be trampled by trolls or zapped by radioactive space goo.

The series includes discs for each grade, kindergarten to fifth. See www.blasternaut.com.

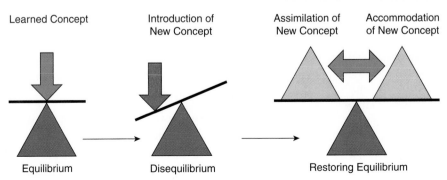

Learned Concept   Introduction of New Concept   Assimilation of New Concept   Accommodation of New Concept

Equilibrium   Disequilibrium   Restoring Equilibrium

Figure 2.5 Learning as a process of disturbing and restoring equilibrium.
Source: Adapted from Sund (1976, 7–8).

new information into existing mental structures. *Accommodation* modifies an existing structure or structures to fit new information (Piaget and Inhelder 1973). For example, suppose a child has developed mental structures to understand addition of single-digit numbers. When she begins adding double-digit numbers, she might first try adding the different columns separately.

$$
\begin{array}{c|c}
1 & 9 \\
+\,1 & 4 \\
\hline
2 & 13
\end{array}
$$

If she uses concrete objects such as counting blocks or sticks to explore her answer, she will find a result of 33 rather than 213. Reconciling this answer with her understanding of adding single-digit numbers will require adjustment to the earlier mental structures as well as connections with ideas about place value and carrying.

Constructing Mathematical Knowledge

A major effect of encouraging teachers to see children as thinkers has been to challenge the copy machine model of education. According to the copy machine model, knowledge consists of a body of facts and skills; the teacher's job is to transmit those facts and skills, and the student's or learner's job is to duplicate the facts and skills. Presumably, the more exact the copy, the greater the learning. However, constructivist views of learning and thinking have led to a different, more complex model.

Basically, constructivists believe that "ideas are not given from one person to another like so many packages but, rather, are actively constructed by each person" (Biehler and Snowman 1993, 16). Children learn mathematics, then, from active experiences that enable them to develop mathematical knowledge structures. According to Piaget (1967), who is considered a founder of constructivism, these structures are not copies of something objective and unchanging but an interpretation of experience.

Even the structures most necessary to the adult mind, such as the logico-mathematical structures, are not innate in the child; they are built up little by little. . . . There are no innate structures: every structure presupposes a construction. All these constructions originate from prior structures.
(149–50).

A preservice teacher once called this view the Lego model of learning mathematics. Children build their understanding of mathematics little by little like a Lego construction, and the activity never really ends. The process of building, changing, adding to goes on and on.

Bruner (1966) touches on the idea of building knowledge with his spiral curriculum. He also emphasizes the importance of learning-as-process.

To instruct someone in [a] discipline is not a matter of getting him [or her] to commit results to mind. Rather, it is to teach him [or her] to participate in the process that makes possible the establishment of knowledge. We teach a subject not to produce little living libraries on the subject, but rather to get a student to think mathematically for himself [or herself], to consider matters as an historian does, to take part in the process of knowledge-getting. Knowing is a process, not a product.

(72)

The Idea File, "Constructivism Applied to Learning Mathematics," shows some of the key principles of constructivism and their applications to learning mathematics. Generally these ideas have underscored the mathematics reform movement. Implementing them is changing not only how we teach mathematics but also what mathematics we teach.

 **Idea Files**

Constructivism Applied to Learning Mathematics

Principles of Constructivism	Applications to Learning Mathematics
1. Knowledge is acquired through exploration.	1. A problem-solving approach can make learning concepts an adventure.
2. Curiosity, enthusiasm, and interest open the gates for learning.	2. Tying mathematics learning to children's interests and worlds engages and motivates.
3. Social interaction and collaboration are important ingredients for both learning and development and are essential for constructing social knowledge.	3. Working together on projects and activities makes learning mathematics a social rather than a solitary effort. Collaboration may also foster cognitive conflict and decentering as children learn to deal with conflicting viewpoints.
4. Children need intellectual autonomy to find their own paths to learning.	4. Encouraging children to develop and test their own algorithms liberates mathematics learning from teacher- and textbook-driven models.
5. Construction of knowledge builds on previous structures.	5. Learning to ask *why* rather than *what*, to reason mathematically rather than to memorize mathematical facts allows knowledge to be structured on a solid foundation.
6. Knowledge structures are continually modified to reflect changing interpretations of experience.	6. Substituting open-ended problem solving for close-ended exercises, such as calculation sets, promotes reflective thinking and accommodation.
7. Meaningful learning emphasizes process rather than product.	7. Emphasizing effective problem-solving processes rather than getting the right answer allows for thinking outside set paths.
8. Meaningful learning allows for ambiguity—multiple answers and representations.	8. Understanding that there may be more than one way to solve a problem and even more than one correct answer encourages children to think like mathematicians instead of calculators.
9. Meaningful learning is active rather than passive.	9. Hands-on learning with manipulatives, lab experiences, and fieldwork makes mathematics three-dimensional and real.
10. Teachers need to be models and guides rather than transmitters of knowledge.	10. Teachers who love mathematics and are confident about their own knowledge are more likely to have students who are motivated to learn and confident about their ability to learn mathematics.

Sources: Wadsworth (1996, 147–61); Biehler and Snowman (1993, 428–30); Martinez and Martinez (1996, 27–40, 55–68).

Matching Teaching to Learning: Models for Diversity

For an activity that emphasizes diversity in working with whole numbers, see Activity 36, Calculating with Chinese Stick Math, on the CD-ROM that accompanies this text.

Research about learning offers a number of useful insights for teaching every student meaningful and important mathematics. One of the most fundamental involves recognizing the value of diversity in learning strategies and understanding that no one learning theory or method will provide a perfect fit for all students. From behaviorism we can gain useful insights for defining learning outcomes, setting performance standards, and sequencing instruction. From cognitive theories come insights about learning processes and developmental states; and from constructivism, ways to make learning active and personal so that students build or construct knowledge in ways that make sense to them and give them a degree of control over the learning process as well as a kind of ownership of the knowledge itself.

Using these insights effectively calls for developing teaching/learning models that respond directly to issues of diversity and accessibility as well as to concerns about standards and goals. Characteristics of effective models include flexibility, multiplicity, and accountability:

- **flexibility** to change methods and materials to match the needs of different students and student groups;
- **multiplicity** to provide more than one way to approach learning tasks and outcomes;
- **accountability** to ensure universal access to instruction and opportunity to excel.

Models that apply what we have discovered from research, meet the needs of diverse student populations, and set high standards for all students include Mastery Learning, Inquiry-Based Learning, and Universal Design for Learning Mathematics.

Mastery Learning

Learning for mastery, as the name suggests, assumes that all students can master mathematics. It draws on behaviorists' concerns with defining and assessing learning outcomes and sequencing learning with step-by-step objectives. Key principles include the following:

1. Setting specific goals and objectives for learning
2. Allowing for differences in pace of learning
3. Providing compensatory instruction where needed
4. Providing multiple opportunities to succeed
5. Individualizing learning plans

(Martinez and Martinez 1996, 131)

For self-paced computer-based lessons about equivalence, see Activity 66, Equivalence, on the CD-ROM that accompanies this text.

Teachers set goals, provide support and direction, and evaluate outcomes. Students work for the most part individually, at their own pace. Learning materials might be sequenced, step-by-step instructions in texts or computer programs that similarly introduce concepts and demonstrate procedures step by step. Feedback on tasks is immediate, whether from a computer, teacher assessments, or self-assessment as students check their own work.

A distinguishing feature of Mastery Learning is high standards. Usually students must achieve a score of 80% or higher on tests to demonstrate mastery and proceed to the next task or concept. Repeated testing (different versions of each test or measure) lets students continue the learning process until they achieve mastery.

Mastery Learning is flexible because it allows students to work at their own rate and in their own way. It allows teachers to individualize instruction, fitting learning to student needs. And it applies high standards universally with multiple opportunities to excel.

As a model for teaching mathematics, Mastery Learning has a long and generally successful record. Many computer programs, especially those that emphasize learning math facts and basic skills, use this model. (For an overview of Mastery Learning and discussions of its advantages and disadvantages, see Keller 1968; Martinez and Martinez 1988, 1996).

Inquiry-Based Learning

Using inquiry to engage students and shape the learning process lets learners select and use problem-solving techniques that work best for them as well as to some extent set their own pace and direction for learning. Compared to traditional models, Inquiry-Based Learning appears to turn instructional patterns upside down. Traditionally, mathematics classes begin with answers—algorithms or concepts to be learned, facts to be memorized—and end with questions in exercises and tests. Teaching mathematics as inquiry follows a different pattern and calls for different types of mathematical thinking. Instead of beginning with answers, Inquiry-Based Learning begins with questions and contexts. These guide students toward discovering and constructing their own answers and meanings.

Key components of successful Inquiry-Based Learning include

- questions that connect and engage students;
- meaningful contexts or problems that challenge and demand critical thinking;
- tools and materials, both virtual and actual, that promote hands-on or active investigations.

The activities on the CD-ROM, *Activities for Developing Mathematical Thinking,* that accompanies this text follow a three-stage process of guided inquiry (Martinez 1988, 2001; Lawson and Renner 1975):

Stage 1 **explore** the concepts
Stage 2 **invent** or construct mental structures and tools to deal with the concepts
Stage 3 **discover** ways to understand, connect, apply, and extend the concepts.

In the classroom, this strategy allows teachers to focus tightly or broadly, to end or extend the investigative process, and to match learning objectives to the performance and assessment goals of a variety of mathematics curricula. Study begins with questions that engage students, set a context, and help focus the inquiry process. Students work first to understand and relate to the mathematical situations. They **explore** relationships and meanings with hands-on methods and manipulatives that let them model and visualize mathematical situations and in effect experience them directly. As students work, they **invent** and test problem-solving strategies and even construct their own procedures and algorithms. And through the process of investigating, students **discover** the meanings implicit in mathematical situations and learn to extend, connect, and apply their discoveries.

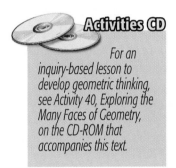

For an inquiry-based lesson to develop geometric thinking, see Activity 40, Exploring the Many Faces of Geometry, on the CD-ROM that accompanies this text.

For an inquiry-based activity to explore standard and nonstandard units of measurement, see Activity 50, Making Measurement Tools with Nonstandard and Standard Units, on the CD-ROM that accompanies this text.

Universal Design on the Web

Several Web sites offer updated information on universal design.

The Center for Applied Special Technology (CAST) emphasizes Universal Design for Learning. Its site offers get-acquainted tours on theory, practice, research, and related topics. It also provides Bobby software to help users assess the accessibility of homepages. Available at http://www.cast.org.

The National Center to Improve the Tools of Educators (NCITE) provides some background information but includes projects and reviews of research. Particularly interesting for mathematics education is a review of research devoted to "efficient math instruction." Available at http://idea.uoregon.edu/~ncite/.

TRACE, which focuses on technology and disability, gives general information about universal design, including the seven major principles. Available at http://www.trace.wisc.edu/.

Universal Design for Learning Mathematics

Another model for effective math teaching and learning is based on the idea that we can and should develop a flexible approach that avoids the inequities of multitracking and makes mathematics universally accessible. A concept borrowed from architecture, Universal Design, suggests a way to do this. The key word here is *universal*. "What makes the design 'universal' is that the adaptations . . . not only allow access to those who have disabilities but they make it easier for everyone to use the space" (Orkwis and McLane 1998, 8). In architecture, this concept means designing and building sidewalks that, on the one hand, allow wheelchair access and, on the other hand, make access easier for everyone else as well—parents with baby carriages, people with shopping carts, workers with heavy loads, walkers, runners, and so forth. In learning mathematics, Universal Design means a teaching/learning model that incorporates the many and diverse needs of students and at the same time provides for common goals and standards. It means a model that recognizes there is more than one way to teach and learn concepts, more than one way to solve problems, and more than one way to demonstrate competency and assess progress.

Figure 2.6 shows how flexibility is built into a Universal Design teaching/learning model. Each element of instruction—engagement, representation, expression, assessment—includes not one but many methods and strategies (see Orkwis and McLane 1998, 3). (For more about Universal Design for Learning, see the Math and Technology feature "Universal Design on the Web.")

Multiple methods of engagement or of getting students involved in the work allow teachers to draw "materials, experiences, and supports . . . from a

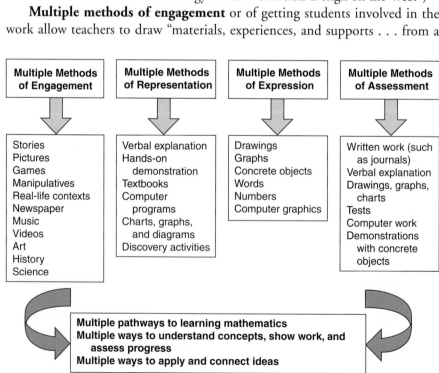

Figure 2.6 Universal Design for Learning Mathematics
Source: Adapted from **www.cast.org**.

wide range of sources," making learning experiences more current, relevant, and "real" (CAST 1998, 2). **Multiple methods of representation** provide different perspectives so that each student can find the explanation or illustration that speaks to her or him as well as broaden understanding by seeing the material from different perspectives. This flexibility similarly allows students to show or express the work in different ways. **Multiple expressions** improve the reliability of evaluation since students can help select the means that best demonstrate their accomplishments (See, for example, Caycel's use of computer graphics to illustrate her word problem about monkeys in Figure 2.7 and Michael's drawings of geometric shapes in Figure 2.8). And **multiple methods of assessment** ensure that understanding in its many shapes and manifestations is both recognized and credited.

To universally design mathematics learning experiences, we need to—

- develop activities that can be approached at different levels;
- build into learning materials the potential for different learning patterns and outcomes;
- make students major players in the learning process by allowing them to choose problem-solving strategies and representations that fit individual learning styles and needs;
- select themes and contexts that engage students' interest and emphasize real-life applications of concepts;
- involve parents and the world of information and resources outside the classroom;
- take advantage of technology for resources and cognitive learning tools or "mind tools" that "enable learners to represent and express what they know" (Jonassen, Peck, and Wilson et al. 1999, 152–153; see also Harvey and Charnitski 1998);
- build in flexibility to enable materials to be updated and revised continually, allowing them to remain current and responsive—both to changes in the world and to individual strengths and interests (CAST 1998).

Many of the key ideas of a universally designed model for learning mathematics parallel those of the mathematics reform movement, including the NCTM Standards. The Idea Files feature on page 44 outlines some of the key principles of Universal Design applied to Universal Design for Learning Mathematics. The chart suggests how NCTM's Standards 2000 equity principle and commitment to developing teaching strategies and materials that make learning mathematics accessible to all students closely match Universal Design's central vision: "to achieve best instructional practices and meet the needs of diverse learners and learning contexts" (CAST 1998, 1).

The mathematics and sports module featured in the Lesson Pro-File of this chapter maximized student involvement by matching medium and message to the audience—a fourth-grade class with special needs students, including both those with learning and with physical challenges. In previous

There were 3 monkeys swinging on the rainbow. Two more monkeys came. Then seven more came, and two left. Now how many monkeys are there?
$3 + 2 + 7 - 2 =$

Figure 2.7 Caycel's word problem represented on the computer.

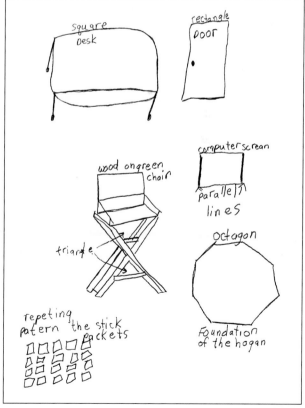

Figure 2.8 Michael finds geometric shapes and properties in the classroom.

Idea Files

Principles of Universal Design Applied to Universal Design for Learning Mathematics

Universal Design (UD)*	Universal Design for Learning Mathematics (UDLM)
Principle 1: Equitable Use	
The design is useful and marketable to people with diverse abilities.	The curriculum design for mathematics is usable and user-friendly, engaging students with diverse abilities and educational backgrounds.
Principle 2: Flexibility in Use	
The design accommodates a wide range of individual preferences and abilities.	The curriculum design accommodates students with different learning styles and abilities and is responsive to both cognitive and affective dimensions of learning mathematics.
Principle 3: Simple and Intuitive	
Use of the design is easy to understand, regardless of the user's experience, knowledge, language skills, or current concentration level.	The curriculum design allows for engagement at a variety of levels, with learning opportunities spiraling from the simple to the complex. Methods and materials are designed to "make sense" to multiage and multiability groups.
Principle 4: Perceptible Information	
The design communicates necessary information effectively to the user, regardless of ambient conditions or the user's sensory abilities.	Information is presented in different modes—pictorial, verbal, tactile—for multiple access. Responses to information are also flexible, with multiple representations and also multiple assessment.
Principle 5: Tolerance for Error	
The design minimizes hazards and the adverse consequences of accidental or unintended actions.	Errors in reasoning and answers to math problems are accepted as learning opportunities, continuing rather than ending the learning process.
Principle 6: Low Physical Effort	
The design can be used efficiently and comfortably with a minimum of fatigue.	The curriculum offers multiple means of both physical and cognitive access to mathematics, providing technology as mind tools as well as physical tools to extend learners' reach and support their efforts.
Principle 7: Size and Space for Approach and Use	
Appropriate size and space are provided for approach, reach, manipulation, and use regardless of user's body size, posture, or mobility.	Appropriate materials, methods, and opportunities are provided to allow learners to approach and explore concepts, including important mathematical ideas and applications, regardless of their background or attainments in mathematics.

Source of Principles: TRACE, University of Wisconsin, http://www.trace.wisc.edu. (click on "Designing a More Usable World")

activities, nearly a fifth of the class had not participated. All of the students participated in this activity, with the special needs students doing their best work of the semester. Overall, the module helped students develop a new perspective on mathematics as a real-world rather than a textbook subject and at the same time to discover the importance of mathematics to themselves personally.

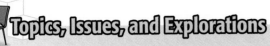
Topics, Issues, and Explorations

Observe two mathematics lessons taught by different teachers. Discuss the level of student involvement. Who participated the most? The least? Why? Was there a difference in the level of participation between the classes? Why or why not? What efforts did the teacher make to encourage all students to participate?

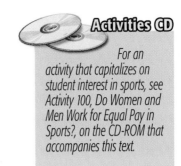
Activities CD

For an activity that capitalizes on student interest in sports, see Activity 100, Do Women and Men Work for Equal Pay in Sports?, on the CD-ROM that accompanies this text.

Lesson Pro-File

The Mathematics and Sports Module

Overall goals for the project were to help students develop a new perspective on mathematics as a real-world rather than a school and textbook subject and at the same time to discover the importance of mathematics to themselves personally. Other goals included

- engaging students who were underachieving in mathematics,
- developing a learning module that could be customized to match a variety of learning styles and goals,
- involving parents in the learning process,
- providing context and themes for multistep problems and extensions—problem-solving that builds on problem solving and works in contexts,
- allowing for flexibility in both accessing resources and representing outcomes, and
- making students part of the selection process for learning materials and outcomes.

The learning experience was essentially open ended, with a set of related activities to shape and direct students' study. Students could work alone or in groups, but all were encouraged to seek help from parents, siblings, or friends who had direct experience of the sport they were researching. The resources to be used and the form of the outcome were also open. Students were encouraged to write, draw, graph, discuss, and act out their findings. The final activity was a show-and-tell-style presentation, with the methods and materials again left up to the students. Scoring for the project was by a point system—20 points for each activity.

Assignment

Mathematics and Sports
A Universally Designed Learning Module

Activity 1 Choose a sport to research for math ideas. Find information about the sport from newspapers, magazines, the Internet, or interviews with people who play the sport.   20 points

Activity 2 Describe the math you find in the sport. Look for things like the size and shape of the field, the scoring systems, and the size or weight of equipment.   20 points

Activity 3 Does the math in this sport make sense to you? Explain it as though you were teaching a friend to play.   20 points

Activity 4 Think about what you learned from this activity. What did you learn about this sport? What did you learn about math?   20 points

Activity 5 Tell the class what you learned. Describe the sport. Explain the math.   20 points

Procedure

A fourth-grade class of 20 students, 11 boys and 9 girls, was given 10 days to complete the project.

For Activity 1, children photocopied, printed, or made handwritten copies of their source materials, including articles from encyclopedias, newspapers, magazines, books, and the Internet. Several watched games on television and wrote their own commentaries.

Activity 2 resulted in detailed descriptions of scoring systems, equipment needed to play, and numbers related to players, innings, and playing time.

Activity 3, which focused on making sense of the mathematics in the sport, drew some interesting responses. While their discussions of the mathematics content in sports focused on reporting numbers, students' explanations for this activity seemed to emphasize problem solving and operations.

In Activity 4, students tied what they had learned about sports math to some of the things their class had been working on, including division, averages, and fractions.

For Activity 5, the show-and-tell exercise, children used visual displays such as maps, charts, models, and drawings.

Overall, the class seemed surprised by the amount of mathematics content in sports. One student wrote, "It turned out that you really half [sic] to work as well as think." And another wrote, "I learned more about math and how to put math in sports. . . . I figured out how to do it and I understand it."

Outcomes

The mathematics-in-sports project fulfilled the objectives set for it and at the same time demonstrated the effectiveness of the Universal Design for Learning concepts. Previously the participation rate for students in this fourth-grade class averaged no more than 80 percent for math activities. Participation for the sports-math activities was 100%, with most parents involved, interested, and helping their children gather and make sense of information. Enthusiasm for the project was high; several children asked for additional activities of this type. And children's levels of engagement and understanding were equally high. None expressed frustration or confusion about concepts or information. All were confident that they had discovered and understood the mathematics in their sports, and all were able to reflect on, explain, and apply what they had learned.

> *Margarita*
>
> Dimensions of the playing field – a rectangular area ranging in size from about 29 meters by 15 meters (about 94 ft by 50 ft) to about 22 meters by 13 meters (about 74 ft by 42 ft.)
>
> At each end of the court is a vertical backboard measuring usually about 2 m by 1 m (about 6 ft by 4 ft) The baskets are attached firmly to the backboards about 3 m (about 10 ft.) above the playing surface. Each basket is about 46 cm (about 18 in.) in diameter and consists of a horizontal hoop, or metal ring, from which a fringe of wide-meshed white netting is hung. The regulation basketball is an inflated, leather- or nylon-covered sphere that weighs from 567 to 624 g (20 to 22 oz) and has a circumference of about 76 cm (about 30 in.)

◀◀◀ LOOKING BACK

At the turn of the century, legislative acts and mathematics reformers called for sweeping changes in mathematics education. Instead of multiple curricula to match differing needs and educational objectives, educators began to work toward providing all students with access to the mainstream curriculum. Emphasizing "important" mathematics—foundation ideas, concepts, processes, life applications—became not only a goal but also a benchmark for curriculum development; instead of skills development and mathematics facts, the focus shifted to mathematics problem solving and reasoning for students of every age and ability level.

At the same time, ideas about how children learn mathematics changed dramatically. An emphasis on student behaviors gave way to an emphasis on student thinking and learning processes. Constructivism led to major changes in teaching methods and materials, including a tolerance for ambiguity, emphasis on hands-on learning, and changes in roles for both teachers and students. Models for mathematics teaching including Mastery Learning, Inquiry-Based Learning, and Universal Design for Learning Mathematics emphasize the ideals of flexibility and equity in mathematics instruction.

Questions for Further Thought, Discussion, and Research

1. Critics sometimes claim that teaching all students mathematics means teaching no one mathematics well. Does teaching important mathematics to all students somehow dilute the educational experience for the majority? Does it in fact rob the gifted few of a quality education? What do you think?

2. "Important" mathematics has often been considered an elite subject—something for the gifted or the college bound. How might this view have contributed to some current attitudes about learning mathematics, including math anxiety? How might a change in curriculum lead to changes in attitude? Do you think this is already happening? Why or why not?

3. Many math computer games and activities use programmed learning techniques. Review one or more software programs (such as Math Blaster), and evaluate them as learning experiences.

4. Is there a place in today's classroom for memorizing math facts? Educators disagree about the importance of memorization in learning mathematics. Many agree that rote learning can tend toward meaningless repetition and imitation without understanding. Nevertheless, some teachers and curricula continue to ask children to memorize facts, including the times tables. Is there any value to this type of activity? Would another kind of learning experience achieve the desired ends—such as learning facts about multiplication—but in a different way? What do you think?

CHAPTER 5

Preparing Students to Think Mathematically

LOOKING AHEAD >>>>>

Who has learned the most: the student who has memorized a hundred math facts or the student who can think through a single math problem and understand it? Using memorized facts as the measure of math proficiency requires students to function like recording machines. Solving math problems calls for students not only to think but also to think mathematically. Learning mathematics is more than memorizing or recording information. It is a complex, multidimensional process that involves a wide range of interacting and sometimes conflicting factors. At the heart of the process is mathematical thinking or reasoning.

Key processes in mathematical thinking include recognizing patterns and relationships in mathematical situations, developing and accessing a web of math concepts including math facts, and constructing arguments and problem-solving strategies based on those concepts.

To prepare students to think mathematically, we as teachers need to understand how the cognitive and affective domains of learning interact to influence what students learn and how effectively they learn. We need to know how to combat mathematics anxiety and develop mathematics confidence. At the same time, students need to apply mathematical thinking in problem solving and construct effective strategies for solving mathematics problems and for using mathematics to problem solve in other areas.

Learning to Think and Reason Mathematically

When mathematics focuses on memorizing facts and algorithms, thinking and reasoning mathematically take a backseat to programmed or conditioned responses. "Often we teachers assume that if students can perform certain number operations, follow established algorithms or procedures or solve problems, then they must be able to explain or justify their actions. Unfortunately, this is often not the case" (Stiff 1999, vii). Learning for understanding, problem solving that goes beyond fill-in-the-blank templates, learning that takes advantage of the wonderfully complex workings of the mind—these approaches to mathematics education go beyond *what* and *how* to *why, why not, what if, what for,* and *what's next.* In other words, they take us away from doing mathematics in a paint-by-numbers style to exploring *real* mathematics, an endeavor that calls for creativity as well as discipline (see Sternberg 1996).

Consider the following classroom scenarios.

Windows on Learning

The Math Minute

Ms. Leyba's third-grade class had been studying division. To keep students from forgetting math facts they had learned earlier, Ms. Leyba developed a math-minute activity. At various times during the day, she would call students to the board and give them one minute to write down all of the math facts they could remember about a number or combination of numbers.

Two important ingredients of the math minute were the surprise and the race—both against time and against classmates. No one knew when Ms. Leyba would call a math minute or what the topic would be. And winning or losing—writing the most or fewest facts correctly before Ms. Leyba called, "Time!"—had important consequences. The winner earned extra class "bucks" to use in the class store; the loser paid a fine in class "bucks."

It was 11:50 and students' eyes were wandering toward the clock as they began to think about lunch and a soccer game scheduled for the noon hour.

"Math minute!" Ms. Leyba called suddenly. "Go to the board. Don't think. Don't stop. Write all of the multiplications facts for the number 6."

The students scrambled to get out of their seats and find a place at a chalkboard or whiteboard.

Tommy ran to the chalkboard, picked up a piece of chalk, and began writing: "$6 \times 3 = 18, 6 \times 2 = 12, 6 \times 4 = \ldots$"

"Don't forget to write the numbers in correct order, and don't forget to include times 1."

Tommy erased his numbers and started over again: "$6 \times 1 = 6, 6 \times 2 = 12, 6 \times 3 = 18 \ldots$"

Kim was writing on the whiteboard with an erase-pen that was almost dry. She pressed hard to make the numbers, reading aloud as she wrote: "Six times 1 is 6. Six times 2 is 12. Six times 3 is, um, 15, times 4 is 20, times 5 is 25."

Next to her Julian wrote quickly for a few seconds: "$6 \times 1 = 6, 6 \times 2 = 12, 6 \times 3 = 18, 6 \times 4 = 24.$" He glanced at Kim's work and then seemed to lose his place in the list of numbers he was reciting. He quickly went through the numbers on the board again before he picked up where he left off: "$6 \times 5 = 30, 6 \times 6 = 36, 6 \times 7 = 42 \ldots$"

When Ms. Leyba called, "Time," the students hurried back to their seats. Kim and Tommy ducked their heads and did not watch as the teacher's aide checked their work. Julian watched and smiled. He knew that he had won again. He was already thinking about how he would spend his prize in the class store.

Total class time: one minute

Facts in Equations

Mr. Abeyta's third graders have also been studying division. Like Ms. Leyba, Mr. Abeyta wants his students to remember previous lessons as well. Also like Ms. Leyba, he has students show their work on the chalk- and whiteboards.

"Everyone to the board for fact equations."

The students formed teams of two or three and took their positions at the boards.

"The number today is 30," said Mr. Abeyta. "Write as many equations as you can think of that result in 30. Try to use division, multiplication, addition, and subtraction."

A student asked, "Can we add and subtract in the same equation?"

"Sure. Use as many operations as you want. Now take your time and think about your answers. Talk with your teammates before you write. Make as many changes as you want. You all have erasers as well as something to write with."

At first no one wrote anything. The students discussed the task. Then some put the number 30 on the board. Others began to try out combinations of numbers, writing and erasing several equations before they shared the results with their teammates.

Finally, each team had compiled a list and written it carefully on the board. Mr. Abeyta moved from group to group, asking questions, making suggestions.

"That looks good for multiplication. Are you sure about the division? You may want to doublecheck your results here. Try reversing the addition equation to give you another subtraction equation."

After a few more minutes of consulting, writing, and revising, the groups were ready to share and explain their results.

"For an addition equation," explained Amy, "we added three 10s to get 30."

"We multiplied 10 by 3 to get 30. That's the same thing," said Jorge, a student in a different group.

As the students discussed and justified each equation, Mr. Abeyta compiled a list of the workable equations. Any equations that were not accepted by the class or adequately justified by the groups were examined and revised until everyone understood and approved.

Total class time: 40–45 minutes

Activities CD

For an activity that builds on students' ability to write and understand equations, see Activity 65, Playing Algebra with Equate, on the CD-ROM that accompanies this text.

As a test of memorized facts, Ms. Leyba's Math Minute is time-efficient, taking no more than one minute of student time plus a few more minutes of the teacher's aide's time for assessment. The carrot-and-stick consequences motivate students to try hard, and the minute format allows Ms. Leyba to test a variety of topics without devoting extensive class time to review. At the same time, the activity discourages thinking. Ms. Leyba even specifically tells students, "Don't think," meaning their responses should be as automatic as a knee-tap reflex (see Paragraph 4 of "The Math Minute"). An obvious problem with this strategy is demonstrated by Kim's response. A few facts into the recital, she shifted from multiplication facts for 6 ($6 \times 1 = 6$, $6 \times 2 = 12$) to facts for multiplying 5 ($\times 3, = 15$, $\times 4 = 20$, $\times 5 = 25$). Because the facts are rote-memorized rather than constructed and because she is not thinking about the numbers, they do not need to make sense to her. She continues mismatching products and multipliers.

Mr. Abeyta's equations, on the other hand, take more class time, both for the activity itself and for discussions of the activity. However, as students compose, justify, and revise equations, they review and integrate what they have learned about math facts in ways not possible with timed recitations. His encouragements to think and rethink as well as his questions show students that what is important here is concepts and reasons, that results are possibilities to be examined rather than etched-in-stone end products.

In both classes students are motivated, although Ms. Leyba's class may be prompted more by the potential for reward or punishment than by engagement in the topic. The quality and degree of student engagement constitute a significant difference between the two approaches to learning and reviewing math facts—a difference mirrored in student work from two other classes (see Figures 3.1 and 3.2). The multiplication and division worksheet shown in Figure 3.1 suggests the student Nicole's lack of involvement. Most of the missed items are simply not completed; moreover, even the teacher's assess-

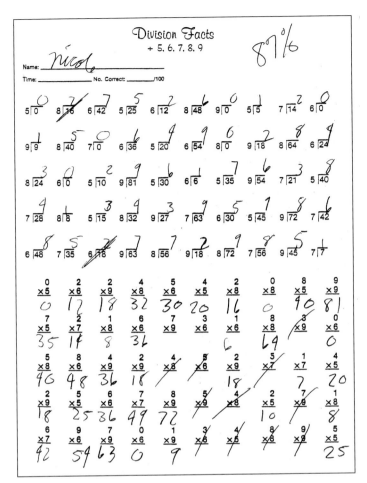

Figure 3.1 Nicole's division/multiplication worksheet.

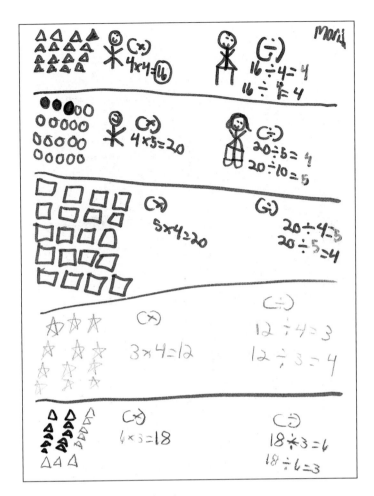

Figure 3.2 Marida's fact-family arrays.

ment appears perfunctory, with two of the uncompleted problems not marked at all. The teacher's reflection describes students' attitudes about the day's math lesson: "This day in math was not very eventful. The students were not excited to review and the day was very blah. Review is a must but the students were not into the lesson."

Figure 3.2 shows a different teacher's approach to the same topic—reviewing multiplication and division facts. Earlier in the year, the students had built the facts with manipulatives. For the review, they used arrays to rebuild the facts and then wrote number sentences. To make a clear distinction between multiplication and division, the teacher puts numbers operations in a family context: she calls multiplication the "little brother" of the fact family and division, the "big sister:" "The little brother wants to be bigger so he always groups small numbers together to get a bigger one (multiplication). But the big sister is very mean and always tries to break his big number apart into smaller ones (division)."

In addition to the arrays and mathematical symbols for multiplication and division, Marida draws stick figures of the little brother and big sister to help group her number sentences. Reflecting about the activity, the

Topics, Issues, and Explorations

Discuss the advantages and disadvantages of the drilling and building concepts approaches to learning math facts. Are there times when one method might be preferred over the other? Can you think of ways to improve or adapt the methods?

Googol: BIG IDEAS in Mathematics

Fact Families, Division, and Multiplication

Understanding the relationship between math facts is an important step toward understanding the meaning of the facts themselves. Seeing division and multiplication facts as part of a fact family helps students make connections and develop a "sense" for both the facts and the operations.

To introduce the concept of fact families, we can begin with general ideas and then place them in a family context.

1. Multiplication and division are opposite operations that undo one another. When we write number sentences for fact families, we use the same numbers for multiplication and division but put them in a different order.

2. Multiplication and division are like siblings in the math-facts family.

   Little Brother Multiplication wants to be bigger, so he always groups small numbers together to get a bigger number.

$$8 \times 7 = 56 \text{ or } 7 \times 8 = 56$$

Source: Adapted from a lesson developed by Jessica Briggs.

Big Sister Division is very mean. She always tries to break her little brother's big number into smaller numbers.

$$56/8 = 7 \text{ or } 56/7 = 8$$

Activity

Use arrays to build the math facts for five fact families. Then use drawings and number sentences to show how Multiplication builds larger numbers and Division breaks down the larger numbers into smaller numbers.

Extension

Have students act out the concept of fact families including Little Brother Multiplication and Big Sister Division as well as perhaps Aunt Addition and Uncle Subtraction. Students can choose and make their own number or symbol signs from 8 × 10 cardstock and hang them on string or yarn around their necks. To act out number sentences, they should show their number or symbol signs and also explain their roles in words.

teacher wrote, "The students felt so successful with multiplication, that when they saw division in terms of multiplying, they felt they could do it." The students not only were engaged in the activity but also understood and knew that they understood the underlying concepts. (See the Googol feature for the entire activity and extension.)

The Importance of Mathematical Thinking

According to Susan Jo Russell (1999), both what children learn and how children learn determine that "mathematical reasoning must stand at the center of mathematics learning" (1).

Mathematics is a discipline that deals with abstract entities, and reasoning is the tool for understanding abstraction. From the very beginning, children encounter the abstraction of mathematics—not only five fingers or five rabbits but the *idea* of "fiveness," not just that circular clock or this circular penny but the *idea* of a circle. Reasoning is what we use to think about the properties of these mathematical objects and develop generalizations that apply to whole classes of objects—numbers, operations, geometric objects, or sets of data.

(Russell 1999, 1)

Activities CD

For an activity that builds relationships between the facts and concepts of multiplication and division, see Activity 33, *Writing Mathematics: Telling Tales by the Numbers,* on the CD-ROM that accompanies this text.

Thinking and reasoning mathematically are integral to children's construction of mathematical knowledge. As children collect, organize, interpret, apply, and evaluate information in problem-solving activities, they are developing pathways and memory structures. As they extend, extrapolate, identify patterns, and make connections, they integrate and reinforce their knowledge. As they conjecture and test, not only do they learn how to confirm or reject trains of thought, but they also develop inquiry skills and the "habits" of questioning and justifying. "Reasoning mathematically is a habit of mind," write the authors of NCTM's *Principles and Standards for School Mathematics*, "and like all habits, it must be developed through consistent use in many contexts" (NCTM 2000, 56).

The Processes of Mathematical Thinking

But what does it mean to "think mathematically?" Does it mean students must learn to think and talk in number sentences? That math facts and algorithms become topics for discussion and reflection? ("How about that multiplication algorithm? I was doing some multiplying the other day and remembered that $9 \times 9 = 81$. I can recite my multiplication tables through 9, but I have some trouble with 7's and 6's.") Mathematical thinking is much more complex. It combines a perspective—a way of looking at the world mathematically—with strategies for approaching, interacting with, and interpreting that world mathematically. Rather than a one-dimensional thought process, mathematical thinking is a rich combination of thinking processes and strategies. These include:

- recognizing mathematical patterns and relationships;
- developing and accessing a foundation of mathematical knowledge, concepts, facts, and skills;
- constructing, expressing, and justifying mathematical arguments and problem-solving strategies;
- reflecting about, testing, and revising arguments and strategies to fit new mathematical situations, information, or perspectives;
- developing and exercising math sense—a feeling for the mathematical potential of a situation and the mathematical "rightness" of problem-solving strategies or solutions. (compiled from Stiff and Curcio 1999; Ball and Bass 2003).

Recognizing Mathematical Patterns and Relationships

Finding the mathematics in situations begins with a habit of questioning. What is alike, what is unlike? Is there repetition, progression, regression? What are the numbers in the situation? How do they relate to numbers in similar or dissimilar situations? What are the spatial relationships? Asking the questions is a starting point for mathematical thinking; searching for answers continues the process—a process that often includes representing the patterns or relationships to be explored for mathematical meaning.

For example, when Marida creates her arrays in Figure 3.2, she identifies patterns that underlie fact families for different numbers. The arrays help her understand that in the fact families she is exploring, the number relationships can be described in different ways—that is, as division or multiplication—but the operations are simply different ways of describing and arranging the same numbers.

Activities CD

For an activity that emphasizes posing and exploring mathematical questions, see Activity 47, How Much Time Does It Take to _____?, on the CD-ROM that accompanies this text.

Activities CD

For an example of mathematical investigations, see Activity 31, Jumping Critters: Kids, Frogs, and Bugs, on the CD-ROM that accompanies this text.

Developing and Using a Foundation of Mathematical Knowledge

An important part of mathematical thinking involves matching situations with the concepts that will help you make sense of them—for example, matching a compute-the-sales-tax situation with information about money notation, percentages, decimals, and multiplying and adding with decimals.

To be accessible, mathematical knowledge must be not only remembered but also organized in ways that make sense mathematically—that is, with connections among concepts and facts (such as multiplication and division facts) clearly understood and even visualized.

For example, the arrays of dots in the adjacent diagram provide a visual dimension for the numerals and for the operations signaled by the mathematical symbols for multiplication, division, and equals.

Russell (1999) compares this foundation to a web:

Mathematical reasoning both leads to and builds on a web of mathematical knowledge—a hammock-like structure in which knots are joined to other knots in an intricate webbing. Even if one knot comes undone, the structure does not collapse but still bears weight—as opposed to what might happen if each individual rope was strung only from one point to another, with no interweaving.

(4)

Topics, Issues, and Explorations

Brainstorm about all of the information you need to know to write these numbers sentences: $9 \times 9 = 81$; $81 \div 9 = 9$; $7 \times 4 = 28$; $28 \div 7 = 4$; $28 \div 4 = 7$. How could you represent the interlocking ideas with a diagram or drawing of a web?

Using Russell's metaphor, memorizing information might be seen as creating a foundation of individual ropes. When Kim dropped the rope for multiplication facts for the number 6, she picked up the rope for the number 5 (see "The Math Minute" Windows on Learning feature on p. 49). Because she had rote-memorized the information as separate lists of facts rather than developing a web of related and visualized information, Kim would not notice her mistake until her answers were marked wrong by Ms. Leyba's aide.

Constructing, Expressing, and Justifying Mathematical Arguments

Breaking out of the mechanical, nonthinking mode of doing mathematics also begins with a question: Why? Developing the ask-why habit is both a mathematical-thinking skill and a prompt for the problem-solving process:

Why is this a mathematical situation?

Why did you choose one perspective, one strategy over another?

Why does your approach work (or not work)?

Why is your solution accurate (or not accurate)?

Why might there be more than one way to look at, work through, explain, justify the mathematics of the situation?

A key result of the "why" habit is a mathematical discourse with classmates, teachers, and even oneself that adds depth and breadth to mathematical thinking. And, as with any type of discourse, to be successful, students must first master the language and conventions of that discourse. Ball and Bass (2003) describe mathematical language as not only words and symbols but also ways of expressing mathematical ideas such as equations or number sentences.

> In our analysis, mathematical language is the foundation of mathematical reasoning that is complementary to the base of publicly shared knowledge. . . .
>
> Mathematical language is central to constructing mathematical knowledge; it provides resources with which claims are developed, made, and justified.
>
> *(32–33)*

As students express their mathematical ideas, they develop a deeper understanding of those ideas. At the same time they reinforce the foundation needed to draw inferences and take the next steps to new conjectures and more complex concepts.

Figure 3.3 shows part of Lucretia's discourse about coins and fractions. She began with an Everyday Math activity, a Math Message.

> If D (dime) is one, then what is N (nickel)?
>
> If a dollar is one, then what is Q (quarter)?

Lucretia wrote pictorial equations to represent the messages and then shaded parts of the whole or one to show the fraction. In her journal she explained how she shaded one of two nickels to show that one nickel is half of a dime and shaded one of the four quarters to show a quarter is one fourth of a dollar. Later in a follow-up discussion, Lucretia and her classmates experimented with other ways to represent the fractions and relationships of the coins.

$$\frac{5\cent}{10\cent} = \frac{1}{2} \qquad \frac{5\cent}{10\cent} + \frac{5\cent}{10\cent} = \frac{10\cent}{10\cent} = 1$$

$$4\,(25\cent) = 100\cent$$

$$25\cent + 25\cent + 25\cent + 25\cent = 100\cent$$

They then extended the discussion to look at additional math messages:

> If D (dime) is one and N (nickel) is ½, then how many ones and halves are there in Q (quarter)?
>
> If a dollar is one, what part of a dollar is D (dime)?

Responding to the Math Messages and then discussing their responses and variations of their responses engaged the students in a multisided discourse that took them beyond the original objectives of the activity and helped them refine and extend their thinking.

Reflecting, Testing, Revising

At its best, mathematical thinking is neither linear nor one-dimensional; it is a recursive, reflective process that continually turns back upon itself. The flow charts in Figure 3.4 and 3.5 contrast linear and recursive models of mathematical

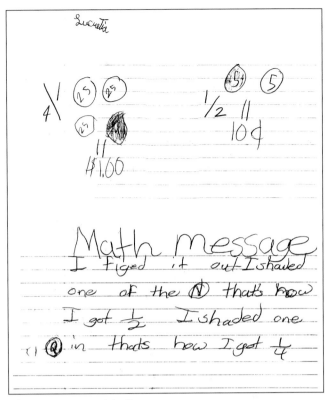

Figure 3.3 Lucretia's discourse.

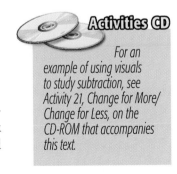

Activities CD

For an example of using visuals to study subtraction, see Activity 21, Change for More/Change for Less, on the CD-ROM that accompanies this text.

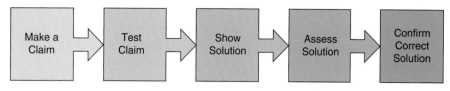

Figure 3.4 Linear model of mathematical thinking.

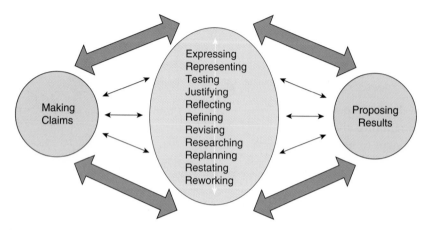

Figure 3.5 Recursive model of mathematical thinking.

thinking. In the former, the process is essentially product driven, with each step geared toward producing and evaluating a solution. In the latter, making claims, working with claims, proposing solutions are part of a continuous process. Testing a claim could lead to a result or to revising the claim or even to making a new claim. Proposing a result is not so much an end product for the process but a new starting point to be tested, justified, and refined and to prompt and support new claims and new cycles of mathematical thinking.

In a project designed to develop mathematical reasoning in third graders, Betsy and her classmates followed a recursive rather than a linear process as they dealt with the question: Does an odd number plus an odd number always equal an even number? (Ball and Bass 2003, 33). Betsy's conjecture responds in the affirmative:

$$odd + odd = even$$

At first the students tried to prove Betsy's conjecture by using examples. Ofala tried out "almost 18" combinations. Because they "all worked," she said she thought that "it can always work." However, Sheena and Jeannie found a flaw in that approach: "Because, um, there's, um, like numbers go on and on forever, and that means odd numbers and even numbers go on and on forever, so you couldn't prove *all* of them work" (Ball and Bass 2003, 35).

Responding to this objection, Betsy and several other classmates rethought their strategy and developed a different way to test and represent Betsy's conjecture: they drew two sets of seven marks on the board and then drew circles around seven sets of two marks. Betsy explained: "If you added two odd numbers together, you can add the 1's left over and it would always equal an even number" (Ball and Bass 2003, 36).

Through a process of reflecting, testing, and revising, the students discovered not only the complexity of an apparently simple mathematical idea but also the open-ended nature of many mathematical conclusions.

Using "Math Sense"

Developing and exercising "math sense" is not so much a separate process of mathematical thinking as a combination of processes. To "feel" the accuracy of a strategy or solution, students must recognize connections and relationships and draw on webs of mathematical information. They need to think critically about facts and strategies and draw on their understanding of how things work in mathematics. For Kim in the Math Minute scenario, this critical thinking might mean recognizing the difference between multiples of an even and an odd number—that is, sensing the wrongness of the odd number 15 as a multiple of 6. Instead of proceeding by reflex without thinking, she needed to reflect about and revise her strategy and ask herself, "Do these numbers make sense?"

Activities CD

For an activity to develop number sense, see Activity 6, The Revolving Jar, on the CD-ROM that accompanies this text.

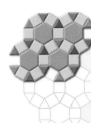

Mathematical Thinking

Mathematical Conjectures

Posing mathematical conjectures can provide the starting point for a chain of mathematical thinking processes that stretch students' understanding of concepts and encourage them to develop new ways of looking at and working with those concepts.

The concept of even and odd numbers is the focus of a mathematical task developed by Deborah Ball and Hyman Bass (2003, 35–37).

Activity 1

Explore what happens when we add even and odd numbers. What happens when we add even and even numbers? Even and odd numbers? Odd and odd numbers? Propose conjectures that summarize your conclu-sion (for example, even + even = even). Discuss and evaluate the conjectures.

Activity 2

Develop strategies to test and justify the conjectures proposed in Activity 1. Record your calculations and thoughts for each conjecture.

Activity 3

Develop, represent, and explain in writing proofs for one or more of your conjectures. Discuss the proofs, looking for strong and weak points. Then rethink, re-fine, and revise the proofs.

Source: Adapted from Ball and Bass (2003, 35–37).

Russell, who uses the terms *mathematical intuition* or *insight,* sees math sense as a function of a special kind of mathematical memory. "It is," she writes, "a memory of essences and core relationships. . . . a memory in which the whole web of ideas has become more than the sum of its parts" (Russell 1999, 6). Developing this sense of insight or memory is itself an ongoing process for which students need a curriculum that goes beyond facts and algorithms. That curriculum should include

- mathematical tasks that defy quick and easy answers;
- time to think and reflect;
- freedom to take chances and make mistakes; and
- flexibility to try multiple pathways to multiple solutions.

Topics, Issues, and Explorations

Evaluate your own "math sense." Without doing the actual calculations, explain why each solution does or does not "feel" right:

$2{,}025 \times 25 = 50{,}620$ $22 + 11 + 22 + 11 = 55$

$1/2 \times 1/2 = 1/4$ $1/2 \div 1/2 = 1/4$

$\frac{666}{66} = 11$ $\frac{555}{5} = 111$ $.25 \times .25 = 6.25$

Understanding Interactions That Affect Mathematical Thinking and Learning

If learning mathematics were a simple linear procedure, we could dispense with teachers and schools and program children as we program and operate our computers: input data, store data to memory, access data, output data, print data—all at the touch of a button or a simple set of commands. In this case, the data itself would be our focus rather than the students and their processes of acquiring, thinking about, and using information. But learning mathematics is neither simple nor linear, and, as we have seen, thinking mathematically is a complex, multidimensional process. As they develop their mathematical thinking skills, learners interact

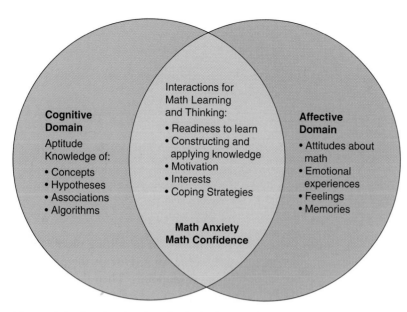

Figure 3.6 Overlapping domains in thinking mathematically and learning mathematics.

with a host of variables. One group of variables—aptitude, concepts, hypotheses, associations, algorithms—comprises the **cognitive domain**. Another group of variables—attitudes, experiences, feelings, some memories—comprises the **affective domain** (Martinez and Martinez 1996, 2–9; see also McLeod and Adams 1989). These domains overlap to influence the processes as well as the products of mathematical thinking and learning (see Figure 3.6). Whether that influence is positive, negative, or something in between depends not only upon individual factors but also upon how those factors interact.

The Cognitive Domain

We might describe the cognitive domain as the logical component of mathematical thinking and learning. Aptitude for learning mathematics, logical thought processes, storage and retrieval of information from a "web" of math knowledge, the match of teaching strategies and students' learning and thinking styles—all belong to the cognitive domain. What makes a learning experience cognitively effective? Two things are important here:

- what the children bring to the experience and
- what the experience offers in terms of meaningful learning.

Children are ready to learn when they have acquired the necessary background and mind tools (idea structures, thinking skills to interact with and manipulate information) to work productively with new information or ideas. For example, children need to have constructed schema or mental structures about "more than" and "less than" before they are ready to develop algorithms for addition and subtraction. Similarly, meaningful thinking and learning build on previous knowledge structures, extending and challenging without losing touch with what children already know. A lesson, "Money Counts," from the popular PBS program *Mathline*, illustrates this point.

In "Money Counts," children in a combined first and second grade explored the value of pennies, nickels, dimes, and quarters. The children had already had experiences with shopping, both with their parents and in a classroom store. They brought to the activity an appreciation for the greater buying power of a dollar over a quarter and a dime over a penny. But they were not clear about counting back change after a purchase. Some tended to confuse more coins of any type with more money value.

> Through a collection of hands-on activities, students gain experience in counting, exchanging, and comparing money. Students begin the lesson by finding all of the possible combinations of coins that can be used to equal a specified amount of money. They then compare two amounts of money and use number sense skills and problem solving strategies to move coins from one group to another so that both groups are equal in value.
>
> *(Public Broadcasting System[PBS] 1997, 1)*

The children understood the number values of the individual and combined coins; however, they had yet to be introduced to the idea of decimals. Conse-

Activities CD

For an activity exploring decimals and percentages in the context of shopping, see Activity 91, Shopping by the Numbers, on the CD-ROM that accompanies this text.

quently, working with calculators became problematic when the teacher said to emphasize "exact . . . placement of decimals" and when she warned the children not to "forget to push the decimal point key on the calculator as it will affect [your] answers" (PBS 1997, 4). The hands-on tasks were cognitively meaningful because they built on understanding; entering decimal points by rote did not.

Students are working in the cognitive domain as they make conjectures, attempt to justify and prove claims, and develop strategies for making sense of mathematical situations. Optimally, they will be challenged with mathematical tasks that stretch them cognitively—that is, tasks that bring together a variety of mathematical information and require them to make connections, test a variety of hypotheses, and pose and evaluate a variety of arguments.

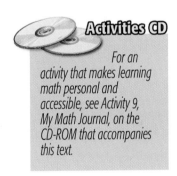

Topics, Issues, and Explorations

What does it mean to be "ready to learn" cognitively? What do the experts say? What do you say? How can we match readiness to preparation for activities? Compose and discuss several guidelines to follow.

The Affective Domain

The affective domain is the emotional or "feelings" component of mathematical thinking and learning. Do you like math? Do you dislike math? Do you feel you are good at math? Do you enjoy learning math? Are your memories of studying math happy or sad? Do people you know—your family, friends, teachers—have positive or negative feelings about math? In *Math without Fear*, we write, "This is the province of attitudes about learning math, of memories of past failures and successes, of influences from math-anxious or math-confident adults, of responses to the learning environment and teaching styles." (Martinez and Martinez 1996, 6).

The affective domain provides a context for learning and thinking about mathematics. If the context is positive, students may be motivated to think mathematically and learn effectively, whatever their math aptitude. If the context is negative, even students with superior math aptitude may dislike math and avoid developing the habits and skills of mathematical thinking.

Often the affective domain works at an unconscious level. A negative situation, such as a 50-problem math test or a pop quiz, produces a negative response such as dislike or dread. Or success and good grades could lead to rewards, satisfaction, and more positive emotions. Key processes at work here are **association** and **repetition.**

Activities CD

For an activity that makes learning math personal and accessible, see Activity 9, My Math Journal, on the CD-ROM that accompanies this text.

> I once observed a math teacher who used a pointer like a whip throughout the lesson. He jabbed at the board, emphasized points with sharp whacks, and underscored class discussion by beating a tattoo on his desk. The teacher saw the pointer as an attention getter and keeper: "No one falls asleep in my class." The students do pay attention, but many of them winced repeatedly throughout the class.
>
> *(Martinez and Martinez 1996, 7)*

Students in that class came to associate the pointer's repeated strikes with learning math. At an emotional level, the subject was linked to a symbolic whipping. Other, more pleasant associations are made by teachers who connect learning math with a special treat. In Chapter 5 we will look at a teacher who used what she calls "edible manipulatives"—candy hearts, jelly beans, even Cheerios—to motivate and create positive associations for learning math in kindergarten.

Interactions

Interactions between the cognitive and the affective domains might be positive, negative, or a combination of the two. Positive affect combined with a solid cognitive foundation can promote students' readiness to learn, while negative affect and gaps in knowledge have the opposite effect. Developing the habits of mathematical thinking will be encouraged or discouraged as factors work against or with each other to affect motivation and interests. Students who like math will probably be more ready to identify mathematical situations in their own worlds and apply concepts in problem solving. Students who dislike math sometimes develop coping strategies such as avoidance or rationalizations: "I'm not a numbers person" or "I'm left-brained, not right-brained."

Two major types of interaction result in the "constructs" of math anxiety and math confidence. Neither is a discrete condition based on a straightforward, single-cause/single-effect progression. Both are called *constructs* because they have multiple causes and multiple effects, tangled together in a way that defies simple diagnosis, simple remedies, and simple how-to instructions. Both affect mathematical thinking and impact the process of learning mathematics.

Math Anxiety

This construct might best be described as a combination of cognitive and affective factors that together impede math learning. The anxiety might begin with a gap in knowledge, such as not understanding fractions, that leads to poor grades and punishment or ridicule. Or it could begin with a teacher or parent who dislikes math, avoids it, or even uses math problems as punishment: "Step out of line, and instead of recess, you'll do 100 multiplication problems." Figure 3.7 shows how different factors work together to create math anxiety. The student begins with what seems like a simple problem (17 + 4 = ?). Then a web of ideas, memories, and feelings complicate the situation.

Although many adults recognize and readily admit that they are math anxious, diagnosing a math-anxious child can be more difficult. Instead of saying they are math anxious, children will say, "I hate math. It's boring. Subtraction is dumb. I can't do fractions. My teacher is stupid. Who needs math?" (Martinez and Martinez 1996, 41). Generally, prevention works better than therapy. Teaching strategies that emphasize understanding and develop a positive math attitude improve students' chances of maintaining a positive thinking and learning process. However, once anxiety has developed, teachers need to intervene. The Idea Files feature suggests techniques for dealing with specific symptoms you observe during

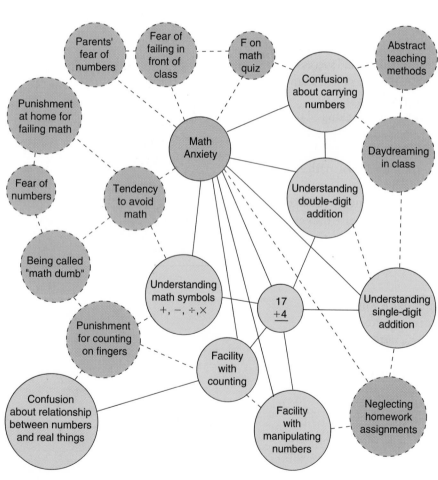

Figure 3.7 Mapping math anxiety.
(Adapted from Martinez, Joseph, and Nancy Martinez, Math without Fear: Anxiety in Children. Published by Allyn and Bacon, Boston, MA. Copyright © 1996 by Pearson Education. Adapted by permission of the publisher.)

Idea Files

Helping the Math-Anxious Student

Math-Anxiety Symptoms	Remedial Techniques
Emotional distress during math activities	1. The spoonful of sugar: teaching with stories, games, or jokes; combining study with treats or privileges 2. Mary Poppins in the classroom: role playing, performing, clowning 3. Music and aroma therapy
Physical distress during math activities	1. Physical exercise before, during, and after study 2. Lessons held outside on grass or among trees 3. Laughing, smiling exercises: Who can laugh the loudest? Who can smile the biggest? Who can grin the widest?
Hostility/anger	1. Write-it-out exercises: "I hate math because . . ." 2. Venting activities such as beating on a punching bag or a Bobo doll, growling, scowling
Lack of attention	1. Shock treatment: wearing a clown nose and wig during lessons, staging slapstick demonstrations 2. Participation activities: singing or chanting multiplication tables, talking out problems, round-robin problem solving (first student does first step, second student second step, etc.)
Fear of numbers	1. Desensitizing activities—numbers linked to relaxing and pleasant activities or things, songs about numbers, food with numbers (such as cupcakes, sweets, or popcorn, etc.), pleasant pictures associated with numbers, a cutout numbers zoo

Source: Adapted from Martinez, Joseph and Nancy Martinez, Math without Fear: Anxiety in Children. Published by Allyn and Bacon, Boston, MA. Copyright © 1996 by Pearson Education. Adapted by permission of the publisher.

math lessons. In addition, teachers may need to develop a treatment plan that responds directly to the causes of math anxiety. The plan might include

- filling in gaps in learning;
- replacing bad learning habits with good learning habits;
- countering a history of math failures with math successes;
- replacing negative with positive attitudes.

Note: For more about assessing and coping with math anxiety, see *Math: Facing an American Phobia*, (Burns 1998), *Math without Fear* (Martinez and Martinez, 1996), and *Overcoming Math Anxiety* (Tobias 1993).

Math Confidence

Like math anxiety, math confidence develops as a variety of factors from the affective and cognitive domains interact. Math confidence is more than an attitude; it is at the same time a perspective, a motivation, an emotional and intellectual readiness to tackle the challenges of thinking mathematically and learning math. Figure 3.8

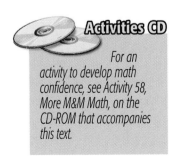

Activities CD

For an activity to develop math confidence, see Activity 58, More M&M Math, on the CD-ROM that accompanies this text.

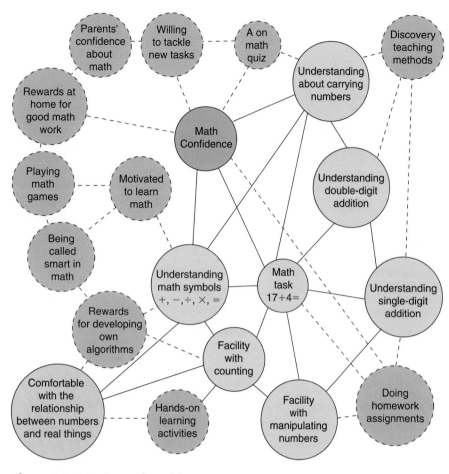

Figure 3.8 Mapping math confidence.

maps the math confidence of a student whose math task, as in the task in Figure 3.7, is to add 17 and 4. The student draws on a web of positive learning experiences including understanding major concepts and completing other tasks successfully.

Teaching strategies that promote math confidence are listed below. Significantly, they include some of the same methods we suggest for coping with math anxiety.

1. Teach a challenging curriculum that calls for maximum rather than minimum efforts.
2. Build on successes; extend effective activities in ongoing studies.
3. Model flexible learning strategies that encourage tolerance for unknowns and ambiguity.
4. Rewrite negative learning histories by substituting good experiences for bad and successes for failure.
5. Encourage "fight" rather than "flight" responses to difficult concepts or problems.
6. Emphasize process and understanding without losing respect for accuracy and exactness.
7. Demonstrate the equal opportunity of learning mathematics by placing concepts and achievements in historical and cultural contexts.
8. Continue working with topics until students experience the "ah-ha!" moment—the point when information or actions come together and make sense.

Games that emphasize mathematical thinking and the process of playing rather than winning can be effective confidence builders. The Mathematical

 Mathematical Games

Developing Math Confidence with Math Smart

Playing games can offer students an engaging and non-threatening context for mastering math facts and operations skills—especially if the emphasis of the game is on the playing rather than on competing with other students.

The Math Smart card games (available from Mind Ware, www.mindwareonline.com) help students develop and extend their knowledge of math facts and at the same time deepen their understanding of what the facts mean.

Math Smart is played like dominoes. Each card has a solution and an equation. Players match solutions to equations in a dominoes-style chain that can grow in several directions—ends, middle, anyplace that a solution and equation can be connected.

There are six decks of Math Smart cards: addition, subtraction, multiplication, division, fraction addition, and fraction subtraction.

Play can focus on one deck and one operation or on a combination such as addition and subtraction (either of whole numbers or of fractions) or multiplication and division. Advanced play can include all of the decks.

Because of the many different combinations of equations and solutions, players recognize relationships, make connections, and select from a variety of options. In other words, they must think mathematically to play the game.

Figure 3.9 "I Was Math Anxious!"

Figure 3.10 "I Am Math Confident!"

Games feature describes a series of card games that help students make sense of math facts.

Given the complexity of the interactions, many students will react to mathematical tasks with a combination of anxiety and confidence. Asked to use concept maps and drawings to explore interactions in their own math thinking, preservice teachers often identify both areas of math confidence and math anxiety. Figures 3.9 and 3.10 were drawn by the same teacher. "I Was Math Anxious!" focuses on negative experiences in elementary school. "I Am Math Confident!" shows not only positive experiences and influences but also the understanding that even if anxiety

occurs, it can be dealt with: "I still feel a little anxious at times but I can overcome it" and "I still get stressed but I get A's." Other preservice teachers combine math confidence and anxiety in single maps or focus and elaborate on a single type of interaction.

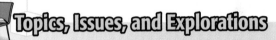

Topics, Issues, and Explorations

Are you math anxious, math confident, or both? Create a concept map or web that reflects your knowledge, experiences, memories, and feelings about math. Share the results and discuss what you discovered about yourself. How can what you discovered help you become a better math teacher?

Applying Mathematical Thinking in Problem Solving

The multiple processes of mathematical thinking, including the cognitive foundations and affective context, come together in problem solving. Problem solving is both an application of mathematical thinking and a vehicle for extending, revising, and refining that thinking. Like mathematical thinking and even learning itself, problem solving is essentially a process in which *doing* is primary; *having done*, or completing a product, is secondary. To experts such as Karl Popper, learning, thinking, and problem solving are in fact synonymous. Problem solving, according to Popper, is a response to "cognitive hunger," an innate drive to understand the world we live in (see Berkson and Wettersten 1984, 16).

Polya's Four Steps to Problem Solving

How to satisfy this "hunger" in learning mathematics was perhaps best described by a mathematics teacher, George Polya. From observations of his students, he developed a four-step method for solving problems (Polya 1973, 1981).

Activities CD

For a problem-solving activity, see Activity 55, Measuring Pi, on the CD-ROM that accompanies this text.

Step 1 **Understanding the problem.** This step includes identifying the parameters of the problem, discovering what has been included and what has been left out, and representing the problem effectively.

Step 2 **Devising a plan.** Here we both mobilize our materials—what we know about the problem as a whole or as individual parts as well as what we know about comparable problems—and organize them in a way that makes sense. As Polya explains:

> *Solving a problem is similar to building a house. We must collect the right material, but collecting the material is not enough; a heap of stones is not yet a house. To construct the house or the solution, we must put together the parts and organize them to a purposeful whole. (Polya 1981, I, 66).*

Step 3 **Carrying out the plan.** Polya's advice here includes the following tips: Put together the pieces of the puzzle, a few at a time. Work forward; work backward; work sideways. "Use what you have, you cannot use what you have not" (Polya 1981, 7).

Step 4 **Looking back.** Reassessing progress is more complicated than just checking your work. It means evaluating the effectiveness of the plan as well as evaluating your execution of the plan. Did you use all the information? Did you follow the plan as a whole or in part? Is your work taking you in the wrong or the right direction? Do you understand more about the problem now than when you began? (Polya 1981, II, 82–83).

Figure 3.11 places these steps within the context of the cognitive and affective domains of learning and thinking. The result is an interactive process. Like the Recursive Model of Mathematical Thinking shown in Figure 3.5, it

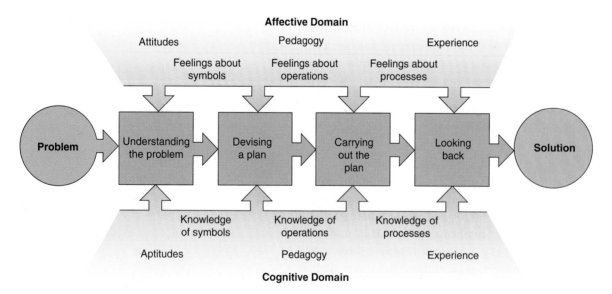

Figure 3.11 The process of solving math problems. (Adapted from Martinez, Joseph and Nancy Martinez, Math without Fear: Anxiety in Children. Published by Allyn and Bacon, Boston, MA. Copyright © 1996 by Pearson Education. Adapted by permission of the publisher.)

is more cyclical than linear and more process than product oriented. Polya emphasizes the "guess and test" dimension of problem solving—the importance of repeatedly devising and testing plans and approaching problems from every possible direction (Polya 1981, II, 56–57).

Earlier we looked at Betsy's conjecture: odd + odd = even (Ball and Bass 2003). Betsy and her classmates used Polya's guess-and-test approach as they first tried proving the conjecture with examples and then developed a more complex proof. The students worked from a strong cognitive foundation: they understood the difference between odd and even numbers, were able to use operations effectively, and were developing the mathematical thinking skills needed to think through the problem and make mathematical sense of the information. The students also worked in a classroom environment that promoted positive affect. They were encouraged, for example, to propose and test a variety of solutions, to collaborate, and to continue to work on complex problems until they felt satisfied with the solution.

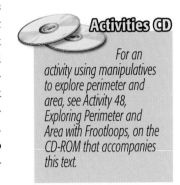

Activities CD

For an activity using manipulatives to explore perimeter and area, see Activity 48, Exploring Perimeter and Area with Frootloops, on the CD-ROM that accompanies this text.

Problem-Solving Approach to Learning

What does it mean to adopt a problem-solving approach to learning mathematics? The videotaped portion of the Third International Mathematics and Science Study (now known as the Trends in International Mathematics and Science Study [TIMSS]) presents good examples of what is and what is not learning by problem solving. Compare, for example, transcripts from two geometry lessons: a Japanese lesson about the area of triangles (Figure 3.12) and a U.S. lesson about angles (Figure 3.13).

Time	Description of Activity	Description of Content
00:01	Prelesson Activity	
00:27	Whole-class work: Working on Tasks/Situations (59 sec)	(Teacher shows a figure on computer screen.) The triangles between two parallel lines have the same areas.
01:26	Whole-class work: Setting Up Tasks/Situations (2 min 39 sec)	(Teacher draws a diagram on chalkboard.) There is Eda's land. There is Azusa's land. And these two people's border line is bent, but we want to make it straight. Eda ⟩ Azusa Try thinking about the methods of changing this shape without changing the area.
03:34		
04:05	Seat work: Working on Tasks/Situations Individually (2 min 59 sec)	
07:04	Seat work: Working on Tasks/Situations in Small Groups (12 min 16 sec)	People who have come up with an idea for now work with Mr. Ishikawa, and people who want to discuss it with your friends, you can do so. And for now I have placed some hint cards up here so people who want to refer to those, please go ahead.

Figure 3.12 Japanese lesson—area of triangles.

Time	Description of Activity	Description of Content
00:01	Whole-class work: Working on Tasks/Situations (2 min 15 sec)	(Chalkboard) 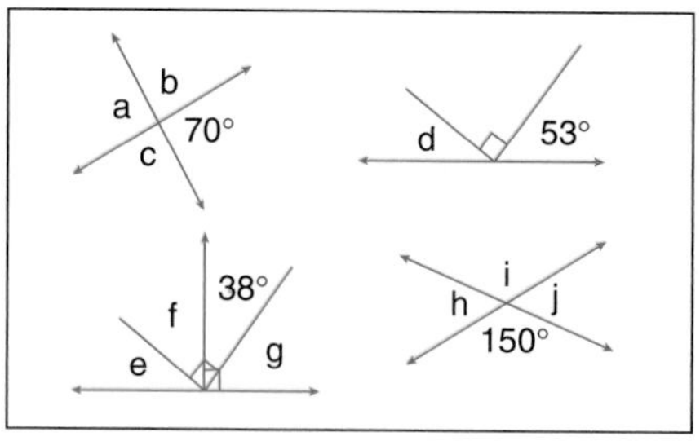 m<a = m<b = m<c = m<d = m<e = m<f = m<g = m<h = m<i = m<j = What is the angle that is vertical to the 70-degree angle? (No answer) Which angle is vertical to angle A? Students: angle 70. Teacher: Therefore, angle A is 70 degrees. What is the supplementary angle to angle A? Student 1: angle B. Teacher: angle B and angle C. What do the supplementary angles add up to? Students: 180 degrees. What is the other angle that I indicated in the diagram besides the 53-degree angle? Student 2: Right angle. What is the size of a right angle? Student 2: 90 degrees. Teacher: Right angle is 90 degrees. What other angle is left in the diagram? Student 3: 37 degrees. Why is it 37 degrees? Student 4: Because 53 degrees and 37 degrees add up to 90 degrees, and with the other 90 degrees, it adds up to 180 degrees.

Figure 3.13   U.S. lesson—angles.
Source: USDE 1997, 102.

Activities CD

For more puzzles and math challenges, see Activity 107, Real Numbers, Math Games, and AlphaNumeric Puzzles, on the CD-ROM that accompanies this text.

The Japanese lesson begins with a problem. The students explore the problem, trying out strategies and developing reasoned solutions. Then they explain, discuss, and reflect while their teacher probes their thinking and asks questions that help them refine and extend the problem-solving process. The American lesson, on the other hand, focuses on vocabulary and identification. The teacher asks students to recite facts rather than to use concepts to solve a problem.

Designing mathematical tasks that engage students in the problem-solving process should begin with what students know and then build step-by-step to more complex concepts and thinking processes. For example, the classic Water Jar problem can become a series of problems, each building on and extending concepts explored in the previous problem.

Water Jar Problem 1

You have two empty water jars. One will hold five gallons and the other, one gallon. Your task is to fill one of these containers with exactly four gallons of water. You have an unlimited supply of water but no other measuring devices. Explain in everyday language and in mathematical language how you solved the problem. You might also want to illustrate your answer with drawings.

Water Jar Problem 2

You again have two empty water jars and an unlimited supply of water but no other measuring devices. This time, one jar can hold five gallons and the other, two gallons. What do you need to do to fill the large jar with exactly four gallons of water? Explain and demonstrate how you solved the problem using both words and symbols.

The first two problems let students work with what they already know about volume and three-dimensional objects such as cylinders. That knowledge provides the foundation for the first step in problem solving: *understanding the problem.* Then, as students *devise and work through various plans for addressing the problem* as they understand it (Steps 2 and 3 in Polya's method), they are beginning to think in terms of proportion and relationships—in other words, to think mathematically about the problem. Finally, they verbalize and represent their work using mathematical language, diagrams, and drawings; they **look back** (Step 4) and begin to "develop multiple perspectives and find the multiple solutions inherent in the problems" (Martinez 2001, 118).

Problem solving for Water Jar 1 and 2 lay the groundwork for the classic version of the problem, Water Jar 3. More challenging than the first two problems, Water Jar 3 requires a more complex problem-solving strategy. Instead of simply pouring water from the smaller to the larger container, students must find a way to isolate one gallon of water in the five-gallon container so that gallons can be added from the smaller container for a total of four gallons. To provide fresh motivation for the task, students can watch an edited episode of the action movie *Die Hard III* in which the main characters, McClane and Zeus, must solve the classic problem to prevent a bomb from endangering a park (see the Math and Technology feature).

Water Jar Problem 3

Help McClane and his assistant, Zeus, save the people in the park from the bomb. They have two empty containers, one that will hold five gallons of water and one that will hold three gallons. To stop the bomb from detonating, they have to put a container with exactly four gallons of water on a pressure-sensitive plate. A fountain filled with water is nearby but no other containers. What should they do? Explain and show how to solve the problem. Do you think McClane and Zeus can solve the problem in five minutes?

Math and Technology

The Water Jar Problem in *Die Hard III*

Engaging students in the problem-solving process may require breaking out of classroom math routines. Videos can expand the context of a mathematical situation, add visual and aural dimensions to written problems, and connect with students on an imaginative level.

To help students see and make sense of the classic Water Jar problem, teachers can use an episode from an edited version of the popular action movie *Die Hard III*.

In the movie a group of terrorists makes the Water Jar problem part of a bomb trap in a busy park. To keep the bomb from detonating, the main characters in the movie have five minutes to put a container with exactly four gallons of water on a pressure-sensitive device. To work with, they have a three-gallon container, a five-gallon container, and an unlimited supply of water from a fountain.

Activity

Watch the first part of the movie clip for the context and basic elements of the problem. Talk about the problem as a class, making sure everyone understands the conditions and limits of the problem (for example, the need for exact rather than approximate measurements).

Then in small groups devise and work out one or more plans for solving the problem. Keep a record of what you do—what works, what does not work, and why—and of the time it takes you to arrive at each answer.

Watch the rest of the movie clip. Compare your group's solution with those of the movie characters and of other class groups. Compile a list of all of the workable solutions. Discuss which solution (or solutions) would have worked best in the movie. Pay special attention to the time it takes to pour the water, the number of gallons poured, and the number of steps to reach the solution.

Topics, Issues, and Explorations

See how many solutions you can find to the classic Water Jar problem. There are at least three and possibly more. Use Polya's multistep process, and diagram or record your work at each stage of the process.

Problem-solving tasks, such as the Water Jar problems, require students to think mathematically. At the same time they take math out of the textbooks and make its processes and outcomes seem more real and even more important and meaningful to students. And they help students not to expect quick, one-step answers when they do math but to expect and be willing to work through a complex, multistep process to solve math problems.

Multiple Solutions/New Beginning

As students work through the steps of the problem-solving process, they soon discover that the process involves many beginnings (and beginnings-again) but few endings. Even the solution, a supposed ending point for the process, often presents a new set of problems and a new set of beginnings.

For example, the classic Water Jar problem (number 3) has a classic solution—the one used by McClane and Zeus in the *Die Hard* movie:

1. Fill the five-gallon container.
2. Fill the three-gallon container with water from the five-gallon container, leaving two gallons in the five-gallon container.
3. Empty the three-gallon container.
4. Pour the two remaining gallons from the five-gallon container into the three-gallon container.
5. Refill the five-gallon container.
6. Top off the three-gallon container with one gallon from the five-gallon container, leaving exactly four gallons.

Once students have discovered and tested the classic solution, they should continue to search for faster ways to solve the problem. Not all of the alternatives will work in the five minutes set by the movie scenario. The following solution, developed by students, works for the problem but would take longer than the classic solution since it involves pouring a total of 23 gallons instead of the 19 gallons (Martinez 2001).

1. Fill the three-gallon container.
2. Empty the three gallons into five-gallon container.
3. Refill the three-gallon container.
4. Pour two gallons into the five-gallon container, leaving one gallon in the smaller jug.
5. Empty the five-gallon container.
6. Add the one gallon from the smaller jug.
7. Fill the three-gallon container, and empty it into the five-gallon container for four gallons. (Martinez 2001, 118)

The dialogue that follows is a transcript of students' search for a third solution. The students worked hands-on with actual containers at a sink. Their geometric solution—using right angles to find half of each container and then adding the halves—would take less time than the classic solution since fewer gal-

Activities CD

For another multi-step, problem-solving activity, see Activity 106, The Golden Ratio, Phi (Φ) and Physical Beauty, on the CD-ROM that accompanies this text.

lons (13½) are poured. As they solve and resolve problems, evaluate and test solutions, students develop a more flexible view of mathematical situations and the problem-solving process.

Diane: Well, we saved the day—sort of. Our solution is the same as the one in the movie.

Don: But it takes longer than five minutes.

Diane: That's only because you took too long to pour the water. McClane does it better.

Teacher: Maybe there's another, quicker solution. Why don't you try something else?

Diane: We already found two solutions, and the correct one has to be the one in the movie.

Teacher: But it took you a long time to pour all of that water. What if there's a quicker way? Why not keep looking?

[To restart their thinking, the teacher showed the students two right-circular cylinders and suggested they recall what they knew about the geometry of cylinders.]

Diane: I just don't see anything. . . .

Don: What if we fill both containers with water and determine if the concept of displacement applies.

Teacher: Remember that in the movie McClane and Zeus had containers that wouldn't fit inside each other. Let's try to stick within the parameters of their problem.

Chelsea: Okay, what if we just filled each container to half full? Then we could add the halves together and get four gallons.

Rachel: But how would you know that exactly half of each container was filled with water?

Sam: Beats me. You can't just look at it and tell.

Haley: Remember, like with McClane, he had to be accurate or the bomb would go off.

[A long pause followed, as students tried to think through the problem again. Some students complained that the teacher was tricking them, that there were no other solutions.]

Teacher: Let's go back to Chelsea's suggestion. Is there a way to determine that each container is exactly half full?

[Another pause. Then Chelsea went up to the sink and filled both containers.]

Teacher: Remember that both containers are right-circular cylinders.

Don: Which means that a line from the bottom of the container straight up makes a right angle with a straight line across the bottom of the container.

Haley: Doesn't that mean that you have a 90-degree angle?

Activities CD

For another hands-on, problem-solving activity, see Activity 75, Are You Hot? Are You Cold? Finding Mean, Median, and Mode, on the CD-ROM that accompanies this text.

Activities CD

For another activity about volume and space, see Activity 52, Estimating Length, Volume, and Weight, on the CD-ROM that accompanies this text.

Topics, Issues, and Explorations

Go back to Water Jar problem 1 in the section on problem solving. How many solutions can you find to this simple version of the problem? Then write a set of questions you might use to guide students to think deeply about the problem and work out a reasoned approach and solution.

Chelsea: Which means, I think that . . . I'm not sure, but if you tilt the container while it is filled. . . . Could you make a 45-degree angle with the water?

[Chelsea got help from Don and Haley to tip the container she had filled.]

Haley: Look! It makes a 45 degree angle if we pour out just enough water to make a straight line from one side of the top to the other side of the bottom.

Teacher: Which tells us what?'

Elaine: It means the thing is half full. It has exactly half as much water.

Chelsea: And if you do the same thing with both containers, you will have half and half.

Don: So we have half of the five-gallon container and half of the three-gallon container. You end up with 2½ + 1½ gallons or 4 gallons.

Diane: And it's faster, too, because you don't have to pour so much water back and forth.

Teacher: So there was another solution, and you found it!

Developing a Mathematical Worldview

How can we as teachers help students think and reason mathematically? Step 1 might be to encourage the development of a mathematical worldview. "Math is everywhere," says Jason in the *Foxtrot* cartoon. The heroine of Scieszka and Smith's (1995) *The Math Curse* begins to "think math" when a teacher named Fibonacci tells the class, "You know, you can think of almost everything as a math problem" (see Mathematics in Literature). Taking mathematics out of the textbooks and finding it in the bigger worlds around us and the smaller worlds of home, playground, and daily lives make it a "living" subject, something we must come to grips with in thought and actions to function effectively.

Fox Trot

"Math is everywhere you look!" From Bill Amend, *Fox Trot.* Used by permission.

Outside the classroom students can be encouraged to think mathematically with activities that help them focus on shapes, patterns, numbers, comparisons, unknowns, problems—the real-world mathematics that is "everywhere" around them. The Jacksonville Woodlands Project featured in this chapter's Teacher Pro-File involved fifth graders in an environmental project that connected math, science, and community life in meaningful ways. The students had to think mathematically and problem solve as they planned trails and reforestation projects and raised and budgeted money. Larry Smith, the students' teacher, writes about the "life impact" of his lessons that extend "their learning and influence beyond their classroom."

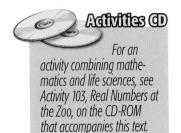

Activities CD

For an activity combining mathematics and life sciences, see Activity 103, Real Numbers at the Zoo, on the CD-ROM that accompanies this text.

Inside the classroom, teachers can encourage children to think and reason mathematically by adopting a discover-explain, guess-and-test approach to learning. "From children's earliest experiences with mathematics, it is important to help them understand that assertions should always have reasons" (NCTM

2000, 56). When we ask for reasons and encourage reflection, evaluation, and justification, both as individuals and in collaborative groups, we are modeling the initial steps toward reasoning mathematically.

For younger children reasoning is informal, with explanations represented verbally or with objects and drawings. As they progress through the curriculum, children add more formal types of reasoning that build on more sophisticated mathematical knowledge. Some guidelines taken from NCTM's *Principles and Standards for School Mathematics* follow:

Early Grades	**Encourage Children To—**
Pre-K–2	• reason from what they know,
	• use trial-and-error strategies for justification,
	• prove by contradiction,
	• explore reasoning through class discussions.

Middle grades	**Encourage Children To—**
(3–5)	• expand thinking from individual mathematical objects to classes of objects,
	• move from unsystematic to systematic exploration of cases,
	• explain and evaluate their own reasoning and that of others,
	• learn to revise previous understanding based on new discoveries,
	• move toward explanations that use mathematical statements and definitions.

Upper grades	**Encourage Students To—**
(6–8)	• deepen evaluations of conjectures and assertions,
	• develop effective deductive arguments based on mathematical truths,
	• deepen understanding of the appropriate uses and limitations of inductive arguments,
	• broaden their use of different types of mathematical reasoning, including algebraic and geometric reasoning, proportional reasoning, statistical reasoning and so forth.

(NCTM 2000, 56–59; 188–92; 262–67)

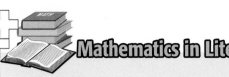

Mathematics in Literature

The Math Curse by Jon Scieszka and Lane Smith

"Mrs. Fibonacci has obviously put a Math Curse on me. Everything I look at or think about has become a math problem."

The main character in *The Math Curse* suffers from a heightened awareness of mathematics in her world. To break the curse, she must solve and solve problems until she can say, "I can solve any problem."

Early elementary students will enjoy the story and illustrations; middle to upper grades will be able to work with more of the concepts.

Activity 1

Read *The Math Curse* aloud; then ask the students to make up their own math problems from the worlds around them.

Activity 2

The girl in the story gives five different ways to count. Ask the students to explain what Russell, Molly, and the others are doing when they count. Ask them to think of other examples of ways to count.

Activity 3

Have the students write their own math-is-everywhere story in round-robin fashion. Divide the class into groups of four or five. Begin the story, "Today we discovered that math is everywhere." Have each member of the group add a place to find math and write a math problem; then pass the story to the next person to write about a different place and compose different problems. When all of the groups have completed their stories, read and discuss them as a class.

Diversity in Learning and Thinking Mathematically

In a roundtable discussion on math anxiety, Kyle remembered her seventh-grade math teacher:

> I would get the same answer he did, but I would get it in a different way, so he would count me wrong. It always had to be his way. That's when I started hating math.

Misha agreed and added a memory of her own:

> I needed to "see" the problem and work it out with my hands, but Mrs. Velarde said that was cheating.

Blue nodded vigorously:

> In Mr. Day's class, he would walk around and watch your fingers. If they moved even a little, like you were using them to count or something, he would take away your quiz and give you an F.

For each of the students in the roundtable, the memories contributed to a negative attitude about math—the affective dimension of learning and thinking mathematically. But the memories also affected the cognitive side. The restrictions on how they could solve math problems limited their thinking and also their options for solution paths and solutions—usually to standard algorithms and their products.

Freeing students to explore and think creatively is a cornerstone of a curriculum that prepares students to think mathematically and problem-solve effectively. Foundational ideas include the following:

- Multiple strategies for solving problems are better than a single strategy.
- Math problems may have more than one solution.
- Any tool that helps students understand, make sense of, and work through a problem is a legitimate tool.
- Solutions to math problems can best be seen as new beginnings, not endings.
- Problem solving is a multistep process.
- Problem solving and mathematical thinking are recursive, looking back as much as forward, drawing on a complex context of information, experiences, and feelings.

Activities CD

For an activity that emphasizes diversity, see Activity 15, Quipus, on the CD-ROM that accompanies this text.

Activities CD

For an activity with multiple solutions, see Activity 17, What if You Had a Million Dollars?, on the CD-ROM that accompanies this text.

Teacher Pro-File

**Larry Smith
Fifth Grade**

The Jacksonville Woodlands Project

Larry Smith of Jacksonville Elementary teaches functional mathematics in the context of an ongoing effort to preserve the Jacksonville Woodlands. For years students in his fifth-grade classes have raised and invested the money to preserve and develop a nature trail and park; they have also lobbied state and local leaders for support for their projects.

Objectives

The learning goals for Smith's classes cross disciplines. Students explore the natural and historical forces that shaped their community and work to understand forest dynamics and the forces of change operating in the woodlands. At the same time they use mathematics as a discovery and planning tool, measuring trail lengths for construction and maintenance, as well as finding the number of trees they will need to reforest a drought-stricken area (and then planting the trees).

Fifth graders preserve Oregon woodlands. © 2005 Bob Pennell/*Mail Tribune*.

Project

In 1992, Brian Mulholland, a student in Smith's class, persuaded a nearby city to sell Jacksonville a 10-acre wooded lot for its original 1916 price of $1,060. That lot became part of a trail system that has won national recognition and awards and also provided a learning laboratory for Jacksonville students. In 1997, Smith's fifth graders' efforts won $12,500 in the Pledge and Promise Environmental Awards. In 2000, Jacksonville was cited in the government's Earth Day report for preserving natural treasures, and during the same year part of the trail system was listed in the National Register of Historic Places.

Smith's students learn firsthand about finances and value. They collect data to help them plan activities as well as budget their money. They apply concepts of measurement and geometry in mapping activities such as those from Smith's *The Jackson Creek-Sarah Zigler Interpretive Trail Resource and Activity Guide.* They communicate what they have learned in creative publications, such as a coloring book, brochures, and videos, that also help raise money for the park.

© 2005 Jim Craven/*Mail Tribune*.

MAPPING

Time: 20-30 minutes

Materials needed: Sketch pads, pencils, calculators, measuring tape, stop watch, 6-inch rulers.

Lead in: Explain that early explorers drew maps. Ask students why maps are important. What kinds of information did they need to include on their maps (water sources, passes, impenetrable thickets, human settlement, fur sources)? Tell the student that they are going to practice these skills.

Procedures: Pair up students and send them to a string loop other than their own. Each couple should be insulated from others. Tell them to draw maps in their notebooks which show the terrain (mountains and valleys) inside the boundaries of their loops.

Reassemble into one group and go over each map as a whole, emphasizing ways to show depth. Take out a topographical map and explain what a topo map is. Explain contour line intervals. How can you tell how steep the slopes are? How can the direction of flow of a stream be found?

Wrap up: Explain that each of you is an expert at observing the small things around you, but as explorers you need to communicate your findings. Early explorers were from different countries. What they saw had to be precisely explained so that the people back home could imagine and feel what this new land was like.

Additional mapping Activity #1: Have the students return to the spot of their first mapping and map the area inside their string loop (without hand lens), using contour lines and shading. Students will need to select areas with uneven ground.

Additional Mapping Activity #2: Have the class sit down on the gravel bank of Jackson Creek about 75 feet up stream from the AmeriCorps Bridge (Post #26). Ask the class to sketch a cross section of the little valley created by Jackson Creek. Place the bridge and the creek slightly below center. Concentrate especially o showing the steepness of the slope to their right.

Additional Mapping Activity #3: Remaining upstream fro the bride, ask the class to draw a topo map of the ravine. Pretend they are flying over the bridge. What would they see? Use inter lines of about 50 feet. Shade to show elevation changes and stream flows.

Measuring the rate of stream flow of Jackson Creek: Measure off one hundred feet of creekbank. Throw a floating object into the creek and record the length of time it takes the object to cover the measured distance of 100 feet, to the nearest whole minute and decimal fraction. Divide 100 feet by the recorded minutes. This will give the rate of stream flow in feet per minute. Multiply the rate in feet by 60 and then divide by 5,280. This will give you the rate of flow in miles per hour. (This will work for Km/hr. Measure out 25 meters, divide by 1,000 instead of 5,280 and work using the same method as above.)

Mapping activities mix math and biology.

Outcomes

Overall, Smith's students have been instrumental in raising more than $40,000 for the woodlands. They have planted 3,000 native trees and cleared forest areas of nonnative shrubs such as Scotch broom. Their coloring book features drawings that represent space, proportion, and perspective and also miniessays about the history of their community with many number-related details.

Smith cites the video *If Trees Could Talk, What Would They Say?* as another of his "kid successes." The 20-minute production conceived by Nate Bennett, one of Smith's fifth graders, features a giant Sequoia planted by Peter Britt, whom the children also write about in a coloring book essay describing him as a "pioneering photographer . . . responsible for capturing history in pictures."

Other successes include what Smith calls a "life impact" on individual students. A newspaper article about the class that won a $12,500 environmental award highlights what these children have learned about the value of money. The reporter writes:

At the going rate of up to $10 per week, that $12,500 prize would represent some 24 years of the fifth-grader's allowance. But don't look for the kids to spend it down at the local video arcade.

As 10-year-old Missy Barron explains, "We're going to build bridges and buy a new piece of land!" (Enriquez 1997)

The GOLDEN YEARS for Jacksonville were the years from 1860 through 1890. During these years, families came from all over. They came in wagons and some people even walked!. People built more stores, churches with steeples and bigger schools. The discovery of gold had made people rich and happy. Jacksonville became the cultural and commercial center for all of Southern Oregon. (Tawnee Ivens, Amanda Warner, Rachel Neff) (Artist: Patrick Johnson)

One of the first churches in Jacksonville was called the Methodist Episcopal Church. It was built because some women wanted a place to worship. The women were angry because there were twelve taverns in town and not a single church. So, the women raised some money and built two churches so the men would not be in the taverns all weekend.
(Angelena Bigham, Sky Sevcik) (Artist: Andy Riggs)

Students illustrate the history of their town with drawings for a coloring book.

Fifth graders make a video, *If Trees Could Talk.*

Extensions and Reflections

Smith says he tries "to design lessons that . . . extend their learning and influence beyond their classroom. We have extended our classroom activities to Washington, D.C.; Orlando, Florida; and numerous speeches to community groups, city councils, state conventions, school boards, senior citizens. We have conducted fund-raisers, which required selling skills and fiduciary responsibility" and successful writing campaigns "requesting people to sell us land.

"I have found that motivation is the number one factor in getting students to internalize and buy into their lessons. When they see that their actions are affecting their whole community and that what they have done will have lasting value, they really get excited."

◀◀◀◀ LOOKING BACK

Mathematical thinking is integral to all mathematics learning. Instead of focusing on memorizing math facts, students need to develop the habits and perspectives of math thinkers. Mathematical thinking combines ways of looking at the world with ways of interpreting what we see and experience mathematically.

Thinking mathematically goes beyond identifying and applying appropriate algorithms. It calls for finding patterns, building a foundation of knowledge, reflecting about and testing solutions, and developing "math sense." Thinking effectively also involves working within a context of aptitudes and attitudes, knowledge of and feelings about mathematics.

Polya's four-step problem-solving method puts mathematical thinking to work. When mathematical tasks challenge students to plan and work through a multistep, problem-solving process, they can begin to develop the flexibility and persistence needed to do "real" mathematics and to understand the importance of process as well as product in dealing with math problems.

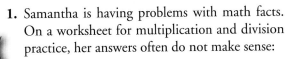

Questions for Further Thought, Discussion, and Research

1. Samantha is having problems with math facts. On a worksheet for multiplication and division practice, her answers often do not make sense:

   $$7 \times 4 = 28,\ 7 \times 5 = 35,\ 7 \times 6 = 36,$$
   $$7 \times 8 = 48,\ 7 \times 9 = 54$$
   $$35/5 = 6,\ 35/5 = 7,\ 64/8 = 7,\ 48/6 = 7$$

   Look at Samantha's errors. Do you see any patterns? What do you think is happening? How might you as a teacher help Samantha?

2. What is math anxiety? What is math confidence? Develop working definitions that explain what these concepts really mean to students and teachers in the classroom.

3. What do you think it means to have a mathematical worldview? Do you have this type of view? Why or why not? How might you go about developing such a worldview for yourself and for your students? You might suggest activities that ask students to collect and interpret information about the neighborhood or community they live in as well as about their homes or schools.

4

One-way mathematics instruction is like a room painted and furnished in one dark color. The dark, bland design makes the room not only dull but also obscure. Without planning for a dynamic design for mathematics instruction, the result is the same, dull and obscure.

Building a mathematics curriculum on principles of diversity and universal accessibility enables us to accommodate the needs of all learners—tapping into the intellectual excitement and challenges that diversity affords—something we might call the rainbow effect.

Developing such a curriculum also requires the planning of supportive day-to-day classroom activities and assessment strategies. A guideline for setting up this planning process is the redundancy principle: multiple means of engagement, representation, expression, and assessment.

Enhancing Mathematics Learning Through Instruction and Assessment

Flexible Mathematics Instruction

How many different ways can you think of to add 2 and 2? There's the traditional way: $2 + 2 = 4$. The count-aloud method: start with 2 and count 2 more, 3, 4. The finger method: one, two fingers plus one, two fingers for one, two, three, four fingers. The stick-math method: start with two sticks, add two more; then count one, two, three, four sticks. Or how about $\frac{1}{4} \times 3$? We can count by fourths: one fourth, two fourths, three fourths. We can multiply the fraction numerator by 3. We can add: $\frac{1}{4} + \frac{1}{4} + \frac{1}{4}$. Or we could use fraction circles or squares, fitting three pieces together to make three-fourths of a circle or three-fourths of a square. We could go on and on. Which method works best depends upon the individual, but helping students see and understand that there are multiple methods for accomplishing the same task encourages mathematical thinking and a problem-solving process that is rich with possibilities.

A flexible instructional design might also provide several avenues of access or a special approach that improves access for everyone—like the ramps or curb indentions at the ends of sidewalks that provide wheelchair access but also make it easier for parents with baby buggies, workers with handcarts, and even skateboarders to cross the street (Center for Applied Special Technology [CAST] 1998). In mathematics instruction, technology can be the equivalent of the indented curb—a tool that improves access for students with and without special needs. Video and audio presentations to support printed text, Internet links to extend and reinforce study, computer programs and languages that develop thinking and problem-solving skills, calculators to streamline operations and encourage self-assessment—all of these applications improve the learning process for everyone. In each area of the curriculum—engagement, representation, expression, assessment—multiplicity and flexibility promote learning experiences that are multidimensional, with something for everyone, as well as multiple-learning opportunities. The overall effect is like refracting light through a prism—a rainbow of colors and multiple perspectives.

Multiple Means of Engagement

Before students learn mathematics, they must focus on mathematics. Engaging students cognitively begins with catching their interest. Visuals such as comic strips, pictures, and videos first engage students through their physical senses, then through their imaginations. For example, comics have a built-in interest factor since students will read the strips for themselves. When the comics introduce math topics or attitudes, they serve as effective hooks, pulling students into discussions or making concepts meaningful.

Topics, Issues, and Explorations

Consider a simple mathematics problem: $1 + 2 + 3 + 5 + 8 = ?$ or $\frac{1}{2} + \frac{1}{2} + \frac{1}{2} = ?$ Then write out all the different strategies you can think of for solving the problem. Which strategies do you think would work best for which students? Which strategies work best for you?

Mathematics Across the Curriculum

A Writing and Design Project

While reformers often focus on curriculum access, the classroom itself needs to be a friendly, supportive learning environment for all students.

Imagine that you are teaching a third-grade class of varying backgrounds and needs. One student is in a wheelchair; one is deaf; two have attention-deficit disorder. You also have 3 English Language Learners (ELL) whose first language is Spanish, 2 ELL students whose first language is Vietnamese, 2 gifted students, and 12 students whose backgrounds and abilities are described by the school counselor as "average." How would you design a classroom to provide a friendly environment for all of the students to learn mathematics?

How would you arrange the classroom and your mathematics learning materials? What kinds of materials would you select? How would you group the students for cooperative learning activities?

Create a map of your idea of a student-friendly classroom environment. Then write about your ideas in a short paper to be shared and discussed with classmates.

Calvin and Hobbes

Calvin falls off the planet to avoid doing his math homework.
(From Calvin and Hobbes, by Bill Watterson. Used by permission of Universal Press Syndicate.)

Fox Trot

Paige is distracted by personalities as she tries to solve a word problem.
(From Fox Trot, by Bill Amend. Used by permission of Universal Press Syndicate.)

The comic strips reprinted here introduce not only some common issues in mathematics education—math anxiety, math avoidance, low expectations—but also some important ideas such as ways to approach word problems.

Calvin of the classic *Calvin and Hobbes* strip is notorious for his ability to avoid, ignore, or reject learning and mathematics. In one strip, he refuses to do a math test because it is "against his religious beliefs" (Watterson 1988, 40). In another series of strips, Calvin is living through fantasy episodes about becoming weightless and growing to Googol-sized proportions. His adventures in these strips have the potential for exploring concepts about size, weight, and gravity, but Calvin uses them to avoid doing his math homework. In class discussions of the strips, students are quick to criticize Calvin's attitude and to advise him to "do his math" or "quit messing around"—advice that can be applied as well to work habits in their own classroom.

To capture students' interest, the subject matter and modes of mathematics presentations need to be meaningful to them. Remember the Mathematics and Sports module profiled in Chapter 2? It succeeded in part because students were interested in sports, and the activity enabled them to link mathematics to something they valued. Basically the task for mathematics engagement calls for establishing two things:

- the **need** to learn mathematics and
- the **desire** to learn mathematics.

Both conditions motivate. "Making Learning Mathematics Fun," in the Idea Files, lists some effective strategies for engaging students and making learning mathematics enjoyable. When students play a math game, read a math story, or solve a math puzzle, they enter a world in which understanding and applying

Activities CD

For an activity in which students write their own story problems, see Activity 61, *Writing Story Problem Equations*, on the CD-ROM that accompanies this text.

Activities CD

For an activity that uses a math story to engage students' interest, go to Activity 7, *Walking on the Googol Side*, on the CD-ROM that accompanies this text.

Activities CD

For an activity related to engaging children cognitively in mathematics, see Activity 27, $100 Shopping Spree, on the CD-ROM that accompanies this text.

math concepts matters because it affects who wins the game or solves the puzzle or how the story's plot develops.

Keep Students on Task

Once interest is established and imagination engaged, we need to keep students on task. To do this, their minds must be caught up in the problem-solving process. Engaging students cognitively calls not only for focusing on the subject matter but also for focusing in a productive way. Paige in the *Foxtrot* cartoon is distracted from solving a word problem by her ongoing feud with her little brother Jason—that is, her personal world diverts attention from the impersonal world of the word problem. Personalizing the story is one solution. Rewriting the problem so that Paige shares with friends instead of family might have kept her on track, or Paige herself might rework the problem so that it is meaningful and makes sense to her. The rewritten problem could look something like this:

> Paige has baked a lemon meringue pie, but she forgot to add sugar. She didn't tell her brothers about her "mistake," so they begged her for pieces of her pie. Her older brother Peter wants a piece twice as big as her younger brother Jason's piece. Jason's annoying friend Marcus wants a piece twice as big as Jason's pesky friend Morton. Morton wants a piece two-thirds as

Idea Files

Making Learning Mathematics Fun

Strategy	Applications
Manipulatives	Hands-on activities with blocks, rods, sticks, straws, and other manipulatives take doing math out of the textbook and make it akin to playing with Legos or tinker toys.
Stories	Reading and writing math stories not only lets children look at concepts through the red, yellow, or purple glasses of the imagination but also emphasizes the connections between mathematics and the humanities.
Art	For preschoolers and children in the early grades, showing math ideas with drawings or other art projects provides a means of expression unrestricted by limited knowledge of mathematics or verbal symbols. For older children, mathematics in art can create a bridge between work they consider creative and liberating and subject matter that may seem restrictive or rigid.
Puzzles/mysteries	Seeing math problems as puzzles or mysteries to be solved adds adventure to the problem-solving process and eliminates the dullness of cookie cutter–style exercises.
Games	Computer games, board games, number games, games of chance and probability—all present learning mathematics as play. Games allow children to explore concepts and develop skills within a flexible, challenging format with competition as an added motivator.
Newspapers	Finding mathematics in newspapers works for children of all ages. Preschoolers can find numbers and shapes; older children can find material about percentages, measurement, basic statistics, and probability.
Videos	Favorite actors and exciting adventures provide a stimulating context for learning mathematics. The Indiana Jones adventures have been used as a source of visually and mentally challenging word problems (see Bransford et al. 1996).
Field trips	Finding mathematics in unexpected places—the park, a gym, the subway, the zoo—as well as in more usual places such as stores and banks helps children understand that mathematics is everywhere, a real part of real life.

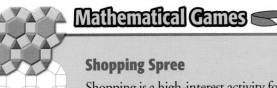
Mathematical Games

Shopping Spree

Shopping is a high-interest activity for students of all ages. Turning shopping into a game lets students explore money values and equivalencies, making change, budgeting, and spending money wisely within the context of play.

Shopping Spree can be played as a board game or in a store as a treasure hunt activity.

Game 1

A Shopping Spree board game is available as an Educa product (www.educaborras.com). It features a shopping mall with six stores, parking space, and various hazard spaces where shoppers can lose money. Players use their "pockets full of money" to fill shopping carts with items from the different stores. The first player to buy something from each store wins.

Game 2

As a class make a shopping list of items needed for school: notebook, scissors, pencils, crayons, calculator, ruler, and so forth. Visit a store that sells school supplies, and find the best price for each item. List and total the costs. The player with the lowest total wins.

Extension

Your class is planning a 100th-day party. Each student in your class has contributed 100 pennies or $1 to buy refreshments. Make a shopping list and then visit a grocery store to see what you can buy with your classmates' contributions. To find the winner, vote on who made the best use of the money.

---

big as Peter's piece. Paige will gladly divide the pie so that no extra pieces remain. What fraction of the pie will go to each of the greedy, unknowing boys?

A major strategy for engaging students cognitively and keeping them on task involves matching learning materials and situations to *learning style.*

Address Different Learning Styles

Children learn in different ways. What works best for one student may not work at all for another. A mathematics learning style is actually a complex construct influenced by physiology, educational background, attitudes, and preferences. Figure 4.1 shows some of the elements that work together to influence how each child learns mathematics.

A learning style may be *aural/oral,* with an emphasis on hearing and speaking; *tactile,* with an emphasis on hands-on experience; *pictorial/symbolic,* with an emphasis on the written word and/or visual representation; or a combination of various types. For example, a student might be a visual, hands-on learner (pictorial and tactile) who needs to both see and do to understand. Or a student's learning style might rely heavily on verbal explanations and on restating problems and concepts in her or his own words (aural/oral).

Matching learning tasks to learning styles is like using computer programs made for your operating system. When there is a match, everything makes sense; when there is a mismatch, nothing connects.

Topics, Issues, and Explorations

NCTM's *Principles and Standards* sets expectations as well as standards. An expectation for preschool to second grade is for children to "understand and represent commonly used fractions, such as ¼, ⅓, and ½" (NCTM 2000, 392). What kinds of materials and strategies could you use to engage children at these levels in learning fractions?

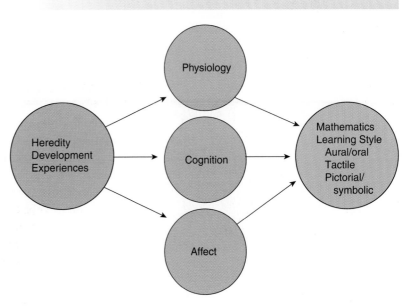

Figure 4.1 Developing a mathematics learning style.

Topics, Issues, and Explorations

How do you learn best? Collect data on your own learning preferences. Keep a log for one week on what you have learned and how you have learned. Include informal learning activities—those outside school, such as learning to use a new toaster or a new computer program—as well as classroom experiences. Record how the material was presented, including the learning environment; how you were engaged in the experience; and how well you understood the ideas or operations.

Activities CD

For an activity that uses a digital format to represent concepts, go to Activity 93, Connecting Fractions, Decimals, and Percents with Virtual Manipulatives, on the CD-ROM that accompanies this text.

Multiple Means of Representation

Students see the world in different ways. Representing material to be learned in a variety of modes allows each student to develop a working perspective—an access route to the information or concepts that fit individual learning styles and abilities. This will mean teaching methods that encourage redundancy rather than efficiency, but the overall effect will be to add depth and breadth to instruction, with children who learn best with one approach nevertheless receiving reinforcement from the other approaches.

Orkwis and McLane (1998) in "A Curriculum Every Student Can Use" emphasize the need to provide learning materials in multiple formats. They propose five "first steps" to ensure all children have access to learning—steps that we have adapted specifically to learning mathematics:

Step 1   Provide all mathematics text in digital as well as any print format—books, handouts, and so forth.

Step 2   Ensure captions or transcripts are available for any audio formats.

Step 3   Provide educationally relevant descriptions for images and graphical layouts, including problems, charts, maps, and other math-related visuals.

Step 4   Verify that captions and educationally relevant descriptions are part of any videos and overheads.

Step 5   Provide cognitive supports for mathematics content and activities:

- Summarize big ideas and concepts related to exercises and problem solving.

- Scaffold or structure support for the learning of new ideas and generalize from specific problems to types of problems.

- Assess background knowledge and attitudes toward mathematics.

- Include explicit strategies to identify the goals and methods of mathematics instruction clearly.

(Adapted from Orkwis and McLane 1998, 6–7)

This ambitious program creates several avenues of access to the curriculum—printed word, digitized word, spoken word, visual images, and oral and written descriptions and interpretations. It also creates an instructional process that underscores connections and patterns, putting ideas in contexts, summarizing, interpreting, and revisiting and highlighting the knowledge structures students are building.

Of the different formats Orkwis and McLane suggest, digital may be the most promising for classroom teachers. With the availability of inexpensive scanners, teachers can quickly digitize printed pages or handwritten worksheets. Because of its flexibility, digital format can be especially effective in diversifying and even individualizing representations for learning mathematics. The size, color, and intensity of numbers and other text can be easily changed. Programs can customize learning plans and track progress. And the rate and level of material can be altered to fit individual needs and preferences.

To match representation to learning styles, levels, and needs, we need to develop multiple-format, multiple-strategy teaching methods. A mathematics lesson that uses representations from each category—pictorial/symbolic, aural/oral, and tactile—will be more accessible to more students. It will also help teachers overcome students' perception of mathematics as a two-dimensional textbook subject and encourage them to look at concepts from a variety of learning perspectives. "Representing Mathematics" in the Idea Files lists a variety of ways to represent concepts, some of which offer opportunities for mathematics learning across the curriculum.

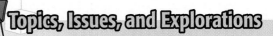

Topics, Issues, and Explorations

Refer to the NCTM objective for learning fractions in the Topics, Issues, and Explorations box on page 81. How would you represent the concepts involved, using means that address the needs of pictorial/symbolic, aural/oral, and tactile learning styles? How would you ensure that each child has a multidimensional learning experience?

Idea Files

Representing Mathematics

Mode of Representation

Pictorial/Symbolic	Aural/Oral	Tactile
Written words	Spoken words	Manipulatives
Written numbers	Spoken numbers	Rods
Mathematics symbols	Discussion	Base-10 blocks
Graphs	Explanation	Pattern blocks
Pictures	Reading aloud	Building blocks
Charts	Thinking aloud	Dice
Equations	Problem-solving aloud	Tangram pieces
Computer graphics	Teaching tapes and CDs	Measuring devices
Videos, TV	Music	Spoons
Artwork	Sound patterns	Cups
Visual dimension	Audio of computer	Rulers
of crafts	programs, videos, TV	Protractors
Maps		Compasses
		Weights
		Scales
		Abacus
		Counting board
		and sticks
		Artwork
		Crafts
		Quilting
		Cooking
		Carpentry
		Musical instruments

Activities CD

For another activity using food to explore fractions, see Activity 78, Tortilla Fractions, on the CD-ROM that accompanies this text.

Multiple Means of Expression

Critics have accused reformers of teaching "fuzzy math" in part because of the way we encourage students to develop and use multiple problem-solving strategies and to express the results in a variety of ways. That there may be more than one correct answer to a problem and more than one way to find and show those answers challenges etched-in-concrete approaches to learning mathematics. "I never have understood math," a preservice teacher told us recently. "In my math classes, I would get the right answer, but I would get it in my own way instead of the teacher's! And that made the whole thing wrong."

What happens when students are not only allowed but also encouraged to find and express answers in the ways that work best for them? What happens when innovation and individuality are discouraged? Consider the following teaching scenarios, Cutting the Pizza 1 and Cutting the Pizza 2 in the Windows on Learning box on this page and the next.

Windows on Learning

Cutting the Pizza 1

Ms. Simpson's fourth grade was studying fractions. With an overhead projector, Ms. Simpson showed the class a large pizza cut into 10 pieces.

"Here's our problem," she said. "We have one large pizza. It has already been cut into 10 pieces, but there are 20 students in the class. How can we get enough pieces for all the students?

"Here's what we do. We take those 10 pieces and we divide them in half like this."

She put another overhead with the worked-out problem on the screen:

$$\frac{10}{1} \div \frac{1}{2} \qquad \frac{10}{1} \times \frac{2}{1} = 20$$

"See? When we divide by ½, we invert the fraction and multiply by 2, so we get 20 pieces, enough for everybody.

"Now you try it. This time we have a pizza cut into eight pieces. Work it out so that we have enough for 16 children. Look on your worksheet. It's the first problem."

The children worked individually with pencil and paper.

After a few minutes, Ms. Simpson said, "All right. That should be enough time. What did you get?"

Rory held up his worksheet. He had drawn a round circle and 10 intersecting lines.

Ms. Simpson shook her head.

Celeste raised her hand. "I added 8 twice and got 16."

Ms. Simpson shook her head again.

Aura showed her paper. She had imitated the procedure on the overhead:

$$\frac{8}{1} \div \frac{1}{2} = \frac{8}{1} \times \frac{2}{1} = 16$$

"That's it. That's the answer I wanted."

The children then continued doing the worksheet exercise, using the same method.

Cutting the Pizza 2

Mr. Lee's second-grade class was also studying fractions. Like Ms. Simpson, Mr. Lee started the lesson with an overhead of a large pizza.

"Do you like pizza?" he asked.

The children nodded.

"Would you all like a piece of this pizza?"

Some of the children nodded, but one boy, Brandon shook his head. "Not unless it's a cheese pizza. I only like cheese."

"Uh oh. This one looks like pepperoni. Oh, well, let's divide the pizza so that there are enough pieces for everyone—even Brandon, just in case he changes his mind. Find whatever you want to work with and work together if you wish."

The children began to work in pairs, groups of three or four, or individually. Some worked with construction paper, some with fraction circles, some with pencil and triangular grid paper. All carefully counted the number of students in the class—16.

Susie cut out a construction-paper circle and began folding it to see how many pieces she could make. After folding it in halves, fourths, and eighths, she raised her hand.

"Mr. Lee, I can't fold this small enough for 16 pieces."

"What would you like to do then?"

"Order two pizzas!"

"All right. Fine. You can make this a two-pizza problem if you want to."

The class worked noisily for 10 minutes, discussing their solutions and problem-solving strategies. Mr. Lee moved around, asking questions, making suggestions, giving a nudge here, a boost there.

Then Mr. Lee asked the children to explain their solutions.

Susie had cut out two circles and folded each into eighths.

Eloy had worked with blocks. "Mine is a square pizza," he said. "I have 16 blocks in four rows of four."

Amy and Rupert had tried drawing a circle on triangular grid paper, then bisecting the angles, but they had come up with 12, then 24 pieces. Then they had drawn a circle on plain paper and divided it in half, fourths, eighths, and sixteenths.

Jeremy, Letetia, and Samantha had worked with numbers and found that 8 plus 8 equals 16. Like Susie, they suggested the best idea was to order two pizzas.

Other solutions included a drawing of the pizza cut into 16 pieces and fraction circles with the eighths carefully divided into sixteenths with blackline tape.

Mr. Lee discussed each one, explaining to the class why the different solutions worked and asking the children how the solutions were alike or different. Were any the same but shown in different ways? Completely different but arrived at in a similar way?

Finally, he threw in his bombshell. "You all did great. You all get a piece of pizza, but what about me? I'm the 17th member of the class, and I'm a lot bigger than you. Can you cut your pizza to give me two pieces?"

Both Ms. Simpson and Mr. Lee use the old favorite cutting-the-pizza problem as a context for studying fractions. Both introduce the problem orally and visually. But Ms. Simpson's class is actually learning a procedure: a specific way to divide a fraction by a fraction. Cutting the pizza is simply window dressing. Mr. Lee's students, on the other hand, are discovering multiple ways to divide a pizza and in the process learning what the fractions they are discovering really mean in terms of size, relationships, and patterns.

Encouraging multiple means of expression adds depth and breadth to learning activities. When students express concepts in the means that best fits their learning styles, they reinforce their access to and understanding of the concepts. When they observe or try additional means of expression, concepts that may have seemed one- or two-dimensional become multidimensional.

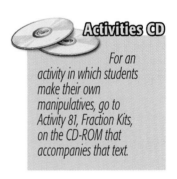

Activities CD

For an activity in which students make their own manipulatives, go to Activity 81, Fraction Kits, on the CD-ROM that accompanies that text.

Using Various Learning Tools

Facilitating diversity in expression are the different learning tools that students use to access and manipulate mathematics concepts. Technology such as computers and calculators serve as **mind tools** when students use them to think with rather than to bypass thinking (Papert 1982, 1993). **Sensory tools,** such as math manipulatives and audio or visual representations, become tools for mathematics expression when students use them to show problem-solving and thinking processes. And **cognitive tools,** such as a math journal, concept maps, or math dialogues (written and spoken), not only help students understand and reflect on their own thinking but also serve as an expression of what and how they have learned (Martinez and Martinez 2001).

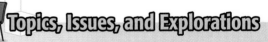

Topics, Issues, and Explorations

Return to the pizza-cutting problem. Find as many ways as you can to solve the problem of cutting the pizza for each situation, including cutting a pizza to give Mr. Lee one or two slices. Express your solutions in a variety of ways. Then discuss what the different means of expression tell you about thought processes, learning styles, and learning tools.

Math Manipulatives

Fractions with Virtual and Actual Counters

Working with actual and virtual (computer-screen) counters to express math problems facilitates the process of moving from concrete objects to abstract ideas. Counters in the shape of frogs are more concrete than images of frogs on the computer screen. You can make your own virtual counters with clip art that allows students to move objects such as frogs around on the screen.

As students work with both means of expression—manipulating the counters by hand and with the mouse—they develop flexibility in seeing and working out a problem as well as showing solutions.

Activity

Consider this story problem:

Twelve frogs were on the streambank. A fourth of the frogs were trying to catch flies; a third were taking a nap. The rest of the frogs were croaking. They croaked and croaked until they disturbed the napping and fly-catching frogs.

"Gallumph!" croaked a fly-catching frog, "You're scaring away the flies."

"Garrumph!" grumped a napping frog, "Be quiet!"

What do you think happened? Are there enough quiet frogs to make the noisy ones be still? What if they took a vote? Who would win?

In small groups show the problem-solving process and solution(s) to this story problem with actual and with virtual or computer counters. Then discuss which way you prefer and why. How many different ways are there to solve this problem? Could there be more than one answer?

In a very real sense, the medium students use to express mathematics learning becomes part of the message—denoting not only learning style but also type and even degree of understanding.

Multiple Means of Assessment

An immediate and automatic outcome of students' using different means to express mathematics learning and problem solving is the need for multiple means for assessing their work. How can teachers tell whether a student really understands a mathematics concept? Does one means of expression indicate greater understanding than another? What does it mean when a student uses an effective problem-solving strategy but does not arrive at an effective solution?

Frequently teachers and education students preparing to teach have told us, "At least grading math is easy, not like grading writing or projects. Either they get the right answer, or they don't." This restricted view of assessment handicaps both teacher and learner and promotes skewed evaluations. A student who does a good job of setting up a problem but makes an error in calculations may actually know more about the concepts involved than a student who imitates a procedure and arrives at a solution given in an answer key. Assessing the entire problem-solving process instead of just the product or outcome provides a broader picture of what children understand or do not understand. It also helps pinpoint trouble spots—the misstep or missteps that led to inadequate conclusions. Similarly, assessing students' progress with a variety of tools rather than a single type of measure such as tests and quizzes provides multiple perspectives, a kind of three-way (or four- or five-way) mirror on learning.

Topics, Issues, and Explorations

Think about the role of grades in assessing achievement in mathematics. What roles have grades played in your own progress? What roles have grades played in the progress of others you know? Do you consider grades to be incentives to learn or punishments for not learning? Discuss your ideas; then write several paragraphs to explain your position.

The challenge for teachers, according to Richard Stiggins (1998), is "the creation of an assessment world that is the antithesis of the one in which most of us grew up" (13). To use assessment to enhance student learning, he recommends involving students in the assessment process in three ways:

- student-centered classroom assessment, which makes students "partners in monitoring their own level of achievement";
- student-involved record keeping, which asks students to track their own performance, "build portfolios of evidence of their success," and reflect "about changes they see";
- student-involved communication, which asks students to prepare and "tell the story of their own success (or lack thereof)" (Stiggins 1998, 13).

Classroom Observations

Teachers, according to Stiggins (1998, 4), make assessments on an average of every three to four minutes. Most of these judgments are necessarily informal and unrecorded. They comprise part of an ongoing mental image of what is working or not working in their classes and help with the minute-by-minute decisions that respond to students' immediate needs and questions and keep the learning process spontaneous and alive. When it is necessary to make a record, a written comment is often more effective than a chart or checklist since descriptions trigger memories more effectively than checkmarks or scores. Figure 4.2 provides a brief example. (See Appendix A, Make Your Own Manipulatives, for a complete form.)

Rubrics

Finding a working balance between quantitative and qualitative assessments can be particularly challenging in mathematics education. Because both teachers and students tend to see quantitative assessments as more authoritative for mathematics work and even to prefer number scores (96%, +47 points, and so forth), a scoring rubric is an effective solution. *Rubric* literally means "written in red" after highlighted headings or titles in medieval manuscripts. A scoring rubric is a series of analytic headings with attached scores. Leitze and May (1999, 307) used a rubric similar to the one in Figure 4.3 to score a problem-solving activity. The main headings represent phases of the problem solution; the subheadings, levels of work within each

Classroom Observation

Name _Lorinda_ Class _2nd grade_
Date _10/9_
Activity _Mathline puppet-making_

Lorinda had trouble using her dollar budget to buy material for her puppet. She wanted to take materials without paying for them. She also had trouble understanding the connection between the prices on the puppet materials and the money she had to spend.

When I attempted to go over the amounts with her and try to set up a budget, she confused quarters and nickels.

Lorinda will need to do some extra work on identifying coins and understanding money values and equivalencies.

Figure 4.2 Observation for Lorinda's understanding money values.

Analytic Scoring Rubric for Problem Solving

Circle the score that best identifies student's understanding of the process described.

Understand or formulate the question in a problem	• Complete understanding	4
	• Part of the problem misunderstood or misinterpreted	2
	• Complete misunderstanding	0
Select or find data to solve the problem	• Found appropriate data	4
	• Found some data	2
	• Found no data	0
Formulate subproblems, and select appropriate solution strategies to pursue	• Identified and applied effective problem-solving strategies and subproblems	4
	• Accounts for one strategy and subproblem	2
	• Does not adopt effective strategy or identify subproblems	0
Correctly implement the solution strategy or strategies, and solve subproblems	• All processes for all phases of the problem	4
	• Correct processes for all phases of the problem	3
	• Some, but not all, processes correct	2
	• No correct processes chosen or used	1

Record Student's Total Score _____pts

Figure 4.3 Evaluating math work with a rubric.
(Adapted with permission from Leitze, A. R., and May, S. T., *Mathematics Teaching in the Middle School* (1999) by the National Council of Teachers of Mathematics. All rights reserved.)

Portfolio Checklist

Name _____Joey_____   Class _____3rd grade_____

Assignment	Date	Score	Comments
Numbers Identity Project	9/12	10/10	Showed number sense, represented concepts visually, in numbers and in words
Multiplying two-digit numbers	9/13, 9/14	5/5, 2/5	Showed understanding with hands-on but had trouble with calculations
Multiplication homework	9/15	5/5	Effective process, accurate product

Figure 4.4   A partial portfolio checklist for Joey.

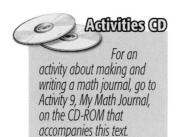

For an activity about making and writing a math journal, go to Activity 9, My Math Journal, on the CD-ROM that accompanies this text.

phase. (For more about scoring rubrics, see Charles, Lester, and O'Daffer 1987).

Portfolios

Increasingly, portfolios are becoming a popular tool for mathematics assessment. A *portfolio* is a collection of materials, often prepared by the students themselves or in partnership with teachers. The materials might include activity worksheets, tests with makeup exercises for areas of poor performance, projects, written explanations, and charts or graphs to map progress. Portfolios can present a complete or a selective record of a student's work in mathematics—the latter compiled in partnership with a teacher or aide to best represent learning; the former organized in order of assignments or by topic. Both types can be evaluated with a checklist, such as the one in Figure 4.4 (see Appendix A, Make Your Own Manipulatives for complete form). Asking students to keep the list up to date frees teachers from some record-keeping chores and also encourages students to reflect about their progress and assume some of the responsibility for seeking help when they need it.

Journals

How can we tell whether students are arriving at solutions by imitating procedures or by understanding and applying concepts? One way is to have them explain what they did and why they did it in a journal. Writing in *Teaching Children Mathematics,* Norwood and Carter (1994) describe the mathematics journal as a means to gain "insight into students' understanding" (146). They cite the example reproduced here. The student's writing shows she can perform the calculations but does not understand the concepts involved:

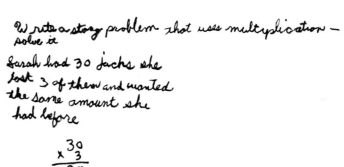

On the other hand, the journal entry in Figure 4.5 demonstrates both the student's understanding of concepts and the ability to multiply effectively.

In *Reading and Writing to Learn Mathematics,* we emphasize using language activities, such as journals and other written work, to help shape future study, to focus on individual progress rather than group comparisons, and to encourage reflection:

Reading their own work and that of their classmates can also take our students to the next level: self-evaluation. The written explanation allows them to second-guess themselves and ask: "What was I thinking here?" "Why did I do this?" "Should I have done that instead?" "Am I sure I want to do this?" "What gave me the idea to do that?"

For all of us, reading and writing assignments add depth and meaning to evaluation, taking us beyond mechanical input/output approaches and in effect making assessment a more human and humane activity.

(Martinez and Martinez 2001, 197–98)

Figure 4.5 Writing about multiplication in a math journal.

Performance Outcomes

Assessing performance outcomes begins with objective criteria—usually a series of specific expectations for students at each grade level. Once the expectations are established, teachers can use a scoring rubric and benchmarks to evaluate student work. For example, Figure 4.6 shows an algebraic activity for K–2 entitled "Mary Quite Contrary." The benchmarks for each performance level are described in the Teacher Instructions excerpted here.

Novice-Level Response: The student work at this level shows rudimentary understanding of the problem.

Apprentice-Level Response: The apprentice shows some understanding of the problem, and the student has some correct work.

Practitioner-Level Response: The work shows complete understanding of the task.

Expert-Level Response: The expert will have in-depth understanding of the task.

Research, Development, and Accountability, (Albuquerque Public Schools, 2002, 3)

Figure 4.7 shows examples of benchmark work at each level.

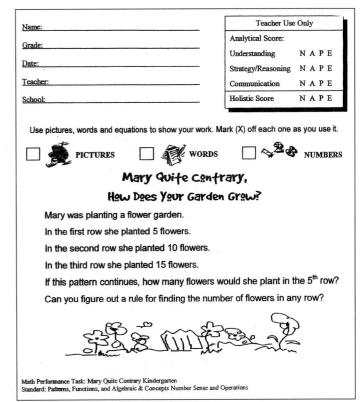

Figure 4.6 Mary Quite Contrary assignment sheet.
(© Exemplars, 2005. Visit www.exemplars.com to view free sample tasks and rubrics.)

Tests

We come last to the assessment measure most people think of first. Both classroom and standardized tests are and will continue to be facts of life in American education. Developing, administering, and interpreting tests so that they enhance education are additional challenges for mathematics educators.

Classroom tests might be taken from texts or supplementary material, or they can be made by the teacher. An advantage of using premade tests is reliability. Usually printed materials, including tests, have been classroom tested, and

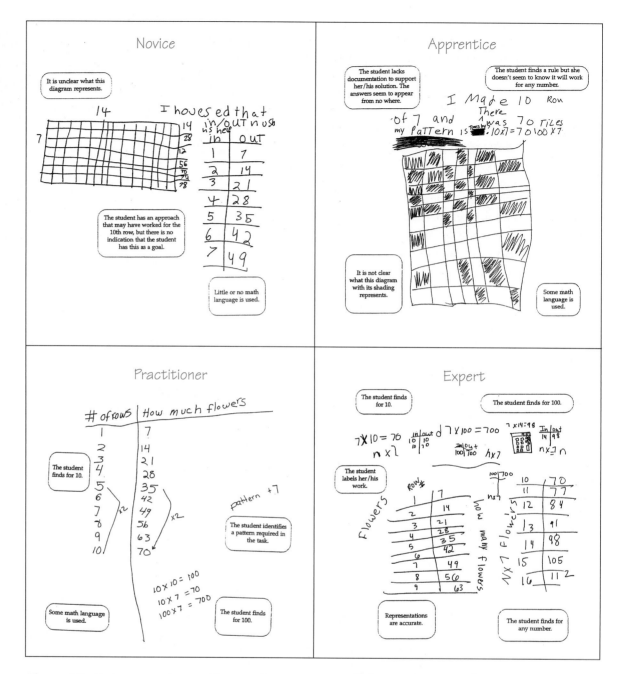

Figure 4.7 Novice, apprentice, practitioner, and expert responses for "Mary Quite Contrary."
(Research, Development, and Accountability, Albuquerque Public Schools, Christina Fritz, Assessment Manager. Used with permission.)

instructional manuals may contain data for comparing student performance. Of course, printed tests also have the advantage of providing answer keys and sometimes multiple forms for retesting.

Teacher-Made Tests   Teacher-made tests also have several advantages, including specificity, flexibility, and accessibility.

Specificity   The items can be composed to reflect the specific material covered in class.

Flexibility The content of the tests can be adjusted to give different emphases—for example, to include review questions or a problem students had difficulty with in class.

Accessibility Many students find teacher-made tests less intimidating than more official-looking printed tests. Moreover, the teachers, knowing the special needs of students in their classes, can make adjustments, such as larger type or more explicit directions, to improve access.

The teacher-made test shown in Figure 4.8 demonstrates some of these advantages. The test covers several new topics—placing parentheses and multiplying multidigit numbers—but it also includes a fact-family review. The teacher has varied representations—using a math box as well as word and number sentences. The result tells her not only how well Jacob understood the new material but also what he remembered from previous lessons and how well he was able to integrate new and old material.

Because test anxiety can be a major factor in mathematics anxiety overall, we need testing strategies that minimize distress. Repeated testing and mastery learning systems, which allow multiple opportunities to succeed, are now regaining popularity as computers relieve teachers of the extra chores these methods bring in grading and individualizing instruction (see Chapter 2; also Martinez with Martinez 1996, 129–32). Involving children in the grading process, either to help define criteria or to apply those criteria to their own work and that of their classmates, encourages them not only to feel more in control but also to accept more responsibility for their performance. This shared responsibility for evaluation creates what Stiggins (1998) calls "classrooms in which there are no surprises and no excuses" (13). Moreover, grading the process as well as the product in tests (how an answer was arrived at as well as the answer itself) helps refocus scoring; it changes the emphasis from punishing failure to rewarding successes.

Standardized Tests What about the role of standardized tests, including state competency exams and national tests such as the National Assessment of Education Progress (NAEP)? These large-scale tests "provide information about student achievement that can inform important programmatic and policy-level decisions" (Stiggins 1998, 4). They also can suggest specific areas for us to work on in the classroom. For example, the 1996 NAEP Mathematics Assessment found that students at all levels had trouble with "complex multistep problems, even those that require only simple computational skills at each step of the problem" (Mitchell et al. 1999, 2). Figure 4.9 shows a portion of a multistep problem about planning a butterfly booth for a science fair. This NAEP result suggests the need for more multistep and extended problems in the curriculum as well as for more experience interpreting and developing strategies to solve complex word problems.

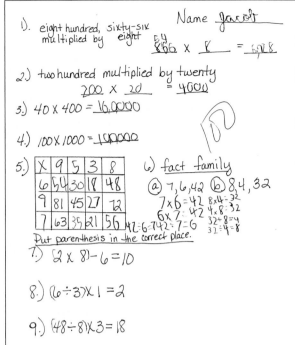

Figure 4.8 Jacob's test.

Topics, Issues, and Explorations

Study the Butterfly Booth problem and responses in Figure 4.9. The headings for the responses suggest one method of assessment. How would you evaluate the responses? Qualitatively? Quantitatively? Are several assessments possible? Discuss the different possibilities in your small group or class.

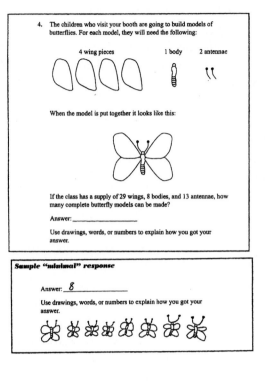

Figure 4.9 The Butterfly Booth problem.

Diversity in Learning and Thinking Mathematically

Diversity in learning styles and tools needs to be an integral part of lesson planning rather than add-on adjustments. The difference is akin to the example given earlier of built-in dips in curbs instead of add-on curb ramps. Both provide wheelchair access, but the former is part of the original curb design, improving access for everyone without creating a hazard for drivers or bicyclists and without altering the original design (CAST 1998).

Designing a mathematics lesson for everyone means incorporating the ideas discussed in this chapter—multiple means of engagement, representation, expression, and assessment—throughout the process. While traditional lesson plans focus on procedures, a plan that ensures access for everyone must be broader and more inclusive, comprising what we call a *teaching/learning plan* (see Appendix A for form).

Some of the key ingredients of an effective teaching/learning plan include the following:

- **A clear focus**—an idea, concept, or skill that involves all children in learning important mathematics;
- **Flexible access**—a variety of tools and methods to involve children in tasks and enable them to work to the best of their abilities and in their best styles;

- **Multidimensional strategies** to develop multiple perspectives on mathematics, including concepts and procedures;
- **Clear but open-ended objectives** that encourage learning connections and extensions; and
- **Flexible evaluative measures** that emphasize understanding (see, for example, Bernadetta's use of oral language and one-on-one discussion to assess Understanding in the "How Tall Is My Dino?" activity, featured in the Teacher Pro-File).

The plan for "Metric System Conversions" in Figure 4.10 uses a popular subject, sports, as a context for activities that emphasize "doing" mathematics. The plan involves tactile, pictorial/symbolic, and aural/oral experiences and creates a learning environment that emphasizes real-life applications of concepts.

Metric System Conversions

Class and/or grade level: *4th grade*

Concepts to be learned: *Conversions to the metric system, decimals, and fractions, time, distance*

Learning objectives: *The students will convert distances to the metric system. Lengths that are not exact will be recorded in decimals or fractions.*

Materials needed: *paper, pencils, calculators*

Procedure:

1. Describe how you will introduce the activity or lesson and how you will motivate students to be interested.
The class will run races and/or time different distances that the students run.

2. Explain the teaching method(s) you will use—problem solving, discovery learning, demonstrating/explaining, etc.
Students will convert different "set" distances to metric or metric to American system. Students will time each other and compare the time and distances in fractions of a minute or represent in decimals.

3. Write out the activities and/or problems you will give the students.
The students will race and time different distances. The distance can be converted—the time can be est., rounded, recorded on charts and timed to the decimal or fraction of a second or fraction of a length.

Assessment:

1. How will you assess process?
The students can brain storm various lengths, estimating of converted lengths and various jobs of recorded runner.

2. How will you assess product?
The class will record all times conversions decimals, etc. and create a class average or chart of findings.

Extensions:

1. How can you extend this activity or lesson to the next level—another concept, degree of difficulty, etc.?
Compare and contrast ourselves to well-known runners world records and Olympic times.

2. How can you connect this activity or lesson to other learning?
We could research famous times-distances w/ other runners—also we could research history of an athlete or sport history.

Figure 4.10 Metric system conversions.

Topics, Issues, and Explorations

Develop a teaching/learning plan to teach basic fraction concepts to students in a combined first- and second-grade class. Be careful to include material and strategies for the different age groups and skills levels. Use the teaching/learning plan outline located in Appendix A.

Teacher Pro-File

**Bernadetta Crawford
Kindergarten**

"How Tall Is My Dino?"

"Kindergartners love dinosaurs," says Bernadetta Crawford, "and they love hands-on learning." She took advantage of these preferences in an activity she has shared with many other kindergarten teachers, "How Tall Is My Dino?" The activity combines counting with measurement and comparison. It introduces students to a metric standard measurement, the centimeter, and it lets them explore the meanings of vocabulary about size, words such as *tall, short, long, big, little.*

Procedures

Bernadetta began the lesson with pictures of dinosaurs. She talked about the size of dinosaurs and about the world they lived in. She answered questions about what their world looked like, what they ate, and what scientists believe happened to them. Then she introduced a song, "How Big Is a Dinosaur?"

After students sang the song several times, each student chose a dinosaur to measure and draw. Some students worked directly from the illustrations; others, from their imaginations. Once they had drawn a dinosaur, they measured it with centimeter cubes, drew a stack of centimeter squares to represent the measurement, and counted and wrote the number of squares in the stack. Then they wrote a description of the sizes of their drawings.

Tall dinosaur illustration.

Short dinosaur illustration.

After discussing and comparing their dinosaurs, the students made a second dinosaur drawing. If they described the first dinosaur as tall, they chose, drew, and measured a short dinosaur; if their first dinosaur was short, they drew a tall dinosaur.

Outcomes

In the process of drawing and measuring their dinosaurs, students worked with several important mathematical concepts and topics:

- They counted and read and wrote numerals.
- They connected numbers to quantities measured.
- They demonstrated one-to-one correspondence by keeping track of quantities.

- They organized and made sense of data by using measurements to evaluate size.
- They used a standard unit of measurement and began to discover the importance of standards in making comparisons.
- They learned and used vocabulary to describe numbered quantities.

Bernadetta relied heavily on oral language to assess what students had learned. Throughout the activity, she encouraged them to verbalize, to talk about what they were trying to do and describe the results. She asked each student to explain to her, one-to-one, his or her drawing and the measurement and description. Then, in a circle, they talked about their dinosaur drawings, noting similarities and differences and comparing their measurements and descriptions. For example, most students called a 10-centimeter dinosaur tall and a 5-centimeter dinosaur short, but some made drawings so small that 5 centimeters was tall and 2 centimeters, short. Talking about the differences helped students understand the importance of standard measurement units in making comparisons.

Commentary

"How Tall Is My Dino?" is a favorite activity—both in Bernadetta's classroom and in the classrooms of the teachers with whom she has shared her lesson plan. Asked why the activity works so well, Bernadetta identified several reasons:

- Students enjoy the work. The dinosaur topic catches their interest and gets them involved in the lesson.
- The hands-on work—drawing and coloring their dinosaurs as well as the measuring blocks—keeps students interested and helps them stay on task.
- The activity integrates a variety of concepts and areas—mathematics, science, language—for a holistic learning experience.
- Students do both individual and group work, giving teachers different contexts for encouraging effort and for assessing understanding.
- The drawings of different dinosaurs make an excellent classroom or hallway display—a means of recognizing and rewarding the entire class's accomplishments.

Activities CD

For more about this activity, go to Activity 3, How Tall Is My Dinosaur? on the CD-ROM that accompanies this text.

◂◂◂◂ LOOKING BACK

Teaching mathematics in the 21st century is not and cannot be a one-dimensional process. The diversity in our classrooms must be met with diversity in our teaching methods and materials. Students with different learning styles need teachers whose professional repertoires incorporate a variety of teaching styles and approaches. Using a variety of methods to engage children cognitively and affectively, to represent content, and to express and assess learning increases the depth of the learning experience and at the same time involves more children in the learning process. To make diversity an integral part of mathematics instruction, classroom teachers can begin with teaching/learning plans that emphasize "doing" mathematics and include multidimensional learning experiences.

Questions for Further Thought, Discussion, and Research

1. Teaching mathematics to everyone challenges teachers to be versatile as well as inventive. But what about teachers who feel more comfortable with one type of representation or assessment than another? How might they fill in the gaps to make their teaching of mathematics more well rounded and diverse?

2. The connection between test anxiety and mathematics anxiety is clear, although researchers have yet to define the exact parameters of each. Interview several people you know who are math anxious. Are they also anxious about taking tests—other types of tests as well as math tests? What about your own experiences?

3. Working in a small group, brainstorm ways to diversify instructional methods. Select a specific concept or skill; then develop methods to represent information to match pictorial/symbolic, tactile, and aural/oral learning styles. How would you use technology to meet this challenge? What other resources might you use?

4. Explore various Web sites such as http://pbs.org/teachersource/math.html or http://server2.greatlakes.k12.mi.us/ that feature lesson plans for mathematics. Select two or three plans to review. How do these plans measure up to the challenges of a universal design for learning mathematics? How might you alter one or more of the plans to meet the challenge?

5. Make a list of the advantages and disadvantages of various traditional and nontraditional assessment methods. Discuss ways to integrate traditional with nontraditional methods to meet the needs of students, schools, and others.

5

Understanding Numbers

What are numbers? Why do we need numbers? Do numbers mean the same thing to a child as to an adult?

Children experience and work with numbers in different ways than adults. They develop a "sense" of number as a mathematical concept as they explore the language of numbers and discover numerosity or number-ness in the worlds around them.

The number skills that children are expected to learn may be basic but not necessarily simple. We expect children to learn to tell time—in hours, minutes, and seconds—measures inherited from Babylonian number systems but marked in Arabic and sometimes Roman numerals. Children measure quantities using English and metric systems. They learn about the names and value of American or Canadian coins and paper money, which are part of a base-10 system, but they might also hear a quarter referred to as "two bits," a term derived from a Spanish "bit" coin worth 12½ cents.

Making sense of the many numbers that affect children's lives is a complex process. Concepts such as base 10 or the decimal number system, place and face value, and part–whole relationships underscore numbers applications in the real world as well as the formal mathematics children study in school.

Understanding The Mathematics of Young Children

Adults, including those who claim to be mathphobes, have a relatively sophisticated grasp of numbers. Few adults would be confused by statements such as the following:

> The Garcias welcomed their second child on 4/1/04. The boy, Eduardo Garcia III, weighed 7 pounds, 8 ounces. Well-wishers may call the Garcias at 265-4748 or send congratulations to 807 Wellesley Avenue, Apt 199, Grand Junction, CO 77106-4950.

Although the announcement includes cardinal and ordinal numbers, numbers related to time and to weight, and identification numbers for addresses and telephones, the meanings are made clear by the contexts. Children, on the other hand, have not yet developed the knowledge structures necessary to read and understand the contextual clues that tell adults how to interpret the different numbers. They may be able to read the numbers, but they lack the experiences necessary to make sense of them.

Some mid-20th-century researchers, such as Jean Piaget (1969), believed that children do not develop a sense of number and cannot engage in numerical reasoning until around age 7. More recent work, however, points to a much earlier awareness. According to Wynn (1992, 1998), children as young as eight months are capable of reasoning numerically although they have not yet learned counting words. Although Ginsburg (1996) describes children's early efforts to "speak math" as rote memorization, Fuson's (1988) studies of children's counting suggest a different perspective. She writes:

> Children very early (almost all 3-year-olds and most 2-year-olds) do learn to differentiate number words from nonnumber words and use only the former when saying the [number] sequence. . . . Children's uses of the number-word sequence after they can produce it display an orderly succession of new abilities. . . . This elaboration [of the sequence] is a lengthy process ranging at least from age 4 to age 7 or 8.
>
> (58)

Because children's understanding of numbers is "in process"—that is, developing and fluid—over several years, how children deal with number tasks and information may differ not only from child to child but also from activity to activity. As children build, test, and stabilize their number-idea constructs (the mental structures that enable them to work effectively with numbers), their behaviors may sometimes appear illogical to adults but nonetheless follow patterns that make sense from the children's perspective and experience (Ginsburg 1996). For example, in the *Baby Blues* cartoon, the child's response to the pieces-of-candy word problem may seem illogical to her father. He clearly expects a mathematical solution, but she tries to make sense of the problem situation from a social perspective (the value she places on her friends versus the value she places on her candy) as well.

Activities CD

For an activity related to connecting numbers to everyday life, see Activity 1, Finding the Numbers in Your Life, on the CD-ROM that accompanies this text.

Baby Blues

Zoe shares her candy.

(Baby Blues Partnership. Reprinted with permission of King Features Syndicate.)

Children who have experienced numbers primarily as words or as positions in a sequence or number line might respond to a problem such as "add 8 and 5" either by "saying numbers," seemingly at random, or by reciting numbers in the sequence after 8 or 5. Whether the answer is mathematically correct or not, the children are attempting to deal with the numbers in ways that are meaningful to them, ways that grow out of their own experiences.

Young children might experience the meaning of numbers as words, as parts of wholes, as positions on a number line, and as units that can be composed and decomposed (for more about how children experience and handle numbers, see Ahlberg 1997; Marton and Booth 1997; Neumann 1987; Ekebald 1996). Therefore, to a child, the number 8 might mean the vocabulary word *eight*, two thirds of 12 or half of 16, the number between 7 and 9 on the number line, the number that results when you add 3 and 5, or the number that divided by 2 gives us 4.

Children might use different ways of handling numbers in different situations, and they might use different methods to arrive at the same conclusions.

> When trying to grasp numerosity children handle numbers in a vast array of ways, and thereby experience different aspects of numbers. However, in spite of using different ways of handling numbers, the numbers may appear in the same way to them and they may experience the same meaning. Consequently, there is not only one pathway, but many pathways to numbers.
>
> *(Ahlberg 1997, 109)*

Encouraging the development of number sense calls for exploring those "many pathways to numbers." This means not only frequent and varied experiences with numbers but also opportunities to interact with classmates and reflect about problem-solving strategies and outcomes.

Topics, Issues, and Explorations

Talk about numbers with a child. Ask questions to discover *what* the child knows and also to discover *how* the child thinks and feels about numbers. Take notes; then think about the responses. What do they suggest to you about the child's development of number sense?

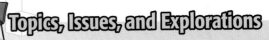

Learning The Language of Numbers

Children begin to develop a sense of number even before they have learned words to express numerosity or number-ness. Nonetheless, learning the language of numbers plays a complex and ongoing role in the developmental process. As children learn number words and accumulate number experiences, they build and weave a knowledge web. Number words, experiences, and ideas cluster and interact to create patterns of understanding (see Fuson 1988).

As early as two years, children are beginning to learn words and concepts about equivalence and order—what is more than, less than, the same as. Before 3½, most are learning the number sequence to 10 and at the same time dealing with numbers found on clocks, televisions, telephones, and addresses. Between 3½ and 4½, children are working on the next decade in the number sequence 10 to 20 and relating the numbers to counted objects—physical, mental, and imaginary. By age 6 most have learned the sequence through 70, and some are already working on the sequence above 100. Refining their understanding of numbers in sequences, in counting, and in measurement and of

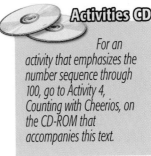
Activities CD

For an activity that emphasizes the number sequence through 100, go to Activity 4, Counting with Cheerios, on the CD-ROM that accompanies this text.

Activities CD

For an activity related to exploring the many contexts for numbers, see Activity 2, Making Numbers Books, on the CD-ROM that accompanies this text.

cardinal and ordinal numbers continues through the early grades. Many children develop their own algorithms for working with numbers before they are introduced to formal operations in school—for example, inventing counting-up and counting-down strategies to solve addition and subtraction problems (Fuson 1988, 56–58).

Language plays a role not only in identifying and describing number concepts but also in thinking through the problem-solving process (see Figure 5.1). The "Double Sums and More" and "Two-Digit Problems" scenarios are taken from diaries that Fuson kept of her daughters' use of number words. The dialogues show two 6-year-olds talking out their strategies and in the process developing a better understanding of concepts.

Fuson's daughter, Adrienne, used what she had learned about double sums to invent a strategy for solving the 7 plus 5 problem. She doubled the 5 and then counted up 2. As she explained her strategy, she made sense of it—a major factor in "owning" the knowledge. Fuson used a similar approach to help a second daughter, Erica, understand the idea underlying a procedure learned in school.

Verbalizing helped Erica identify the pattern behind a procedure she had learned by rote (adding 1s and 10s columns). Fuson's questions served primarily as road signs—signals pointing the way and guiding the child not only to think aloud but also to recognize what she knew. In a clinical interview excerpted in the "Toby's Math" scenario, Herbert Ginsburg (1996, 199) guided another 6-year-old, Toby, to move from her own informal knowledge of addition to the formal symbols and operations of mathematics. As Toby talked about what she was thinking, she began to coordinate her manipulation of the counting chips and her understanding of the mathematical idea of "plus."

Ginsburg builds on Toby's language and intuitive grasp of mathematics. In the process he leads her to an "ah-ha" experience—a moment when she connects words and ideas and advances beyond her initial understanding (201). By helping her relate what she does with the chips to the words and symbols of formal mathematics, he not only "ascends to the concrete"—that is, uses what Toby knows as a foundation—but also encourages her to reflect about her own thinking, an important step toward metacognition or thinking about thinking and toward learning to think mathematically (Ginsburg 1996, 201, 188).

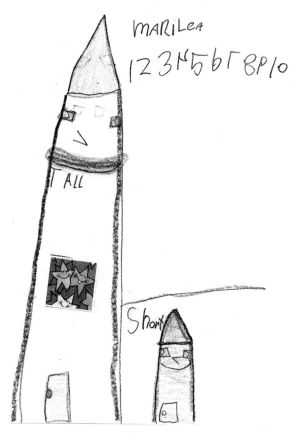

Figure 5.1 A kindergartner's rendering of "What is tall?" and "What is short?"

Windows on Learning

Double Sums and More

You know most of the double sums (3 + 3, 7 + 7, etc.). I asked you some tonight and then asked nine plus nine. You closed your eyes and scrunched up your face and thought and then said, "Eighteen." I asked how you figured it out. "Well, I knew eight plus eight was sixteen, and I knew there had to be one in the middle, so it was eighteen" (i.e., you knew the double sums went up by skipping every other num-

ber). I then asked you five plus seven. You thought for a while and then said, "Now don't ask me to describe it because it is very difficult." You closed eyes, etc. and after a while said "Twelve." I was surprised. "Could you give me a clue?" "Well, I had one five and there was another five in seven with two left over, so that made one eleven and two was twelve." Big smile. Me too.

Source: Fuson (1988, 23)

Windows on Learning

Two-Digit Problems

You had been doing some two-digit problems without trading (carrying) in first grade. I wrote down the problem 42 + 35 (with the 35 under the 42) and asked you to do it. You wrote 77. I asked you, "How does this work?" You said, "I don't know. The teacher just told us how to do it." "But why does it work?" "Mom, I don't . . . Oh, because you are adding the tens and adding the ones." You drew a 1 with a circle around it above the ones column and a 10 with a circle around it above the tens column.

Source: Fuson (1988, 25).

Windows on Learning

Toby's Math

Herbert: What if we do, ah, four plus two equals . . . what should it be? [After a pause, she writes "6."] Six, OK. Now, what does the plus mean in here?

Toby: The plus?

Herbert: Yeah, what does plus mean there? [She shrugs.] OK, and the equal means. . . .

Toby: I think coming up.

[. . .]

Herbert: Something's coming up. Can you show me with these chips what this means?

Toby: Four. . . . [She counts out four chips.]

Herbert: OK.

Toby: And two. . . . [She counts out two chips.]

Herbert: OK.

Toby: Lemme have these chips altogether, 'cause four: one, two, three, *four*, and two, equals six. . . . I would count it: one, two, three, four, five, six, and I would get six altogether.

Herbert: OK, so that's what that means, huh? OK, very good. You see when . . . you were doing this . . . counting, you said "four" and then you said "*and* two more". . . . The "and" is like the plus . . . right?

Toby: Ooooohhhhh . . .

Source: Ginsburg (1996, 198).

Topics, Issues, and Explorations

In another part of Ginsburg's (1996, 189–90) interview, Toby had difficulty with a word problem: "Rabbit has five carrots, squirrel has three carrots, how many do they have all together?" Toby answered, "Seven," explaining, "I counted seven, I counted three [uses hands to gesture toward each animal . . .]." What do you think Toby might have been thinking that led her to that answer? If you were Toby's teacher, what questions might you ask, or what tasks could you set to help her understand and work through the word problem?

Developing Verbal and Nonverbal Mathematical Skills

Children need to learn the language of numbers as they learn mathematics; however, they also need to learn nonverbal mathematical skills such as skills tied to visualizing mathematics and mathematical situations and manipulating numbers (Nunes, Schliemann, and Carraher 1993; Nunes and Bryant 1996). Nonverbal cognitive processes also play an important role in developing numerical thought. In fact, verbal and nonverbal mathematical skills may work independently, with different types of mathematical information being processed by different systems and different parts of the brain (Gallistel and Gelman 1992; Dehaene and Cohen 1995; Donlan 1998). For example, spoken numbers and written Arabic numerals may be processed by different cognitive systems; and different tasks, such as rote counting or identifying place values, may also involve different methods of numerical information processing (Donlan 1998, 257, 273–74).

Therefore, asking children to use language to explain what they are thinking may be only one way to advance their mathematical thinking. Asking them to represent concepts in a variety of ways not only encourages overall development but also helps children construct multidimensional idea worlds. A child whose mathematics learning consists primarily of memorized words tied to memorized symbols and imitated procedures will tend to see mathematics as one-dimensional and linear and to restrict problem solving to narrow, set patterns. Children who develop both the verbal and nonverbal aspects of their mathematics thinking are better able to think creatively and find multiple pathways to solutions.

In the scenarios quoted earlier in the Windows on Learning boxes, the researchers used primarily spoken representations, but the children expressed their thoughts by speaking and writing. Ginsburg in the third scenario used questions and verbalized concepts to prompt Toby's learning process, but he also represented concepts concretely with counting chips. He asked Toby to use the chips as a thinking tool as well as a means of expression.

Concrete Mathematics and Nonverbal Skills

Whether you believe the capacity to learn mathematics is innate or acquired, early concrete experiences can be essential to develop understanding. Infants respond meaningfully to numbers of objects, sounds, and physical actions and may even be able to compute the results of some simple numerical operations, such as adding 1 and 1 or determining that 5 is larger than 2 or 3 (Wynn 1998, 5–17).

Concrete mathematics—mathematics that can be experienced with the five senses—allows young children to explore ideas they may not have learned to name or talk about. For infants this may mean seeing different groupings of objects such as puppets or colored lights, feeling different shapes and sizes of rings or blocks, and hearing patterns of sounds as in measures of drumbeats or music. Older children can explore more complex concepts with the aid of base-10 materials, pattern blocks, rods, and other manipulatives.

Activities CD

For an activity about the language of numbers, go to Activity 7, Walking on the Googol Side, on the CD-ROM that accompanies this text.

Topics, Issues, and Explorations

Do you know someone (yourself, a friend, a child) who can solve mathematics problems but cannot explain what she or he has done? Explore the reason for this. Consider whether the person is simply imitating a procedure learned by rote or understands the concepts involved but has difficulty putting them into words.

Spoken and Written Mathematics and Verbal Skills

Verbalizing the problem-solving process reinforces the hands-on learning of concrete activities and at the same time helps learners shape the information to be stored in and eventually retrieved from memory (Donlan [1993] discusses the role of verbal skills in numerical information processing at length). Integrating language experiences with learning mathematics supports the construction process needed to make sense of mathematical knowledge, formal and informal, and to make it accessible for application. Reading and writing mathematics are in fact "essential to both the problem-solving and concept-discovery processes" (Martinez and Martinez 2001, 1).

Activities CD

For an activity that integrates mathematics and language as learning experiences, see Activity 18, Discovering Eight World, on the CD-ROM that accompanies this text.

> They help bridge the gap between ordinary language and the specialized language of mathematics. Writing-to-learn mathematics enhances the development of effective problem-solving strategies and inductive reasoning. It promotes metacognition—thinking about mathematical thinking. It also facilitates assessment by documenting the problem-solving process. Reading-to-learn mathematics helps break down barriers between mathematics learning and learning across the curriculum. Students become better math-readers and, at the same time, they develop cognitive structures and contexts for processes and procedures.
>
> *(Martinez and Martinez 2001, 1)*

Similarly, speaking mathematics helps children focus and work through their thoughts, as we saw in the scenarios quoted earlier. And a dialogue can be used to prompt children to reflect about the reasons for their actions and even to experience the kind of "ah-ha" moment Ginsburg highlights, when concept or procedure suddenly makes sense.

Topics, Issues, and Explorations

Brainstorm in small groups about a task that integrates nonverbal and verbal mathematics skills. Begin with concrete activities to help preschoolers explore concepts such as the number line or counting by 5. Then add a verbal task, such as counting aloud or explaining what they are doing with the manipulatives in the concrete activity. What did you discover?

Discovering Number in Patterns and Relationships

What is alike? What is not alike? What is the same as—same amount, same size, same shape or color? What is more than, less than, the biggest, the smallest, the longest, the shortest? These are questions that help children define their worlds, and answering them begins in the cradle. Infants viewing moving checkerboard patterns of objects on a screen have accurately discriminated 2 from 3 and 3 from 4, and 6- to 9-month-old babies have connected numbers of items on a screen to numbers of drumbeats (Wynn 1998, 6–7).

From infancy throughout early childhood, children are drawing mental maps of their worlds and setting benchmarks by which they can measure and orient themselves within those worlds. In the process they are learning to process and interpret information collected by their senses about size and quantity as well as comparative sizes and quantities.

What Is More, Less, or the Same?

While children need to learn the language of number and quantity comparisons, the concepts themselves may fall within the domain of nonverbal mathematical skills. In a series of studies based upon a nonverbal discrimination-learning paradigm, Siegel found that preschoolers could choose among numerically greater, smaller, or equivalent sets of dots before they could respond to questions such as "Which is bigger? or Which has the same number?" (Siegel 1982).

To develop these skills, children need multiple experiences with not only visual representations of number and quantity but also physical and aural representations. Pairing these representations with verbal expression—often in a descriptive dialogue of questions and statements—helps interpret and encode information so that it can be anchored within a child's knowledge framework for later retrieval.

 Mathematics in the Real World

More and Less Bugs and Crawly Things

Number concepts become real to students when they discover and work with ideas in the real world. When the real-world context is something they enjoy, such as a garden, students will be engaged and ready to learn. Tying the concepts "more" and "less" to the bug life of a garden also opens the way for connections with science and allows for artistic representations.

Activity 1

A garden is home to many bugs and crawly things. Some are helpful. Some are not. Some ladybugs help in a garden by eating harmful bugs. Earthworms dig up the dirt and make plants grow. Bees spread pollen from flower to flower.

Grasshoppers and caterpillars eat the leaves of green plants. Snails eat young plants. Cutworms attack roots.

What kind of bugs do you want **more of** in your garden? What kind do you want **less (or fewer) of**? Draw a garden in which you have more of one kind of bug and less of others. Is your garden filled with growing things or have the green things been eaten by bugs?

Extension

What is the difference between a caterpillar and a centipede or a millipede? When might a caterpillar be welcome in a garden?

Activity 2

Decide whether you want a flower or a vegetable garden. What would you plant? Gather packages of seeds for the garden you want. How many seeds are there in each package? How can you decide how many seeds you will need to plant in your garden? Which plants do you want more of? Which plants do you want less of?

Googol: BIG IDEAS in Mathematics

Creating a Standard for Measurement

In this activity, students learn to set and use a standard for measurement. They begin with the measurement concepts "tall" and "short," and then measure with nonstandard units such as paperclips before re-measuring with standard units represented by centimeter blocks.

Activity: Tall and Short Rabbits

Draw and color a tall rabbit and a short rabbit. Explain which is which. Measure the height of each rabbit with a nonstandard unit, such as paperclips. Then re-measure with centimeter blocks. Trace around the measuring units. Count and write the numbers.

How many units (nonstandard and standard) tall is the tall rabbit? The short rabbit?

Use a ruler to measure your rabbits. Compare the ruler measurement with the number of nonstandard and standard units. Are they the same? Is one more or less than the other? Why? Which measurement unit is most useful? Why?

For another measurement activity using centimeter blocks, see the Teacher Pro-File in Chapter 4.

Feeling, seeing, hearing, saying—these simple processes work together to create a learning paradigm that is dynamic rather than static. They also combine nonverbal and verbal learning patterns for a learning experience that can be accessed and enjoyed at several levels. Kindergartners drawing butterflies or rabbits are exploring symmetry, sameness, and proportion as they observe their models, try to match butterfly wings or rabbit legs, and hear and use phrases such as "the same as," "equal to," "as long as," " as wide as," "just alike, "tall, taller," and "short, shorter" (see the Googol activity "Tall and Short Rabbits"). Older children who do mirror and fractal activities continue to refine upon the concepts and language, adding phrases such as "repeated pattern" and "reversed image."

Why Is Something More, Less, the Same?

Identifying what is more, less, or the same, may involve making some fine and even complex distinctions to understand why. For example, quantity or amount comparisons might overlook other likenesses or differences such as color, texture, or even shape—as in a comparison of quantities of mixed-shape and colored pattern blocks. In the "Money Counts" *Mathline* scenario in Chapter 2, one of the children says a numerically equivalent but differently ordered set of coins is unlike a previous arrangement because of the sequence of the coins—a distinction that affects the pattern but not the total amount.

Activities CD

For an activity related to the number systems involved in measuring sizes, see Activity 11, How Big Am I? How Big Are You?, on the CD-ROM that accompanies this text.

Helping children understand these distinctions begins with discovery. Activities that allow children to explore the relationships of size and number can lead to some surprisingly sophisticated observations. For example, a kindergartner had two small balls; her classmate had one large ball. Asked who had "more," both replied, "Me"—the first because two is "more" than one, the second because big is "more" than small.

Generally, children understand more before less, possibly for the same reason that addition and multiplication are more easily grasped than subtraction and division. Piaget, whose developmental theory pays special attention to the order of learning, found reverse thinking (counting backward, subtracting to check addition, dividing to check multiplication) to take longer to develop and to require a different level of mental operations (Sund 1976). The Idea Files chart suggests several activities that challenge and teach the concepts of more, most, less, and least through perceptual processes involving touch, sight, and sound.

Like more and less, the concept of sameness or equivalence is a foundational idea. When children compare and match objects, sounds, and movements, they are learning to make judgments about size and shape and laying the groundwork for

Activities CD

For another activity related to quantity or size comparisons, see Activity 3, How Tall Is My Dino? on the CD-ROM that accompanies this text.

Idea Files

Exploring More/Most/Less/Least

Perceptual Processes	Activity 1	Activity 2	Activity 3
Feeling	**Use fingers** to explore two piles of beans—one with a cupful and one a handful of beans. **Pile** them up. **Spread** them out. **Put** each pile in a separate envelope and lift, one in each hand.	**Touch, feel,** lift two identical glasses—one filled to the top with liquid, the other partially filled. **Use** string, tape, or paper strips to help you measure the liquid. **Mark** your measurements.	**Explore** the amounts in three different piles of colored disks. **Arrange** the disks in various ways—lines, circles, stacks, empty squares, filled-in squares. Arrange the piles from most to least.
Seeing	**Observe** and compare the piles of beans. **Notice** how tall, how wide, how much space each pile occupies.	**Compare the size** of the glasses. Are they the same? **Notice** how close the liquid comes to the top. **Compare** the marks on the string, tape, or paper strips you used to measure.	**Look at** how long a line the disks make, how big a circle, how large a square, how tall a stack. **Compare** these figures visually; then use a measuring device.
Hearing/Saying (Ask and answer questions aloud.)	QUESTIONS: **Which** pile feels larger/smaller? **Which** looks larger/smaller? **Which** pile has more/less—the cupful or the handful?	QUESTIONS: **Are** the glasses the same size? How do you know? **Which** glass has more/less? How do you know? **How much** more/less—a little, a lot?	QUESTIONS: **Which** piles have more/less? Why? **Which** pile has the most/the least? **Which** pile is in the middle—less than one and more than the other?

the formal mathematical idea of equivalence. Discovering sameness calls again for a young-scientist approach. Children need not only to "see" sameness with traditional match-the-dots-or-pictures activities but also to "feel" and "hear" sameness in activities that ask them to match objects by feeling them and sounds by hearing them. Consider the following examples:

See the same   (Choose the starbursts that look alike.)

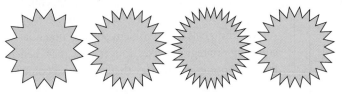

Feel the same   (Blindfolded, choose the shapes that feel alike.)

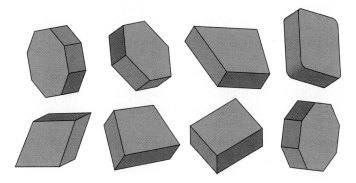

Hear the same   (Choose the bars of music that sound alike.)

Topics, Issues, and Explorations

Comparisons of size and amount are not strictly a child's concern. Adults continue to make judgments about more, less, and the same throughout their lives. Many adults wrestle daily with the paradox of the less-that-is-more. Every year the popular cartoon strip *Cathy* includes several episodes about weight. In Cathy's world, less weight would make her feel more attractive, more desirable, more worthy. What kinds of more, less, and same evaluations are part of your life? What kinds of criteria do you use to make those judgments? How do these comparisons differ from the ones you made as a child?

Counting and Number Sense

Because counting is one of the first mathematical skills children acquire, we tend to think of the process as simple and even unsophisticated; however, counting is both complex and cognitively sophisticated. "Counting is the successive assignment of a sequence of number words to items" (Fuson and Hall 1983, 55). Gelman and Gallistel (1978) identify five underlying principles that describe how children count:

1. **One-one principle.** Each item counted is represented by one and only one counting word or symbol.
2. **Stable-order principle.** The sequence of counting words or symbols must be repeatable and unchanging.
3. **Cardinal principle.** The word or symbol for the last item in a counting sequence represents the total number of items.
4. **Abstraction principle.** A variety of items may be collected and counted.
5. **Order-irrelevance principle.** Items may be counted in any order.

(77–82)

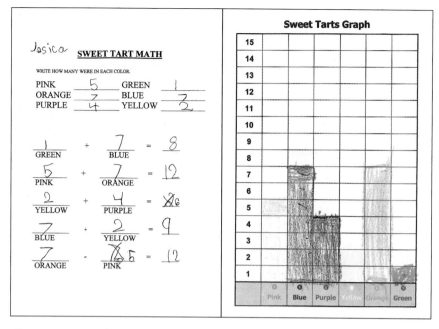

Figure 5.2   Jesica's Sweet Tart worksheet and graph.

The first three principles generally describe *how to count*. The abstraction and irrelevance principles describe *what to count*. Children's application of the principles vary not only with age but also with the set size of the items counted with larger sets taking longer to master (Fuson 1988). Younger children may show breaks in the counting sequence or problems with reversing order; nonetheless, even preschool children demonstrate considerable competence in counting (Fuson 1988; Ahlberg 1997). Learning *why to count*—the goals and problem-solving potential of counting strategies—takes longer and may benefit from counting experiences that make the counting goals both explicit and understandable to children. In the Mathematics Across the Curriculum feature, the immediate purpose of counting is a census of tadpoles and frogs; a second, related purpose is to demonstrate an important biological fact—that tadpoles turn into frogs. (See Sophian 1998 for more about the goal structure of counting.) In the classroom, it makes sense to children to count classmates to see whether there are enough chairs or treats for everyone. Counting cats or fish or bugs can be more meaningful if the number counted is then used for some specific purpose, such as making a drawing or creating a graph. For example, after Jesica counted the different-colored Sweet Tarts and wrote the totals on her worksheet, she used the numbers and colored markers to create a graph that represents what she did visually (Figure 5.2).

Mathematics Across the Curriculum

Counting All, Counting On, Counting Down in the Tadpole Census

This activity provides a social science context for counting (a census) and also a scientific reason for applying the counting-on and counting-down processes (the changing of tadpoles into frogs). The problem involves readers in the census-taking process by having them identify and count missing tadpoles and help Werner with his census report. To solve the mystery of fewer tadpoles and more frogs, the students must learn about biology. To understand the problem, they also need to discuss why a census is taken and how it is taken.

> Students *count all* as they follow Werner's head count.
>
> They *count on* as they discover more frogs in the pond.
>
> They *count down* as they identify missing tadpoles.

Story Problem

Werner the Tadpole is in charge of taking a census of Farmer Susan's pond. Although he counts carefully, Werner's results for the frogs and the tadpoles in the pond keep changing. At first Werner counts 10 tadpoles and 5 frogs; then 9 tadpoles and 6 frogs. As the census proceeds, Werner finds more frogs and fewer tadpoles. He must adjust his census numbers by counting on for frogs and counting down for tadpoles.

Continue the story, keeping track of the diminishing number of tadpoles and increasing number of frogs. Does any number not change?

Because the Tadpole Census problem is open-ended with no set conclusion, students may continue the narrative and the counting activities until Werner himself changes from a tadpole to a frog.

Particularly in the early stages, learning to count is as much a physical as a mental activity. Children count with their fingers, by pointing at or touching objects, by looking and tapping, by looking at or touching and saying numbers, by using objects or marks to show and group numbers. In Figure 5.3, Alen draws, counts, and groups fish.

Counting all is a basic children's counting strategy that calls for applying the how-to-count principles. Items to be counted are linked one-to-one with the numbers in the stable number sequence; the number for the last item is the total number of items. Children often use this strategy to answer questions about how many and how much.

Counting on is a strategy for dealing with a change in the number that results in more (Fuson 1988). Children start with a number and then count on through the number sequence until they "count out" the change and arrive at a new total. For example, to find 2 more than 5, a child might say: "Five, six, seven."

Counting down calls for reverse thinking and, therefore, may be more common in the early grades than preschool or even kindergarten (see Baroody 1992 for more about reverse counting). The strategy enables children to deal with changes in number that result in less by counting down from a starting number (Fuson 1988). For example, to find 2 less than 5, a child might say, "Five, four, three."

Many children develop their own counting-on and counting-down strategies for simple addition and subtraction before they are introduced to the operations in school.

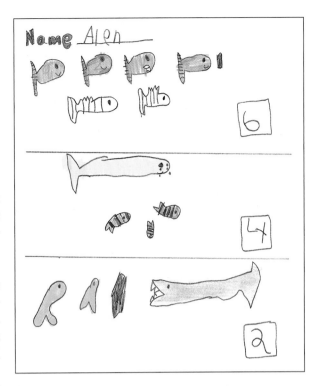

Figure 5.3 Alen's counting and grouping of fish.

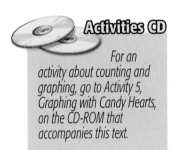

Activities CD

For an activity about counting and graphing, go to Activity 5, Graphing with Candy Hearts, on the CD-ROM that accompanies this text.

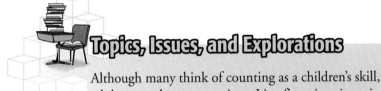

Topics, Issues, and Explorations

Although many think of counting as a children's skill, adults are always counting. List five situations in which adults count. Why is it important to be accurate? How might you use these situations to connect counting to life skills?

Mathematical Thinking

Counting Fish

Students explore the relationship between objects and numbers as they draw, count, and write totals. Grouping fish according to size and counting by group helps students discover the different meanings of the numbers—total number of fish, number of blue fish and striped fish, comparable numbers of large and small fish, and number of fish eaten and not eaten by the shark. In the process they begin to incorporate counting into their thinking, using counted numbers both as an analytical tool and as a means of expression.

Activity

1. Draw some blue and some striped fish swimming in an ocean. Count the fish. Put the number in a box.
2. Draw a bigger fish and three smaller striped fish. Count all of the fish, and put the number in the box.
3. A shark ate some of the small fish. How many small fish are left? Write the number in the box.

See Figure 5.3 for an example.

Understanding Number Systems

We often hear it said that mathematics is a universal language. This statement may be true in a sense. The concepts and thought processes that comprise mathematical thinking, both informal and formal, seem to transcend culture and nationality. In the 21st century, at least, students in Japan, Romania, Germany, the United States, and many other countries all study similar topics and solve similar problems in mathematics. Because of this commonality, we are able to compare performance in research studies such as the ongoing Trends in International Mathematics and Science Study (TIMSS).

However, common practice in the 21st century may be more a byproduct of globalization than a reflection of true universality of expression. The history of mathematics shows many number systems, and current global practice includes ideas from several systems. Even among societies that appear to share number systems and the vocabulary that describes those systems, there are differences. For example, both the United States and Great Britain use the words *billion* and *quart,* but in the United States, a billion is a thousand millions (1,000,000,000), and a quart is 16 fluid ounces; in Great Britain, a billion is a million millions (1,000,000,000,000), and a quart is 20 fluid ounces. In the United States and France, a trillion is a million millions, while in Great Britain and Germany, a trillion is 1 followed by 18 zeros (1,000,000,000,000,000,000).

What Is a Number System?

Basically, a *number system* is a way of organizing and representing numerosity or number-ness. A number system has two major components:

- a method to represent number, and
- an overall structure, including sequence and relationships, that allows users to work with the numbers in an organized way.

Mathematical Games

Kanji

Kanji is a numbers game in which players learn to count and recognize Japanese symbols for the numbers 1 to 10.

Before the game, players study a number chart with numerals, dots, Japanese words with phonetic pronunciations, and the Kanji or visual representations of the words.

Levels of play build from simple recognition and matching to discrimination and rapid translation of Japanese and English symbols. At Level 1 players match phonetic pronunciation of Japanese words and standard numerals. At Level 2 players match dots and Kanji or symbols. At Level 3, matches may involve any of the four representations—numerals, dots, Japanese words, or Kanji.

Players accumulate points by matching and winning cards. In case of a tie, the player who is first to write the 10 Japanese words for the numbers in correct order wins.

Playing Kanji helps students connect words, symbols, and number concepts. They develop visual, verbal, and symbolic skills necessary to understand mathematics and at the same time work within a different cultural context.

Kanji is a product of Mindware, www.mindwareonline.com.

At early stages in a civilization's development, number systems are often tied to concrete referents such as parts of the body. For example, anthropologists in the 19th century found that some Pacific Islanders used parts of their bodies in a specific order to count from 1 to 33 (Ifrah 2000, 13). The Islanders counted visually and physically (see Figure 5.4). Beginning with the little fingers, they touched the fingers of the right hand (1–5), then the wrist (6), elbow (7), shoulder (8), and sternum (9) before moving to the left shoulder (10) and reversing the process down to the little finger on the left hand (17). Amounts from 18 to 33 used the feet, legs, and hips in a similar up-down progression, beginning with the little toe of the left foot (18) and ending with the little toe of the right foot (33).

Other systems use pebbles, sticks, or shells as counters, sometimes in sophisticated patterns, suggesting that the culture's understanding of number is neither primitive nor rudimentary. For example, in the 20th century shepherds in West Africa used a system of shells and white, blue, and red straps to tally sheep passing through a gate.

> As the first one went through the gate, the shepherd threaded a shell onto a white strap, as the second went through, he threaded another shell, and so on up to the ninth. When the tenth went through, he took the shells off the white strap and put one on a blue strap, which served for counting in tens. Then he began again, threading shells on the white strap until the twentieth sheep went through, when he put a second shell on the blue strap. When there were ten shells on the blue strap, meaning one hundred sheep had now been counted, he undid the blue strap and threaded a shell onto a red strap, which was the "hundreds" counting device. And so he continued until the whole flock had been counted. If there were for example two hundred fifty-eight head in the flock, the shepherd would have eight shells on the white strap, five on the blue strap, and two on the red strap.
>
> *(Ifrah 2000, 24–25)*

As Ifrah points out, the shepherd uses different symbols for the numbers and his ability to deal with large numbers is limited; however, his system is essentially the same one that we use.

Figure 5.5 shows how several ancient civilizations represented numbers. Some, like the Chinese, had more than one way of showing numbers. The stick numbers given here show the arrangement of the sticks they used as manipulatives for calculations on a counting board. The Hebrew and Greek numerals are actually letters of their alphabets denoting a level of abstraction beyond the simpler representation of concrete objects. The Incan numbers are knots in strings.

Why Do We Need Number Systems?

The development of number systems has been an integral part of the development of civilizations. With numerosity or number-ness organized into shared

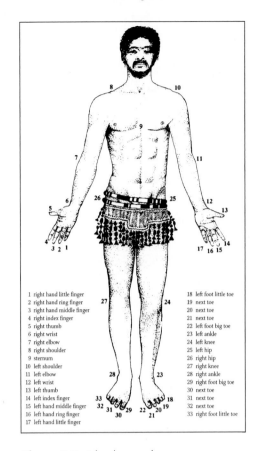

Figure 5.4 Islander numbers.
(Georges Ifrah, *The Universal History of Numbers: From Prehistory to the Invention of the Computer,* (New York: John Wiley & Sons, 2000), 12. Used by permission.)

1 right hand little finger
2 right hand ring finger
3 right hand middle finger
4 right index finger
5 right thumb
6 right wrist
7 right elbow
8 right shoulder
9 sternum
10 left shoulder
11 left elbow
12 left wrist
13 left thumb
14 left index finger
15 left hand middle finger
16 left hand ring finger
17 left hand little finger
18 left foot little toe
19 next toe
20 next toe
21 next toe
22 left foot big toe
23 left ankle
24 left knee
25 left hip
26 right hip
27 right knee
28 right ankle
29 right foot big toe
30 next toe
31 next toe
32 next toe
33 right foot little toe

Topics, Issues, and Explorations

The ancient Incas represented numerical concepts with knotted strings called *quipus*. The number and position of knots in the string and the colors and number of strings conveyed numerical information, including place value, since the Incas had developed a verbal decimal system. Do some research about quipus; then try your hand at representing numbers with knots. Show the numbers 1 through 10, 58, 234, 1,624, and so forth. Are there any advantages to the system? Any disadvantages?

Arabic	Incan	Chinese	Mayan	Greek	Hebrew	Roman
0			⬯			
1	(knot)	∣	•	α	א	I
2	(knots)	∥	••	β	ב	II
3	(knots)	∣∣∣	•••	γ	ג	III
4	(knots)	∣∣∣∣	••••	δ	ד	IV
5	(knots)	∣∣∣∣∣	—	ε	ה	V
6	(knots)	T	–•–	ς	ו	VI
7	(knots)	TT	–••–	τ	ז	VII
8	(knots)	TTT	–•••–	η	ח	VIII
9	(knots)	TTTT	–••••–	θ	ט	IX
10	(knots)	—	═	ι	י	X

Figure 5.5 Numbers across cultures.

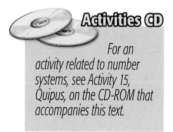

Activities CD

For an activity related to number systems, see Activity 15, Quipus, on the CD-ROM that accompanies this text.

systems, doing business could go beyond simple trading of items to value-based exchanges using money. Societies could count and tax their members, structure time and space, and grow into nations. Builders could design larger and more complex structures. For mathematicians and scientists, number systems are foundational, providing basic concepts and tools. For average citizens, yesterday and today, number systems are part of the fabric of daily living—unnoticed much of the time, but so fundamental to our behaviors that we can use them automatically, almost without thinking, like a natural reflex.

Unfortunately for children just learning to use numbers, modern civilization draws upon several different historical systems. We use Arabic numerals (0, 1, 2, 3, 4, 5, 6, 7, 8, 9) and a base-10 system for mathematics and money. However, for measuring time, circles, longitude and latitude, we use a base-60 (or sexagesimal) system, inherited from the Sumerians and Babylonians. We occasionally put Roman numerals (I, II, III, IV, and so forth) on clock faces and in date lines (McLeish 1991). Our calender is Roman, and its numbers are related to movements of the sun and the moon (Gullberg 1997). The United States clings to a base-12 (or duodecimal) system in measurement (12 inches in a foot, 12 units in a dozen, 12 × 12 dozen in a gross) but also uses some base-20 (or vigesimal) concepts such as a score, which is 20 units (Ifrah 2000; Gullberg 1997).

A traditional approach to teaching these disparate systems was rote memorization of the numbers involved. Some of you may remember being drilled on tables of weights and measures, answering questions such as "How many feet in a mile?" "How many inches in a square foot?" "How many quarts in a peck?" You may never have experienced a mile, one foot at a time, or visualized a square foot built an inch at a time, but memorizing and drilling conditioned the information like a reflex—a factor that probably contributes to many people's continued resistance to the universal and uniform metric measures.

Nonetheless, children can learn and apply the different components of our number systems with understanding and without resorting to what some consider the drill-and-kill method (drilling facts, killing motivation). When children experience a curriculum that emphasizes multiple approaches and multiple outcomes to problems, they tend to respond favorably to learning activities that call for them to shift perspectives or devise different strategies. Some guidelines for teaching number systems effectively follow:

1. Emphasize the usefulness of numbers as tools and the multiple uses for those tools.

2. Show how the different kinds of math applications or "maths"—clock math, calender math, measurement math, money math—help us organize and make sense of the world around us.

Mathematics Across the Curriculum

The Metric System in History

The history of most number systems is long and complex, with applications and advances tied up with historical and cultural events and following the serpentine pathways typical of constructs evolving from convention. The metric system is different. Instead of growing up topsy-turvy with a society, it was created to be an agent of social and intellectual order.

Activity

Research and draw a historical time line showing key dates, events, and people in the development of the metric system. Include the answers to questions such as these:

Who proposed the development of the system?

Who worked to create the system?

What nations have adopted the system legally and when?

When did the United States become involved? What standards were adopted?

Write a brief assessment of the system, including advantages for science, commerce, and other fields including education.

Extension 1

In 1999 a problem involving dual measurement systems (English and metric) resulted in the loss of a Mars-orbiting spacecraft. Search the archives of newspapers or news magazines to discover what the error was and its effect on the spacecraft.

Extension 2

How is the International System of Units (SI) related to the metric system? How was SI developed, and what are its key standards? What do this system and its standards tell us about modern requirements for measurement? Why do we need SI as well as the native system?

3. Make applications practical and meaningful, tied to events and phenomena in children's worlds.

4. Use inquiry-based activities to involve the children in the ideas and encourage them to figure out for themselves how things work or operate.

Number Systems and Time

Teaching children to "tell time" has become both simpler and more complex with the advent of digital clocks. On the one hand, children who have learned the first six decades in the number sequence can read a digital clock easily. On the other hand, a digital clock does not provide the visual image for the passage of time that a traditional clock gives us. Nor does the digital clock lend itself readily to explorations of the relationship of seconds, minutes, and hours.

"Telling time" means more than learning to read a clock face, digital or round; it means tapping into a system that organizes and spaces daily events. What does time mean to children? For children time is keyed to things happening—time to get up, time to eat, time to go to school, time to go to bed. For adults time is often exact and demanding—a taskmaster driving our days. Children's first experiences with time are softer and less precise. They may tie time to specific events—lunch time, bedtime, playtimes—and they explore the meaning of time-related expressions such as "a little while," later," and "now."

Working from a child's perspective on time, we have both a knowledge starting point and a contextual starting point:

- numbers 1 to 60 and beyond
- daily activities tied to time

Topics, Issues, and Explorations

How many different kinds of math applications (clock, calendar, money, and so forth) do you use regularly? What ideas or features do these maths share? What ideas or features are unique to each math? Do you remember which you learned first—the common or the unique features—or was learning simultaneous? Why?

Activities CD

For an activity that connects time standards and the relationship between degrees of a circle and longitude and latitude, see Activity 16, The Circle of Time, on the CD-ROM that accompanies this text.

Many preschoolers know the number sequence through 10 and are working on the teens; most kindergartners are working on the decades from 20 to 70; most first graders and nearly all second and third graders know the 1 to 100 sequence and are working on the next century of numbers (Fuson 1988, 57). Moreover, all children experience activities that happen at specific times or have timed durations. These foundations give children both a reason and some tools for telling time.

Children build on what they know by first reading the familiar numbers for hours and then connecting specific hours to specific activities. A traditional round clock works well for identifying numbers and exploring the concepts of hours, minutes, and seconds. Action questions, such as the following, help connect concepts to children's experiences and also encourage them to discover the meaning of time for themselves:

When is it time to _____?

What time is it when _____?

When is the best/worst time to _____?

Clocks with chimes, cuckoos, or animal noises provide an aural dimension to telling time, while clocks with raised numerals provide a tactile dimension, so that children learn to see, hear, and feel the time. Of course animal clocks are a favorite; clocks that use bears' growling or birds' singing to mark the hours offer an opportunity for cross-disciplinary extensions of time-telling activities as well as built-in mnemonic devices: What does the clock say at two? Cuckoo, cuckoo or cockle doodle doo, cockle doodle doo.

The Idea Files chart, "Teaching 'Time,'" outlines some basic telling-time activities.

Parts and Whole

Traditionally we have thought of telling time as a kindergarten and early-grades activity, a matter of drills that follow a basic pattern. "When the little hand is on _____ and the big hand is on _____, what time is it?" However, with the advent of digital clocks, some children in the middle grades are still working on reading time, especially minutes. Big-hand, little-hand approaches are too much like "kid stuff" to these older children, but learning how seconds, minutes, and hours fit together in a part–whole relationship is not. In addition, the clock and the language of time provide an effective way to link basic fractions to a familiar subject and images—half hour, quarter hour, three-quarters of an hour.

Calendar Time

Reading and interpreting the numbers on a calendar involve not only another way to use numbers but also an important link to science. What makes a day and a night? What is a month (or a "moon"th), a year, a decade, a century, a millennium?

We have all seen the maps with an *x* to mark the spot where we are standing. A daily *x*-marks-my-spot calendar activity helps children tie actual days to the numbers and months of the calendar. For a hands-on rather than a point-and-name experience, you can use a blank calendar with magnetic months and numbers. A different team of children can be in charge of adjusting the calendar each

---

Activities CD

For an activity about measuring time in other cultures, go to Activity 53, Boiling Potatoes for Inca Time, on the CD-ROM that accompanies this text.

Topics, Issues, and Explorations

Some teachers feel that digital clocks have made the old round-clock math obsolete; others ban digital clocks from their classrooms and work exclusively with round clocks. What do you think? What are the advantages and disadvantages of each kind of clock for teaching children to tell time? Are there any concepts that the digital clock is better suited to teaching than the round?

Idea Files

Teaching "Time"

Activity/Level	Materials	Procedure	Goals
Time Dice (pre–grade 2)	Dice Cardboard clocks with removable hour, minute, and second hands	Work in small groups with a cardboard clock with removable hands. Start with the small hand only. Roll two dice; then position the hand on the clock at the number rolled and name the hour. Continue until all hours have been named. Add the large hand for minutes. Roll two dice for the hour, then a handful of dice for minutes. Count minute by minute, then by 5s, 10s, 15s to read minutes. With older students, add third hand and work on reading seconds.	Recognizing clocks as symbols of passing time Identifying hours, minutes, seconds as measures of time Developing strategies to "count up" to hours and minutes Laying groundwork for understanding part–whole relationships of time— seconds as parts of whole minutes and so forth
Feeding Time at the Zoo (grades 2–3)	Paper Crayons, colored pencils, or paints Clock-face cards with zoo animals and clock hands, but no numbers	The animals at the zoo have to be fed on time. Divide into small groups. Each student receives a card with an animal to feed and a time to do it. Some of the times might not be appropriate, leading to hungry animals and chaos at the zoo. Identify the feeding time. Then make up a story about what happens when you feed the animal. Illustrate the story with a picture. Write out or tell your story.	Identifying time by position on the clock Connecting time to responsibilities and consequences Understanding the concept "on time"
How Much Time? (grades 2–4)	Stopwatches or clocks with hour, minute, and second hands Log paper	How long is a second, a minute, an hour? Working in pairs, search for five things that take a second, five that take a minute, and five that take an hour. Then identify and time 10 common activities—how long it takes to open and close a door, to drink a glass of milk, and so forth. Have one member of the team do the timing; the other, log the results. Be sure to include things you can see, feel, and hear.	Understanding the relationship of seconds, minutes, and hours Developing "time sense" Defining time in personal or real-life terms

day, adding numbers, changing month names, or making other adjustments to mark the day. The teacher or the children themselves can ask, "What is today?" Saying the answers aloud and writing them in various ways reinforces learning. Other calendar questions might have children count forward or do some basic operations such as adding and subtracting. The students whose work appears in

Figure 5.6 How many days are left in April?

Activities CD

For an activity related to math journals, see Activity 9, My Math Journal, on the CD-ROM that accompanies this text.

Figure 5.6 wrote the question and drew calendars of the month of April. One used a subtraction strategy to find an answer; the other, counting on. The calendars suggest the students do not yet understand the concept of seven-day weeks.

The days-in-April activity was recorded in the students' math journals—an ongoing project that fits neatly with calendar study since *journal* literally means "daily." Children make the journals their own by designing unique and colorful covers (see Figure 5.7); then they fill the pages with problems of the day, drawings, and other material. The result is an active involvement that is difficult to achieve with preprinted activities.

Number Systems and Measurement

Many schoolchildren in the United States have problems with measurement. In the TIMSS, both fourth and eighth graders scored below the international average in measurement (U.S. Department of Education 1997, 32). At the eighth grade only four countries had scores that were significantly lower than ours, and all of our major trading partners including Japan, Canada, England, and Germany scored higher (U.S. Department of Education 1996, 29). Since the United States is the only one of these nations that has not fully adopted the metric system, it makes sense to suggest that at least some of the problem is societal. Often children learn the foot-pound system informally, the metric system formally, and perhaps neither system well.

Nonetheless, children are as capable of learning multiple systems of measurement as they are of learning multiple languages or the rules to dozens of games. Whether the system is base-12 like the feet-inches system or base-10 like the metric system matters less than whether the system makes sense to children and connects with their reality. The "Tall and Short Rabbits" activity in the Googol feature uses base-10 blocks to measure drawings of rabbits; the children work directly with centimeters, and the idea is also there in the blocks them-

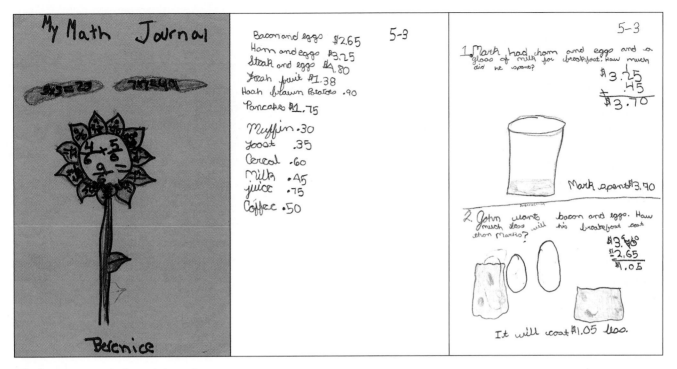

Figure 5.7 Berenice's math journal.

selves, ready to be built on and extended. The draw-and-measure activity in Figure 5.8 has children draw a picture and then use a ruler to measure in inches. The "Measure Me" activity in the Math Manipulatives feature has children measure each other with colored strings and then measure the strings with both a tape and a yardstick.

Each activity is hands-on. Children measure something meaningful to them. And they learn to apply various standards of measurement, using tools such as the blocks, measuring tape, or ruler. The result is learning experiences that rate high for understanding and also lay the foundation for more complex measurement tasks. (See Chapter 9 for discussion of measurement and more activities.)

Figure 5.8 Drawing and measuring with a ruler.

Topics, Issues, and Explorations

What were your own experiences with learning about measurement? Did you memorize tables or conduct measuring experiments? Did you measure in both English and metric systems? Have you memorized conversion formulas? What have been the effects, cognitive as well as affective, of your learning experiences with measurement?

Activities CD

For more measurement activities, see Activity 50, Making Measurement Tools, on the CD-ROM that accompanies this text.

Math Manipulatives

Tapes, Yardsticks, and Rulers

Making standard units of measurement meaningful to students can begin with making them personal. In the "Measure Me" and "Measure My World" activities, students provide the subjects for measurement—first themselves and then their drawings.

Manipulatives in the activities are lengths of colored string, lines and shapes drawn on paper, and the measuring tools.

Activity 1: Measure Me

1. Work in teams. Use lengths of colored string to measure each other.

2. Measure and cut string for height, length of arm and leg, distance around head, and so on.

3. Use a tape measure and yardstick to measure length of string pieces in both centimeters and inches.

4. Compare measurements.

Activity 2: Measure My World

1. Draw and color a picture of some part of your world (such as your home, classroom, playground).

2. Use a ruler to help you draw lines.

3. Use a ruler to measure the number of inches in some of the lines.

4. How does the size of the drawing compare with the size of the real thing?

Activities CD

For an activity related to explaining the concepts of money, especially coins, see Activity 10, How Much Money?, on the CD-ROM that accompanies this text.

Number Systems and Money

In kindergarten and the early grades, students spend considerable time and effort learning about money. Is this an appropriate topic for small children? Do they need to know and are they able to understand about value and exchange? Equivalence—the idea that five pennies equal a nickel and two nickels equal a dime—may be difficult for some children to grasp at first, but most understand early on that money can be exchanged for things that they want. Carmen, a teacher whose class is described in Windows on Learning, was surprised to find that her kindergartners knew about quarters and dimes before they had learned about pennies and nickels.

Windows on Learning

Making Connections with Money

Carmen's kindergartners were studying coins. She sat on the classroom floor with the children in a circle around her. Each child had a baggy with 10 pennies, 2 nickels, 1 dime, and 1 quarter. As Carmen held up each coin, the children were asked to identify each coin and find the same coin in their bags and hold it up.

"What do I have in my hand?" Carmen asked, holding up a dime.

All of the children answered, "Dime," and held up the appropriate coin.

"What do I have now?" She held up a nickel.

Two children said, "Nickel." One said, "Penny." The rest didn't answer.

"How about this coin?" This time she showed them a penny.

Half of the children identified the penny, but two of the children called it a nickel, and several did not respond at all.

Next Carmen held up a quarter.

The answer was quick and almost unanimous.

Carmen stopped and looked around the circle. "Why do you know about quarters?" she asked.

Moodi, who had lost several of his 10 pennies and was spinning one of his nickels like a top, grinned and said one word, "Pickles!"

Carmen was mystified, but Paola nodded and added, "Popcorn!"

Carmen began to get the idea. Pickles and popcorn sold for a quarter in the lunchroom.

"How about dimes?" she asked.

"Fruit rollups!" the children answered.

The children in Carmen's class did not know how many pennies were in a quarter or how many nickels in a dime, but they understood that dimes and quarters were valuable; they could be exchanged for treats the children wanted in the lunchroom. With this "hook," Carmen had the perfect tie-in to explore equivalencies: If you don't have a quarter, how many other coins do you need to buy popcorn? If you spent your dime, how many nickels do you need to buy a fruit rollup?

In the early grades, children are usually ready to work with money in terms of part–whole relationships—100 pennies in a dollar and so forth. Because our money system uses base 10, understanding the relationship of dollars and cents helps children with mathematical concepts such as place value and decimal points. As children work with the values of coins, they begin the grouping and regrouping processes (group of 5, 10, 25, and so on) that underscore base-10 processes.

The Decimal Number System

For most of us the decimal or base-10 number system feels so natural that we assume it is natural. In fact, some historians see a biological connection with humans' 10 fingers.

> The almost universal preference for base 10 comes from nothing more obscure than the fact that we learn to count on our fingers, and that we happen to have ten of them. . . .
>
> If nature had given us six fingers, then the majority of counting systems would have used base 12. If on the other hand . . . [we had] four fingers on each hand . . . , then we would doubtless have long standing traditions and habits of counting on base 8.
>
> *(Ifrah 2000, 44)*

Of course, nature not only gave us 10 fingers but also 10 toes—an arrangement for using a base-20 or vigesimal system such as the Mayans and Inuits developed. But remembering 20 distinct number symbols is more difficult than remembering 10, and performing simple operations, such as multiplication, is more complicated when you are working with 20 rather than 10 symbols (see Ifrah 2000, 40–42).

Two of the big ideas in our number system are *face value* and *place value*. In English the meaning of a sentence has two components: the meaning of individual words and the order in which they occur in a sentence. "The elephant scared the mouse" means something different

Activities CD

For an activity that explores the complexities of financial commitments such as pet ownership, see Activity 13, How Much Is That Pet?, on the CD-ROM that accompanies this text.

Mathematics in Literature

How Much Is That Guinea Pig in the Window?

Joanne Rocklin gives a well-rounded picture of money math in her book, *How Much Is That Guinea Pig in the Window?* (New York: Scholastic, 1995). The book is about a class that earns money from a bake sale and then spends the money for a classroom pet. The children have a budget of $50, which turns out to be too little to buy a guinea pig and everything it needs. To make extra money, they collect bottles and cans for recycling.

Activity 1

Read the story aloud to the class, or have the students read aloud in round-robin fashion. Talk about the costs associated with pets. Provide some price lists, and ask the students to figure out the cost of buying, feeding, and caring for a class pet.

Activity 2

The children in the story had a bake sale and collected bottles and cans to raise money. What are some other ways for children to raise money (holding car washes, selling candy, and so forth)? How much could children make in a day, a week, two weeks, or a month? Be sure to include the cost of supplies (soap for the car wash, candy, and so forth) since those costs will have to be deducted from the total to find the profit.

Activity 3

Cut out pictures and items from catalogs, advertisements, or construction paper to set up a pet store. You will need cut-outs for pets, pet supplies, and pet food. Use empty cartons for pet carriers, dog houses, and cages; yarn for leashes; paper cups of sand or paper strips for cat or cage litter; and felt pieces for toys.

Give each student $50 in play money to buy and outfit a pet.

Topics, Issues, and Explorations

Try an experiment with two or three children in the preschool to second grade range. Ask each child some questions about money: What is it? What is it used for? Then ask each child to choose coins from various combinations—penny or dime, nickel or dime, nickel or quarter, four nickels or quarter, and so forth. Record their choices and the reasons the children give. Then look for patterns. Do the children choose by size or quantity over value? Do they know more about some coins than others? Speculate why.

Activities CD

For an activity showing how other cultures use a base-10 system, see Activity 28, Adding and Subtracting with Chinese Stick Math, on the CD-ROM that accompanies this text.

Activities CD

For an activity to help with understanding the base-10 through the use of calculators, see Activity 14, Filling-Up or Filling-Out, on the CD-ROM that accompanies this text.

from "The mouse scared the elephant." Similarly, number meaning has two parts:

- **face value**, the meaning of individual numbers, and
- **place value**, the meaning of the numbers' placement or order.

In our base-10 system, place value increases by a factor of 10 as we read from right to left, so that 264 means

$$2(100) + 6(10) + 4(1) \text{ or } 200 + 60 + 4.$$

Integrating face and place value is easiest for numbers we are accustomed to working with, but even adults sometimes have difficulty reading the place value of numbers with more than six digits.

Understanding the decimal system has been described as "the most difficult and important instructional task in mathematics in the early years" (Resnick 1983, 126). Essentially it involves interpreting numbers, not just as individual units or as points in a sequence but as parts of other numbers.

> The development of decimal number knowledge can be understood as the successive elaboration of the Part-Whole schema for numbers so that numbers come to be interpreted by children as compositions of units and tens (and later of hundreds, thousands, etc.) and are seen as subject to special regroupings under control of the Part-Whole schema.
>
> *(Resnick 1983, 126)*

In other words, children learn that numbers can have more than one meaning. They have meaning as individual units, and they have meaning as parts of larger numbers (the face value–place value distinction). And they learn that the pattern for the larger numbers builds by 10s.

Resnick identifies three major stages in children's understanding of the base-10 system. In **stage 1** children move from counting to combining and learn to interpret a two-digit number as a combination of a 10s value and a units value. In **stage 2** children build on counting and combining experiences to structure information about decades and other base-10 patterns. And in **stage 3** children formalize their understanding in mathematical applications such as carrying and borrowing (Resnick 1983, 127–45; see also Ahlberg 1997 for a discussion of children's handling of numbers with counting and structuring and experiencing numbers as individual and composite units).

Stage 1: From Counting to Combining

Even if a child can count to 100, that does not mean that she or he understands the numbers as anything other than units in a sequence. The child might understand that 47 is larger than 37 because the 40s are further along the number line in counting than the 30s, but thinking in terms of decades and units of 5, 10, and more calls for a different strategy.

How do we move from understanding that 10 ones give us a total quantity of 10 (see Chapter 6 for more about this principle of counting) to seeing 10 as a unit and ten 10s as equal parts making up a whole 100? The process of constructing this new way of seeing and working with numbers begins with patterning and grouping.

Children need to discover the meaning of number patterns and groups empirically. When they count aloud by 2s, 3s, 5s, or 10s, they are trying out number patterns and at the same time laying the conceptual foundation for factoring. When they show their numbers with manipulatives or drawings, they process and interpret the information in a way that is meaningful to them (see Figure 5.9).

Grouping activities with counting objects and interlocking blocks help children visualize the quantities and components involved in two-digit numbers and also prepares the way for work with base-10 materials in Stage 2. Grouping with plastic cats, bears, or blocks into 10s and ones puts children on the path to constructing the concept of sets. Building 10s from interlocking blocks underscores the partitioning process (10s from 1s) and the composing process (1s into 10s). See, for example, Figures 5.10 and 5.11.

Stage 2: From Combining to Structuring

As students work with the patterns discovered in Stage 1, they begin to understand base-10 structure. They learn that it is in effect a repeating structure, that not only can ten 1s be combined to make a unit of 10, but also that 10 units of 10 can be combined to make a unit of 100. They continue to work empirically

Figure 5.9 Drawing on circles to make count-by-5 pictures.

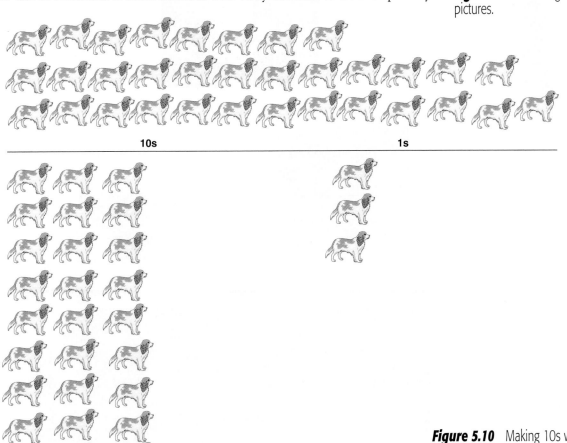

Figure 5.10 Making 10s with counting objects. A long line of dogs is waiting to be fed at the animal shelter. They can be fed more quickly if you can break up the line into smaller lines of 10 dogs. How many lines of 10 can you make? Are there any dogs left over?

and inductively, counting up to establish that three 10s and seventeen 1s gives us the same number as four 10s and seven 1s (Resnick 1983, 127). And they learn that ten 1s can be exchanged for one 10 unit and ten 10s for a hundred without reducing the value of the whole.

Base-10 blocks provide effective visual and tactile tools by exploring the base-10 structure. Students can see the proportional relationships of unit blocks, rods, flats, and cubes; with their hands they can line up units to make rods and rods to make flats and stack flats to make cubes until they understand the part–whole relationships (Figure 5.12).

Stage 3: From Structuring to Formalizing

The third stage, which may continue throughout elementary school and into middle school, involves applying knowledge of base-10 structure to formal

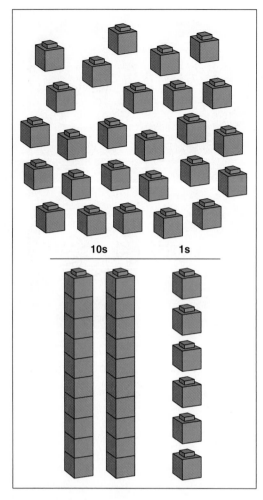

Figure 5.11   Making 10s with interconnecting centimeter cubes.
Use a paper cup to scoop up some centimeter cubes. See how many rods of 10 cubes you can make. Are there any cubes left over?

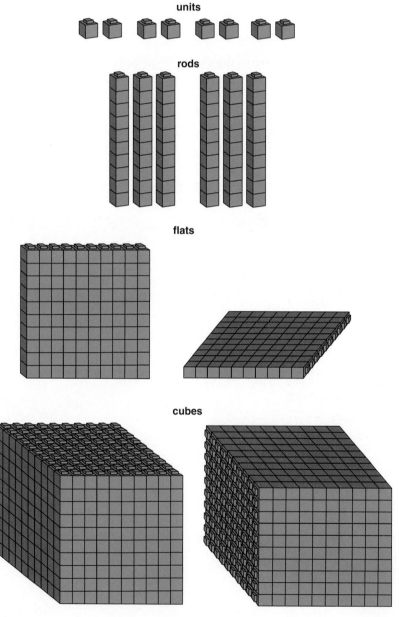

Figure 5.12   Tactile tools for exploring structure.

cubes	flats	rods	units
1	2	5	2

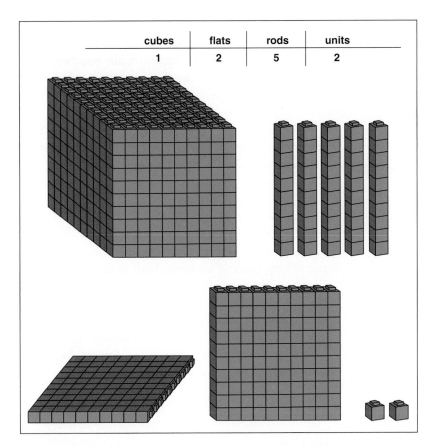

Figure 5.13 How many units, rods, flats, and cubes are in the box?

mathematics. A first step is often to represent with numbers a quantity built with blocks. The students might start with blocked-off columns for place value to help them visualize quantities (Figure 5.13). Early activities might start with two places for units and rods (1s and 10s) and then add places for flats (100s) and cubes (1,000s) (see Nortman-Wolf 1990 for activities that progress from simple to complex tasks with base-10 blocks).

Exchange principles, developed to show equivalencies and to work with more-than, less-than tasks, are applied to written numbers at this stage. Students continue to work empirically, exploring relationships with manipulatives and other visual representations, but they are learning to represent concepts symbolically with numerals. One result is the conceptual basis needed to construct algorithms for mathematical operations such as addition and subtraction and for procedures such as exchanging one 10 for ten 1s or one 100 for ten 10s, the basis for the traditional algorithms of borrowing and carrying (Resnick 1983, 127).

Diversity in Learning and Thinking Mathematically

The tactile and visual pathways to interpreting number systems are rich and plentiful. Measurement has natural hands-on applications in cooking, sewing, building, and other crafts. Coins can be distinguished by design and size, and in Canada denominations of paper money can be also. Time adds an aural dimension to counting with clocks' chiming, cuckooing, meowing, or twittering on the hour. The result is number systems we can see, touch, and hear and a plethora of ready-made teaching devices to engage students with a variety of learning styles.

Deborah Kahler, featured in the Teacher Pro-File, uses what she calls "edible" manipulatives to combine visual and tactile learning with taste experiences. Her manipulatives not only engage the students but also make numbers more meaningful to them. They "care" about the number of candy hearts in their cups, and counting and grouping hearts or Cheerios are both enjoyable and worthwhile activities to them.

Topics, Issues, and Explorations

Can you read music? Musical time is written as a ratio (3/4 time, 4/4 time). The names of musical notes are fractions (whole note, half note, quarter note, eighth note, sixteenth note), and playing measures of music involves not only interpreting notes on a scale but also reading note values and keeping time. Develop a teaching idea that uses music to teach number patterns, part–whole relationships, and equivalencies. You might start with a metronome, or use sticks to set times.

While teachers have frequently used rhymes as a mnemonic device or memory aid, sound and music may be underutilized in understanding number systems. In addition to the usual counting songs, music can help teach number patterns and relationships. The concepts of measure and time are expressed with numbers and can be heard as well as felt in drumbeats and notes on a scale.

Tapping or keeping time is a method many children use to keep track of counting, both in sequences and in simple operations such as counting on to add and counting down to subtract (Ahlberg 1997). Learning experiences that link sound patterns to number can build on children's own strategies to provide another perspective on numerosity and improve access for children with aural/oral learning styles.

Teacher Pro-File

Deborah Kahler
First Grade

Math with Edible Manipulatives

When Deborah Kahler begins a math lesson, her first graders sit up straighter in anticipation, and some begin to lick their lips. Because Mrs. Kahler finds her school's printed math lessons boring, she "livens up" the class sessions with math experiments and edible objects.

Mrs. Kahler makes math colorful and active. For patterning she uses "Ocean and Sea Life" as an overall theme. Children make a pattern with heads of fish, dolphins, and turtles; then they draw and name the shapes in their patterns. Samuel created a pattern of four turtles, four dolphins, and four fish, while Victoria created a dolphin, fish, and turtle pattern.

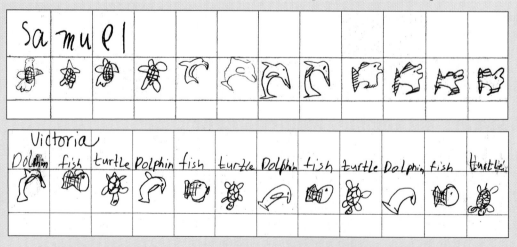

Samuel and Victoria create patterns.

Mrs. Kahler uses what she calls "edible manipulatives" in many of her lessons. She reads Barbara McGrath's *The M & M's Counting Book* and *The Cheerios Counting Book* aloud in activities that help children count, group, and sort by color.

When given edibles to work with, the children usually ask, "Can we eat them?" Mrs. Kahler's standard reply is "Yes, on your way to recess, after all of the children have finished the activity, some will be distributed for eating. We don't want to eat the ones we are working with. They will be dirty." Of course, there are always a few who eat some of their manipulatives, creating an opportunity to work with less-than and counting-down concepts.

In the "Counting Hearts" project, Mrs. Kahler integrates counting, ordering, and classifying with graphing. The students work in small groups to encourage collaborative learning, but each child has a cup with 20 candy hearts, graph paper with rows labeled by color, and crayons matching the colors of the hearts. First, the children sort the hearts by color; then they put them on the graph paper one heart to a block. They count the candies and color in the corresponding number of spaces to make a graph.

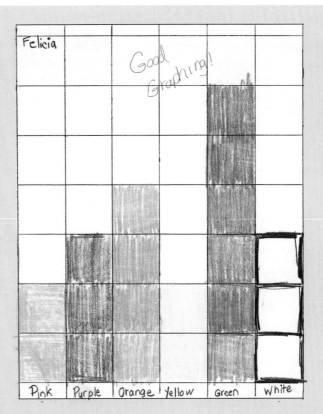

Graphing candy hearts.

Mrs. Kahler asks questions that help children relate the activity to a variety of related concepts:

Who has more of each color?—The most pink, purple, and so forth?

Does anyone have the same number of any colors?

If you all started with 20 hearts, why do your graphs look different?

What colors did each of you show the most of and the least of in your graph? How many more do you have of one color than another?

The activity not only encourages children to work collaboratively in groups but also provides experiences to fit different learning styles: *auditory* as the children listen to directions, answer questions, and talk about results; *visual* as they observe the one-to-one correspondence between candy and squares on their graphs; *kinesthetic* as they use small motor skills to manipulate the candies and make their graphs.

Mrs. Kahler identifies two major learning outcomes.

- The children learn how a graph can express quantities and relationships.
- They learn the concepts and language of graphing with vertical towers.

Activities CD

Mrs. Kahler's math activities are included as Activity 4, Counting with Cheerios, and Activity 5, Graphing with Candy Hearts, Jelly Beans, or Gumdrops, on the CD-ROM that accompanies this text.

‹‹‹‹LOOKING BACK

Making sense of the many ways we use numbers and our multiple number systems can be a daunting task. Children must learn different systems for time, measurement, money, and mathematics—the latter two requiring the mastery of an abstract numbers structure based on 10.

Making numbers real to children is the first step. Tying clock time, calendar time, measurement, and money to children's worlds makes interpreting those numbers accurately important to the children and meaningful. Making the base-10 system real begins with counting and hands-on activities. As children explore the concepts empirically with counting objects, connecting centimeter cubes, or base-10 blocks, they establish foundations for constructing algorithms and learning formal mathematics.

Questions for Further Thought, Discussion, and Research

1. Teachers have long realized the value of using familiar and even edible objects to help children learn and expand their counting skills. Jelly beans and M&M's can be counted and sorted by color. Cheerios, because they are inexpensive and plentiful, can be used to count large numbers. Select several other edible objects to develop counting exercises and problems for your students.

2. Is there a better way to tell time—a better clock, a better calendar, a better system? What would happen if we changed from a base-60 to a base-10 system for clock time? How would it work? Can we have a base-10 calendar? Why or why not?

3. Make a list of terms and standards related to measurement—*inch, centimeter, score, gross, twofold,* and so forth. Use your dictionary and other sources to help you find origins and meaning. How many different number systems or origins can you identify? What are some of the effects of this seemingly random collection of ideas? Why do we keep some of the terms and standards? For example, is the concept of a score or a ream useful today?

4. How might you use money to teach place value, including the value of places to the right of the decimal point? Develop a series of lessons that use money as manipulatives to teach the value of places from 1,000s to 100s.

5. Explore the meaning of place value in the base-20 or a base-60 number system. Apply the ideas with Arabic numerals; then try the same thing in Mayan or Babylonian symbols. What would it be like to add or subtract numbers in those systems?

6

Working with Whole Numbers: Addition and Subtraction

Children begin to work with whole numbers long before they enter school. Most preschoolers have invented strategies for adding single-digit numbers, and many kindergartners understand basic addition concepts.

Children's early mastery of numbers work depends to a large extent on rich, fluent learning experiences. The more opportunities they have to use numbers and explore applications, the more they understand and can do. Generally conceptual and procedural knowledge seem to develop in tandem in the early years, but procedural knowledge sometimes outpaces conceptual knowledge as children encounter the broad curriculum and fast pace of school mathematics.

Instruction that explicitly maps concepts to procedures increases children's understanding of the big ideas. At the same time it promotes their ability to invent and execute effective procedures. Some of the important concepts include cardinal and ordinal numbers and the commutative principle of addition. Some of the important procedures include counting all and counting on models of addition, mental calculators, and multidigit addition and subtraction.

The Changing Faces of Whole Numbers: Cardinal, Ordinal, Measurement

What is a **whole number?** A student once described a whole number as "a number that hasn't been broken up into pieces." That is, she defined a whole number by what it is not. It is not a fraction like 1/10, a percentage like 10%, or a decimal fraction like .10. That may not be the entire story, but it is close enough for a beginning. Whole numbers consist of 0 and all of the counting numbers. They respond to questions such as "How many? Which one? How much? How big? What size?"

Many of the standards and expectations for children's early learning focus on whole numbers. In NCTM's *Principles and Standards for School Mathematics*, expectations for grades pre-K–2 make working with whole numbers the starting point for understanding numbers, operations, and computation:

In prekindergarten through grade 2 all students should—

- Develop understanding of the relative position and magnitude of whole numbers and of ordinal and cardinal numbers and their connections;
- Develop a sense of whole numbers and represent and use them in flexible ways, including relating, composing, and decomposing numbers;
- Understand various meanings of addition and subtraction of whole numbers and the relationship between the two operations;
- Understand the effects of adding and subtracting whole numbers;
- Develop and use strategies for whole-number computations with a focus on addition and subtraction.

(NCTM 2000, 78)

Expectations for grades 3–5 continue and build on this early work.

In grades 3–5 all students should—

- Understand the effects of multiplying and dividing whole numbers;
- Develop fluency in adding, subtracting, multiplying, and dividing whole numbers;
- Develop and use strategies to estimate the results of whole-number computations and to judge the reasonableness of such results;
- Select appropriate methods and tools for computing with whole numbers from among mental computation, estimation, calculators, and paper and pencil according to the context and nature of the computation and use the selected method or tool.

(NCTM 2000, 148)

Working with whole numbers goes beyond identifying and naming the numbers themselves. Students must also understand the context for the numbers—whether we are using them to show quantities such as a number of objects; to show order such as what comes first, second, or third; or to show measurements such as the length of an object in inches or centimeters and its weight in ounces or grams. These three contexts provide the basis for what we call the three "faces" of whole numbers:

Activities CD

For an activity about whole numbers, go to Activity 2, Making Numbers Books, on the CD-ROM that accompanies this text.

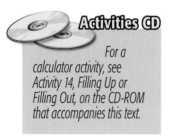

Activities CD

For a calculator activity, see Activity 14, Filling Up or Filling Out, on the CD-ROM that accompanies this text.

Cardinal numbers—whole numbers that represent quantities

Ordinal numbers—whole numbers that represent order

Measurement—whole numbers that represent a comparison between something measured and a standard of measurement

Cardinal Numbers

Children's earliest learning experiences emphasize cardinal numbers or numbers tied to quantities—one frog, two frogs, three frogs, and so forth. These numbers are called *cardinal* (*chief* or *primary*) numbers and are used in counting and totaling. When we ask young children, "How many?" we are in fact asking them to do two things:

1. **to count**—that is, to make a one-to-one correspondence between a set of items and the number sequence

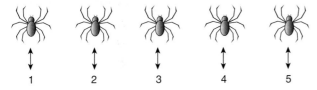

2. **to total**—that is, to regroup the individual items conceptually into a whole that can be described with a single number.

   (Fuson 1988, 8–9; see also Copeland 1974, 108–9)

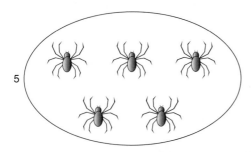

Usually children can provide some accurate answers to the how-many questions long before they understand the cardinal concept of matching things to numbers and then totaling them (Rittle-Johnson and Siegler 1998, 84–85). To develop understanding, children need opportunities that help them break away from inflexible procedures and construct flexible problem-solving strategies. One way to do this is to add new learning perspectives by posing a series of questions. Each builds conceptually on the one before and increases in difficulty (Frye et al. 1989). For example:

Pose a question that starts at the beginning. Ask students to start with number 1 and count until they have a total:

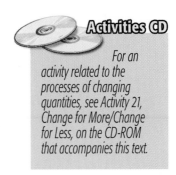

Activities CD

For an activity related to the processes of changing quantities, see Activity 21, Change for More/Change for Less, on the CD-ROM that accompanies this text.

How many chipmunks are there?

Pose a question that starts at the end with a total. Ask students to use counting to test that total.

Are there 15 fish?

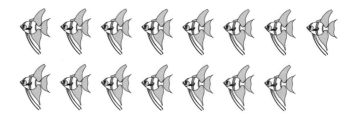

Activities CD

For another activity about counting and totaling, see Activity 4, Counting with Cheerios, on the CD-ROM that accompanies this text.

Pose a question that begins with the same total found to be correct in the previous task, but pair it with a counting task that groups items differently and will have a different total.

Do we still have 15 fish?

Pose a question that asks students to count and total. Then ask them to regroup the items for a new set of totals.

How many doves are there? Please circle each group of 4.

Make a claim and pose a question that students must use counting and totaling to confirm.

I think there are 16 cats here. Are there?

Make a claim and pose a question that students must use counting and totaling to reject and find the correct answer.

I think there are 22 dogs here. How many are there?

The progression of questions encourages students to think beyond the traditional how-many situation and use counting as a tool to explore the cardinality of sets. Asking students to represent their answers in a variety of ways (explaining, writing in words and numerals, and showing with pictures or manipulatives) reinforces thought processes and also gives students a chance to revisit and reflect about their problem-solving strategies.

Figure 6.1 shows the work of two kindergartners. The Grab Bag counting activity engaged their interest immediately as they chose and explored the contents of different bags. For each bag the students first emptied the contents and then grouped the items by type. They represented each group with drawings, counted the items in the group, and wrote the total number.

In Bag E, Marissa drew and wrote numbers beneath a row of disks, establishing visually the one-to-one relationship of the disks to the number sequence, before she wrote the final number and total. Jaime explored the contents of Bag D. Like Marissa, who reversed the 4 when she wrote the total of a group of buttons, Jaime had difficulty with reversing the number 6; however, he counted and totaled accurately. Both students show a solid grasp of the relationship between counting objects and finding the total number—an important foundation for arithmetic operations such as addition.

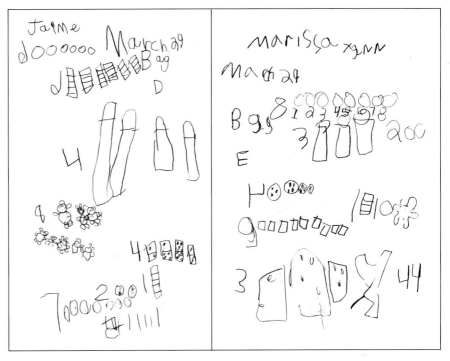

Figure 6.1 Grab bag counting.

Ordinal Numbers

With cardinal numbers the order of items is irrelevant. Ordinal numbers, on the other hand, reflect an organizational pattern or order. The order might be from smallest to largest or vice versa, from youngest to oldest, from earliest to latest. The order might be a ranking, like the Olympic gold, silver, and bronze medals for first-, second-, and third-place finishes. The easiest way to distinguish cardinal from ordinal numbers (first, second, third, fourth, and so forth), according to Ifrah, is to use the hand.

Topics, Issues, and Explorations

Design a hands-on lesson to help kindergartners explore counting and totaling with cardinal numbers. Use prepared manipulatives, such as plastic counters or blocks and rods, or homemade manipulatives such as beans, paper cut-outs, chenille wires, and sticks. Be sure to include perspectives for visual, aural/oral, and tactile learning—that is, something to see, something to hear and say, something to touch and do. (For cutouts of counters, see Appendix A, Make Your Own Manipulatives.)

[The hand] serves as an instrument permitting natural movement between cardinal and ordinal numbering. If you need to show that a set contains three, four, seven, and ten elements, you raise or bend *simultaneously* [at the same time] three, four, seven, or ten fingers, using your hand as cardinal mapping. If you want to count out the same things [ordinally], then you bend or raise three, four, seven, or ten fingers *in succession* [one after another], using the hand as an ordinal counting tool.

(Ifrah 2000, 22)

The numeral representation of the numbers stays the same, but the number words change:

numerals—1, 2, 3, 4, 5, 6, 7, 8, 9, 10

cardinal words—one, two, three, four, five, six, seven, eight, nine, ten

ordinal words—first, second, third, fourth, fifth, sixth, seventh, eighth, ninth, tenth (abbreviated 1st, 2nd, 3rd, and so forth)

Generally children's understanding of ordinal numbers develops later than cardinal numbers by two or even three years, although children may be working

Activities CD

For an activity related to bilingual math and reading, see Activity 20, Animals, Numbered and on the Town: A Bilingual Lesson in Spanish and English, on the CD-ROM that accompanies this text.

Math and Technology

Putting Cardinal Numbers in Context with *Dora the Explorer*

To avoid mechanical approaches to numbers situations, children need to see concepts in meaningful, engaging contexts.

Counting blocks or objects aloud or by hand can fall into a classical conditioning loop—point or touch/say the number, point or touch/say the next number, and so forth. To replace conditioned with reasoned responses, the context for learning must be interesting enough to engage and keep the children's attention, and the learning process should proceed meaningfully within that context in a cause-effect pattern.

Dora the Explorer (Viacom International) is an interactive cartoon with strong math content. The hero is a Hispanic girl, and the setting suggests semitropics.

In the various episodes, learning math is a natural outcome of the problem-solving narrative. For example, in one episode Dora asked the children watching to help her find out how many sections of train track needed to be replaced to repair the track and allow the explorers to win a race.

The tracks were blue blocks that the children had to find, count, and total "to make sure." As viewers help Dora, they use cardinal numbers and begin to understand why giving an exact answer to a how-many question can be important.

(See also http://www.nickjr.com.)

with ordinal numbers in preschool (see Fuson 1988, 404). Children begin working with ordinal numbers in calendar math and in comparisons. They learn to read numerals on a calendar as ordinal rather than cardinal numbers since it is the succession rather than the quantity of days that is important. *January 1* and *April 30* could be read "January first" and "April thirtieth" rather than "January one" and "April thirty." Children learn early to want to be "first" in line and in competitive situations.

For some children understanding comes after application. The activity featured in this chapter's Mathematics in Literature feature and in Figure 6.2 is from Susan Elya's (2000) bilingual story *Eight Animals on the Town*. After drawing the eight animals and writing about them in her own book, one child experienced an "ah-ha" moment. She told her teacher, "That's what they mean when they say 'first,' 'second,' 'third'!" The activity calls for children to read, illustrate, and talk about numbers and words in the story.

Measurement

Strictly speaking, measurement numbers are not different from other whole numbers, but they may *seem* different to children. In measurement situations, number is a continuous rather than a distinct quantity. Fuson (1988) describes measurement this way:

> In a measure situation the entity to be measured is a continuous quantity (e.g., length, area, volume, time). A unit for that kind of quantity must be selected (e.g., a centimeter, a square mile, a cubic centimeter, a swing of a pendulum, 1 *m* in length) and repeatedly applied to the particular continuous quantity until the quantity is used up. The measure number word tells how many units are required to cover (fill) the continuous quantity.
>
> *(7–8)*

As with ordinal numbers, measurement calls for more complex thinking than cardinal numbers. The child must be able to follow a multistep conceptual process:

1. Identify the quantity to be measured (such as length).
2. Relate it to an appropriate tool (such as a ruler).
3. Divide the quantity to be measured into subunits (such as centimeters).
4. Apply the standard (centimeters on the ruler) an appropriate number of times to the measured object.

In laboratory experiments, Piaget observed, "The ability to measure develops later

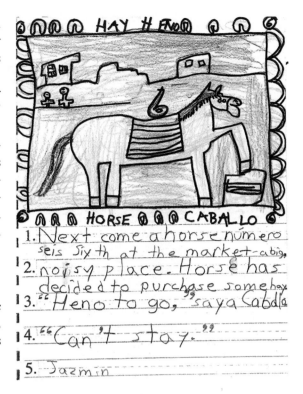

Figure 6.2   Horse is sixth.

Mathematics in Literature

Ordinal Numbers in Susan Elya's *Eight Animals on the Town*

Susan Elya's (2000) bilingual story follows eight animals that visit a market, dance, and ride in cars. The animals shop one at a time with their order counted in Spanish number words and English ordinal words. Spanish and English are combined in the text, with translation following the story line naturally and rhymes to reinforce pronunciation.

Activity 1

Make a book with construction paper covers and pages that are half lined for text and half unlined for illustrations. Rewrite and illustrate the story, writing numbers in words in the text and numerals in the illustrations.

Activity 2

Act out an expanded version of the story adding enough animals for every student in the class. Use construction paper to make and decorate paper hats for each animal. Write the animal's name and number, in numerals, Spanish, and English ordinal words on a sign or tag to be worn around the neck.

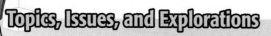

Topics, Issues, and Explorations

Reflect about your own use of numbers. Identify and record the cardinal, ordinal, and measurement numbers you use every day. Which do you use most? Least? Why?

Activities CD

For an estimation activity, see Activity 6, The Revolving Jar, on the CD-ROM that accompanies this text.

than the number concept . . . because it is more difficult to divide a continuous whole, such as an object being measured, into interchangeable subunits than it is to count a set of objects that are separate and discrete from each other, such as beads and blocks" (Copeland 1974, 252).

Children begin to construct the necessary strategies for measurement with activities that ask them to build a measuring system from common objects such as centimeter blocks and use a simple counting procedure to apply it to an object for drawing. A good example is the "How Tall Is My Dino?" activity (see Chapter 4 Teacher Pro-File). Children draw a tall and a short dinosaur; then they draw and count a stack of centimeter blocks to show the dinosaur's height.

Estimation exercises also help children develop measurement strategies as they guess-and-test to find the number of jelly beans, M&M's, or peanuts in a jar or the number of animal crackers in a bag. A creative variation of the traditional estimation activities is the pig-in-a-poke. Fill an opaque bag with one kind of a common object (crayons, gum sticks, Ping Pong balls); have the children guess the contents and estimate the number.

Single-Digit Addition and Subtraction

Very young children may show an impressive knowledge of counting and basic arithmetic, especially when they work with very small numbers. Even before they begin school, many children can count, add, and even do simple subtraction. This does not mean, of course, that children are born with that knowledge. Most have had ample opportunities for learning math informally from adult caregivers, siblings, and the world around them. Even more important, they have opportunities and the desire to make sense of their worlds in mathematical terms.

In a study to discover how children learn math, children reported learning by watching and listening to others but also by working out ideas for themselves. Generally they do not count "just being told" as learning but insist on the primary importance of their own efforts to learn (Ekeblad 1996, 213–20). Asked how they had learned to count or do simple addition and subtraction, children in the study suggested that for them *real* learning was an independent achievement. A first grader, Josie, said she taught a younger friend to count, but she herself had learned on her own (see Windows on Learning, Who Taught You Math?).

Although young children recognize the role of others in learning mathematics, they see that role and responsibility as secondary to their own. Ekeblad explains it this way:

Children [. . .] certainly assign a role for others in their learning (as informants and monitors) but there is a crucial part of learning that is the exclusive responsibility of the learner—others can do a lot to help and inform, but there is something that they cannot do for you. Learning by oneself means figuring the answers out on one's own, as opposed to getting ready-made solutions, which would have been an

Who Taught You Math?

Interviewer: Did anybody teach you before when you were little?

Josie: No. I had to teach myself.

Caroline also said she had taught herself.

Caroline: . . . You do the counting yourself then nobody else tells you what the an-what it is. . . . What the answer is like.

Carl explained that he figured out things for himself by thinking.

Interviewer: Umm . . . How did you know that it [three horses plus five horses] made eight?

Carl: . . . I counted in my head.

Interviewer: Yes. And how did you count 17 in your head?

Carl: . . . I thought.

Source: Ekeblad (1996, 216–18).

alternative possibility—but one where you could not truly claim to have learned.

(Ekeblad 1996, 217–18)

Children's view of their own math learning reaffirms the need for instructional methods that let students explore and discover mathematical ideas, invent and test problem-solving strategies, and create meanings that make sense to them. Mapping instruction to student learning begins with acknowledging students' perspectives, their own ideas about how their learning works. The students in the dialogue quoted in the Windows on Learning feature identified several key components of successful math learning:

Activities CD

For an activity showing how to use fingers to count and do basic calculations, see Activity 22, One-Handed Fingermath, Part I: Counting All and On to Add Single-Digit Numbers, on the CD-ROM that accompanies this text.

- **teaching themselves**—or taking the lead in their own learning;
- **working with concepts (doing the counting or calculations) until they understand the process and the product**—knowing, according to Caroline, "what the answer is like";
- **thinking about and working out problems mentally**—as opposed to applying an algorithm and arriving at an answer automatically.

The bottom line here is a fundamental principle for teaching children mathematics:

The mathematics of children is first and foremost mathematics they create for themselves.

What they create and discover, including their own informal strategies for working with whole numbers, provides a foundation for building the conceptual framework of school mathematics. If we as teachers acknowledge the value of and work with students' own strategies, school mathematics will make more sense to them, and they can continue to claim ownership of their math learning.

Children's Strategies for Adding

Before they start school most children understand that to add means to join two quantities. Most have worked out a strategy or informal algorithm for adding small

Figure 6.3   Robby counts all the children.

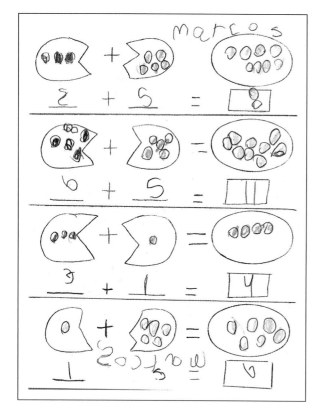

Figure 6.4   Jelly bean addition.

numbers (Rittle-Johnson and Siegler 1998, 187). Usually they begin by inventing a counting-all algorithm. They start with the first number in the problem, count it out, and then continue counting until they have counted out the second number.

Adding by Counting All

$$5 + 5 = 10$$

1. Begin with 1 and count out the first five numbers.
2. Continue from 5 and count out the next five numbers in the number sequence.
3. The last number, 10, is the total.

A problem like 5 + 5 becomes "1, 2, 3, 4, 5" plus the next five numbers in the sequence, "6, 7, 8, 9, 10." Often students use fingers, drawings (see Figure 6.3), or objects and either touch or move them to keep track of their counting.

Figure 6.4, Jelly Bean Addition, is the end point in a kindergarten-level discovering-addition activity. The assignment builds on children's counting-all strategy, then takes the next step to represent their thinking and answers. The students begin by rolling pairs of dice and counting jelly beans to match the numbers rolled. Each roll of a pair gives the students two groupings for the jelly beans—3 on one die resulting in a group of three jelly beans; 4 on the other, a group of four jelly beans. It also gives students a ready-made addition problem, 3 + 5 = ?, that can be worked out by counting all of the jelly beans.

Figure 6.4 shows the next step—representing the quantities in the problem and the solution with drawings and numbers. The students' teacher describes the counting-all strategy and the concepts of grouping and joining groups to find the total number of jelly beans:

> The children count the dots on the dice and duplicate the numbers with jelly beans. They then group and join the jelly beans to figure out the total. They draw the jelly beans and numbers they figure out on their worksheets. They read the problems and explain them to me while I ask questions. (Finally, they are able to enjoy their jelly beans.)

By kindergarten many children have also invented a counting-on strategy for adding. This simplifies their task by letting them count on from the larger number. In the 5 + 5 problem, instead of counting out the first number, they begin with "5," then count on in the number sequence from there, "6, 7, 8, 9, and 10," for the total.

Both of these strategies could be represented by the drawings in Figure 6.5. The student has shown each number with a group of individual objects. Counting all (sometimes called the *sum procedure* of doing the addition) would mean counting each object. Counting on (sometimes called the *min procedure*) would mean naming one number and then continuing to count the objects in the second group individually to arrive at the total.

Young children usually work out some of the primary concepts of addition on their own:

1. Adding means joining quantities to get a larger quantity or more of something.
2. Each number added should be represented only once.
3. Changing the order of numbers does not change the total.

(Rittle-Johnson and Siegler 1998, 88; see also Cowan and Renton 1996 and Siegler and Crowley 1994)

The third concept is often called the *commutative principle of addition.* Understanding it allows children to simplify the counting-on process. Instead of beginning with the first number, they can start with the largest number and count on from there.

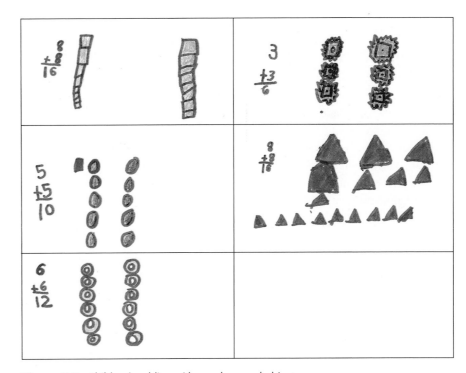

Figure 6.5   Children's adding with numbers and objects.

Adding by Counting On

$$9 + 3 = ?$$

1. Identify larger addend, 9.
2. Count on from 9, three places: 10, 11, 12.
3. The last number, 12, is the answer.

Children's Strategies for Subtracting

Instead of approaching subtraction as the reverse of addition, children often adapt the counting-all strategy. As they explore a subtraction situation with counting manipulatives, they will count all of the manipulatives, count out and take away the number to be subtracted, and then count all of the manipulatives that are left.

Subtracting by Counting All and Taking Away

$$6 - 3 = ?$$

1. Count all, 1 to 6.
2. Count and take away, 1 to 3.
3. Count what is left, 1 to 3, for the answer 3.

Interestingly, children discover counting up to subtract before they develop counting down or backward strategies. As teachers in the early grades soon discover, "The backward counting-down procedures are much more difficult for children than the forward procedures" (Fuson 1988, 278; see also Baroody 1984 and Fuson 1984). A child who can count forward in sequence by 2s, 5s, and even 10s will often stumble over the reverse process, skipping numbers and altering intervals in the sequence. When children invent a counting-up strategy to subtract, they have actually found a way to subtract by adding. In other words, they have avoided the problem of reversing

Activities CD

For an activity showing how to use fingers to perform simple subtractions, see Activity 23, One-Handed Fingermath, Part II: Counting Up and Down to Subtract Single-Digit Numbers, on the CD-ROM that accompanies this text.

Googol: BIG IDEAS in Mathematics

Plus (+) for Add/Minus (−) for Subtract

Knowing when to add and when to subtract is a foundational concept for working with whole numbers. Connecting the symbols + and − with the actions of adding and subtracting begins with doing. Gingerbread House Math is an activity that helps students understand these key ideas for working with whole numbers.

Materials for the activity include:

One gingerbread house
Die marked +1, +2, +3, −1, −2, −3
Pathways marked in steps
Baggies of pieces of bread or croutons
Story: "Hansel and Gretel"

To set an imaginative context for the activity, teachers can read the Hansel and Gretel fairy tale aloud.

Activity

You are trying to escape from the witch's cottage. To find your way home, you need to cover all of the steps on your path with bread crumbs.

Take turns rolling the die. If you roll a number with a plus, then put that number of crumbs on your path starting at the gingerbread house and leading away from the house along the path. If you roll a number with a minus, remove that number of crumbs from the path.

Keep rolling the die and adding and subtracting bread crumbs until all of the students have covered all of the steps on their paths with crumbs and have escaped from the witch's gingerbread house.

Extension

Answer these questions:

What number lets you put the most bread crumbs on the path?
What is the worst number you can roll? Why?
What if you roll +3, then −2? How many bread crumbs would that leave on the path?
What if you roll +2, then −3? Would there be any bread crumbs left?

Source: From an activity created for kindergarten by Donna Waid.

Kindergarten teacher Donna Waid shows a group of preservice teachers her Gingerbread House Math activity.

direction and turned the problems into a procedure that moves forward along the number line.

Subtracting by Counting Up

$$9 - 6 = ?$$

1. Identify the smaller number, 6.
2. Count up from 6 to 9: 7, 8, 9.
3. Identify the number of spaces counted up.
4. The number of counted-up spaces is the answer.

(For a description of these procedures that emphasize language, see Fuson 1988, 279.)

Children take the next step toward a more conceptually complex reverse or backward procedure when they explore and develop strategies for take-away situations. Figure 6.6 shows Dustin's response to the take-away problem:

Teresa has 13 animals—6 snakes, 3 lizards, 2 turtles, 1 dog, and 1 cat. She gave 7 animals to her friends. How many does she have left?

Dustin drew the 13 animals and also three girls, Teresa and two friends, but he did not represent in his drawings a full counting/taking-away/counting strategy. Asked how he got his answer, Dustin said, "I thought it in my head. I went backward like—13 animals, take away 1, 12 take away 1, 11 take away 1...." Dustin used what amounts to a rough backward counting or counting-down strategy.

Counting down to subtract literally means reversing the number sequence. The process requires both different cognitive structures and a more advanced level of development in mathematical thinking (Fuson 1988; Fuson and Fuson 1992; Copeland 1974). Students must understand first that counting can go up or down the number sequence. They must also understand that counting up results in more, counting down in less—a conclusion that will be obvious to adults but not necessarily so to children. Dustin's rudimentary counting-down process is less streamlined but follows the general pattern of a counting-down subtraction algorithm.

Subtracting by Counting Down

$$9 - 6 = ?$$

1. Identify the larger number, 9.
2. Count down from 9 to 6: 8, 7, 6.
3. Identify the number of spaces counted down.
4. The number of counted-down spaces is the answer.

Fingermath

Because of the importance placed on memorizing math facts for addition and subtraction, many teachers

Figure 6.6 Dustin's subtraction.

Topics, Issues, and Explorations

Some of the strategies discussed in this chapter—such as counting on fingers and encouraging children to invent their own strategies for adding and subtracting—run contrary to traditional instructional practices. Even today, in some schools students caught counting on their fingers might be punished, and answers arrived at in any way but the one taught by the teacher might be considered wrong, even if the numbers are correct. What do you think? Does counting on the fingers or developing their own algorithms help or hinder students' learning mathematics?

Two-Handed Fingermath

Right-hand numbers:

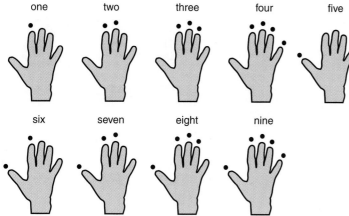

Left-hand numbers:

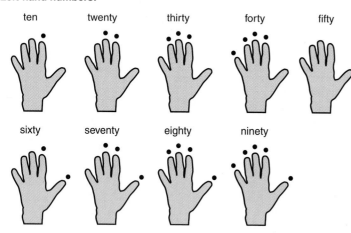

Numbers with both hands:

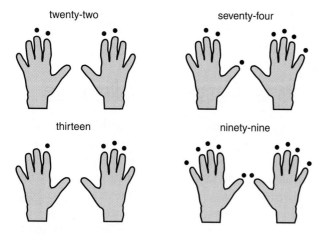

Figure 6.7 Finger patterns for 1 to 99.
(Adapted from Lieberthal 1979.)

discourage counting on fingers when children add or subtract. However, research and classroom practice have shown that using the fingers can work like manipulating counters or other concrete objects. The objects themselves as well as the act of manipulating them help anchor concepts in the concrete and keep students on task.

Karen Fuson, a noted researcher in early math learning, has found that finger-counting strategies improve young children's understanding of addition and subtraction. She recommends using counting, counting up, and counting down with one-handed finger patterns to teach addition and subtraction in the early grades (Fuson and Willis 1988; Fuson and Fuson 1992).

Figure 6.7, Finger Patterns for 1 to 99, shows how the thumb on the right hand is the pivotal 5; on the left, 50. The other fingers work alone or in combinations with 5 and 50 to form the numbers through 9 with the right hand and through 90 with the left (Lieberthal 1979). The finger patterns for counting down are reversed, beginning with the largest numbers, 9 or 90, and showing the numbers in order from largest to smallest, 8, 7, 6 (right hand) or 80, 70, 60 (left hand). Children often keep track of the number of spaces counted down by saying the numbers and remembering how many.

Mental Addition and Subtraction

For very young children, adding and subtracting small numbers mentally probably begins with estimation (Baroody 1984). Children use what they know about numbers and mathematics to make educated guesses. For example, they might look at the largest number in an addition problem and name a number they know represents more as a possible sum; or in a subtraction problem, they will look at the largest number and guess a number that is less (Baroody 1989). If estimation does not produce an acceptable answer, they look for a way to represent the situation concretely. They make drawings and tally marks, model numbers with their fingers, and count out the numbers (Siegler and Shrager 1984).

After many school experiences with single-digit numbers, students develop number sense for the combinations and relationships possible. That is, they have worked with triplets of numbers such as 5, 3, 8 (5 + 3 = 8, 8 − 5 = 3, 8 − 3 = 5) and 7, 3, 10 (7 + 3 = 10, 10 − 7 = 3, 10 − 3 = 7) so often in both addition and subtraction that they "can find any missing number if two are known" (Fuson 1988, 283). Fuson (1988) calls this a "cardinal triplet conceptual structure" because of the grouping of related facts by threes (283). At that point they may not need to perform the actual calculations mentally but instead simply recall the results of past problem solving. The facts have become part of their math knowledge web, and drawing on that web has become a working part of their mathematical thinking.

Topics, Issues, and Explorations

Many teachers ask children to add or subtract in their heads as a kind of mental gymnastics. What role, if any, do you think mental calculations can play in developing mathematical thinking? What are your own experiences? Do you ever do calculations in your head—for example, when you are shopping? If you do, do you use exact or estimated numbers? Do you ever use your fingers or other concrete counters to help you keep track of numbers? Why do you think this skill is (or is not) important for children to learn?

Activities CD

For an activity in which mental calculations play a role, see Activity 27, $100 Shopping Spree, on the CD-ROM that accompanies this text.

Mathematical Games

'SMATH

'SMATH is an award-winning board game (*Woman's Day*, Best Educational Toys 2000) for first grade and up. Like Scrabble, the game uses tiles with point values and a board with bonus squares. Game pieces include number tiles; equals-sign tiles; blank tiles; parentheses; and tiles for addition, subtraction, multiplication, and division. Play proceeds in a crossword-puzzle style. However, instead of creating words, players make math statements.

10	+	10	=	20		
×				−		
1		3	+	14	=	17
=				=		
10			6	÷	2	=	3

Players draw on their knowledge of math facts to form math statements and also to compute and record scores—the sum of the point value for all the tiles in the statement plus any points allowed by covering bonus squares on the board.

Play can be adjusted to fit students' levels of learning. For example, first and second graders might use only the addition and subtraction tiles for operations, while third and fourth graders could add multiplication and division.

Building math statements from tiles available for play and those already played on the board promotes flexibility in math thinking. To score the highest number of points, players must compose and test a variety of valid statements, calling for them to compare and make judgments.

(For a similar game with an algebra focus, see the Mathematical Games feature in Chapter 10, "Playing Algebra: Equate.")

Multidigit Addition and Subtraction

Working with multidigit whole numbers comprises a significant portion of the mathematics curriculum during the early grades. Emphasis on procedures rather than concepts may prolong the learning process and lead to "buggy" applications, such as subtracting smaller from larger numbers regardless of where they appear in the problem—for example, reversing the numbers in $11 - 22 = ?$ to read, $22 - 11 = 11$ (see Van Lehn 1983 for a description of common procedural "bugs"; also Lindquist 1989 and Fuson 1990 for discussion of U.S. students' application of procedures they do not adequately understand).

Students show a better grasp of both concepts and procedures when teachers map instruction to concepts instead of procedures—that is, when teachers pair reasons for doing something with the steps for doing it. With multidigit addition and subtraction, this means instruction "that emphasize[s] concepts of place value and how they relate to steps in a procedure" (Rittle-Johnson and Siegler 1998, 95, 96). Significantly, when concepts and procedures are tied together, students usually learn more about both. Because the procedures make sense, they can be applied more appropriately and efficiently.

Activities CD

For fingermath activities with multidigit numbers, go to Activity 30, Two-handed Fingermath, on the CD-ROM that accompanies this text.

Building Concepts for Working with Multidigit Numbers

The starting place for understanding and working with multidigit numbers is the base-10 system and place value. Early experiences with numbers emphasize one-to-one correspondences and single units. Children work with single-unit manipulatives such as counting dinosaurs or frogs, and they draw or make a mark for each item. However, for numbers larger than 20, "children need to think in terms of multiunits—of groups of 10, 100, 1,000, and so forth " (Fuson 1990, 273).

> Both English number words and written number marks for multidigit numbers are built up of increasingly larger multiunits related to ten (ten hundred, thousand, etc.). Understanding multidigit numbers requires being able to think about these various sizes of multiunits, and understanding operations on multidigit numbers requires understanding how to compose and decompose multidigit numbers into these multiunits in order to carry out the various operations.
>
> *(Fuson 1990, 273)*

How do children deal with multidigit numbers such as 114? Do they read the symbols and think first of the words *one hundred, ten,* and *four*? Do they envision objects that, when counted, will add up to a total of 114? Or do they think of a long number line with 114 being the final number in the sequence? With a number as large as 114, they often think of the words and not the concrete numbers. However, dealing successfully with multidigit numbers calls for a well-rounded understanding of the numbers themselves:

1. Children need to be fluent in the language of numbers—being able to translate from words to numerals and numerals to words.

2. They need to know what the numbers mean in a cardinal sense—that is, as quantities of concrete objects or other entities.

3. They need to understand the numbers in terms of the base-10 system—as a composite of different types of units with the specific type identified by the order of the numbers.

4. And they need to be able to show their understanding with words, symbols, concrete objects, and other patterned representations such as schematic drawings.

Representing quantities with base-10 blocks (sometimes called *Dienes blocks*) is a good place to begin to build the concepts of multiunits, base-10, and place value (Dienes 1960; Fuson 1990; Baroody 1990). Students explore until they understand the relationship of the different blocks—that 10 units make one rod, that 10 rods make one flat, and that 10 flats make one cube. Once the visual/tactile referent is firmly established, they can translate quantities into number words and symbols. After that they are ready to experiment with equivalencies—how many rods equal 20 units and how many flats, 20 rods. Trading units for rods of 10 and rods for flats of 100 gives children a conceptual basis for carrying. Figure 6.8 shows the tiering of activities as children move from exploring to showing to comparing quantities (for cut-out patterns for base-10 blocks, see Appendix A).

Another type of manipulative that encourages multiunit thinking is Cuisenaire rods. Based roughly on Chinese math sticks and the abacus, the rods use color and size to represent units from 1 to 10 centimeters in length (see the Math Manipulatives feature for more about Cuisenaire rods and the Teacher Pro-File feature in this chapter for more about Chinese math sticks).

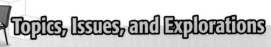

Topics, Issues, and Explorations

Base-10 blocks have been an important teaching tool for many years. Did you use them in school? What kind of activities did you do with blocks? Or, have you observed block activities? What works and what does not work? How would you use base-10 blocks in your own classroom?

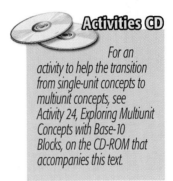

Activities CD

For an activity to help the transition from single-unit concepts to multiunit concepts, see Activity 24, Exploring Multiunit Concepts with Base-10 Blocks, on the CD-ROM that accompanies this text.

Math Manipulatives

Cuisenaire Rods

Cuisenaire rods develop multiunit concepts with a building-block model. There are 10 different rods, each with a square centimeter base. The lengths increase from 1 to 10 centimeters and are color coded—white, 1 centimeter; red, 2 centimeters; green, 3 centimeters; purple, 4 centimeters; yellow, 5 centimeters; dark green, 6 centimeters; black, 7 centimeters; brown, 8 centimeters; blue, 9 centimeters; orange, 10 centimeters. To work with the rods, students need to think in terms of multiunits—of two red rods or four whites to equal one purple, for example.

Activity 1

Explore the relationship of the different rods by finding equivalencies. Find all of the different combinations that will equal each of the following:

> one orange rod,
> one orange and one yellow rod,
> four purple rods, and
> three black rods.

Represent the combinations with drawings, words, and numbers.

Activity 2

Use rods to model simple addition and subtraction; then write the problems in both words and numbers.

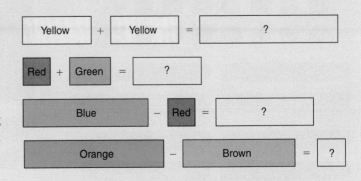

(For more activities with Cuisenaire rods, see Welchman-Tischler 1992.)

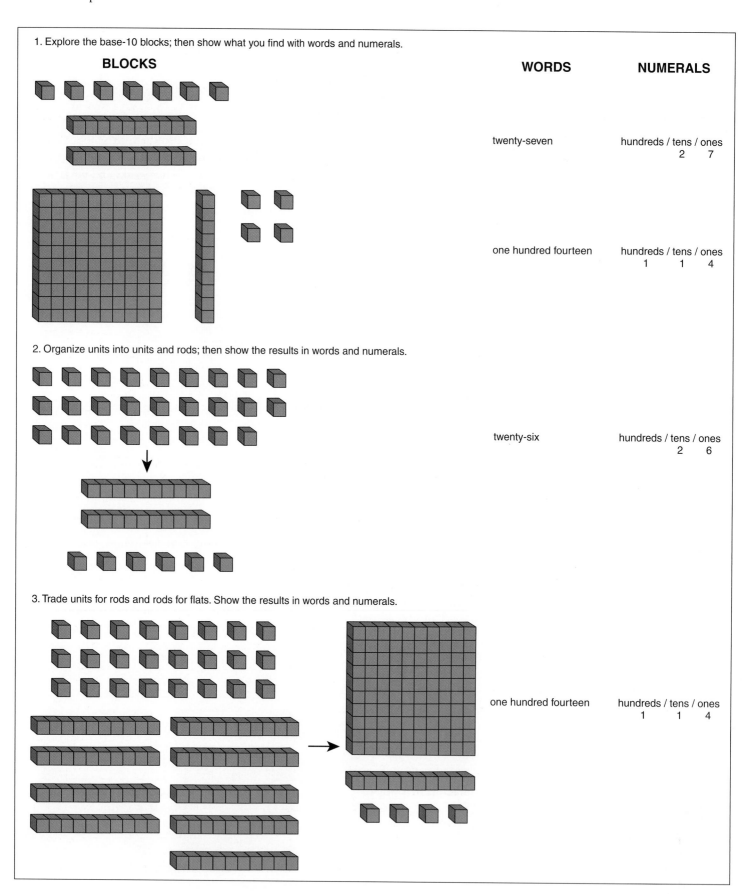

1. Explore the base-10 blocks; then show what you find with words and numerals.

BLOCKS   **WORDS**   **NUMERALS**

twenty-seven

hundreds / tens / ones
                2   7

one hundred fourteen

hundreds / tens / ones
         1   1   4

2. Organize units into units and rods; then show the results in words and numerals.

twenty-six

hundreds / tens / ones
                2   6

3. Trade units for rods and rods for flats. Show the results in words and numerals.

one hundred fourteen

hundreds / tens / ones
         1   1   4

Figure 6.8 Using base-10 blocks to explore multiunit concepts.

Adding and Subtracting Multidigit Numbers

Students' own algorithms for working with multidigit numbers are often adapted from problems with single-digit numbers. Shawntel's addition strategy in Figure 6.9 is an adaptation of a single-digit algorithm. First, she treats the two columns as separate single-digit problems. She even represents the numbers with circles or dots to count. She adds the columns separately, possibly working from left to right. Then she reconciles the numbers by adding a 1 to the 10s column and erasing or writing over the initial sum for that column.

Making the transition from single-unit to multiunit strategies for adding and subtracting requires students to think in larger terms than those of their early experiences. Base-10 blocks work better than single-unit counters for modeling problems with multidigit numbers because they incorporate multiunit concepts. Nevertheless, some students will attempt to use counting-all and counting-on strategies when they begin to work with block addition. The difficulty of applying those strategies increases with the size of the numbers. Few students will count the blocks in a flat of 100, and the 1,000-block cube cannot be dismantled. Working with large combinations helps even very young children think in terms of base-10, multiunit structures and to make the connections needed to move from concrete representations to more abstract ideas and schemes (see Baroody 1990, 282).

Two fundamental concepts for adding and subtracting multidigit numbers are **trading** and **regrouping**. Shawntel's method of working with two-digit addition (Figure 6.9) is to treat the problem as two single-digit problems, then regroup and reconcile the answers. To develop a more effective strategy than Shawntel's, students must first construct a "10-for-1 trading scheme . . .: trading 10 units for one next larger unit, that by position only denotes a tenfold increase in size" (Baroody 1990, 283).

Figure 6.8 shows a series of concrete-to-pictorial activities with base-10 blocks aimed at establishing the 10-for-1 scheme. Once students understand the equivalence of the different representation as well as the ascending-by-10s structure of the decimal number system, they are prepared to see trading as part of a *re*grouping strategy—that is, a way to reorganize and order quantities.

To make the links among trading, regrouping, and the operations with numbers, children need to work back and forth from hands-on models to pictorial representations to numerals. Figures 6.10 and 6.11 show examples for addition and subtraction. Students begin by modeling their work with manipulatives; then they represent the models with drawings of blocks and squares. Circles show the trading and regrouping—for example, in the addition problem ten 1s traded for one 10 and ten 100s traded for one 1,000. Finally, the problem is rewritten as numerals.

Children need to understand that multiple ways for solving problems and multiple representations for their solutions are both permissible and desirable. The more perspectives they can create, the more flexible their thinking becomes and the more problem-solving strategies they develop. Thinking creatively, Molly developed a concrete strategy that used counting and trading to subtract.

Molly was asked to use Dienes [base-10] blocks to subtract 29 from 47. She began by constructing the block display that matched the larger number—that is, 4 tens and 7 units. She then tried to remove 9 units and, of course, could not. . . . Asked if she could find any way to get more units[,] Molly

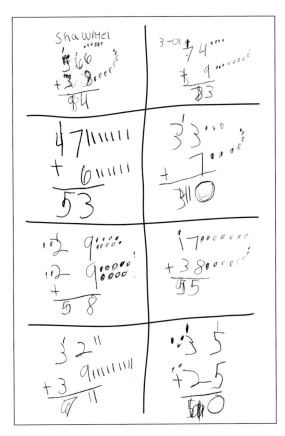

Figure 6.9 Shawntel adds multidigit numbers.

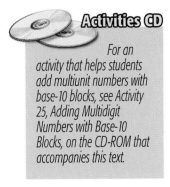

Activities CD

For an activity that helps students add multiunit numbers with base-10 blocks, see Activity 25, Adding Multidigit Numbers with Base-10 Blocks, on the CD-ROM that accompanies this text.

Activities CD

For an activity that helps students subtract multiunit numbers with base-10 blocks, see Activity 26, Subtracting Multidigit Numbers with Base-10 Blocks, on the CD-ROM that accompanies this text.

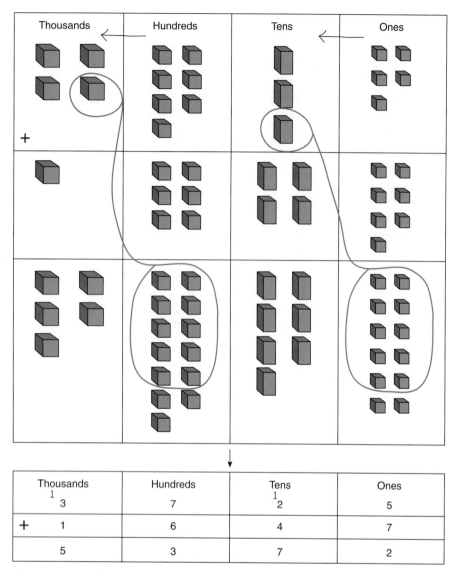

Thousands	Hundreds	Tens	Ones
1 3	7	1 2	5
+ 1	6	4	7
5	3	7	2

Figure 6.10 Addition: Adding 1647 and 3725.
(Adapted from Fuson 1988, 289.)

responded by putting aside all of the units blocks and one of the tens in her display, leaving just 3 tens. She counted these by tens ("10, 20, 30") and then continued by ones adding in a units block with each count, up to 47.

(Resnick 1983, 136)

Once Molly had regrouped her blocks, she had 17 units and 3 rods from which she could easily take away 9 units and 2 rods. After more practice with this invented strategy, "she stopped counting up and began simply to trade—that is, discard a tens block and count in 10 units, or discard a hundreds block and count in 10 tens" (Resnick 1983, 137). In other words, Molly moved from a unitary to a multiunit strategy and in the process developed a concrete representation for trading one 10s block for 10 unit blocks.

Like the trading-up strategy in addition (10 smaller for 1 larger unit), trading down in subtraction (1 larger for 10 smaller units) can best be understood as a regrouping of quantities. Multiunit numbers are decomposed to accommodate subtracting larger numbers in one or more digits of the number subtracted. Understanding the process can begin with blocks and proceed to working side-by-side with schematic drawings and numerals. Vertically aligning multidigit numerals can be a problem for some children. Using columns or lines (as in Figures 6.10 and 6.11) helps guide the placement visually and also reinforces place-value concepts.

Understanding Standard Algorithms

Working with the standard algorithms is a goal of many state and local school districts. Once students have constructed a foundation of concepts—understanding the base-10 system, the relationship of place and face value, addition as a process to increase, subtraction as a process to decrease, the 10-for-1 trading scheme—teachers can introduce the standard algorithms as meaningful processes instead of memorized procedures.

The standard algorithms for both addition and subtraction of multidigit numbers are right-to-left procedures. First, we add or subtract the 1s, then the 10s, then the 100s, and so forth. At each step, if the numbers add up to more than 9 or if the face value of the number subtracted is greater than the number it is subtracted from, we must stop, make a trade (10 for 1 or 1 for 10), regroup, and continue. This procedure makes sense to students if they see it as an effect of the base-10 structures they have built with blocks or other manipulatives. Also, understanding the relationship of face and place value makes trading from right to left work conceptually for students.

Standard Procedure, Addition

111	Add 1s:	$1 + 2 = 3$
+ 92	Add 10s:	$10 + 90 = 100$
203	Trade up:	ten 10s for one 100
	Add 100s:	$100 + 100 = 200$
	Total: 203	

Standard Procedure, Subtraction

211	Subtract 1s:	$1 - 0 = 1$
− 90	Subtract 10s:	$10 - 90 = ?$
121	Trade down:	one 100 for ten 10s
	Subtract 10s:	$110 - 90 = 20$
	Subtract 100s:	$100 - 0 = 100$

For students who have built a strong conceptual base, the standard algorithms can work as shortcuts—a kind of mathematical shorthand that is meaningful and useful because the students understand the processes behind the procedures.

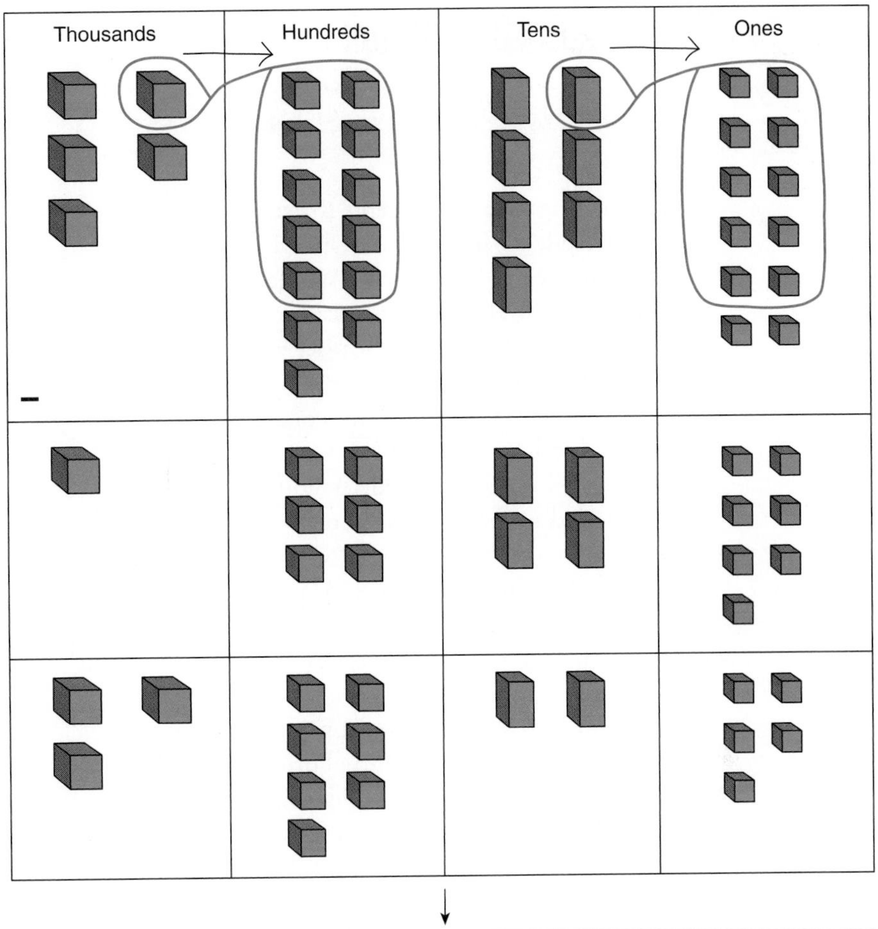

Understanding Alternative Algorithms

Knowing more than one way to work a problem has several advantages:

1. Multiple methods help us understand both problems and solutions better by letting us see them from different perspectives.

2. If we are not able to solve a problem with one method, we may be able to do so with a different method.

3. We can use alternative methods to rethink problems and test solutions.

Thousands	Hundreds	Tens	Ones
⁴$\not{5}$	¹$\not{3}$	⁶$\not{7}$	¹$\not{2}$
− 1	6	4	7
3	7	2	5

Figure 6.11   Subtraction: Subtracting 1647 from 5372. (Adapted from Fuson 1988, 290.)

Topics, Issues, and Explorations

How many different ways can you find to solve the problems $144 + 64 = ?$ and $144 - 25 = ?$ Which method seems easiest? Which makes the most sense? Which shows the processes of addition or subtraction most clearly?

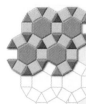

Mathematical Thinking

Using Extended Notation to Reinforce Base-10 Concepts

Understanding base-10 concepts is a major challenge for many students. The ideas implicit in a three-digit number such as 111 are neither simple nor immediately obvious. Students must interpret both the face value of individual digits and the place value of the digits in relation to each other.

After students have "built" the concepts with base-10 blocks or other manipulatives, we can use extended notation to reinforce their understanding.

Extended notation breaks down a number into terms that make base-10 place value explicit. For example, the number 111 can be extended to $100 + 10 + 1$; 222 can be extended to $100 + 100 + 10 + 10 + 1 + 1$.

Extending the number in this way spells out the meaning of both face value and place value. It also helps students build a conceptual bridge for adding and subtracting multidigit numbers. For example, $43 + 26 = ?$ can be extended as follows:

$$10 + 10 + 10 + 10 + 1 + 1 + 1$$
$$+ \; 10 + 10 + 1 + 1 + 1 + 1 + 1 + 1$$
$$\overline{\; 10 + 10 + 10 + 10 + 10 + 10 + 1 + 1 + 1 + 1 + 1 + 1 + 1 + 1 + 1}$$

OR   6   tens   and   9   ones   **OR**   69

Counting the 10s and 1s and rewriting in standard form underscores the meanings of the numbers as well as showing what happens when we add multidigit numbers.

Activity

Use extended notation to explore and work out these problems. Explain what you did and how you got your answer:

1. $34 + 45 = ?$ 2. $16 + 20 = ?$
3. $90 + 10 = ?$ 4. $73 + 82 = ?$
5. $23 - 10 = ?$ 6. $62 - 12 = ?$
7. $46 - 33 = ?$ 8. $111 - 11 = ?$
9. $222 - 111 = ?$

Extension

Use extended notation to explore exchange or trading and regrouping concepts. Work out and discuss what happens when face values exceed 9 in addition or when the face value of the number subtracted is larger than the number it is subtracted from. Discuss how extended notation can help you see and understand the 10-for-1 trading scheme of the base-10 system.

1. $65 + 65 = ?$ 2. $89 + 89 = ?$
3. $82 - 23 = ?$ 4. $111 - 22 = ?$

The alternative algorithms outlined in the Idea Files chart range from simple to complex. Interestingly, the standard European algorithm is the left-to-right rather than the right-to-left method. It also resembles the invented student algorithm featured in Figure 6.9.

Diversity in Learning and Thinking Mathematically

Although more and more teachers are using manipulatives, a significant proportion of mathematics instruction still focuses on practice worksheets and pencil-and-paper calculations. When the emphasis is upon memorized

Idea Files

Alternative Algorithms for Addition and Subtraction

Addition	Subtraction

LEFT-TO-RIGHT ALGORITHM

Starting at the left, add column by column; then adjust the result.

```
      2  6  8
   +  4  8  3
```

1. Add   6 14 11
2. Adjust 10s and 100s.   7   4 11
3. Adjust 1s and 10s.   7   5   1

LEFT-TO-RIGHT ALGORITHM

Starting at the left, subtract column by column; then adjust the result.

```
      9  3  2
   -  3  5  6
```

1. Subtract the 100s.   - 3 0 0
                            6 3 2
2. Subtract the 10s.   -   5 0
                            5 8 2
3. Subtract the 1s.   -   6
                            5 7 2

PARTIAL-SUMS ALGORITHM

Add the numbers in each column.
Then add the partial sums.

```
      2  6  8
   +  4  8  3
```

1. Add 100s.   6 0 0
2. Add 10s.   1 4
3. Add 1s.   1 1
4. Add partial sums.   7 5 1

PARTIAL DIFFERENCES ALGORITHM

Subtract the numbers in each column.
Then add the partial differences.

```
      4  8  3
   -  2  9  5
```

1. Subtract the 100s.   2 0 0
2. Subtract the 10s.   -   1 0
3, Subtract the 1s.   -   2
4. Add partial differences. 1 8 8

Source: Compiled from the Algorithms Website, http://www.millburn.org/math/mathweb/ALGORITHM/add.html.

procedures rather than mathematical thinking and concepts, students may in fact be practicing operations they do not fully understand. Moreover, in the process they may be conditioning flawed or "buggy" processes (see Van Lehn 1983).

Shifting emphasis from procedures to concepts can be as simple as emphasizing word problems. An effective word problem provides a context for problem solving. It links math to communication, combining verbal and quantitative skills. It also leaves devising a strategy, setting up the problem, working through the problem-solving process, and representing solutions up to the students. This means that students may choose the approaches that make the most sense to them, and then let new understandings emerge as they test and accept or reject ideas. In the subtraction with blocks example discussed earlier, Molly began with

Activities CD

For an activity that applies adding and subtracting multidigit numbers to a real-life situation, see Activity 27, $100 Shopping Spree, on the CD-ROM that accompanies this text.

For an activity that shows how to add and subtract using Chinese stick numbers, see Activity 28, Adding and Subtracting with Chinese Stick Math, on the CD-ROM that accompanies this text.

a counting-on strategy that many teachers would consider inadequate to deal with multidigit subtraction problems; however, she used her invented strategy to find her way to the more sophisticated 10-for-1 trading scheme.

Changing starting points, context, representations, or expression of solutions may not be enough to provide all children with access to a topic. When past learning experiences have resulted in numerous practice-conditioned bugs, your best option may be to find a new medium for your message. In this chapter's Teacher Pro-File, Connie Wattenburger teaches multidigit addition and subtraction from the fresh perspective of Chinese math sticks. Other teachers have used Chinese math sticks to engage older students who have not yet mastered the place-value concepts and the 10-for-1 process of trading and regrouping. (For more about using math sticks in the classroom, see Martinez and Martinez 2004.)

Teacher Pro-File

**Connie Wattenburger
Second Grade**

Chinese Math Sticks

Connie Wattenburger likes to emphasize active learning in her second-grade classroom. She believes that spending too much time on workbooks and pencil-and-paper exercises limits her students' thinking and makes math less real—a school subject rather than everyday, meaningful knowledge.

Because her assigned workbook introduces place value in an abstract way, Ms. Wattenburger starts with a hands-on activity that gives a different view of the base-10 system—Chinese math sticks.

Background

Chinese math sticks present an active, concrete approach to the abstract topics of base-10 and place value. Predating the abacus, stick math was used by Chinese merchants more than 2,000 years ago. The system works like a manual calculator. Numbers are laid out with sticks on a counting board and then added, subtracted, and so forth.

In Ms. Wattenburger's activity, a large sheet of paper, divided into columns, serves as the counting board where the stick numbers can be laid out and manipulated for calculations. Colored "sticks" made of chenille wires form the digits 1 to 9. Zero is represented by a blank space. The Chinese number system uses base-10, so the columns on the counting board increase by multiples of 10 from right to left. The stick numbers are easy to learn and use and can be quickly translated into Arabic numbers.

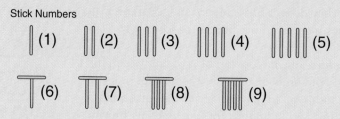

Stick Numbers

Procedure

Each student has a large piece of blue paper, divided into rows and columns, with the 1s, 10s, and 100s columns labeled. In addition, each student has a handful of chenille wires, cut in lengths to fit within the squares. Chinese stick numbers are written on the whiteboard for students to refer to.

First, Ms. Wattenburger has students practice making one-digit, two-digit, and three-digit numbers on their sheets. She has students explain why they put the numbers in the different columns and what the columns mean in terms of place value.

She introduces stick-math addition and subtraction with one-digit problems, and then moves on to bigger numbers. Students form the numbers to be added on their counting sheets, and then add another row of numbers for totals. As the students work, Ms. Wattenburger walks around the classroom asking questions and making suggestions. She asks for volunteers to show the class how each problem would look with standard numerals.

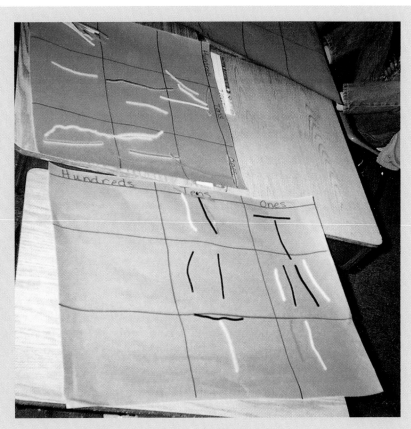

Problem: 3 + 2 = 5

Problem: 61 + 23 = 84

Problem: 211 − 10 = 201

Outcomes

As students work with forming the stick numbers in the different columns, they begin to understand the relationship between face values and place values. One student showed his knowledge with a stick-math 3:

> I put the three sticks here [pointing to the first column on the right]; that's 3. If I go here [lining up the sticks in the second column], that's 30. And here [moving the sticks to the left] that's 300.

Students also get a different perspective on addition and subtraction. The math sticks demonstrate the joining of quantities in addition and the taking away in subtraction in a way similar to working with counters; however, the stick numbers are also symbols, and using them helps students make the connection between quantities and symbols for those quantities.

Commentary

Ms. Wattenburger writes:

> Chinese math sticks fit in perfectly with our study of place value for 1s, 10s, and 100s. Before I introduce math sticks, students sort of understand why numbers are placed in a certain order, but they really grasp the concept after doing Chinese math sticks.

> Not only do students think it is something completely new, but they think Chinese math sticks are cool because of the name. They love the thought of learning something so exotic.

> I feel fortunate to have discovered this activity for teaching place value. Second graders really need some kind of stimulus and some concrete way to approach this abstract topic. I truly believe students enjoy this type of math experience, and hopefully they will never forget it.

◀◀◀◀ LOOKING BACK

Children's experiences with whole numbers before school often include opportunities to learn about cardinal and ordinal numbers, counting, and informal addition and subtraction. Generally preschoolers have a good grasp of the concepts behind the procedures they use.

Children move from informal, invented algorithms to more formal algorithms for single- and multidigit addition and subtraction gradually. By working with concrete, pictorial, symbolic, and other representations, they are able to explore concepts and test problem-solving strategies. Activities with base-10 blocks can help children move from unitary to multiunit conceptual structures and understand place values.

Word problems are an effective way to engage children in mathematical thinking and problem solving. When children select their own strategies and modes of expression, they can devise procedures that make sense to them. Also they can explore and often discover for themselves the algorithms they need to do formal mathematics.

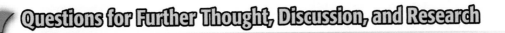

Questions for Further Thought, Discussion, and Research

1. Watch a children's television program, such as *Dora the Explorer*, that attempts to teach mathematical concepts. How effective do you think the program is? Why? Are there any television programs that you would recommend to help older students learn mathematics?

2. Do you ever count or do simple math with your fingers? Fingers are often called the first calculators. How many different calculations can you do on your fingers? Can you subtract as well as add? Can you add multidigit as well as single-digit numbers?

3. A number of different methods, such as Chisenbop and Fingermath, attempt to organize using fingers to do math into a system. Explore one of these methods; then evaluate its usefulness for the classroom.

4. Using math symbols and ideas from other cultures is an effective way to broaden students' perspective and help them appreciate the universality of math concepts. Explore the math of another culture such as that of the Incas, Mayans, Egyptians, Babylonians, and so forth. How might you use that information in the classroom? (An Internet search will give you both information about the math itself and ideas for lesson plans and activities.)

CHAPTER 7

Working with Whole Numbers: Multiplying and Dividing

LOOKING AHEAD >>>>

When should children begin to multiply and divide? As soon as they can understand the concepts and develop working procedures.

Very young children find an entree to multiplication through grouping and adding and to division through partitioning and subtraction. The more formal algorithms build on work with base-10, place value, and the 10-for-1 trading schemes developed from working with multidigit numbers.

Learning to multiply and divide with understanding grows out of meaningful contexts and problem-solving experiences that allow children to inquire, to experiment, and to make and test judgments.

Not only are children capable of constructing their own algorithms for multiplication and division, but they also can use those algorithms as bridges to understanding and mastering the more traditional procedures introduced in the classroom.

Discovering Multiplication and Division in the Early Grades

Multiplication and division were once considered to be too complex conceptually for young children. Early in the 20th century, educators recommended delaying study of these concepts until high school. More recently, research has emphasized the matching of instructional methods rather than subject matter to learning readiness. In fact, epistemologists such as Piaget suggest that children are ready to multiply as soon as they are ready to add and that multiplication and division "must both be understood if either is to be understood" and, therefore, "should be taught simultaneously" (Copeland 1970, 143).

As early as kindergarten, children can use *direct modeling* to explore problem situations involving multiplication and division. Often they will begin by identifying the problem as a change-for-more or change-for-less situation, linking them conceptually to addition and subtraction; then apply grouping, sorting, or counting strategies.

For example, in the Windows on Learning scenario, Gina modeled the cookies in the multiplication/sharing problem with grouped counting disks and counted all of the disks to find the answer; Jon counted the cookies and passed them out for the division/sharing problem.

In the scenario, both Gina and Jon used direct modeling and counting. For Gina, the final number was large enough that she felt more comfortable counting all of the items one at a time rather than double-counting or adding. For Jon, dividing followed a simple sharing plan—one for you, you, and you . . . ; two for you, you, and you; and so forth. The strategies the children used are conceptually closer to addition and subtraction than to multiplication and division; however, they mark the beginning of a process that can lead to more sophisticated strategies and idea structures.

Early experiences with multiplication and division should emphasize holistic learning. Burns (1989) writes:

> Children do not develop mathematical understanding through a bit-by-bit approach in which concepts are broken into pieces and presented to them in manageable "bites." Such an approach reinforces the notion that mathematics is a collection of unrelated ideas, rules, and skills. Instead, children learn by being surrounded by concepts in a variety of ways and encouraged to make sense out of their experiences, see connections in their ideas, and look for relationships among mathematical concepts.

(125–26)

To develop understanding in a holistic manner, students can begin with experiences in which multiplication or division emerge naturally as tools to solve a meaningful problem, as in the sharing cookies scenario. Or the concepts might be part of cross-disciplinary studies. Burns (1989, 128–29) recommends writing stories to fit a mathematics sentence such as $7 \times 3 = 21$ or $21 \div 7 = 3$. The Mathematics in Literature feature on page 157, Pinczes's *A Remainder of*

Activities CD

For an activity that builds on children's ability to add and subtract to understand multiplication and division, go to Activity 30, Two-handed Fingermath, on the CD-ROM that accompanies this text.

Activities CD

For an activity on how to use writing to engage students with mathematics, see Activity 33, Writing Mathematics: Telling Tales by the Numbers, on the CD-ROM that accompanies this text.

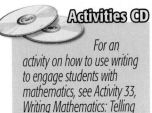

Topics, Issues, and Explorations

Discuss children's readiness to learn and the early introduction of multiplication/division concepts. What do you think? How old were you when you learned to multiply? To divide? Did you "discover" the concepts for yourself, or did you learn specific procedures?

Windows on Learning

The Sharing Activity

Once a week Angela Liu's combined first- and second-grade class has a sharing time. Teams of two to four students plan and bring a treat to class for all of the students to share. This week's team was Gina and Jon.

Monday

Ms. Liu gave Gina and Jon some time to get together and make a plan.

"You will need to choose a treat and figure out how many of that treat you will need for the whole class," Ms. Liu told them.

Gina looked at Jon and Jon looked at Gina. Each was waiting for the other to make a start.

Finally, Gina said, "I guess we could have cookies."

Jon shrugged. "Whatever." He wasn't that interested in the planning stage.

"My dad makes the cookies at our house," Gina said, "but he will want to know how many he should make."

Using her fingers to keep track, Gina counted 21 students, then she selected counting disks from the manipulatives box and counted 1 to 21 once, 1 to 21 twice. "That's for two cookies for everyone," she told Jon. Then she counted all of the disks again. "Forty-two," she said. "We need 42 cookies."

"You forgot Ms. Liu and the aide," Jon commented.

"Oh, yeah." Carefully, Gina laid out four more disks. "One, two, one, two." Then she counted on from 42, touching each of the additional disks in turn. "Forty-three, 44, 45, 46."

Friday

Friday was sharing day. Gina and Jon would be responsible for dividing up the cookies so that everyone got an equal share.

That will be easy, Gina thought, knowing that she had counted out exactly 46 of the peanut butter cookies her dad had made and put them in the bag she was carrying in her backpack.

She had forgotten, though, about Jon. He had not helped much with the planning, but he did like cookies; he had asked his mom to make 46 cookies also.

"Now everybody will have lots of cookies to eat," he told Gina.

To figure out how many cookies everyone should have, he again counted the number of students in the class. Today there were only 20 children because one had stayed home sick; the regular aide was also absent, but one mother had come to class to help out.

Jon counted, putting down a napkin on the table for each person. He carefully put one cookie on each napkin, and then two, three, and four cookies. "Everyone gets four cookies," he told Gina.

"But you have four left over," she told him. "No, I don't. We forgot Mr. Sanchez, the janitor." And he counted out the remaining four cookies.

One, incorporates whole-number problems that can be solved by repeated addition and subtraction but also lead logically to grouping and partitioning strategies and ultimately to multiplication and division. The Mathematical Thinking feature on page 158 also suggests ways to adapt fairy- and folk tales to explore concepts and develop number sense.

Understanding Multiplication

Do you understand multiplication? Too often, both children and adults answer that question with an inventory of multiplication facts that they have memorized or by describing a specific procedure for calculating. But multiplication is more than facts and procedures; it is a process in which a variety of concepts and knowledge bases play a role. To understand multiplication,

Mathematics in Literature

A Remainder of One by Elinor J. Pinczes

Elinor Pinczes's story combines mathematics concepts with a social component meaningful to children. The main character is Joe, an infantry bug. When his troop marches in even rows in the Queen's parade, he is left out, "a remainder of one."

There are 25 bugs in Joe's troop, and they try different marching combinations—2 rows of 12, three of 8, four of 6—until Joe suggests the 5-by-5 combination that includes him.

Most students can understand and sympathize with the idea of being left out. Finding a mathematical solution to Joe's problem engages children at all levels. Younger students can explore intuitive approaches to multiplication and division; older students can work with their own or learned algorithms as well as explore factors, factor pairs, and prime numbers.

Activity 1

Listen to the story as it is read aloud in class. With each new marching order, answer the question "Will this marching order let Joe march with the others?" In small groups, use manipulatives or peel-and-reuse stickers to model the marching bugs, or draw the bug parades with colored markers. Add combinations that leave a larger remainder, such as two rows of 11 to leave a remainder of 3 or three rows of 7 to leave a remainder of 4.

Activity 2

After the concepts in the story have been explored, you are ready to extend your study by learning "The Ants Go Marching" song (to the tune of "When Johnny Comes Marching Home Again"). The lyrics and tune are easy to remember, but you may want to write out the words and start by singing along to a recording.

> The ants go marching, one by one, hurrah, hurrah.
> The ants go marching, one by one, hurrah, hurrah.
> The ants go marching, one by one,
> The little ant stops to suck his thumb,
> And they all go marching down, to the ground, to get out of the rain.
> Boom, boom, boom, boom, boom, boom, boom
>
> The ants go marching, two by two, hurrah, hurrah.
> (And so forth)

Once you are familiar with the song, you can model the number combinations by marching 2 by 2, 3 by 3, and so on. With each combination you can stop and ask, "Is there a remainder?" Then write the numbers on the board.

Reference: Elinor J. Pinczes, *A Remainder of One*, illustrated by Bonnie McKain (New York: Scholastic, 1995).

---

children need to build on the one-to-one correspondence scheme developed while learning to count; they need to be able to visualize and think in terms of two-to-one, three-to-one, and other multiple correspondences—that is, to move conceptually from one-to-one to two-to-one to three-to-one relationships as in the following arrays:

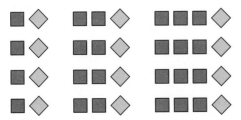

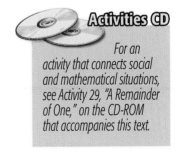

Activities CD

For an activity that connects social and mathematical situations, see Activity 29, "A Remainder of One," on the CD-ROM that accompanies this text.

They need to extend their understanding of the commutative law (the idea that changing the order of added numbers will not change the sum) to include multiplication ($2 + 4 = 4 + 2$ and also $2 \times 4 = 4 \times 2$). They need to extend their grasp of the 10-for-1, base-10 trading scheme to include exchanges

Mathematical Thinking

"Mathematicizing" Fairytales and Folk Tales

Fairytales and folk tales, in both original and revised versions, have a high interest level for children. Some of the classic tales already include a math element—for example, the clock striking 12 for midnight and the ritualized actions in triplets in both the Russian and the German versions of Cinderella. However, even tales that do not originally include math can easily be "mathematicized" to introduce a variety of concepts.

Adding math content to well-known stories promotes mathematical thinking by making mathematics part of students' imaginative worlds. Finding ways to use math knowledge to present and solve problems in those worlds calls for using both problem-solving and creative thinking processes as well as using math concepts to make sense of situations in the stories.

Teachers may want to rewrite the stories themselves or have students come up with their own math versions of familiar tales. Some simple methods of "mathematicizing" stories follow:

1. **Add mathematics to an existing story.** For example, "The Three Little Pigs" can be used to develop money sense if you add price tags to the pigs' building materials and labor—least for the straw, more for the sticks, most for the bricks.

2. **Use mathematics to highlight and expand an episode of the story.** In "Red Riding Hood's Race," the Wolf's hurrying to get to Grandmother's house can become a race between Red Riding Hood and the Wolf. Create a map of the different ways to get to Grandmother's house, and use math to decide which path Red should follow to beat the wolf (See Martinez and Martinez 2000).

3. **Rewrite a story with a math focus.** In "Red Riding Hood Turns the Times Tables on the Wolf," Red uses her knowledge of multiplication facts to trick the Wolf into shoveling snow at her grandmother's house. The following is an excerpt:

"Wolfie, I'll make you a deal. If you will shovel the walks and the driveway, you can have all of the cookies and cider left from our party."

The wolf was suspicious. "How do I know you will leave any?" he growled.

"Figure it out for yourself," said Little Red. "We have 48 cookies and 48 ounces of cider. There are just 4 of us and we each want 2 helpings of 6 cookies and two 6-ounce mugs of cider."

The wolf, adding the numbers instead of multiplying them, thought, "$4 + 2 + 6 = 12$ cookies; that leaves 36 cookies for me. And $4 + 2 + 8$ equals 14 ounces of cider; that leaves 34 ounces all for me."

(Martinez and Martinez (1996, 122–24.

Activity

Choose a favorite fairytale or folk tale. Rewrite, revise, or add to the story to explore specific concepts or to develop number sense. Create a story booklet with construction paper and paper that is half blank, half lined. Illustrate your story with colored pencils, crayons, or markers. Develop word problems for each story. Explain how you would solve each problem you write.

Read one or more of your classmates' stories. Work out their word problems on a separate piece of paper. Discuss your answers.

Activities CD

For another example of a "Mathematicized" fairy tale, see Activity 33, Writing Mathematics: Telling Tales by the Numbers, on the CD-ROM that accompanies this text.

(ten 1s for one 10, ten 10s for one 100, and so forth) in multiplication algorithms. And they need to develop facility in reading and interpreting multiplication "sentences." For example, $3 \times 4 = 12$ can also be written, "Three sets of four is twelve."

Having children memorize the facts first and then tie the facts into a conceptual framework—the ideas behind the facts and procedures—is akin to throwing an unassembled kite into the air and expecting it to fly. The kite materials may have the potential to fly, but before that can happen comes a period of construction and testing. In learning to multiply, this means a period of hands-on exploration with children free to work out solutions and develop their own algorithms for multiplying.

What Is a Multiplication Algorithm?

An *algorithm*, as we saw in chapter 6, is a basic step-by-step procedure for solving a problem. "An algorithm is a precise, systematic method for solving a class of problems. An algorithm takes *input*, follows a *determinate* set of rules, and in a *finite* number of steps gives *output* that provides a *conclusive* answer" (Maurer 1998, 21).

The standard or common algorithm for a two-digit multiplication problem, like the standard algorithm for adding multidigit numbers, is a right-to-left process. This multiplication algorithm has three phases: For example:

32   multiplicand or number multiplied

× 41   multiplier

Phase 1: (1×2) then (1×30) First, multiply the numbers in the 1s column; then the number in the 1s column of the multiplier with the number in the 10s column of the number multiplied.

Phase 2: (40×2) then (40×30) Next, multiply the 1s, then the 10s number of the number multiplied by the 10s number of the multiplier.

Phase 3: $32 \times 41 = (1 \times 2) + (1 \times 30) + (40 \times 2) + (40 \times 30)$

$$= (2 + 30) + (80 + 1,200)$$
$$= 32 + 1,280$$
$$= 1,312$$

Add the 1s and 10s from phases 1 and 2 for the answer.

Following the step-by-step procedure results not only in a predictable and repeatable answer but also in a common representation of both the procedure's process and its product. Those who talk about the "universal language" of mathematics are often referring to the commonality resulting from shared algorithms (see the Mathematics Across the Curriculum feature for a historical note on the Arab mathematician Al-Khwarizmi and the source of some of our standard procedures and the word *algorithm*).

Educators disagree about the value of learning standard algorithms; however, most feel that step-by-step procedures may be worthwhile if they are learned with understanding and within the context of other methods, including children's invented algorithms. One way students can demonstrate understanding is by representing mathematical situations with drawings like that in Figure 7.1, a word problem from Tino's math journal.

What Kinds of Multiplication Algorithms Do Students Invent?

Asking students to invent their own algorithms has the initial advantage of letting them make sense of their own experiences. Students who have worked out and tested their own procedures for multiplying are more likely to

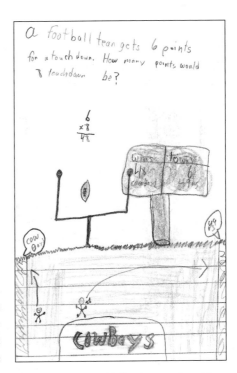

Figure 7.1 A multiplication word problem from Tino's math journal.

Topics, Issues, and Explorations

What do you think? Is it worthwhile for children to learn step-by-step procedures? Why or why not? What ideas do you have about how to teach procedures with understanding?

Mathematics Across the Curriculum

Al-Khwarizmi and Algorithms

Why is a step-by-step routine for solving mathematical problems called an *algorithm*?

One student, trying to connect the sound of the word with its meaning, suggested the interpretation "all goes in rhythm" to reflect the interlocking, by-the-numbers order of algorithmic problem solving.

The word *algorithm*, however, comes not from the action it describes but from the name of the mathematician whose books impacted the study of mathematics for more than a millennium.

Al-Khwarizmi was a noted scholar in Baghdad's House of Wisdom, a scientific academy, during the 9th century. He wrote two books that helped shape the development of world mathematics (McLeish 1991, 138–39). His book on arithmetic explained the decimal system and the use of 0. It also described and illustrated "rules" or procedures for adding, subtracting, multiplying, and dividing (McLeish 1991, 139). The scholar's name, which is sometimes given as Algorism, eventually led to the word *algorithm*.

Activity

See what you can find in the library or on the Internet about Al-Khwarizmi and algorithms.

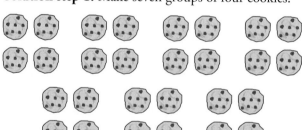

Activities CD

For an activity on how to model multiplication, see Activity 34, Modeling Multiplication, on the CD-ROM that accompanies this text.

recognize and understand other methods for accomplishing the same thing and even to identify and adopt methods that may be more efficient or accurate than their own.

Since students are in control of their own learning in the invention process, the teacher's role is less one of transmitting or demonstrating knowledge than of providing the conditions and guidance for its discovery or construction as well as assistance in interpreting and reflecting about the results. Encouraging students to invent algorithms such as those described here not only allows them to explore multiplication on their own terms but also prepares them to understand and even appreciate standard algorithms.

Direct Modeling

Young children begin to understand multiplication by creating a concrete model (Baek 1998; Carpenter et al. 1999; Kouba 1989). They can use counters, blocks, tally marks, or drawings to represent the quantities and relationships involved. The experience is both tactile and visual, letting them act out what has been described as an "intuitive" two-step process: (1) "make several equivalent sets," and (2) "put them together" (Kouba 1989, 156; see also Fischbein et al. 1985).

Direct modeling usually begins with grouping or matching and concludes with counting, as in the following example.

Problem: *You are having a party. Seven people will be at the party—yourself and six guests. If each person is given four cookies, how many cookies do you need altogether?*

Solution step 1: Make seven groups of four cookies.

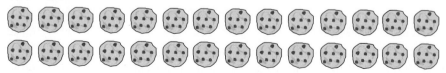

Solution step 2: Put the groups together and count all.

Answer: 28 cookies

Figure 7.2 shows students' use of tally marks, drawings, and a grid to figure the distance of five, 9-foot frog leaps.

Repeated Addition

This strategy follows naturally from modeling. Like modeling, it involves building sets and putting them together (Kouba 1989, 156). It also builds on students' early experiences with skip counting—counting by 2s, 5s, 10s, and so forth. Some students set up a repeated addition procedure as a chain of addition problems; some use doubling.

Problem: *There are five butterfly bushes in the garden. Each bush has 11 butterflies on it. How many butterflies are on the bushes?*

Solutions:

1. Chain of addition:

```
   11
  +11
   22
  +11
   33
  +11
   44
  +11
   55
```

2. Doubling:

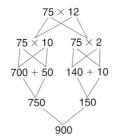

3. Skip-counting: 11 ⟶ 22 ⟶ 33 ⟶ 44 ⟶ 55

Part-Whole Strategies

Often students will rewrite a problem into two or more simpler problems, and then combine the solutions (Baek 1998, 154–58).

Problem: *"Pretend you are a squirrel. There are 12 trees. If you find 75 nuts under each tree, how many nuts do you find altogether?"* (Kouba 1989, 150).

Solution:

```
           75 × 12
         /         \
    75 × 10      75 × 2
     /    \      /    \
  700 + 50    140 + 10
      |           |
     750         150
        \       /
          900
```

Some part-whole strategies combine other methods including counting and repeated addition. For example, in the nuts-under-the-trees problem, a student might use counting by 25 to find the number of nuts under two trees and then double that amount six times for the total.

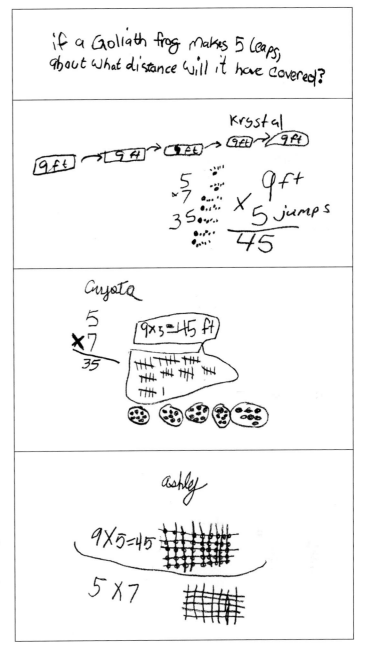

Figure 7.2 Modeling a frog's leaps.

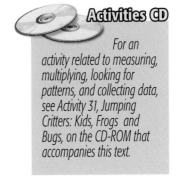

Activities CD

For an activity related to measuring, multiplying, looking for patterns, and collecting data, see Activity 31, Jumping Critters: Kids, Frogs and Bugs, on the CD-ROM that accompanies this text.

In some cases, students will work from facts they know and adapt the results. Baek (1998) gives the example of Kathy, who adapted her knowledge of the multiplication fact 12 × 5 = 60 and counting by 5s to solve a problem that asked her to multiply 16 times 5.

Problem: *"If there are 16 packs of gum with 5 pieces of gum in each pack, how many pieces of gum are there altogether?"*

Topics, Issues, and Explorations

Do you use any invented algorithms when you multiply? For example, do you use a part-whole algorithm to figure out the 15% tip on a restaurant bill (10% of total + ½ of 10%)? If you use invented algorithms, when are you most likely to use them—when you calculate with pencil and paper, with calculators, or in your head?

Kathy's Solution: "12 × 5 is 60, so 13 × 5 is 65, 14 × 5 is 70, 15 × 5 is 75, and 16 × 5 is 80. It's 80." (Baek 1998, 156)

Baek suggests that "through the process of inventing algorithms, children develop a deeper and more flexible understanding of multiplication" (1998, 159). Equally important, they build conceptual bridges from mathematical concepts they understand to the new ideas and processes introduced with multiplication.

How Might Teachers Introduce Other Multiplication Algorithms?

Studies of students' invented algorithms have found that students begin with direct modeling and strategies tied to addition and gradually develop methods that are more abstract and reflect multiplicative thinking. "When teachers understand children's invented algorithms and their developmental paths, they can help students move to more sophisticated algorithms" (Baek 1998, 160). It is important to approach these "more sophisticated algorithms" with the same multiple representations and expressions—visual, tactile, oral—that children themselves use to explore and shape their learning. This will mean continuing to use manipulatives and drawings, to verbalize the problem situation and solution processes, and to provide realistic or interest-catching contexts. It will also mean avoiding a sudden shift from hands-on problem solving to worksheets and pencil-and-paper calculations.

An initial step in making the transition from intuitive to more abstract algorithms involves becoming comfortable with the language and symbols of mathematics. Marilyn Burns (1989) explains that "it is important for the teacher to present the mathematical notation for multiplication so that children begin to connect the situation to the symbolism" (127). A three-point process helps students build a conceptual bridge from a concrete situation to a symbolic representation of the situation:

1. **model** the problem situation by using objects or drawings or by acting it out physically;
2. **verbalize** the solution;
3. **symbolize** the solution in a mathematical sentence.

Burns illustrates the concrete-to-abstract progression with a word problem about eyes:

> For example, the problem "How many eyes are there on six children?" can be posed. Six children come to the front of the room, and the others count their eyes. They count by ones and by twos. . . . Each child has 2 eyes, so with 6 children there are 12 eyes all together, or 2 × 6 = 12.
> *(127)*

Also important in making the transition from additive to multiplicative thinking is understanding that the numbers in addition and multiplication problems function differently. In addition the numbers are all addends and can be represented concretely and counted collectively. In multiplication the number multiplied—the multiplicand—can be shown with a set of concrete objects but the number multiplied by—the multiplier—has a different meaning and function. It "represents a set of equivalent sets" and indicates "the number of times the 'build a set' action is performed" (Kouba 1989, 156).

Students who rely on counting methods to solve multiplication problems often have trouble keeping track of the two levels of counting—counting items in sets and counting number of sets. To help them visualize the difference in concrete representations, they can use different kinds of counters or marks—for example, disks for the multiplicand, sticks for the multiplier; or tally marks for the multiplicand and *x*'s for the multiplier. As they verbalize and symbolize the process, teachers can ask, "Which number are we multiplying? Which number are we multiplying by? What is the difference?"

Because the more sophisticated multiplication algorithms rely heavily on understanding the base-10 number system, modeling multiplication with base-10 blocks is also an effective transitional activity. Continuing the three-point strategy—model, verbalize, symbolize—we can establish a strong link between the action of multiplying and the meaning of the multiplication algorithm.

Problem: *You are having a birthday party. If you invite 11 friends and each friend brings two presents, how many presents will you receive?*

Model

	Words	**Numbers**
	Each friend brings 2 presents, so with 11 friends, there will be 22 presents altogether.	$2 \times 11 = 22$

For more complex multidigit problems, students can use squared centimeter paper to build arrays (Burns 1989). For example, to model the problem 21×11, they can start by making a rectangular array on the centimeter paper. Counting 21 down and 11 across results in a rectangle that shows the result as a composite of individual squares, which can be counted. We could also build arrays to show the role of place value in the multiplication process:

1×1 for an array of one square;

1×20 for an array of 20 squares by 1;

10×1 for an array of 10 squares by 1;

10×20 for an array of 10 squares by 20.

Topics, Issues, and Explorations

Write a word problem for a multiplication situation involving two-digit numbers. Work out the problem using centimeter paper and base-10 blocks; then think about what you did. Did you learn anything new or gain a clearer mental picture of any part of the multiplication process? How do you think your insights might differ from those of your students? (See Appendix A for centimeter paper and base-10 block patterns.)

Building Multiplication Facts with Arrays

Making sense of multiplication facts begins with understanding how the facts are arrived at and what they mean.

Multiplication arrays use centimeter paper to show what the facts look like. For example, 3 × 8 gives us an array 3 centimeter squares wide and 8 centimeter squares long.

The arrays are simple and inexpensive to make. Creating the arrays reinforces understanding of the multiplication process. The arrays can also be used to link multiplication and finding area.

Activity 1

Working in small groups, use centimeter paper to create a set of multiplication arrays to represent multiplication facts for the numbers 1 through 10. On each array you make, write the number sentence that describes it. For example, the array 3 centimeters wide and 7 centimeters long will have the number sentence 3 × 7 = 21. Color and cut out each array.

Activity 2

Use a sheet of centimeter paper to create a grid for multiplication facts. Place the colored, cut-out arrays, one at a time, at the top left corner of a 10 × 10 square (numbered left to right and top to bottom). Identify the number of squares covered by each array. Write the number of squares covered by each array in the bottom right square of the area covered on the 10 × 10 grid. Continue until you use all of the arrays and put numbers in all of the squares on the grid.

Extension

Apply what you have learned about creating arrays to finding the area of rectangles. Develop a procedure or algorithm that will tell you how many square units are in a rectangular area.

Source: From a make-your-own-manipulatives lesson developed by Becca Rainey.

Adding the different arrays together will give us 231 squares on the sheet of centimeter paper. (For patterns for multiplication arrays, see Appendix A, Make Your Own Manipulatives.)

Marilyn Burns (1989) suggests covering the centimeter squares in the arrays with base-10 blocks to reinforce base-10 concepts. For the array in Figure 7.3, we would need two flats of 100 units each, three rods of 10 units each, and a single-unit block. Modeling the operation with arrays and blocks not only gives students a visual and tactile multiplication experience but also demonstrates concretely the logic behind the procedures of the standard algorithm, including the 10-for-1 trading scheme.

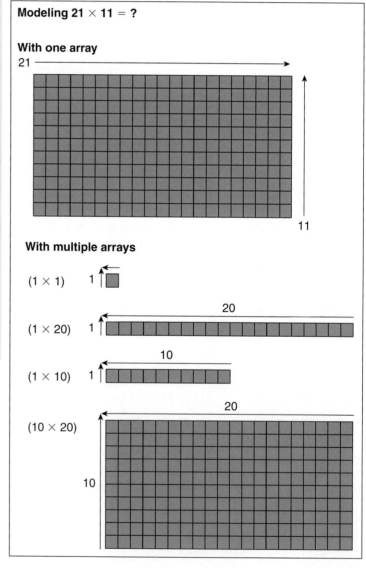

Figure 7.3 Showing multiplication with arrays.

Understanding Division

Because division is a reverse process, it is both conceptually and procedurally more difficult, especially for young children (see chapter 6 for a discussion of children's difficulties with reverse processes in subtraction). As with multiplication, the focus in division is upon things that come in or can be put into groups or sets; however, the beginning point of division is the end point of multiplication, and the conventional algorithm calls for complex reverse-order thinking as well as deconstructing the place values of multidigit numbers.

Children sometimes learn division facts as a variation of memorized multiplication facts; that is, if they have memorized the multiplication sentence $5 \times 6 = 30$, they can supply any of the sentence's parts, in whatever order they are presented in. In this case, $30 \div 5 = ?$ triggers the recollection of a missing component of a multiplication fact rather than a mental process of dividing or partitioning.

Students may also learn the conventional division algorithm without "making sense" of the procedures. Asked why she started working at the left instead of the right side of the number in the problem $363,636 \div 6$, a fourth grader answered, "Because teacher said to." Students in a British study of 12-year-olds claimed that "divided by," "divided into," and "shared among" meant the same thing, and "asked to interpret the division of a smaller number by a larger one, they often inverted the numbers" (Lampert 1992, 232).

Teaching division for understanding might be described as exploring a web (see Figure 7.4). Lampert (1992) writes about "avoiding the straight and narrow path through the subject" and having "students work on the sorts of problems that take them into the web of concepts related to division" (278, 275). Figure 7.4 shows some of the ideas and relationships involved.

Students and teachers together can make a pathway through the web—what Lampert (1992) calls a "journey" into the "division region." Lampert's guidelines for the journey include—

- **beginning** with concepts students *do* understand;
- **encouraging** students to invent and test their own division algorithms;
- **using** interactive learning strategies to engage students and shape instruction;
- **using** stories, not for motivation, but for putting ideas and procedures in meaningful contexts;
- **connecting** students' invented algorithms and the reasoning behind them to the concepts and symbolism of formal mathematics.

Because different groups of students may have different starting points and invent different algorithms, "many alternative journeys through this region are possible" (Lampert 1992, 249). However, if these journeys do not

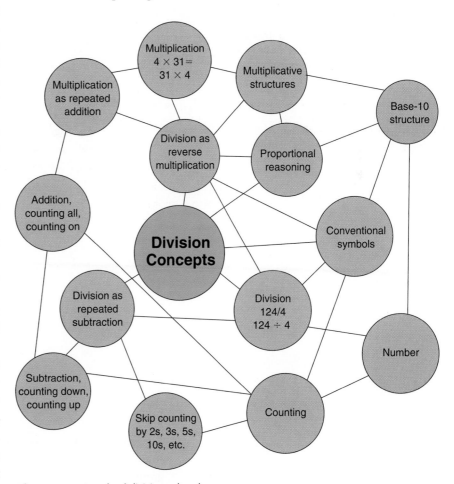

Figure 7.4 A web of division-related concepts.

share a common path, they do share some common methods: an emphasis upon investigation rather than procedures and process rather than product, and a willingness to let students find their own answers and construct their own ways of understanding division.

What Kinds of Division Algorithms Do Students Invent?

Children's intuitive algorithms for division may vary with the type of division, measurement (finding number of sets) or partitive (finding number of objects in sets) (Fishbein et al. 1985; Kouba 1989; Carpenter et al., 1999). In *measurement division* we start with a total number of objects and then divide (or measure out) that number by the number of objects in each set, and find the number of sets.

> Tomas has 24 apples. He puts 2 apples on each of his friends' desks. How many desks does Tomas put apples on?

In *partitive division* we start again with the total number of objects but divide by the number of sets to find the number of objects in each set.

> Tomas has 24 apples. He wants to put the same number of apples on each of his 12 friends' desks. How many apples will he put on each desk?

Intuitive strategies for solving both types of problems begin with direct modeling and counting and then move on to more abstract methods.

Direct Modeling

The *direct modeling* algorithms for division are essentially counting methods. Given the earlier measurement division problem, a student will first count out 24 objects to represent the 24 apples, divide into groups of 2, and count the number of groups.

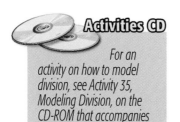

For an activity on how to model division, see Activity 35, Modeling Division, on the CD-ROM that accompanies this text.

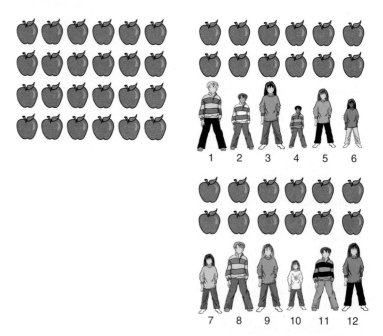

For the partitive division problem, the student will use a count-and-share strategy: start with 24 objects, create 12 groups, "share" the objects among the groups, and count the number of objects in a group.

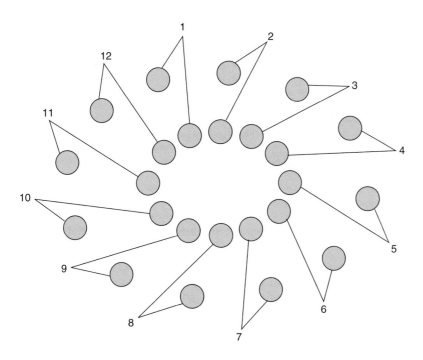

Structured Counting

This strategy works best for measurement division but is sometimes adapted with a guess-and-test approach to partitive division (see Kouba 1989; Carpenter et al. 1999). Often children will use their fingers to keep track of the number of multiples. The following examples are from *Children's Mathematics* (Carpenter et al. 1999):

Measurement Division

A restaurant puts 4 slices of cheese on each sandwich. How many sandwiches can they make with 24 pieces of cheese?

Susan counts, "Hmmm, 4, 8, 12, 16, 20, 24." With each count Susan extends one finger. When she is done counting, she looks at the six extended fingers and says, "Six. They can make six sandwiches."

Partitive Division

There are 24 children in the class. We want to divide the class into 6 teams with the same number of children on each team. How many children will there be on each team?

Susan counts, "Let's see, 3, 6, 9, 12, 15, 18." With each count, Susan extends one finger. When she has extended 6 fingers, she pauses. "No, that's not big enough. Let's try 4, 4, 8, 12, 16, 20, 24." Again, Susan extends a finger with each count. When she reaches 24, she sees that there are 6 fingers extended. "That's it. There would be 4 in each group." (Carpenter et al. 1999, 41–42)

Repeated Subtraction

Children develop *repeated subtraction* or repeated take-away algorithms for both types of division. They write out the number to be divided and remove equivalent groups until the dividend is exhausted (Kouba 1989, 156).

Activities CD

For an activity that uses repeated subtraction to divide, see Activity 30, Two-Handed Fingermath, on the CD-ROM that accompanies this text.

There are 28 M&M's in a package. If you eat 7 M&M's at a time, how many times will you eat M&M's?

$$\begin{array}{r} 28 \\ -7 \\ \hline 21 \\ -7 \\ \hline 14 \\ -7 \\ \hline 7 \\ -7 \\ \hline 0 \end{array}$$

one time

two times

three times

four times

The answer is four times.

As with structured counting, the procedure for partitive division may include a guess-and-test component.

There are 28 M&M's in a package. If you eat M&M's four times, how many M&M's will you eat each time?

$$\begin{array}{r} 28 \\ -5 \\ \hline 23 \\ -5 \\ \hline 18 \\ -5 \\ \hline 13 \\ -5 \\ \hline 8 \end{array} \rightarrow \begin{array}{r} 28 \\ -6 \\ \hline 22 \\ -6 \\ \hline 16 \\ -6 \\ \hline 10 \\ -6 \\ \hline 4 \end{array} \rightarrow \begin{array}{r} 28 \\ -7 \\ \hline 21 \\ -7 \\ \hline 14 \\ -7 \\ \hline 7 \\ -7 \\ \hline 0 \end{array}$$

The answer is 7.

Topics, Issues, and Explorations

Write a word problem like those in Figure 7.5 for measurement division. Then rewrite it for partitive division. Which intuitive algorithm works best for each problem?

Intuitive models for division, like intuitive models for multiplication, seem to follow a concrete-to-abstract progression, with children relying more upon symbolic representations as they internalize relationships and processes.

How Do Students Handle Division Problems with Remainders?

Traditionally division problems with remainders have presented an extra level of difficulty, particularly for students who use the standard division algorithm (Silver, Shapiro, and Deutsch 1993). However, it may be the procedures rather than the concepts that children find more difficult. When problem situations are concrete and meaningful, a remainder may make the solution strategy less cut-and-dried and the outcome more real. For example, the following task not only calls for dividing but also asks students to make a judgment about the remainder:

The Clearview Little League is going to a Pirates games. There are 540 people, including players, coaches, and parents. They will travel by bus, and each bus holds 40 people. How many buses will they need to get to the game?

(Silver et al. 1993, 121).

Students are less likely to give inadequate whole-number answers, such as 13, or non-whole-number answers, such as 13½, if they map the situation concretely and keep the real-life ramifications in mind: the 20 remaining people need transportation to the game, even if they will not completely fill a bus, and we cannot plan in terms of ½ of a bus.

Carpenter and his team (1999) suggest that division "problems with remainders are not a great deal more difficult than corresponding problems without remainders" (43). They can be solved with the basic strategies described earlier plus a simple focus question. In the Pirates-game task, we have a measurement division problem: we know the total number of passengers and the number who will fit in each bus. Grouping by 40 will give us 13; then we ask the focus question "How will the remaining 20 passengers get to the game?" The answer might be to partially fill a bus or to take them in a van or several cars.

Other Examples

Problem   It takes 5 apples to make an apple cake. You have 23 apples, and you want to make 5 cakes.

Strategy   Take away 5 apples at a time; count the number of groups and the number of apples left over.

Focus question   How many more apples will you need?

Problem   You have 14 cookies and 4 friends. You want to share the cookies so that each friend will have an equal number. How many cookies will you give each friend?

Strategy   Deal cookies to make 4 equal groups.

Focus Question   How many cookies will be left over for you to eat?

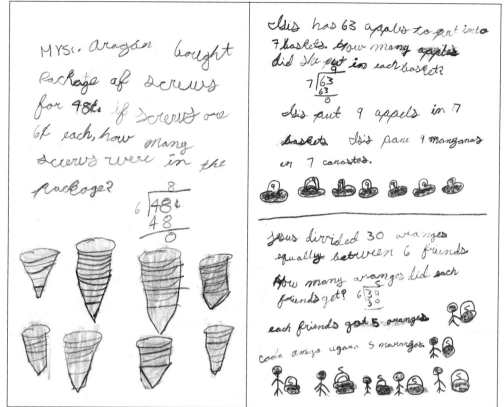

Figure 7.5   Modeling division for word problems.

How Can Teachers Help Students Understand Other Division Algorithms?

Whether mathematics curricula should include the long-division algorithm has been debated for decades. While some reformers have recommended deemphasizing long division, other members of the education community, often including parents and the students themselves, believe it has value. In fact, many consider it to be an "important milestone in measuring mathematical accomplishment within the school culture" (Lampert 1992, 222).

One approach is to teach the conventional algorithm in the context of a variety of methods that connect procedures to important mathematical concepts. Students at the fourth-grade level and above, who have worked out division concepts for themselves and can arrive at the same results in a variety of ways, can be introduced to the conventional algorithm as a viable but not exclusive method for representing the division process. For example, in his

Figure 7.6 Tino's division problem.

math journal (Figure 7.6), Tino writes and illustrates one of the word problems from Figure 7.5; however, instead of using direct modeling as a division strategy, he uses long division.

Methods such as writing stories, applying base-10 concepts, and mapping multiplicative relationships provide a conceptual context for making sense not only of the conventional algorithm but also of the division process itself.

Writing Stories

The importance of contextualizing mathematical situations in word problems has been well established; however, frequently the stories themselves are written by teachers or even textbook authors. When students write their own stories for problems, they are working to make sense of the problems at more than one level: first, they are translating mathematical symbols into natural language; second, they are concretizing the abstract, making a two-dimensional representation into a three-dimensional scenario. For example, fourth graders Dillon, Ariel, and Cassey wrote word problems for the division sentence "18 ÷ 3 = ?" as follows:

Dillon   Will wants to ride the ferris wheel. It costs 3 tickets for a ride. He has 18 tickets. How many times can he ride?

Ariel   Mr. Ramos rides the bumper cars. He has 18 tickets. He gives 3 tickets for a ride. How many times can he ride?

Cassey   Jenny wants to buy gumballs at the refreshment tent for her and her friends. She has 18¢. Gumballs cost 1¢. She gives 3 gumballs to each friend. How many friends does she have?

Dillon and Ariel stick close to the problem and to the text theme of fun rides. Cassey's problem is a bit more complicated, taking her beyond the initial situation and involving more steps. She must first divide 18¢ by 1¢ to find out how many gumballs she can buy. Then she has to divide 18 gumballs by 3 gumballs. Cassey answers her problem first with a 6 but quickly erases the 6 and writes 5 when she remembers to deduct herself from the total.

Topics, Issues, and Explorations

Pick a theme topic such as a county fair, a field trip to a museum, or a basketball game. Write several division story problems to learn how to model writing them with students. Include problems that call for both measurement and partitive division. You might also write at least one problem in which there will be a remainder.

Applying Base-10 Concepts

Working out division with base-10 blocks provides a tactile and visual demonstration of breaking down multiplicative structures. It also shows concretely how division is an inverse process of multiplication. Figure 7.7 illustrates both the decomposing of base-10 elements and the left-to-right procedures of division (the reverse of multiplication's building up and right-to-left operations).

Decomposing numbers to divide can also be done on paper with circles or squares to serve as posts or containers. A class of fourth graders approached the division problem 765 ÷ 5 = ? by first thinking of 765 in terms of monetary

Problem: There are 124 students in your grade. All want to attend the State Fair on Students-Get-in-Free Day. If your school has 4 buses, how many students will need to ride in each bus?

Procedures:

1. Represent the total with base-10 blocks.

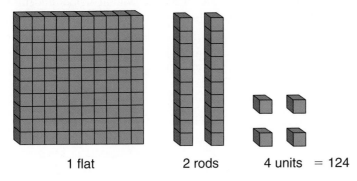

1 flat   2 rods   4 units   = 124

2. Starting at the left, decompose the blocks using a 10-for-1 trading scheme for regrouping.

12 rods   4 units   = 124

3. Put the blocks in four equal groups.

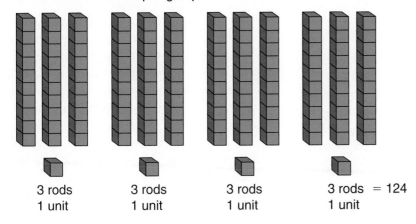

3 rods   3 rods   3 rods   3 rods   = 124
1 unit   1 unit   1 unit   1 unit

4. Count the number in one group of blocks for the answer.

31 students per bus

Figure 7.7   Dividing with base-10 blocks.

| 1 hundred
1 ten
1 one | 1 hundred
1 ten
1 one | 1 hundred
1 ten
1 one |

| 1 hundred
1 ten
1 one | 1 hundred
1 ten
1 one |

With 2 hundreds and 1 ten left over

units: seven $100 bills, six $10 bills, and five $1 bills. Then they dealt out the bills into five "pots" of money (Lampert 1992, 259).

Mapping with a Function Chart

The roles of proportionality and estimation in the division process can be explored with a function chart like the one presented here. Middle-school students who have begun working with fractions will be better prepared to understand the proportional reasoning involved, but elementary school students who understand multiplicative relationships can use the estimation process to "build up" an approximate answer. Lampert uses the example of 1,536 ÷ 73 and asks, "What multiples of 73 come close to 1,536?"

$$\frac{73}{1} = \frac{146}{2} = \frac{1,460}{20} = \frac{1,533}{21} = \frac{1,606}{22}$$

or

x	$f(x)$
1	73
?	1,536
2	146
20	1,460
21	1,533
22	1,606

Googol: BIG IDEAS in Mathematics

Estimating Division

Two of the important ideas underlying division are proportionality and multiplicative structures. Magdalene Lampert (1992, 266–71) developed an estimation game to encourage fourth graders to connect proportional reasoning to division. Students learn to estimate by guessing and testing multiples of different numbers to build up approximate answers.

The game is played in teams of two. One member of the team serves as estimator; the other uses a calculator to multiply the estimates and the divisor and to coach the student making the estimates. The game begins with the two students posing a division problem to solve.

$$4,644 \div 86 = ?$$

The students compose a story to provide a context and make sense of the problem situation. Then the estimator makes a guess. The multiplier checks the guess using a calculator, records the results on a chart, and gives the estimator feedback, such as "too much" or "not enough."

Guess	Multiplication	Answer
15	15 × 86	1,290
70	70 × 86	6,020
45	45 × 86	3,870
50	50 × 86	4,300
55	55 × 86	4,730
54	54 × 86	4,644

The game is over when the estimator arrives at the correct answer. The partners then reverse roles for the next division problem. At the end of the game period, the largest number of solved problems wins.

Students "build up" the approximate answer (between 1,533 and 1,606 but closer to 1,533) by guessing and testing multiples of 73. For an exact answer, they can subtract (1,536 – 1,533 = 3, so the answer is 21 with a remainder of 3) or use a calculator (21.041095).

Interpreting the language of word problems, modeling with base-10 blocks, and mapping with a function chart help students make sense of their own division experiences, but they also prepare the way for using conventional algorithms when appropriate. Students work out for themselves the rationales for working from left to right, decomposing large numbers, and thinking in terms of multiples of the divisor.

Not all versions of the conventional algorithm are the same. In the U.S. version, each step in the procedure is shown; in the version taught in Mexico, the multiplication and subtraction are done mentally (Midobuche 2001, 501).

United States	Mexico
313	313
5⟌1565	5⟌1565
15	6
6	15
−5	0
15	
−15	
0	

Interestingly, middle school students who have learned the conventional algorithm often use it as a representational rather than a problem-solving method. In division work with sixth, seventh, and eighth graders, teachers found a difference between their students' "scratch" work and the handed-in written work. On the scratch work students used grouping, drawings, and other intuitive algorithms to solve division problems, but their final papers showed only the long-division algorithm. Apparently, although the students used their own algorithms to solve the problems, they considered the conventional algorithm more suitable for written responses, perhaps even using the familiar format as a way of checking and validating their work (Silver et al. 1993, 130–31).

Topics, Issues, and Explorations

Identify the various positions and explore the issues in the debate over teaching the long-division algorithm. Which position(s), if any, do you agree with? Why? Tie in your own experiences as a learner or as an observer of children's learning.

Diversity in Learning and Thinking Mathematically

The emphasis in this chapter upon understanding multiplication and division represents a significant shift in teaching philosophy as well as a change in the way we look at these operations. Instead of mechanical actions, we see multiplication and division as important mathematical processes that require thought and understanding and may even involve creativity.

Traditionally, the goal of learning in these areas has been to turn students into human calculators, able to calculate by hand or by head quickly and accurately with a minimum of thought or problem solving. Memorizing tables and drilling in multiplication and division facts provided a shortcut to mastering the operations that in many ways also resulted in a short circuit. Not only did many students who mastered the facts not understand the concepts behind them, but also many students who were capable of understanding the concepts were sidetracked by the method's narrow, lock-step approach to learning.

Research with children and adults who have special needs calls for a broader perspective: the inclusive view that begins with realizing that "there is no such thing as mathematical *ability*, only mathematical *abilities*" (Dowker 1998, 275–76). The ability to perform as a human calculator may actually rely upon lower-order mathematical abilities than those required to understand mathematical situations and to develop and test algorithms to fit those situations.

Encouraging students to invent, test, and use their own rather than prescribed algorithms makes multiplication and division more universally accessible. Students with learning disabilities such as dyslexia or developmental dyscalculia often have difficulty with the types of representations typical of the conventional algorithms as well as with the transcoding processes implicit in the calculating procedures (see Macaruso and Sokol 1998 for an in-depth discussion of mathematics and learning disabilities). Also, students from other cultures may become confused and disaffected if the algorithms taught in other countries are considered incorrect in U.S. classrooms.

Activities CD

For an activity to help discover patterns in multiplication and division, see Activity 32, Multiplication and Division: Maps of Facts, on the CD-ROM that accompanies this text.

Mathematics in the Real World

Creating Patterns with Addition and Multiplication

Students often ask, "Is this relevant? Is it something I can use?" The obvious answers for using basic calculation skills, such as addition and multiplication, involve such everyday tasks as shopping—adding up costs, buying multiples of some items, and so forth. However, there are other, more creative uses for these skills. For example, students can use addition and multiplication to create attractive patterns for such real-world tasks as quilting and tiling, as show here in Luis's tiling.

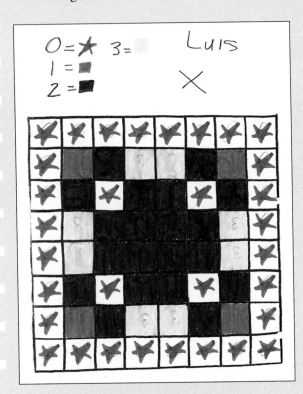

Activity 1

Create a pattern using addition. Make a grid with the numbers 0 to 3 across the top and the left side. Fill in the grid by adding the numbers, as in the following example. Since you are working with the numbers 0 to 3, if the numbers add up to more than 3, compensate by substituting a 0 for a 4 and a 1 for a 5, and so forth.

+	0	1	2	3
0	0	1	2	3
1	1	2	3	0
2	2	3	0	1
3	3	0	1	2

Flip and rotate the grid until you have four quadrants for your design. Then select a different color for each number and fill in the design.

Activity 2

Follow the same procedure as in Activity 1, but instead of adding the numbers, multiply them. If you want to limit the number of colors in the pattern, start again with 0 whenever the number exceeds 3: that is, use 0 for 4, 2 for 6, 1 for 8, 2 for 9, and so forth. A full design of four quads might look like this:

Quad 2				Quad 1			

×	0	1	2	3	3	2	1	0	×
0	0	0	0	0	0	0	0	0	0
1	0	1	2	3	3	2	1	0	1
2	0	2	0	2	2	0	2	0	2
3	0	3	2	2	2	2	3	0	3
3	0	3	2	2	2	2	3	0	3
2	0	2	0	2	2	0	2	0	2
1	0	1	2	3	3	2	1	0	1
0	0	0	0	0	0	0	0	0	0
×	0	1	2	3	3	2	1	0	×

Quad 3				Quad 4			

Assign a number for each color in the design. Make a model of the quilt pattern or tiling design by coloring in the squares on a grid of paper.

Eva Midobuche (2001), whose family came from Mexico to the United States when she was a child, describes an elementary teacher's rejection of the division algorithm she had learned from her father:

> One evening, my father had helped me solve my division homework problems. To my surprise, the next day, the teacher counted every single problem wrong. The answers were right, but the teacher assumed that because I had not shown all the steps in solving the problems, I had copied the answers. I tried to explain to him, in my limited English, that my father had helped me solve the problems. Not only did I get a zero for a grade, but I was also given a public lecture on cheating and copying someone else's work. My family, my home, my values, and my way of doing things were not respected nor even acknowledged.
>
> *(500)*

Are all algorithms, then, equally useful? Not necessarily. But making and learning alternative algorithms extends students' ability to make judgments about the methods that work best or make sense of mathematical situations for them. Teachers and students can work together to assess the effectiveness of individual algorithms by asking three questions:

1. **Is the method mathematically valid?** Does it result in accurate answers? Do the procedures make good mathematical sense?

2. **Is the method generalizable?** Can it be applied effectively to other problems of the same type?

3. **Is the method efficient?** Does it take a long time to do? Can the procedure be streamlined or represented in a different way to take less time but still record mathematical thinking?

(Campbell et al. 1998, 52–53)

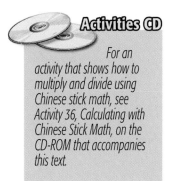

Activities CD

For an activity that shows how to multiply and divide using Chinese stick math, see Activity 36, Calculating with Chinese Stick Math, on the CD-ROM that accompanies this text.

⟨⟨⟨⟨ LOOKING BACK

Children often learn about multiplication and division long before they study these subjects in school mathematics. Kindergarten experiences with grouping and sharing lay the groundwork for understanding. Children's intuitive and invented algorithms let them explore and make sense of multiplicative structures and prepare them for the introduction of more efficient or sophisticated methods.

The process of inventing and testing algorithms is an important step toward understanding multiplication and division. Students build understanding first by direct modeling and concrete representations that rely on their knowledge of counting, addition, and subtraction; then gradually they develop more abstract and symbolic methods that reflect multiplicative thinking.

How students arrive at answers may vary. However, to become part of their mathematical toolkits, a method should be mathematically valid, generalizable, and efficient.

Questions for Further Thought, Discussion, and Research

1. What is additive thinking? What is multiplicative thinking? Why might it be important to develop the latter?

2. Although Piagetian researchers claim children are ready to learn multiplication and division as soon as they understand addition and subtraction, many school curriculums delay introducing multiplication until the third grade and division until the fourth or even fifth grade. What do you think of this timing? Can you think of some ways to introduce the basic concepts less formally but earlier?

3. How do you feel about teaching multiplication and division facts? Although research emphasizes the value of understanding over memorizing, some members of the education community, including school boards and parents, may expect children to be able to recite facts as well as to explain concepts. How might you teach facts in a way that makes them meaningful and perhaps even fun?

4. Do some research on different cultures' multiplication and division algorithms. You might look, for example, at the procedures in Chinese stick math (see Martinez and Martinez 2001; McLeish 1991). Look for elements in these alternative algorithms that seem more or less efficient and effective than the methods you learned or expect to teach in school.

CHAPTER 8

Geometric Thinking Across the Grades

LOOKING AHEAD >>>>

Geometry can and should be one of the most accessible areas of mathematics. Literally the mathematics of earth *(geo)* measurement *(metry)*, geometry is everywhere—in the shapes and structures of the Earth's topography, in the ways we arrange our communities, in architecture, in the games we play, in the arts we enjoy, and in many of the professions we practice.

Understanding geometry starts with direct, physical experiences. When children see, touch, and manipulate three- and two-dimensional shapes and figures, they begin to develop spatial reasoning. As they represent and reflect about their experiences, they begin to construct the big ideas of geometry. And as they use those ideas to solve problems, they lay the foundations needed to make formal geometry meaningful.

Two Dutch researchers, Pierre Van Hiele and Dieke Van Hiele-Geldof, identified five levels in the progression from informal to formal geometric thinking. The Van Hiele levels have become influential in developing a preschool to high school geometry curriculum that emphasizes hands-on experiences with space, shapes, and relationships and encourages children to think about and apply the big ideas of geometry.

Geometry as the Mathematics of Living Space and the Living World

Children love geometry, but some teachers do not. The difference in attitudes probably has its roots in contrasting perspectives. For children, working with geometric shapes and relationships follows naturally from playing with building blocks or Legos. For too many teachers, geometry recalls struggles with the disembodied theorems, axioms, and proofs of high school or college geometry classes.

A group of preservice teachers discussed their misgivings about teaching geometry in a recent math methods class. Their comments suggest a view of geometry that is both limited and limiting.

Gina: I can't see teaching geometry to third graders. It's too abstract.

Valerie: My cooperating teacher hates geometry, so she's having me teach that unit. It's for fifth grade.

Chris: We can't teach geometry in kindergarten. The kids have to learn to count and tell time before they can learn about squares, triangles, and circles.

Instructor: Is that what geometry means to you? Squares, triangles, and circles?

Chris: Sure. And other geometric figures.

Valerie: I'll also be teaching about solids in my unit. They have to know what prisms, cubes, and cones are.

Tiffany: But geometry is more than that. It's about finding areas and volume and figuring out angles.

Gina: And Euclid. In our college class, we used Euclid's book and about half of it had to do with logic and proofs. We had to memorize a lot. Too much for little kids.

Clearly the preservice teachers were defining geometry in a very narrow sense. They saw it as abstract exercises dealing with plane and solid figures and using a formal system of deductive reasoning. In other words, geometry to them was the curriculum of their high school and college classes—a textbook subject divorced from the real world and student interests. In Figure 8.1, this view reflects only one cell in the diagram—academic geometry—and only a fraction of the ideas, activities, images, and thought systems that make up the totality of geometry (Shirley 1995).

The diagram divides geometry into pure and applied areas, and also formal and informal areas. Roughly, *pure* geometry emphasizes structures and systems in the abstract; *applied* geometry emphasizes uses and concrete models. *Formal* geometry is usually complex and taught in advanced high school and college courses; *informal* geometry is more accessible to students at every level of geometric thinking and is universal with examples and uses around the world and across the ages.

GEOMETRY	Pure	Applied
Formal	Academic	Technical
Informal	Recreational	Everyday

Figure 8.1 A broader view of geometry.
(Adapted from Shirley 1995, 35. Adapted with permission from *Connecting Mathematics Across the Curriculum*, NCTM Yearbook 1995, by the National Council of Teachers of Mathematics. All rights reserved.)

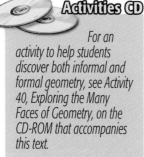

Activities CD

For an activity to help students discover both informal and formal geometry, see Activity 40, *Exploring the Many Faces of Geometry*, on the CD-ROM that accompanies this text.

The Four Faces of Geometry

Geometry has four faces: academic, technical, recreational, and everyday. While the academic face is the one most people (such as the preservice students) think of first, the other three faces may come closer to demonstrating the importance of geometry in our lives. Examples of technical geometry are all around us—in the engineering of bridges, the architecture of buildings, the networks of streets and highways that structure communities and guide movement within them. We enjoy recreational geometry in art, puzzles, and games, and when we cook, plan a garden, fill boxes or bags, plan a trip, make a paper hat, or design a quilt like the one in Figure 8.2.

The geometry of these three faces—technical, recreational, and everyday—seems to come closest to Hans Freudenthal's (1973) description of geometry in school. In *Mathematics as an Educational Task*, he described studying geometry as experiencing and interpreting "the space in which the child lives, breathes, and moves" (403). Combine this description with the more global idea of using one's own world or body as a measuring stick for Gaia or the "living world," and we can then describe geometry as *the study of living space in the living world* (Davis 1996, 120). The result is a subject that is both attractive and accessible and fits snugly into the curriculum at *every* level.

In fact, introduced to this broader view, the preservice teachers in the earlier discussion changed their minds about teaching geometry in the early grades. Chris, who had believed there was no time to teach geometry in kindergarten, realized that he was already teaching it. His students frequently worked with spatial relationships and patterns—for example, sorting blocks by shapes and colors and exploring symmetry by folding paper and cutting out butterflies with matching wings. Gina's third graders had been using interlocking blocks to model number operations; she realized that she was neglecting the geometry dimension of the activities and the opportunity to connect number concepts to geometric shapes. Valerie developed an activity using tangram pieces and puzzles to serve as an introduction to her fifth-grade geometry unit. Her cooperating teacher admitted that she did not hate tangram geometry. Another preservice teacher, Jamie, summed up the class reaction with a question: "Why didn't somebody tell us that geometry can be fun?"

Mathematics in the Real World

Exploring the Four Faces of Geometry

In the interactive television program *Dora the Explorer*, Dora charts her course through a variety of experiences by using maps to guide her course and to interpret the world around her. Like Dora, students live in a world of geometric shapes and applications. Discovering the geometry in their worlds and using maps to help them understand spatial relationships make learning geometry an adventure.

Activity

Go exploring to find the four faces of geometry. You might start with a map of your school or community and mark your discoveries on it as you make them. Or make up your map as you go along.

Represent discoveries on your map with symbols of your own choosing or drawings. If you are using a large fold-out map or making a map on rolled butcher paper, you might affix original photographs or pictures cut from magazines and newspapers.

You might look for technical geometry in architecture or engineered structures, for recreational geometry in art and games, for everyday geometry in a library or on a Web site. Try to find as many examples of each type of geometry as you can.

When you have finished your explorations, use what you found to write a response to the statement "Geometry is everywhere, everyday for everyone."

Activities CD

For an activity that combines geometry and measurement with art and design, see Activity 37, Friendship Quilt, on the CD-ROM that accompanies this text.

Figure 8.2 Kindergartners make a friendship quilt.

Topics, Issues, and Explorations

Explore the idea that geometry is the study of living space in the living world. What is meant by "living space"? By the "living world"? How are the two related? How might we use geometric concepts to understand and represent that relationship?

Geometric Thinking from Level to Level

What does it mean to think geometrically? Does it mean seeing the world as a Picasso painting or translating information into geometric figures? Or does it mean using geometric concepts to help us interpret and understand our worlds?

Pierre Van Hiele and Dieke Van Hiele-Geldof describe geometric thinking as a building process with five distinct levels (Van Hiele 1986). The process begins with the simple and concrete and builds to the complex and abstract. Figure 8.3 shows the Van Hiele levels in a pyramid-style flowchart.

The foundational level, which the Van Hieles call Level 0, ties thinking to the physical world—what students perceive and represent with the senses. Levels 1 and 2 build on Level 0 with increasingly complex mental processes. Students continue to observe, manipulate, and represent physical objects, but the emphasis shifts from naming and recognizing to understanding the nature of the objects and their relationships or understanding the space in which the objects occur. Generally, geometric thinking from preschool through grades 7 or 8 will begin with Level 0, hands-on observations, and progress through a Level 1 stage of analyzing and describing in the early grades to a Level 2 stage of informal arguments and application of theory in the upper grades. Levels 3 and 4, which emphasize formal logic and abstract geometry, are usually attained in high school and college geometry courses.

The Van Hiele levels form a ladder of learning. Whatever the age, whatever the background knowledge, new geometric concepts are best approached from the ground up, one rung of the ladder at a time. Pierre Van Hiele (1986) writes, "The ways of thinking . . . have a hierarchic arrangement. Thinking at the second level is not possible without that of the base level; thinking at the third level is not possible without thinking at the second level" (51).

One result of this hierarchical arrangement is a staged learning process—that is, learning that proceeds by steps or stages rather than in a continuous, unbroken line. Moving from one thinking level to the next, according to Van Hiele, "is not a natural process; it takes place under [the] influence of a teaching-learning program (50). To be effective, that program must match students' current level of geometric thinking, then provide the experiences and language needed to evolve to the next level.

Van Hiele describes five stages of teaching behaviors and learning experiences that make up an effective teaching/learning program. The Idea Files, "Van Hiele's Teaching/Learning Program for Reflection," applies these stages to moving up the learning ladder from Level 1 to Level 2 for a specific concept, reflection. Students begin their study with hands-on explorations, and then proceed to analyze and generalize their findings until they can apply, explain, and draw conclusions about the concept. The learning experiences in the example show analysis and description (Van Hiele Level 1) as a starting point and informal deduction and theory as the concluding point. In other words, in this example the teaching/learning program is designed to move students from Level 1 thinking about reflection and symmetry to Level 2 thinking.

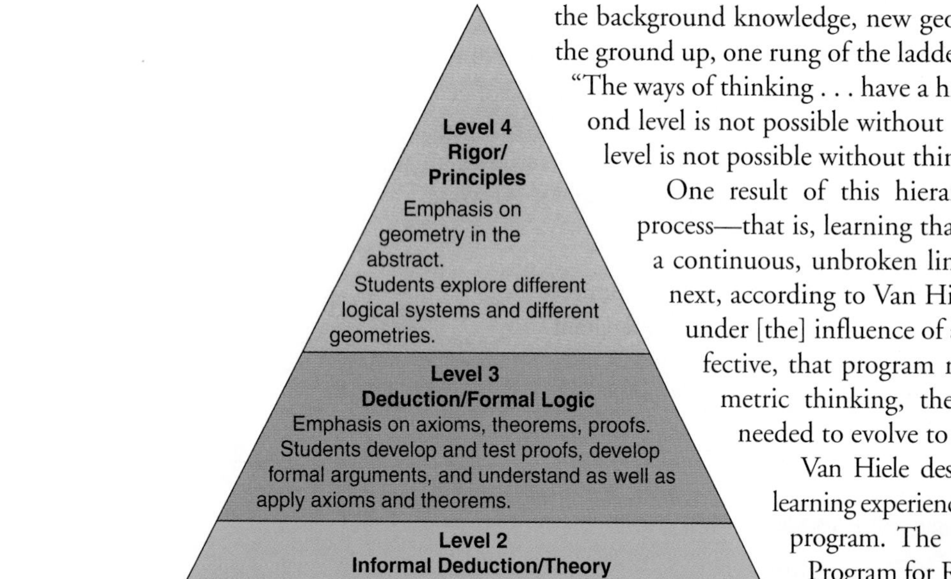

Level 4
Rigor/Principles
Emphasis on geometry in the abstract.
Students explore different logical systems and different geometries.

Level 3
Deduction/Formal Logic
Emphasis on axioms, theorems, proofs.
Students develop and test proofs, develop formal arguments, and understand as well as apply axioms and theorems.

Level 2
Informal Deduction/Theory
Emphasis on interrelationships of properties, meaningful definitions and informal arguments.
Students build on empirical data to understand properties of figures and classes of figures.

Level 1
Analysis/Description
Emphasis on properties, concepts, and generalization.
Students observe and experiment, draw conclusions about classes of shapes, and describe findings in geometric terms.

Level 0
Visualization
Emphasis on recognition, identification, and direct representation.
Students explore shapes as whole entities, learn basic vocabulary, and reproduce what they see.

Figure 8.3 The five Van Hiele levels of geometric thinking.
(From Van Hiele 1986.)

Idea Files

Van Hiele's Teaching/Learning Program for Reflection

Teaching/Learning Strategies	Learning Experiences
First stage: information	Students fold paper or look in a mirror.
Second stage: guided orientation	Students examine many geometrical figures and attempt to find their reflections on a grid or by folding paper.
Third stage: explicitation (making explicit)	Students discuss various ways to recognize geometrical figures as reflections of each other.
Fourth stage: free orientation	Students explore complex and open-ended tasks, such as exercises with geometrical figures with axes of symmetry.
Fifth stage: integration	Students explain how symmetry can be recognized and summarize characteristics of geometrical figures with axes of symmetry.

Source: Adapted from Van Hiele (1986, 54–55).

In addition to learning experiences, Van Hiele emphasizes the importance of language not only to the learning process but also to identifying students' levels of geometric thinking. Moving from one level of geometric thinking to the next must be preceded by learning "a new language"—that is, by learning the words and meanings that characterize thinking and communication at that level.

Teachers can apply their knowledge of the language used at each level of thinking to identify their students' understanding of concepts. In "The Van Hiele Model of the Development of Geometric Thought," Crowley (1987) writes, "The nature of a student's geometric explanations reflects that student's level of thinking" (14).

As an example, consider responses to the questions "What type of figure is this?" ⬚ "How do you know?" Students at each level are able to respond "*Rectangle*" to the first question. (If a student does not know how to name the figure, he or she is not at Level 0 for rectangles.) Examples of level-specific responses to the second question are given here. In parentheses is a brief explanation of why the statement reflects the assigned level.

Level 0: "It looks like one" or "Because it looks like a door." (The answer is based on the visual model.)

Level 1: "Four sides, closed, two long sides, two shorter sides, opposite sides parallel, four right angles . . . ." (Properties are listed; redundancies are not seen.)

Level 2: "It is a parallelogram with right angles." (The student attempts to give a minimum number of properties. If queried, she would indicate that she knows it is redundant in this example to say that opposite sides are congruent.)

Level 3: "This can be proved if I know that this figure is a parallelogram and that one angle is a right angle." (The student seeks to prove the fact deductively.)

(Crowley 1987, 14–15)

Topics, Issues, and Explorations

The Van Hiele levels can be applied to geometric thinking concept by concept or to one's overall thinking about geometry. How would you rate your own thinking? Does the level vary or remain fairly consistent across the subject matter? For example, are you at different levels working with the concepts of two-dimensional or plane geometry than working with three-dimensional or solid geometry? Explain.

Teachers can model the language and explain the concepts involved at each level of thinking, but students themselves must construct the network of ideas and relationships that result in understanding. They do this through a combination of experiences and language—experiences that let them discover, test, and apply concepts and language that help them reflect about and express their discoveries.

Van Hiele suggests that his theory can be extended beyond geometry to all mathematics education; nonetheless, the Van Hiele levels and stages of learning continue to be most influential in the area of geometric thinking.

Early Experiences with Shapes and Space

Children begin learning about geometry long before they enter school; in fact, some of their earliest learning experiences match Freudenthal's (1973, 403) description of studying geometry—exploring the space in which they live, move, and breathe. When babies see, reach, and touch, they are beginning to map the world around them—to understand the differences between something far away and close at hand, open or closed, inside or outside.

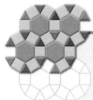

Mathematical Thinking

Reading and Modeling Geometric Concepts in Math Stories

Mathematical thinking means more than just thinking about mathematics. It means thinking in a mathematical way.

In geometry, mathematical thinking calls for making geometric concepts part of the process of seeing and understanding, interpreting, and representing our worlds.

To develop geometric-thinking skills, we can use a combination of learning tools: (1) math stories to provide an imaginative context and engage students in problem solving; (2) math manipulatives to model and make problem situations as well as the problem-solving process tangible.

When geometry is fundamental to plotting a storyline, problem solving becomes part of the reading and thinking processes involved in comprehension. Modeling the story's geometric concepts with manipulatives anchors both storyline and mathematical thinking in the concrete and provides a focus for trying different problem-solving strategies and solutions.

Activity 1

Read and model the geometric shapes in the story *Sir Cumference and the First Round Table* by Cindy Neuschwander (1997). Help Sir Cumference answer the question "What geometric shape will work best for King Arthur's conference table?" Make a drawing or cut-out of each table shape Sir Cumference tries. Discuss why some shapes make King Arthur's knights feel trapped, cornered, squished, or poked by a sharp point.

Activity 2

Work in small groups. Read enough of the story *A Cloak for the Dreamer* by Aileen Friedman (1994) to understand the problem: making a cloak with polygons. Working with templates for drawing different polygons, choose one or more polygons per group. Try to draw a cloak without gaps and holes with the polygon(s) you chose. Share the results with the class. Discuss the advantages and disadvantages of each design. Then finish the story. Compare your solutions with those in the book.

For more about reading and modeling geometric concepts in literature, see Martinez and Martinez (in press).

The geometry of young children is neither static nor rigid; rather, it is a "rubber" geometry in which shapes are perceived as changing instead of fixed (Copeland 1984, 21). To an infant, a mother's face changes shape with proximity and angle. Squares, rectangles, circles, and triangles are seen as essentially the same—enclosed spaces that can be stretched or squeezed in various shapes.

The big ideas of these early experiences include **proximity, separation, enclosure, order,** and **continuity.** What is closest? What is farthest? What is side by side? What is touching or not touching, in, out, between, next to? What is left, right, up, down, forward, backward? What is the difference between a point in space and a line that goes on and on?

Answering these questions and constructing the big ideas begin with hands-on explorations. Children sort, match, and order colored blocks, beads, and cut-out shapes. They fit pieces in puzzles, arrange objects, real or imagined with Legos, Tinker Toys, or Lincoln Logs. And they draw what they see—shapes, objects, animals, people. Often these drawings are as much commentary as snapshots. For example, if children are fascinated by earrings or braided hair, they might inflate their size or make them the predominant feature of the drawing (Copeland 1984).

Parents and teachers can help children interpret and refine their discoveries with questions that encourage reflection:

Is that where the hat (or nose) should be?

Is your picture like this drawing?

Is the dog in the right place?

Is the door on the house in the right place?

(Copeland 1984, 234)

Asking questions such as these without supplying readymade answers encourages children to look again and compare what they see with their own representations. It also reinforces an important corollary of hands-on learning experiences: thinking about what is being done so that interpreting, making judgments, and formulating and testing concepts are an integral part of the learning process.

Activities CD

For an activity to give students experience with working with shapes, see Activity 42, Building Polygons and Polyhedrons with Gumdrops and Toothpicks, on the CD-ROM that accompanies this text.

Topics, Issues, and Explorations

Informal recreational geometry is an important type of geometry in many childhood games and toys. Visit a toy store and make an inventory of early childhood toys and games that use geometric concepts. Discuss ways these materials might be used to teach the big ideas of early childhood geometry.

Later Experiences with Shapes and Space

Making the transition from the "rubber" geometry of early childhood to the practical geometry of daily life as well as school geometry is a gradual process, ongoing throughout the elementary years. By kindergarten and the early grades, children are ready to conceptualize size and shapes as constant rather than elastic, but they may not understand some of the basic ideas taught in school geometry until middle school—for example, the concept of a line as an infinite set of points (Piaget and Inhelder 1963).

Throughout this transitional period, effective learning experiences will include three key components:

- **sensory/motor activities** (such as seeing, touching, handling, manipulating pictures and models);
- **thought and imagination** (as in discussions, question-answer dialogues, story and literature connections);
- **representation** (including tracing outlines, drawing pictures, building models, creating symbols, and composing explanations and descriptions for math journals).

Because the evolution of spatial ideas occurs at two levels, perceptual and mental, children need activities that combine sensory/motor and the thoughtful or imaginative elements to ensure development. Representation adds a bridge to connect perceptions and thoughts into a meaningful whole (Piaget and Inhelder 1963; Copeland 1984).

At this stage important topics for the development of spatial reasoning include symmetry and transformations.

Symmetry

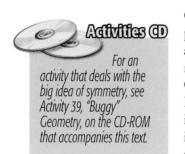

For an activity that deals with the big idea of symmetry, see Activity 39, "Buggy" Geometry, on the CD-ROM that accompanies this text.

Children begin exploring ideas of symmetry early. When they draw pictures of people, animals, houses, or other symmetrical objects, they are learning about balance and matching reverse images. Paper folding and cutting, drawing with mirrors, and making quilts and rug patterns provide sensory/motor experiences with symmetry. Questions such as "How are the two [or three or four, and so forth] sides alike? How are they different?" help children conceptualize what they are seeing and doing. And reproducing the patterns identified in another medium, such as a drawing or geoboard design, and explaining the idea behind the patterns in words underscore connections between doing and knowing and reinforce understanding.

From preschool through the early grades, children explore line symmetry when they fold paper and then cut out butterflies, hearts, stars, or crawly things. The objects show line symmetry when the same image shows on each side of a line or space as in Figure 8.4 or Figure 8.5.

The lines or axes of symmetry for the objects in Figure 8.4 are easy to identify because they follow the paper fold. Children can test already cut-out objects such as geometric shapes, leaves, sunbursts, animals, or human figures for sym-

Figure 8.4 Folded paper cutouts and line symmetry.

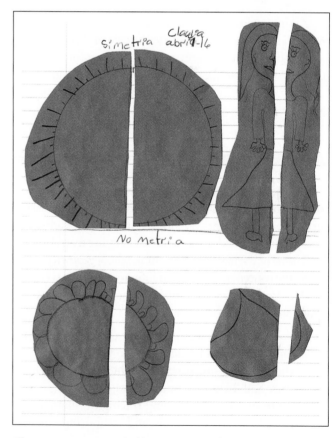

Figure 8.5 Symmetrical/not symmetrical.

metry by folding them in various directions or cutting them in half, as in Figure 8.5. If the sides match exactly, the fold is the line of symmetry. They can also use mirrors or a plexiglass Mira. They place the mirror or Mira on the object tested, adjusting the position until the mirror image reflects exactly half of the object, and draw a line at the base to show the axis of symmetry.

Objects, of course, may have more than one line of symmetry. In **rotational symmetry** an object will have multiple lines of symmetry and show an order of symmetry equal to the number of matching sides. Rotate an equilateral triangle and it will look the same from three different perspectives; rotate a square and it will look the same from four perspectives; therefore, we can say the equilateral triangle has order 3 rotational symmetry and the square, order 4.

Finding axes of rotational symmetry in geometric figures is an effective bridge activity. It helps children make the transition from the multiple perspectives/ multiple shapes thinking of rubber geometry to the multiple perspectives/single shape understanding needed to interpret spatial relationships in the real world and to study school geometry. It also helps build a bridge between Van Hiele Level 0 of geometric thinking (identifying and naming shapes) to Level 1 (understanding the properties of shapes, the characteristics that make a square a square or a triangle a triangle).

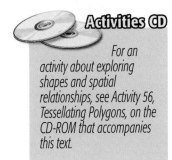

Activities CD

For an activity about exploring shapes and spatial relationships, see Activity 56, Tessellating Polygons, on the CD-ROM that accompanies this text.

Transformations

Children continue to make the transition from the rubber geometry of early childhood as they explore transformations and geometric motions. Young children who have learned to identify triangles and other geometric shapes often do not recognize them if the position or orientation is changed. For example, they may not recognize a triangle or square that has been rotated from position A to position B.

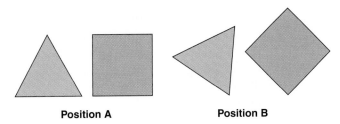

Position A   **Position B**

The geometric motions are basic in transformational geometry: slides, flips, and turns. A *slide* transforms a figure by moving it from one place to another without changing its orientation.

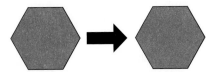

A *flip* transforms by reversing the figure to create a mirror image.

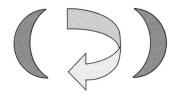

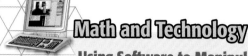

Using Software to Manipulate Shapes

Popular software such as Microsoft Word provides features for making and manipulating various geometric shapes. For example, Autoshapes in Microsoft Word include triangles, rectangles, circles, and other polygons.

Shapes can be manipulated for size—to become larger, smaller, taller, shorter. They can be changed for perspective and dimension. And they can be rotated, moved, colored, copied, and even used to create designs.

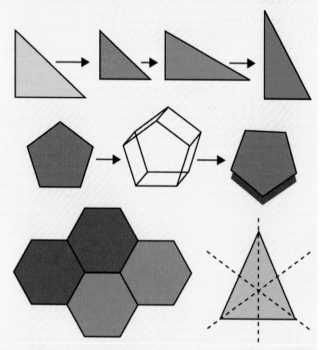

Activity

Use the Autoshapes feature and tools of Microsoft Word or another software package to explore the properties of polygons.

Start with a triangle. Make it larger. Make it smaller. Rotate it to the right, the left; turn it upside down. Using the line button on the toolbar, draw lines to show different axes of symmetry. Do the axes change or stay the same as you rotate the triangle? What happens if you make the triangle taller? Shorter? Longer in the base?

Explore other shapes such as rectangles, octagons, pentagons, and circles.

A *turn* transforms by rotating the figure.

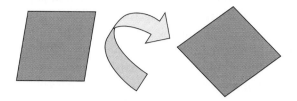

Children develop an intuitive understanding of these motions as they solve puzzles or create tessellations (designs that replicate geometric shapes such as hexagons or triangles in a solid pattern) with attribute blocks (see Appendix A for cut-out patterns). Turning pieces or blocks, flipping them over, and sliding them into place "help students become aware of the motions and the result of each one. They also learn that changing an object's position or orientation does not change its size or shape" (Clements and Sarama 2000, 85).

Moving from an intuitive to a more mature understanding can begin with interactive computer programs that let children manipulate puzzle pieces or blocks. To solve puzzles or create patterns on the computer screen, children "must choose each motion deliberately" (Clements and Sarama 2000, 85). The process of choosing encourages both visualization and application—important steps in the development of spatial thinking. Representing transformations with drawings (as in Figure 8.6), paper quilts, or tiling projects takes the next step; as children represent mental images in creative ways, they not only demonstrate but also deepen their understanding of the concepts.

Symmetry, Transformations, and NCTM Standards

NCTM Standards call for students at all levels to "apply transformations and use symmetry to analyze mathematical situations" (National Council of Teachers of Mathematics 2000, 96). Becca Rainey's students used transformations as well as symmetry to create the frieze shown in Figure 8.7.

The frieze responds to a problem that is both mathematical and aesthetic: creating a decorative border for the classroom's rectangular doors. Rebecca Kennerly's fifth graders combined their study of polygons with rotational transformations to create rotating designs such as those in Figure 8.8. The activity begins at Van Hiele Level 0

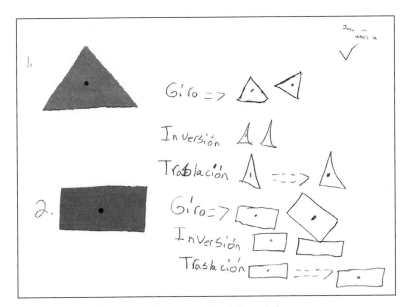

Figure 8.6 Exploring transformations in a bilingual class.

Figure 8.8 Rotating polygons.

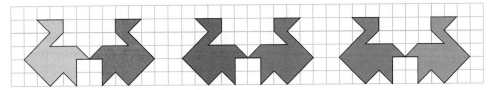

Figure 8.7 From transformations to frieze.

as students identify polygons visually and by name. It continues to Level 1 as they experiment with patterns created by rotating the different polygons and even touches on Level 2 as they analyze and discuss their designs, speculating about why some designs that started with the straight lines and angles of polygons resulted in circles.

Topics, Issues, and Explorations

Multicultural mathematics offer rich opportunities for studying geometry. Research the art forms of Native Americans and various ethnic groups such as Mexican or African Americans. What kinds of symmetry or geometric designs are used in their rugs, baskets, pottery, or jewelry? Discuss ways you might use your discoveries to create multicultural learning experiences.

Activities CD

For an activity to use for experimenting with polygons to create artistic designs, see Activity 44, Spinning Polygons, on the CD-ROM that accompanies this text.

Activities CD

For an activity that shows students how to apply geometric principles in decorative patterns, see Activity 43, Symmetry and Geometric Transformations: Creating a Frieze Pattern, on the CD-ROM that accompanies this text.

Explorations in Two and Three Dimensions: Plane and Solid Geometry

Children's early explorations with shapes and space are three-dimensional. They experience their own bodies, those of their caregivers, and the world around them in terms of solids (some moving, some not, some alive, some not) and space (sometimes maintaining the same relationships but often flowing and changing as things move or alter position). Preschool and kindergarten activities continue these experiences with three-dimensional counting objects, building blocks, puzzles, or other manipulatives.

Adding two-dimensional shapes requires a shift in perspective. It can begin with picture books and games and continue with representing images in drawings and cutouts such as the tangram animals shown in Figure 8.9.

Although the traditional curriculum imposes a linear development of concepts from plane to solid geometry, children's own experiences and intuitive grasp of geometry make it important for them to explore both two- and three-dimensional shapes early on. NCTM's (2000) geometry standard calls for students at all levels to "analyze characteristics and properties of two- and three-dimensional geometric shapes and develop mathematical arguments about geometric relationships." (41).

Similarly, the AAAS Project 2061 Benchmarks call for students not only to identify and describe geometric shapes but also to use them to solve practical problems and "to describe and predict things about the world around us" (www.project2061.com).

In terms of the Van Hiele levels, children in the early grades focus on visualizing and describing geometric shapes and properties (Level 0) and begin to understand the properties that form classes—what makes a square a square or a triangle a triangle (Level 1). In the middle grades they continue to visualize, describe, and generalize about classes (Levels 0–1) but also begin to develop informal arguments using geometric concepts and data (Level 2). And in the upper grades they visualize, describe, generalize, develop arguments (Levels 0–2), and prepare for the next stage of development (Level 3, Deduction/Formal Logic) by exploring more complex geometric concepts and applications.

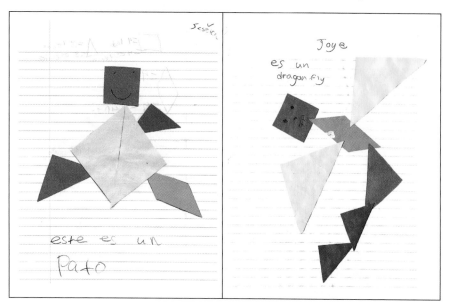

Figure 8.9 Tangram animals.

Activities CD

For an activity that shows how to make tangrams, see Activity 38, 7 "Magic" Pieces: Tangrams, on the CD-ROM that accompanies this text.

The Early Grades

From preschool to second grade, meeting NCTM and AAAS goals means identifying, representing, and describing shapes such as triangles, squares, cubes, and pyramids and exploring their characteristics both individually and in groups. Effective activities build on children's intuitive geometry, including using their bodies, step size, hand size, arm length, and so forth, to measure their worlds. The "Activities to Develop Geometric Thinking" in the Idea Files chart use sensory experiences as a starting point and then form connections to language, concepts, and the imagination.

Clements and Sarama (2000, 83) suggest using questions and pretend activities to help children make those connections. For example, as children explore the shapes in a "feeling box," teachers ask questions that encourage them to think about what they are doing and draw conclusions:

What are you feeling? How are you feeling it? How do you know this is a triangle instead of a square? How are these shapes alike? How are they different? Children can extend their exploration of three-dimensional shapes by pretending to be inside one.

After displaying an oatmeal box, say to the children, "Pretend that you are inside a cylinder like this. Your fingers are touching the inside of your cylinder. Close your eyes, and touch your cylinder. Now touch the top of the cylinder. Go around the top with your hands. What shape do you trace? Go around the bottom of your cylinder with your foot. What shape do you trace? Move all around inside your cylinder."

(Clements and Sarama 2000, 83)

Also effective to engage children's imagination and thinking processes are math stories such as Marilyn Burns's (1994) *The Greedy Triangle.* Stories help children master the language of geometry and at the same time place words and concepts in a context meaningful to them.

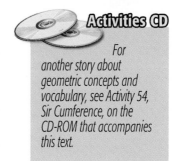

Activities CD

For another story about geometric concepts and vocabulary, see Activity 54, Sir Cumference, on the CD-ROM that accompanies this text.

The Middle Grades

From third to fifth grade, NCTM Standards emphasize analysis and experimentation. Students continue to visualize and represent two- and three-dimensional objects, but the vocabulary and context of their descriptions are more mathematical.

As they describe shapes, they should hear, understand, and use mathematical terms such as *parallel, perpendicular, face, edge, vertex, angle, trapezoid, prism,* and so forth, to communicate geometric ideas, with greater precision. For example, as students develop a more sophisticated understanding of how geometric shapes can be the same or different, the everyday meaning of *same*

Idea Files

Activities to Develop Geometric Thinking

Grade/Van Hiele Levels	Activity/Procedure
Preschool–2nd Grade **Van Hiele Level 0 (Visualization)** **and Level 1 (Analysis/Description)**	**"Feely" bag or box** Students select two- or three-dimensional shapes and explore them by feeling, first with eyes closed, then open. They describe the objects, match them to other like shapes, and learn names.
	Make-a-shape skits Students working in small groups use their bodies and a Chinese jump rope (or other stretchable cord) to form shapes and learn the properties of various polygons. A variation of the activity—I'm in a _____ (box, pyramid, cone, and so forth)—lets students feel solids from the inside out and prepares them to learn about volume.
	Build a shape/take it apart/build again Students use pattern blocks, building blocks, Tinker Toys, toothpicks and marshmallows, straws and string to explore two- and three-dimensional shapes and patterns. Taking their designs and constructions apart lets them rethink the process, understand the properties of the shapes, and revise or build on patterns.

(continues)

3rd–5th Grade

Van Hiele Level 0 (Visualization), Level 1 (Analysis/Description) and Level 2 (Informal Deduction/Theory)

Paper hats and origami zoos

Students explore the relationship between two- and three-dimensional shapes by building three-dimensional objects from two-dimensional sheets of paper. They can start with a large square of newsprint and follow seven classic steps to make a triangle-shaped hat, and then create a mini-zoo using some of the simpler origami shapes, such as the frog, swan, whale, and peacock. Or, they can use fold-by-number materials such as Yasutomo's Fold'Ems printed on origami paper to make giraffes, lions, and elephants. Creating habitats for the animals extends study to include concepts such as area and perimeter and connects with science and the study of animal habitats.

Geoboard polygons

Students use geoboards to create as many different three-sided, four-sided, five-sided, and so forth, polygons, as they can; then draw the different shapes on dot paper. Comparing their work in small groups encourages reflection and development of informal arguments about congruence and similarity (for a geoboard pattern, see Appendix A, Make Your Own Manipulatives).

Make-your-own tangrams

Students follow a pattern to cut out their own sets of tangram pieces from construction paper or card stock. After identifying and comparing each of the seven pieces, students see how many geometric shapes they can form using all or some of the pieces. Younger children can form shapes such as rabbits, foxes, and birds by covering printed patterns with tangram pieces. Older students can work from sheets of classic puzzles, form and name their own shapes, or use several sets of tangrams to tell a story (see Appendix A for pattern, classic puzzles and solutions).

6th–8th Grade

Van Hiele Level 0 (Visualization), Level 1 (Analysis/Description), Level 2 (Informal Deduction/ Theory), and Level 3 (Deduction/Formal Logic)

Tessellating polygons

Students use stencils of polygons to make 10 triangles, squares, pentagons, and hexagons and 5 heptagons, octagons, nonagons, decagons, and dodegons. They work with individual polygons and then combinations to see which will tessellate and which will not and explain in mathematical language why (Peterson 2000; for patterns for polygons, see Appendix A).

Building polyhedra

Students work in groups to construct solids from sheets of card stock and masking tape. Groups of five or six students use triangles, pentagons, and squares to construct regular polyhedra; then they use combinations of shapes to create semiregular polyhedra—for example, combining pentagons and hexagons to make a truncated icosihedron. Students answer the questions "What are the angle measures?" and "Why are they important?" (Peterson 2000, 356).

Designing paper airplanes

Students apply their knowledge of geometric shapes to design and test-fly paper airplanes. The activity connects with science lessons about flight and lift. Students can start with folded-paper designs; then move on to card stock cutouts and even rubber-band-driven propeller craft. Competition to see which plane flies the farthest should include discussions using scientific and mathematical language of why and how.

is no longer sufficient, and they begin to need words such as *congruent* and *similar* to explain their thinking.

(NCTM 2000, 166)

The AAAS Project 2061 Benchmarks for this level also focus on describing shapes geometrically, including understanding and using "geometric concepts, such as *perpendicular, perimeter, volume*" (www.project2061.com). In addition, the Benchmarks underscore the importance of anchoring concepts in real-world applications such as describing the world around us and helping "explain how the world works and how to solve practical problems."

The "Activities to Develop Geometric Thinking" in the Idea Files on p. 189 start as activities for earlier grades, with hands-on explorations and visualization. Building three-dimensional shapes from two-dimensional sheets of paper in the paper hats and origami zoos activity helps students visualize the connection between two and three dimensions and also gives them a tactile understanding of the space relationships involved. Students move to the next level of geometric thinking—analysis and description—as they connect activities with real-world applications in the origami zoo or discuss and reflect about geoboard shapes. Also, as students develop and explore the properties of various shapes and explain their reasoning, they take their understanding to the next level of thinking and apply meaningful definitions and discover relationships among geometric shapes. For example, as students make squares, triangles, and other shapes from the seven tangram pieces, they are applying knowledge of the properties of each piece and of pieces working together. Older students might take this development further by investigating and developing informal arguments about a question such as the tangram conundrum: Why is it impossible to make a square from six tangram pieces? (Thatcher 2001, 394).

Part of the challenge at this level is keeping students' learning of vocabulary and definitions from becoming exercises in by-rote memorization. Literacy connections such as Cindy Neuschwander's (1997) *Sir Cumference and the First Round Table* present complex concepts in ways that can be both humorous and memorable. For example, students will understand that the circumference, diameter, and radius of a circle are not really named after a knight named Sir Cumference, his wife Lady Di of Ameter, and their son

Mathematics in Literature

The Greedy Triangle

Marilyn Burns's (1994) *The Greedy Triangle* animates the two-dimensional world of polygons in a way children find delightful and memorable.

The story is about a triangle who at first enjoys its life of supporting bridges, being a piece of pie or a boat sail, and eavesdropping on people's conversations when they put their hands on their hips to form triangles. Then the triangle becomes bored. It thinks it would have more fun as a quadrilateral, so it visits a shape shifter and begins a cycle of searching for fulfillment by adding sides and angles to its shape. Eventually it has added so many sides and angles that it cannot stand up straight. The shape shifter turns it back into a triangle, and the triangle is happy again.

Throughout the story vivid images tie geometric shapes to real-world objects so that children will develop a habit of looking for and identifying polygons everywhere. The triangle's step-by-step increase in sides and angles structures the polygon family in a way that makes names and basic characteristics easy to remember.

Activity 1

Use toothpicks and miniature marshmallows to create as many of the triangle's shape changes as you can. The length of the sides will stay the same, but the angles will change. The first few shapes will be easy to make, but after the octagon it will be more and more difficult to make a regular, stable shape. Discuss why having so many sides might make it difficult for the shape to keep its balance.

Activity 2

Make a shapes log by folding five or more 8 1/2 × 11 sheets of paper in two and stapling them in the middle. Write the name of a polygon at the top of each page and draw the shape. Then do a shape survey. Write down each shape you find in the world—for example, in traffic signs, architecture, clothes, plants. Which shapes do you find the most examples of? The least? Are there any shapes with no examples?

Activities CD

For an activity linking math with art and science through origami, see Activity 46, Origami Zoo, on the CD-ROM that accompanies this text.

Activities CD

For an activity to explore the nine ways to form a square from a set of seven tangram pieces, see Activity 57, on the CD-ROM that accompanies this text.

Radius, but the fantasy will help them understand the concepts and remember terms and definitions.

The Upper Grades

From sixth to eighth grade, students refine and sharpen the tools needed to study formal geometry. Their definitions and descriptions of geometric properties become more precise and mathematical. They continue to explore the physical properties of two- and three-dimensional objects, but they begin to understand the larger picture of relationships and concepts. NCTM (2000) expectations for the Geometry Standard show a shift in emphasis from concrete experiences like manipulating objects to more abstract experiences such as creating and critiquing "inductive and deductive arguments concerning geometric ideas and relationships such as congruence, similarity, and the Pythagorean relationship" (232). The AAAS Project 2061 Benchmarks call for students to "make and understand logical connections" and also to understand how mathematicians represent things abstractly with propositions and formulas (www.project2061.com).

The connection between geometric representation and abstract ideas can be demonstrated effectively by exploring a basic concept such as the Pythagorean Theorem:

The square of the hypotenuse of a right triangle is equal to the sum of the squares of the adjacent sides.

Students can demonstrate the relationships described by first drawing a right triangle on centimeter or graph paper and then extending each side of the triangle into a square of squares (see the Googol feature). The number of squares generated by the long side or hypotenuse will equal the sum of the squares generated by the other two sides.

Learning continues to be anchored in hands-on experiences but moves beyond the *what* of naming and describing shapes to *how* and *why*. For example, students explore *how* to apply and combine shapes to create a tessellation—a repeated pattern that covers an entire space without leaving any gaps—and also *why* some shapes tessellate and some don't (Peterson 2000). The activities with polygons and polyhedra outlined in the Idea Files on p. 190 do not bypass the first rungs but use them to prepare for the next rungs and climb up higher in the ladder of geometric thinking. Students still visualize and name shapes such as octagons or hexagons, and they still analyze and describe their properties (Van Hiele Levels 0–1), but they also construct meaningful definitions about classes of objects and develop arguments to explain their observations.

Developing arguments and working with generalizations such as the Pythagorean Theorem also prepare students for the next level of geometric thinking: deduction and formal logic (Van Hiele Level 3). Moreover, building geometric squares from the sides of a right triangle forms the basis for one of many formal proofs of the theorem. As students use the squares to visualize and describe the relationships represented by the theorem, they are also being introduced to the Level 3 concept of geometric proofs.

Since encouraging students to reflect about concepts and to deal with geometric ideas in the abstract is important at this level, Edwin Abbot's (1983)

Students and teachers build three-dimensional objects with the Zometool system.

Googol: BIG IDEAS in Mathematics

The Pythagorean Theorem

Understanding some of the basic ideas in geometry begins with understanding the connection between the ideas and spatial relationships.

The Pythagorean Theorem was named after the Greek mathematician, Pythagoras, who lived around 580–500 B.C. The development of the ideas embedded in the theorem, however, dates back around 1,500 years before Pythagoras (Gullberg 1997, 435). It describes a relationship among the sides of a right triangle:

In a right triangle, the square of the length of the longest side will equal the added squares of the lengths of the other two sides.

Or, $c^2 = a^2 + b^2$

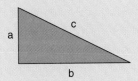

The idea is called a *theorem* because it is a general statement that applies to all right triangles and can be proved mathematically.

One way to prove it is to build squares from the lengths of each side.

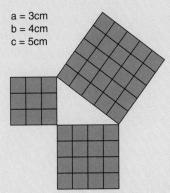

a = 3cm
b = 4cm
c = 5cm

The largest square is the size of the two smaller squares put together:

$$9 \text{ cm}^2 + 16 \text{ cm}^2 = 25 \text{ cm}^2$$

You can check the figures by counting the boxes in each square and adding the numbers.

Activity

Explore the Pythagorean Theorem by drawing several right angles of different sizes. Use a ruler to measure and draw the squares of each side then use a calculator to find the squares of the lengths. What did you find?

Flatland: A Romance of Many Dimensions and its various offshoots such as Ian Stewart's (2001) *Flatterland: Like Flatland Only More So* provide an enjoyable reading connection. *Flatland* and the works written in its tradition combine geometry with philosophy and pose significant questions from both areas. Younger students might be introduced to the stories in abbreviated or edited versions, but older students can read the originals.

Activities CD

For an activity to engage students in exploring dimensions, see Activity 45, Dimensions: Exploring Flatland, on the CD-ROM that accompanies this text.

Topics, Issues, and Explorations

Although traditionally formal geometry has been a high school and college subject, we hear increasingly a call to offer it in middle school. In fact, more and more schools are offering formal geometry in the eighth grade. What do you think of this trend? Did you or would you have taken geometry in the eighth grade if it were offered? Why or why not?

Math Manipulatives

Zometools

For years manipulatives such as pattern blocks have been an important tool for exploring geometric concepts in the early grades. However, the need for hands-on learning experiences is equally great in the middle and upper grades.

Zometools, used by NASA for space-station research, present an effective way to introduce older students to solid geometry. Students build three-dimensional objects with a system of struts and connecting balls or nodes. Each length of strut is a different color, and the end of each type of strut is shaped differently to fit the various holes in the connecting balls. Students can focus on building specific polyhedra or let their imaginations take over and create towers or other fanciful structures.

Activity 1

Use the Zometool system to build a two-dimensional triangle; then add more struts to make the shape three-dimensional.

What kind of figure results? How many sides does it have? How many edges? How many joining points or vertices? Repeat the process for other geometric shapes.

Activity 2

In a large bucket or sink, mix detergent with water to create a bubble solution. Dip your Zometool structure in the solution. What happens? How many surfaces or planes are formed by the bubble solution?

Extension

Take the Zometool tetrahedron challenge. See how many different tetrahedra you can make using Zometool struts and nodes. The Zometool instruction booklet describes about 70 possible combinations.

(For more about Zometool, Inc., go to http://www.zometool.com)

Diversity in Learning and Thinking Mathematically

The many informal and creative dimensions of geometry as well as its numerous real-world connections make geometry an ideal equal-opportunity subject. Because concepts can be approached from so many different directions—visual, tactile, pictorial, symbolic—they are accessible to students with a variety of learning styles. Numerous applications in art, crafts, sciences, sports, and practical skills such as carpentry can be used to engage and motivate students with a wide variety of interests. Moreover, geometry provides opportunities for many "success" activities such as math art projects that enable students to experience and even develop a taste for doing well.

Thelma Aragon, who is featured in this chapter's Teacher Pro-File, used tangrams to teach both geometry and English in her ESL classes. Among her students was a first-grader who had been diagnosed as learning disabled in kindergarten and showed little interest in either math or language arts. His response to the tangram activities was both immediate and startling. He manipulated the seven pieces quickly and accurately to form a square and other geometric shapes. As Ms. Aragon read *Grandfather Tang's Story* (Tompert 1990) and modeled the tangram figures, he was able not only to form the shapes but also to help other students—a significant step toward developing confidence and understanding spatial relationships at a higher level (for a tangram pattern and puzzles, see Appendix A, Make Your Own Manipulatives).

Activities CD

For an activity involving Ann Tompert's classic work, see Activity 41, Tangrams and Grandfather Tang's Story, on the CD-ROM that accompanies this text.

Teacher Pro-File

Thelma Aragon
K–Fifth, ESL

Tangrams in an English as a Second Language (ESL) Class

As a bilingual ESL teacher, Thelma Aragon faces multiple challenges in the classroom. She must teach the content areas of the curriculum, such as mathematics, but also provide learning bridges for students whose home language is not English and whose background may make the American school culture seem strange and intimidating.

Background

Ms. Aragon often mixes language study with math, history, art, and other subjects for a holistic style of instruction. Her tangram unit begins with a discussion of Chinese culture including the invention of tangram puzzles. Students explore the puzzle pieces, learning both vocabulary and the properties of each geometric shape, and they manipulate the pieces to create squares and other shapes.

Procedure

Ms. Aragon reads *Grandfather Tang's Story* (Tompert 1990) to the class, stopping wherever necessary to discuss story elements, such as the myth of magic foxes, and to explain new words or expressions. Once the students understand the story, they are ready to apply what they have learned. They rewrite the story in their own words, sometimes in both English and Spanish, and illustrate the different episodes with tangram puzzles.

Instead of using commercial products, the students make their own tangram pieces from construction paper. Since they will be using tangrams to illustrate all of the animals in the story, they need multiple sets, each in a different color to avoid mixing pieces.

Ms. Aragon models each animal on an overhead projector and also gives examples of sentences they might write as they retell the story. At the end of the activity, each student has produced a version of the story that can be bound and taken home to show their families. Most also retain at least one set of construction paper tangrams that they can use to form other classic tangram shapes.

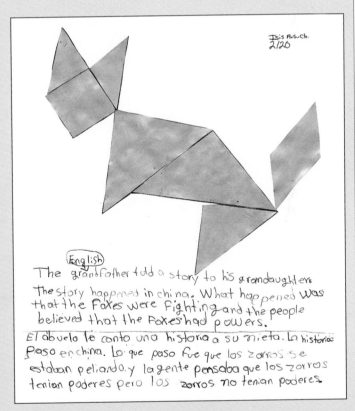

Iris's tangram fox and explanation.

hou changed
from a fox
to a dog.

Tangram dog.

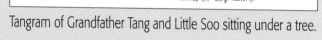

El abuelo
le djo a su
nieta, Esto fue
el cuentode los
dos zorrosque
cambiaron a varios
animales? La nieta le
preunto, y los zorros
lo vellvieron a jogoros
otra? El abuelo dijo,
"claro que si, pero con
moto guidado.

The grandfather said "This is the story of two
foxes that changed into many animals." The
granddaughter asked, "Did the foxes ever play
that game again? the grandfather replied, "OF
course but very carefully."

Tangram of Grandfather Tang and Little Soo sitting under a tree.

Outcomes

The learning outcomes from these activities are numerous and stretch across the curriculum. According to Ms. Aragon:

> The students learn geometric concepts and vocabulary. They develop spatial reasoning as they manipulate tangram pieces into various shapes and patterns. They learn something about ancient Chinese culture and begin to realize that many cultures have contributed to geometry specifically and mathematics generally. And they learn to succeed in math, to understand spatial relationships involved in forming puzzle shapes, and *to know* that they understand.

Ms. Aragon assesses students' work by reviewing the products—the text and illustrations of their booklets and their accuracy in creating and identifying various geometric figures—but she also asks questions and makes observations during the learning process. For example, she might ask why a student is using the tangram square instead of two triangles to form a fox's head. The student's answer would not only tell her whether the student could identify the shapes but also whether she or he understood the spatial relationships involved.

◀◀◀◀ LOOKING BACK

The creative and recreational dimensions of geometry make it a favorite math subject for many elementary and middle school students. Approaching the subject from its informal dimensions and building a foundation for later more formal study increases accessibility and motivation to learn.

As students explore concepts and extend their experiences with shapes and spatial relationships, they progress step-by-step from simple to more complex patterns of reasoning. The Van Hieles described five basic levels of geometric thinking, the first three of which apply to the elementary and middle school curriculum. From preschool to second grade, students begin at Level 0, Visualization, and work toward Level 1,

Analysis/Description. From third to fifth grade, they move from Level 0 to Level 1 and work toward Level 2, Informal Deduction/Theory. And from sixth to eighth grade, they move from Level 0 to Levels 1 and 2 and work toward Level 3, Deduction/Formal Logic.

Throughout the elementary and middle school grades, students can study geometry in connection to a variety of other subjects including art, history, science, and literature. Students from across cultures will find geometry an equal-opportunity subject that opens doors to learning other subjects and motivates them to excel in other areas of mathematics.

Questions for Further Thought, Discussion, and Research

1. If geometry is the mathematics that describes the world we live in, that means geometry is everywhere around us. Use the language and concepts of geometry to describe your own world—your home, your workplace, your possessions, your daily commute or other travel patterns.

2. Cubist painters used geometric shapes to reflect their own interpretation of their worlds. Research the cubists—how they worked and what they were trying to say. Then draw a cubist self-portrait. Discuss how the geometric shapes you use reflect your perspective, attitudes, or self-image.

3. Use blocks or other manipulatives to explore the relationships between squared numbers and geometric squares. Compare the advantages of manipulating numbers and manipulating blocks to calculate squares and to find square roots. Can

you extend what you have learned to include cubes?

4. Edwin Abbott's (1983) classic, *Flatland: A Romance of Many Dimensions,* includes biting satire about the status of women in the 19th century as well as the class structure of Abbott's native England. Read *Flatland;* then discuss his choice of geometric forms for women and the various social classes. For example, discuss why he chose a straight line to represent women and triangles for soldiers and workmen.

5. Select a favorite application of recreational geometry, such as solving two- and three-dimensional puzzles or creating quilts and rugs. Find or make examples of the art, game, or craft you choose. Then explain to the class what geometric concepts are involved and what kind of reasoning skills are exercised.

CHAPTER 9

Understanding and Using Measurement Concepts

Measurement may be the most user-friendly area of mathematics. It is practical, with everyday applications in cooking, shopping, building, sewing, decorating, gardening, travel, art, and sports. Its basic tools for the most part are simple and easy to use—rulers, measuring spoons and cups, tape measures, clocks, scales and weighing machines, even protractors, compasses, and angles.

Measurement standards and methods are rich in history and culture, often bridging the gap between formal and informal mathematics with folk wisdom such as "An inch is the distance between the first two knuckles of the index finger" and "A yard is the distance from the tip of your nose to the tip of your fingers."

Because measurement concepts help structure contemporary life, children need to master them early. From preschool through middle school, learning objectives in measurement emphasize hands-on experiences, aimed at understanding and using measurement standards, including both the metric and common systems.

Measurement Sense

How much, how big, how many, how far, how wide, how soon, how often, how tall, how short, how deep—these are some of the questions measurement systems attempt to answer. The answers are important to us not only as individuals but also as a society. Who we are individually can be described in part by our vital or "life" statistics—measurements of our age, weight, height, size, accomplishments. Who we are collectively, nationally, and even globally emerges from a complex web of measurements—geographic, economic, and social.

Children begin developing measurement sense early. When infants reach and touch, lift and throw, they are learning about the length of their arms, distances in space around them, and the size and even weight of objects. When young children compare heights or compete to throw a ball or jump the farthest, they are not only developing their individual measurement sense but also preparing to understand measurement standards—the commonly used units of length, weight, and size that let us share our measurement perceptions with others.

Activities CD

For an early-childhood measurement activity, see Activity 11, How Big Am I? How Big Are You? on the CD-ROM that accompanies this text.

Early Stages in Understanding Measurement

There are basically three stages in children's early learning about measurement:

Stage 1 measuring with "self" as the unit of measurement—the length of "my" arm or foot, size of "my" hand or head and so forth;

Stage 2 measuring with nonstandard units and tools such as unifix cubes, paperclips, Froot Loops, and so forth (see Figure 9.1);

Stage 3 measuring with standard units—centimeters, inches, grams, ounces— and with standard tools—rulers, tapes, scales (see Figure 9.2)

Stage 1, using self as the measurement scale, is tied closely to children's exploration of spatial relationships and development of spatial sense. Stage 2, using common items as nonstandard units of measurement, links the concept of measurement with the concept of number (see Figure 9.1). Children might build

Figure 9.1 Measuring an elephant's trunk with paperclips.

Draw a dinosaur that is 17 centimeters tall. Make sure her tail is 6 centimeters wide.

Figure 9.2 Measuring a dinosaur with centimeter paper.

Activities CD

For an activity in which students explore nonstandard and standard units of measurement, see Activity 50, Making Measurement Tools with Standard and Nonstandard Units, on the CD-ROM that accompanies this text.

a column of unifix cubes to the height of the object they are measuring (as in the "Tall and Short Rabbits" activity in chapter 5) and then count the number of cubes to get a total. Stage 3, using standard measurement systems, builds on the previous two. Children who have measured dinosaurs with unifix cubes can draw their own dinosaurs on centimeter paper (see Appendix A), using specific sizes for height and width (see Figure 9.2). An assignment to measure the width and length of a classroom can start with an individual task, stepping off and counting the number of shoe or foot lengths in each direction, and move to a group activity using a meter- or yardstick. Comparing the individual with the group results lets children discover for themselves the greater reliability of standard measures as well as the value of using shared standards.

In the Windows on Learning Box, "How Big Is My Foot?", Ms. Sandoval's first graders explore the difference between personal and objective measurements and between standard and nonstandard measurements.

The first graders in Ms. Sandoval's class used the procedure she demonstrated for measuring with a standard ruler and arrived at an accurate answer. Nonetheless, some of them, including Luisa, seemed uncomfortable, preferring the more direct and personal method of measuring with their own or a classmate's footsteps. In a similar activity, Young and O'Leary (2002) helped students get past that point by starting not with their own feet but with newsprint cutouts of footprints. Measuring with the cutout footprints encouraged their first graders to begin to objectify the measurement process and to think in terms of community rather than personal space. In both Ms. Sandoval's and Young and O'Leary's activities, the students discovered some critical conditions for effective measurement:

- the need to measure exactly without leaving gaps or overlapping;
- the need to count the units of measurement carefully without skipping or starting over;
- the inverse relationship between the size of the measurement unit and the final count;
- the importance of using a meaningful unit of measurement.

Instead of memorizing names and figures (such as 12 inches = 1 foot) that may have no meaning for them, these students are bringing together elements of the three different knowledge bases (physical, social, logical-mathematical) that work together to make measurement an effective learning tool.

The Three Knowledge Bases of Measurement

Like learning most areas of mathematics, learning measurement is not a simple, linear process. Figure 9.3, The Areas of Measurement Knowledge, shows how measurement involves the intersection of three different types and sources of knowledge—physical, social, and logical-mathematical (Piaget, Inhelder, and Szeminska 1960). Children acquire physical knowledge related to measurement when they make direct, empirical observations—handling objects

Topics, Issues, and Explorations

As adults we use standard measurements almost without thought. Nonetheless, nonstandard measurements also play a role in speech and behavior. We ask for a "pinch" of salt or a "smidgen" of dessert. We promise to be somewhere in "two shakes" or to serve a "dollop" of whipped cream. In some situations we might even prefer nonstandard measurements—for example, in cooking, building, or decorating. Do you or someone you know use nonstandard measurements on a regular basis or even instead of a standard system? Give some examples and discuss why a nonstandard measurement might be preferred in some cases.

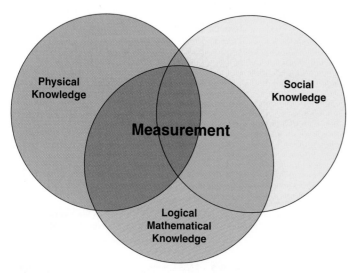

Figure 9.3 The areas of measurement knowledge.

Windows on Learning

How Big Is My Foot?

The class had been comparing foot sizes. First, each student looked for three classmates with larger and three classmates with smaller feet than her or his own. They "measured" foot sizes by standing side by side to see whose foot stuck out further. Then they removed their shoes and, using the classroom wall as a straight edge to put the heels against, tried to line up all the shoes in order from smallest to largest. There was some disagreement about several pairs of shoes that seemed to be the same size. Those were placed in a vertical row jutting out from the wall so that the final lineup of shoes looked something like a broken comb with all but a few teeth missing.

Teacher: All right! The shoes are in a line, but what does it mean?

Arturo: That there are a lot of stinky feet in this class! (Laughter)

Teacher: Okay, but besides that. What does the line say about the size of your feet?

Luisa: There are a lot of different sizes.

Teacher: Good. How many?

The students counted quickly. Most forgot that shoes come in pairs and counted each shoe. Once they discussed and worked through that problem, Ms. Sandoval shifted the focus back to comparing sizes.

Teacher: Whose feet are the smallest? Whose feet are the biggest?

After the owners of the shoes at opposite ends of the line had been identified, Ms. Sandoval suggested another activity.

Teacher: Let's see what happens if we use Luisa's feet (the smallest) and Eduardo's feet (the largest) to measure the length of this room. The length is the distance from the whiteboard to the door.

She demonstrated how to walk heel-toe, heel-toe so that there was no space between steps. As Luisa and Eduardo stepped off the distance, half the class counted Luisa's steps; the other half counted Eduardo's. The final count was higher for Luisa's steps than Eduardo's—something that several students found confusing.

Iris: That can't be right. The number for Luisa is bigger, but her feet are littler.

Arturo: No, that's okay. It took Luisa more steps, but they were littler. They can't count as much.

Teacher: So what's the answer? How long is the room? Is it the number of Luisa's steps or Eduardo's?

Jamal: Both.

Meesha: No, we need a ruler. Then we can really measure it.

Luisa: A ruler's too short. You would have to have a lot of them.

Teacher: What if you "walked" the ruler down the room, turning it end over end? Sort of like Luisa's and Eduardo's steps.

After Ms. Sandoval demonstrated the procedure, the students followed it to find the length of the room in standard feet. Several, though, seemed less than satisfied with the result.

Luisa: We needed someone with really big feet to get it right. Then we would know for sure.

directly and making observations about size, shape, weight, and so forth. They acquire social knowledge about measurement as they learn the conventions of measurement systems. And they draw upon the physical data and conventional systems to construct the logical-mathematical concepts (such as transitive reasoning and unit iteration) that make measurement applications meaningful (see Reece and Kamii 2001 for further discussion).

Constructing those concepts is neither automatic nor instantaneous. Children may be using rulers to measure objects before they truly understand measurement scales, and they may repeat and even use some measurement facts before they fully understand the idea structures that generate the facts.

Activities CD

For a real-life example activity of using nonstandard and standard measurements, see Activity 51, Cooking on the Oregon Trail with Nonstandard and Standard Measurements, on the CD-ROM that accompanies this text.

Effective measurement activities integrate the three areas of knowledge in contexts that children find meaningful. For example, Reece and Kamii (2001) suggest a measuring activity for first and second graders that involves an event or decision that directly impacts the children.

> Show the class two different drinking cups that have different shapes . . . and say, "We're going to have a Coke party tomorrow, and the class needs to decide which one of these two cups you want me to buy more of. . . ." Each cup, along with a pitcher or bottle of water or rice, and extra large container should be provided during the day so that children can cast their votes at the end of the day. . . . It is also important that enough time be given for all students to handle the materials, discuss the problem together, and come to their own decision. At some point toward the end of the day, it is beneficial for the class to have a group time to discuss why they are convinced that one cup is better than the other.
>
> *(360)*

For an activity that combines social, physical, and mathematical knowledge in the study of time measurement, see Activity 16, The Circle of Time, on the CD-ROM that accompanies this text.

The promised treat, a Coke party, engages the students' interest and gives them a stake in the outcome. Handling and testing the cups provides physical knowledge, and discussions with classmates add a social criterion—the better cup is the one that will hold more Coke. Then as the children "think and exchange points of view . . . [they] construct logico-mathematical knowledge" about shape and volume and about comparisons between containers (Reece and Kamii 2001, 360).

The Mental Tools of Measurement

An important outcome of meaningful measurement activities is the development of mental tools and abilities that help children make sense of measurement information and also use measurement to make sense of the world around them. Two key abilities are developed early in elementary school:

For an activity about using centimeter cubes as units of measurement, go to Activity 3, How Tall Is My Dino? on the CD-ROM that accompanies this text.

- the ability to use a third object (such as a ruler) to compare objects that cannot be placed side by side or compared directly, and
- the ability to think of a unit (such as a centimeter cube) as part of a whole and use it repeatedly in measuring

(Kamii and Clark 1997)

The first ability, called **transitive reasoning** by Piaget, enables children to use standard measurement tools such as rulers effectively. The second, called **unit iteration**, helps them measure and understand the measurement of objects that are larger than a single ruler or meterstick. In the scenario from Ms. Sandoval's first-grade class, the children's discomfort with using the ruler measurement may be tied to a lack of development in these areas. Because Luisa was more comfortable with direct measurement, she tended to prefer steps to rulers as a measurement tool, and perhaps because she was not yet thinking of the units as parts of a whole, she found the total of individual steps more meaningful as a measure of distance than the whole derived from repeating ruler lengths.

Building Mental Tools from Concrete Experiences

Constructing other mental tools, such as conceptual rulers and connections between number and geometry, contributes to the development of measurement sense (Clements 1999). A first step toward constructing a conceptual ruler could be making and using an actual ruler or measuring tape with standard or nonstandard units (see the Googol feature). The concrete activity encourages students to identify and work their way through some of the basic concepts of measurement tools: developing a scale, using the same-sized unit for each interval in the scale, assigning numbers to the intervals, and understanding the greater efficiency of tools such as a meterstick or foot-long ruler rather than a centimeter- or inch-long stick (Young and O'Leary 2002, 400, 403). Exploring these major concepts helps students reach what Clements calls "a critical point in their development of measurement sense"—the point when they have constructed "an 'internal' measurement tool . . . [that] is not a static image, but a mental process of moving along an object, segmenting it, and counting the segments" (Clements 1999, 8).

Googol: BIG IDEAS in Mathematics

Create a Tape Measure with Nonstandard and Standard Units

Some of the big ideas of linear measurement are embodied in a simple tool, the tape measure. Making tape measures, first with nonstandard and then standard units, demonstrates vividly the importance of using units of equal size as a basis for measurement and of numbering units consistently. Applying a variety of measurement tools and units to the same objects shows that there can be different but equally valid measurements, each contributing valuable information.

Activity 1

Link colored paper clips to create a chain. Use the chain as a tape measure to measure objects in your classroom. Answer questions such as these: How many paper clips long is the chalkboard? How many paper clips tall are you? Compare results.

Activity 2

Use markers and rolls of adding machine, cash register, or other narrow paper to create a paper tape measure. Decide on units of measurement, and develop a method for marking the tape at regular intervals. Number the intervals consecutively. Then use the tape to measure the same objects you measured with the paper clip chain. Compare the results. Was using the paper tape easier or harder than using the paper clip chain? Were the results more or less satisfying?

Activity 3

On the reverse side of the paper tape, make a measurement scale with centimeters and decimeters as the base units. Use a manufactured ruler or meterstick as a model to help you mark off and number the intervals. Remeasure objects in your classroom with the centimeter side of the tape. Compare and discuss the results.

Topics, Issues, and Explorations

Test your own measurement sense. Estimate the length, width, volume, and weight of a variety of objects. Make your estimations using both common and metric measurements. Then use standard tools to measure the objects directly. How did you do? Were you more successful at estimating length and width than volume or weight? Were your estimates closer for common or for metric units? Compare and discuss the results with your classmates. On a scale of 1 to 10, how would you rate your own measurement sense and that of your class as a whole?

Activities CD

For an activity about using measurement tools to compare lengths of jumps, see Activity 31, Jumping Critters: Kids, Frogs, and Bugs, on the CD-ROM that accompanies this text.

Math and Technology

LOGO's Turtle Math

The LOGO computer language gives students a simple but effective way to interact with computers. Developed by Seymour Papert and a group of MIT researchers in the 1970s, LOGO uses a series of basic commands that allow even very young children to write computer programs. Commands pair direction (Forward, Backward, Right, Left) with numbers (turtle steps, angle of turn) to move a cursor called a turtle around the screen. A LOGO program to draw an equilateral triangle might look like this:

Commands	Graphic
PD	
FD 40	
RT 120	
FD 40	
RT 120	
FD 40	
PU	

PD (Pendown) prepares the turtle to draw a line segment. FD (Forward) 40 moves the cursor forward 40 turtle steps. RT (Right) 120 rotates the cursor 120 degrees to a new heading that will create an internal angle of 60 degrees. FD 40 again draws a 40-turtle-step line segment followed by another RT 120-degree turn and a final FD 40 command for the third 40-step line. PU (Penup) ends the drawing feature.

There are many different versions and applications of LOGO. *Turtle Math* (Clements and Meredith 1994) includes tools such as Label Line to provide feedback and assist children's mathematical thinking.

Activities CD

For an activity that uses LOGO and a turtle-cursor to introduce computer logic and allow students to explore the properties of polygons, see Activity, 49, LOGO's Turtle Math, on the CD-ROM that accompanies this text.

Building Mental Tools from Virtual Experiences

Virtual manipulatives such as LOGO's turtle graphics continue the development of measurement sense and mental tools by encouraging students to connect numbers, segmented lines, and geometric shapes. For example, to create a figure such as a triangle, students use mental measurement tools to visualize the figure and then estimate the number of turtle steps and angles of turtle turns needed to construct the figure. (See the Math and Technology feature for an example of a simple program for constructing a triangle.)

Building Mental Tools with Estimation

Estimation also plays a key role in developing the cognitive skills and thinking tools involved in measurement sense. Making and testing conjectures about size, weight, or volume help students refine their mental measurement tools. With repeated estimations followed by direct measurement techniques, they arrive at a "sense" of how a foot or a meter looks and how a pound or a kilogram feels. Since physical development affects perception, estimation work should continue throughout the grades. What appears large and heavy at 6 years old may seem small and light at 12. Coordinating sense data and the cognitive processes that result in interpretation, including measurement sense, will in fact be part of life-long learning—the process of continually refining and updating everyday math skills.

Measuring with a ruler.

Measurement Systems

We use many basic measurement facts so frequently and automatically that they seem like a natural and inevitable part of life, something that always has been and always will be. Most of us do not need to think twice to answer questions such as "How many hours are there in a day? How many minutes in an hour? How many seconds in a minute? How many months in a year?" The facts may seem simple because of their familiarity, but when we begin to probe the whys behind them, the ideas behind the facts are more complicated. The lengths of days, months, and years are tied to the scientific phenomena of the Earth's turning on its axis, the moon's revolving around the Earth, and the Earth's revolving around the sun. But the 60 seconds in a minute and 60 minutes in an hour as well as the 360-degree measurement for a circle have their roots in the Babylonian base-60 number system. A typical table of common weights and measures is a historical and sociological hodgepodge, combining ideas from a variety of cultures and number systems.

By contrast, the metric system is relatively simple. Its controlling ideas are multiplying or dividing by 10 and relating units across properties such as length, volume, and mass. Richard Deming (1974), who calls the metric system "a universal language of measurement," emphasizes the step-by-step logic by which the system was "built" rather than "grown" as the common system grew from disparate sociological and historical forces (58).

> [T]here is no logical relationship between a yard and a gallon, or between a gallon and a pound.
>
> The metric system, on the other hand, is so orderly that one quantity relates to another in a logical and easily understood manner. The keystone of the system is the length unit. The unit of capacity is built upon it, and originally the mass unit was based on volume.
>
> . . . When the metric system was first devised the mass unit of the gram was defined as the mass of a cubic centimeter of distilled water at sea level and at a temperature of 4 degrees centigrade (now called Celsius), the temperature at which it had the most density. . . . This original relationship is still a handy teaching device because it points up the step-by-step logic on which the metric system was built.

(Deming 1974, 57–58)

Table 9.1 highlights the commonalities in vocabulary and number among metric measurements of length, volume, and mass, including shared prefixes and formulae for converting units:

> To change to a larger unit, multiply by 10.
>
> To change to a smaller unit, divide by 10.

Activities CD

For a measurement activity related to history and art, see Activity 106, The Golden Ratio, Phi, and Physical Beauty, on the CD-ROM that accompanies this text.

TABLE 9.1	Metrics: A System of 10s		
Length	**Volume**		**Mass**
10 millimeters = 1 centimeter	1,000 (10 × 10 × 10) cubic millimeters = 1 cubic centimeter		10 milligrams = 1 centigram
10 centimeters = 1 decimeter	1,000 (10 × 10 × 10) cubic centimeters = 1 cubic decimeter		10 centigrams = 1 decigram
10 decimeters = 1 meter	1,000 (10 × 10 × 10) cubic decimeters = 1 cubic meter		10 decigrams = 1 gram
10 meters = 1 dekameter	1,000 (10 × 10 × 10) cubic meters = 1 cubic dekameter		10 grams = 1 dekagram
10 dekameters = 1 hectometer	1,000 (10 × 10 × 10) cubic dekameters = 1 cubic hectometer		10 dekagrams = 1 hectogram
10 hectometers = 1 kilometer	1,000 (10 × 10 × 10) cubic hectometers = 1 cubic kilometer		10 hectograms = 1 kilogram

Topics, Issues, and Explorations

In their efforts to ensure children learn the metric system of measurement, some countries such as Australia adopted a Think Metric approach. Instead of teaching dual systems or techniques for conversion, this approach calls for teaching only the metric system (Deming 1974, 59–60). Proponents of Think Metric believe parents will be forced to learn the system to help their children with homework, and the end result will be a complete and nationwide change from common to metric measurement. What do you think of this idea? Would it work in the United States? Do you agree with the goal? Why or why not?

Figure 9.4   The clown clock.

Teaching the Metric System

Because most of the world uses the metric system, it is imperative that schoolchildren in the United States become proficient in metrics. At the same time, because inches, gallons, pounds, and other common units continue to be popular, they must also be proficient in the common system. Fortunately, learning multiple systems, like learning languages, is not difficult for children, especially if all of the systems being learned are presented in experiential, hands-on contexts.

To ensure that children see both the metric and the common measurement systems as useful, measurement activities should be frequent and meaningful. For example, measuring oneself (checking height, weight, length of arms, feet, and so forth) can be an ongoing activity, with children keeping a log of common and metric data. Entries can be recorded both as numbers and in line graphs to show growth patterns. Games to estimate height, weight, and capacity of familiar objects and containers help children build their conceptual measurement skills, particularly when the children themselves test their estimates using common and metric tools. Measurement tasks with manipulatives such as centimeter cubes can reinforce the learning of dual systems when a point is made of translating data and comparing/contrasting the results. Overall, emphasis should be on actual, repeated measurements using the two systems rather than on converting measurements from one system to the other by using conversion formulae.

Measuring Time and Temperature

"Telling" time or temperature is not the same thing as measuring it (see Figure 9.4 for the result of a kindergarten-level, telling-time activity in which children make their own clock with movable hands). The former involves primarily reading numbers on a scale and connecting them to the appropriate vocabulary such as *o'clock* or *degrees*. The latter involves comparing and contrasting and making judgments based on actual physical phenomena. Developing measurement sense for time and temperature begins with simple qualitative comparisons (hot, cold, a long time, a short time) and continues with experiences that draw finer distinctions and relate judgments to quantitative scales (for example, 5 hours = a long time, 5 minutes = a short time, and so forth).

To be effective, experiences with measuring time and temperature should include three basic elements:

- hands-on measurement activities,
- reflection about the process and results,
- comparison and discussion of results.

Children might use a stopwatch, sand timer, or mental device (such as reciting "1-1,000, 2-1,000, 3-1,000") to measure the time it takes to sing a song, boil an egg, or endure a commercial break in a favorite television program. Thinking about the process and the results begins the process of developing mental timers. Comparing and discussing results with classmates help refine perceptions and share viewpoints—an important prerequisite of effective communication.

Time

We have all heard or even said ourselves, "Is it time yet?" "Are we there yet?" "Will this or that special day ever come?" Time can seem relative in more than just an Einsteinian sense. Young children will often gauge time by feelings rather than clocks, and even as adults we talk about time "dragging" or the clock "creeping," even though we know objectively that each second or minute on the clock is exactly the same as every other second and minute. The tie between what is important to people and their measurement of time is illustrated by the Mathematics in the Real World activity "Boiling a Potato for Inca Time." The Incas grew more than 200 varieties of potatoes, and the potato was a staple in Incan diets; therefore, how long it takes to boil a potato was their basic unit of time, akin to our hour. Having students boil a potato and then use potato time to create clocks and schedules gives them not only a different perspective on time but also a better understanding of time's sociological components and complexity (PBS Teacher Source).

Because of the widespread use of digital clocks, some children in the early grades have difficulty seeing time as a progression with equal units and, therefore, as something that can be measured. Telling-time activities can be helpful with developing a measurement sense of time when they tie time to the number line and emphasize sequence and continuity. For example:

- Keep an hour-by-hour, minute-by-minute log of a day's activities.
- Create a 24-hour, round clock. Use poster board for the face and black card stock for hour and minute hands. Write in numbers for both hours and minutes with felt-tip pens.
- Make a time line for a celebration or event, such as the Fourth of July. Draw the time line in black; then mark key moments, such as the scheduled times for a picnic and fireworks, in red and other bright colors.
- Tie time to other areas of measurement by measuring your shadow's length at different times of the day (see Figure 9.5).

Temperature

Touching objects or feeling the air can give us a general sense of whether something is hot, cold, lukewarm, and so forth; however, to get a more precise measurement, we take an indirect approach. Temperature scales are based on the

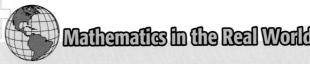

Mathematics in the Real World

Boiling a Potato for Inca Time

The potato is an Incan contribution to the world. In Incan society, the potato was central to agriculture, diet, and even time. The basic unit of Incan time (like our hour) was the time it takes to boil a potato.

Activity 1

Put a medium-sized potato in a saucepan, cover with water, and boil until the potato is soft enough to insert a fork easily. Use a clock with both minute and second hands to mark the time. Then use the time it took to cook the potato to make a potato-time clock, with cooking time rather than hours as major divisions.

Activity 2

Use the potato-time clock to create a daily schedule for yourself, your school, or a television channel you enjoy watching.

Compare your results with those of classmates. Discuss any difficulties you have identified in setting a potato-time standard and in using potato time to make a clock and develop a schedule.

(*Source:* Adapted from PBS Teacher Source, "Lesson Plan 9: One Potato, Two Potato, Inca Style!" *Mathline,* www.pbs.org/opb/conquistadors/teachers/teachershtm.)

Activities CD

For an activity to help students discover the relativity of time, see Activity 47, How Much Time Does It Take To _____?, on the CD-ROM that accompanies this text.

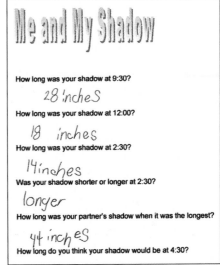

Figure 9.5 Me and my shadow.

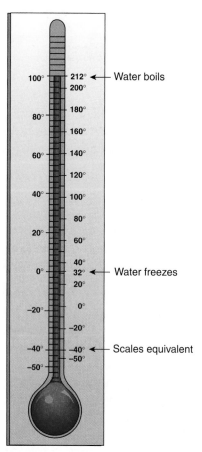

Celsius (°C)   Fahrenheit (°F)

Figure 9.6 The Celsius and Fahrenheit scales.
(Adapted from Deming, 1974, 88.)

Activities CD

For an activity to explore different systems of time measurement, see Activity 53, Boiling Potato for Inca Time, on the CD-ROM that accompanies this text.

Topics, Issues, and Explorations

An effective way to keep measurement studies concrete and meaningful is with an ongoing project that uses a variety of measurement skills in interesting ways. A project used by many schools is the WeatherNet Classroom. Students collect data from their own WeatherNet station and post the information on their own Web site. Visit the WeatherNet Classroom at http://classroom.aws.com/login.asp. Then discuss the different types of measurement students might learn with this project as well as the crossovers with other subject matter areas.

effect temperature has on the liquid element in the tube of a thermometer. To get beyond simply reading a thermometer and understand the measures involved, students need first to see taking a temperature as a comparison of physical effects—an effect that we can feel on our skin and an effect that we can see reflected in the liquid's rising and falling in the tube.

Mood stones or other novelties that respond to body temperature with physical changes can serve as an introduction to seeing and interpreting the effects of temperature. Experimenting with a thermometer's tube without the scales—observing what happens when the tube sits on ice cubes or is held over a steaming teakettle—encourages students to make their own judgments about changes in the liquid that show hot, cold, or just warm. In an activity for first graders, Young and O'Leary (2002) covered the Celsius and Fahrenheit scales on thermometers and had students make their own marks and nonstandard scales.

> The students were asked to draw a mark on the tape alongside the glass tube to indicate the initial level of the liquid; this measurement was room temperature. Then the students recorded four more marks for the level of the liquid when the thermometer was placed (1) in hot water (be careful), (2) in ice water, (3) in ice water with salt added, and (4) under the arm to take body temperature.
>
> *(404)*

The students used colored dots to create a numerical scale for temperature, with smaller numbers of dots at the bottom of the scale because, according to the children, "when the red [liquid] goes higher, the numbers should go higher" (405).

Two Scales for Measuring Temperature   As with most other areas of measurement, students need to learn at least two scales for measuring temperature: the Fahrenheit scale, named for its 18th-century developer G. Daniel Fahrenheit, and the Celsius scale, named for another 18th-century scientist, Anders Celsius. Both scales measure in degrees and use the freezing and boiling points of water as standard reference points (32°F, 0°C; 212°F, 100°C). For the most part, students understand the relationship of the scales better if the readings are taken by the students themselves and reflect information they can verify at least generally with their senses—for example, that 0°C and 32°F temperature feels cold and causes water to freeze. Lesson plans for older students frequently focus on applications of conversion formulas such as the following:

$$F = \frac{9C}{5} + 32 \qquad C = \frac{(F - 32)}{9} \times 5$$

Using calculators and an equivalency scale such as the one in Figure 9.6 can help keep these exercises from becoming too abstract and repetitive.

Measurement and Geometry

Geometry is about measurement (*geo* = earth, *metry* = measure), and most measurement tasks (including using the changes in a tube of liquid to reflect temperature) involve geometry. Measuring length, width, perimeters, area, angles, and other properties of polygons is basic to plane or two-dimensional geometry. In the past an emphasis on memorizing and using formulas has sometimes made these aspects of measurement seem abstract and even unreal. Using everyday and recreational geometry as contexts for measurement helps make the concepts real and the applications meaningful.

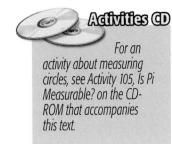

Activities CD

For an activity about measuring circles, see Activity 105, Is Pi Measurable? on the CD-ROM that accompanies this text.

Plane Geometry

Although some researchers worry that working with two-dimensional shapes may seem unreal or abstract to children, most are experienced at representing three-dimensional objects in two dimensions at an early age. How they deal with the problems of proportion, symmetry, and orientation as they draw people or objects plays an important role in children's understanding of spatial relationships.

Children's own drawings and representations are a good place to introduce measuring two-dimensional objects. The drawing "My House" in Figure 9.7 resulted from a combined social studies, art, and math project for first graders. After talking about the different types of dwellings built by different societies, the children drew their own homes from memory. Most did some creative things with color that had more to do with art than fact—for example, the pink roof and orange door on a yellow house. Then they used rulers to measure lines in their drawings and tried to identify lines that were the same length, longer, shorter, and so forth.

Activities CD

For an activity about symmetry and spatial relationships, go to Activity 43, Symmetry and Geometric Transformations, on the CD-ROM that accompanies this text.

Measuring with understanding involves several key components:

- Defining the limits of the object to be measured—that is, identifying a beginning and ending point for lines or spaces measured
- Selecting an appropriate standard for measurement
- Applying the standard consistently and thoroughly
- Interpreting and representing the results

Some of the difficulties children might have with these components are shown in the "My House" drawing. Briseida's measurements overlap the lines, mix common and metric measures, and are represented in a confusing manner because the symbol for inches (″) looks like the number 11.

Becoming proficient requires more than practice; it requires measuring, assessing, remeasuring, and reassessing until both the process and the results of measurement achieve the level of precision and accuracy called for by the task.

Figure 9.7 My house.

Some questions you as a teacher can ask to guide learning and encourage reflection include the following:

- Have you measured all of what you wanted to measure? Have you missed any parts or gone too far?
- What measurement standard are you using? Have you used it consistently?
- If you are using more than one standard, do you have two complete sets of data and conclusions?
- What tools did you use to measure? Were there any gaps or overlaps in the way you used them?

Two of the big ideas for measurement in plane or two-dimensional geometry are **perimeter** and **area**. NCTM's (2000) *Principles and Standards* suggests that children in the early grades (K–2) should explore these ideas as characteristics of objects and students in the middle grades (3–5) should not only develop strategies for estimating and calculating perimeter and area but also "explore what happens to measurements of . . . perimeter and area when the shape is changed in some way" (398). Manipulatives, both physical and virtual, encourage students to approach these explorations like experiments, testing different strategies, collecting data, and drawing conclusions.

In the Math Manipulatives activity, Froot Loops Perimeter and Area, students in the early grades use nonstandard and standard measures to find the perimeters and areas of irregularly shaped objects, their handprints. Comparisons and discussions move the activity beyond gathering and recording facts to thinking about the characteristics of the shapes they are working with and beginning to generalize about size and its relationship to perimeter and area. Because students, even in the middle grades, sometimes confuse these concepts, Malloy and Friel (1999) asked students to manipulate the area of a figure made up of plastic tiles to change the perimeter to 16. Looking for and discussing a variety of answers to the problem helped students conceptualize the meanings of the terms *perimeter* and *area* and understand the relationship between the concepts.

Malloy and Friel used both manipulatives and cooperative learning to make the concepts and terms of plane or two-dimensional geometry seem real and meaningful. Another strategy is to use imaginative literature as a context, both for the ideas

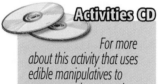

Activities CD

For more about this activity that uses edible manipulatives to measure perimeter and area, see Activity 48, Exploring Perimeter and Area with Froot Loops, on the CD-ROM that accompanies this text.

Math Manipulatives

Froot Loops Perimeter and Area

Students explore perimeter (the distance around a two-dimensional object) and area (the space inside the object) using handprints and Froot Loops.

Activity 1

Spread your fingers wide and draw around them and beneath the wrist to make a handprint. Outline the handprint with Froot Loops, and count the Froot Loops to get a number for the perimeter. Then compare handprints and numbers, and talk about the differences the size of the print makes in the perimeter.

Activity 2

Fill your handprint with a layer of Froot Loops; then count the Froot Loops to get a number for area. Talk about size of handprint and its effect on area.

Activity 3

Use string to outline your handprints; then cut and measure the string with a centimeter ruler or tape measure. Next fill your handprint with centimeter blocks, and count the blocks. Compare and evaluate the results with Froot Loops and centimeters as measurement units.

Source: Adapted from an activity by Tim Conly.

and for manipulative or other activities (Moore and Bintz 2002; Moyer 2001; Martinez and Martinez 2001). Math stories engage students on several levels:

- **Images** of geometric shapes, such as the polygons in Marilyn Burns's (1994) *The Greedy Triangle;*
- **Words**, such as *circumference, radius,* and *diameter* in Cindy Neuschwander's (1997) *Sir Cumference and the First Round Table;*
- **Math concepts**, such as pi in Neuschwander's (1999) *Sir Cumference and the Dragon of Pi;*
- **Storylines**, like the struggle of the two-dimensional characters in Abbott's (1983) *Flatland* to understand and believe in the three-dimensional reality of Spaceland.

In the Sir Cumference series of math adventures by Cindy Neuschwander, the names of the major characters are math concepts—Sir Cumference, Lady Di of Ameter, and their son Radius. The math adventures usually involve discovering a math idea or application as a way to resolve the story's major complication. For example, in *Sir Cumference and the Dragon of Pi,* Sir Cumference turns into the Pi Dragon, and Radius must discover the number pi in order to mix a potion to cure him.

Sir Cumference and the Great Knight of Angleland introduces another big idea of plane geometry, **angle**. The major concepts and terms—*degrees, right angle, acute* and *obtuse angles*—are represented by characters' names (Sir D'Grees), exercises in Radius's training to be a knight (the Knightly right angle), and geographic features of Angleland (the Mountains of Obtuse and a "cute," steep-roofed design in village houses). Radius uses a family heirloom, a circular protractor/medallion with half of the circle cut out and divided into 180 degrees to guide him on his quest to find King Lell. A copy of the medallion is inserted at the end of the book so that readers can measure degrees of angle for themselves (Neuschwander 2001). Other stories tied to plane geometry concepts are listed in the Mathematics in Literature feature.

For some students, the physical skill and practice needed to work successfully with protractors, rulers, and pencils may limit early explorations of angles. Working with virtual manipulatives such as Turtle Math or Geometer's Sketchpad allows them to test and revise without the tedious and often lengthy process of drawing and redrawing figures. For example, to draw a square manually requires them to draw a line, measure a 90-degree angle, draw another line of exactly the same length, measure another 90-degree angle, draw another line, measure still another 90-degree angle, and draw another line to connect with the starting point and form a fourth 90-degree angle. To make the same shape with LOGO requires only a simple set of commands: REPEAT 4 [FD 50 RT 90].

Solid Geometry

Encountered first in the pages of a textbook, the shapes and concepts of solid or three-dimensional geometry might seem to belong primarily to the academic face of geometry. However, with learning experiences that help them discover applications and examples in the real world, students are quick to recognize everyday applications. Sent on a shapes hunt, they will find cone shapes in hats, waffle cones for ice cream, even a well-trimmed evergreen or garden shrub. They will see cubes and pyramids in architecture, prisms in light fixtures, and cylinders in soft drink cans and oatmeal boxes.

Once students recognize solid geometric shapes visually (Van Hiele Level 0, Visualization), they are ready to explore the shapes' properties (Van Hiele Level 1,

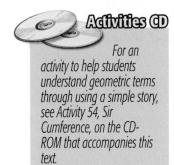

Activities CD

For an activity to help students understand geometric terms through using a simple story, see Activity 54, Sir Cumference, on the CD-ROM that accompanies this text.

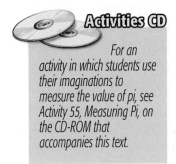

Activities CD

For an activity in which students use their imaginations to measure the value of pi, see Activity 55, Measuring Pi, on the CD-ROM that accompanies this text.

Activities CD

For a hands-on activity to explore angles and related properties of polygons, see Activity 56, Tessellating Polygons, on the CD-ROM that accompanies this text.

Mathematics in Literature

Stories for Teaching Geometry Measurement Concepts

Concept	Story	Description
Perimeter and area	Burns's (1997) *Spaghetti and Meatballs for All*	Rearranging tables for guests shows how an area may have different perimeters.
Circumference	Lasky's (1994) *The Librarian Who Measured the Earth*	The circumference of the Earth is measured as the distance around the equator and the prime meridian.
Polygons	MacCarone's (1996) *The Silly Story of Goldie Locks and the Three Squares*	The story shows the relationship between the number of sides of a polygon and the size of the interior angles.
Two dimensions	Brown's (1992) *Flat Stanley*	Stanley is flattened by his bulletin board and discovers what it is like to be a two-dimensional figure in a three-dimensional world.
Three dimensions	Abbott, Burger, and Asimov's (1994) *Sphereland*	The story is a companion for Abbott's *Flatland* and explores the properties of three-dimensional figures.
Multiple dimensions	Stewart's (2001) *Flatterland: Like Flatland, Only More So*	Square's granddaughter Victoria Line voyages through the Mathverse, exploring 10 dimensions.

(For more stories tied to geometric concepts, see Moore and Bintz 2002.)

Activities CD

For an activity about building models of solids with everyday objects, see Activity 42, Building Polygons and Polyhedrons with Gumdrops and Toothpicks, on the CD-ROM that accompanies this text.

Analysis/Description). One way to do this is with virtual manipulatives like those at NCTM's Illuminations Web site (see the Mathematical Thinking feature). In the Exploring Geometric Solids activities, students use e-tools to rotate solids, to change the colors of different faces, or to highlight edges by making the images transparent. Properties are listed on an e-worksheet as students discover them.

Building models of the solids with either everyday materials or manufactured manipulatives such as Zometools and MAGZ prepares students to move to the next level of understanding (Van Hiele Level 2, Informal Deduction/Theory). As they construct, compare, and contrast shapes, they discover relationships among the shapes and begin to classify and develop abstract definitions (Van Hiele 1986). Koester (2003) used 1,000 straws and plastic twists as connectors in a building-solids activity for fourth graders.

> These simple materials . . . allowed students to construct knowledge about three-dimensional shapes in an active way. As they built, students also were engaged in talking about their models, so they learned and used new vocabulary in meaningful context. Instead of simply memorizing definitions, students were developing precise ways to describe and classify shapes based on their own observations and experiences.

(442)

Mathematical Thinking

Exploring Geometric Solids and Their Properties with NCTM'S Illuminations

NCTM's e-resource Illuminations lets students explore geometric shapes and concepts with interactive activities for each grade band (pre-K–2, 3–5, 6–8). Students manipulate geometric solids by rotating them, changing the colors of different faces, and altering images from opaque to transparent.

At each stage of the investigation, questions set an inquiry-based context for students' work. Tasks for grades 3–5 include studying different solids and making a table of their different properties, constructing solids with gumdrops and toothpicks and explaining their construction, and making a shape jacket. Tasks for grades 6–8 include building and manipulating shapes with an isometric grid, comparing isometric drawings, drawing mat plans, and building figures from mat plans.

Math investigations feature interactive math applets, suggestions for student activities, discussion and questions for teachers, as well as links to Web site resources.

Activity

Visit the Illuminations site at http://illuminations.nctm. org/imath/3–5/Geometric Solids/GeoSolids4.html. Copy and fill out the worksheets for Exploring Geometric Solids and Cubes Everywhere. Use the tools provided to examine the properties of solids and build cubes.

Other everyday materials that work well to build geometric solids are toothpicks with gumdrops or marshmallows as connectors and chenille wires. With Zometools, MAGZ, and several other commercial products, students use colored struts and connecting balls to build polyhedra or a variety of other structures such as bridges and domes. To highlight faces and show relationships, Zometool (1999) suggests dipping constructions in a bubble solution and then popping unwanted bubbles with a dry finger or moving bubbles around with a wet finger. Young students might use bubbles to show the six faces of a cube, while more advanced students might use bubbles to explore the shadows of four-dimensional figures.

Three of the big measurement ideas of solid geometry are **weight**, **volume**, and **surface area**. Each of the ideas has everyday applications that will help engage students' interest and make the ideas meaningful to them personally.

Topics, Issues, and Explorations

Working with four or five other students, construct a giant polyhedron. Select either a regular solid such as a dodecahedron (pentagon faces) or icosahedron (20 triangle faces) or a semiregular solid such as an icosido-decahedron (a combination of pentagons and triangles as faces). Begin by making a small version of your polyhedron to serve as a model. Then use cardboard and 2-inch-wide masking tape to build the giant polyhedron. Work to scale from your model, making side lengths as long as 12 inches for all edges. Your construction could be gigantic—as much as 6 feet in diameter—so be sure you have enough room to work (Peterson 2000; see also Zillox and Lowrey 1997).

Understanding Weight

Like height, **weight** is a measurement concept children encounter early. They are weighed each time they visit the doctor. They probably have heard adults discussing weight gains or losses. They might have purchased a bag of candy or nuts and noticed how much more a pound is than a quarter pound—as well as how much more a pound costs. In the early grades, experiences with weights can begin with lifting and comparing objects to decide which ones feel light or heavy and which ones feel lighter, lightest, heavier, and heaviest. A bathroom scale that shows both metric and common measures works well weighing large objects; a postage meter, for small objects (although most of those use only ounces and pounds). Students in the middle

How much would you weigh on the moon and the planets of our solar system?

How much you weigh is an effect not only of your size but also of the gravity of the planet or space body you are on. Astronauts in space feel weightless because they do not feel the effects of gravity.

To determine your weight on the moon or other planets, you can use Earth's gravity as a starting point (Earth = 1); then multiply your weight by the percentage of Earth's gravitational attraction you would feel if you stood on that surface. For example, on Mars you would feel 38% as heavy as you feel on Earth, so multiplying your Earth weight by .38 would give your weight on Mars.

Planet	Weight on Earth in Pounds or Kilograms	Multiply Earth Weight by Surface Gravity—	Your "New" Weight
Mercury		× 0.38 =	
Venus		× 0.9 =	
Earth's Moon		× 0.16 =	
Mars		× 0.38 =	
Jupiter		× 2.87 =	
Saturn		× 1.32 =	
Uranus		× 0.93 =	
Neptune		× 1.23 =	
Pluto		× 0.03 =	

1. On which planet would you feel lightest? Heaviest?
2. Which planets have the same surface gravity?
3. On which planet would you feel closest to your weight on Earth?
4. Judging from surface gravity, which planet is probably the largest? The smallest?

Figure 9.8 Determining how much you would weigh on the moon and the planets. (Adapted from PBS Teachersource, "Space Odyssey 2000," *Mathline*, **http://www.pbs.org/ teachersource/mathline/concepts/space2/activity/2.shtm**).

Activities CD

For an activity to help students develop the mind tools needed to estimate size, see Activity 52, Estimating Length, Volume, and Weight, on the CD-ROM that accompanies this text.

and upper grades can explore the difference between the weight and the mass of objects and the connections between weight and gravity. An effective context for studying mass and weight is a combined math–science unit on gravity and the solar system. For example, students might explore the effect of gravity on weight by calculating their weight on the moon or various planets (see Figure 9.8).

Understanding Volume

A good beginning point for exploring **volume** is estimating with nonstandard units. For example, middle-grade students were asked to estimate the numbers of M&Ms in a transparent rectangular container (a prism). The estimate was for the M&M volume of the container—that is, its capacity to hold M&Ms. Some students counted all the M&Ms they could see and guessed at the rest. Others used a layering strategy to develop an algorithm:

Number of M&Ms in one layer	$\times$	Number of layers in a container	$=$	M&M volume of container

Testing the algorithm with base-10 blocks not only confirms the strategy but also shows more clearly than the irregular M&M shapes the way the number of blocks in the base area can be calculated by multiplying the blocks in two adjacent sides. Discovering a workable formula for the volume of a rectangular solid (length $\times$ width $\times$ height) is only a step away.

Since base-10 blocks are based on the centimeter cube and show a direct relationship between linear measurements and volume, they are an excellent tool, both visually and mentally, for exploring volume. Everyday cooking tools, such as measuring cups and spoons, also work well, although the common measurements will not show the same easy-to-conceptualize relationship of linear and volume units as the metric measurements.

Understanding Surface Area

Surface area measurements have everyday applications in upholstering furniture, wallpapering a room, or deciding how much paint is needed to cover a house. Students get hands-on experience with making and using surface area measurements by "wall"papering different-shaped boxes—cylinders, cubes, and other prisms. To paper flat-sided boxes, students will need several pieces of information:

- number of sides of the box,
- shapes of sides and number of each shape, and
- length and width of each shape.

To paper cylindrical boxes, students will need to know—

- circumference of the cylinder,
- height of the cylinder, and
- diameter of the cylinder.

Students might start by tracing around the surfaces to make patterns and then use rulers or other tools to find standard measurements. Having students develop their own formulas for finding the surface area of different solids encourages them to generalize and think in terms of classes of shapes rather than individual objects. It also prepares them for working with the standard formulas for areas by providing both context and perspective for the problem-solving processes that formulas represent.

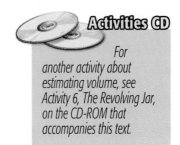

Activities CD

For another activity about estimating volume, see Activity 6, The Revolving Jar, on the CD-ROM that accompanies this text.

Topics, Issues, and Explorations

Why is a pound cake called a pound cake? Find a from-scratch recipe for pound cake. Then use a kitchen scale to identify the pounds in the cake. Does the name reflect the total weight of the ingredients, the weight of some ingredients, or the weight of the final product? (To answer the last question, you may need to actually bake the cake.)

Diversity in Learning and Thinking Mathematically

A core principle of contemporary methods of teaching mathematics is flexibility in learning methods, materials, and outcomes. Because of its multiplicity in systems, tools, and uses, measurement is an excellent subject area for diversity. Activities designed to explore a specific area such as volume can use actual or virtual manipulatives and engage students with images, things to feel, sounds (as in the different tones made by glasses filled to different levels), and even smells (as in a cooking application). Outcomes might be written in words or numbers, built with hands-on or computer tools, or explored and discussed in cooperative learning groups.

Susan Mercer, a California middle-school teacher, designed a series of activities with pentominoes for her seventh-grade classes (Germain-McCarthy 2001). The classes included mainstream students, students with limited English proficiency (LEP), and special education students. Working cooperatively in multi-skills-levels groups, students first used tiles to form the pentomino shapes of five touching but not overlapping squares (see Figure 9.9). Then they replicated pentominoes on graph paper, cut, and folded them to discover which make open boxes and which do not.

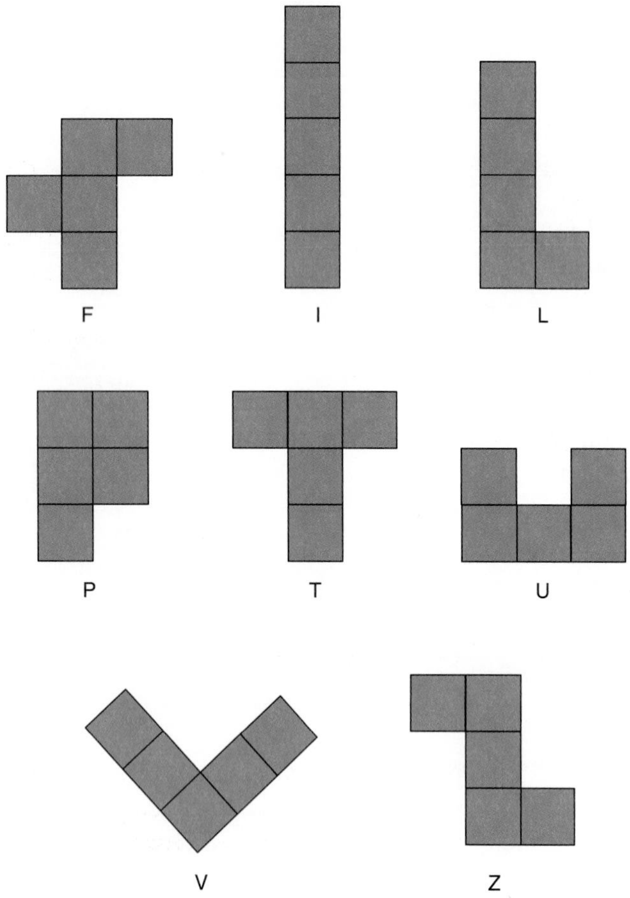

Other activities in the series included the following:

- Using 1-inch tiles to construct a pentomino with 2-inch sides; then replicating the larger pentomino with graph paper, cutting it out, and computing its area and perimeter
- Finding the volume of 1- and 2-inch pentominoes that form open boxes
- Making a poster to show 1-, 2-, 3-, 4-, and 5-inch pentominoes in order with their length, perimeter, area, and volume as well as the methods used to make each calculation

Throughout the activities, Mercer asked students to construct their own procedures and to defend their answers. Students brainstormed in their groups, tested their answers with manipulatives and on paper, and worked at coming to a consensus about concepts. Mercer writes:

Figure 9.9 Pentominoes in letter shapes.

During the project it is very interesting to observe how students moved from using manipulatives to the abstract so as to calculate the volume. . . . As they found procedures, students would test their "theories" using the cubes, but I also observed students getting excited for having "discovered" procedures they were able to explain. At the end of the project, most groups were finding the volume by calculating the base, then multiplying by number of "layers going up." In one of the groups having one LEP Vietnamese student and five LEP Hispanic students, the Vietnamese student "informed" the rest that he knew how to calculate the volume without cubes, but the Hispanic students were not convinced so they checked the answers with the cubes. After doing four of the five pentominoes, they were convinced and started using the algorithm.

(Germain-McCarthy 2001, 30)

Overall, Mercer found that students with a variety of skills levels and special needs were able to participate in the activities and contribute to the cooperative learning process. All of the students worked on the same problems, and all were expected to succeed (Germain-McCarthy 2001, 38). As a result, according to Mercer, "this unit allowed all students to feel successful because it provided them with an opportunity to experience important mathematics concepts through participation in a challenging project (Germain-McCarthy 2001, 25).

‹‹‹‹LOOKING BACK

Measurement forms an important part of the pre-K–8 curriculum. Understanding the way time, temperature, length, volume, and weight are measured prepares children to live in a society that measures almost everything. We use time measurements as a way to orchestrate and order the interactions of daily life. We use other measurements as important criteria in buying or selling, building, making decisions, or communicating perceptions about the world and environment. How big? How small? How long? How short? How light? How heavy? These questions are asked every day in thousands of contexts and in hundreds of different ways. Shared measurement standards mean we can calculate answers knowing the meaning will remain constant.

Children need to learn both common and metric systems in order to understand the measurement language and standards of everyday U.S. society and of the world.

Measurement also provides essential tools for exploring and constructing concepts in both plane (two-dimensional) and solid (three-dimensional) geometry.

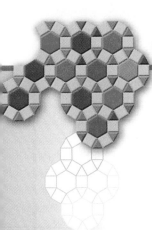

Questions for Further Thought, Discussion, and Research

1. Explore the time zone concept as a way to order time around the world. Are the zones based strictly on scientific facts, or are social/political factors involved? How about Daylight Savings Time? Is that idea scientific or social/political?

2. The theory of multiple intelligences suggests that there are many different ways of being "smart" and many different contexts for assessing intelligent behavior. Is it possible for a student whose general math achievement has been low to excel in geometry and measurement tasks? Why or why not?

3. Quilting is an excellent recreational application of geometry concepts. Quilters even have their own measurement tools and strategies. What kinds of measurement and geometry ideas can you identify in a popular quilting pattern? You might select a pattern from a catalog, quilting magazine, or a quilt you own.

4. Measurement is obviously important in old-fashioned, from-scratch cooking. Is it also important in more modern styles of cooking using microwaves and prepared foods? Explain.

5. How about arts and crafts? What types of arts and crafts use measurement as essential artistic strategies? What types of measurement tools and units might they use?

CHAPTER 10

Algebraic Thinking Across the Grades

In the 19th century algebra was primarily a college subject; in the 20th century, a high school subject. Now in the 21st century, we are teaching algebraic thinking across the grades. The change calls for new content such as working with equations in the early grades but also for a new way of looking at and extending work with standard curriculum areas such as classifying, discovering patterns, or factoring to begin to construct the big ideas of algebra.

Algebraic thinking is more than being able to work with unknowns or writing and solving equations. It involves "habits of mind" that facilitate understanding and applying the big ideas of algebra, including equality, variables, functions, symbolic representation, and proportion.

Learning to think algebraically in the early grades smooths the transition from the elementary to the middle and high school math curricula and at the same time provides students with the cognitive or mind tools needed to deal effectively with important mathematics.

Changing "Algebra for Some" to "Algebra for All"

The place of algebra in the mathematics curriculum has undergone dramatic changes over the years. During the 19th century, algebra was seen as "advanced" mathematics and primarily a college-level subject. During the 20th century, Algebra I and Algebra II became fixtures in the high school curriculum—courses for those who had more or less mastered the K–8 arithmetic curriculum and were preparing for college. Now in the 21st century, mathematics educators are working to make algebra an integral part of learning mathematics across the grades—what Kaput (1998, 25) calls "algebrafying" school mathematics.

Factors motivating this effort highlight both the social and the intellectual challenges of teaching mathematics today. These include the following:

The equity principle—the idea that everyone should have the opportunity to do important mathematics (NCTM 2000)

Mathematical reasoning—the recognition that algebraic thinking is fundamental to many areas of the mathematics curriculum

Problem solving in the real world—the understanding that the habits of mind necessary for algebraic thinking are important in problem-solving situations that involve mathematics

Does this mean that first graders will be expected to solve complex equations or that polynomials will replace multiplication and division as elementary math topics? Not at all. Instead, "algebra for all" and "algebra across the grades" mean exploring basic ideas and developing a cognitive framework for studying algebra long before students enroll in a formal course. "One of the central purposes of algebra is to model real situations mathematically" (Driscoll 1999, 119). When children identify patterns in collections of objects (as in Figure 10.1), represent the patterns pictorially and symbolically, and even predict what comes next in the pattern, they are developing and using mathematical models and in effect thinking algebraically. When they examine geometric shapes and construct and explore algorithms such as $a = lw$ for finding area, they are not only thinking algebraically but also using the language of algebra to summarize and represent their thoughts.

Topics, Issues, and Explorations

Think about your own early experiences with algebra. When did you first encounter algebraic concepts such as equations and variables? Was your experience formal, as in an algebra course, or informal, as in activities or readings outside the classroom? How accessible did these concepts seem at the time? Did you feel well prepared or unprepared to deal with them?

Figure 10.1 Patterns in shapes.

Understanding Algebraic Thinking

What does it mean to "think algebraically," and how might we as teachers foster algebraic thinking? Someone who remembers primarily the symbols and equations of algebra might speculate that thinking algebraically means thinking in algebraic statements such as $5x - 4 = 6$. But algebraic thinking involves more than translating situations into algebraic language; it involves patterns of thought or what can be called "habits of mind" (Driscoll 1999, 1–2).

Students develop these habits or patterns as they explore situations with algebraic potential and reflect about their meanings and implications for additional problems and problem solving. The result is a set of mental tools that become increasingly refined and sophisticated as students deal with more and more complex mathematics. However, the starting points are already basic to much of the pre-K–8 mathematics curriculum and well within the reach of students in the early grades (see Moses 1999; Chambers 2002; Kaput 1998).

Mathematics Across the Curriculum

A Prealgebra Art Activity

Representing numbers and number relationships on a two-dimensional plane is a foundational idea for algebra. Paired coordinates are plotted on the x-y axes to create a pattern that is basically a picture of meaning.

Teachers can introduce this idea with prealgebra art activities. Students use paired coordinates to create two-dimensional pictures. As they plot the coordinates, students develop facility in working with the x-y axes. At the same time, they begin to understand the connections between numbers and visual representations in graphs.

Activity 1

Plot the following paired coordinates on graph paper. Connect the dots with straight lines. Identify the picture.

Outside lines: $x = 1$, $y = 5$; $x = 2$, $y = 3$; $x = 4$, $y = 1$; $x = 6$, $y = 1$; $x = 8$, $y = 3$; $x = 9$, $y = 5$; $x = 8$, $y = 7$; $x = 7$, $y = 9$; $x = 6$, $y = 7$; $x = 4$, $y = 7$; $x = 3$, $y = 9$; $x = 2$, $y = 7$

Inside lines: (a) $x = 3$, $y = 5$; $x = 4$, $y = 5$, $x = 4$, $y = 6$; $x = 3$, $y = 6$
(b) $x = 6$, $y = 5$; $x = 7$, $y = 5$; $x = 7$, $y = 6$; $x = 6$, $y = 6$
(c) $x = 5$, $y = 3$; $x = 6$, $y = 4$; $x = 4$, $y = 4$
(d) $x = 3$, $y = 3$; $x = 4$, $y = 2$; $x = 6$, $y = 2$; $x = 7$, $y = 3$

Extension

Plot additional coordinates adding details to the picture.

Activity 2

Create your own picture on graph paper using paired coordinates. List the x and y coordinates for each dot in the picture. Connect the dots with straight lines. Have a classmate use your coordinates to duplicate your picture.

Identifying Patterns in Algebraic Thinking

Some of the basic patterns of early algebraic thinking are as follows:

Generalizing—finding patterns in objects, shapes, or numbers and identifying or constructing principles and rules that underlie the patterns

Symbolizing—constructing pictorial, symbolic, and numerical representations

Equating/balancing—building on the comparing/contrasting processes that identify like and unlike to see or construct equivalencies in symbols as well as objects, shapes, and numbers

Working forward and backward—starting at the beginning or the end, with the problem itself or with the solution to the problem, and being able to problem solve in either direction

These mental habits are also important to other areas of mathematical reasoning. For example, students generalize when they develop algorithms for solving problems, and they represent ideas symbolically or pictorially when they use drawings to help them understand concepts such as the base-10 number system. Equating or balancing underscores early-grades activities such as finding the different ways to make 15 cents from nickels, dimes, and pennies. And students begin to develop the reversibility skills that enable them to work backward as well as forward when they count backward, count down to subtract, or add to check their subtraction and subtract to check their addition.

As students become more skilled in thinking algebraically, the patterns or habits of mind become more complex as well as more mathematically sophisticated. Driscoll identified "three habits that seem to be critical to developing power in algebraic thinking" in the later grades:

1. **Doing-undoing**—"being able to undo mathematical processes as well as do them. . . . Algebraic thinkers cannot only solve an equation such as $9 \times 2 - 16 = 0$, but also answer the question, 'What is an equation with solutions 4/3 and $-4/3$?' "

2. **Building rules to represent functions**—"the capacity to recognize patterns and organize data to represent situations in which input is related to output by well-defined functional rules."

3. **Abstracting from computation**—"the capacity to think about computations independently of particular numbers that are used."

(Driscoll 1999, 1–2)

Fostering Algebraic Thinking

Whether students are in the early or later grades, teachers can foster algebraic thinking by "algebrafying" the mathematics curriculum—that is, by "seeding" "aspects of algebra . . . through relatively ordinary, elementary mathematical activity" (Kaput 1998, 26). Many activities that are already part of the curriculum can be seeded, including those that call for

(a) learning about the use of symbols,
(b) using patterns to look for generalizations, and
(c) understanding the use of independent, systematic relationships to model situations and make predictions.

(Williams and Molina 1998, 41)

Williams and Molina also describe many natural contexts as "steeped in algebra": "determining gas mileage, predicting the amount of food to prepare for a party, and figuring costs of renting videos" (41). "Seeding" these mathematical situations with algebra becomes more a matter of emphasizing and exploiting what is already there than of radically changing or adding something new to the mathematics involved. For example, sharing a pizza—a favorite division or fraction activity for elementary students—emphasizes the algebraic concept of function when students explore "what happens if [the] pizza must be shared among larger and larger groups of picnickers" (Burrill and Ferrini-Mundy 1998, 162). Similarly, finding the relationship between the amount of juice and ginger ale or sparkling water used in making punch—a favorite fractions or percentage activity for older students—can be refocused and extended to explore proportionality, a linear function (Burrill and Ferrini-Mundy 1998).

Activities CD

For an activity about functions and planning a party, see Activity 91, Shopping by the Numbers, on the CD-ROM that accompanies this text.

Problem Solving and Algebraic Thinking

Developing algebraic habits of thought begins with problem solving in mathematical situations that elicit algebraic reasoning; it continues and strengthens as students reflect about the problem-solving process and its outcomes. Questions can play a key role not only in triggering reflection but also in extending students' thinking beyond assimilation to accommodation—that is, beyond integrating information into

Topics, Issues, and Explorations

Examine your own algebraic thinking by exploring different aspects of the classic "how many pizzas" problem: How many pizzas will you need to feed 8, 16, 32, 64, and so forth, picnickers? How many picnickers will you need to eat 8, 16, 32, 64, and so forth, pizzas?

You might use a *t*-table or other aid to help you identify patterns. For example:

Express your findings in algebraic sentences. Then in small groups brainstorm about your experience. Consider the use of different "habits of mind" and levels of algebraic thinking. Assess comfort levels as well. Did the thinking involved seem natural or unnatural, smooth or awkward, comfortable or uncomfortable? Use your findings to write goals for developing algebraic habits of mind.

1	8
2	16
4	32
8	64

what they already know to understanding and learning something new. In many cases "the full algebraic potential . . . will go unexploited unless the teacher asks questions that are used to extend students' thinking about the problem" (Driscoll 1999, 7). Questions might probe understanding the problem situation, setting up the problem, representing outcomes, or generalizing results. For example:

- What's the problem asking you to find?
- Is there a rule or relationship here?
- How does the rule work, and how is it helpful?
- How can you describe the steps?
- What are other ways to write that expression?
- How can you check your answer? What if you start at the end?
- When you do the same thing with different numbers, what still holds true? What changes?

(selected and adapted from Driscoll 1999, 2–6)

The Idea Files feature lists some activities and questions that teachers have used to foster algebraic thinking at different grade levels.

Mathematical Thinking

Writing-the-Process in Problem Solving

Writing-the-process means explaining in words how we look at, set up, and work through a problem. It helps students think through the problem and at the same time helps teachers understand and assess students' thinking.

In addition, when students explain what they did and why they did it, they engage the important learning tool of **reflection**. They begin to review and self-assess, preparing the way for finding and correcting their own errors as well as discovering better or more efficient ways to solve problems.

A series of questions or thought "prompts" can be used to shape the process and encourage students to think mathematically. For example:

What is the problem asking you to do?

What do you know about the problem?

What do you not know about the problem?

How can you represent the situation mathematically?

What will you do first, second, and so forth? Why?

How do you know your solution is accurate?

Activity

Draw a line down the center of a sheet of paper. On the left side, set up and work out the following algebraic word problem. On the right side, explain what you are doing and why you are doing it.

Problem

Juan has five times as many girlfriends as Pedro. Carlos has one girlfriend less than Pedro. The total number of girlfriends [among] them is 20. How many does each gigolo have? (from the motion picture *Stand and Deliver*, 1988)

Extension

As background for the word problem, watch segments of the motion picture *Stand and Deliver* (1988) about the famous East L.A. math teacher, Jaime Escalante. Discuss the problem within the context of the movie. Talk about the various solutions offered by the film characters.

Idea Files

Activities and Questions to Foster Algebraic Thinking

Grade Bands	Activities	Questions
Pre-K–2	**Monkeys Playing in the Trees** Show students a picture of five monkeys, a large tree, and a small tree. Explain that all of the monkeys want to play in the trees. Ask the students to find all of the ways the monkeys can play in the trees. Create a two-column *t*-table to record each combination of monkeys at play (Cobb et al. 1977; Yackel 2002).	How many monkeys are there? How many trees? How many different ways can the five monkeys play in the two trees? If there are _____ monkeys in the big tree, how many monkeys will be in the small tree? How can you be sure you have all the possible combinations?
Grades 3–5	**Paper Folding to Make Name Cards** Ask students to make name cards for everyone in the class by folding a large sheet of paper repeatedly in half to create a card for each name. Have students draw a picture of the paper after each fold and think about how the number of cards increases (adapted from Burrill and Ferrini-Mundy 1998, 167–69).	What does the fold line do to the paper? How many cards do you have when you have no folds, one fold, two folds, three folds? How many folds do you need to make name cards for the entire class? How many cards would you make if you folded the paper 20 times? How many folds would it take to make 64 cards?
Grades 6–8	**Trapezoid Problem** Show students a diagram of a trapezoid ABCD with height h and bases b_1 and b_2. Ask students to explore different ways to find the area of the trapezoid. Have them express their methods for finding area in terms of height h and lengths of bases b_1 and b_2 (Burrill and Ferrini-Mundy 1998, 176–79).	What different methods did you find? What symbolic expressions did you use to express your reasoning? Are your symbolic expressions equivalent to each other? How can you decide? Can you show that the expressions are (are not) equivalent by symbolic manipulation?

Understanding the Big Ideas of Algebra

The patterns and habits of mind of algebraic thinking give students the mental tools they need to deal with the big ideas of algebra, including the following:

- Equality
- Variables
- Functions
- Symbolic representations
- Proportion

These ideas establish a foundation or framework for understanding algebra conceptually (Greenes and Findell 1999; Woodbury 2000). For many students in

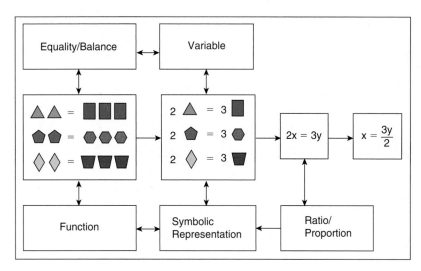

Figure 10.2   Big ideas of algebra interact in an algebraic sentence.

formal algebra classes, "the essence of algebra is memorizing rules and procedures" (Woodbury 2000, 227; see also Kieran 1992/1999). According to Skemp (1978), this "rules without reason" approach leads to only a partial or "instrumental understanding" of algebra. By contrast, a fuller, "relational understanding" results when students build up "a conceptual structure (schema) from which . . . [they] can (in principle) produce an unlimited number of plans for getting from any starting point within [their] schema to any finishing point" (14; quoted in Woodbury 2000, 22). In other words, studying the big ideas of algebra not only gives students a context for rules and procedures but also helps them "build conceptual structures to which future information and procedures can be added" (Woodbury 2000, 227).

Figure 10.2 shows how these big ideas act as a framework for composing a simple algebraic sentence such as $x = 3y/2$. First, we have **equality** and a linear-**function** pattern in a list of shapes. Then **variables** and quantities are identified and **represented** symbolically with numbers and letters. And finally the relationship is expressed as a ratio (**proportion**) in the algebraic sentence.

The big ideas of algebra and the patterns of algebraic thinking discussed earlier connect in meaningful ways. For example, generalizing and building rules underscore the big idea of functions; equating and doing and undoing prepare the way for working with ideas in the equations of algebraic sentences.

Equality/Balance

The concept of equality or balance is fundamental to both understanding and working with equations. Basically, "an equation is a mathematical sentence with an equals sign in it" (Long 1998, 71). That equals sign means "the same as," and it guides both our reading of the sentence expressions and our modifications of them. Whatever is done on one side of the equals sign (addition, subtraction, and so forth) must be equaled or balanced on the other side.

These concepts can be difficult for students to grasp, in part because many read the equals sign as a signal to "do it" or complete a computation. Asked to solve a simple problem, $8 + 4 = \square + 5$, many students will work linearly, adding 8 and 4 to get 12 or extending the addition to add the 5 and get 17 (Falkner et al. 1999, 232). Vance (1998) explains:

Many children view the equals sign only as an instruction to compute. This misconception is reinforced early on when they are shown the vertical computational format for $3 + 2 \left[\begin{smallmatrix} 3 \\ +2 \end{smallmatrix}\right]$; the bar under the lower number is a signal to find an answer. It is also true that pressing $3 + 2 =$ on a calculator results in the standard form of the answer.

(282–83)

Similarly, students may insist that the mathematical sentence's proper order is left to right (as in a sentence of words), with components of the problem first

Activities CD

For an activity in which students get hands-on experience with the basic ideas of balance and equivalence, see Activity 66, Equivalence, on the CD-ROM that accompanies this text.

followed by the solution. Given the sentence $7 = 3 + 4$, students in a combined first and second grade agreed that $3 + 4$ equals 7 but objected, "The sentence is wrong" and "It's backward." Even after the teacher explained that "the equals sign means that the quantity on each side of it has to be equal," one student persisted, "Yes, but it's the wrong way" (Vance 1998, 234).

To understand the concept of equality and its applications in algebra, students need learning experiences that not only dispel or avoid misconceptions about procedures but also demonstrate the ideas of balance and balancing concretely. In the early grades, this means *modeling* problems with cubes, counters, or tiles; then experimenting with operations that disturb and restore balance. For example, we might remove a block from one side of a modeled equation and then ask, "How can we make both sides equal again?"

It also means exploring different ways to write mathematical expressions ($4 + 3 + 2$ or $2 \times 5 - 1$ for 9) and sentences ($5 = 3 + 2$ and $3 + 2 = 4 + 1$) (Vance 1998, 283). In the middle and upper grades, students can build on and extend these early experiences with equality as they "learn ways to transform expressions and equations to equivalent forms and to modify inequalities to achieve equality" (Greenes and Findell 1999, 129). Figure 10.3 shows how a seventh grade student, Battersly, solved the problem of balancing a scale.

At all grade levels, work with hands-on manipulatives, such as algebra tiles, or virtual manipulatives, such as NCTM's interactive scales, helps students visualize and concretize the abstract concept of equality and balance (see the later Math Manipulatives feature on p. 234 and the Math and Technology feature). Composing and decomposing equations for a game such as Equate (described in the Mathematical Games feature) encourages students to think creatively as well as critically about algebraic expressions and sentences and to develop flexibility in the way they see and write those expressions and sentences.

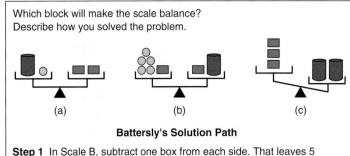

Which block will make the scale balance? Describe how you solved the problem.

(a)   (b)   (c)

Battersly's Solution Path

Step 1 In Scale B, subtract one box from each side. That leaves 5 spheres balancing 1 cylinder.

Step 2 In Scale A, substitute 5 spheres for the cyclinder. That makes 6 spheres balancing 2 boxes. Each box is equal to (6 ÷ 2), or 3 spheres.

Step 3 In Scale C, put in 3 spheres for each box and 5 spheres for each cylinder. That makes 9 spheres on the left and 10 spheres on the right. Add one sphere to the left pan to make the scale balance.

Figure 10.3 Balancing the scale.

Topics, Issues, and Explorations

Working in pairs, compose equations with geometric shapes, weights, and other measured quantities, numbers, and letters. Then take turns unbalancing and restoring balance in the equations. Talk about the ideas involved, both in the equations and in your modifications.

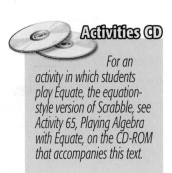

Activities CD

For an activity in which students play Equate, the equation-style version of Scrabble, see Activity 65, Playing Algebra with Equate, on the CD-ROM that accompanies this text.

Mathematical Games

Playing Algebra: Equate

Equate, developed by mathematician Mary Kay Beavers, is a math version of Scrabble. Students create algebraic sentences horizontally or vertically on an Equate board that, as in Scrabble, has squares for double and triple scores. Scores are determined by the equations' positioning on the board and by numbers written as subscripts on the tiles.

Level of play is determined by the types of tiles used. For the early grades, the tiles emphasize whole numbers, addition, and subtraction; for the middle grades, multiplication, division, and fractions; and for the upper grades, more fractions, positive and negative integers, and exponents.

Playing Equate encourages students to think creatively and critically. They must develop strategies for using their own tiles and those of the other players to their best advantage. And they must work backward as well as forward as they build equations upon equations.

The game underscores the role of equality and balance in composing and working with equations. Equa-

tions can be formed vertically as well as horizontally and can be expanded.

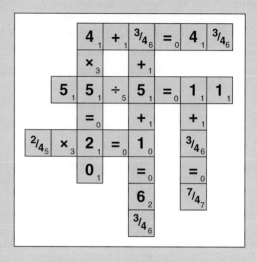

Equate is produced by Conceptual Math Media. See www.PlayEquate.com.

Variable

Activities CD

For an activity in which identifying variables plays a key role, go to Activity 107, Real Numbers, Math Games, and Alphanumeric Puzzles, on the CD-ROM that accompanies this text.

Understanding the big idea of the variable is essential both to understanding algebra and to applying algebraic ideas in problem-solving situations (Phillip 1992/1999; Schoenfeld and Arcavi 1988/1999). Moreover, "understanding the concept provides the basis for the transition from arithmetic to algebra and is necessary for the meaningful use of all advanced mathematics" (Schoenfeld and Arcavi 1988/1999, 150).

Procedurally, the definition of variable is relatively simple: "A variable is a letter [or other symbol] that is used to represent a number" (Long 1998, 71). Conceptually the idea is more complex. Greenes and Findell (1999) identify several uses for variables in algebra, including two that are particularly important in the pre-K–8 curriculum:

- representing "a specific unknown number or numbers as in the equations $5x + 3 = 13$ and $x^2 = 36$";

- representing "a varying quantity that has a relationship with another variable, as in $y = 4x$."

(130)

In early experiences with variables, the letter or symbol functions basically like a place saver, something to hold the spot of a component and call attention to filling in the spot with a number. In the examples to the right, question marks, orange triangles, and letters are used to represent variables.

$$5 + 6 + 3 = ?$$
$$14 = ? + 6 + 3$$
$$\triangle + \triangle + \triangle = 15$$
$$\triangle + \triangle + 5 = 15$$
$$15 = 3\triangle$$
$$x + 6 = 12$$
$$9 = x + 3$$

Math and Technology

Exploring Equivalence with a Pan Balance: NCTM'S Illuminations E-Resource

Equivalence is the subject of a series of interactive applets at NCTM's Illuminations Web site (http://www.illuminations. nctm.org/imath/across/balance).

The i-Math investigation uses a virtual pan balance for exploring the equivalence of objects, numbers, and symbols. The investigations become gradually more abstract and complex as students complete tasks successfully and as the level increases.

The investigation of equivalence has four parts:

Balancing Act, which explores the equivalence of collections of objects;

Stability in Numbers, which balances numeric expressions;

Extending to Symbols, which puts symbolic expressions on the scales; and

Exploring Equations Further, which extends the investigation to systems of equations.

In each task students use the balance as a research tool, exploring questions such as "What combination of shapes weighs the same as a yellow diamond?" or "What number sentences can you create using the number 12?"

Activities CD

For an activity that emphasizes equivalence concepts, go to Activity 80, Writing and Identifying Fractions, on the CD-ROM that accompanies this text.

Later experiences can explore using symbols or letters to represent varying quantities. Everyday life provides ample material for demonstrating and exploring this type of variable: the varying weights, heights, and sizes of classmates; weather facts such as temperature or barometer levels; batting averages and games scores. The everyday variable of house numbers also creates a context for discovering the idea of the series, which students can represent with a combination of numbers and letters: $x \pm 1$ (if numbering is consecutive), $x \pm 2$ (if numbering is even or odd).

Using two variables can be introduced with a basic math-facts task, such as the following:

Students will discover that there are multiple values for ● and ■, and finding values results in a table of the numbers that can be added to get 12.

Functions

Many believe that function is the cornerstone idea for teaching algebra and making it accessible to all students (Fey and Good 1985; Coxford et al. 1996; Hirsch 1998; Yerushalmy and Schwartz 1991). "Functions are everywhere," writes Susan Davidenko (1997/1999, 206), who uses everyday activities such as shopping, interacting with friends, and reading the newspaper to teach functions from

Activities CD

For an activity in which students develop an understanding of patterns by identifying and making them, see Activity 63, Patterns and Functions, on the CD-ROM that accompanies this text.

kindergarten to college. The Idea Files, "Finding Functions in the Real World," suggest everyday contexts for identifying and representing functions.

Greenes and Findell (1999, 132) identify several key components in the concept of function:

- A function is a relationship.
- The relationship involves sets of objects, numbers, shapes, and so forth.
- The sets are linked by a rule.
- The rule pairs elements in the sets.

A function, according to Greenes and Findell, operates like a machine with inputs and outputs. "If the rule is known, students can find an output value for each input number. Similarly, outputs may be given and students can determine the corresponding inputs . . . by using inverse operations" (132). For example, if the rule is squaring, the output for 2 will be 4 and for 4, 16; if the output is 25, the input is 5; and if the output is 144, the input will be 12. When the rule is doubling, if the in-

Idea Files

Finding Functions in the Real World

Activity	Representation
Finding Functions on the Street	
Study the way address numbers are assigned to houses, businesses, and buildings. Look for patterns in the numbers. Do they increase by one? By two? Are there even numbers on one side of the street and odd numbers on the other, or is there a different arrangement?	Make a map of your findings. Describe what you discovered in a sentence or two. Write a numbers sentence or an equation that shows the pattern.
Finding Functions in Shopping	
Your older sister has just given birth to quintuplets. You have been asked to buy what the new babies need at the shopping center, but you will need five of each item. Look for items in the infants' department. Write down the items and the prices.	Write a number sentence or equation to show how you would compute the price for five of any one item. Then write a number sentence or equation to show how you would compute the total price for all the items.
Finding Functions in the Kitchen	
Plan a birthday party for one of your closest friends. Your friend has told you that he does not like big parties, so you will need to keep it small, including your plans for refreshments. Find a recipe for a birthday cake; then cut the recipe to make it smaller—for example, by half or a fourth.	Write out the original recipe. Explain how you want to reduce the recipe. Then write a number sentence or equation to show how you will reduce the amount of each ingredient. Rewrite the recipe with the reduced amounts.
Finding Functions in Basketball	
You have been asked to keep score for a basketball game in the gym. To discover the patterns in the scoring, make a map of the court. On the map indicate where a basket would earn two and three points. What is the relationship between distance from the basket and the number of points scored? How about scores of one point? Do they fit the pattern?	Describe in one or two sentences the relationship between points scored and distance from the basket. Write number sentences or equations to describe how each type of score is computed; then write number sentences to show how you would determine the number of baskets scored in each scoring category. Explain where most of the scores in the game came from.

put is three purple circles, the output will be six purple circles; if the input is one square, the output will be two squares. See Figure 10.4, for example.

Comparing sets of objects to find patterns in their relationships prepares the way for understanding functions and for constructing the mental tools for making these function "machines." As children identify patterns in colored shapes, objects, or numbers, they are developing strategies for abstracting organizational principles. Extending their thinking to predict the next or previous component of the pattern and even further, to alter the pattern and create new ones calls not only for identifying but also for composing and testing the principles that in effect "rule" the pattern.

Figures 10.5 and 10.6 show how teachers used a situation from NCTM's Algebra Working Group to build a learning ladder from patterns to functions (Ferrini-Mundy et al. 1997/1999). In the activity, students used blue and white tiles to build square swimming pools with borders. Students in the early grades focused on sorting and counting tiles and made observations about the shape of the pool and the relationship between the number of blue tiles in the center and the number of white tiles around the edge. For example, they used blue and white tiles to build the fourth pool in the series with 16 blue tiles in the center surrounded by 20 white tiles.

Students in the middle grades not only explored patterns in color, shape, and number but also worked at representing the patterns in tables like the one below and making connections between physical models and definitions of concepts such as "squaring."

Number of White Tiles	Number of Blue Tiles
8	$1 \ (1^2)$
12	$4 \ (2^2)$
16	$9 \ (3^2)$
20	$16 \ (4^2)$
24	$25 \ (5^2)$

In the later grades, students identified variables and graphed data. The graphs showed a straight line for the white tiles (a linear function to show four times the number of blue tiles on a side plus four for the corner tiles) and a curved line for the blue tiles (a quadratic function to show squaring of the blue tiles). Students used the graphs to predict the structure of larger and larger pools (Ferrini-Mundy et al. 1997/1999).

Representation

In algebra, representing information is more than a way of communicating; it is also a tool for exploring and understanding. Plotting data in tables, maps, or graphs creates a structure or frame for the information that helps us see and understand relationships.

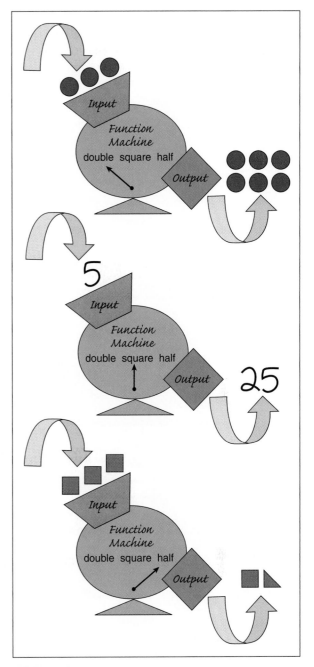

Figure 10.4 Function machine for doubling, squaring, and halving.

Activities CD

For an activity to represent patterns with colors and shapes, see Activity 59, Making and Guessing Patterns, on the CD-ROM that accompanies this text.

Figure 10.5 Pool problem.
(From Ferrini-Mundy et al. 1997/1999, 13. Adapted with permission from *Algebraic Thinking, Grades K–12*, copyright 1999 by the National Council of Teachers of Mathematics. All rights reserved.)

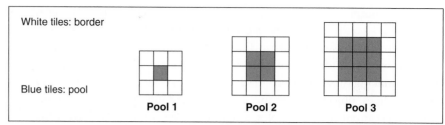

Pool Problem: Identify the pattern for building square swimming pools of blue tiles with a border of white tiles. Then use the pattern to find out how many blue and white tiles you will need to make larger pools.

For an activity in which students model pools to help understand models and patterns, see Activity 62, The Pool Problems, on the CD-ROM that accompanies this text.

For an activity in which students use M&Ms to write equations and explore equivalencies, see Activity 58, More M&M Math, on the CD-ROM that accompanies this text.

Grades K–2

- **Sorting, classifying** tiles
- **Modeling** structures in Pool Problem
- **Counting** tiles
- **Describing** shapes
- **Exploring** patterns in color, shape, and number

Grades 3–4

- **Modeling** structures in Pool Problem
- **Exploring** patterns in color, shape, and number
- **Identifying** relationships
- **Recording** numbers in tables
- **Generalizing** about number relationships and proportion

Grades 5–6

- **Generalizing** about number relationships and proportion
- **Identifying** and exploring variables
- **Representing** patterns in graphs
- **Comparing** patterns for increases in blue and white tiles
- **Predicting** data about larger pools

Figure 10.6 Learning Ladder: patterns to functions.
(Summarized from Ferrini-Mundy et al. 1997/1999, 112–19.)

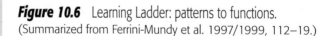

Topics, Issues, and Explorations

Look for patterns in the world around you—for example, in the arrangement of leaves on a rose bush, the prices in a grocery store, the price and size of servings at a fast-food restaurant. Record what you find in tables, diagrams, or numbers. Describe the patterns you discover in a mathematical expression or sentence; then compare and discuss your findings in class. Talk about Davidenko's statement "Functions are everywhere." Did you find this statement to be true?

Algebra uses three major types of representation:

- **pictorial** representation—including drawings, maps, pictographs, and diagrams;
- **graphical** representation—including bar, line, and circle graphs;
- **symbolic** representation—including variable expressions, tables and formulas.

Understanding this big idea of algebra can begin in the early grades with bar graphs of colors from a sorting activity such as the M&M's color activity in Figure 10.7, or tables of tally marks like the two-column table in Figure 10.8 that shows how many different combinations of five monkeys can play in two trees (see the Idea Files on p. 223 for a description of the "Monkeys Playing in the Trees" activity).

The Googol feature on p. 232 combines pictographs and tables to represent a variety of relationships among

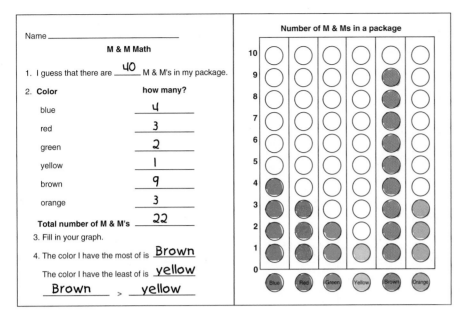

Figure 10.7 M&M's colors.

Figure 10.8 Table of tally marks for combinations of five monkeys in two trees.
(Adapted from Yackel 2002, 198).

objects, numbers, and classes of ideas. Younger students might work with one-to-one relationships as in "How We Love Apples." Chelsea used a pictograph of one apple to represent one person's vote. Older students, like Bryan whose work is shown in "Old MacDonald's Farm," can use relationships such as one animal to represent four animals in a pictograph to work with larger numbers. Bryan also drew his table on a computer, choosing art clips as pictographs.

Dominic combined drawings with arrays to organize and represent the information explored in a series of equations (see Figure 10.9). With each equation, Dominic exercises the important algebraic thinking of working forward and backward or doing and undoing as he reverses the multiplication sentences to write two division sentences for each equation.

Finally, middle- and upper-level students can explore the relationship between numbers and coordinate points on a graph as a prelude to understanding line graphs. To create the smiling block shape in Figure 10.10 on p. 233, Mayra first developed a set of coordinates; then she plotted the coordinate points on graph paper and connected the points. The project showed not only that information can be represented in a variety of ways but also that a graphic representation can reveal information hidden in a set of data—in this case, the picture hidden in Mayra's list of numbers.

Proportion

Proportion is both a big idea of algebra and a connecting idea for the mathematics curriculum specifically and the academic curriculum generally. In their discussion of the foundations of algebraic reasoning, Greenes and Findell (1999) describe the importance of proportion in this way:

> Fractions, unit costs, rates, percents, similar triangles, and right-triangle relationships are all examples of proportions that students confront in their mathematics programs. . . .
>
> Proportion is also a big idea in other areas of the curriculum. In geography and history, students reason proportionally when they interpret map scales and time lines. In science, in the study of simple machines students

Figure 10.9 Representing with drawings and arrays.

Activities CD
For an activity to represent quantities with pictures, see Activity 60, Pictographs, on the CD-ROM that accompanies this text.

Googol: BIG IDEAS in Mathematics

Pictographs

In these activities, students learn how to represent data with pictographs or representative drawings and how to organize that information in tables. The pictographs take an important step toward using symbols to represent numbers, objects, or ideas and toward understanding the concept of variables. Each pictograph can represent one, two, or more people, animals, objects, and so forth.

Activity 1

As a group, discuss your favorite ways to eat apples. Make a list of the ways: applesauce, juice, apple pie, caramel apples, plain, and so forth. Then vote and do tallies. Individually, work with the concept of one apple equaling one person or vote and draw a pictograph table of the vote.

Activity 2

Working individually as investigative reporters, survey the class to discover classmates' favorite animals, soft drinks, TV shows, games, or other activity. Make a list of the favorites mentioned, and keep tallies of the numbers for each. Then create a pictograph table to show the results. Work with the concept of two for one so that two votes for dogs as favorite animals is recorded as one dog pictograph and so forth.

Extensions

Discuss the pictograph tables in class, exploring questions such as these: Which pictographs represent the most votes, the least, the same, or almost the same? What is the relationship between the most and the least?

Use a computer to draw the table. Experiment with different values for the pictographs—5 to 1, 10 to 1, and so forth. Devise a way to represent remainders and fractions.

Pictograph, "How We Love Apples"

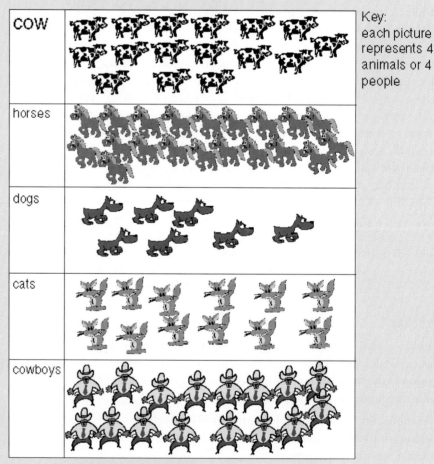

Pictograph, "Old MacDonald's Farm"

explore the proportional relationships illustrated by gears, pulleys, and levers. In art, students make use of proportions when drawing the human figure or constructing scale models. In music, students use proportions to transpose melodies from one key to another.

(134–35)

Understanding proportional relationships plays an important role in our discussion of part–whole relationships later in this text (see Chapters 12–13). Activities that lay a foundation for studies of proportion might include the following:

- **Making pictograph tables** with varying number-to-pictograph relationships (one-to-one, two-to-one, three-to-one, and so forth)
- **Comparing prices** of products to find the better buy
- **Drawing maps** of places and things to scale
- **Creating a fractal design** with triangles or other shapes
- **Making models** of square and round swimming pools with tiles, compass and paper, or other tools; then doubling, tripling, and so forth, the size

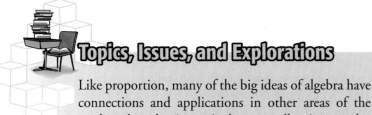

Topics, Issues, and Explorations

Like proportion, many of the big ideas of algebra have connections and applications in other areas of the math and academic curriculum as well as in everyday life. Brainstorm in small groups to identify connections and applications for each big idea. Then discuss the implications of what you found for the place of algebra in the pre-K–8 mathematics curriculum.

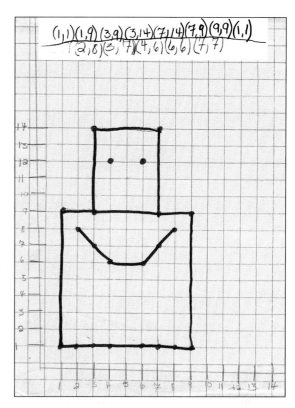

Figure 10.10   Picture graph.

Building Bridges from Arithmetic to Algebra

Although algebraic thinking and ideas are integral to the mathematics curriculum throughout elementary and middle school, the transition from the number-based operations of arithmetic to the more symbol-based problems of algebra can be difficult for many students. Several factors contribute to students' discomfort: the increased abstractness from arithmetic to algebra, a tendency for learning materials in algebra to minimize real-life applications and imaginative contexts, and students' feeling that the procedures and rules of algebra are radically different from any they have studied before.

To make the transition to algebra as seamless as possible, students need to continue the hands-on experiences that helped make number operations concrete. They need real-life and imaginative contexts for learning that make both problems and outcomes meaningful. And they need to understand the connections between working with numbers and working with variables so that they can see algebra as a continuation of rather than a departure from the mathematics they already know (see Kiernan 1991/2002).

Hands-on Algebra

Some educators have suggested that manipulatives and hands-on learning experiences should be deemphasized in algebra and even in prealgebra in order

Activities CD

For an activity about proportion, go to Activity 106, The Golden Ratio, Phi, and Physical Beauty, on the CD-ROM that accompanies this text.

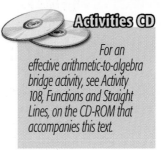

Activities CD

For an effective arithmetic-to-algebra bridge activity, see Activity 108, Functions and Straight Lines, on the CD-ROM that accompanies this text.

to emphasize symbols and abstract ideas. "How can you model variables like *x* or *y*?" they ask. "Won't concrete models change algebraic expressions into simple number expressions?"

Of course, it is not only possible to model variables with manipulatives, but it is also an effective way for students to visualize and explore relationships. Earlier in this chapter, we saw how students modeled swimming pools with blue and white tiles as they explored patterns and constructed the concepts basic to functions. On the other hand, Alge-tiles are manipulatives developed specifically for studying algebra (see the Math Manipulatives feature). Students use the tiles to model relationships as represented by equations. The tiles make modifying the equations a visual and tactile experience as well as a mental exercise.

Real-Life and Imaginative Contexts

Tying algebra concepts to the world students know makes them seem more meaningful and real. For example, deciding on the best buy for soda pop, 12 cans for $3.60 or 6 cans for $2.40, is a real-life proportion problem that many students can relate to at several levels—physically with sight, touch, and taste; mentally with previous knowledge of price per item and value; and even emotionally when students have a personal interest in the purchase, such as buying the soda pop for a class party.

Stories that engage students' imaginations put concepts in a meaningful and also memorable context. Story lines serve as organizers for the information while story elements such as characters and themes help students see the concepts as important. For example, in the story *A Remainder of One* by Elinor Pinczes, factoring 25 is important to the left-out ant because it helps him find a way to march in the Queen's parade with the other ants (see the Mathematics in Literature feature in chapter 7). In *Anno's Magic Seeds* by Mitsumasa Anno (1995), understanding the "magic" of the multiplying seeds involves algebraic reasoning. The plot develops a pattern of increases that students can draw, graph, and represent algebraically as a linear function.

Connections

Students frequently object to the apparent alien-ness of algebra. "Math is supposed to be about numbers," one student complained. "Letters are for English class"

Activities CD

For an activity in which there is an imaginative context for exploring variables and number patterns, see Activity 64, Anno's Magic Seeds, on the CD-ROM that accompanies this text.

Math Manipulatives

Alge-tiles

Alge-tiles are hands-on materials for investigating ratios, integers, polynomials, factors, and equations. A central idea of using Alge-tiles is "how your fingers do a lot of thinking for you" (Scully, Scully, and Le Sage 1991, i). The authors of the Alge-tiles handbook suggest a reflective approach to studying algebra with manipulatives: "Students will DO something with the materials, REFLECT on what they have done, formulate some theories (THINK), DO something with a model of the materials, REFLECT on what they have done, formulate a definite strategy or algorithm (THINK), and DO (using the strategy, algorithm, etc.)" (Scully et al. 1991, iii).

A set of Alge-tiles consists of red and white *1* tiles, green and white *x* and x^2 tiles, orange and white *y* and y^2 tiles, and gray and white *xy* tiles.

Represented in tiles, the equation $3x - 2 = 4$ looks like this:

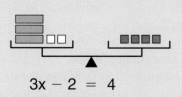

$$3x - 2 = 4$$

The solution $x = 2$ looks like this:

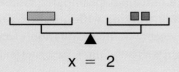

$$x = 2$$

Alge-tiles are produced by Exclusive Educational Products of Ontario, Canada, **www.exclusiveeducational.ca**.

(Martinez 2002, 326). To dispel this misconception, we need to help "students make explicit links between their arithmetic and the nonnumerical notation of algebra" (Kieran 1991/2002, 221). Physical models such as Alge-tiles make this link by connecting algebraic expressions with quantity. However, many students become disconnected at the level of written expressions. Numbers in mathematical expressions look familiar and right; letters do not.

We can build bridges from arithmetic to algebra by following these guidelines:

1. Start with what the students know.

2. Sequence activities from where students are now to where they need to be.

3. Reinforce links by paralleling numerical and nonnumerical expressions.

Figure 10.11 demonstrates a sequence of exercises designed to show the similarities between operations with numbers and operations

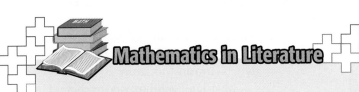

Mathematics in Literature

Anno's Magic Seeds

Anno's Magic Seeds by Mitsumasa Anno (1995) is written in the tradition of "Jack and the Bean Stalk"; however, in this case, the "magic" involves the number of seeds rather than the size of the plant.

A wizard gave Jack two magic seeds and told him to eat one seed and plant the other to give him two seeds—one for eating, one for planting—for the next year. Jack followed the wizard's advice for several years; then he decided to plant both seeds. That gave him two new plants, each bearing two seeds, and he ate one seed and planted three. The story continues with Jack eating and planting and the number of plants and seeds increasing each year.

Activity 1

Listen to the story as a class. Use a calculator or pencil and paper to try to keep track of the number of seeds by multiplying, adding, and subtracting as the story progresses. At the end compare answers. Discuss the "magic" involved.

Activity 2

In small groups, use beans to model the changing number of seeds. Draw a branching-tree diagram to show the changes.

Activity 3

Explore the concept of doubling with beans or other objects. Develop a graph to show the concept. Then develop a graph to show the changing number of seeds in the story. Compare the story graph to the doubling graph. How are they alike? How are they different?

Exercise Set 1: Carry out the operations indicated, and explain.

1. $2 + 2 + 2 =$ _____ $a + a + a =$ _____
2. $3 + 3 + 3 + 3 =$ _____ $b + b + b + b =$ _____
3. $2 \times 2 \times 2 =$ _____ $a \times a \times a =$ _____
4. $3 \times 3 \times 3 \times 3 =$ _____ $b \times b \times b \times b =$ _____

Exercise Set 2: Carry out the operations indicated, and explain.

1. $2 + 2 =$ _____ $2a + 2a =$ _____
2. $3 + 6 =$ _____ $3b + 6b =$ _____
3. $2 + 3 + 6 =$ _____ $2c + 3c + 6c =$ _____

Exercise Set 3: Carry out the operations indicated, and explain.

1. $3 \times 3 =$ _____ $a \times a =$ _____
2. $2 \times 2 \times 2 =$ _____ $b \times b \times b =$ _____
3. $4 \times 4 \times 4 \times 4 =$ _____ $c \times c \times c \times c =$ _____

Exercise Set 4: Carry out the operations indicated, and explain.

1. $2^2 \times 2^3 =$ _____ $a^2 \times a^3 =$ _____
2. $2^2 \times 2^3 \times 2^1 =$ _____ $a^2 \times a^3 \times a^1 =$ _____
3. $3^2 \times 3^2 \times 3^1 =$ _____ $b^2 \times b^2 \times b^1 =$ _____

Exercise Set 5: Carry out the operations indicated, and explain.

1. $2 + (4 + 6) =$ _____ $2a + (4a + 6a) =$ _____
2. $(2 + 4) + 6 =$ _____ $(2a + 4a) + 6a =$ _____
3. $(2 + 6) + 4 =$ _____ $(2a + 6a) + 4a =$ _____

Exercise Set 6: Carry out the operations indicated, and explain.

1. $2 \times (4 \times 6) =$ _____ $2a \times (4a \times 6a) =$ _____
2. $(2 \times 4) \times 6 =$ _____ $(2a \times 4a) \times 6a =$ _____
3. $(2 \times 6) \times 4 =$ _____ $(2a \times 6a) \times 4a =$ _____

Test Set: Carry out the operations indicated, and explain.

1. $3^2 \times 3^2 \times 2^2 =$ _____   2. $a^2 \times a^2 \times b^2 =$ _____
3. $1^3 \times 2^3 \times 3^3 =$ _____   4. $a^3 \times b^3 \times c^3 =$ _____
5. $1^2 + 2^3 =$ _____   6. $a^2 + b^3 =$ _____
7. $1^2 + 2^3 + 3^3 =$ _____   8. $a^2 + b^3 + c^3 =$ _____

Exercise Set 7: Carry out the operations indicated, and explain.

1. $2^2 \times 2^1 + 2^3 =$ _____ $a^2 \times a^1 + a^3 =$ _____
2. $3^1 + 3^1 \times 3^2 =$ _____ $b^1 + b^1 \times b^2 =$ _____
3. $1^2 + 1^3 \times 1^4 =$ _____ $c^2 + c^3 \times c^4 =$ _____
4. $2 \times (4 + 6) \times (1 + 2) + (3 + 4) =$ _____
5. $2a \times (4a + 6a) \times (b + 2b) + (3a + 4b) =$ _____

Figure 10.11 From arithmetic to algebra.

with letters. It also helps students distinguish between factors and terms and understand the use of parentheses in simplifying (Martinez 2002, 329).

Diversity in Learning and Thinking Mathematically

Responding to the traditional view of algebra as advanced mathematics for exceptional students, James Kaput (1998) argues for "transforming algebra from an engine of inequity to an engine of mathematical power" (25). To do this, we need to make an important distinction. Studying algebra needs to be deinstitutionalized and made part of every student's mathematics curriculum. We must exchange, according to Kaput, our commitment to "Algebra, the Institution" for a commitment to "Algebra, the Web of Knowledge and Skill" (25).

Lusher, a middle school in New Orleans, has designed an eighth-grade algebra curriculum that makes algebra accessible for all students. All students take either a prealgebra or an algebra course. The school uses multiple assessment measures, and students are encouraged to discover and understand concepts rather than memorize and apply rules (Germain-McCarthy 2001).

Madeline Landrum, who teaches at Lusher, believes that "all students can learn mathematics." She applies this belief to teaching algebra by creating a cooperative and flexible learning environment. Her students are given the time and the tools to work with concepts, and she employs a variety of teaching techniques to "break down the walls that hinder their learning" (Germain-McCarthy 2001, 68).

Because Lusher has an art focus, Landrum uses art to engage her students. The proportion activities described in the Mathematics in the Real World feature incorporate art historically with the Greek idea of the Golden Rectangle and directly as students make the calculations for a Golden Rectangle picture frame and measure themselves and each other for Golden Rectangle proportions.

Amy Johnston is another teacher who works to make algebraic concepts accessible to all students. Her lessons on equations, representation, and functions are described in this chapter's Teacher Pro-File.

Mathematics in the Real World

Golden Rectangle

The Golden Rectangle is a Greek idea of a rectangle of perfect proportions. Those proportions are found in nature in pine cones, eggs, and shells. Greek architects used the Golden Rectangle to design the Parthenon, and sculptors have based the proportions of their creations on it.

Activity 1

"Artists often use the golden rectangle because it is considered to be pleasing to the eye. The length of a golden rectangle is about 1.62 times its width. Suppose you are making a picture frame in the shape of a golden rectangle. You have a 46-inch piece of wood. What are the length and width of the largest frame you can make? Round your answers to the nearest tenth of an inch" (*Algebra* 1997, 193; quoted in Germain-McCarthy 2001, 63).

Activity 2

Use a tape measure and the Golden Rectangle to search for "divine" body proportions (Germain-McCarthy 2001, 66). Measure classmates, family members, and others in two places: (1) head to the navel and (2) navel to the feet. Use the first measure for the numerator of a fraction and the second for the denominator. How close is the result to the divine proportion of 1.62?

Extension

Read Theoni Pappas's (1993, 45–47) story "Penrose & the Golden Rectangle." Apply Pappas's method for creating Golden Rectangles without measuring. Then use a ruler and calculator to look for examples of Golden Rectangles in art, nature, and everyday life.

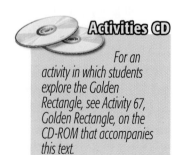
Activities CD

For an activity in which students explore the Golden Rectangle, see Activity 67, Golden Rectangle, on the CD-ROM that accompanies this text.

Teacher Pro-File

Amy Johnston
First and Second Grade

Amy Johnston Teaches Algebraic Concepts in First and Second Grade

Amy Johnston's class at Tomasita Elementary School combined first and second grades in a cooperative learning environment. Amy described her own role as counselor and friend as well as teacher and emphasized the importance of her students' working out ideas for themselves and becoming skilled mathematical thinkers rather than repositories of math facts.

Amy's algebra lessons focused on algebraic thinking and big ideas. Her students wrote equations, used drawings to represent relationships, and discovered patterns. She encouraged them to reflect about their thinking by writing explanations as part of the problem-solving process.

Procedures for Writing Story Problems and Equations

Amy began the story problem/equation activity by reading a story problem aloud: "I was walking in the park and I saw some squirrels playing together. There were nine squirrels; then four got scared and ran away." She had several students retell the story and explain the order of events. Then she asked questions: How many squirrels are left? Are there more or less? How do you know? Are they separating or combining?

Once they understood the major ideas, the students worked on representing the situation with drawings, words, and a number equation. Then they created their own story problems.

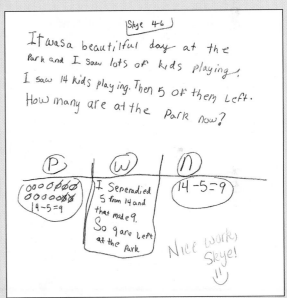

"It was a beautiful day. . . ."

Procedures for Exploring Patterns and Functions

Amy used several lessons to explore patterns and functions. Each lesson began with a story that she read aloud and tied into the topic.

1. **Making Patterns.** Amy read *The Napping House* and then asked students to identify different patterns in the classroom. She introduced specific types of patterns: AB, AAB, ABB, ABC, AABB. For examples, she used sound and motion (snapping, clapping, stomping) as well as colors, letters, blocks, and the students themselves (boy, boy, girl). Students first identified patterns and then made their own using construction paper.

2. **Guess My Pattern.** This lesson began with the story *Bring the Rain to Kapiti Plain.* Amy used manipulatives to create patterns and had students identify and continue the patterns. Then in groups of two, the students played Guess My Pattern. Partners took turns at creating patterns and guessing and explaining what comes next. For variety, teams changed the type of manipulative they were using every 5 minutes.

3. **T-charts and Dot Patterns.** Amy began by reading two stories, *The House That Jack Built* and *I Know an Old Woman Who Swallowed a Fly.* She used an overhead to show dot patterns and to draw a t-chart. She explained the use of the t-chart in identifying functions. Then students completed t-charts for number of eyes for 1–10 children, number of fingers for 1–10 children, number of legs for 1–10 dogs, and number of toes on one foot for 1–10 children.

4. **The Functionator.** The story for this activity was *Two of Everything.* Students worked with a Functionator, a box with two holes, one labeled "This Goes In," the other labeled "This Comes Out." Students put a number such as 2 on one hole and pulled a number such as 4 out the other end; then they deduced the pattern or function.

Daniel's worksheet 1. (Page 219 from *Investigations, Number Games and Story Problems Gr. 1*) by Marlene Kliman and Susan J. Russell. Copyright © 2004 by Pearson Education, Inc. Reprinted by permission.)

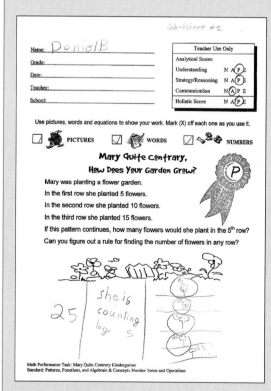

Daniel's worksheet 2.
(© Exemplars, 2005. Visit www.exemplars.com to view free sample tasks and rubrics.)

Outcomes

Amy's students were comfortable with multiple representations of concepts. They verbalized answers and explanations and worked effectively from beginnings (write an equation to solve the problem) or endings (write a problem to fit the equation).

They were able to identify and make different patterns. They could continue patterns with manipulatives or t-charts, and they could deduce the functions behind the patterns. For example, in the "Mary Quite Contrary" problem, Daniel projected 25 flowers in the fifth row of the garden and wrote a rule to cover the increases: "She is counting by 5."

Commentary

Reflecting about teaching algebraic concepts to first and second graders, Amy explained that she prepared her own materials to fit her district's standards and benchmarks. She was particularly pleased with the literature component of the pattern and function activities. The stories engaged the students' interest and helped them to stay on task during the group work.

For the future, she identified several challenges:

- broadening the range of difficulty so that students stay involved and productive longer;
- encouraging students to think about problems rather than rushing to find concrete answers;
- emphasizing algebraic concepts rather than procedures.

Amy writes:

I want my students to think about a problem before solving it and I want them to be able to tell me how they solved it. When I asked my students how they got their answer, I got a lot of responses like "I just knew it" or "I don't know. I just added." I want them to tell me *how* they knew it or *why* they knew to add instead of subtract [or to double numbers or to count by fives]. Thinking about math is the first step to understanding it and I want my students to understand math as much as possible.

. . . I am absolutely in my element when I am in my classroom, and when I am not there I am thinking about it and wishing I were. I love doing and teaching math and I hope my enthusiasm shows in the classroom. I think that if my students see that I am not anxious about math, but instead excited about it, they too will learn to enjoy it—or at least not fear it. My ultimate goal as a classroom teacher is to produce students who are independent learners as well as excellent problem solvers not only in school but also in the real world.

Pictures of Amy's students at work.

◀◀◀ LOOKING BACK

The place of algebra in the mathematics curriculum is expanding. Instead of being introduced in high school as a course in advanced mathematics, algebra is being studied across the grades. In elementary and middle school, students develop their algebraic thinking skills as they learn to find patterns, generalize and deduce principles, and represent mathematical ideas in a variety of ways, including drawings, tables, and equations. They develop the mental tools that enable them to understand and work effectively with the big ideas of algebra such as equality, variables, functions, proportion, and symbols.

Although unfamiliar aspects of algebra such as variables continue to puzzle some students, teachers can smooth the transition from numerical to nonnumerical expressions by continuing to use hands-on methods, by presenting concepts in meaningful and imaginative contexts, and by making the links between arithmetic and algebra explicit.

Questions for Further Thought, Discussion, and Research

1. For many people, algebra is the mathematics of x's and y's; however, for centuries algebra used words rather than letters or symbols to express ideas. Do some reading about the history of algebraic expressions. How were variables expressed in the early years? When did mathematicians begin to use letters and symbols? What was the effect on algebra?

2. Increasingly, school districts are becoming committed to the "algebra for all" philosophy; however, some students ask, "Why do I need to know this?" Brainstorm as a group to answer that question. Make a list of examples from the worlds of work and commerce, everyday life, art, hobbies, sports, and music as well as school subjects including mathematics.

3. Putting algebra in contexts is an important way to tie the concepts to everyday experience and the reality of students' own worlds. Frequently texts ask students themselves to write word problems to fit a situation or idea. Sharing their work demonstrates the many situations that can be summarized in a mathematical sentence and in effect reverses the process of generalizing by reconstructing specific instances. Individually write two or three word problems for each of the following mathematical sentences. Share your problems in a group. Discuss the potential for student learning from the activity.

$$7 + 19 - 10 = 16$$

$$2x - 6 = 0$$

$$\frac{x}{3} = 4$$

CHAPTER 11

Working with Data

LOOKING AHEAD >>>>

Data are everywhere—behind every object, around every corner, in front of your nose, under your feet, and above your head. Data are any kind of information that can be counted, measured, or quantified and displayed in charts, tables, or graphs.

Understanding data comprises not only important mathematical skills but also essential life skills. We use data to interpret and make decisions about the world around us—to choose the best buys in cars, groceries, clothes, and health care; to spend or invest our earnings; to select candidates to vote for or schools we and our families want to attend.

Succeeding in a 21st-century world of data calls for a sophisticated grasp of what numbers mean in a variety of contexts as well as how data can be displayed, interpreted, and even manipulated to influence decisions. To develop this level of understanding, students need to work with data from the earliest grades. They need to collect and analyze their own data, to read and interpret data collected by others, and to use data to draw inferences and make predictions.

Activities CD

For an activity that helps students see data everywhere in their worlds, see Activity 69, Collecting Data in Our Worlds, on the CD-ROM that accompanies this text.

Worlds of Data

We often say that we live in the information age. It would be equally accurate to say we live in an age of data, data, and more data.

More than 250 homes destroyed by 6,500-acre wildfire!

Highs will be in the 90s; lows in the 60s.

Unemployment hits 7.5%, the highest level since 1991.

The DOW rose 280 points; the NASDAQ fell 12.8 points.

The price of a gallon of unleaded averages $2.79 in the city; $2.82 across the state.

Less than half (39%) of those polled said they recycled at home; less than a quarter (22%) said they recycled at work.

Mathematics in the Real World

Data in Newspapers

Newspapers are filled with data. Reporters use numbers to support points and to ground their stories in facts. Data help reporters describe who, what, when, where, how, and why and to make their information credible to readers.

Activity 1

Find a newspaper story with data that seems important or interesting to you. Summarize the story; then explore the data by asking these questions:

What kinds of numbers do you find?
Are the numbers exact or approximate?
What do the data tell you?
Do the data seem reliable? Why or why not?
Do the data add to or detract from the story?
What makes the data memorable or not memorable?

Activity 2

In small groups, survey a newspaper for data. Assign a section of the paper to each group member. Devise tally charts to keep track of the kinds of data you find and the number of stories with and the number without data. Pool the chart information to create a data profile of the edition of the newspaper. Then use the profile to answer questions, such as these:

Which section of the paper uses the most data and the least data? Why?

What types of data are most often found in sports, business, health, food, and other sections?

What do you need to know about numbers to understand the different types of data?

For more math-in-newspapers activities, see Martinez and Martinez (2001).

Our personal worlds of home, school, work, and play take direction and stay afloat on a river of data-filled information—data about money, time, weather, test scores and grades, game scores and standings. Similarly, our public worlds including society, the nation, and the world surround us with data about the economy and the environment, politics, cultures, science, and history.

Understanding and living successfully in our worlds depend in a large part on understanding and working effectively with the data and data systems of those worlds. We need—

- **to read data accurately** (to know numbers' values, to distinguish percentage points from decimal points and whole numbers from fractions);
- **to place data in appropriate contexts and relationships** (to distinguish money numbers from measurement numbers, exact numbers from approximate numbers);
- **to use data to infer and predict** (to understand the effect of a 15% drop or rise in price, population, temperature, opinions);
- **to evaluate data and make judgments based on its reliability** (to get beyond numbers as facts to numbers as indicators and evidence);
- **to recognize manipulated data** (to tell the differences between statistical truth and statistical half-truths and lies).

The importance of working with data is reflected in the NCTM *Principles and Standards*:

Mathematical Thinking

The Counting Activity

Developing statistical reasoning skills can begin with a process as simple as counting. The counting is used to collect data for analysis. As students count, analyze, interpret, and represent their data, they are describing that data in greater detail and depth; therefore, the activity can be called an exercise in descriptive statistics.

Activity

Select something to count. Choose from people, animals, objects, behaviors, events, and so forth. Identify at least four categories within your subject to count; for example, if your topic is hair color, you might look for people with brown, blonde, red, and black hair. Make a counting log and keep a tally as you collect your data. Use your categories to help you organize your findings.

Begin analyzing your data by computing totals—total number counted, numbers counted for each category. Calculate the percentage of the whole represented by each category. Then calculate means and medians.

Make a bar graph and a pie chart to represent your findings.

Answer these questions: What does your data tell you? Do you see any patterns? Can you draw any conclusions from the data? Do the results raise any questions?

The amount of data available to help make decisions in business, politics, research, and everyday life is staggering: Consumer surveys guide the development and marketing of products. Polls help determine political campaign strategies, and experiments are used to evaluate the safety and efficacy of new medical treatments. Statistics are often misused to sway public opinion on issues or to misrepresent the quality and effectiveness of commercial products. Students need to know about data analysis and related aspects of probability in order to reason statistically—skills necessary to becoming informed citizens and intelligent consumers.

(NCTM 2000, 48)

Unlike practice in many countries, NCTM proposes a Data Analysis and Probability Standard that spans the grades. From prekindergarten to grade 12, the standard proposes an emphasis on "gathering and using data wisely" and "reasoning about data and statistics [that] will serve students well in work and in life" (NCTM 2000, 48).

Students develop statistical reasoning skills as they "work directly with data" (NCTM 2000, 48). They learn how to collect and organize, display and analyze data and in the

Googol: BIG IDEAS in Mathematics

Lying by the Numbers

Can numbers lie? Perhaps not the numbers themselves—but they can be used to distort the truth. We have all heard Disraeli's famous statement "There are three kinds of lies: lies, damned lies, and statistics." Darrell Huff, author of *How to Lie with Statistics*, even coined a new word for manipulating people with lying numbers: *statisticulation* for *statistics* + *manipulation*. Here are some ways data can be used to lie:

The lying average—averaging high numbers with low numbers to skew perceptions of the whole (for example, averaging a $100,000 salary with a $20,000 salary to give an average of $60,000);

The lying sample—generalizing the results of a small, favorable sample (for example, when 7 out of 10 children in a sample of 10 choose Cap'n Crunch for breakfast, suggesting that 70% of all children prefer it);

The misleading decimal point—using numbers to the right of the decimal point to make approximate numbers seem exact (for example, asking 100 people for the approximate hours they sleep, getting a total of 783.1, dividing by 100, and "announcing that people sleep an average of 7.831 hours a night (Huff 1993, 106);

The lying visual display—manipulating a visual image to make numbers look more impressive than they really are (for example, showing the federal government's share of our national income by shading all of the states with small populations and large areas instead of states with large populations and small areas (Huff 1993, 101–3).

Activity

Develop and share some statistical lies of your own. Discuss what these lies suggest about reading, collecting, and using data in your own life.

Preservice teachers' "My Data" project.

process how to interpret and use data to make decisions and predictions and to answer the question "What are the meanings of the data in my life?" A group of preservice teachers used a variety of charts, graphs, and collages to try to answer that question for themselves. The resulting displays ranged from straightforward lists of vital statistics to complex charts and graphs (see "My Data" photos).

The Process of Working with Data

Although data collection may rely on methods as simple as counting and measuring, making sense of the information can be both complex and challenging, particularly when data sets are massive and multilayered such as an opinion poll or a marketing survey. It is helpful to approach working with data not as a collection of independent procedures to be learned and practiced, but as a process with a range of applications, simple to complex.

Figure 11.1 shows the flow of activity in the working-with-data process. It begins with **identifying a topic**, then proceeds to **collecting and organizing data**—steps that interact when organizing tools such as tables and tally sheets help shape and guide the collection of data. **Analysis** is a reflective stage in the process, involving searching the organized data for patterns and meanings. And **displaying and interpreting the data** also interact as data are graphed or charted to show the analyzed patterns and to give an interpretive picture of meaning. The final stage—**understanding, concluding, predicting**—might have the general heading: "Using the Data." It suggests applications that encompass the topic represented by the data as well as other related data sets—for example, concluding from a class survey of eye colors that there are mostly brown eyes in the class and, by implication, that brown may be the most common eye color.

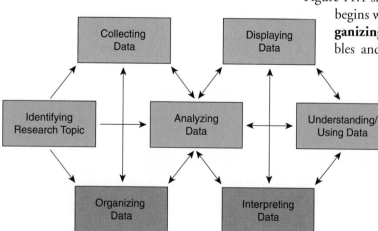

Figure 11.1 The process of working with data.

Instead of a piecemeal approach to statistical reasoning skills, students need to work with the entire process but at different levels, "becoming increasingly sophisticated across the grades so that by the end of high school students have a sound knowledge of elementary statistics" (NCTM 2000, 48). Very young children might select a topic such as eye color, survey the class and keep a tally sheet, and then count the tally marks and make a bar graph to show the results. Interpretation and prediction would probably be limited to explaining the most and least colors and perhaps speculating about eye color in the rest of the school. Older students might choose a slightly more complex topic such as hours of television watched per day, do a survey tally and frequency count, display the results in a graph (see Figure 11.2), but then use mathematical tools to find the average hours watched (the mean), the midpoint of hours (the median), and the most frequently given number (the mode).

Collecting and Organizing Data

Some of the earliest-learned math skills such as counting, sorting, and classifying provide useful tools for collecting and organizing data. Children are naturally curious about everything around them. Observant teachers, such as Judy Taylor, build on this natural curiosity and children's eagerness to use their developing math skills to create an investigative classroom environment. "Walk into a second-grade classroom in my school, and you will likely be greeted with a question: 'Would you rather read fiction or nonfiction?' 'Which football team do you think will score the most points this weekend?' 'How far away from school do you live?' " (Taylor 1997, 146).

With questions as a beginning point, Ms. Taylor's young scientists collect raw data about favorite rocks, parts of speech, preferences for white or chocolate milk, favorite snacks, zoo animals for a papier-mâché project, bedtimes, heights, and lunch choices. "Dealing with data," she writes, has "become a natural part of their daily lives" (Taylor 1997, 149).

Collecting the raw data involves three key elements:

the question (an inquiry or topic to shape and guide the investigation);

the count (by object, time, or occurrence);

the record (tallies, logs, surveys).

For younger students, questions about things touching their own lives usually generate the most enthusiasm, while the counting process may be one-by-one with a record of tally marks or drawings. Older students often pose questions related to the larger world, such as concerns about time or costs. They may still count and tally, but they often work with larger numbers and distinguish between values of data and frequency of occurrences (NCTM 2000, 49).

An effective plan for collecting data, such as a tally chart or a survey log marked with categories, begins the process of organizing raw data:

- data about objects can be organized by physical characteristics such as color, size, or weight;
- data about actions, by frequency, duration, or actor;
- data about opinions, by *pro, con*, and *indifferent* or on a scale, such as 1–5.

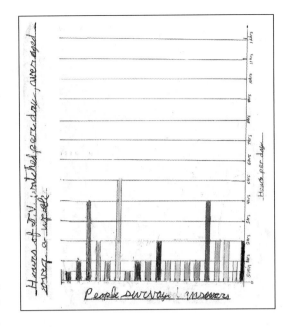

Figure 11.2 Hours watching TV.

Topics, Issues, and Explorations

Choose a topic for collecting data; then work stage by stage through the working-with-data process. Write a log explaining your use of tools and concepts at each stage of the process. Discuss the value of the data you found and the value, limits, and applications of the conclusions you reached.

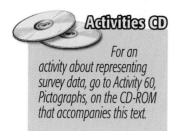

Usually the organizing principle for the data is more or less defined by the research question. For example, the question "What is your favorite animal?" points to an organizing principle of kinds of animals; the categories for data could be animals' names in the survey (cats, dogs, horses, and so forth) or animals named by those questioned (snakes, monkeys, crocodiles, and so forth). Data from a more complex question, such as "How many hours of television do you watch each week?" could be organized by individuals (as shown in Figure 11.2), by average hours over a period of several weeks, or by total hours for one week. Important questions to ask in helping students identify an organizing principle include the following:

- What categories or groups can you identify in the data?
- Do any categories overlap?
- Are any data left out?
- Can the data be organized in more than one way?

In addition to charts and survey sheets, students use drawings, pictures, manipulatives (physical and virtual), and letters of the alphabet to organize data. On the computer, Chris organized a data set of 21 flags into seven rows by type of flag, with three flags in each row (see Figure 11.3). Allison used drawings and letters of the alphabet to organize the data about streets and houses and to answer questions about the data (see Figure 11.4). Nicholas cre-

Topics, Issues, and Explorations

Observe a group of people (such as students in a class you are taking). Explore the different ways you might collect data and categorize them (eye or hair color, type of shoe, left handed or right handed, color of backpack or book bag, color or style of clothes, and so forth). Discuss which ways yield the most interesting information and best fit the group.

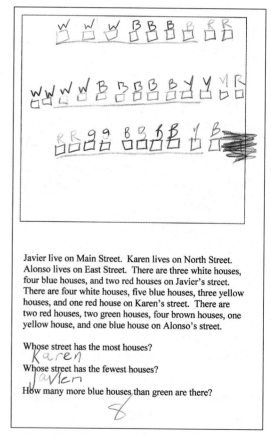

Javier live on Main Street. Karen lives on North Street. Alonso lives on East Street. There are three white houses, four blue houses, and two red houses on Javier's street. There are four white houses, five blue houses, three yellow houses, and one red house on Karen's street. There are two red houses, two green houses, four brown houses, one yellow house, and one blue house on Alonso's street.

Whose street has the most houses?
Karen
Whose street has the fewest houses?
Javier
How many more blue houses than green are there?
8

Figure 11.4 Organizing streets and houses.

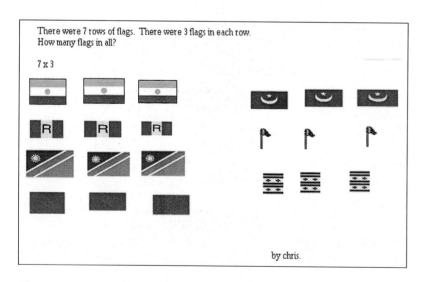

There were 7 rows of flags. There were 3 flags in each row. How many flags in all?

7 x 3

by chris.

Figure 11.3 Organizing 21 flags.

ated the problem in Figure 11.5, then he used tally sheets to explore different ways of organizing the people: by male and female (two groups), standing still or doing something (two groups), and (most successfully as shown in the figure), by type of figure (seven groups).

Analyzing Data

Making sense of data collected and organized may be as simple as adding the tallies and comparing the totals in each category. For example, the major purpose of an eye color survey might be fulfilled by finding the totals for brown, blue, green, and hazel eyes. Comparisons to find most, least, and same or similar require nothing more than a knowledge of the number line. However, more complex data and purposes call for more sophisticated analyses. Toward this end, the mathematical area of statistics provides us with a wide variety of concepts, ideas, relationships, and organizational schemes to help investigators make sense of data.

Three of these statistical concepts are **the mean, the median,** and **the mode**—often referred to as **measures of central value** because they describe three ways of looking at the center of sets of data (Spatz and Johnston 1989, 35). All three measures are "ways of summarizing data" (Spatz and Johnston 1989, 35). Attempts to teach these three measures beginning in the fourth grade have met with difficulties, according to Russell and Mokros (2002):

> Children in fourth grade and beyond learn to apply the algorithm for finding the mean fairly easily, but what do they understand about the mean as a statistical idea?
>
> Many students do not have opportunities to learn about various kinds of averages as statistical concepts. They view an average as a number found by a particular procedure rather than as a number that represents and summarizes a set of data. Students may learn to find a mode, median, or mean . . . but they do not necessarily know how these statistics relate to the data being represented.
>
> *(226)*

Providing the opportunities students need to understand and construct these core, "measure of center" concepts is listed in NCTM's *Principles and Standards* as an important expectation for students in the third- to fifth-grade strand (NCTM 2000, 176). When these opportunities are presented within the context of the working-with-data process, they encourage students to forge and maintain the links between the concepts and actual data.

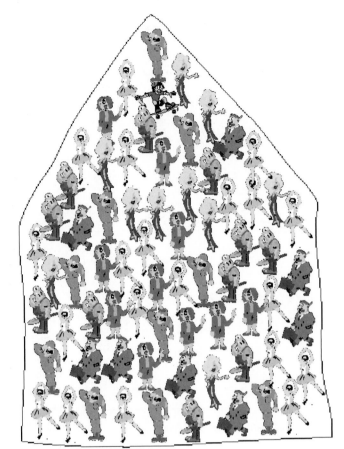

There are 68 people at a party. How many different groups?

Figure 11.5 Nicholas's People at a Party problem.

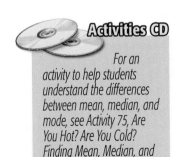

Activities CD

For an activity to help students understand the differences between mean, median, and mode, see Activity 75, Are You Hot? Are You Cold? Finding Mean, Median, and Mode, on the CD-ROM that accompanies this text.

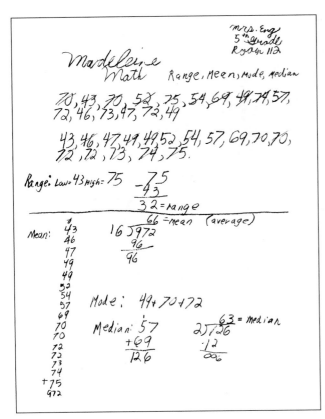

Figure 11.6   Finding mean, median, and mode.

Mean

Of the three measures of central value, the **mean** is probably the most widely used and recognized. Basically, the mean is the arithmetic average of a set of quantities such as scores on a test, annual salaries, or prices of homes or any commodity. The mean is used in summarizing weather-related information such as average precipitation and average high and low temperatures (as in Figure 11.6). Students often encounter the concept first in athletics. Many sports utilize the mean to understand how an individual player, an entire team, and even an entire league are performing. For example, Figure 11.7 shows examples of different types of means in the sport of baseball; they include such averages as the following:

- batting average—"the measure of how often a batter gets a hit";
- slugging average—which "measures a batter's power hitting" including "home runs, triples, and doubles";
- earned run average (ERA)—which "represents the number of runs given up by a pitcher during a 9-inning game" (Muschla and Muschla 1995, 295–96).

In each case, the baseball average, or mean, is computed by division. Generally, you add the scores and divide the sum by the total number of possible scores. With batting average and slugging average, the larger the number, the better; however, with the earned run average or ERA, the lower the number, the better the pitching—something that demonstrates for students the importance of context and purpose in using the concept of mean.

Median

"The **median** is the *point* that divides a distribution of scores exactly in half" (Spatz and Johnston 1995, 38). Three concepts emerge from this definition: distribution, median, and point. **Distribution** in this context refers to ordering scores either from largest to smallest or from smallest to largest. Median and point go together. The median is not necessarily one of the scores in the distribution; it might occur between two scores.

The median is always a point on the distribution separating half of a distribution from the other half. See for example, Table 11.1.

In the Distribution of Physical Weights part of Table 11.1, five weights are ordered from top to bottom, the heaviest weight to the lowest weight. The median separates the top two weights from the bottom two weights; therefore, the median is 221 pounds. The Distribution of Physical Heights shows six heights ordered from top-down, tallest to shortest. The median, or midpoint, of the distribution is not one of the heights; the median must separate the top three heights from the bottom three heights. Adding together the two middle heights, 72 inches and 71 inches, and dividing this sum by 2 gives us the

---

Finding Averages (or Means) in Baseball

Batting average: number of hits divided by the number of official at-bats

> **Examples:** 1 hit in 3 at-bats = 1/3 = .333 batting average
> 12 hits in 48 at-bats = 12/48 = 1/4 = .250 batting average
> 132 hits in 268 at-bats = .493 batting average

Slugging average: total number of bases reached divided by the number of official at-bats

> **Examples:** 10 bases reached with 15 at-bats = 10/15 = .667 slugging average
> 53 bases reached with 60 at-bats = 53/60 = .883 slugging average

Earned run average (ERA): the number of runs given up multiplied by 9, then divided by the total number of innings pitched

> **Examples:** 6 runs given up in 7 innings pitched = 9(6)/7 = 7.714 ERA
> 5 runs given up in 20 innings pitched = 9(5)/20 = 2.25 ERA

Figure 11.7   Applications in sports.

TABLE 11.1	Finding the Median		
	Distribution of Physical Weights (in pounds)		Distribution of Physical Heights (in inches)
	242		78
	235		76
Median ➡	**221**		72
	215	Median ➡	**(71.5)**
	198		71
			68
			65

Activities CD

For an activity in which students use statistics to analyze data, go to Activity 103, Real Numbers at the Zoo, on the CD-ROM that accompanies this text.

average of the two heights, or 71.5 inches—which is the median of the second distribution.

Mode

The third measure of central value is the **mode.** "The mode is the most frequently occurring score—the score with the greatest frequency" (Spatz and Johnston 1995, 39). In the distributions of weight and height in Table 11.1, no number is repeated; therefore, neither set of numbers has a mode. However, if we repeat some numbers, the situation changes. We can add a frequency column to each distribution and find the mode, as shown in Table 11.2.

In the first distribution, a weight of 235 pounds appears twice and is the most frequent weight; therefore, 235 pounds is the mode of the distribution. In the second distribution, the height of 68 inches appears three times and is the most frequently occurring height; therefore, it is the mode for the second distribution.

Displaying and Interpreting Data

Even organized and analyzed data sets can be difficult to read and understand. Displaying the results of analysis in a graph or chart is like the "picture that's worth a thousand words"; the visual representation shows the information and starts the process of interpretation that might include a written or oral explanation.

Bar graphs are a good beginning point. The relationship between frequency counts on the vertical axis and survey categories on the horizontal axis are easy for

Topics, Issues, and Explorations

Work in a group and find examples of averages in a daily newspaper, from the sports page or any page. Then describe what these averages "mean"—their significance, implications within the context of the story, and so forth.

Topics, Issues, and Explorations

Order the following heights (in inches); then find the median of the distribution:

54	55	81	76	63	71	65	59	42
48	57	79	51	61	58	73	75	66

TABLE 11.2	Finding the Mode		
Distribution of Physical Weights (in pounds)	Frequency	Distribution of Physical Heights (in inches)	Frequency
242	1	78	1
235	2	76	1
221	1	75	1
215	1	72	1
198	1	68	3

Activities CD

For an activity about showing data with a bar graph, see Activity 5, Graphing with Candy Hearts, Jellybeans, or Gumdrops, on the CD-ROM that accompanies this text.

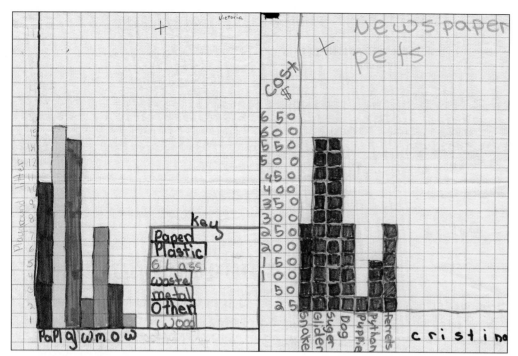

Figure 11.8 Students' bar graphs.

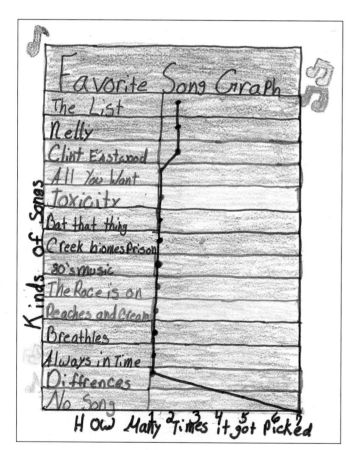

Figure 11.9 Favorite songs dot-and-line graph.

Activities CD

For an activity in which students explore the science, social issues, and math of garbage, see Activity 71, Waste Collection and Graphing, on the CD-ROM that accompanies this text.

students to conceptualize and execute. In the early grades, bar graphs can be built around objects such as the kindergartner's M&Ms graph in Chapter 10 (see Figure 10.7). In the middle and later grades, students are able to generalize the relationship of bar height to frequencies rather than seeing bars as a direct representation of physical objects. In Figure 11.8, Victoria uses a bar graph to show the different types of litter she found on the school playground. She uses abbreviations and color coding with a key to explain. Cristina graphs the costs of pets she found advertised in the paper. Instead of frequencies on the vertical axis, she lists costs.

Graphs of lines and dots, like Leslie's favorite songs graph in Figure 11.9, can also be used to show frequency. The line creates a different type of picture and emphasizes the differences between the highest and lowest frequencies. Older students who are studying algebra will discover the importance of more complex lines-and-dots graphs to represent functions. For example, in the square pool problem described in Chapter 10, students at the middle school level discovered that data for the increases in blue pool tiles and white border tiles created different graph patterns—a straight line to show the linear function of the increasing number of white tiles and a curved line to show the quadratic function of the increasing number of blue tiles (Ferrini-Mundy et al. 2002, 213–14).

Students who have learned to work with percentages and degrees of angle can display data in a **pie chart**. To create a pie chart, students need to—

- convert data to percentages (for example, finding the percentage of the total students surveyed for each eye color option or total surveyed for each category);
- multiply 360° by each percentage figure to convert percentage to degrees of a circle (for example, 72° of the pie chart for hazel eyes if 2 out of 10 students surveyed had hazel eyes);
- use a protractor to plot the different angles on the circular pie chart.

Figure 11.10 shows a successful and an unsuccessful attempt to display data with a pie chart. Natalie's survey of colored folders has a number and color key and is clearly marked, but percentages ex-

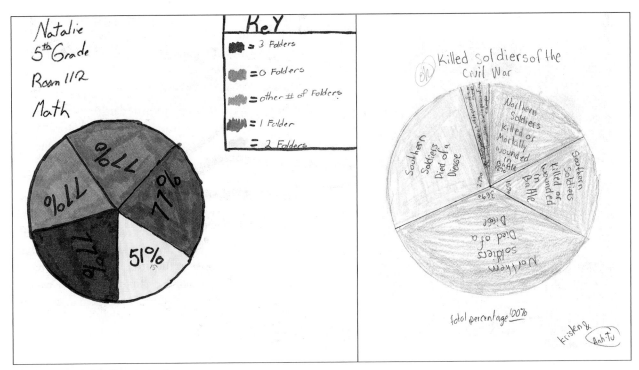

Figure 11.10 Students' pie charts.

ceed 100, and there seems to be little or no relationship between the numbers and the pie segments. Kristen's pie chart works better. Working with data from a unit on the Civil War, Kristen accurately computed and charted percentages for northern and southern fatalities.

Students' interpretation of data often focuses on reading their charts or graphs. For example, asked to explain her graph of pet costs in a newspaper, Cristina simply wrote, "Snake costs $250. Sugar Gliders $550. Dogs are $250 each," and so forth. In other words, she translated the chart line by line. Questions can help us get past translation to a deeper level of meaning:

- Which category shows the largest amount or highest frequency (tallest bar, highest point, largest pie slice)?
- Which category shows the smallest amount or frequency (shortest bar, lowest point, smallest pie slice)?
- What is the range from highest to lowest?
- What are the center points? Would it be helpful to find the mean, median, and mode? Why or why not?
- What does this data tell you about _____?
- What do these data mean (or not mean) to you? To others?
- Is there a message in the data? How would you summarize it?

Range

A key concept for interpretation of data is **range.** Basically, *range* means the distance between the highest and lowest numbers in the data set and can be computed with simple subtraction. Range sets the context for the data, establishing parameters within which comparisons can be made and other numbers understood. Range can be particularly important when you are working with measures of central value. For example, if a company has an average salary of $50,000, but the median salary is

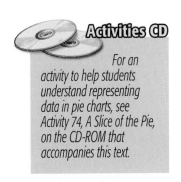

Activities CD

For an activity to help students understand representing data in pie charts, see Activity 74, A Slice of the Pie, on the CD-ROM that accompanies this text.

Topics, Issues, and Explorations

Do some reading and thinking about the concept of the average or mean and its application in schools through the bell curve. What does the mean suggest in terms of grades and achievement? Why is the concept represented with a bell curve? What are the implications for grading on the curve? Is it fair? Why or why not?

Activities CD

For an activity to help students see data in the larger world, see Activity 72, Exploring Data in the Bigger World, on the CD-ROM that accompanies this text.

Activities CD

For an activity in which students pretend to play the stock market, see Activity 76, $10,000 Stock Market Contest, on the CD-ROM that accompanies this text.

$40,000, the mode is $30,000, and the range is $1,500,000 to $15,000, that tells us that there are a few very high salaries but a preponderance of low salaries.

Understanding and Using Data

Closely tied to the interpretation of data is use or purpose. How can we use the information found to form judgments, make decisions, set goals, or take action? One way is to use the information to decide what people want. If a class party committee collected data on favorite foods, they might find out that most of their classmates like pizza and burgers and, therefore, could order those foods for the party. Another way is to identify problems and suggest solutions. Victoria's survey of litter on the playground (see Figure 11.8) not only showed her that there was too much litter but also revealed that most of the litter was recyclable paper, plastic, and glass, suggesting the need for outdoor recycling bins. Other ways to use the information are to identify products such as game consoles that peers with similar tastes and values prefer; to test the market for services, such as a car wash or a bake sale as a fund-raiser; and to match options with available resources, such as the cost of a class visit to a theme park with money in the class fund.

Questions to guide and encourage applications extend the line of thought of the questions for interpretation:

- Do the data suggest a course of action?
- Do the data confirm or contradict currently held beliefs or opinions?
- How can you relate the data to other knowledge and experiences?
- Who else needs to know this information? Who else might find it interesting or important?
- Is there enough information to prove or disprove a point?
- What is new or helpful in the data?

Both the Mathematical Games and Mathematics in Literature features emphasize the importance of using data effectively to make decisions. In *Pigs Will Be Pigs*, the amount of money the pigs find determines the amount and kind of food pur-

Mathematical Games

Stock Market Made Easy

Stock Market Made Easy is a Newspapers-in-Education game (Quigley 2003) played each year by students in elementary, middle, and high schools.

Students work in teams of three or four. The object of the game is to invest an imaginary $10,000 in stocks traded on the New York Stock Exchange.

For their portfolios, students research companies and develop a log to record the progress of their stocks. Students check and record data about their stocks for each day of trading. At regular meetings of each team, students review their portfolios, discuss investment strategies, and write team journal entries about their decisions.

The game continues for eight weeks. The winning team is the one that makes the most money. Earnings should be reported in dollars and percentages of increase.

(For more about Stock Market Made Easy, go to http://www.abqjournal.com. Search "Youngsters Beat New York Stock Exchange Index.")

Variations Research and select a portfolio of stocks and stick with them for the entire eight-week period. Or "manage" the portfolio by buying and selling stocks throughout the eight weeks, being careful to record the reasons for each transaction in the team journal.

Mathematics in Literature

Pigs Will Be Pigs: Collecting Data and Money

Pigs Will Be Pigs by Amy Axelrod (1994) combines data collection with organization and use as well as experiences with counting and spending money. The plot follows the attempts of a family of four hungry pigs to find enough money to eat at the Enchanted Enchilada. The pigs search their house, finding change and bills in coat pockets or toy boxes and under the bed. The book includes a complete menu so the pigs can match their resources with prices.

Activity 1

Develop a money tally sheet to help the pigs organize and record the money they found. Make different vertical columns for each coin and each denomination of bill. As the story is read, tally the money found. You may also want to make horizontal columns to have a record of each place money is found. At the end of the book, use a calculator to figure out the amount of money in each vertical column; then add to find the total amount the pigs have to spend.

Activity 2

Help the pigs spend their money. Study the Enchanted Enchilada menu. Figure out the cost if the pigs order four specials or order four different meals. Subtract the cost of the meal from the total amount the pigs found to discover how much they had left.

Activity 3

The pigs' refrigerator is still empty. With the money left from their meal, how much takeout can the pigs order to eat later at home?

Activities CD
For a more detailed description of this activity about managing money, see Activity 70, "Pigs Will Be Pigs": Collecting Data and Money, on the CD-ROM that accompanies this text.

Activities CD
For another activity about budgeting money, go to Activity 13, How Much Is That Pet? on the CD-ROM that accompanies this text.

chased. In the Stock Market game, winners emphasize the importance of buying what you know and buying low and selling high. The Waffle-Stompers, a middle school team that won in its division, bought familiar names such as Toyota and The Gap (Quigley 2003).

Probability

The concept of probability plays an important role in interpreting and using data to plan and make decisions. Probability deals with uncertainty. It focuses on the role played by chance in events. And by doing so, the concept of probability helps investigators work with data and analyze it from a different perspective—the perspective of prediction. Prediction is one of the key activities of all science, and the concept of probability is central to this activity.

Toward this end, the statistical concept of probability provides us with a wide variety of concepts, ideas, relationships, rules, and organizational schemes to help investigators make predictions.

Historically, determining probabilities had its beginnings in games of chance, especially gambling (Stigler 1986, 63). In education, exploring the language and basic notions of probability prepares students for a world in which answers may be fuzzy rather than clear-cut and tentative rather than final. "Some things children learn in school seem to them predetermined and rule bound. In studying . . . [probability], they can also learn that solutions to some problems depend on assumptions and have some degree of uncertainty" (NCTM 2000, 48).

Talking About Probability

Before children can understand and explore mathematical schemes tied to probability, they need a foundation in words and basic ideas. What does it mean to be certain or uncertain? How can we decide whether an event is probable or unlikely?

A good place to begin is probability words:

Unlikely	might not
Likely	might
Certain	will happen
Uncertain	might or might not happen
Possible	might happen
Impossible	will not happen
Opinion	a belief or idea that we think
Fact	something tested and proven
Prediction	educated guess
Chance	different possibilities

Matching words to situations students can relate to helps anchor the concepts in their worlds and at the same time provides examples for comparisons. Second graders matched words such as *possible* and *certain* to sentences such as "It will rain at my house today" and "The cafeteria menu for tomorrow is fish sticks and tater tots." Then they came up with their own examples for *likely* and *unlikely*.

Likely	Unlikely
It is likely we will have library today.	It is unlikely that we can fly without wings.
It is likely I will take a shower.	It is unlikely I will eat a cockroach.
It is likely there will be worms in my apple.	It is unlikely a kid can drive a car.
It's likely that I can bend my finger back.	It's unlikely that someone could run 200 miles.
It's likely that the world will turn.	It's unlikely the dice would roll 6 all the time.

Later as an assessment exercise, the same group of students divided a sheet into four boxes and filled in each box with word and number sen-

Activities CD

For an activity about using data to make predictions, see Activity 31, Jumping Critters: Kids, Frogs, and Bugs, on the CD-ROM that accompanies this text.

Activities CD

For an activity that involves prediction and M&Ms, see Activity 111, M&M Count and Crunch, on the CD-ROM that accompanies this text.

tences to illustrate the terms *likely, unlikely, impossible,* and *certain.* Barbara's paper, shown in Figure 11.11, demonstrates a better grasp of the concepts for everyday events than for mathematics. Her major distinction between *likely* and *certain* and *unlikely* and *impossible* in number sentences seems to be a matter of degree rather than kind; she simply uses bigger numbers for *impossible* and *certain.*

Calculating Probability

Students can begin exploring the mathematical implications of probability with simple manipulatives such as dice, spinners, and coins. The Math Manipulatives feature describes a simple activity for one and two dice: roll dice, tally results, graph results, and test predictions. Spinning an arrow on a card marked with numbers is a very basic version of roulette. After tallying and charting the number of times the arrow lands on each number, students try their hand at predicting the next number and discover how very difficult it is to select the right one and how soon educated guessing based on tally results becomes wild guessing based on nothing.

Coin tossing offers an excellent introduction to some of probability's mathematical concepts and computations. If we tossed a nickel in the air, would it land heads up or tails up? Either it lands heads up or tails up (barring a landing on its edge). The nickel toss should favor neither outcome; therefore, the probability of a heads-up landing or a tails-up landing should be equal. Mathematically, the probability is 1/2 for either outcome: one, divided by the total possible number of outcomes. The probability of heads showing up is 1/2; and the probability of tails showing up is also 1/2.

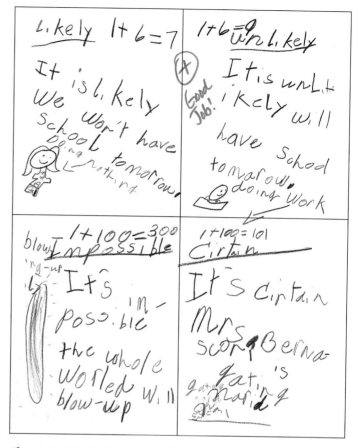

Figure 11.11 Barbara's probability boxes.

Activities CD

For an activity that discusses probability, see Activity 73, Rolling the Dice, on the CD-ROM that accompanies this text.

Math Manipulatives

Rolling the Dice

Almost everyone has rolled dice. Dice are part of many board games, and rolling the highest number often determines who goes first, how many steps to advance, or what score to record.

Some believe there is a trick to rolling the dice or that "luck" decides the numbers you roll. But rolling dice is a game of chance. Probability, not luck or skill, determines the results.

Explore the possibilities first with one die, then two dice.

1. Make a tally sheet with columns for each possible number—a column for each number on the single die, a column for each combination of the two dice.

2. Roll at least 25 times.
3. Keep a tally of the numbers.
4. Add the tallies.
5. Make another tally table with two columns, "Correct" and "Incorrect."
6. Guess the number before you roll. Tally your answers, correct or incorrect.
7. Add the tally marks to see whether there are more correct or incorrect answers.

Share the results of the experiments. Talk about any patterns or lack of patterns in individual and in pooled results. Discuss the implications of what you found for opinions about luck and skill in gambling.

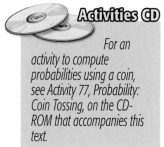

Activities CD

For an activity to compute probabilities using a coin, see Activity 77, Probability: Coin Tossing, on the CD-ROM that accompanies this text.

Topics, Issues, and Explorations

Determine the probabilities of the following situations involving tossing three different coins:

1. Three heads
2. Three tails
3. One head and two tails
4. Two tails and one head
5. Two heads and one tail
6. One tail and two heads

With two coins, the situation becomes more complicated. What is the probability of both coins landing heads up? First, we determine all possible outcomes:

Heads, Heads   Heads, Tails   Tails, Heads   Tails, Tails

Since there are four possible outcomes, the probability that two heads will face up is "one out of four," or $\frac{1}{4}$. The probability that two tails will land face up is also $\frac{1}{4}$. But if we toss both coins and one lands heads up while the other lands tails up, what is the probability? Of the four possible outcomes, two outcomes combine heads up and tails up. In other words, we have one out of four or $\frac{1}{4}$ for each of two outcomes; therefore the probability is $\frac{1}{4} + \frac{1}{4} = \frac{2}{4} = \frac{1}{2}$. If we toss two coins enough times, we will eventually get $\frac{1}{4}$ or 25% of the time either two heads or two tails landing face up, but $\frac{1}{2}$ or 50% of the time we will get one coin landing heads up while the other lands tails up. The key here is tossing enough times. Probability works by something called the *law of averages,* and it requires "a substantial number of trials"—perhaps as many as 1,000—to be useful in describing or predicting (Huff 1993, 40).

The Process Plus Probability: The M&Ms Project

Suppose you want to apply the working-with-data process to the colors of M&Ms in a regular-sized package (a favorite activity with students from kindergarten to middle school). The first thing to do is collect the data. Open the package and determine how many colors of M&Ms it contains. Then count and record the number (or frequency) of each color. Figure 11.12 gives us this information from five third graders from left to right: Bobby, Jaime, Tony, Ty, and Minette.

Note the differences in relative frequencies across different colors and across different students. Figure 11.13 gives the same information but displays it in graph form.

Apparently, no two packages of M&Ms are the same in terms of the distribution of numbers of different colors. A few patterns emerge from both figures:

- There were fewer blue M&Ms in each package than any other color, except for Tony's package; Tony found a greater number of blue-colored candy than orange-colored candy.
- Bobby's package showed the greatest range: 5 blue and 15 green M&Ms.
- Most packages contained about 60 candies per package. Whose package was the exception?

Table 11.3 examines Bobby's data more closely, looking at frequencies in terms of percents and probabilities determined from the percents.

M & Ms					
Brown	12	10	13	12	9
Blue	5	6	11	10	6
Orange	12	11	10	9	13
Red	11	12	12	13	10
Green	15	12	14	13	12
Yellow	8	9	15	10	12
Student Name	Bobby	Jaime	Tony	Ty	Minette

Figure 11.12 Frequency count of M&Ms by color and by student name.

Because the word *percent* means "per hundred," the wording for probability will go something like this: "———chances in a hundred." Bobby converted the frequency for each color to a percent and then interpreted what each percentage means in terms of the "chances in a hundred of finding an M&M of _____ color," which will give the probability of each color.

These data point toward several conclusions. First, if other M&M bags of candy are similar to the five the students analyzed, then they would expect to find fewer blue and more green M&Ms than other-colored candies. Second, they should not expect to find equal numbers across different colors. And third, they might also expect the range from the least frequent to the most frequent number to be in the vicinity of 5 to 10.

Summary of the Process

- Identifying color as a distinguishing feature of M&Ms
- Counting by color
- Graphing by color
- Developing a table that includes
  frequency counts,
  frequency counts converted into percentages, and
  percentages converted into probability statements
- Drawing conclusions about M&Ms from the findings

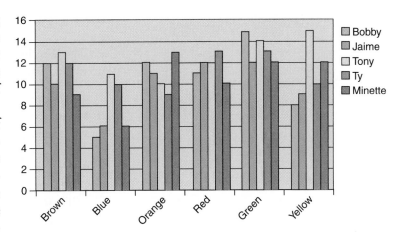

Figure 11.13 Graph of frequency count of M&Ms by color and by student.

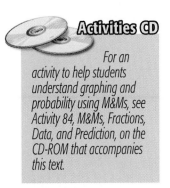

Topics, Issues, and Explorations

Obtain a bag or can of munchies—mixed candy, crackers, and so forth—and apply the data-gathering and analysis process. Use a table or tally sheet to organize your data; then represent it with a graph or pie chart.

TABLE 11.3	Bobby's Color Frequencies and Percentages of Each Color of M&Ms, and Probability Statement for Each Color		
Color	**Frequency**	**Percentage**	**Probability Statement**
Brown	12	12/63 = .19	We have 19 chances in a hundred of finding a brown M&M in the given package.
Blue	5	5/63 = .08	We have 8 chances in a hundred of finding a blue M&M in the given package.
Orange	12	12/63 = .19	The chances of finding an orange M&M is the same as finding a brown M&M in the given package.
Red	11	11/63 = .17	We have 17 chances in a hundred of finding a red M&M in the given package.
Green	15	15/63 = .24	We have 24 chances in a hundred of finding a green M&M in the given package.
Yellow	8	8/63 = .13	We have 13 chances in a hundred of finding a yellow M&M in the given package.

Activities CD

For an activity to help students understand graphing and probability using M&Ms, see Activity 84, M&Ms, Fractions, Data, and Prediction, on the CD-ROM that accompanies this text.

Diversity in Learning and Thinking Mathematically

Working with data lends itself to what we call "success" activities. Success activities are those that encourage students by letting them experience and enjoy succeeding at a meaningful, mathematical task. Success activities have a high interest level. They can be adapted to fit a variety of abilities and learning styles. And they have not one preferred method and outcome, but multiple methods and outcomes.

The Weather Data project, described in this chapter's Lesson Pro-File, is a success activity with multiple dimensions:

- It engages students personally (everyone has connections with the weather).
- It makes connections students can identify and appreciate (meteorology is a science, and weather impacts social studies areas such as geography and economics).
- Students can draw on a variety of resources to collect data (they can research weather in person, on the Internet, in print, on television, and so forth).
- There are many ways to organize, analyze, and display weather data (range of high and low temperatures, averages, measures of precipitation and humidity, maps, graphs, charts, and so forth; Figure 11.14 shows a fifth grader's compilation of temperature statistics to compare April weather in two cities).
- There are many ways to interpret and use weather data (deciding whether to carry an umbrella or plan a picnic, understanding the need to conserve water, predicting floods or other disasters).

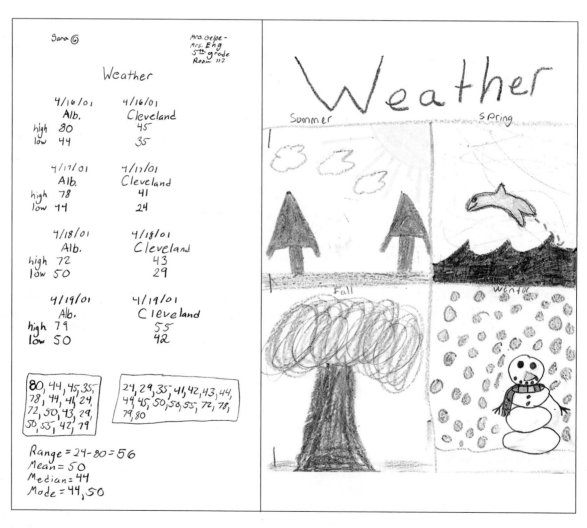

Figure 11.14   Observing the weather.

Math and Technology

Instant Weather on the 'Net

Want to know the temperature in Cairo? See if it's raining in Hawaii or smoggy in LA? Like to get an instant forecast for your city without waiting for the news on television or the radio?

Log onto the Internet. Weather sites let you check forecasts by city, state, Zip code, or country. Many sites show live radar and satellite images. Some connect to cams that show live or updated pictures of different places and often include temperatures and other weather data. Many sites will log data over a period of time and even compute averages.

Some popular sites:

Wunderground.com—The site features Fast Forecast and a variety of radar and satellite links.

AreaGuides.net/weather.html—The site gives forecasts for more than 30,000 cities and all 50 U.S. states.

AccuWeather.com—The site includes animated maps, international and world forecasts, and historical weather research.

Information from these sites can be printed to create weather logs or to compile data for classroom activities such as the following:

Select your hometown and another place you would like to visit. Log high and low temperatures for a week. Find range, mean, median, and mode. Describe the weather in each location for the period. Do you still want to visit the second location?

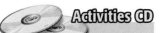

Activities CD

For another activity that involves collecting weather data, go to Activity 68, Mini Gardens, on the CD-ROM that accompanies this text.

Lesson Pro-File

Understanding the Weather Through Tables and Graphs

Working with weather data presents learners with areas of knowledge that cut across mathematics, physics, geography, topology, and history. Weather data provide learners of all school ages an understandable wealth of information—from temperatures to elevations, from information about sunny days to blizzards, from pollution to pollen counts, from local forecasts to worldwide forecasts, from values indicating exposure to the sun's ultraviolet rays to local almanacs filled with statistics.

Context and Weather Data Collected

The geographic context for this project is a small fictional town in the Southwest, Sunnyside, Arizona. The weather information table lists data for the year 2005.

The first data entries involve temperatures. Since weather reports typically report daily highs and lows, the entries include the average highs across all 12 months of the year. The average highs for each month were computed by dividing the sum of each daily temperature for a given month by the number of days in that month. The figure, "Average High Temperature," gives us a bar graph of the table's first column. On the vertical axis, the ordinate, temperatures range from 0° to 100°. On the horizontal axis, called the *abscissa,* the bar graph includes the 12 months from the table.

The second data entry involves average precipitation. Like the calculations for temperature, the average rainfall for each month was computed by dividing the sum of each daily measure of precipitation for a given month by the number of days in that month.

The next entry is pollen count. When pollen count is reported, it is reported for a 24-hour period that ends on the previous morning at 10:00 A.M., which means that the 24-hour period actually covers 10:00 A.M. on the previous day to 10:00 A.M. on the day before it is reported. This means—from a practical point of view—that if you're hit by the pollen truck in terms of allergic reactions, you won't know what truck hit you until the day after.

Also, pollen levels are typically reported as low, which is 0–3; moderate, 4–7; and high, 8 or more. As the table

	Average Highs– Temperature	Average Precipitation– in inches	Average Pollen	Average Pollution
January	50	0.03	34	61
February	56	0.05	44	54
March	65	0.43	48	56
April	68	0.55	50	66
May	70	0.6	55	70
June	75	0.55	65	80
July	85	0.63	71	89
August	93	1.02	74	101
September	82	1.03	70	87
October	65	1.45	66	80
November	56	1.55	58	100
December	42	1.5	45	150

Pollen: 0–3, Low; 4–7, Moderate; 8 or more, High
Pollution: 0–30, Good; 31–54, Moderate; 54+, High

Table of weather information—Sunnyside, Arizona, 2005.

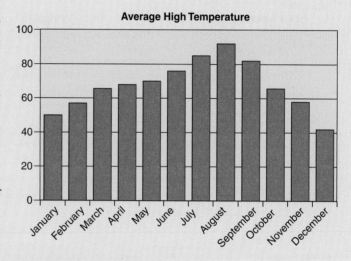

Average highs–temp.

shows, the pollen levels for Sunnyside are through the ceiling in terms of average pollen for 12 months. Average pollen for each month is computed by dividing the sum of each daily measure of pollen for a given month by the number of days in that month.

The last table entry is pollution. Pollution is typically reported as good, 0–30; fair or moderate, 31–54; and bad, 54+. Pollution is divided into the following categories: Smog, Dust, and Carbon Monoxide. Pollution can also be divided into Coarse Particulates, Fine Particulates, Carbon Monoxide, and Ozone.

One way to determine the pollution level in a specific geographic setting, such as a town or a city, is to add the numbers for each category given. For Sunnyside, we can add the numbers from the three categories—Smog, Dust, and Carbon Monoxide—for each day in each month of 2005; then compute the average pollution for each month by dividing the sum of each daily measure of pollution for a given month by the number of days in that month.

Integrated Weather Bar Graph

The bar graph integrates all of the information from the table, giving a visual representation of the weather facts for Sunnyside. On the vertical axis, the *ordinate,* the range is from 0 to 160; this range takes into account the smallest number from the column on average precipitation, which was 0.03 inches, and the largest number, which was a measure of 150 for the average pollution for the month of December. The horizontal axis, the abscissa, represents the weather data for all 12 months.

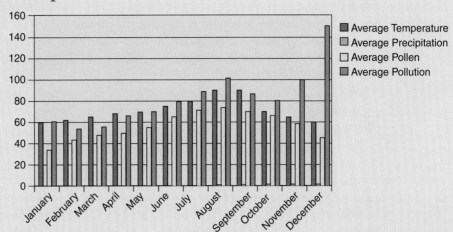

Integrated weather bar graph of average temperature, average precipitation, average pollen, and average pollution.

Basic Findings from Integrated Weather Data

A number of relevant findings about Sunnyside emerge for 2005:

- **Very little precipitation on any given month.** The most rainfall is in November—and that is only 1.55 inches on the average; in some months, such as January, there is almost no rain at all.
- **Ranges in the average highs for temperature from a low of 42° in December to a high of 93° in August.** There are five months, from May to September, when the average temperature is 70° or warmer.
- **High average pollen for all of the months measured.** The range is from 34 in January to 74 in August.
- **Very high average pollution for every month.** The range is from 54 in February to a high of 150 in December.

Trends from Integrated Weather Bar Graph

Taking into consideration all four measures per month, the bar graph shows some trends:

- From January to August there is an increase in average daily temperature coupled with miniscule rainfall and increasing average daily pollen and pollution.
- From August to December, there is a decrease in average daily temperature while the pollen average decreases and the pollution generally increases (except for October) to a year's high pollution reading in December of 150.

Conclusion and Class Projects

For 2005, Sunnyside was a moderately hot to hot city with very little rainfall and a lot of pollen and pollution. These data and analysis form the basis for a number of class activities:

1. Compare Sunnyside with towns in California, New Mexico, and Texas that are geographically at a similar latitude. Determine what *latitude* means, what it has to do with mathematics and navigation, and what, if anything, it has to do with the four measures discussed in this project profile: temperature, precipitation, pollen, and pollution.

Note: *Latitude* is a navigational term that refers to the angular distance in degrees, north or south from the equator. A related navigational term is *longitude,* which refers to the "distance east or west on the earth's surface, measured as an arc of the equator (in degrees up to 180° or by the difference in time) between the meridian passing through a particular place and a standard or prime meridian, usually the one passing through Greenwich, England" (*Webster's New World Dictionary of the American Language* 1980, p. 834).

2. Compare Sunnyside to three other cities, but this time change the latitude to cities in the northwestern part of the United States from states such as Washington, Oregon, Idaho, and Montana. What do you think will happen?

3. Find out how cities actually measure rainfall, temperature, pollen, and pollution, and describe your findings.

4. Find out about and describe other mathematical and scientific measures taken to determine weather-related phenomena. For example, how are tornados or hurricanes spotted and measured?

5. Come up with your own weather-related project: define the terms used and describe your project; then carry it out. Describe your findings.

◀◀◀◀ LOOKING BACK

Working with data provides rich and varied learning experiences. Students learn to collect and organize, analyze, display and interpret, and understand and use data. They also begin to explore the element of uncertainty in their own actions and the world around them and to understand the role of probability in interpreting and predicting events.

Data collection and analysis make it possible for learners to explore their different worlds and make sense of them in ways that can be constructed, understood, and communicated—all critical for continued growth in mathematics learning beyond elementary and middle school.

Questions for Further Thought, Discussion, and Research

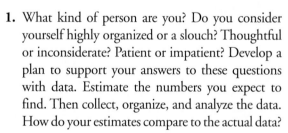

1. What kind of person are you? Do you consider yourself highly organized or a slouch? Thoughtful or inconsiderate? Patient or impatient? Develop a plan to support your answers to these questions with data. Estimate the numbers you expect to find. Then collect, organize, and analyze the data. How do your estimates compare to the actual data?

2. Annual salary is often a touchy subject for teachers whose low pay and high workloads are axiomatic. Search the virtual archives of a newspaper in an area where you would like to teach. Look for data about averages and entry-level salaries as well as information about pay scales and increases. Evaluate the data. What does it tell you? What doesn't it tell you?

3. Are you a big eater? Collect data on your daily food consumption. For a period of seven days collect data on what and how much you eat.

Find information on the amount of calories for each of the foods you consume over the seven days. Calculate a mean, median, and mode after the seven days, and graph your results. Describe your findings. What do they signify?

4. Compare your findings from item 3 to local, regional, or national averages for a person of your gender and age. How do you compare?

5. With legalized gambling finding its way into more and more states, the incidence of gambling among young people seems to be rising dramatically. A study of 6,753 eighth graders in Delaware found that nearly one-third admitted to gambling, and trends point to higher incidence of compulsive gambling (8%) among young gamblers (Crary 2003, A3). Discuss learning about probability as a way to prepare students for the dangers and uncertainties of gambling.

CHAPTER 12

Exploring Part–Whole Relationships: Fractions

LOOKING AHEAD >>>>

Fractions have always been one of the most challenging parts of the K–8 mathematics curriculum. Children come to the formal study of fractions with experiences and intuitive strategies for working with parts of wholes that may not mesh easily with classroom procedures.

To integrate children's constructed knowledge of fractions with instructed knowledge, teachers must build on current understanding, then expand and deepen that understanding with frequent and varied hands-on learning experiences.

Emphasizing real-life contexts and problem-solving strategies rather than procedures and memorized solution paths helps students see fractions as a meaningful way of describing objects in the world around them and as a useful tool for manipulating quantities.

Some of the big ideas of fractions include ideas about their properties—order, equivalence, part-whole relationships, and divided quantities or quotients—and ideas about fraction operations—additive and multiplicative structures and reversed structures with subtracting and dividing. Understanding and using these ideas to work and think mathematically is a developmental process that continues from grade to grade.

Activities CD

For an activity that uses cooking applications to apply fractions, see Activity 82, Introduction to Fractions, on the CD-ROM that accompanies this text.

Students, Teachers, and Fractions—Complex Topic, Complex Relationship

Asked to identify their least favorite math topic, both students and teachers often respond, "Fractions!" Surprisingly, some of the same students and teachers cite individual fraction activities as among their most creative and successful. Especially in the early grades, activities—such as Hershey Bar Fractions, Tootsie Roll Fractions, making quesadillas from fractions of tortillas—frequently build on children's experiences with sharing a treat and connect with their understanding of equal-sharing as a division task.

So what happens to make fractions a bear to study and to teach? And when does the disconnect between students' constructed knowledge of fractions and instruction occur?

Part of the answer to these questions can be found in the subject itself. "*Fraction* is such a powerful mathematical idea," writes Smith (2002), "because it can be used to express so many different kinds of relationships" (4). Fractions can be used to express quantities or ratios. They are often connected to and represented with geometric shapes. They can be used to build whole numbers, but to do so, we need to understand the complex property of equivalence. Moreover, working with fractions involves reversing some of the assumptions that underscore working with whole numbers. For example, with fractions a larger number in the denominator means a smaller, not a larger, segment or quantity, and the outcomes of whole-number multiplication and division can be reversed with fractions. In short, fraction concepts are complex and in some cases appear to

Mathematics in the Real World

Quesadilla Fractions

Making quesadillas lets students explore two different relationships expressed by fractions: (1) parts of whole objects as they divide tortillas to make the quesadilla pieces and (2) parts of quantities as they divide the condiments into equal segments to spread on the tortilla pieces.

For the activity, students will need two 12-inch tortillas for each group of three or four; salsa; guacamole; cheese slices; scrambled eggs; a microwave or toaster oven.

Activity

Divide the tortillas into fractions so that there are an equal number of slices for each member of the group. For example, if there are four in the group, you might divide the tortillas into fourths or eighths; if there are three, thirds or sixths.

Share the toppings equally among the slices of one tortilla. Start with eggs, then add salsa and guacamole. Top with cheese and toast or microwave until cheese melts. Then add salsa and guacamole, and top with slices of the second tortilla.

Draw and write about the process in words and numbers. Be sure to explain what fractions the group used and how the students divided the tortillas and toppings.

contradict students' previous learning and intuitive understanding of numbers. This complexity and its potential for confusion make fractions one of the most challenging parts of the K–8 mathematics curriculum. Smith (2002) goes even further when he claims that "*no area* of elementary school mathematics is as mathematically rich, cognitively complicated, and difficult to teach as fractions, ratios, and proportionality" (3; emphasis added).

Linked closely to the cognitive challenge of understanding fractions is a pedagogical challenge: How do we teach fractions without confusing students? A common response, especially in the middle and upper grades, is to emphasize procedures and drill rather than concepts and problem solving (see Kamii and Warrington 1999; Litwiller and Bright 2002; Kieren 1988). "Teaching Fractions Scenario 1" in Windows in Learning demonstrates this approach in the classroom.

When the teacher in the scenario asks a student to explain an answer, what he really wants her to do is explain how she applied the standard algorithm for addition that he demonstrated: Find the lowest common denominator, convert the fractions, and add numerators. An ideal response from this perspective would be to describe the procedure step by step. His students might write something like the following on the board and explain: "The lowest common denominator for $\frac{1}{3}$ and $\frac{2}{6}$ is thirds, so I converted $\frac{2}{6}$ to $\frac{1}{3}$ and added $\frac{1}{3}$ to $\frac{1}{3}$ to get the answer $\frac{2}{3}$."

$$\frac{1}{3} + \frac{2}{6} = \frac{1}{3} + \frac{1}{3} = \frac{2}{3}$$

"Teaching Fractions Scenario 2" shows a different approach. Students work collaboratively and make drawings to discover how to divide fractions. As a group they find different ways to represent the problem, and they follow a process of inquiry guided by questions that leave room for multiple answers. Students are encouraged to experiment and think rather than imitate and memorize.

The hands-on, discovery approach may take longer initially, and there is no guarantee that the algorithm students construct will be the standard one. However, the additional time needed for students to understand and construct fraction concepts is usually offset by less time spent in review and remediation. Moreover, encouraging students to develop and use a variety of algorithms, including their own, helps them see fractions from multiple perspectives and in effect to think outside textbook procedures when they work with fractions.

Windows on Learning

Teaching Fractions Scenario 1

A class of fifth-graders sits in rows of desks facing a chalkboard. On each desk are an exercise sheet and a #2 pencil (no calculators allowed).

A teacher, armed with a pointer and chalk holder with a long piece of yellow chalk, walks to the board and writes:

$$\frac{1}{4} + \frac{1}{2} =$$

Still facing the chalkboard, he explains in a monotone, "Adding fractions is easy. First, find the lowest common denominator and convert fractions. Second, add the numerators. And you have it: the answer is three-fourths."

In the back row, a student leans toward her neighbor and whispers, "How did he do that?"

The teacher turns quickly and jabs the pointer in her direction: "You, Miss Silva, come to the board and show us homework problem number 6: $\frac{1}{3} + \frac{2}{6}$. Move quickly now. Write clearly and be ready to explain your answer."

(Martinez and Martinez 1996, 27)

Windows on Learning

Teaching Fractions Scenario 2

Several fifth graders are working at a large table. They have been using compasses to draw circles of various radii.

The teacher has been moving around the table, looking over shoulders and making suggestions. Now she calls for the students' attention and asks, "How many circles have you made?"

The students count quickly and answer, "Five."

"All right. Now take a ruler and draw a line through the center of each circle."

The students draw the lines.

The teacher is ready with her next question, "When you draw a line through the middle of a circle, what do you get?"

"A half."

"Just one half?"

"No, two halves for each circle."

"How many halves for the five circles?"

"Two, 4, 6, 8, 10!"

The teacher moves now to the whiteboard. "How would we write that in words?"

"Five circles divided in half make 10 halves."

"Or two halves of a circle times five circles makes 10 halves."

"Or one circle divided in half makes two halves times 5 makes 10."

The teacher writes and then asks, "How would we write that in numbers? Try it on your own paper."

The students scribble for a minute, look at each other's papers, and then write some more.

Finally, one student speaks up, "We didn't all do it the same way."

"That's fine. Let's look at all the ways."

After several minutes of discussion, the whiteboard shows three different ways to write the problem in numbers:

$$\frac{5}{\frac{1}{2}} = 10 \qquad \frac{1}{2}\overline{)5} = 10 \qquad 5 \div \frac{1}{2} = 10$$

Once the students have repeated the process with quarters, eighths, and sixteenths, the teacher calls their attention to the whiteboard, now covered with numbers.

"Whenever we divide a fraction, what happens? Do we end up with a larger number than we started with or a smaller number?"

"Larger!"

"How much larger?"

More scribbling. A minute passes.

"As much as if we multiply by the fraction."

The teacher writes quickly on the whiteboard:

$$5 \times \tfrac{1}{2} = \tfrac{5}{2}$$

"Is this what you mean?"

"No, turn the fraction over. Then multiply."

$$\tfrac{5}{1} \div \tfrac{1}{2} = \tfrac{5}{1} \times \tfrac{2}{1} = 10$$

Source: Adapted from Martinez and Martinez 1996, 35–36.

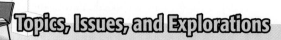

Topics, Issues, and Explorations

How did you learn fractions? Were you taught to imitate procedures or to discover concepts? Did your teacher follow a textbook approach or use real-life applications? Think about the effect of the way you learned on how you think about fractions today. Is the effect positive or negative? Why?

A Hands-on Pedagogy for Teaching Fractions: Connecting Constructed Knowledge and Instructed Knowledge

Because fractions form a significant part of the mathematics curriculum from fourth or fifth grade through middle school, many think of fractions as primarily a topic for older students as well as a topic that belongs for the most part to the formal study of mathematics. Most teachers expect young children to enter school with intuitive knowledge about whole numbers and whole-number operations. However, Empson (2002b) writes, "You might be surprised to learn that first graders know a lot about fractions" (122). Smith (2002) concurs and makes an important distinction between children's intuitive understanding of fractions and the formal instruction they receive in school:

> Students' experience with these concepts begins early—even before formal schooling. . . . Before they learn anything in our classrooms, students engage in activities in the everyday world where they generate ideas about fractions, ratios, and proportionality. Some activities take place in the home (e.g., how to divide up an object among friends); some in organized practices in the wider culture (e.g., tracking baseball batting averages). In these activities children construct knowledge about relational numbers. They bring this *constructed* knowledge into our classrooms where it interacts with what our curriculum and teaching offer (*instructed knowledge*). Mathematically successful students manage to connect these two bodies of knowledge; students who never really understand do not. *(3)*

Making the connection between constructed knowledge and instructed knowledge is a foundational task. It calls for teaching strategies that not only build on students' previous experiences with fractions but also ensure that students accommodate new concepts-that is, that new ideas are fully integrated with the old. Successful teaching strategies incorporate several key components:

- **real-life or familiar contexts** to engage and to connect;
- **hands-on explorations** to keep learning active and to ground the abstract in the concrete;
- **multiple representations** including models, drawings, notation, and words to encourage a variety of perspectives;
- **emphasis on language connections** to stimulate and deepen understanding.

Real-Life Contexts

Children begin to build fraction concepts early as they explore size and shapes and develop strategies for measuring and comparing. Even as toddlers, children may notice whether their milk or juice bottles are full or only partially full, whole or part of a whole. Preschoolers observe the larger portions of food and shares of treats given to older siblings. And children learn early the principles and strategies of equal sharing—slicing a cake or pie so that everyone gets the same size, and cutting an extra cookie into halves, thirds, or fourths so that each child receives an equal share. Learning to work with fractions in a more systematic sense

Activities CD

For an activity that presents fractions in visual form, see Activity 83, Learning Fractions with Pictures, on the CD-ROM that accompanies this text.

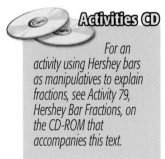

Activities CD

For an activity using Hershey bars as manipulatives to explain fractions, see Activity 79, Hershey Bar Fractions, on the CD-ROM that accompanies this text.

Idea Files

Familiar Fraction Activities

Grade Levels	Activity/Procedur	Questions for Inquiry-Based Learning
K–2	**Orange fractions**—Peel an orange; then count and separate the sections. Make a drawing to show the number of sections that make up a whole orange. Learn the fraction words to show one, two, three sections and so forth.	How many sections are there in one orange? Does each orange have the same number of sections? What number shows all the sections? What fraction shows one, two, three sections?
3–4	**Apple fractions**—Begin with paper cut-outs of apples. Fold to show $\frac{1}{2}$, $\frac{1}{4}$, $\frac{1}{3}$, and other fractions. Write the fraction on each folded part, then cut along the folds. Compare and combine fractions to discover relationships.	If you fold the apple once, how many parts do you have? Twice? Three times? Which is bigger, $\frac{1}{2}$ or $\frac{1}{3}$? How many apple halves, fourths, thirds does it take to make one whole apple?
5–6	**Pizza fractions**—Draw plans for dividing a pizza into pieces so that each person in your group can have one, two, three, or more pieces. Calculate the number of pizzas you will need for each person to have different sizes and numbers of pieces ($\frac{1}{8}$, $\frac{1}{6}$, $\frac{1}{4}$, two or three of each size, and so forth).	How will you divide your pizza for even numbers? For odd numbers? How many different ways can you find to give eight people $\frac{1}{4}$ of a pizza? To divide two pizzas among five people?
7–8	**Crazy-cake fractions**—Bake a cake in a square or rectangular pan. Decorate it with three different kinds of frosting. Make a model for cutting the cake so that each person receives an equal portion with equal parts of each flavor of frosting. Can you make a model for equal portions but with one flavor of frosting for each piece?	What size and shape are your cakes? How many will share it? What fraction of the cake will each share? If two do not want any cake, what fraction will each share?

should begin with these familiar and well-understood experiences and then build to more formal and complex applications.

Equal-sharing activities provide an effective bridge from informal, intuitive knowledge about fractions to the more formal knowledge of the mathematics classroom (Empson 1999, 2001, 2002a, 2002b). Because sharing is a familiar situation at all grade levels, students see the activities as meaningful—something they can relate to and engage on their own terms. Moreover, students often bring to the activities an intuitive knowledge of concepts and problem-solving strategies that can serve as a foundation for understanding and working with fractions formally. Sharing a cake or pizza calls for students to—

- **see** the cake or pizza in terms of a whole and parts of the whole;
- **quantify** the whole/part–whole relationship in terms of number of those sharing the cake or pizza; and
- **develop strategies** for partitioning the cake or pizza into equal parts.

From this beginning point, students can explore properties of fractions such as equivalence and operations such as addition and subtraction. Empson (2002b), whose work with fractions spans more than a decade, emphasizes the importance of fraction activities like equal sharing that make sense to the students.

Equal-sharing problems fostered a sound conceptual foundation for understanding how fractional quantities are related by prompting children to reflect on different ways to partition the same amounts. . . . If teachers spend a great deal of time developing concepts of equivalence through equal-sharing problems, children will eventually be able to solve . . . [fraction] problems using their own strategies based on concepts that make sense to them.

(124)

Making the transition from informal to formal knowledge of fractions is neither automatic nor guaranteed. Students need learning experiences that encourage them to "use their informal knowledge to give meaning to fraction symbols and procedures" (Mack 2002, 138; see also Mack 1990). This approach may mean presenting real-world problems with corresponding symbolic problems (as in Figure 12.1) and using inquiry and discussion to help students make the connections. Or it may mean using the real-world problem as both a laboratory for discovering fractions concepts and as a model for developing and solving new problems.

Hands-on Explorations

For the most part, students' understanding of number is based on experiences with whole numbers. Predictably, their whole-number sense can adversely affect students' reasoning about fractions. In a long-term series of studies with fourth and fifth graders, the Rational Number Project (RNP) found that frequently students would attempt to apply whole-number concepts to fraction situations (Cramer et al. 1997).

> Children reasoned that one-third is greater than one-half because three is greater than two. Children often regressed to additive or subtractive strategies when comparing fractions. Two-fifths equaled five-eighths because $2 + 3 = 5$ and $5 + 3 = 8$. They considered three-fourths and two-thirds to be equal because the difference between the numerator and denominator in each fraction was one.

(Post and Cramer 2002, 141)

RNP researchers found that the most important factor in constructing a new, rational-numbers sense was frequent and extended experiences with fraction manipulatives.

> In order to develop fraction sense, most children needed extended periods of time with physical models such as fraction circles, Cuisenaire rods, paper folding, and chips. These models allow students to develop images for fractions, and these mental images enable students to understand about fraction size. Students can use their understanding of fraction size to operate on fractions in a meaningful way.

(Cramer and Henry 2002, 41)

Many commercially produced manipulatives can be used to explore fractions. The Idea Files, "Fractions with Manipulatives," describes activities for

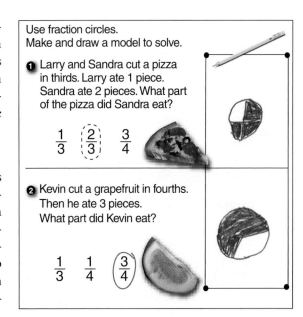

Figure 12.1 Integrating fraction symbols and real-world application.

(From Worksheets for Fraction Circles, Harcourt Brace Jovanovich n.d., 369.)

Topics, Issues, and Explorations

Work in small groups to brainstorm about everyday situations that involve fraction concepts. Make a list of the situations; then rate the situations for familiarity at different grade levels (early, middle, upper, and so forth). Discuss how these situations might be used to introduce fractions, to explore fraction equivalence or order, and to apply operations.

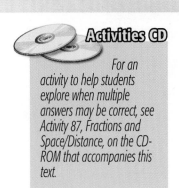

Activities CD

For an activity to help students explore when multiple answers may be correct, see Activity 87, Fractions and Space/Distance, on the CD-ROM that accompanies this text.

several products. Some such as fraction tiles and circles are made especially for modeling fractions; others such as pattern blocks and geoboards model a variety of math concepts.

Students or teachers can also make their own fraction kits with construction paper or other materials. Models might be fraction circles, squares, or strips and use different colors to denote different sizes of fractions. Teach-

Idea Files

Fractions with Manipulatives

Manipulative	Activities
Fraction Circles	Order fractions of circles from smallest to largest. On a strip of paper, make a number line to reflect the order. Compare and combine parts of circles to find equivalent fractions and to explore adding and subtracting fractions.
Cuisenaire Rods	Use rods to represent and name fractions. Place one rod over or above the other to compare size. Explore relationships by using different-colored rods to represent denominators and, selecting appropriate rods, to represent numerators (http://teachertech.rice.edu/Participants/silha/Lessons/cuisen2.html).
Geoboards	Work with rubber bands and geoboards to construct fractional parts of a square. Find as many halves, fourths, thirds, and so forth, as possible, including "crazy fractions" in irregular shapes. Transfer the fractions to geoboard recording paper and explain in words.
Pattern Blocks 	Use pattern blocks on triangular grid paper to identify fractions, find equivalent fractions, and perform basic operations. Place different pattern blocks on the grid and identify number of grid triangles covered. Use the grid to compare sizes of the blocks, to divide blocks into parts of wholes, and to explore and show combinations such as $\frac{1}{2} + \frac{1}{3}$ (Welchman-Tischler 1992, 20).
Fraction Tiles 	Identify equivalent fractions by comparing tiles. Start with a tile such as $\frac{1}{2}$. Then look for all of the combinations that make up the same size. Continue, finding equivalent fractions for $\frac{1}{3}$, $\frac{3}{4}$, and other numbers. Make a list of all equivalent fractions. Look for patterns in the fractions (Abrohms, n.d., 3).
Tangrams	Make a set of tangrams by folding and cutting a square. Identify the fractional part of each tan. Compare and combine the tans to explore size and equivalence (www.pbs.org/teachersource/mathline/concepts/asia/activity2.shtm).

Math Manipulatives

Make a Fraction Kit

Having students create their own fraction manipulatives has two major advantages:

- It is less expensive than manufactured materials and allows each student to make and keep her or his own kit.
- The process of dividing and labeling the fraction strips allows students to discover for themselves fraction properties such as size, order, and equivalence.

Activity 1

Begin with 10 strips, each duplicated on a different color of card stock. Leave one strip whole. Use a ruler to divide the second strip into halves, the third into thirds, the fourth into fourths, and so forth. Label each strip section with the fraction it represents.

Activity 2

Working in pairs, explore all of the different combinations of fraction parts that you can find to make $\frac{1}{2}, \frac{1}{4}, \frac{1}{3}, \frac{3}{4}, \frac{2}{3}$, and other fractions. Write down the combinations; then compare lists with classmates.

Variations

Make a second set of fraction strips from white card stock. Develop fraction sense by identifying and combining unlabeled segments to form $\frac{1}{2}, \frac{1}{4}, \frac{1}{3}$, and other fractions.

---

ers in the early grades often use tactilely friendly materials such as velvet or felt and focus on the larger fractions ($\frac{1}{2}, \frac{1}{3}, \frac{1}{4}$). Rand Barker, the teacher featured later in this chapter's Pro-File, used strips of colored paper cut to show a whole and fractions up to $\frac{1}{16}$. The fraction kit described in the Math Manipulatives feature is made up of fraction strips, but the process could also be used to construct fraction circles, the manipulative that the Rational Numbers Project calls "the most powerful of the models" (Cramer and Henry 2002, 42). The Make Your Own Manipulatives section in the Appendix A of this book includes models for fraction squares, circles, and strips.

Multiple Representations

How many different ways can you show or represent one third? Draw a circle or rectangle, and block off one third. Create an array of dots or diamonds, and draw a line around one third of them. Connect dots on geoboard recording paper. Color in sections of polygons on centimeter grid paper or triangular grid paper. Write "one third" in words. Write "$\frac{1}{3}$" in numbers. Write or draw a number or shapes sentence that yields $\frac{1}{3}$:

$$\frac{1}{6} + \frac{1}{6} = \frac{2}{6} = \frac{1}{3}$$

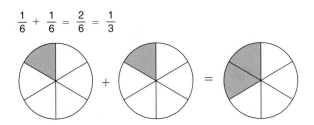

Multiple representations of fractions are important not only because they help teachers understand students' thinking about fractions but also because

Activities CD

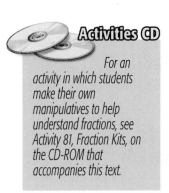

For an activity in which students make their own manipulatives to help understand fractions, see Activity 81, Fraction Kits, on the CD-ROM that accompanies this text.

they help students themselves to construct concepts and refine their thinking about those concepts. In a teaching experiment with Cuisenaire rods, Steencken and Maher (2002, 59) asked fourth graders to represent fractions situations in three ways:

1. physical models with Cuisenaire rods,
2. pictures of the models, and
3. notation.

In seven sessions over three months, students' knowledge of fractions grew from a basic level of name recognition to a more sophisticated level of understanding magnitude and equivalence. The researchers concluded, "It is clear that young children can build a deep understanding of fraction ideas and enjoy doing it" (60).

Empson (2002a) emphasizes the need for representation tools that are "a combination of student-generated and teacher-provided" (35).

> On the one hand, teachers need to tell children about some of the conventional aspects of representation, such as fraction symbols. On the other hand, . . . [b]ecause [problem-solving] strategies are closely coupled with the use of representations, encouraging the development of student-generated representations can enhance and deepen the meaning of representations.
>
> *(35)*

In Figures 12.2 to 12.4, students use a combination of arrays, drawings of geometric figures, geoboard recording dots, and fraction symbols to represent fractions.

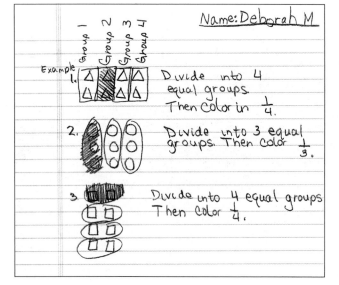

Figure 12.2 Representing fractions with arrays.

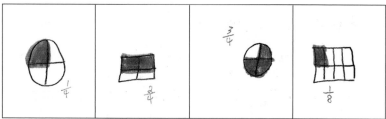

Figure 12.3 Representing fractions with geometric drawings.

Topics, Issues, and Explorations

Write a number sentence with fractions. Then explore all of the different ways to represent your problem-solving process. Share the results with classmates. Discuss which representation strategies might be appropriate for you as a teacher to provide and which you might expect to see as student-generated responses.

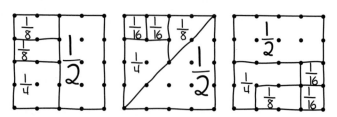

Figure 12.4 Representing fractions with geoboards and recording paper.
(From *Investigations, Different Shapes, Equal Pieces* Grade 4 by Cornelia Tierney, Mark Ogonowski, Andee Rubin, and Susan Jo Russell. Copyright 1998 by Dale Seymour Publications. Reprinted by permission of Pearson Education, Inc.).

Language Connections

Successful fraction learning is rarely silent seat work. Verbalizing thinking about fractions stimulates and deepens understanding and allows students to enjoy the gestalt advantage of cooperative learning (the whole's being greater than the sum of its parts).

Teachers play a major role in making discussion of fractions mathematically productive. According to Empson (2002a), "The way teachers talk with students about the fractional amounts they have created is central to the development of children's fraction conceptions" (36). Teachers can model fraction terminology by being specific about naming fractions-that is, specifying $\frac{1}{2}, \frac{1}{3}, \frac{1}{6}$ instead of saying "a piece" or "a part." We can also model ways of thinking about fractions, of comparing sizes and calculating equivalence, by phrasing questions that generate a process of inquiry rather than instant cut-and-dried responses. Productive questions usually require students to look and think before they answer—for example, "How big is that fraction?" or "How much brownie [or other shared item] does one person get?" or "How many of that fraction would fit into the whole?" (Empson 2002a, 37).

As students use fraction terminology and explore paths of inquiry in discussions with each other as well as with their teachers, they are able to compare and test their own ideas and broaden their perspective to include a variety of strategies and representations. In the study with Cuisenaire rods mentioned earlier, an argument about the comparative sizes of two-thirds and one-half led to a better understanding of fraction equivalence.

Teacher 1:	And you got two thirds to be bigger than one half?
Matt:	[Politely impatient] Yes.
Teacher 1:	By how much?
Matt:	[Deliberately] By one sixth.
Meredith:	Or, or two twelfths.
Matt:	[Shaking his head in dissent] No. [Mutterings in the classroom of "no"]

Meredith defended her idea and provoked a lively debate among her classmates. Ed offered his understanding of Meredith's solution.

Ed:	Yeah, but see just the two whites together. That's right, it would be two twelfths. But you have to combine them. You can't call them, you can call them separately, but you can also call them combined and if you combine them it would be a, a, one sixth.

(Steencken and Maher 2002, 58)

In the discussion, the students presented and developed arguments to support their solutions, discovering that two apparently different solutions were in fact the same answer because two-twelfths and one-sixth are equivalent fractions. Whether students support their ideas orally or in writing, putting fraction concepts into words helps students reflect about and revise or reaffirm their thinking (see Figure 12.5 for an example of a fifth grader's written explanation of fractional parts).

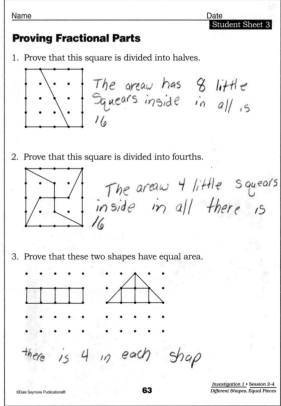

Figure 12.5 Proving fractional parts.
(From *Investigations, Different Shapes, Equal Pieces* Grade 4 by Cornelia Tierney, Mark Ogonowski, Andee Rubin, and Susan Jo Russell. Copyright 1998 by Dale Seymour Publications. Reprinted by permission of Pearson Education, Inc.).

As with other areas of mathematics, the language connection of literature serves two purposes:

- to engage and motivate, and
- to provide contexts for learning and situations for exploring concepts.

For younger students, *The Doorbell Rang* by Pat Hutchins (1986) contextualizes and then presents variations of an equal-sharing problem: how to divide a plate of cookies among two children, then four, then seven, with the number of sharers changing each time the doorbell rings (see the Mathematics in Literature feature). For older students, Alice's *Adventures in Wonderland* can work as a metaphor for their own bewilderment in the "wonderland" of fractions. Alice's experiments with shrinking and enlarging herself as she drinks from the White Rabbit's bottle or nibbles on opposite sides of the Wonderland mushroom provide material for exploring multiplication of fractions (Taber 2002). In these and other stories, students encounter fractions in an imaginative, creative context. The context makes the fractions themselves seem more meaningful and solving fraction problems seem more important.

Topics, Issues, and Explorations

There is a strong connection between fractions and measurement. A working knowledge of fractions is important in cooking, and most recipes include fractions. Select a favorite recipe. Discuss how much knowledge about fractions you need to read and follow the recipe. What if you want to make a half or a double recipe? Could you do that without knowing anything about fractions?

Mathematics in Literature

The Doorbell Rang

Pat Hutchins's (1986) *The Doorbell Rang* incorporates a variety of math concepts including division, patterns, equal-sharing situations, and fractions.

The story is about two children whose mother baked a batch of cookies for them to share. They divided the cookies in half, but before the children could eat the cookies, the doorbell rang, and two more children arrived to share the cookies. The children then divided the cookies into fourths, but the doorbell continued to ring; more children arrived calling for more sharing until the children's grandmother came with another batch of cookies.

Activity

Use construction paper and markers to create a batch of paper cookies. As the teacher reads the story, model the task—children's sharing of the cookies. After the teacher shows and discusses the words and notations for writing $\frac{1}{2}$, $\frac{1}{3}$, and $\frac{1}{4}$, divide the paper cookies into two, three, and four equal parts, then represent the equal sharing with drawings, words, and fractions.

Extension

In groups of three or four, bake giant cookies. Divide each cookie equally among members of the group, representing the sharing plan with drawings, words, and fractions.

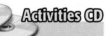

Activities CD

For another activity that uses concrete objects to explore fractions, see Activity 84, M&M Fractions, Data, and Prediction, on the CD-ROM that accompanies this text.

Big Ideas of Fractions

Opinions differ about how much work with fractions should be required. NCTM Standards recommend introducing concepts early and including fraction work in each grade (NCTM 2000). However, some educators argue that younger children are not developmentally ready to understand fractions. In a 2001 article, Watanabe wrote, "Let's eliminate fractions from primary curricula," and he went on to argue that student development and issues of curriculum and instructional materials make fraction work in the early grades unproductive (70). Powell and Hunting (2003) disagree, calling for more rather than less fractions:

> The concept of fractions is important; the earlier it is taught, the more personal the mathematical power that children will bring to higher education and discovery. The development of fraction concepts should not be delayed until the intermediate grades but rather nurtured and built on throughout students' school careers.

(7)

Integral to the more-rather-than-less position are several basic assumptions:

- that younger students as well as students in the middle and upper grades can construct meaningful fraction concepts;
- that fraction concepts are foundational, an essential part of mathematical thinking rather than a refinement or enrichment of the curriculum;
- that the big ideas of fractions, including the properties of fractions and operations with fractions, are accessible to all students.

Research strongly supports these assumptions but at the same time points toward shortcomings in the way students are introduced to the properties of fractions and to applying operations with fractions. Riddle and Rodzwell (2000) found that traditional emphases on finding common denominators, adding, and simplifying were "completely at odds with the way in which the students were thinking" (205). When students used concrete objects in the problem-solving process and developed their own algorithms for adding fractions, including adding with mixed numbers, the results were more positive. They gave students from kindergarten to sixth grade the addition problem $2\frac{1}{2} + \frac{3}{4} = $ _____. "In all grades, students displayed a solid understanding of fraction concepts. For instance, they used equivalencies with ease to build a whole" (205).

Some of the big ideas important to the fraction curriculum include concepts related to the **properties** of fractions (ideas about order, equivalence, part-whole relationships, and divided quantities or quotients) and **operations** (additive and multiplicative structures as well as reversed structures with subtracting and dividing). Understanding these ideas begins with discovery as students explore fractions concretely. Using these ideas to build new ways to think and work mathematically—that is, constructing new tools for their mathematical toolboxes—is a developmental process. In the early grades, the process might emphasize naming fractions and showing how parts fit together to make a whole; in later grades, incorporating formal symbolism and notation.

Activities CD

For an activity to help make fractions meaningful to students, see Activity 88, Finding Fractions in Your Life, on the CD-ROM that accompanies this text.

Ordering Fractions with Colored Circles

Ordering fractions is a foundational activity. As students compare and work with fraction sizes and relationships, they develop the concepts needed to understand equivalence and operations.

Fraction circles serve as a frame of reference for constructing and understanding fraction order.

Activity

Duplicate the pattern for fraction circles on card stock (see masters in the Appendix A). Cut out the patterns; then use a different color of construction paper to make each circle.

Develop a fraction-order table by organizing and filling in the information for the following:

Color
Number of pieces
Fraction notation for one piece
Fraction notation for all pieces
Color with smallest pieces

Source: Adapted from Post and Cramer (2002, 143).

Properties of Fractions

What makes a fraction a fraction? How do fractions differ from whole numbers? How does working with fractions compare to working with whole numbers? Answering these questions is essential to understanding fractions, but the answers challenge students to develop a larger and more complex knowledge framework for numbers—one that allows them to reconcile inverse relationships. For example, with whole numbers, larger figures mean larger quantities or size; with fractions, larger numbers in the denominator mean smaller portions of quantities or smaller size.

Order

Building an understanding of fraction order begins (like earlier efforts to understand whole numbers) with hands-on experiences. Organizing fractional pieces of circles, squares, or other shapes in descending or ascending order of size establishes a visual and tactile foundation for a fraction number line akin to the whole-number lines with which students are familiar. The illustration of fractions on a number line shows pieces of fraction circles ordered by size and paired with fraction numbers on a line. Understanding that $\frac{1}{6}$ is smaller than $\frac{1}{2}$, even though 6 is a larger number, or that $\frac{2}{3}$ is larger than $\frac{2}{6}$ emerges slowly as students learn to think quantitatively about fractions.

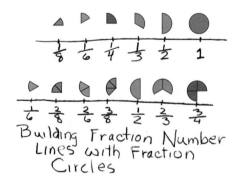

Building Fraction Number Lines with Fraction Circles

Thinking quantitatively about fractions, according to Post and Cramer, (2002) means that students have developed "internal images" of fractions, fraction relationships, and order. To develop those images, the authors recommend "extended instruction with a variety of manipulative materials" as well as activities with both identical numerators and identical denominators (142). For example, working with fraction circles cut from different colors of construction paper, students explore order and at the same time discover the concepts implicit in the terms *numerator* and *denominator* (see the Googol feature, "Ordering Fractions with Colored Circles").

Equivalence

Closely related to order is the property **equivalence**. Ordering fractions calls for comparing sizes and developing internal images about which fraction is larger, smaller, and so forth. Finding equivalent fractions builds on the same process and images. To find fractions equivalent to $\frac{1}{2}$, $\frac{1}{4}$, or $\frac{1}{3}$, students continue to use physical referents to compare sizes but also to construct new images with combinations of fractions.

Using colored-paper fraction circles, 11-year-old Jordann first explored the ways she could create a whole and common fractions such as $\frac{1}{2}$ and $\frac{1}{3}$ with same-colored pieces. She found that three orange $\frac{1}{6}$s, two butterfly-printed $\frac{1}{4}$s, and four green $\frac{1}{8}$s all covered one half of a whole circle. Then she tried a variety of combinations—two orange $\frac{1}{6}$s and one pink $\frac{1}{3}$ to make two thirds; a pink $\frac{1}{3}$, four green $\frac{1}{8}$s and two flowered $\frac{1}{12}$s to make a whole, and so forth. Asked to reflect about what she had learned, Jordann wrote, "I did not understand equivlent fractions before the lesson. The lesson helped me by using the fraction circles because they were fun and they gave me a visaul [*sic*] picture of what I was doing with fractions."

As Jordann moved from manipulating pieces of the circles to working with number notation, those mental pictures helped her begin to construct a strategy for reducing fractions. At the same time she was able to extend her thinking beyond the concrete objects and work with fractions such as $\frac{25}{45}$ and $\frac{14}{24}$ for which she had no fraction-circle examples (see Figure 12.6).

Comparison tasks play an important role in developing a sense for fraction equivalence. Smith (2002) gives students "carefully selected pairs and groups of fractions" and asks, "Which of the following two (or more) fractions is greater, or are they equal?" (9). Initially, students tend to make visual judgments based on their own attempts to draw or sketch the divided quantities; however, they soon develop more abstract strategies such as using reference points and relying on numerical rather than visual representations.

For example, they may get fed up with trying to draw out "elevenths" and "thirteenths" to decide if "$\frac{7}{11}$ or $\frac{7}{13}$" is greater. In their frustration, they come to see that the only thing that matters is that "thirteenths" are smaller than "elevenths," so $\frac{7}{11} > \frac{7}{13}$.

With lots of experience reasoning about fractions with divided quantity diagrams, students can shift almost seamlessly to reasoning directly about the given numerators and denominators.

(Smith 2002, 10).

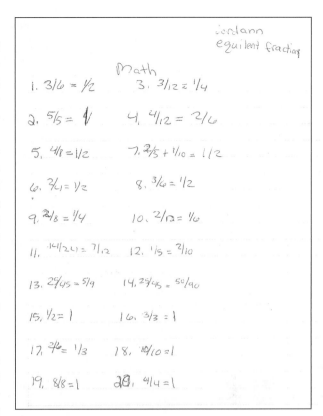

Figure 12.6 Jordann's fraction worksheet.

Part–Whole Relationships

Fractions are often defined as numbers representing parts of wholes; however, the apparently simple definition may obscure the complexity of a concept that is both abstract and multifaceted. Children who use prefractional concepts in working with fractions frequently have learned some fraction terms but do not yet understand the relationships implicit in the terms. For example, asked to divide a candy bar into thirds, Teresa measured three equal parts, but asked to represent the amount of candy with fractions, she responded "one and one third" (Steffe and Olive 2002, 129).

> Because she usually interpreted fractional situations in terms of halving and doubling, she combined two pieces to make a whole and then combined this whole with the remaining piece, which she had already named as *one-third*. *One-third* for Teresa had no meaning with respect to the fractional whole. It was simply one of three pieces that she had made.
>
> *(Steffe and Olive 2002, 129)*

Moving from prefractional to fractional concepts depends to a significant extent on students' understanding the part–whole relationships represented by fractions. This means—

- understanding that a fraction may represent a part of a single item;
- understanding that a fraction may represent a part of a set of items; and
- understanding that a fraction is a relative number, that it represents a relationship independent of size.

Students build this understanding as they identify fractions in the world around them (half a globe, half a cup, half a class), construct fractions (half a square, half a circle, half a dozen), and produce wholes from different parts (a whole Hershey bar from a third, a whole pizza from an eighth) (see Steffe and Olive 2002 for more about constructing wholes from parts).

Divided Quantities or Quotients

The mathematical process that produces a fraction is division: one item or set of items is divided by 2 to produce $\frac{1}{2}$, by 3 to produce $\frac{1}{3}$, and so forth. Students conceptualize fractions as quotients when they divide an item or set of items into equal parts to help them visualize fraction relationships.

Looking at fractions from the perspective of divided quantities or quotients helps students understand an apparently contradictory characteristic of fractions: the larger the number in the denominator, the smaller the fraction. Students know from their informal experiences with equal sharing that the greater the number of sharers, the smaller the quantity for each share. This perspective also prepares students to interpret fractional notation accurately and to understand the importance of position as a component of meaning. Initially students might refer to the parts of a fraction informally as "the top number" and "the bottom number," but the formal terms, *numerator* and *denominator*, help reinforce and define differences.

> **Numerator**   (tells number or how many)
> **Denominator** (names fractional part)

The bottom part or denominator of a fraction is its name. It tells us "which" or "what" fraction we are talking about—halves, thirds, fourths, sixths, and so forth. In fact, inside the word *denominator* is another word, *nom*, which means "name". The top part or numerator of a fraction is the number part. It tells us "how many" halves, thirds, fourths, and so forth we're talking about. Notice the word (almost) *numer* or number inside the longer word *numerator* (Martinez and Martinez 2001, 32).

Activities CD

For an activity connecting fractions to common objects, see Activity 80, Writing and Identifying Fractions, on the CD-ROM that accompanies this text.

Activities CD

For an activity to help make pi more than a number to be memorized, see Activity 85, Pi as a Fraction, on the CD-ROM that accompanies this text.

Operations with Fractions

Most mathematics curricula call for students to perform all of the same operations with fractions that they have learned to perform with whole numbers (addition, subtraction, multiplication, division). However, students may become confused when they discover that the procedures they have learned for working with whole numbers cannot be applied directly to working with fractions. Attempting to force-fit whole-number algorithms to fractions results in problems such as adding or subtracting numerators and denominators:

$$\frac{1}{2} + \frac{1}{2} = \frac{2}{4} \qquad \frac{6}{8} - \frac{2}{4} = \frac{4}{4} = 1$$

Before students are ready to learn conventional algorithms for operations with fractions, they need to develop a conceptual foundation. They need to be able to visualize what is happening when fractions are added, subtracted, multiplied, and divided. And they need to understand how operations with fractions can be both alike and different from operations with whole numbers. Table 12.1, "Comparing Conventional Algorithms for Whole Numbers and Fractions," outlines procedures that are different in detail but still alike in direction and meaning.

Developing a conceptual base begins with doing, representing, and reflecting about the mathematics rather than memorizing vocabulary and procedures.

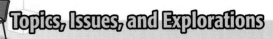

Topics, Issues, and Explorations

Working with students from fifth grade through college, Smith (2002, 11–12) identified four major strategies students use to make sense of fractions: (1) looking at fractions as divided quantities, (2) focusing on numerical components, (3) using reference points, and (4) performing various conversions such as fractions to decimals or percentages and denominators to lowest common denominators.

Do you use any of these strategies when you work with fractions? If so, which ones, and how do they help you understand fraction properties? If not, what strategies do you apply? Do you find that you rely primarily on procedures or concepts to understand fractional relationships?

TABLE 12.1	Comparing Conventional Algorithms for Whole Numbers and Fractions			
Operation	**Whole Numbers Problem**	**Standard Algorithm**	**Fractions Problem**	**Standard Algorithm**
Addition	$\overset{1}{18}$ $+\,93$ 111	Add numbers from right to left, one column at a time. When sum in a column is double digit, carry left digit to next column on left.	$\frac{1}{2} + \frac{2}{8} = \frac{4}{8} + \frac{2}{8} = \frac{6}{8} = \frac{3}{4}$	Find lowest common denominator. Convert fractions. Add numerators. Reduce.
Subtraction	263 $-\,99$ 164	Subtract from right to left, one column at a time. Borrow from left when digit to be subtracted is larger than digit subtracted from.	$\frac{1}{4} - \frac{4}{32} = \frac{8}{32} - \frac{4}{32} = \frac{4}{32} = \frac{1}{8}$	Find lowest common denominator. Convert fractions. Subtract numerators. Reduce.
Multiplication	$\overset{2}{44}$ $\times\,55$ 220 $\underline{220}$ 2420	Multiply one digit at a time from right to left. Line up calculations under multiplier digits. Carry second digit of two-digit results to the left. Add for total.	$\frac{1}{6} \times \frac{3}{4} = \frac{3}{24} = \frac{1}{8}$ $\frac{1}{\underset{2}{6}} \times \frac{\overset{1}{3}}{4} = \frac{1}{8}$	Multiply numerators and denominators. Reduce. OR Prime factor. Cross cancel. Multiply numerators and denominators.
Division	$3\overline{)465}$ with quotient 155 $\underline{3}$ 16 $\underline{15}$ 15 $\underline{15}$ 0	Divide from left to right, one digit at a time. Record answer above each digit divided. Multiply each number of answer by divisor, subtract from number divided. Bring down next digit and repeat process.	$\frac{1}{8} \div \frac{1}{2} = \frac{1}{8} \times \frac{2}{1} = \frac{2}{8} = \frac{1}{4}$ $\frac{1}{8} \div \frac{1}{2} = \frac{1}{\underset{4}{8}} \times \frac{\overset{1}{2}}{1} = \frac{1}{4}$	Invert divisor. Multiply numerators and denominators. Reduce. OR Invert divisor. Prime factor. Cross cancel. Multiply numerators and denominators

Frequently teachers have objected to informal, student-generated algorithms for fear that the often cumbersome personal strategies will interfere with students' learning more efficient, conventional procedures. Yet for many students, inventing an algorithm is a critical step in understanding the mathematics and in making sense of and being able to work meaningfully with the conventional algorithm.

Once children have developed their ideas in personal, informal ways with mathematical integrity, teachers should help students connect their ideas and procedures to conventional algorithms. Classroom discourse should be rich with conventional symbols and language. Lessons should connect concepts and procedures and culminate in the use of symbols.

(Sharp, Garofalo, and Adams 2002, 27)

Addition, Subtraction, and the Least Common Denominator

Adding and subtracting fractions with manipulatives encourages students to visualize fraction relationships before they work with notation. On Jordann's fraction worksheet (see Figure 12.6), she used her fraction circles to help her add $\frac{2}{5}$ and $\frac{1}{10}$. She put two $\frac{1}{5}$ pieces and a $\frac{1}{10}$ piece together, then, comparing them to other fraction pieces, she found that they covered the same amount of space as the $\frac{1}{2}$ piece. She concluded, therefore, that the answer was $\frac{1}{2}$. Another student, asked first to find the number of $\frac{1}{10}$s equal to $\frac{2}{5}$ and then to add that number, $\frac{4}{10}$, and $\frac{1}{10}$, commented, "I see. You make them the same, then add the tops together. That's easier." In a group effort, Reyes, Danny, Adam, and Jose used a combining process to add the different segments of a geoboard square (see Figure 12.7). They added $\frac{1}{16}$ and $\frac{1}{16}$ to get $\frac{1}{8}$ and then added that $\frac{1}{8}$ to the $\frac{1}{8}$ blocked out on the board. The resulting $\frac{1}{4}$ was added to the blocked-out $\frac{1}{4}$ on the board to get $\frac{1}{2}$, which they then added to the board $\frac{1}{2}$ to give them 1. In the process, the boys discovered the ease of adding numbers with like denominators as well as a way numbers with different denominators can be combined.

In each case—Jordann, her classmate, and the geoboard group—manipulating physical objects such as fraction circles and spaces on the geoboard encouraged students not only to visualize the process and results of adding fractions but also to begin to understand the value of working with fractions that have common denominators.

Finding the **least common denominator (LCD)** is a major difference between the conventional algorithms for adding and subtracting whole numbers and fractions (see Table 12.1). Initially students might experiment with fraction pieces to find the common ground—for example, overlaying a $\frac{1}{3}$ piece with $\frac{1}{6}$s to find common ground for subtracting $\frac{1}{6}$ from $\frac{1}{3}$. As problems become more complex, teachers can introduce methods that rely more on manipulating numbers than concrete objects. In Figure 12.8, Kyle looks for the least common denominator by finding the **least common multiple (LCM)** of the denominators. In his fraction worksheet, Kyle first calculates multiples for the denominators, then circles the smallest (or least) numbers the denominators have in common (hence, least common denominator). He converts the fractions by multiplying the numerator by the same number as the denominator.

Once students understand the concept of least common denominators and least common multiples, they can streamline the process or use shortcuts such as the prime-factors method illustrated here: For example, to find the least common multiple for the numbers 8, 10, 12, follow these steps:

Step 1.   Prime-factor each number in the given set.
8 can be prime factored as $2 \times 2 \times 2 = 8$.

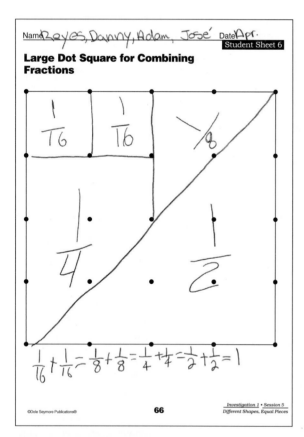

66   *Investigation 1 • Session 5*
Different Shapes, Equal Pieces

Figure 12.7   Adding geoboard fractions.
(From *Investigations, Different Shapes, Equal Pieces* Grade 4 by Cornelia Tierney, Mark Ogonowski, Andee Rubin, and Susan Jo Russell. Copyright 1998 by Dale Seymour Publications. Reprinted by permission of Pearson Education, Inc.).

10 can be prime factored as $5 \times 2 = 10$.

12 can be prime factored as $3 \times 2 \times 2 = 12$.

Step 2. Select each unique prime factor the greatest number of times it appears in any given factorization: 2, 2, 2, 3, 5.

Step 3. Multiply these unique prime factors: $2 \times 2 \times 2 \times 3 \times 5 = 120$ to give you the least common multiple for the set of numbers 8, 10, and 12.

Find the least common multiple of the following numbers: 4, 6, 12, and 18.

Step 1. 4 can be prime factored as $2 \times 2 = 4$.

6 can be prime factored as $2 \times 3 = 6$.

12 can be prime factored as $3 \times 2 \times 2 = 12$.

18 can be prime factored as $2 \times 3 \times 3 = 18$.

Step 2. 2, 2, 3, 3

Step 3. $2 \times 2 \times 3 \times 3 = 36$, which is your least common multiple for the numbers 4, 6, 12, and 18

Finding the least common denominator is integrated meaningfully into adding and subtracting fractions when students have constructed the mental tools that make the procedures involved more than just a sequence of memorized steps. Those steps might include mental images of the process or a thorough grasp of the "whys" behind each step. Asking students to write out procedures in a math journal helps them focus and reflect about their own mathematical thinking. The following examples of adding and subtracting fractions may be more "wordy" than some traditional mathematics teachers prefer, but the explanations underscore the importance of thinking through the procedures when we apply algorithms.

Add: $\frac{1}{2} + \frac{1}{3} + \frac{1}{6}$

First find the least common multiple:

Step 1 Prime-factor all denominators: $2 = 2 \times 1$; $3 = 3 \times 1$; $6 = 3 \times 2$

Step 2. Select each unique prime factor the greatest number of times it appears in any factorization: 2 and 3

Step 3. Multiply these unique prime factors: $2 \times 3 = 6$

Step 4. Identify the least common denominator. Given that 6 is the least common multiple, 6 is also the least common denominator.

Therefore, $\frac{1}{2} + \frac{1}{3} + \frac{1}{6}$ becomes:

$$\frac{1}{2} \times \frac{3}{3} = \frac{3}{6} \qquad \frac{1}{3} \times \frac{2}{2} = \frac{2}{6}$$

$$\frac{3}{6} + \frac{2}{6} + \frac{1}{6} = \frac{6}{6} = 1$$

Visually what happens is this:

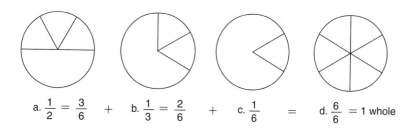

a. $\frac{1}{2} = \frac{3}{6}$ + b. $\frac{1}{3} = \frac{2}{6}$ + c. $\frac{1}{6}$ = d. $\frac{6}{6} = 1$ whole

Figure 12.8 Kyle's fraction worksheet.

Add and subtract: $\frac{1}{2} - \frac{1}{3} + \frac{2}{5} - \frac{1}{6}$

First find the least common multiple:

Step 1. Prime-factor all denominators: $2 = 2 \times 1$; $3 = 3 \times 1$; $5 = 5 \times 1$; $6 = 3 \times 2$

Step 2. Select each unique prime factor the greatest number of times it appears in any factorization: 2, 3, and 5

Step 3. Multiply these unique prime factors: $2 \times 3 \times 5 = 30$

Step 4. Identify the least common denominator. Given that 30 is the least common multiple, 30 is also the least common denominator.

$$\frac{1}{2} \times \frac{15}{15} = \frac{15}{30} \qquad \frac{1}{3} \times \frac{10}{10} = \frac{10}{30} \qquad \frac{2}{5} \times \frac{6}{6} = \frac{12}{30} \qquad \frac{1}{6} \times \frac{5}{5} = \frac{5}{30}$$

$$\frac{15}{30} - \frac{10}{30} + \frac{12}{30} - \frac{5}{30} = \frac{12}{30} = \frac{2}{5}$$

All that adding and subtracting resulted in $\frac{2}{5}$.

Multiplication

Asked whether multiplication always results in more, most students will draw on their sense of whole-number operations and answer, "Yes, always." Operating with fractions, as Huinker (2002, 75) points out, requires students to reexamine their expectations and at the same time to broaden and synthesize their "operation sense" or ways of thinking about operations to include fractions.

Building a new way of thinking about multiplication can begin with the familiar and follow a path of discovery to the unfamiliar. For example, multiplying fractions with whole numbers involves the familiar idea of multiplication as repeated addition. Multiplying $3 \times \frac{1}{4}$ means that you add three $\frac{1}{4}$ths as shown below.

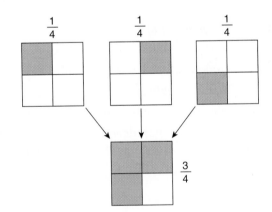

Three $\frac{1}{4}$ above equal $\frac{3}{4}$ below.

Three $\frac{1}{4}$s cover $\frac{3}{4}$s of the original square, so it is less than a whole but more than the $\frac{1}{4}$ used as a multiplier. The problem fits the expectation that multiplication results in more but prepares students to see results that are less than a whole.

Warrington developed a series of bridge activities to help students build on and adjust their understanding to include multiplying fractions by fractions. She began with half, which she considers "the easiest fraction," and posed word problems that led students gradually from finding half of whole numbers to finding half of various fractions (Warrington and Kamii 1998, 340).

If Willy had 15 ounces of orange juice in his Thermos, and he drank half of it during lunch, how many ounces of juice did he drink during lunch?

If Willy had drunk one-fourth of 15 ounces during lunch, how much juice would he have drunk?

If you had half of an apple pie and you ate half of it, how much pie did you eat?

(Warrington and Kamii 1998, 340)

Mack's (2002, 147) approach builds on students' informal knowledge of equal sharing and partitioning ("How can we share 10 cookies among four people?") and then moves on to finding fractions of whole numbers and fractions of fractions ("finding one-fourth of four-fifths of a cookie").

Both Warrington and Mack use language and real-life contexts to help students visualize multiplying fractions with fractions. Instead of asking, "What is $\frac{1}{2}$ *times* $\frac{3}{4}$? or "$\frac{1}{4}$ *times* $\frac{4}{5}$?" they ask, "What is $\frac{1}{2}$ *of* $\frac{3}{4}$?" or "$\frac{1}{4}$ *of* $\frac{4}{5}$?". The word *of* encourages students to formulate a problem-solving strategy that involves partitioning a part of a whole into more parts and in the process to understand that the result will not only be less than a whole but less than the part of the whole with which they began.

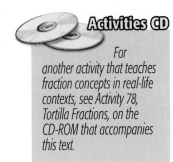

Activities CD

For another activity that teaches fraction concepts in real-life contexts, see Activity 78, Tortilla Fractions, on the CD-ROM that accompanies this text.

Division

As with multiplication, students' experiences with whole-number division may have resulted in expectations that will not directly transfer to fraction division—for example, the idea that dividing always means reducing or making smaller. Traditionally, students are introduced to fraction division with the IM (invert and multiply) algorithm. "Most adults," writes Warrington (2002), " 'invert and multiply' without any notion of why they are doing so, and students usually cannot explain the reasoning behind this frequently used and widely accepted procedure" (150).

Constructing the conceptual framework that culminates in and is summarized by the algorithm is again a building process. The foundation for the framework as well as the starting point for this building process is what students already know—both *constructed* knowledge, what they have learned about division from real-life experiences, and *instructed* knowledge, what they have learned from school mathematics (see Smith 2002).

In a mixed class of fifth and sixth graders, Warrington (2002) started with whole-number division and then proceeded step-by-step from dividing whole numbers by fractions, to dividing fractions by whole numbers, to dividing fractions by fractions. Her students' explanations not only show how students think naturally about fraction division but also how the students tended to create concrete examples to help them visualize new aspects of division. With each expression, Warrington asked the students to think about it and to explain "what it meant to them" (151–52).

Whole-number division: $4 \div 2$
Explanation: "It means how many times does two fit into four or how many groups of two fit into four?"

Division of whole number by fraction: $2 \div \frac{1}{2}$
Explanation: "I think it's four . . . because if you had two candy bars and you divided them into halves, you'd have four pieces."

Division of fraction by whole number: $\frac{1}{3} \div 3$
Explanation: "I think it's one-ninth because if you had one-third of a pie left and you were sharing it with three people [two friends], each person would get one-ninth."

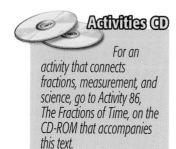

For an activity that connects fractions, measurement, and science, go to Activity 86, The Fractions of Time, on the CD-ROM that accompanies this text.

Division of fraction by a fraction: "I purchased $5\frac{3}{4}$ pounds of chocolate-covered peanuts. I want to store the candy in $\frac{1}{2}$-pound bags so that I can freeze it and use it in smaller portions. How many $\frac{1}{2}$-pound bags can I make?"

Explanations: "You get ten bags from the five pounds because five divided by one-half is ten, and then you get another bag from the three-fourths, which makes eleven bags, and there is one-fourth of a pound left over, which makes a half-pound bag."

"I just doubled it [five and three-fourths] and divided by one . . . to make $11\frac{1}{2}$."

(Warrenton 2000, 151–52)

Building on what they already know about division, Warrington's students created a conceptual framework for understanding that dividing by $\frac{1}{2}$ can be interpreted as doubling—in other words, inverting the fraction and multiplying (the IM algorithm).

That takes us to a key concept for fraction division and the IM algorithm, the **reciprocal.**

> Reciprocals need to be stressed. Students need to realize that $\frac{1}{4}$ is the unit divided into 4 equal parts, and also that the unit is made of four parts of $\frac{1}{4}$ each. Students also need to see that $\frac{1}{4}$ of 4 is 1. These reciprocal relations hold of course for all fractions: $\frac{5}{2}$ is two and a half units, and also two fifths of $\frac{5}{2}$ is 1. Fractions whose product is 1, such as $\frac{1}{5}$ and 5, need to be connected in the students' minds.
>
> *(Flores 2002, 241–242).*

Basically, the reciprocal is the multiplicative inverse of a number—that is, the number we multiply by to get a product of 1. With whole numbers the reciprocal is actually a fraction ($\frac{2}{1} \times \frac{1}{2} = 1$), while with fractions, the reciprocal is a whole number ($\frac{1}{2} \times \frac{2}{1} = 1$). With fraction division, the reciprocal tells us how many groups of a fraction are in 1 (measurement division), or it is the operator needed to reduce the fraction to its component parts and then expand it to 1 (sharing division) (see Siebert 2002, 254). Table 12.2 shows how the reciprocal of $\frac{3}{4}$ or $\frac{4}{3}$ helps shape the meanings of fraction division situations that have the same notation but different contexts.

TABLE 12.2	Measuring and Sharing Interpretations for Division of Fractions	
	Measurement	**Sharing**
Situations	Joel is walking around a circular path in a park that is $\frac{3}{4}$ miles long. If he walks $2\frac{1}{2}$ miles before he rests, how many times around the path did he travel?	Joel is walking around a circular path in a park. If he can walk $2\frac{1}{2}$ miles in $\frac{3}{4}$ of an hour, how far can he walk in an hour, assuming he walks at the same speed?
Guiding question for interpreting $2\frac{1}{2} \div \frac{3}{4}$	How many groups of $\frac{3}{4}$ are in $2\frac{1}{2}$?	If $\frac{3}{4}$ of a group gets $2\frac{1}{2}$, how much does a whole group get?
Meaning of reciprocal	The reciprocal $\frac{4}{3}$ means there are $\frac{4}{3}$ groups of $\frac{3}{4}$ in 1.	The reciprocal $\frac{4}{3}$ is the operator necessary to shink $\frac{3}{4}$ to $\frac{1}{4}$ and then expand $\frac{1}{4}$ to 1.
Reason for multiplying the dividend by the reciprocal of the divisor	There are $\frac{4}{3}$ groups of $\frac{3}{4}$ in 1. There are $2\frac{1}{2}$ times as many groups of $\frac{3}{4}$ in $2\frac{1}{2}$ as there are in 1. Thus, there are $2\frac{1}{2} \times \frac{4}{3}$ groups of $\frac{3}{4}$ in $2\frac{1}{2}$.	Since we shrink/expand $\frac{3}{4}$ by $\frac{4}{3}$ to get 1 whole group, we have to shrink/expand $2\frac{1}{2}$ by $\frac{3}{4}$ in order to find out how much the whole group gets.

Mixed Numbers and Reducing and Simplifying Fractions

Students sometimes find the conventions for working with mixed numbers and also for reducing and simplifying fractions difficult to grasp—not because the conventions are too complex or intellectually challenging but because many students simply do not see the need for turning mixed numbers into improper fractions or for reducing and simplifying fractions. Asked to divide $5\frac{3}{4}$ by $\frac{1}{2}$, Warrington's students divided the chocolate-covered peanuts problem into two parts, $5 \div \frac{1}{2}$ and $\frac{3}{4} \div \frac{1}{2}$. Although the students discovered the foundation for the IM algorithm, "not one child considered converting the mixed numeral $5\frac{3}{4}$ to an improper fraction of $\frac{23}{4}$, which would be the first step in a traditional algorithm" (Warrington 2002, 152). Similarly, students will usually not reduce or simplify fractions. They may know that $\frac{2}{6}$ and $\frac{1}{3}$ are equivalent fractions but not understand why $\frac{1}{3}$ might be preferred over $\frac{2}{6}$ as a final answer.

Before they can understand and apply the conventions, students first must visualize the quantities and relationships they are working with. J.F.'s fractions and mixed numerals worksheet in Figure 12.9 uses segments of pizza and circles to represent mixed numbers. J.F. goes a step further: he puts the segments together in his own drawings and then darkens parts of the circles to help him visualize wholes and parts of wholes.

Games such as Find Grampy—Strict at the Visual Fractions Web site use number lines to help students see and simplify mixed numbers (http://www.visualfractions.com/FindGrampystrict.html). Players use segments of the line to identify whole numbers and fractions, and then enter Grampy's location in lowest terms.

Some key questions to ask in simplifying improper fractions follow:

- How many wholes can you make from the fraction?
- What fraction (if any) of a whole is left over?
- Is that fraction expressed in its lowest terms?

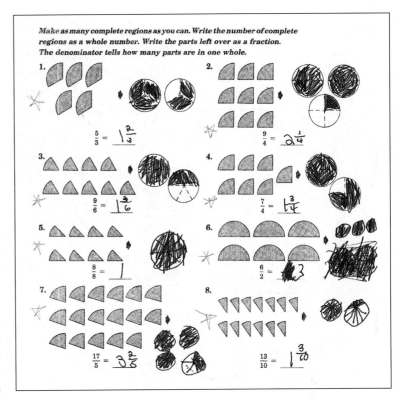

Figure 12.9 J.F.'s Fractions and mixed numerals worksheet. (From Student book 10-10. Charles E. Merrill, 1987, 286.)

Mathematical Games

Grammy and Grampy Fractions

A series of games at Richard Rand's Visual Fractions Web site (http://www.visualfractions.com/) encourages players to visualize fraction order and relationships and to identify and write fractions and mixed numbers.

- In Find Grampy, Grammy uses a number line to help players find Grampy, who is hiding. The game's object is to identify fractions on the number line.
- *Find Grampy—Strict* again features a hiding Grampy. To score, players must use a mixed number and simplify it to lowest terms.

- *Cookies for Grampy* has players build cookies with fractional pieces. Images in the game emphasize circle representations of fractions.
- *Find Grammy* reverses the usual game plot. Players help Grampy find Grammy while Grampy provides two-word clues.

With all four games, students build confidence and flexibility in identifying fractions and performing operations. Other activities at the site give additional instruction and practice with identifying, renaming, comparing, adding, subtracting, multiplying, and dividing fractions.

Like many conventional algorithms, reducing or simplifying fractions can be seen primarily as a matter of efficiency. It is simply easier to work with fractions expressed in their lowest terms. Sometimes arriving at those lowest terms can be challenging, especially if the numbers involved are large. Kimberly, a preservice teacher, used factor trees to help her students map the process of reducing fractions, step-by-step.

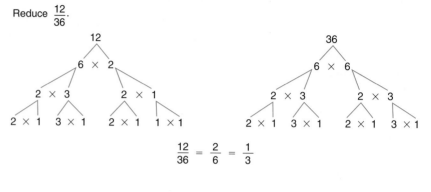

Brandon, a student in Kimberly's class, used the tree method to reduce the fractions in Figure 12.10.

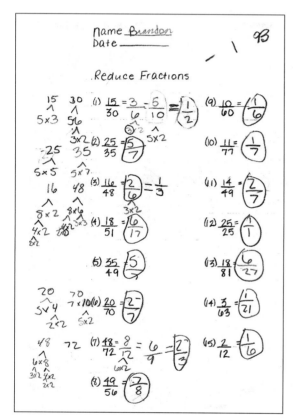

Figure 12.10 Brandon reduces fractions.

Diversity in Learning and Thinking Mathematically

What do you do if cut-outs, virtual manipulatives, and even pizza parties fail to engage your students in the study of fractions? Amy Lein, a classical violinist, jazz singer, and math and science teacher, developed a series of fractions activities that she calls "Jazz and Math: Rhythmic Innovations" (http://www.pbs.org/jazz/classroom/rhythmicinnovations.htm). She introduces students to jazz rhythms by having them watch Ken Burns's PBS documentary about Buddy Burns's Bolden.

The students explore musical notation and fraction equivalents and use fraction pie pieces and fraction bar manipulatives to represent notes (see the Mathematics Across the Curriculum feature).

Rand Barker, who is featured in this chapter's Teacher Pro-File, uses fraction games to engage students and keep them on task. Because his students make their own fraction kits for playing the games, they have fraction pieces to take home and use to model homework problems.

Activities CD

For an activity that connects math an music, see Activity 89, Jazz and Math, Rhythmic Innovations, on the CD-ROM that accompanies this text.

Mathematics Across the Curriculum

Jazz and Fractions

Jazz legend Buddy Bolden is remembered for creating the "Big Four" beat, the basis of jazz's uneven, lilting rhythms. Amy Lein's "Jazzy Lessons and Activities for K–12 Cats" begin with Episode 1, "Gumbo," of Ken Burns's *Jazz* documentary.

Students watch the documentary and discuss the differences between jazz and march rhythms. They duplicate the rhythms by clapping or dancing and then look for ways to represent the rhythms on paper. Students explore the relationship of rhythms, musical notation, and fractions. As a group, they answer questions such as these:

How long does a quarter note last? How many quarter notes make up 1 whole note?

Students practice writing out musical measures in notes and fractions. To add visual and tactile dimensions, they represent notes with fraction pie pieces and fraction bar manipulatives, coloring in different segments to represent different notes and fractions (see figure).

In addition to the video and fraction manipulatives, the lessons call for access to the PBS Jazz Web site, which has a Fraction of a Note chart, a Rhythms Worksheet with fraction and note equivalents, and a variety of visuals and tools.

Musical Note		Number/Fraction	Diagram (Parts of Whole)
whole note		1	
half note		$\frac{1}{2}$	
quarter note		$\frac{1}{4}$	
eighth note		$\frac{1}{8}$	
sixteenth note		$\frac{1}{16}$	

Fractions and musical notation.

From http://www.pbs.org/jazz/classroom/rhythmicinnovations.htm.

Teacher Pro-File

Rand Barker
Fifth Grade

Teaching Fractions with Games

Rand Barker calls himself an "idealistic" teacher who prefers to work outside the box of traditional textbooks and lock-step curricula. Some of his most successful teaching strategies are to introduce difficult or challenging concepts with games and to use computer graphics to help students visualize and represent fractions.

Rand introduces fractions to a fifth-grade class.

Overview

Engaging all of the students and keeping them on task is Rand's first concern when he teaches mathematics. He uses games to introduce fractions because they set concepts in a positive, play context and avoid his students' knee-jerk, instant-boredom reaction to text lessons.

The games, including Cover-up and Uncover by Marilyn Burns, explore fraction equivalence and order. Students identify and compare fractions and make estimations. Computer graphics let students interpret number relationships in terms of shapes and shades.

Procedure

Students begin by creating their own fraction kits from strips of colored paper and labeling them with numbers and words: one red strip for $\frac{1}{1}$ or one whole; two orange strips for $\frac{1}{2}$ or one half; four gray strips for $\frac{1}{4}$ or one-fourth; eight pink strips for $\frac{1}{8}$ or one eighth; sixteen white strips for $\frac{1}{16}$ or one sixteenth. Students use the fraction strips and fraction die to play the games. In the first game, Cover-up, game players roll a fraction die to select fraction pieces to place on the whole strip. In Uncover, players roll the die to select pieces to remove from the whole strip. The first player to cover the whole strip or remove all the pieces wins.

Once students can identify fractions and have made some comparisons, they are ready to create representations on the computer. Students use different shapes and sizes to show that a fraction represents a relationship rather than an exact size or specific form.

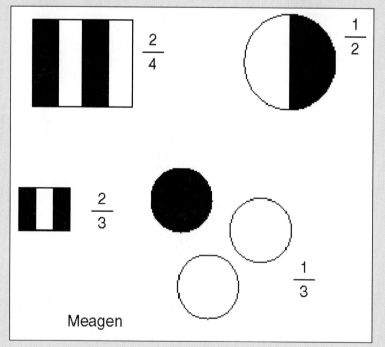

Meagen's computer graphics fractions.

Outcomes

From the games, students learn to identify different fractions, to develop a sense for which fraction is larger or smaller, and to begin to understand fraction equivalence. They then move on to applying concepts—not only in representing fractions with computer graphics but also in using their fraction kits to model mixed numbers and various operations.

Rand introduces additional games periodically to maintain motivation and to keep students focused. The game of Magic Squares has students fill in blanks and columns of whole numbers and fractions to reach the magic sum of $8\frac{1}{2}$. The MARS Fraction Hunt (a game by Paul T. Williams of Phoenix, AZ) mixes words and fractions. And Fraction Conversion Bingo (a game by Mike Wales of Golden, CO) reinforces students' understanding of the relationships among fractions, decimals, and percentages.

Commentary

Rand emphasizes the need to tailor or "dress up" lessons to fit the learning styles and needs of individual students. "Mathematics," he writes, "needs to be anchored to the students' reality and everyday existence for them to want to bite into it and attempt to digest the concepts." He is concerned that math curricula and materials too often force-fit students, falling short of a natural match of learners and learning objectives. Rand's remedy for this approach includes

- creating multiple-level instruction,
- matching instruction to individual styles,
- emphasizing hands-on activities,
- engaging students with high-interest activities such as the fraction games and computer work, and
- keeping students on task with visual and physical stimuli and by thinking and encouraging students to think outside the box of texts and standard procedures.

◀◀◀◀ LOOKING BACK

Fractions are a challenging subject to learn and to teach. Building fraction sense calls for understanding both the similarities and the differences between whole-number and fraction systems.

Students need to create mental tools for working with fractions, including visual images that help them estimate size, order, and other relationships. Multiple experiences with multiple manipulatives seem to be the key to establishing a conceptual foundation for understanding fractions.

Traditionally, operations with fractions have been introduced primarily as step-by-step procedures. However, conventional algorithms make more sense to students when they first develop their own informal algorithms based on hands-on and real-life experiences with fractions.

Fraction concepts are more accessible when students recognize their widespread applications in life—for example in musical notation, equal-sharing situations, cooking, and other measurement tasks.

Questions for Further Thought, Discussion, and Research

1. Many adults who admit to being math anxious cite fractions as a key component of their negative feelings about math. Conduct an informal survey among your classmates, friends, and other adults. Compose a series of open-ended questions about fractions, such as "Do you like fractions? Why or why not?" "What do you know or not know about fractions?" "How did you learn fraction operations?" Discuss the results of your surveys. Are you able to draw any conclusions about fractions and math anxiety?

2. Conventional algorithms are a major focus of some mathematics curricula. Outline the key topics; then explore the importance of each to students' understanding and working effectively with fractions.

3. The Internet offers many different sites to help students learn and teachers teach fractions. Surf the web for the sites you consider the most helpful. Compile an annotated bibliography; share and combine the results to create an Internet Fractions Resource.

4. Use Amy Lein's Jazz Fractions as a model to create a fraction unit tied to a special interest of your own or of someone you know well—music, cooking, quilting, art, puzzles, sports, and so forth.

5. Do some research about the history of fractions as part of our number system. Who among the ancients used fractions? Did they use them in the same way that we do today? How were the conventional algorithms developed? How long have fractions been a focus of school learning? What about pi? Is the $\frac{22}{7}$ fraction as useful as 3.1416 or more accurate computations?

13

LOOKING AHEAD >>>>

Although school curricula often emphasize fractions as a way of representing part-whole relationships, everyday mathematics in the media, financial transactions, and even government documents such as tax forms often represent parts of wholes with decimals and percents. Understanding and using decimals and percents is as much a survival skill as an academic goal. Yet, according to the National Assessment of Educational Progress (NAEP), most students' knowledge is limited. They can identify decimals and percents but not use them effectively in problem-solving situations.

NCTM Standards call for students to work flexibly with fractions, decimals, and percents. To do this, they need to build conceptual bridges including mental tools for visualizing and representing parts of wholes as fractions, decimals, and percents. They also need to make connections with important foundational concepts such as the base-10 number system and develop strategies for applying operations.

NCTM Standards also suggest emphasizing proportionality in the middle grades. However, students' thinking about ratio and proportion begins much earlier. As they compare sizes and explore patterns, students develop informal strategies for working with multiplicative relationships and lay foundations for understanding formal algorithms.

Exploring Part–Whole Relationships: Decimals, Percents, Ratio, and Proportion

Understanding Decimals and Percents

Children encounter decimals and percents at an early age. Usually, they first discover decimals as the dividing point between dollars and cents in money notation. Percents are often connected with evaluation even in the early grades, with benchmarks such as 100% quickly established for exemplary achievement, while another benchmark such as 50% might mean a poor performance or, conversely, as in "50% off," an excellent sale.

Being able to read and interpret decimals in numbers and percents in contexts such as opinion polls, sales, or statistical data is an important survival skill. It might even be considered an essential component of basic literacy (verbal and mathematical). Without this skill, students would have a difficult time reading and understanding many newspaper and magazine articles or sales advertisements, including the pop-up ads that appear on the Internet.

The abundance of practical, everyday applications might lead us to expect students to be able to recognize and read decimals and percents in a variety of contexts. Tests such as the NAEP and TIMSS (Trends in International Mathematics and Science Study) show that most students can identify and interpret decimals and percents correctly in simple diagrams or one-step problems (National Center for Education Statistics [NCES] 2003; Beaton et al. 1996). However, many students have difficulty with multistep problems as well as with some situations that require them to make fraction/decimal/percent conversions.

Figure 13.1 shows examples of NAEP questions and the results for eighth graders. Problem (a), the cost of eggs problem, asks students to multiply with a decimal—something that 85% did successfully. However, just 51% were able to convert the decimal to a fraction in Problem (b), and only 40% could use percent to find cost in Problem (c), the used-car problem. Problem (d) asks students to find 38% of 1,200—something they could do by converting 38% to 0.38 and multiplying or by estimating from benchmarks: 50% of 1,200 = 600 − 10% of 1,200 or 120 to get approximately 480 and make the correct answer *B*, 456. Most students, or 54%, chose the correct answer but still significantly fewer than answered correctly for Problem (a). A mere 1% answered Problem (e), a percent increase problem correctly.

Overall, performance on the NAEP example problems declined significantly as we move from problems that emphasize recognition and simple procedures to those that are more complex and require multistep solutions. Moreover, in the final problem (the one example shown here that is not multiple choice), 21% of students achieved only partial answers, while 18%

Activities CD

For an activity that uses newspapers to help connect decimals and percents to the real world, see Activity 96, Decimals and Percents in Your World, on the CD-ROM that accompanies this text.

Mathematics in the Real World

Decimals and Percents in the Newspaper

Decimals and percents form an important part of newspaper language. They can be used in stories about national or international news, sports, finance, or human interest topics. They often appear in advertisements, including the classifieds.

Activity 1

Working in small groups, survey a local, state, or national newspaper (such as *USA Today*) for decimals and percents. Keep a log of each example found. Write out the sentence or other context for the example and the story, section, and page where you found it. Then explain in your own words what each number means in terms of its context.

Activity 2

Research and write your own news stories using decimals and percents.

Collect information about the costs of various items in your school cafeteria or snack bar or at a popular fast-food restaurant. Then write a story about the costs in dollars and cents of various meals, including your assessment of the best deal for most students' budgets.

Survey classmates or family members about their favorite foods, colors, TV shows, celebrities, or other topic. Convert the data you collect to percents, using the number surveyed as 100% and the number for each selection as percents of the whole. Write a news report about your findings. Include a bar or pie chart.

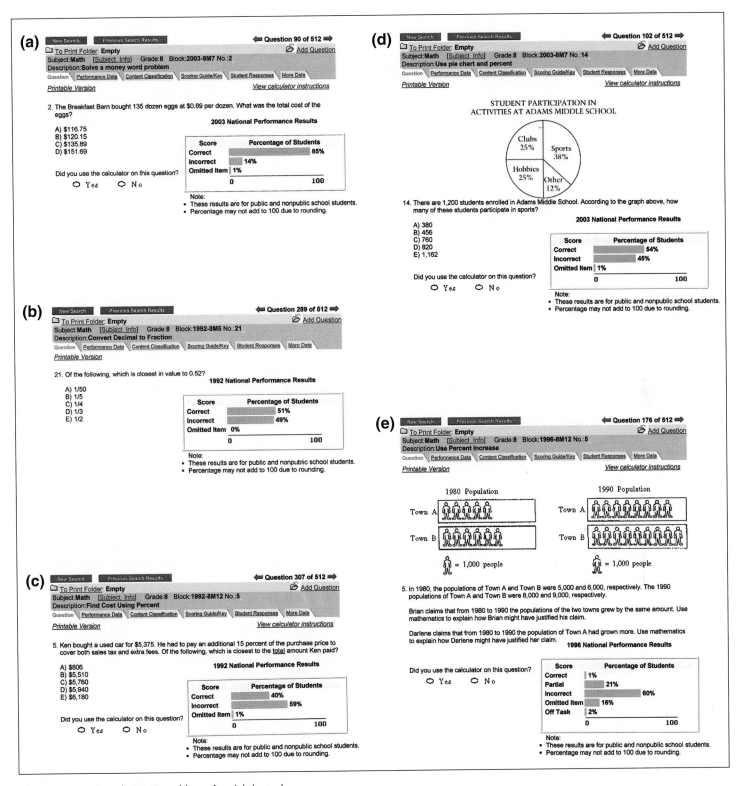

Figure 13.1 Sample NAEP problems for eighth graders.
(NAEP NQT v2.0—Question @http://nces.ed.gov/nationsreportcard/itmrls/qtab.asp)

either omitted the problem or were off task. Similar results for TIMSS show a major decrease in performance as objectives shift from identification to application and from one-step to multistep problems (see Beaton et al. 1996, 57–64, 93–98).

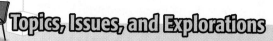

Topics, Issues, and Explorations

Brainstorm in a small group about everyday uses of decimals and percents. List and give examples of uses. Then talk about what you need to know to understand these uses.

Although some interpret test results primarily as an indictment of current curricula and methods, they are more useful as guides for setting goals. In terms of teaching decimals and percents, students' performance suggests some specific needs:

Topics, Issues, and Explorations

Assess your own level of understanding decimals and percents. Work out each of the example problems in Figure 13.1 from NAEP. Talk about how you solved them and what problems the eighth-graders taking the test might have encountered.

- the need to connect fractions, decimals, and percents;
- the need to develop flexibility in using the different ways of representing and working with parts of wholes and in estimating and rounding;
- the need to understand and use decimals and percents in practical, everyday applications;
- the need to understand and explore decimals and percents as mathematical ideas with connections to other mathematical concepts;
- the need to understand and perform basic mathematical operations with decimals and percents.

Connecting Fractions, Decimals, and Percents

NCTM's *Principles and Standards* emphasizes the connections among fractions, decimals, and percents and the importance of underscoring those connections by teaching the concepts in tandem.

In grades 3–5, students should have learned to generate and recognize equivalent forms of fractions, decimals, and percents, at least in some simple cases. In the middle grades, students should build on and extend this experience to become facile in using fractions, decimals, and percents meaningfully.

(NCTM 2000, 215)

Applications will be more meaningful if they are tied to concrete activities and models such as manipulating base-10 blocks, fraction strips and circles, or decimal squares. For example, using coins and dollar bills to model wholes, fractions, decimal amounts, and percents prepares the way for problems such as the following from an Everyday Math worksheet:

How many pennies are in $1?_____

What fraction of $1 is one penny?_____

What percent of $1 is one penny?_____%

(Everyday Math 1999)

Elizabeth Sweeney and Robert Quinn use visual images and a game of Concentration to keep students engaged in a series of lessons designed to develop fluency in identifying and using different representations of part–whole relationships. After assessing students' knowledge, the teachers show them circles shaded to represent parts of the whole. As a group the class compiles a chart of equivalent values including not only decimals, percents, and fractions but also the corresponding degrees of a circle. Students model relationships on geoboards and use calculators to make conversions. Then they build on what they have learned to create the materials and play games of Concentration in which equivalent expressions are matched (see the Mathematical Games feature). "Once the students can determine fractions, decimals, percents, and degrees for a given figure fairly easily, it is time to move forward. Explain to the students that they will be creating their own games of Concentration using fractions, decimals, percents, and circle graphs" (Sweeney and Quinn 2000, 327).

Visual representations are foundational for learning experiences that connect fractions, decimals, and percents. At the National Library of Virtual Manipulatives (http://matti.usu.edu), students in grades 3–8 can use a virtual manipulative that represents part–whole relationships with two graphs. Students choose two of three numbers (whole, percent, and decimal); the manipulative fills in the third number and shows the relationship by coloring portions of a bar and a circle. The manipulative also represents the relationships with formulas that show how to find equivalent expressions (see the Math and Technology feature). Visuals not only make the relationships concrete but also help students develop mental images of parts-of-wholes—images of halves, thirds, fourths, and other benchmark quantities that serve as reference points when they compare and estimate.

Activities CD

For an activity to help students develop a sense for equivalent expressions, see Activity 95, Playing Concentration with Parts of Wholes, on the CD-ROM that accompanies this text.

Topics, Issues, and Explorations

In small groups, create a deck of 32 Parts-of-Whole Concentration cards. Play the game. Then discuss ways you might vary the game to focus on different learning objectives or content.

Mathematical Games

Parts-of-Whole Concentration

Students use fractions, decimals, percents, and circle graphs to create playing cards for Parts-of-Whole Concentration.

To prepare, in groups of four, students are given numbers in fraction, decimal, or percent form. Each group then determines equivalent values and makes a set of four cards—one each for decimal, percent, fraction, and circle graph. Groups may create a complete deck of 8-card sets or 32 cards or combine their sets with other groups.

To play, the cards are shuffled and placed face down on the table in a four-by-eight rectangular array. Students can play as individuals or as groups. Each turns two cards face up. If the cards show equivalent expressions, they form a match and are removed from play. If they do not match, they are returned to the table face down. Play continues until all of the cards have been matched.

Variation

Give each group eight different numbers, and ask them to create a complete set of cards. Have the groups exchange sets of cards one or more times during play to give students practice with the different numbers.

Source: Adapted from Sweeney and Quinn (2000, 327).

For an activity using the National Library of Virtual Manipulatives, see Activity 93, Connecting Fractions, Decimals, Percents with Virtual Manipulatives, on the CD-ROM that accompanies this text.

Math and Technology

Connecting Fractions, Decimals, and Percents with Virtual Manipulatives

Developing facility and flexibility in changing from fractions to decimals and percents and back again requires not only the ability to manipulate the numbers involved but also meaningful practice. To make practice with conversions meaningful, the National Library of Virtual Manipulatives (http://matti.usu.edu) uses a format that mixes visual representations and numbers.

Students using the manipulative fill in numbers for two of the three: decimals, percents, wholes. The display then fills in the third number and represents the relationship with two visuals, a bar and a circle colored to show the part of the whole.

If the student chooses a whole of 1 and a part of 0.5, the display will look something like this:

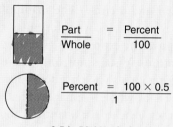

$$\frac{\text{Part}}{\text{Whole}} = \frac{\text{Percent}}{100}$$

$$\text{Percent} = \frac{100 \times 0.5}{1}$$

0.5 is 50.0% of whole

Altering any of the numbers and/or relationships changes the displays. Students can experiment with percents, decimals, or wholes as a starting point.

Topics, Issues, and Explorations

Identify a set of equivalent numbers, such as $\frac{1}{4}$, 25%, and 0.25. Create a set of visuals that show the part–whole relationship from several perspectives.

Exploring Decimals and Percents as Mathematical Concepts

Students often have a great deal of informal knowledge about decimals and percents. They see and use the decimal when they work with money. In fact, asked to give their definition of a decimal, students often say, "It's the period that divides the dollars from the cents." Percents are usually associated with sales—20% off, 50% off, extra 15% off—and are also connected with monetary transactions. Few middle schoolers (and not that many adults) actually perform the calculations to determine how much they are saving.

To introduce more complex decimal and percent applications, we need to move beyond this informal level of knowledge and explore the mathematical concepts. For decimals, this means going back to the ideas of a base-10 number system.

Decimals

Although we often use the word *decimal* to describe the point placed between whole and parts-of-whole numbers, *decimal* actually has a broader meaning. It means "of or based on the number 10." It refers not only to the decimal point and numbers to its right but also to our base-10 number system in general.

Millions	Hundred Thousands	Ten Thousands	Thousands	Hundreds	Tens	Ones
3	4	6	5	2	7	8

The chart above shows the base-10 or decimal system for whole numbers with an example of a whole number in the second row. The number, 3,465,278, can be represented and expanded in several ways. Written in words, the amount would be,

"Three million, four hundred sixty-five thousand, two hundred seventy-eight."

An expanded representation in numbers would look like this:

$3,000,000 + 465,000 + 278$

$= (3 \times 1,000,000) + (4 \times 100,000) + (6 \times 10,000) + (5 \times 1,000) + (2 \times 100) + (7 \times 10) + 8$

$= (3 \times 10^6) + (4 \times 10^5) + (6 \times 10^4) + (5 \times 10^3) + (2 \times 10^2) + (7 \times 10^1) + (8 \times 10^0)$

In the number, 3,465,278, place value increases by a factor of 10 as we move from right to left; it increases from an exponent or power of 0 to an exponent of 6. The following chart shows the progression with exponents.

Millions	Hundred Thousands	Ten Thousands	Thousands	Hundreds	Tens	Ones
10^6	10^5	10^4	10^3	10^2	10^1	10^0

Giving more detail, we have the following:

$10^0 = 1$
$10^1 = 10 \times 1 = 10$
$10^2 = 10 \times 10 = 100$
$10^3 = 10 \times 10 \times 10 = 1,000$
$10^4 = 10 \times 10 \times 10 \times 10 = 10,000$
$10^5 = 10 \times 10 \times 10 \times 10 \times 10 = 100,000$
$10^6 = 10 \times 10 \times 10 \times 10 \times 10 \times 10 = 1,000,000$

All of this information concretizes the relationship of place value to the base-10 decimal system, demonstrating how we can build and represent large numbers using just nine digits and 0.

But what does it mean when there are numbers to the right of the decimal point? The simplest answer to this question is they are fractions or parts of one. Consider, for example, the decimal number 0.125.

Topics, Issues, and Explorations

Try your hand at representing large numbers with expanded notation: 2,305; 33,678; 1,200,000. Write each number in at least two ways. Discuss what the expanded notation makes clear that might be overlooked in reading the numbers alone.

In words, then, 0.125 would be "one hundred and twenty-five thousandths." In expanded notation:

$$0.1 + 0.02 + 0.005$$
$$= (1 \times 0.1) + (2 \times 0.01) + (5 \times 0.001)$$
$$= (1 \times \tfrac{1}{10}) + (2 \times \tfrac{1}{100}) + (5 \times \tfrac{1}{1000})$$
$$= (1 \times \tfrac{1}{10^1}) + (2 \times \tfrac{1}{10^2}) + (5 \times \tfrac{1}{10^3})$$

The next chart shows place values to the right of the decimal point and at the same time gives us another set of equivalent representations for decimal numbers, this time using exponents.

Ones	Tenths	Hundredths	Thousandths	Ten Thousandths	Hundred Thousandths
1	$\dfrac{1}{10}$	$\dfrac{1}{100}$	$\dfrac{1}{1000}$	$\dfrac{1}{10,000}$	$\dfrac{1}{100,000}$
10^0	$\dfrac{1}{10^1}$	$\dfrac{1}{10^2}$	$\dfrac{1}{10^3}$	$\dfrac{1}{10^4}$	$\dfrac{1}{10^5}$

In the following list, each denominator is expanded to show the relationship between the base-10 exponential value and the expanded form of the value.

$$10^0 = 1$$
$$\frac{1}{10^1} = \frac{1}{10}$$
$$\frac{1}{10^2} = \frac{1}{100}$$
$$\frac{1}{10^3} = \frac{1}{1,000}$$
$$\frac{1}{10^4} = \frac{1}{10,000}$$
$$\frac{1}{10^5} = \frac{1}{100,000}$$
$$\frac{1}{10^6} = \frac{1}{1,000,000}$$

Decimals and Visuals

Do visuals help or hinder learning decimals? The answer to that question may seem obvious; however, some educators believe that decimals can best be understood as abstract concepts. In an article in *Teaching Children Mathematics*, the authors analyze TIMSS data that suggest that third and fourth graders in our country do less well on problems involving decimals than on problems focusing on fractions. One culprit, according to this article, may be that our youngsters are unable to work with visual representations of decimals (Glasgow et al. 2000, 89–93).

Representing decimal values visually may in fact be more difficult than representing whole numbers or basic fractions such as $\tfrac{1}{2}$, $\tfrac{1}{3}$, and so forth. An effective manipulative tool is the same base-10 blocks students use to explore place values for whole numbers. The Math Manipulatives feature describes activities that use base-10 blocks to show relationships between the whole number one and parts of that whole represented by numbers to the right of the decimal point. The cube block represents 1; the flat, which is $\tfrac{1}{10}$ of a cube, represents $\tfrac{1}{10}$; a rod, $\tfrac{1}{100}$; and a unit (one part of the cube), $\tfrac{1}{1,000}$.

 **Math Manipulatives**

Decimals and Base-10 Blocks

Most students are familiar with base-10 blocks to represent whole numbers—units for 1s, rods for 10s, flats for 100s, and cubes for 1,000s. Using the same blocks for decimals calls for a shift in perspective and for understanding that the blocks can be used to show relationships as well as whole-number counts.

For decimal activities, we can use the cube as 1, flats for $\frac{1}{10}$s, rods for $\frac{1}{100}$s, and units for $\frac{1}{1,000}$s.

Activity 1

Use base-10 blocks to build numbers that include decimal fractions—for example, 3.4, 1.235, 0.647, 1.938, and 2.001. Write the numbers you build in expanded notation, such as

$2.325 = 2$ cubes $+ 3$ flats $+ 2$ rods $+ 5$ units

$2.325 = 2$ ones $+ 3$ tenths $+ 2$ hundredths $+ 5$ thousandths

$2.325 = (2 \times 1) + (3 \times \frac{1}{10}) + (2 \times \frac{1}{100}) + (5 \times \frac{1}{1000})$

Activity 2

Explore greater than, less than, or equal values for decimal numbers. Count out the blocks in Column 1. Trade blocks to represent a number using the fewest blocks possible. Write the number you build. Use the symbols >, <, and = to compare the number you build with the number in Column 2.

Column 1	Symbol >, <, =	Column 2
11 rods		
16 units		0.12
number =		

Create additional blocks and number situations to cover each relationship: greater than, less than, and equal.

Source: Adapted from Nortman-Wolf (1990, 79–84).

In the following examples, shaded figures like those often used to show fractions represent decimal numbers. In each example,

1. Count the number of cells or parts of the whole.

2. Determine what part or fraction of the whole is shaded.

3. Convert your fraction into a decimal equivalent.

The first example has 10 parts; 2 are shaded; therefore, $\frac{2}{10}$ or 0.20 is shaded.

The second has 8 parts; 2 are shaded; therefore, $\frac{2}{8} = \frac{1}{4} = 0.25$ is shaded.

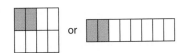

The third has 15 parts; 5 are shaded; therefore, $\frac{5}{15} = \frac{1}{3} = 0.33$ is shaded.

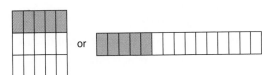

Another approach is to use decimal squares. Students can count the parts of a 10×10 square indicated by the decimal number and then fill in the parts for a visual representation (see Figure 13.2).

 **Activities CD**

For an activity that involves using base-10 blocks to model decimals, see Activity 92, Modeling Decimal Numbers with Base-10 Blocks, on the CD-ROM that accompanies this text.

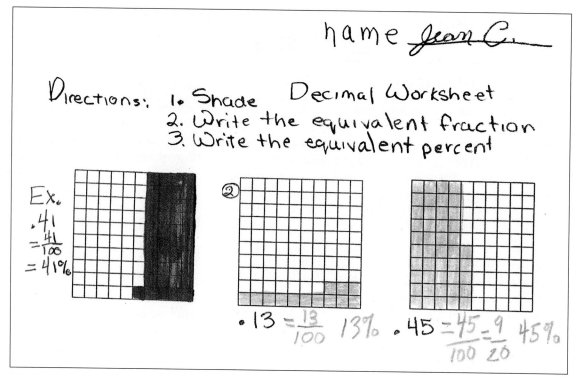

Figure 13.2 Decimal squares from a student's worksheet.

Topics, Issues, and Explorations

Develop visuals and use them to build the following decimals: 0.01; 0.33; 0.25; 0.50; 0.125; 0.80. Write the decimals in expanded notation. Identify and discuss the decimals that can be used as benchmarks for comparisons.

Percents

Informal knowledge can present some special problems for students' understanding the mathematical idea of percent. Most know that a 50% off sale is better than a 30% off sale but not that a 60% off sale is better than 50% off plus an extra 15% off. Moreover, many are not bothered at all by a coach's demanding 125% or a company's promising 200% satisfaction.

Understanding percent as a mathematical idea starts with understanding the word *percent*. It is from the Italian, *per cento*, which means "per hundred." In other words, when we talk about percents and parts of a whole, we are talking about a very specific relationship: a whole divided into 100 parts with the percent constituting a numerical part of that hundred. In addition, the symbol % means "for percent," so that $p\% = \frac{p}{100}$ (Harris and Stocker 1998, 16). Specifically, 7% means 7 out of 100; 40% means 40 out of 100; 100% means 100 out of 100 or a whole.

Any percent can be represented as a fraction and as a decimal.

7% = 7 per hundred or $\frac{7}{100}$ or 0.07

40% = 40 per hundred or $\frac{40}{100}$, which can be simplified to $\frac{4}{10} = \frac{2}{5}$ or 0.40

100% = 100 per hundred or $\frac{100}{100}$, which can be simplified to $\frac{10}{10}$ or 1.0

Visual representations for percents can be 10 × 10 grids, as in Figure 13.2, or segments of circles, such as the graphs used by Sweeney and Quinn in their Parts-of-Whole Concentration game. Significantly, some students have a problem creating a pie chart with percents because they are unclear about the basic parameters for their calculations. That is, they do not understand that—

- the total for the percents must add up to 100;
- the whole on which the percents are based is 360° so that each 1 percent is represented by a 3.6° segment of the circle.

Devon, whose color-of-eyes graph is shown in Figure 13.3, appears to have confused degrees and percents. His percents add up to 368 instead of 100. On the other hand, another student, who surveyed family and classmates for data about pictures, calculates percents that add up roughly to 100, but there appears to be no relationship between the percent and the segment of the circle. The same-size segment is used for 14.3% and 28.6%, except in one case where a 14.3% segment is twice the size of the others. Nonetheless, the student does use the combined percent and decimal notation accurately, with tenths of a percent expressed as 0.6 or 0.3 (see Figure 13.4).

Working with a similar set of survey data, Scott manages to put it all together. His survey of various types of frogs results in a total of 25 frogs. He calculates percents of the total for five different types of frogs, achieving a total of 100%, and the segments of his pie chart for the most part match the percents, with 36% having a larger segment than 24% and 4%, a much smaller segment than 16% (see Figure 13.5).

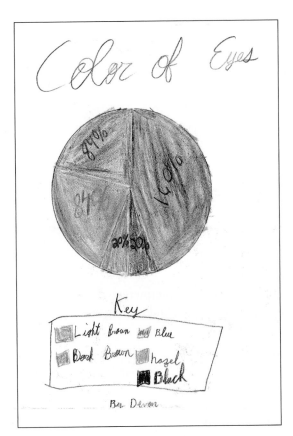

Figure 13.3 Color-of-eyes percent graph.

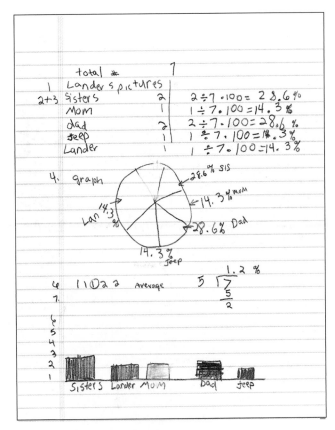

Figure 13.4 Percents for picture survey.

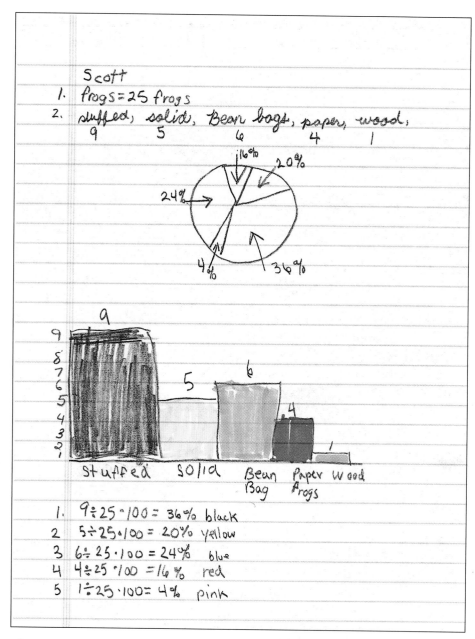

Figure 13.5 Percent of frogs.

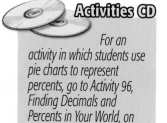

Activities CD

For an activity in which students use pie charts to represent percents, go to Activity 96, Finding Decimals and Percents in Your World, on the CD-ROM that accompanies this text.

Because percents are an important tool in interpreting and representing data, students should become proficient in reading and making pie charts. Some questions to help them evaluate their own work include these:

- What is the total quantity that makes up your whole or 100%?
- If you apply benchmarks to that total, what amount would be half or 50%, a fourth or 25%, a third or $33\frac{1}{3}$%?
- When you have calculated percents of your total, do the percents add up (at least roughly after rounding) to 100%?
- If you were to represent the benchmark fractions and percents on a pie chart, how much of the circle would represent a half, a fourth, a third?

■ When you represent the percent calculations of your total, do the relationships look right? Is 26% a larger segment than 14%, and is 18% shown with a segment twice the size of 9%?

Googol: BIG IDEAS in Mathematics

100% of a Whole and No More

Frequently in the media or conversation, we read statements such as "We give 110%" or "She is 200% correct." The intent, of course, is to emphasize the level of giving or correctness; however, mathematically there is a problem. Strictly speaking, one cannot give more than all or be more than totally correct, and 100% means both all and the sum total.

For students, this distinction between conventional uses and mathematical meaning can be confusing. Linking percents as parts of a whole with the whole itself calls for activities that show the relationships in a variety of ways.

Activity 1

Begin with multiple cutouts of circles, rectangles, squares, hexagons, and other polygons. Cut the figures in halves, fourths, thirds, sixths, and twelfths. Figure out, label, and record the percent for each part. Add the numbers to get 100%. Then mix and match parts of the same shape; that is, combine a half of a circle with two-fourths or combine six-twelfths of a hexagon with three-sixths. Add the percents for each mix-and-match figure to get 100%.

Activity 2

Work with a compass and protractor to explore degrees and percents of a circle. Use the compass to draw circles with various radii. Use the protractor to divide a circle into fractions and percents. Figure out the number of degrees for each segment in two ways—measuring with the protractor and calculating the percent of 360°.

Activities CD

For an activity about the properties of polygons, see Activity 56, Tessellating Polygons, on the CD-ROM that accompanies this text.

Number lines combine visual representation with number notation—an effective partnership for making comparisons as well as for integrating work with parts of wholes and previous knowledge of whole numbers. Moreover, the relationship between the number line and decimals and percents extends our knowledge by allowing comparisons of parts of whole numbers. Typically, a number line used to compare whole numbers looks something like this:

To use the same line to compare parts of whole numbers, we might stretch the space between each whole number.

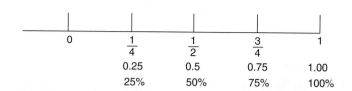

Since there must be an infinite number of fractions between 0 and 1, then an infinite number of decimal numbers and percents exist between 0 and 1. Moreover, between any two whole numbers there can be an infinite number of fractions, decimals, and percents. For example, the following decimals and percents would be placed on the number line between 0 and 1: 0.25, 14%, 33%, 0.045. First we convert to equivalent expressions, decimals or percents; then order the numbers on the line between 0 and 1.

Not only parts of a whole but also mixed numbers can be ordered and compared on a number line. A number line with mixed numbers might look like this:

Theoni Pappas's story "The Day the Number Line Fell Apart" takes the concept of number lines a step further and connects it to the axes of the Cartesian coordinate system (see the Mathematics in Literature feature).

Topics, Issues, and Explorations

Develop several visuals to show benchmark percents: 50%, 25%, $33\frac{1}{3}$, 10%, $66\frac{2}{3}$%, 75%, 80%, and so forth. Then collect survey data on a topic such as eye color, number of pets, or favorite desserts, and represent the data visually. Discuss any problems you encounter in representing the data. Also discuss which visuals work best and why.

Converting Percents, Decimals, and Fractions

NAEP and TIMSS data suggest that most students in the United States understand that they can represent parts of wholes in three different ways:

By a percent form: 38%

By fractional form: 38 per 100 or $\frac{38}{100}$ or $38 \times \frac{1}{100}$

By decimal form: $38 \times \frac{1}{100} = 38 \times 0.01 = 0.38$

However, the same data show that students are less comfortable with selecting and using appropriate forms in problem-solving situations and with identifying the need to convert from one form to another and with performing the necessary calculations.

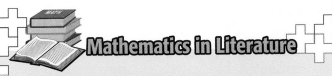

"The Day the Number Line Fell Apart"

Theoni Pappas's (1993, 38–39, 50) short story "The Day the Number Line Fell Apart" features a talking number line, talking numbers, and a battle over who belongs where on the number line. After the quarreling numbers fall off the line, the line itself establishes some rules for position and place: "I will allow each number exactly one point to sit on, and each point will just get one number."

Activity 1

Read the story in groups. Then draw a number line and arrange the numbers from the story along it. Discuss the placement of each number, paying special attention to equivalent expressions. Compare your line with the one at the end of Pappas's book. Then have each member of the group select additional numbers. Place them on the line, explaining the arrangement in terms of the line itself and other numbers.

Activity 2

Write your own story about numbers and the number line. You might deal specifically with the placement of fractions and decimals or address the reason you would not place percents on a real-number line.

Extension

Pappas explains the relationship of the number line to the axes of the Cartesian coordinate system. Explore this connection by plotting a set of numbers on an x and y plane—that is, on two number lines, the x and y axes.

Before students learn to apply a set of mathematical procedures for converting fractions, decimals, and percents, they can build a conceptual framework and the mental tools that will make the procedures meaningful. Activities such as shading squares in a 10×10 grid and representing the visuals with decimals, fractions, and percent numbers combine an image of the part in relation to the whole with a simple method to convert from one form to the other. For example, with the excerpt from the Decimal Squares Worksheet shown in Figure 13.2, the decimal, percent, and fraction can all be found simply by counting squares and then applying the appropriate symbol and forms:

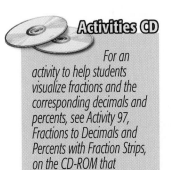

Activities CD

For an activity to help students visualize fractions and the corresponding decimals and percents, see Activity 97, Fractions to Decimals and Percents with Fraction Strips, on the CD-ROM that accompanies this text.

Decimal = period + number of squares

Percent = number of squares + %

$$\text{Fraction} = \frac{\text{number of squares}}{100}$$

Frequently, since many students work with manipulatives labeled with equivalent expressions, such as $\frac{1}{3}$, $33\frac{1}{3}\%$, and 0.3333, they will remember some equivalencies as math facts. Working with those facts as benchmarks results in another informal algorithm for converting expressions. For example:

12.5% is half of 25%.

25% can be written 0.25 and $\frac{1}{4}$.

Dividing 0.25 in half gives us 0.125.

Dividing $\frac{1}{4}$ in half gives us $\frac{1}{8}$.

Once students are comfortable with the idea of converting to find equivalent expressions for parts of wholes (as shown in Figure 13.6), they can be introduced to standard, three-step algorithms outlined here. Notice

| | **1.** Use a calculator to complete the table. (Round the decimals to the nearest hundreth.) | **2.** Complete. Do not use a calculator. |

1. Use a calculator to complete the table. (Round the decimals to the nearest hundreth.)

Fraction	Decimal	Percent
$\frac{3}{7}$	.429	42%
$\frac{10}{11}$	.91	91%
$\frac{8}{15}$	.53	50%
$\frac{7}{9}$	.78	78%
$\frac{6}{14}$	.429	42%

2. Complete. Do not use a calculator.

a. __40__ × 600 = 24,000

b. 90 × 90 = __8,100__

c. 20 × __50__ = 1,000

d. 70 × __700__ = 49,000

e. 500 × __5,000__ = 200,000

Figure 13.6 Converting expressions.

that the fractional form of *per hundred* serves as an intermediary step in all conversions.

To Convert from Percent Form to Decimal Form (or Notation)

1. Change the percent symbol to a *per hundred* notation.
2. Multiply the *per hundred* quantity by the initial p value.
3. Put in decimal notation.
   For example: Convert 14%, 25%, 67%, and 0.25%.

$$14\% = 14 \times \tfrac{1}{100} = \tfrac{14}{100} = 0.14$$

$$25\% = 25 \times \tfrac{1}{100} = \tfrac{25}{100} = 0.25$$

$$67\% = 67 \times \tfrac{1}{100} = \tfrac{67}{100} = 0.67$$

0.25%, note that this percent is a decimal percent; therefore,

$$0.25\% = 0.25 \times \tfrac{1}{100} = \tfrac{0.25}{100} \text{ (moving the decimal point two places to the left)} = 0.0025$$

Topics, Issues, and Explorations

Use informal or standard methods of conversion to create a table of equivalent expressions. Include all of the common and some uncommon quantities in your table. Discuss and make a list of situations in which fractional, decimal, or percent numbers might be most useful. For example:

Fractions	$\frac{1}{4}$	$\frac{33}{100}$	$\frac{3}{4}$
Decimals	0.25	0.33	0.75
Percents	25%	33%	75%

To Convert from Decimal Form to Percent Form (or Notation)

1. Remove decimal notation.
2. Change the decimal form to the *per hundred* fractional form.
3. Change the fractional *per hundred* form to a percent symbol.
   For example, convert 0.34, 0.78, 0.0025

$$0.34 = \tfrac{34}{100} = 34 \times \tfrac{1}{100} = 34\%$$

$$0.78 = \tfrac{78}{100} = 78 \times \tfrac{1}{100} = 78\%$$

$$0.0025 = \text{ (moving the decimal point two places to the right) } \tfrac{0.25}{100} = 0.25 \times \tfrac{1}{100} = 0.25\%$$

Performing Operations with Decimals and Percents

Because percents and decimals look rather more like whole numbers than fractions do, expectations for operations with these numbers often reflect whole-number experiences. Nonetheless, like fractions, percents and decimals are parts of a whole, which means that operations are both alike and unlike whole-number operations. Step-by-step procedures may be more akin to whole-number than fraction operations, but the results, particularly for multiplication and division, may look more like those for fractions than for whole numbers. That is, multiplying with a percent or decimal may result in less rather than more and dividing may result in more rather than less.

Addition and Subtraction

Modeling addition and subtraction with decimals and percents should begin with manipulatives that clearly establish the part–whole relationship. Fraction circles and squares that include equivalent expressions for decimals and percents help students link operations to the concrete and develop mental images as benchmarks for comparing and estimating. However, students soon discover the limitations of manufactured manipulatives for working with numbers not represented specifically by the pieces. It is simple to model addition or subtraction problems such as those in Figure 13.7 with fraction squares or circles.

However, less common segments are not represented by the manufactured manipulatives, so that problems such as the following would be difficult to show:

$$0.10 + 0.30 + 0.15 = 0.55 \qquad 0.55 - 0.30 = 0.25$$
$$10\% + 5\% + 7\% = 22\% \qquad 22\% - 10\% = 12\%$$

Alternative visuals such as the Percent Circle (a circle marked in 1%, 5%, and 10% increments) lets students work with less regular and more realistic numbers. Kyra, whose graph of a sports survey for fifth graders is shown in Figure 13.8, could use her Percent Circle to model and answer addition and subtraction questions, such as "What percent of the students prefer soccer and swimming?" (21% + 10%) or "How many of the students do not prefer football?" (100% − 15%).

Similarly, decimal squares and base-10 blocks let students model more complicated addition and subtraction problems and at the same time keep track of the part–whole relationships involved. With the 10 × 10 grid of a Decimal Square, each segment of the square is 0.01 or $\frac{1}{100}$. Adding and subtracting can be done by simply filling in or taking away the appropriate number of segments. The National Library of Virtual Manipulatives uses base-10 blocks to model adding and subtracting decimals. Ones are represented by rods and tenths by units. The rods can be broken down into units, and units can be combined into rods and moved from column to column.

After working with parts-of-wholes expressed as fractions, percents, and decimals, students also discover that it is generally easier to convert fractions and percents to decimals and then perform calculations with decimals, especially with

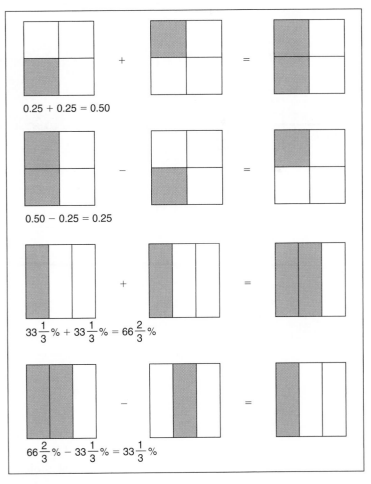

Figure 13.7 Modeling addition and subtraction with fraction squares.

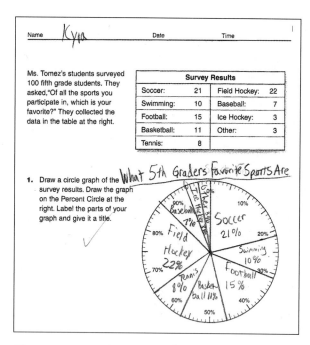

Figure 13.8 Kyra's percent circle
(Everyday Learning, 1999.)

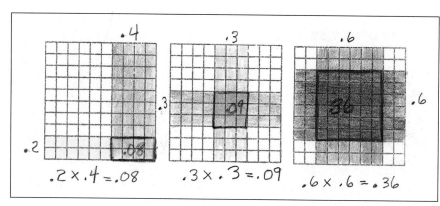

Figure 13.9 Multiplying with Decimal Squares.

$$\frac{2}{1} \times \frac{4}{10} = \frac{8}{10} = \frac{4}{5}$$

$$\frac{40/100}{4} = \begin{cases} \dfrac{10}{100} \\ \dfrac{10}{100} \\ \dfrac{10}{100} \\ \dfrac{10}{100} \end{cases} \qquad \text{or} \qquad \frac{4}{10} \div \frac{4}{1} = \frac{\cancel{4}}{10} \times \frac{1}{\cancel{4}} = \frac{1}{10}$$

multidigit numbers and several addends. The major thing to remember is to line up the decimals to ensure adding tenths with tenths or subtract hundredths from hundredths. Once the decimals are lined up, operations follow the standard whole-number algorithms.

Line up the decimals:

$$\begin{array}{r} 0.25 \\ 0.309 \\ 0.00001 \\ +0.1010110 \\ \hline 0.6600210 \end{array} \qquad \begin{array}{r} 0.6600210 \\ -0.1010110 \\ \hline 0.5590100 \end{array}$$

Multiplication and Division

Like addition and subtraction, multiplication and division with percents and decimals should build on what students already know and use tools with which they are already familiar. This means linking the operations not only to whole numbers but also to fractions. It also means continuing to use manipulatives and visuals such as base-10 blocks, fraction circles and squares, and various grids and circle graphs.

As we saw with fractions, it can be helpful to begin by multiplying or dividing parts of wholes with wholes.

$$2 \times 0.4 = \qquad \text{or} \qquad \frac{40\%}{4} =$$

Students might model the problem with circle or square segments and use repeated addition and repeated subtraction to find the answer.

$$2 \times 0.4 = 0.4 + 0.4 = 0.8$$
$$40\% - 4\% = 36\% - 4\% = 32\% - 4\% =$$
$$28\% - 4\% = 24\% - 4\% = 20\% - 4\% =$$
$$16\% - 4\% = 12\% - 4\% = 8\% - 4\% =$$
$$4\% - 4\% = 0, \text{ meaning 4 will go into } 40\%$$
10 times

They might also convert to fractions and apply the informal or formal algorithms they are comfortable with.

Visuals for multiplication and division with Decimal Squares and base-10 blocks are shown in Figures 13.9 and 13.10. As we saw with fractions, word choice can play an important role in shaping mental images and encouraging understanding. For example, asking students to calculate 0.5 *of*

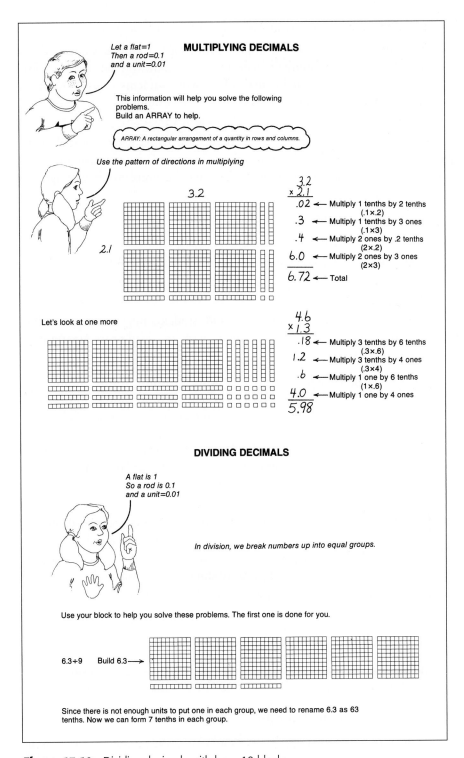

Figure 13.10 Dividing decimals with base-10 blocks.
(From Nortman-Wolf's "Base-10 Block Activities," Copyright 1990, Learning Resources. Used with permission.)

0.8 gives a different and clearer view of a problem than asking them to multiply 0.5 by 0.8. Similarly, asking students to find how many 0.2 or two-tenths there are in 1.0 presents a different picture than just asking them to divide 1.0 by 0.2.

Converting Numbers to Multiply

To work with large numbers or complex, multistep operations, some students might prefer to convert numbers to decimals and some to fractions. Converting to decimals has the added benefit of allowing students to use calculators rather than making the calculations by hand. For example:

$$32\% \times 12\tfrac{1}{2}\% = 0.32 \times 0.125 =$$

If students use calculators, it can be helpful to have them verbalize the process. Putting the numbers and the process into words can maintain focus and keep calculations tied to meaning. Verbalizing the problem above might go something like this:

> Enter decimal, then thirty-two hundredths.
>
> Multiply that by . . .
>
> Enter decimal, then one hundred, twenty-five thousandths.
>
> The result is decimal point, zero four or four-hundredths, which we can convert to $\frac{4}{100}$ or 4%.

Working out the same problem by hand, students might use the standard multiplication algorithm for whole numbers with an added procedure for placing the decimal.

$$
\begin{array}{r}
0.125 \\
\times\ 0.32 \\
\hline
250 \\
375 \\
\hline
0.04000
\end{array}
$$

Algorithm:
Line up numbers.
Multiply, one digit at a time, from right to left.
Line up results under digit used as multiplier.
Add.
Count total number of decimal places in problem.
Count same number of decimal places from right to left of result.
Place decimal.

Instead of converting to decimals before calculating, some prefer to convert percents and decimals to fractions. Fraction notation has the advantage of showing part–whole relationships clearly and underscoring the meaning of the decimal point. For example:

$$0.34 \times 0.45 =$$

Convert decimals to fractions: $0.34 = 34/100$ and $0.45 = 45/100$

Multiply numerators and denominators: $\dfrac{34}{100} \times \dfrac{45}{100} = \dfrac{34}{100} \times \dfrac{45}{100} = \dfrac{1530}{10{,}000}$

Convert fractions to decimals: 0.1530 or 0.153

(How did we know that $\frac{1{,}530}{10{,}000} = 0.1530$? Count the number of zeroes in the denominator; this will tell you how many spaces to count from right to left in the numerator.)

Another example:

Multiply: $0.02 \times 0.67 \times 0.301$

Process: $\dfrac{02}{100} \times \dfrac{67}{100} \times \dfrac{301}{1{,}000} = \dfrac{2(67)(301)}{10{,}000 \times 1{,}000} = \dfrac{134(301)}{10{,}000{,}000}$

$$= \dfrac{40{,}334}{10{,}000{,}000} = 0.0040334$$

Topics, Issues, and Explorations

Create a multiplication problem using decimals or percents. Develop a visual to show the operation. Then explain two or more algorithms students might use to solve the problem.

Converting Numbers to Divide

Students have the same options for division. They can convert numbers to decimals and use the calculator; work out calculations by hand, adjusting a whole-number algorithm for decimal number; or convert to fractions. Many educators feel that the first option is the most important one since it is the one students will probably use most often. Again, verbalizing the process can help keep problem solving on track and meaningful.

For example, reversing the problem we worked out earlier in multiplication, we might begin with percents and convert to decimals.

$$4\% \div 12\tfrac{1}{2}\% = 0.04 \div 0.125 =$$

Enter decimal, then zero four or four hundredths.

Divide that by . . .

Enter decimal, then one hundred, twenty-five thousandths.

The result is decimal point thirty-two or thirty-two hundredths, which we can convert to $\frac{32}{100}$ or 32%.

Typically, division problems with percents are more of an academic exercise than a situation with real-life applications, such as multiplying with percents to find savings on sales. However, including percents in the learning process can help students with constructing and integrating their strategies for working with parts of wholes.

Again, for those who prefer to work with fractions, there is a three-step process. For example: $0.34 \div 0.17$

Convert to fractions: $0.34 = 34/100; 0.17 = 17/100$

Invert divisor and multiply: $\frac{34}{100} \div \frac{17}{100} = \frac{34}{100} \times \frac{100}{17} = \frac{2}{1}$

Convert to decimals (or percentages): $\frac{2}{1} = 2.0$

Another example:

Divide: 1.2505 by 0.05

Process: $12{,}505/10{,}000 \div 5/100$; therefore,

$$\frac{12{,}505}{10{,}000} \times \frac{100}{5^*} = \frac{2501}{100} = 25.01$$

$$*\frac{12{,}505}{5} = \frac{5(2{,}501)}{5} = 2501$$

Here we know that a number that ends in 5 is divisible by 5.

The long-division algorithm can also be used with decimals if we add procedures for placing the decimal point.

$1.2505 \div 0.05$ could be represented by

```
        2501 = 25.01
 .05⟌1.2505
      1 0
       25
       25
        5
        5
        0
```

Move decimal point in divisor and dividend the same number of places to the right.
Divide from left to right, one digit at a time.
Multiply each digit in quotient by divisor to create a running subtraction problem under dividend.
Align decimal in quotient with decimal in dividend.

Understanding Decimals and Percents in Practical Applications

Understanding decimals and percents as mathematical concepts enables students to work with confidence and skill in practical situations. For example, a typical trick for figuring a 15% or 20% tip mentally is to take 10% of the check total, then either halve or double that, and add. For the trick to make sense, students need to understand how things work in a base-10 system (that is, that taking 10% of a quantity is accomplished simply by moving the decimal point to the left).

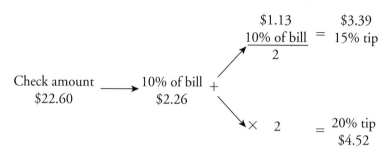

Understanding the base-10 system is also important for rounding numbers. Basically rounding involves increasing or decreasing the face value of a digit by 1. Like the base-10 system itself, rounding works from right to left across place values and can be applied to whole numbers as well as to decimals. Rounding follows two simple rules of thumb:

- **Round up** if the number to the right is 5 or more.
- **Round down** if the number to the right is 4 or less.

Many students are introduced to rounding with division. Instead of giving remainders, they might be asked to round to the nearest whole number. Working with calculators, they might discover that calculations will be given to five or even seven decimal places while a problem calls for rounding to hundredths or tenths. For example, dividing 1 by 3 with the TI-108 (a popular calculator by Texas Instruments for the early grades), the display will read 0.3333333. Rounding to tenths, 0.3 would be accurate, but 0.333 would come closer to indicating that the number here is a decimal equivalent for $\frac{1}{3}$ or $33\frac{1}{3}\%$. Choosing which place value to round to can be an important part of the problem-solving process. Letting students decide the degree of accuracy or precision appropriate to a problem situation extends the learning process and calls for a level of mathematical thinking beyond application of procedures.

Outside the classroom, rounding appropriately can impact the calculations on which we make judgments—for example, whether the $20 bill in your pocket is enough to cover all of the items on a favorite-snacks shopping list as well as any sales tax.

Shopping list	Costs	Rounded
Ice cream	$5.99	$6.00
Tortilla chips	3.69	4.00
Guacamole dip	1.79	2.00
Peanuts	2.45	2.00
Sports drink	3.86	4.00
Goldfish crackers	1.25	1.00
	$19.03	$19.00

For an activity connecting decimals and percents with a social issue, see Activity 100, Do Women and Men Work for Equal Pay in Sports?, on the CD-ROM that accompanies this text.

For an activity reviewing the concept of rounding, see Activity 94, Rounding, on the CD-ROM that accompanies this text.

For an activity to help students understand repeating decimals, see Activity 98, Fractions to Decimals: Repeating Decimals and Rounding, on the CD-ROM that accompanies this text.

Calculating a 6.5% sales tax on the snacks list could begin by rounding the estimated total of $19 to $20 and multiplying mentally by a rounded 0.07. The result, $1.40, suggests you will be short by around 20 to 30 cents and need to look again in your pocket for change or perhaps drop the Goldfish crackers from your list.

Developing facility in rounding and estimating with decimals and percents is an important financial tool and one that most students (as well as their parents) can appreciate. Shopping and budgeting activities, like the Million-Dollar Shopping Spree described in this chapter's Lesson Pro-File, engage students in real-world problem solving at the same time that they forge connections between classroom and everyday mathematics.

Activities CD

For an activity to help students use percents in social studies, see Activity 101, Population Percentages, on the CD-ROM that accompanies this text.

Topics, Issues, and Explorations

When you shop, do you keep a running tally of costs in your head? How do sales prices (20% off, extra 15% off, and so forth) affect your shopping decisions? Do you use coupons? Comparison shop? Pay cash or use credit? Brainstorm in small groups about your shopping strategies. List the strategies for the group and discuss the mathematics involved.

Idea Files

Money Applications for Exploring Decimals and Percents

Applications	Activities
Shopping (Grades 3–5)	**Find the Best Buy** Identify one or more items that you would like to purchase. Describe the items, including details such as features you want or do not want. Find or create pictures of the items. Look for the best buys using catalogs, ads, and eBay. Explain your choices with words and numbers.
Paying Taxes (Grades 5–8)	**Taking an Extra Bite: Sales Taxes** Explore the impact of sales taxes on your purchasing power. Find out the sales-tax rate in your own and two other communities. Then compute the amount of $100 eaten up by taxes in each of those communities. Select five items you purchase regularly. Figure out the tax and total cost for each item, in each of the communities.
(Grades 7–8)	**Computing Income Taxes** In small groups, choose a profession and do some research about salaries. Then get a copy of the IRS Form 1040 and the accompanying instruction book. Make a list of all of the things you would need to know to figure out income taxes, including the math operations you would need to perform. Estimate the tax on the salary for the job you selected if you were using the standard deduction and one exemption.
Paying for Credit (Grades 7–8)	**Using Plastic Money** Buying with a credit card may seem like free money; however, the cost of credit can add nearly 20% to your bill. Imagine that a favorite aunt wants to buy you a very special present. She does not have much cash, so she plans to use a credit card. See whether you can help your aunt by finding something you want on sale. If your aunt's credit card rate is 18.2% per year, estimate the percent off you will have to find for your aunt to use her card and still save money on your present.

For an activity that connects fractions and ratios, see Activity 111, M & M Count and Crunch, Fractions and Ratios with M & Ms, on the CD-ROM that accompanies this text.

Understanding Ratio and Proportion

What is a *ratio*? What is *proportionality*? How are they related? Why are the concepts important? Smith (2002) defines *ratio* as "a multiplicative relationship between two quantities" and *proportion* as "reasoning with ratios" (4–5). How the ideas can be constructed in practical terms is demonstrated in the Windows on Learning scenario.

The students in Ms. Chavez's class were working their way toward an understanding of ratios and multiplicative structures. They established that the

Windows on Learning

How Many Vans?

The four fifth-grade classes at Van Buren Middle School were planning a field trip. None of the district's large buses were available, but several smaller vans could be used to transport the students. Ms. Chavez asked her class to figure out how many students, teachers, and chaperones would be going on the trip and how many vans or other transportation they would need.

Ms. Chavez: I need you to help me figure out how much room we have in the vans. Two vans will take 22 passengers, and we have seven vans available. How do I figure it out? Where do I start?

Jamal: First, you have to know how many will go in one van.

Jaqui: What about drivers? Do they count?

Jamal: No, she said passengers, so that means drivers are extra.

Ms. Chavez: Okay, so how do we find out how many passengers will go in one van?

Roberta: Well, you have two vans and 22 people, so just divide by 2 and get 11.

Ms. Chavez wrote "22 ÷ 2 = 11" on the board.

Jamal: Then you take that 7 times and get 77.

Roberta: Or you could just work with the first number and multiply 22 times $3\frac{1}{2}$ since 7 vans makes $3\frac{1}{2}$ twos. You still get 77.

Ms. Chavez writes "$22 \times 3\frac{1}{2} = 77$."

Ms. Chavez: Uh-oh. I think we have a problem. There are 22 students in our class, and 23 in each of the other three fifth grades.

Shawntel: And parents. Teachers and aides too.

Ms. Chavez: You're right. So for four classes, let's say four teachers, four aides, and maybe two parent-chaperones per class. How many is that? Let's put it all on the board.

She wrote:

22 students in our class
23 students × 3 other classes
4 teachers
4 aides
2 parents for 4 classes

Ms. Chavez: How many does that give us?

The students worked on the problem. Some used tally marks. Others wrote out the numbers in columns for a traditional addition problem:

$$
\begin{array}{r}
22 \\
69 \\
4 \\
4 \\
+\ \ 8 \\
\end{array}
$$

Jamal: I get 87.

Audrea: That's not enough. There are more than that in the four classes.

Jamal: Okay, I see. I forgot to trade up. Add two 10s, and it's 107.

Ms. Chavez: Then how many people still need a ride? We have room for 77, remember.

Roberta: 107 take away 77 is 30.

Jaqui: We'll have to have more than two vans because two can only hold 22.

problem involves a ratio of one van for 11 passengers. Then they used a combination of division and multiplication to find out the capacity of the vans available and compared it to the number of people who would be making the field trip. Applying the 1:11 ratio of vans to people to the overall situation of the field trip involved students in a complex, interconnecting pattern of comparisons and began the process of proportional reasoning or reasoning with ratios and thinking in terms of multiplicative relationships.

The problem Ms. Chavez gave her class was practical and concrete, but at the same time the relationships involved had a complex, abstract dimension. Working with their informal strategies, including multiplying and dividing different quantities represented by the ratios, students laid the foundation for more formal operations as well as an appreciation for the real-life significance of the concepts.

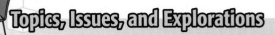

Topics, Issues, and Explorations

Take an inventory of your world. List the examples of ratios you find and situations in which you use proportional reasoning, perhaps without even realizing you are using the concepts. You might start with sales (two-for-one, three-for-one, and so forth) and cooking (making a double, triple, or half recipe).

Ratio

A *ratio* is a mathematical way to describe a relationship involving multiples—that is, it compares quantities that have a multiplicative relationship. When we say that one person is twice the height of another person, we are making a multiplicative statement about two quantities—therefore, a ratio statement. Visually, the twice-as-tall relationship might look like this:

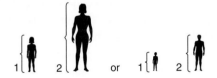

Mathematically, the ratio statement can be given in several ways:

$$\text{“two to one”} \qquad \frac{2}{1} \qquad 2 \div 1 \qquad 2 : 1$$

When we say that one person is half as tall as another person, we are also making a ratio statement but in reverse:

$$\text{“one to two”} \qquad \frac{1}{2} \qquad 1 \div 2 \qquad 1 : 2$$

Ratio statements are often stated in the form of a fraction or division.

Although representing and working with ratios formally may be challenging for students, most will recognize and understand everyday applications. For example, they readily grasp the multiplicative relationship of cost-per-item to number of items purchased and can use it to compute total costs in problems such as the following:

> If one gallon of milk costs $3 and two gallons cost $6, the ratio of price to quantity is 3 to 1. How much milk can we buy for $12?

Activities CD

For an activity about the Golden Ratio, see Activity 106, The Golden Ratio, Phi, and Physical Beauty, on the CD-ROM that accompanies this text.

Activities CD

For an activity about ratios, see Activity 110, Trailmix Ratios, on the CD-ROM that accompanies this text.

Proportion

Since the concept of proportion involves reasoning with ratios (Smith 2002), understanding proportion builds on understanding ratio. We might describe *proportion* as "two ratios that have the same value" (Cai and Sun 2002, 188). Since the *value* of a ratio is the number of multiples it represents, we can compute value easily by dividing, or by performing what can be called the *ratio operation* (see Cai and Sun 2002, 198).

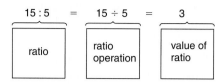

Using this process, the ratios 15:5 and 18:6 have the same value, and the quantities they describe are proportional. Reasoning with these ratios can help us predict other, related data. For example, if Henry drinks one quart of Gatorade for every two miles he jogs, a 1:2 or 1-to-2 ratio describes the relationship of Gatorade he drinks to miles he jogs. Understanding this ratio helps us predict that Henry will drink two quarts of Gatorade if he jogs four miles; three quarts if he jogs six miles, and four quarts if he jogs eight miles. Or if Mrs. Garcia picks up her mail once every four trips to work, the ratio of her mail pickups to her trips to work is 1:4 or 1 to 4. Therefore, we can say that when she picks up her mail twice, she will have made 8 trips to work; three times, 12 trips; and four times, 16 trips.

Proportional reasoning begins with identifying a proportional relationship and then determining whether the quantities involved are increasing or decreasing, scaling up or down. Problem solving with proportional reasoning might involve identifying the relationship or using the relationship to identify missing quantities. According to Lamon (1999), "Problems involving proportional reasoning are of two basic types. The first is a *comparison problem*, [such as which] vehicle has faster average speed. . . . The second kind of problem is one in which three quantities are given and the fourth quantity is missing; hence, they are called *missing value problems*" (224; emphasis added).

Both of these kinds of problems, comparison and missing value, have practical applications. For example, looking at sales taxes in different communities can be shaped as a comparison problem. If Max was charged $1 after spending $25 in one city on an item and Suzanne was charged $2 in tax on the same-priced item in another city, we know that the tax rate is twice as high in the second city, meaning the taxes on items purchased there will be double. Or if the temperature is dropping at the rate of 3° every 20 minutes, and the temperature is currently 89°, what will the temperature drop to in two hours? We can shape the problem to find the missing value.

$$\frac{3°}{20 \text{ min}} = \frac{x}{120 \text{ min}}$$

The missing value is 18°; therefore, the temperature will drop 18° in two hours, so 89° − 18° = 71°.

In each case, proportional reasoning provides a tool for interpreting data as well as for making decisions—Suzanne may want to shop in Max's city; and if the temperature continues to drop, you might need to wear a sweater.

Strategies for Developing Proportional Reasoning

Proportional reasoning is an important mathematical tool that cuts across a variety of content areas including measurement, geometry, algebra, and probability. In practical terms, students who develop proportional reasoning skills are better able to recognize and interpret information in the world around them and to orient themselves and understand their own position within that world. The Idea Files feature outlines some of the practical applications as well

Activities CD

For an activity about proportion and the Golden Rectangle, see Activity 67, Golden Rectangle, on the CD-ROM that accompanies this text.

Idea Files

Applications of Proportional Reasoning

Situation	Use Proportional Reasoning to . . .
Making punch with a ratio of three parts juice to two parts water	. . . **find out** how much water and juice to mix to make five gallons of punch (see Lanius and Williams 2003, 394).
Tossing coins	. . . **predict** how often heads or tails will turn up when you toss one or two coins.
Rolling dice	. . . **understand** the probability of rolling different numbers.
Tipping at restaurants	. . . **calculate** the increase in tips from poor to outstanding service.
Doubling or tripling a recipe in cooking	. . . **figure out** how much more to include of each ingredient in a recipe as well as how much of each ingredient to buy.
Decorating a room with art and arrangements of objects	. . . **understand and apply** proportion in creating aesthetically pleasing art and décor (refer to the Golden Ratio).
Making a model of a playing field	. . **decrease** all parts equally so that the result accurately represents the proportions of the original.
Building a full-scale object (such as a birdhouse) from a model	. . . **increase** all parts equally so that the result accurately represents the proportions of the original.

as suggests connections we as teachers can make to ensure the concepts are both real and meaningful to students (see also Telese and Abete 2002; Pappas 1993; Lanius and Williams 2003).

To develop proportional reasoning skills, students should build on earlier work comparing and ordering by size and quantity. Activities that ask them to work through the foundational ideas—multiplicative relationships, ratios, division as a ratio operation, value as a result of that operation, equal values as an indicator of proportion—anchor understanding in the concrete and at the same time make the abstract algorithms of formal study more meaningful. A student who has explored ratios with concrete models will see the algorithms for finding the value of the ratio and cross multiplying as ways to work with multiplicative relationships rather than as meaningless procedures (See Figure 13.11).

An effective approach to working with proportions in problem-solving situations begins with hands-on explorations and builds from students' current knowledge and skills toward abstract concepts. Figure 13.12 shows a three-step problem-solving process for a money collection problem: (1) model the problem with drawings of quantities; (2) solve the problem with arithmetic; (3) solve the problem with equations based on the proportional relationship.

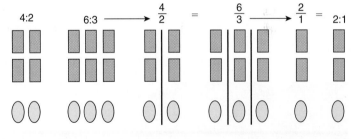

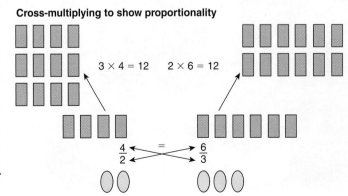

Figure 13.11 Comparing values of the ratios.

Problem: Kim Sue and Augie are collecting money for a local animal shelter. The ratio of Kim's collections to Augie's is 3 to 1. If Kim has collected $12, how much will Augie have to collect to catch up?

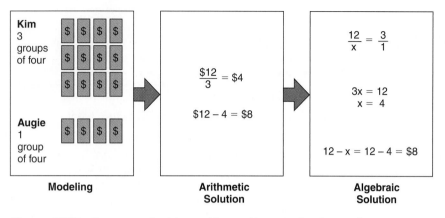

Figure 13.12 Steps toward solving problems with proportional reasoning.

Cai and Sun (2002, 199), who present a Chinese perspective on teaching proportion, describe concrete representation as a way to "experience" proportionality. They explain the value of using both arithmetic and algebraic solution paths in this way:

> The arithmetic approach holds the promise for developing students' proportional sense through qualitative reasoning. . . . The equation approach based on the proportional relationship can facilitate students' understanding of the standard proportional algorithm, which is a useful and efficient tool for problem solving.
>
> *(202)*

In addition, the authors emphasize the need for students to solve problems in a variety of ways and to extend their understanding by working through variations of the same problem and by tackling increasingly complex versions of the problem. Discussing the variations and different solutions "can help students make coherent connections among ratio, proportion, fraction and part-whole relationships" (Cai and Sun 2002, 204).

For students to make those connections, we as teachers need to provide bridges between what students already know and what they are learning and between the meaningful worlds of students' experiences and imaginations and the mathematical worlds of textbooks and classroom activities. Examples of effective teaching strategies for developing proportional reasoning follow.

Scaling

Build on early experiences comparing size and order by having students make scale models. Since proportionality is an important tool for orienting themselves within various environments, they might begin by creating a scaled model of themselves in a familiar place, such as their bedrooms or classrooms.

Cooking

Recipes provide an engaging context for proportional reasoning. As students increase or decrease servings, they must increase or decrease ingredients proportionally. Doubling the recipe for the fraction sundae shown in the photograph will increase the total number of scoops in the recipe to 12, with the number of scoops for each flavor increasing proportionately. (See Kent, Arnosky, and McMonagle 2002 for more about using recipes as a context for proportional reasoning.)

Reading

Stories can help students visualize and make sense of proportional relationships. The classic *Jack and the Beanstalk* as well as the updated *Jim and the Beanstalk* (Briggs 1970) present images to be interpreted with multiplicative ideas. A group of educators asked

A student creates a recipe for Giant Fraction Sundaes.

Mathematical Thinking

Proportional Reasoning in Lilliput

Many students know about *Gulliver's Travels* from watching video or television versions of the story. Swift's story is engaging and leads naturally to math work with measurement and proportion.

Margaret Hodges's (1995) adaptation focuses specifically on Gulliver's visit to Lilliput. The Lilliputians are six inches tall, and Gulliver is six feet tall. Assuming that everything in their land is built for and in proportion to the Lilliputians' height, Gulliver is faced with a variety of problems related to size, including the problem of having clothes made to fit him.

Because the Lilliputian tailors are so small, it would be difficult for them to measure Gulliver exactly for a new suit of clothes. Instead they use a "rule of thumb": "twice around the thumb equals the measurement for the wrist; twice around the wrist, the measurement for the neck; and twice around the neck, the distance around the waist."

Activity 1

Explore the Lilliputians' rule of thumb. Take thumb, wrist, neck, and waist measurements for volunteers in your class. Make a table of the results. Does the 2-to-1 ratio apply? If it does, how would that help the tailors? If it does not, what could happen?

Activity 2

Make a scale drawing of the Lilliputians and Gulliver. You may also want to include other parts of the Lilliputian environment in your drawing, such as houses, trees, or furnishings. To do so, you will need to measure comparable objects in your own world and apply the 12-to-1, Gulliver-to-Lilliputian, ratio.

Source: Adapted from Thompson, Austin, and Beckmann (2002).

fifth-graders to suppose the giant is 9 feet or 108 inches tall compared to one of the students, Lynne, who is 51 inches tall. They asked the students to figure out "how many Lynnes would need to be stacked on top of each other to equal the height of the giant" (Thompson, Austin, and Beckmann 2002, 131). The students approached the problem first with additive strategies—adding Lynne's height twice to come close but not exactly match the giant's height. Then they multiplied Lynne's height by 2, 3, and decimal numbers in between. Finally, they divided 108 by 51 to arrive at 2.12.

The same group of educators have used a modified version of Gulliver's adventures in Lilliput (Hodges 1995) to develop proportional reasoning in middle school students. Their activity is described in the Mathematical Thinking feature.

Topics, Issues, and Explorations

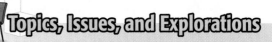

Gulliver's Travels also includes a visit to Brobdingnag, a land of giants. Develop an activity about the proportions involved in Gulliver's adventures among the Brobdingnagians.

Diversity in Learning and Thinking Mathematically

For verbal and visual learners, approaching decimals and percents as abstract concepts can be off-putting. Without images and contexts, the ideas and algorithms may seem disconnected and even unfocused—isolated procedures and facts to memorize rather than tools for structuring and interpreting real-life situations. A preservice teacher, who argued for decreasing the emphasis on decimals and percents in the mathematics curriculum, responded very differently

For an activity involving budgeting for a vacation using percents and decimals, see Activity 99, Percents, Decimals, and the Dream Vacation, on the CD-ROM that accompanies this text.

when the same topics were introduced in the context of shopping. "I know my shopping," the teacher explained. "No one gets more out of a dollar than I do." The preservice teacher as well as others with similar learning styles need more than clear explanations and examples and frequent practice with immediate feedback to become engaged in learning and thinking mathematically about decimals and percents. They need learning experiences that go beyond textbook math and textbook language. They need

- to "see" and represent ideas and relationships with drawings, diagrams, and pictures;
- to "hear" and express ideas in language that makes sense to them;
- to encounter and come to grips with concepts in meaningful contexts;
- to become involved in a problem-solving process that calls for more in-depth thinking and more complex strategies than identifying an appropriate algorithm and plugging in the numbers.

The activities outlined in the two Idea Files allow enough flexibility to fit a variety of learning styles. At the same time, they have the additional advantage of involving students in multistep problem-solving processes resulting in multiple answers. Individually, verbalizing the processes and justifying the outcomes reinforce learning; cooperatively, they demonstrate the diversity of students' perspectives and thinking.

Lesson Pro-File

The Million-Dollar Shopping Spree

Spending money and fantasizing about spending money are favorite pastimes for both young people and adults. To turn the daydreams into learning experiences, we combine dreams-come-true and wish lists with the dollars-and-cents reality of budgets and bookkeeping.

The scenario: You are a participant in a new reality game show. Instead of doing extraordinary things to win a million dollars, your job is to do all of the work of spending $1,000,000—not a penny more, not a penny less.

Materials and Resources

Students will need a spending spree log, pencils, and calculators. They will also need access to a variety of catalogs, advertisements, real estate guides, and financial information. They may need tax tables for states with sales taxes and Internet access with a search feature such as Google.

Procedure

Students begin by making wish lists in their logs of all the things they think a million dollars will buy. For each item, they should make a guesstimate about costs and then find the total to see how close they come to a million dollars. If the total is over or under, they may need to subtract or add items from the wish list.

Once they have a rough plan, students proceed to the research stage. For each item, they will need to comparison-shop, looking for best buys for their money, then compute and log costs for each item. For most items there will not only be up-front costs but also hidden costs such as taxes and various fees. Students may need to interview adults to find out about charges such as closing costs and work-up fees for big-ticket items. If cruises or vacations are on their shopping lists, they may also have to factor in the costs of meals, tips, taxis, souvenirs, and so forth.

For each item students decide to buy, they compile a complete log entry with pictures, itemized list of costs (original cost, sales deduction, taxes, extra fees). Then they enter the cost total in a separate part of the log where they keep a running list of deductions from the $1,000,000.

Outcomes

Students discover quickly that actually spending large amounts of money can be hard work. The wish lists come easy, but finding out the specific details of buying a house or car, paying for a college education, or financing a cruise for friends and family is challenging. Although the math involved is basic, the many steps needed to compute charges for each item (costs minus discounts plus taxes, fees, and so forth) and then deducting that amount from a million dollars provide ample opportunity for small errors that can have big consequences. For example, misplacing the decimal point or making an error in adding, subtracting, or multiplying could result in over- or underspending.

≪≪≪ LOOKING BACK

Decimals and percents are two different, but related, forms for representing part–whole relationships. Understanding and being able to use these forms in a variety of contexts are part of basic mathematics literacy. NCTM Standards emphasize the need for students to develop flexibility in expressing part–whole relationships with decimals and percents as well as fractions. Modeling with hands-on and virtual manipulatives and representing decimals and percents with graphs, charts, and drawings help students visualize relationships and develop mental tools for problem solving. Exploring the concepts as mathematical ideas prepares students to understand applications in real-life contexts.

Similarly, students need to build on early work with size, order, and comparison to construct the important and related concepts of ratio and proportion. A ratio describes a multiplicative relationship between quantities; proportion involves reasoning with ratios that have the same value. NCTM Standards call for using "proportionality as an integrative theme in the middle grades," connecting work in a variety of areas including measurement, geometry, algebra, and probability (NCTM 2000, 212).

1. Some researchers believe that decimals are more difficult for students in the upper elementary grades than fractions. Do you agree? Why or why not? (See Glasgow et al. 2000 for some background.)

2. Rate your competence with decimals, percents, and fractions. Are you stronger working with one of the three forms? Explain. What about friends and members of your family? Are they comfortable working with decimals and percents in the context of money and sales? In other contexts?

3. Brainstorm in small groups about the advantages and disadvantages of working with the three forms: decimals, percents, and fractions. Make a list and give examples on both the plus and minus sides.

4. Explain the rationale for teaching decimals and percents abstractly and the rationale for teaching the topics concretely. Describe each method, and act out a lesson with classmates. Which do you think is the better method? Why?

5. Look for examples of things, objects, or events that are proportional and not proportional. Describe the differences between the two types of examples.

6. Explore the relationship between proportionality and aesthetics. What is the Golden Ratio? The Golden Rectangle? What role do these ideas play in art and architecture?

CHAPTER 14

Building Bridges

The transition from elementary to middle school mathematics can be difficult for some students. Studies suggest that between fourth and eighth grade, students who enjoyed and even excelled in math begin to have problems. Math anxiety increases while understanding and performance on standardized tests decrease.

Bridging the gap between earlier, less formal explorations and the more formal learning experiences of middle and high school mathematics calls for a systematic effort to identify and make connections. Teachers need to continue efforts to make ideas real and concrete but at the same time encourage students to generalize and learn to work with abstractions.

To build affective bridges, we must continue to make learning mathematics accessible to all students and work to promote math confidence.

Building conceptual bridges begins with constructing a strong foundation—understanding and using the big ideas of the elementary mathematics curriculum as well as developing skill and flexibility in mathematical thinking. It continues as students recognize the familiar in new math challenges and work to construct and apply more complex concepts.

Making the Transition: Is Fourth-Grade Math the Beginning of the End?

In a 1994 article, a concerned teacher asked the question: Is fourth-grade math the beginning of the end? (Swetman 1994, 173). The answer could be "yes" or at least "maybe." Until fourth grade, students appear to have positive attitudes about math, and many do well on achievement measures such as standardized tests. After fourth grade, positive attitudes and achievement decline while math anxiety and avoidance increase.

In fourth grade, most students say they like math and believe everyone can do well in mathematics. By eighth grade, the percentages drop sharply; fewer students think they can succeed, and more prefer not to study math or take formal math courses. Fourth graders generally do well on tests, such as TIMSS; 8th graders, less well; and 12th graders score near the bottom (see Mitchell, Hawkins, Jakwerth, Stancavage, and Dossey 1999a, 1999b; Steele and Arth 1998; Swetman 1994; Peak 1996; U.S. Department of Education 1997a, 1997b).

The case of Jaime, a onetime high achiever in mathematics, illustrates the problem:

> In the early grades Jaime liked math. He was a math explorer. When his class made maps of their math worlds, his project was one of the best. He built and furnished a paper carton house for the Math Village, staying within the assigned $1.00 budget. He wrote and illustrated a math story about talking triangles, and in a math play his role was Dr. Googol, the math expert. Because of his enthusiasm and almost intuitive grasp of concepts, his teachers described Jaime as a "gifted math learner" and predicted he would be a mathematician someday.
>
> But something happened. By sixth grade Jaime was avoiding math. His teachers complained that he would throw away his worksheets and did not pay attention to explanations. During seatwork exercises, he would not stay on task. His quiz and test scores ran from average to failing. And Jaime no longer liked math. Asked to rate his subjects on a scale of one to five, he gave math a one for "least favorite" subject. He did not want to take algebra in the seventh grade or geometry in the eighth. He even admitted that some math problems made him feel "anxious."

(Martinez and Martinez 2002, 27)

What happens to change Jaime and other students from eager to reluctant math learners? What changes take place after fourth grade that might account for declines in both attitude and achievement? When we posed these questions to a group of teachers, their responses suggested the complexity of the problem:

"Math gets harder in the fifth grade."

"Yes, there's not as much time to play games."

"Or work with manipulatives."

"They have to get ready for the state tests, so we do more testing."

"They have to learn to work with abstract concepts if they are going to be ready for algebra."

"We do more pencil-and-paper exercises."

"They have to memorize more formulas and use the standard algorithms."

"We have a lot to cover to meet standards. They have to work harder to keep up."

Activities CD

For an activity that helps students make the transition from elementary to middle-school mathematics, go to Activity 111, M & M Count and Crunch, Fractions and Ratios with M & M's, on the CD-ROM that accompanies this text.

The teachers' comments point toward a double-bind situation for students: at the same time that learning objectives become more complex and abstract, the pressure to learn and achieve increase. Moreover, teaching methods and objectives appear to shift toward the traditional. There is greater emphasis on tests, pencil-and-paper exercises, and memorized procedures.

Reviewing the Research

Research, including the TIMSS Videotape Classroom Study, shows the persistence of explain-practice-memorize methods in middle school. In an article on math anxiety, Steele and Arth (1998) write:

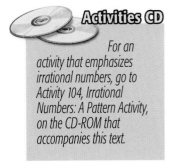

Activities CD

For an activity that emphasizes irrational numbers, go to Activity 104, Irrational Numbers: A Pattern Activity, on the CD-ROM that accompanies this text.

> In the middle grades many teachers begin to focus more on pencil-and-paper drill and practice and measure their students' knowledge with more written assessments. Many of these teachers use a cycle of mathematics lessons: explain the problems, do the problems, memorize the algorithms, correct the problems, and test for correct methods. This teaching approach of explain-practice-memorize is the major source of math anxiety.
>
> *(44–45)*

TIMSS researchers identified a sharp contrast between teaching methods and lesson content in U.S. and Japanese classrooms. In U.S. schools, lessons typically begin with demonstrations of procedures and introduction of vocabulary, and then move on to applications in exercises. Most U.S. teachers describe their classroom goals as skills related, "Being able to do something" (U.S. Department of Education 1997b, 55). In Japan, where eighth graders scored near the top in TIMSS, lessons emphasize inquiry and problem solving. Teachers pose a problem and encourage students to invent and share solutions as well as reflect about their work to deepen understanding (Peak 1996; U.S. Department of Education, 1997a). Most Japanese teachers (71%) described their goals in terms of mathematical thinking and understanding concepts (Peak 1996; U.S. Department of Education, 1997a).

In addition, many U.S. students appear to avoid complex, multistep problems and even seem "to lack the mathematical knowledge needed to solve problems" (Mitchell et al. 1999a, 21). Overall, according to TIMSS researchers, "the content of U.S. middle-school mathematics classes is not as challenging as that of other countries, and topic coverage is not as focused" (Peak 1996, 11).

Topics, Issues, and Explorations

Recall your own middle school experiences with learning mathematics. Do your experiences fit the pattern described by researchers, or do they show something different? Why do you think this is so?

Identifying the Gaps

What the research and the experiences of students and their teachers have identified is not one but a series of gaps in learning mathematics from elementary to middle school:

- **A gap in pedagogy**—a shift in the methods and goals of teaching from the early to middle grades;
- **A gap in content and emphasis**—a change from challenging to less challenging, from complex to simple, from an emphasis on mathematical thinking and problem solving to an emphasis on applying standard algorithms and procedures;

- **A gap in attitude**—a decline in math confidence and enthusiasm but an increase in math anxiety and avoidance;
- **A gap in performance and achievement**—an often abrupt change from meeting to not meeting standards and expectations, including not attempting to solve complex problems (in the National Assessment of Educational Progress, NAEP, many middle schoolers do not attempt "to answer the more complex questions that required them to write explanations or apply concepts in problem solving" [Mitchell et al. 1999a, 2]).

To bridge these gaps, we need strategies that address both the affective dimensions of the problem (such as attitudes and stereotypes) and the cognitive dimensions (such as lesson content and assessment) as well as areas where the dimensions interact (such as learning styles and format).

Building Affective and Conceptual Bridges

How do we ensure that students who like mathematics and are confident about their learning abilities in elementary school continue to excel in middle school? One answer is to continue doing what worked well in the early grades. That is, instead of using explain-practice-memorize methods, emphasize inquiry, mathematical thinking, and problem solving. Instead of dropping manipulatives and focusing on pencil-and-paper exercises, continue to introduce new concepts with hands-on explorations. And instead of limiting assessment to tests, continue to use multiple measures, including portfolios and verbal explanations to determine understanding.

Nonetheless, there will be changes. The mandates to raise standards, increase accountability, and teach important mathematics to all students are apparent at local, state, and national levels. Responding to these mandates without losing the gains of the early years is a multidimensional challenge. It requires teachers to engage all students in learning mathematics, make complex ideas accessible to everyone, and balance the demands of teaching for understanding with the pressure to teach for the test.

Strategies for coping with these new and sometimes intimidating challenges form an integral part of the bridges we need to build from elementary to middle school mathematics.

Affective Bridges

Keeping students from losing their desire and their belief in their ability to learn mathematics is fundamental to ensuring equal opportunity in mathematics learning. Students will continue to enjoy math if they believe it is meaningful and accessible. They will continue to believe in their abilities if they see themselves or others like them succeeding. Figure 14.1 shows a student's responses to learning about geometric figures; the student appears to equate understanding with "having fun." Another student ties understanding with being "able to do geometry" and making her mother proud of her grades. She writes:

Figure 14.1 Not having fun and having fun with geometry.

Before I did not know what symmeitry was but when Mrs. Kennerly came to help me I started getting it. . . . I [wasn't] able to do geometry the way I am doing it now. It was just like a miracle. When my mom saw better grades on my assignments my mom was so proud of me.

Some effective strategies for keeping students engaged and confident follow:

- **Make mathematics real and meaningful.** Emphasize the connections between what students experience with their senses and the mathematical concepts they are learning. Field trips to "find" math at the mall, in a park, at a sports complex provide real-world applications for ideas about geometric shapes and measurement, operations with fractions and decimal numbers, or data collection and analysis.
- **Keep mathematics integrated.** A major change from elementary to middle school is the shift from integrated, holistic study to separate classes devoted to individual subjects. One effect of this change can be to fragment the subjects themselves—to examine, for example, the abstract concepts of geometry apart from their applications in science, art, geography, sports, and so forth. Collaborating with other teachers to create multidisciplinary assignments ensures meaningful contexts for concepts and at the same time helps students make connections and in effect "discover themselves" in the subject.

For an activity to help students discover the importance of real numbers in the workplace, see Activity 102, *Real Numbers in the Workplace*, on the CD-ROM that accompanies this text.

For an activity that combines math and life sciences, see Activity 103, *Real Numbers at the Zoo*, on the CD-ROM that accompanies this text.

Mathematics in the Real World

Do We Really Need Negative Numbers?

Students sometimes think that mathematical concepts are like vestigial organs—oddities to be identified and described but not used. Typical responses to new ideas are "Why do we need to know this?" and "What does that really mean?" We can challenge students to discover the answers to these questions for themselves.

Activity: Discovering Negative Numbers in the Real World

Make a Negative Numbers Log to collect data. Devote separate pages to negative numbers in different areas, such as finance, geography, politics, weather, sports, and so forth. Make pockets by taping a folded page to a full page. Use the pockets to collect newspaper clippings or other examples of negative numbers.

Spend a week collecting information. Then review what you have found and write detailed responses to these questions:

Why do we need to know about negative numbers?
What specifically do we need to know?
How are negative numbers used in the real world?
What do negative numbers really mean?

Discuss what you found, sharing your answers in class.

For other activities in which students "discover themselves" in mathematics, see Activity 1, *Finding the Numbers in Your Life*, and Activity 88, *Finding Fractions in Your Life*, on the CD-ROM that accompanies this text.

For another activity about friezes, go to Activity 43, Symmetry and Geometric Transformations: Creating a Frieze Pattern, on the CD-ROM that accompanies this text.

Mathematics Across the Curriculum

The Geometry, History, and Art of Friezes

A *frieze* is a pattern created along a straight line. It can consist of shapes, designs, or pictures and may be repeated or altered in a variety of ways to create a symmetrical pattern. Friezes are used to decorate the borders of buildings, rooms, rugs, or even clothing.

To make a frieze, an artist starts with a shape, design, or picture; then

repeats the pattern, changing the number of elements (by twos, threes, and so forth);

changes the order of elements of the pattern;

transforms parts of the pattern with reflections, rotations, and slides.

Activity 1

Look for friezes in art, architecture, and the everyday world. Identify and explain the patterns in each frieze. How many different patterns can you identify?

Activity 2

Research and write the history of one of the frieze patterns you discovered in art or architecture. Explain what the pattern represents and its significance historically or culturally.

Activity 3

Use geometric shapes to design a frieze pattern. Then duplicate the pattern on a rolled sheet long enough to form a decoration over a door or a bulletin board or other classroom feature. Identify and discuss the symmetry and transformations (slides, reflections, rotations) in your design.

For an activity about gender gaps and wages, see Activity 100, Do Women and Men Work for Equal Pay in Sports? on the CD-ROM that accompanies this text.

- **Combat stereotypes with diversity.** Both teachers and students can become caught up in stereotyping that negatively impacts math learning. In *Math without Fear*, we wrote:

> In math teaching specifically, some stereotypes come disguised as contemporary wisdom. The obvious one is the idea that boys are inherently math types, whereas girls must be lured from a natural affinity with the arts to study math and science. . . . Students may also generalize and label themselves and each other. "Math dumb," "math nerd," "numbers junky," "computer jerk," "computer geek," "brainiac," "arithmenut"—few teachers use names like these, but students do. . . . Girls neglect math because it is a "boys' subject" . . . [while] boys fall into the good-at-math/poor-at-English-and-reading type of either-or thinking.

(Martinez with Martinez 1996, 142–143)

To avoid harmful stereotypes, we need to broaden our perspective. We need to add women mathematicians such as Emma Noethers to our list of math heroes and models. We need to acknowledge and showcase the contributions of different cultures such as the Mayans and Incas to mathematics. And we need to teach the entire curriculum—the difficult as well as the simple—to all students.

Note: Before we can eliminate harmful stereotypes, we must identify them. The self-test and oral survey in Figures 14.2 and 14.3 have helped teachers recognize potential problems.

- **Build confidence with "success" activities and resources.** When students are fully engaged, they are more likely to do well on a task. Moreover, tasks that place mathematics in engaging contexts and at the same time allow multiple avenues for student responses have a built-in success factor. Students respond positively to activities that ask them to find a cartoon or comic strip with a math theme. Finding and enjoying the joke or humorous situation provide a successful starting point for exploring concepts, attitudes, or even stereotypes. The two Idea Files describe "Resources for Success" and "Activities for Success" that encourage students to enjoy mathematics and lay the foundations of positive attitudes and confidence they need to succeed.

Check the *Yes* or the *No* column for each question. Eight or more checks in the *Yes* column indicates a serious stereotyping problem; four to seven, a problem; and any, the need for corrective action.

	Yes	No
1. Have you ever excused poor math performance or attitude by saying that you (or your students) are right-brained and creative rather than left-brained and quantitative?	____	____
2. Do you expect more from boys than girls in math class?	____	____
3. Close your eyes and call to mind the image of the quintessential math whiz. Is the image a boy?	____	____
4. Close your eyes and call to mind the image of a great mathematician. Is the image male?	____	____
5. Have you ever praised ethnic students for assumed group traits—blacks for good athletic ability, Native Americans for artistic ability, Hispanics for musical abilities, and so forth?	____	____
6. Do you call on boys more often than girls to do math problems?	____	____
7. Do you call on girls more often than boys during writing or reading lessons?	____	____
8. Have you ever attributed poor or good math performance to ethnicity—that is, to Asians' supposed facility with numbers, to Native Americans' supposed problems in dealing with time, and so forth?	____	____
9. Fill in the blanks in the following sentence with the first words that come to mind: _____ is a Ph.D. in mathematics; _____ supervises a computer lab. Does the first word refer to a male? Does the second word refer to a male?	____	____
10. Fill in the blanks in the following sentence with the first words that come to mind: _____ hates math; _____ is very math anxious. Does the first word refer to a female? Does the second word refer to a female?	____	____

Figure 14.2 Teachers' stereotyping self-test.

Source: From Martinez, Joseph, and Martinez, Nancy. *Math Without Fear: A Guide for Preventing Math Anxiety in Children.* Published by Allyn and Bacon, Boston, MA. Copyright © 1996 by Pearson Education. Adapted by permission of the publisher.

This is an oral survey to be administered individually in nonthreatening settings. Use the answers to each question to generate more questions. If possible, tape each session and prepare a transcript rather than trying to write down responses during the interview itself.

1. Do you like math?
2. Do most girls like math?
3. Do boys like math?
4. Which members of your family like math?
5. Who is the best mathematician in your class?
6. Do you think (insert name of minority classmate) is good at math?
7. Repeat question #6 until all ethnic or racial groups in the class have been represented.
8. Who do you think is smarter, a mathematician from the United States or a mathematician from Egypt? From Mexico? From India? From China?
9. Who is the worst mathematician in your class?
10. Who has the hardest job—a math teacher, a reading teacher, or an English teacher?

Figure 14.3 Survey of stereotyping.

Source: From Martinez, Joseph, and Martinez, Nancy. *Math Without Fear: A Guide for Preventing Math Anxiety in Children.* Published by Allyn and Bacon, Boston, MA. Copyright © 1996 by Pearson Education. Adapted by permission of the publisher.

Idea Files

Resources for Success

Resource	Description	Applications
Jasper Woodbury video series	Adventures designed like math mysteries, with data needed to solve problems embedded in the story. Girls and boys who model effective mathematical thinking come from different backgrounds and include children with special needs.	Introduce important mathematical ideas related to statistics, finance, geometry, algebra. Show the diversity of successful mathematical problem solvers. Engage students in complex problem-solving processes that include connections to other disciplines such as science, social studies, and language arts.
Web sites devoted to math-related topics and learning	**Ask Dr. Math:** http://forum.swarthmore. edu/dr.math/ Interactive site devoted to answering questions about math	Compose questions about math. Read and understand answers.
	FunBrain: www.Funbrain.com Games and a quiz lab, with results e-mailed to teachers	Balance math-as-play with assessment activities.
	McRel: www.mcrel.org/connect/math.html Interdisciplinary site with links to literature, Fibonacci numbers, info. about women in math	Connect math with other subjects.
	Math for All: www.learner.org/content/ K12/acplotv/mfa/patterns.html Activities from the interactive TV show	Use multiple representations to engage all learners.
Manipulatives, both homemade and manufactured	**Chinese stick math**—hands-on approach to basic operations that uses home-made counting board, red sticks for positive numbers, black sticks for negative numbers	Develop a new perspective on basic operations. Work hands-on with positive and negative numbers.
	Tangrams—magic square of seven pieces that can be used alone or with grid paper to study shapes, area, fractions, as well as patterns in classic puzzles	Discover patterns and relationships of geometric figures. Develop understanding of fractional relationships and percents.
	Pattern blocks—geometric figures that can be arranged and duplicated in designs to study patterns and relationships, including fractals	Experiment with repeated figures in designs and nature observations.

Source: Used with permission from National Middle School Association, from Joseph Martinez and Nancy Martinez, "Teaching Mathematics in Elementary and Middle School: Developing Mathematical Thinking," *Middle School Journal,* March 2003, 32.

Activities CD

For another "success" activity, see Activity 110, Trailmix Ratios, on the CD-ROM that accompanies this text.

Interestingly, the idea that they can enjoy mathematics and have fun learning may seem strange to some middle school students. In the TIMSS videotape study, U.S. eighth graders observed a tape of a Japanese algebraic problem-solving session. The topic of the lesson was buying cakes, and the Japanese students talked informally with the teacher, worked hands-on, and even laughed. U.S. students were both surprised and disapproving. They considered mathematics about cake too "easy" for middle school—even though the problem itself was complex. They were surprised by the laughter, the informality, and the teacher's emphasis on multiple

Idea Files

Activities for Success

Activity	Procedure	Objectives
Discovering *pi* *Level:* 7th–8th grade, groups of 3–4 *Materials:* measuring tapes, variety of circular objects.	Measure the circumference and diameter of 20 round or circular objects both in centimeters and inches. Keep a log of findings. Divide circumferences by diameters for each item measured to find *pi*. Compute averages for all items. Analyze process and identify sources of variability.	Understand *pi*. Dialogue about the process and results. Understand reasons for variations in process and results. Connect with history of *pi*.
Enjoying math in comics *Level:* 5th–8th grade, individual *Materials:* newspaper, comics, other printed cartoons.	Find a cartoon or comic strip that includes a math-related idea, such as a concept, attitude, or even a stereotype. Explain the idea, and discuss why the cartoon is (or is not) humorous, Discuss your response to the comic.	Engage students' interest. Demonstrate the humorous side of math learning. Uncover some common assumptions about learning math.
Exploring math in writing *Level:* 5th–8th grade, individual *Materials:* looseleaf notebook and paper	Keep a daily journal of math-learning experiences. Write summaries of new concepts. Write your thoughts for solving difficult problems. Compose and answer questions. Explore your attitudes and responses to specific learning experiences. Be creative: write plays, stories, poems about math. Develop confidence: write "I know" and "I can" entries.	Provide a record of thoughts and feelings about math. Work through difficult concepts verbally. Confront negative experiences, attitudes; expand on, reinforce positive experiences and attitudes.
Putting math in imaginative contexts *Level:* 8th grade, individual or pairs *Materials:* Indiana Jones video, pencil, paper	Watch a segment of the Indiana Jones adventure, *Raiders of the Lost Ark,* in which Indiana Jones uses a bullwhip to swing across a pit. Draw a diagram of Indiana, his bullwhip, and the pit. Estimate the width of the pit (from Bransford et al. 1996, 208). Discuss the effect of Indiana's correctly guessing the width of the pit upon the outcome. Discover other math applications in the video and write problems about them.	Put math in action. Estimate from observations and deduction. Emphasize the importance of accuracy. Evaluate problem solving. Develop as well as solve problems to develop greater understanding of the problem-solving process.

Source: Used with permission from National Middle School Association, from Joseph Martinez and Nancy Martinez, "Teaching Mathematics in Elementary and Middle School: Developing Mathematical Thinking," *Middle School Journal,* March 2003, 33.

solutions instead of one correct answer. To the U.S. students, the Japanese students seemed to be having too much fun for an upper-level mathematics class (U.S. Department of Education 1997b; discussed in Martinez and Martinez 2003, 33–34).

Cognitive Bridges

A cognitive bridge has basically three parts:

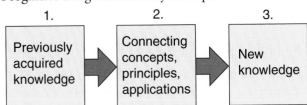

Topics, Issues, and Explorations

Asked about math, most elementary school students respond with feelings. They like or even love math. Math is their favorite or best subject. And they are "good" at math. These responses often change toward the negative in middle school, frequently with an increase in math-anxiety-related responses such as being scared or not being good at taking tests. Explore some of the factors involved in this change. Brainstorm about specific measures, including and in addition to the ones described here to promote positive attitudes about learning math in middle school.

Breaking the Code of an Alphanumeric Puzzle

Alphanumeric puzzles such as the following are math problems written in letter codes. To solve the puzzle, you need to find the number equivalents for each letter and do so in the context of the mathematical operation of multiplication.

There are 10 letters in the problem, and you have 10 numbers, 0 through 9, to work with.

Puzzle: *The 12 C's*

$$
\begin{array}{r}
\text{ABCDEFGH} \\
\times\ \text{AJ} \\
\hline
\text{EJAHFDKC} \\
\text{BDFHAHC} \\
\hline
\text{CCCCCCCC}
\end{array}
$$

(from Summers 1968, #43)

For a similar code-breaking activity with a long-division context, go to http://www.tpgi.com.au/users/puzzles/page19.html.

Activities CD

For an activity working with codes, puzzles, and code breaking, see Activity 107, Real Numbers, Math Games, and AlphaNumeric Puzzles, on the CD-ROM that accompanies this text.

Bridging the gap between previously acquired and new knowledge requires a combination of specially designed learning materials and methods. The materials can make connections explicit:

> "Negative numbers are like positive whole numbers because you can add, subtract, multiply, and divide with them."

Or they can present information in such a way that students make the connections for themselves:

> "What can you discover about negative numbers and positive whole numbers by working with an expanded number line?"

In Chapter 13, we looked at a teaching strategy for ratio and proportion that asked students to first model the problem and then work out an arithmetic and an algebraic solution. The method bridges the gap between familiar and unfamiliar procedures and underscores the value of multiple approaches to mathematical situations.

Effective strategies for building these and similar bridges include the following:

- **Sequenced tasks** such as sets of exercises that start with the familiar and build step by step toward the new;
- **Hands-on explorations** that give learning visual and tactile dimensions;
- **Multiple paths to solutions** that ask students to look beyond the right or "correct" solution—beyond the *what* to the *how*'s and *why*'s of problem solving;
- **Multistep tasks** that call for students to "think through" a complex problem and try out various problem-solving strategies;
- **Imaginative contexts** that engage students cognitively as well as increase motivation.

Some specific content areas that may require special attention as students move from elementary to middle school are integers, algebraic expressions, solid geometry and measurement, and word problems.

Activities CD

For an activity with an imaginative context, go to Activity 45, Dimensions: Exploring Flatland, on the CD-ROM that accompanies this text.

Integers

Students begin working with number concepts before kindergarten and continue to expand and deepen their understanding throughout elementary

Googol: BIG IDEAS in Mathematics

The Divine Proportion

Can physical beauty be measured? Can physical beauty be defined as physical symmetry and measured by approximations to the Golden Ratio?

The ancient Greeks believed that it could. They developed a concept called the Divine Proportion or Golden Ratio to define the symmetry of beauty. Mathematically, their idea can be represented by a line, an equation, and a number.

Activity

Collect photographs or drawings of buildings, objects, people, or faces that are considered beautiful. Use a calculator and metric ruler to look for Golden Ratios. You might compare, for example, a person's height to the length from the top of the head to the navel or the length from the top of the head to the chin to the width of the head (for more ideas about what to measure, go to http://www.markwahl.com/golden-ratio.htm). With rectangular objects look for the *a/b* relationship shown in the Golden Section.

Make a record of any Golden Ratios that you find.

Discuss why measuring some things you yourself consider to be beautiful may or may not have resulted in a Golden Ratio.

Golden Section:

```
A       C    B
|_____|____|
    a      b
```

Golden Ratio:

$$\frac{a + b}{a} = \frac{a}{b}$$

Golden Number:

$$\frac{a}{b} = \frac{\sqrt{5} + 1}{2} \approx 1.618$$

---

school. Broadening their idea of whole numbers to encompass the overall concept of integers, including negative numbers, can begin with a device as simple and familiar as the number line. Most students have used a number line beginning with 0 to help them see the sequence of numbers and to connect counting and simple operations—for example, adding two numbers by counting them in sequence up the number line or subtracting by counting down the number line.

Extending the familiar number line to show negative integers presents a familiar tool for understanding not only the negative sequence but also some operations with negative numbers.

When students realize that the negative part of the number line is a mirror image of the positive side, they soon discover that operations work in reverse. Addition, then, for whole numbers moves to the right along the line while adding negative numbers moves to the left. For example:

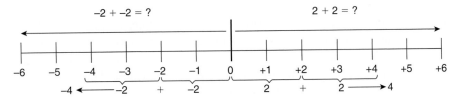

Activities CD

For an activity that discusses the Golden Ratio, see Activity 106, The Golden Ratio, Phi, and Physical Beauty, on the CD-ROM that accompanies this text.

Activities CD

For another activity about the Golden Ratio, go to Activity 67, Golden Rectangle, on the CD-ROM that accompanies this text.

Activities CD

For an activity in which students work with the Cartesian coordinate system, see Activity 109, Functions: Straight Line Graphing Linear Equations Using Intercepts, on the CD-ROM that accompanies this text.

Similarly, students discover that subtracting positive numbers moves right to left, and subtracting negative numbers moves left to right.

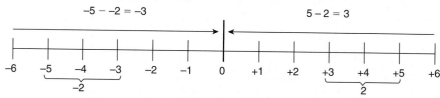

Connections can also be made when students explore adding and subtracting negative numbers with another familiar manipulative—counters. Manipulating counters labeled with negative numbers lets students see relationships and walk through them physically. For example, $-1 + -1 = -2$ might look like this with counters:

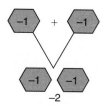

Subtracting negative numbers with counters is a simple take-away process. If all of the counters are labeled -1, the problem $-10 - -2 = -8$ could be represented in this way:

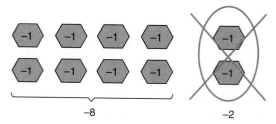

When students move beyond working with terms in addition and subtraction to working with factors in multiplication and division, it becomes even more important to make connections and show the process. Students often have difficulty deciding whether the product or quotient is positive or negative. Memorizing a two-by-two table such as the following may result in accurate answers without ensuring that students truly understand why a negative times a negative results in a positive, but a negative times a positive results in a negative.

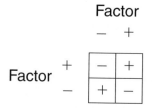

By adding a vertical dimension to the number line, a grid with modified Cartesian coordinates helps students make sense of operations with positive and negative numbers. Plotting the operation lets them visualize the process. They can turn the result into an array of squares on the grid. For example, the problem $-2 \times -2 = 4$ might look like the grid in Figure 14.4.

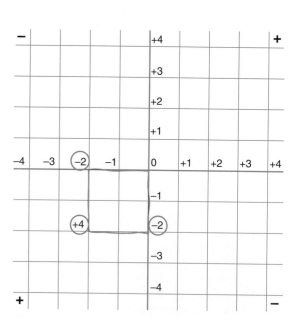

Figure 14.4 Plotting the multiplication of negative numbers.

The operation results in four squares in a + or positive quadrant, so the answer is +4.

The grid also works well as a model for division with positive and negative numbers. To find the answer to the problem $4 \div -2$, start with the grid number 4 and work backward to −2 on the coordinate lines. For a problem such as $6 \div -3$, first locate the −3 on one coordinate line, count out six squares in the array, and follow the squares to the −2 on the other line (see Figure 14.5). Figure 14.6 shows additional examples.

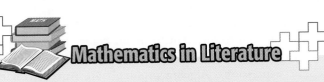

Topics, Issues, and Explorations

Try your hand at working on the modified Cartesian coordinates grid. Copy the grid from the Blackline Masters in Appendix A. Then experiment with multiplying and dividing positive and negative numbers by plotting the operations on the grid. To work with larger numbers, you can extend the grid and add more numbers.

Mathematics in Literature

A Messy Room, a Fly, and the Cartesian Coordinate System

The Cartesian coordinate system is an abstract and challenging concept for students in the early grades. To make it accessible, teachers need to make the ideas both concrete and meaningful.

Julie Glass (1998) does both in her book *The Fly on the Ceiling*. She writes a story about René Descartes's developing the system. She begins with something children ran relate to—being sick at home in a messy room. To avoid looking at the mess, Descartes stared at the ceiling where he observed the antics of a fly. He wondered how many times the fly would land and whether it would land in the same place twice. The result of his observations was a grid and the Cartesian coordinate system.

Activity

Listen as the teacher reads the story aloud to the class. Then use a large sheet of graph paper, a ruler, and a pencil to draw the Cartesian coordinates. Use a penny or other flat object to represent the fly. Toss the object into the air over your sheet of paper. Mark the spot where it falls on your graph. Continue until the object has fallen several times in each quadrant. Use a pencil to connect the marks. What does the result look like? How many times did the object fall in each quadrant? How many times did it fall in the same spot?

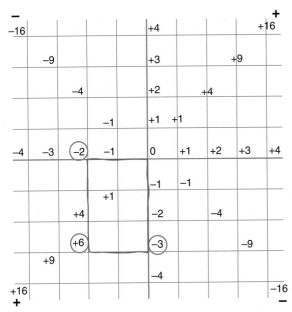

Figure 14.5 Plotting the division of negative numbers.

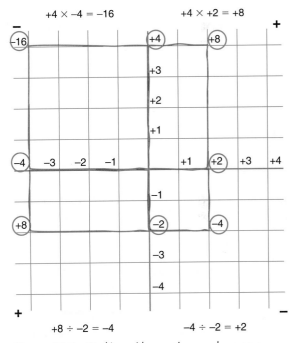

Figure 14.6 Working with negative numbers on a modified Cartesian coordinate grid.

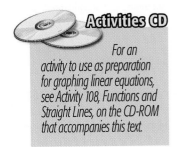

Activities CD

For an activity to use as preparation for graphing linear equations, see Activity 108, Functions and Straight Lines, on the CD-ROM that accompanies this text.

(a) Sample Item 15
Solve linear equation for x

    If $3(x + 5) = 30$, then $x =$

        A. 2   B. 5   C. 10   D. 95

(Performance Category: Performing Routine Procedures)

(b) Sample Item 16
Equivalent algebraic expressions

    If m represents a positive number, which of these is equivalent to $m + m + m + m$?

        A. $m + 4$ B. $4m$ C. m^4 D. $4(m + 1)$

(Performance Category: Knowing)

(c) Sample Item 17
Expression representing number of hats

    Juan has 5 fewer hats than Maria, and Clarissa has 3 times as many hats as Juan. If Maria has n hats, which of these represents the number of hats that Clarissa has?

        A. $5 - 3n$ B. $3n$ C. $n - 5$ D. $3n - 5$ E. $3(n - 5)$

(Performance Category: Using Complex Procedures)

(*Source:* International Association for the Evaluation of Educational Achievement 1996, pp. 77-78)

Figure 14.7 Three sample TIMSS problems on algebra
(From Martinez 2002, 328. Reprinted from *Mathematics Teaching in the Middle School,* copyright 2002, by the National Council of Teachers of Mathematics. All rights reserved.)

Exercise Set 1: Carry out the operations indicated, and explain.

1. $2 + 2 + 2 =$ _____ $a + a + a =$ _____
2. $3 + 3 + 3 + 3 =$ _____ $b + b + b + b =$ _____
3. $2 \times 2 \times 2 =$ _____ $a \times a \times a =$ _____
4. $3 \times 3 \times 3 \times 3 =$ _____ $b \times b \times b \times b =$ _____

Exercise Set 2: Carry out the operations indicated, and explain.

1. $2 + 2 =$ _____ $2a + 2a =$ _____
2. $3 + 6 =$ _____ $3b + 6b =$ _____
3. $2 + 3 + 6 =$ _____ $2c + 3c + 6c =$ _____

Exercise Set 3: Carry out the operations indicated, and explain.

1. $3 \times 3 =$ _____ $a \times a =$ _____
2. $2 \times 2 \times 2 =$ _____ $b \times b \times b =$ _____
3. $4 \times 4 \times 4 \times 4 =$ _____ $c \times c \times c \times c =$ _____

Exercise Set 4: Carry out the operations indicated, and explain.

1. $2^2 \times 2^3 =$ _____ $a^2 \times a^3 =$ _____
2. $2^2 \times 2^3 \times 2^1 =$ _____ $a^2 \times a^3 \times a^1 =$ _____
3. $3^2 \times 3^2 \times 3^1 =$ _____ $b^2 \times b^2 \times b^1 =$ _____

Exercise Set 5: Carry out the operations indicated, and explain.

1. $2 + (4 + 6) =$ _____ $2a + (4a + 6a) =$ _____
2. $(2 + 4) + 6 =$ _____ $(2a + 4a) + 6a =$ _____
3. $(2 + 6) + 4 =$ _____ $(2a + 6a) + 4a =$ _____

Exercise Set 6: Carry out the operations indicated, and explain.

1. $2 \times (4 \times 6) =$ _____ $2a \times (4a \times 6a) =$ _____
2. $(2 \times 4) \times 6 =$ _____ $(2a \times 4a) \times 6a =$ _____
3. $(2 \times 6) \times 4 =$ _____ $(2a \times 6a) \times 4a =$ _____

Figure 14.8 Sequenced exercise sets for understanding equivalent expressions.

(From Martinez 2002, 329. Reprinted from *Mathematics Teaching in the Middle School,* copyright 2002, by the National Council of Teachers of Mathematics. All rights reserved.)

Algebraic Expressions

To many middle school students, algebra seems like a totally new and totally alien subject. They complain that algebra is different from the math they know and like.

> "I like numbers, but these x's, y's, and z's are confusing. They don't mean anything, and math is supposed to mean something."
>
> "Math is supposed to be about numbers. Letters are for English class."
>
> "I like math I can use. I'll never use algebra."

(Martinez 2002, 326)

In TIMSS, U.S. students were generally successful at performing routine procedures, as in Sample Item 15 in Figure 14.7. However, many had difficulty with problems such as 16 and 17 that asked them to demonstrate their understanding of algebraic expressions and use their knowledge in complex procedures (see Martinez 2002 for more discussion and data).

Sequenced activities can help bridge the gap from what students already know to the new concepts or methods of expression that seem so different to them. Figure 14.8 shows a series of exercises designed to develop students' understanding of equivalent algebraic expressions. Algebra problems are paired with more familiar number problems to encourage students to see parallels. The progression of items within each exercise set also guides students to make distinctions "between what only *looks* alike and what actually *is* alike" (Martinez 2002, 329). Asking students to explain the connections they discover and defend their answers reinforces the conceptual bridge they are building.

Figure 14.9 shows another sequence of problems—this time word problems leading conceptually, step by step, to a problem similar to Item 17 in TIMSS. The student work shown with each phase of the sequence demonstrates a steady progression from operations with whole numbers to algebraic thinking and expressions.

Topics, Issues, and Explorations

Try your hand at writing a sequence of exercises to help students understand the equivalent expressions in TIMSS sample item 16: $m + m + m + m = 4m$.

(a) Problem: Clarissa's Hats No. 1
Juan, Maria, and Clarissa collect hats. Juan has 5 fewer hats than Maria and 10 fewer hats than Clarissa. If Maria has 20 hats, how many do Juan and Clarissa have? Explain your thinking in both words and symbols.

Student work
Find the # of hats. Maria has 20. Juan has 5 less, 15. Clarissa has 10 more than Juan. That's 15 plus 10 to get 25.

Maria 20	Juan 15
− 5	+ 10
Juan 15	Clarissa 25

(b) Clarissa's Hats, First Extension
Juan, Maria, and Clarissa have been adding to their collections. Juan and Clarissa now have 15 more hats than they had before, and Maria has 2 times as many hats as she had before. How many hats does each collector have now? How many do they all have together?

Student work
You have to do #1 right for this one to turn out. First I went back and got the numbers, 15 for Juan, add 15 to get 30. Then 25 for Clarissa, add 15 to get 40, and 20 hats for Maria times 2 for 40 hats. 30 plus 40 plus 40 is 110 hats.

Juan	15 hats + 15 = 30 hats
Clarissa	25 hats + 15 = 40 hats
Maria	2(20 hats) = 40 hats
Total	110 hats

(c) Clarissa's Hats, Second Extension
Use the data from *(b)*, but try to represent your work in single sentences, both in words and in symbols. See if you can find more than one way to do this.

Student work
1. Add 15 hats to Juan's 15 hats, 15 hats to Clarissa's 25 hats, and take Maria's 20 hats times 2 to get 30 hats, 40 hats, 40 hats and a total of 110 hats.
   $(15 + 15) + (25 + 15) + 2(20) = 110$
2. Take 15 hats for Juan and 20 hats for Maria times 2 and add 15 to Clarissa's 25 hats and get 110 hats.
   $2(15 + 20) + (25 + 15) = 110$

(d) Problem: Clarissa's Hats; A New Problem
Rewrite the first extension so that you know how many hats Juan and Clarissa have but not how many Maria had to start with. How would you rewrite your explanations in the second extension leaving out that important piece of information?

Student work
Take 15 hats for Juan and ? hats for Maria times 2 and add 15 to Clarissa's 25 hats and get 70 hats plus Maria's 2 times ?
$2 (15 + ?) + (25 + 15) = 70 + 2(?)$

(e) Problem: Clarissa's Hats; A Generalization of the TIMSS Problem
Juan has 5 fewer hats than Maria, and Clarissa has 3 times as many hats as Juan. How many hats does Clarissa have? If we represent the number of Maria's hats with the letter *n* to show it is unknown, how would you write out your approach to solving the problem in words and in symbols?

Student work
Maria has *n* hats. Juan has *n* minus 5 hats. To get the number of Clarissa's hats, we have to take the number Juan has times 3.
n = number of Maria's hats
$n - 5$ = number of Juan's hats
$3(n - 5)$ = number of Clarissa's hats

Figure 14.9 Sequenced word problems.
(From Martinez 2002, 330–31. Reprinted with permission from *Mathematics Teaching in the Middle School,* copyright 2002, by the National Council of Teachers of Mathematics. All rights reserved.)

Geometry and Measurement

Too often middle school and even high school students see geometry and measurement as a collection of theorems and formulas to be memorized: $c^2 = a^2 + b^2$, $a = \pi r^2$, $v_{cone} = 1/3\ \pi r^2 h$, 1 cup = 8 fl. oz. = 16 T = 48 t = 237 ml, and so forth. Like algebra, geometry and measurement seem intrinsically

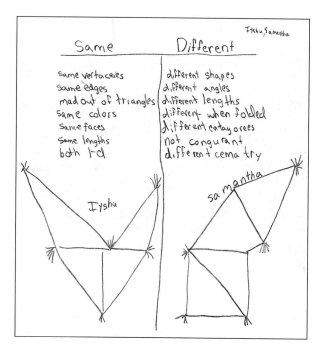

Figure 14.10 Iyshu and Samantha explore the Four Triangles problem.

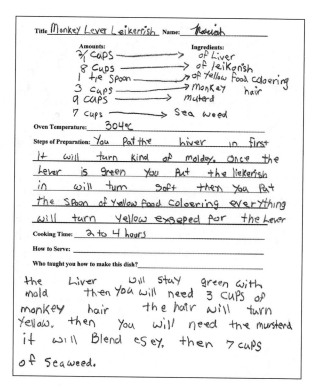

Figure 14.11 An imaginative recipe for Monkey Liver Licorice.

different from the subjects they explored in the earlier grades as they discovered which polygons tessellate and why or what happens when they halve or double a recipe for banana bread (see, for example, the Four Triangles problem explored in Figure 14.10).

To bridge this gap, we need strategies that continue the hands-on approach and creativity that sometimes make early work in these areas and "play" almost synonymous. The imaginative recipe in Figure 14.11 continues the creativity of early studies of measurement used in cooking but updates the activity for middle school interests.

The classic water jar problem discussed in Chapter 3 also serves as a bridge activity as students start with arithmetic strategies and build to geometric thinking and problem solving. Students use cylindrical plastic containers marked in gallons or liters to experiment with solutions—a hands-on approach to solving the problem. The clip from *Die Hard III* sets an imaginative context that engages the students and makes the situation meaningful to them. Students will usually discover three possible solutions—the first two involving pouring and emptying the containers and using addition and subtraction; the third, focusing on spatial relationships and using the geometry of the cylinders to solve the problem (see the Math Manipulatives feature).

Word Problems

In the popular comic strip *Foxtrot,* mathphobe Paige tells her math-genius brother, "I hate word problems" (Amend 1995; see Chapter 3, p. 70). Unfortunately Paige's attitude is probably more common than Jason's (see Bransford et al. 1996, 206; Charles and Silver 1988; Silver 1986; Hegarty, Mayer, and Green 1992; Hegarty, Mayer, and Monk 1995; Mayer and Hegarty 1996). Paige, who dislikes all math, would probably prefer to plug numbers into one of the memorized formulas Jason mentions and be done with the assignment. But a "good" word problem encour-

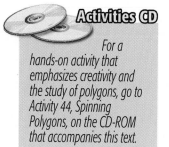

Activities CD

For a hands-on activity that emphasizes creativity and the study of polygons, go to Activity 44, Spinning Polygons, on the CD-ROM that accompanies this text.

Activities CD

For an activity to help demystify word problems, see Activity 61, Writing Story Problem Equations, on the CD-ROM that accompanies this text.

Math Manipulatives

The Water Jar Problem (Again)

The classic Water Jar problem comes alive when students begin the problem-solving process with actual containers and water. To add an imaginative dimension, their work can be set in the context of *Die Hard III*. Like the characters in the movie, students can imagine they have five minutes to solve the problem and keep a bomb from destroying a crowded park.

The Water Jar Problem: you have two empty containers, one can hold no more than 3 gallons of water, the second, no more than 5 gallons of water. You have an unlimited supply of water (as did Bruce Willis and Samuel T. Jackson in *Die Hard III*) to work with. Your task is to fill one of the containers with exactly 4 gallons of water. See if you can find 3 different solutions to this problem.

Hint: both containers are right-circular cylinders.

Cautions: not allowed are the following—anything that can be used to mark either container; any kind of tape or tape measure. And you cannot put one container in the other container.

TIME:_____

ages you to see the math that in Jason's words "permeates everything" and to think mathematically about not only the problem but also the world around you.

Emphasizing word problems is essential if we are going to continue the focus on mathematical thinking begun in the early grades. However, for word problems to be effective as bridge activities, we must overcome negative attitudes and make students want to think about the mathematics involved. We need to—

- **engage** the students' imaginations with creative, thought-provoking problems and
- **involve** the students more directly in evaluating their own word-problem-solving strategies by having them think and write descriptively and critically about their mathematical thinking [Figure 14.12].

(Martinez 2001, 248)

An excellent example of an engaging, thought-provoking word problem is Hogben's (1993) adaptation of the famous Achilles and the Tortoise paradox:

Achilles runs a race with the tortoise. He runs ten times as fast as the tortoise. The tortoise has 100 yards' start. Now, says Zeno, Achilles runs 100 yards and reaches the place where the tortoise started. Meanwhile the tortoise has gone a tenth as far as Achilles, and is therefore 10 yards ahead of Achilles. Achilles runs this 10 yards. Meanwhile the tortoise has run a tenth as far as Achilles, and is therefore 1 yard in front of him. Achilles runs this 1 yard. Meanwhile the tortoise has run a tenth of a yard, and is therefore a tenth of a yard in front of Achilles. Achilles runs this tenth of a yard. Meanwhile the tortoise goes a tenth of a tenth of a yard. He is now a hundredth of a yard in front of Achilles. When Achilles has caught up this hundredth of a yard, the

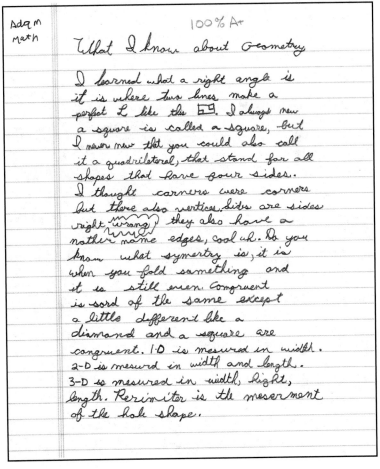

Figure 14.12 Adam describes what he knows about geometry.

Mathematical Thinking

Crossing the Bridge

Two key components of effective mathematical thinking are the abilities to review and revise problem-solving strategies and to find multiple solutions to problems. Crossing the Bridge is a problem with many solutions, some better than others.

The objective of the problem is to create a plan to cross the bridge as quickly as possible. The example solution with a 24-minute total is too long; therefore, we need to find one or more better ways to solve the problem.

Crossing the Bridge Problem: Your task is to get the following four people across a narrow bridge at night as quickly as possible—only two at a time with a sin-

gle flashlight. The first person can cross the bridge no faster than 10 minutes, the second person, 5 minutes, the third person 2 minutes, and the fourth person 1 minute.

How fast can you get all four across the bridge with only one flashlight, without any person carrying another across, and without throwing the flashlight across the bridge—given the length of the bridge?

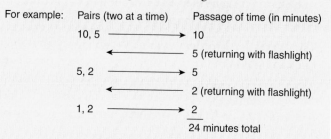

For example:

Pairs (two at a time)	Passage of time (in minutes)
10, 5 ⟶	10
⟵	5 (returning with flashlight)
5, 2 ⟶	5
⟵	2 (returning with flashlight)
1, 2 ⟶	2
	24 minutes total

tortoise is a thousandth of a yard in front. So, argued Zeno, Achilles is always getting nearer the tortoise, but can never quite catch up.

(Hogben 1993, 11)

Topics, Issues, and Explorations

Discuss the attitudes toward word problems of Paige and Jason from the *Foxtrot* cartoon (see Chapter 3, p. 70). Which character do you agree with? Which character would you like to agree with? Why? Does your position change as you change roles from math learner to math teacher? Why or why not?

Students can respond to the problem by acting out the race, making diagrams of the runners' progress, or modeling the situation with manipulatives. Solutions can be logical, arithmetic, or algebraic, with students' problem-solving processes increasing in complexity and sophistication as they write about, evaluate, revise, and discuss their solutions.

The Mathematical Thinking feature focuses on another classic word problem, Crossing the Bridge.

Diversity in Learning and Thinking Mathematically

Some of the teachers that we quoted earlier in this chapter seemed actually to approve of the gaps between elementary and middle school mathematics. They described the traditional format of many middle school classes as "getting down to business" and "getting past the fun and games" of elementary school mathematics. "Real mathematics is about discipline and hard work," said one teacher. "We don't have time for colored manipulatives and touchy-feely activities."

Does this attitude help explain why teaching methods in middle school mathematics appear to resist change? Perhaps. But, more important, the attitude suggests a need for changes in the way we look at serious mathematics—a change, that is, from equating serious with dull and meaningful with obscure. We once tried to persuade a mathematics teacher to revise an item on a math test because the topic, furlongs, was meaningless to most students. His response? Changing the topic would make the item "too easy," and he did not believe in "mollycoddling" students.

Acknowledging that the principles of equity and accessibility that underscore the curriculum in elementary school apply in middle school as well takes a first step toward making middle school mathematics more student- and learning-friendly. Providing multiple means of engagement, representation, expression, and assessment will help ensure access for students with visual, aural/oral, and tactile learning styles as well as the more traditional symbolic style. And making multicultural and interdisciplinary connections will keep learning mathematics on track as a way of interpreting and understanding information in worlds outside the math classroom and math textbook.

Erica Daughetee, the teacher featured in this chapter's Teacher Pro-File, used lessons developed by Julie Murgel of the Goals 2000 Partnership for Educating Colorado Students to teach the Mayan number system to a multiethnic class. The lessons not only deepened students' understanding of our own base-10 number system but also increased their understanding of and appreciation for the contributions made by other cultures to mathematics.

Activities CD

For other activitites about multicultural mathematics, go to Activity 15, Quipus, and Activity 53, Boiling a Potato for Inca Time, on the CD-ROM that accompanies this text.

Teacher Pro-File

Erica Daughetee

Mayan Number System

Erica Daughetee uses a unit developed by Julie Murgel of Goals 2000 Partnership for Educating Colorado Students. The unit combines information about Mayan mathematics, architecture, and history. Students not only learn about Mayan numbers but also use them to perform basic operations and to calculate area, volume, and perimeter. They compare the Mayan, base-20 system with Roman, Egyptian, and Babylonian number systems. As part of the unit's study of Mayan architecture, students create their own models of a Mayan temple, including a computer graphic of a pyramid.

Procedure

The unit begins with an introduction to the Mayan numbers. Students learn to identify and interpret the dots and bars of the different numbers and then to convert from Mayan to Arabic numerals and back again. Students use worksheets to apply and practice what they are learning. They work with calculators to multiply large numbers, although some, like Sara, double-check some calculations in the margin of the worksheets.

To compare the Mayan system to other number systems, students are introduced to the Egyptian, Roman, and Babylonian symbols for different numbers. They compare the systems again in a series of worksheets, including an overview of likenesses and differences.

Finally, students use the Internet to explore Mayan architecture. They look for and make a list of Web sites with information about Mayan buildings. Then they

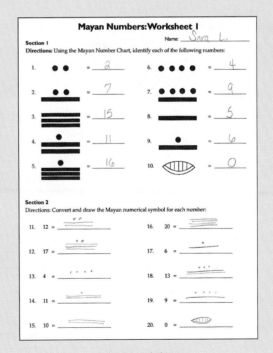

Sara's Mayan numbers Worksheet 1.

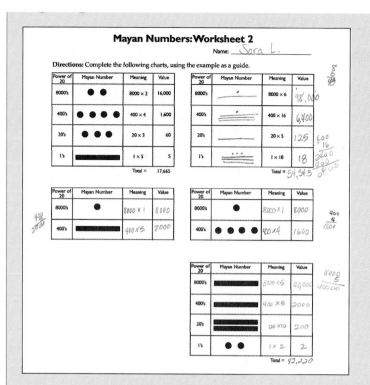

Sara's Mayan numbers Worksheet 2.

focus on El Castillo, a four-stairway pyramid devoted to Kukulcan, the feathered serpent. Students use paper folding to make a replica of the temple; then measure it to find perimeter, area, and volume. Finally, they create their own Mayan pyramids on the computer.

Outcomes

Working individually and in groups, Ms. Daughetee's students are immediately engaged in the unit. Looking at numbers and working with numbers from the perspective of the Mayan and other systems encourages them to see

mathematics in a different way. They also discuss the contributions of ancient cultures to mathematics, learning, for example, to appreciate the Mayans' development of a symbol for zero. Students are particularly fascinated by Mayan architecture and spend hours building and measuring their pyramid replicas and using the computer to design a pyramid.

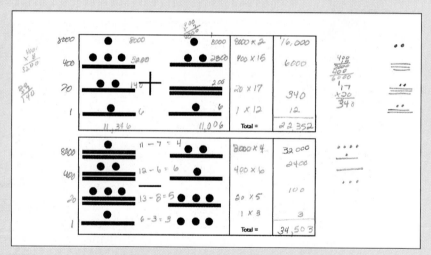

Sara's Mayan numbers Worksheet 3.

Egyptian Number System:
The Egyptians used a base 10 number system. They represented their numbers with hieroglyphics (picture writing). The Egyptian system started at the number 1 and did not include symbols between 2 and 9. The position of the number did not change the value of the number.

Mayan Number System:
The Maya wrote their numbers from bottom to top. They used a base 20 system. They symbolized their numbers with bars and dots. They also had a symbol which represented zero. The Mayan number chart is in Lesson 1.

Arabic	Egyptian	Arabic	Egyptian
1	/	8	//// ////
2	//	9	///// ////
3	///	10	∩
4	////	100	𝄅
5	/////	1000	𝄃
6	/// ///	10,000	↿
7	//// ///	100,000	𝄡

Megan's number systems Worksheet 4.

Directions: Use the number charts on Worksheet 4 and the Mayan number chart to complete this page.

Compare and contrast the Egyptian number system and the Mayan number system.

Likenesses: lines, one symbol is repeated

Differences: Egyptians used 10, Egyptians don't have zero. numbers position in Egyptian doesn't matter.

Megan's number comparison Worksheet 5.

Commentary

Throughout the unit, Ms. Daughetee emphasizes how engaged students are and how much they enjoy the work. Both she and the students are impressed by their ability to apply what they already know about numbers and operations to making calculations with Mayan numbers. Students, she notes, develop a high level of confidence as they work through the unit and at the same time begin to understand that numbers are symbols and that there is more than one way to work with and represent numbers.

Ms. Daughetee describes the unit as "very effective":

The finished products are excellent and I am extremely happy that they gain such a good knowledge of the subject. . . . I think it is very engaging and fun for the students as well as me. I cover several important areas of mathematics and also incorporate history and spatial sense. It is a good experience.

≪≪≪ LOOKING BACK

The transition from elementary to middle school mathematics is rarely seamless. Students encounter major changes in the way math is taught as well as in how they are expected to function as math learners. Test scores fall, math anxiety rises, and students who once liked math avoid it.

Gaps appear in pedagogy, lesson content and emphasis, attitude, performance and achievement. To bridge these gaps, teachers need to adopt strategies that address both the affective and the cognitive dimensions of students' learning.

Affective bridges include emphasizing real-world applications, integrating math with other disciplines, combating stereotypes about who can learn math, and building confidence with "success" activities.

A cognitive bridge connects previously acquired knowledge with new knowledge. Teachers can use sequenced tasks, hands-on activities, multiple solutions, multistep problems, and imaginative contexts to build a path of understanding from what students already know to what they are learning in middle school mathematics.

Questions for Further Thought, Discussion, and Research

1. At one time stereotypes about who could and should study important mathematics influenced many students to avoid formal mathematics courses. Working as a group, make a list of stereotypes that might impact learning mathematics. Discuss any experiences you and other members of the group may have had with these stereotypes.

2. In earlier chapters we discussed ways to use mastery learning or repeated-testing strategies as a way to decrease testing anxiety and to increase students' management of their own learning. Could mastery learning methods be an answer to the call for increased accountability through student testing? Discuss the possibilities.

3. Do you feel that middle school mathematics should or should not be "fun"? Do you think games and hands-on learning activities send the right or the wrong message to math learners? Do you think there should be limits to the fun-and-games approach to learning mathematics? Discuss your answers.

4. Although algebra and geometry were once considered to be high school–level subjects, NCTM Standards now list algebraic and geometric expectations for every grade level, and many middle schools are now offering formal algebra and geometry classes. What do you think about this change? How might it impact efforts to smooth the transition from elementary to middle school mathematics?

Appendix A

Make Your Own Manipulatives

Pattern: ***Fraction Strips***
Directions: Copy the pattern on paper or card stock. Give sheets to each student. Have them cut out the strips. Work with fractions showing at first, then turn over the strips to develop fraction sense.

1

$\frac{1}{2}$	$\frac{1}{2}$

$\frac{1}{3}$	$\frac{1}{3}$	$\frac{1}{3}$

$\frac{1}{4}$	$\frac{1}{4}$	$\frac{1}{4}$	$\frac{1}{4}$

$\frac{1}{5}$	$\frac{1}{5}$	$\frac{1}{5}$	$\frac{1}{5}$	$\frac{1}{5}$

$\frac{1}{6}$	$\frac{1}{6}$	$\frac{1}{6}$	$\frac{1}{6}$	$\frac{1}{6}$	$\frac{1}{6}$

| $\frac{1}{8}$ | $\frac{1}{8}$ | $\frac{1}{8}$ | $\frac{1}{8}$ | $\frac{1}{8}$ | $\frac{1}{8}$ | $\frac{1}{8}$ | $\frac{1}{8}$ |

| $\frac{1}{10}$ | $\frac{1}{10}$ | $\frac{1}{10}$ | $\frac{1}{10}$ | $\frac{1}{10}$ | $\frac{1}{10}$ | $\frac{1}{10}$ | $\frac{1}{10}$ | $\frac{1}{10}$ | $\frac{1}{10}$ |

| $\frac{1}{12}$ | $\frac{1}{12}$ | $\frac{1}{12}$ | $\frac{1}{12}$ | $\frac{1}{12}$ | $\frac{1}{12}$ | $\frac{1}{12}$ | $\frac{1}{12}$ | $\frac{1}{12}$ | $\frac{1}{12}$ | $\frac{1}{12}$ | $\frac{1}{12}$ |

| $\frac{1}{16}$ | $\frac{1}{16}$ | $\frac{1}{16}$ | $\frac{1}{16}$ | $\frac{1}{16}$ | $\frac{1}{16}$ | $\frac{1}{16}$ | $\frac{1}{16}$ | $\frac{1}{16}$ | $\frac{1}{16}$ | $\frac{1}{16}$ | $\frac{1}{16}$ | $\frac{1}{16}$ | $\frac{1}{16}$ | $\frac{1}{16}$ | $\frac{1}{16}$ |

Pattern: *Fraction Squares*
Directions: Copy the squares on card stock or colored paper. Cut out the individual squares; then cut along the lines inside the squares to make fractions of squares.

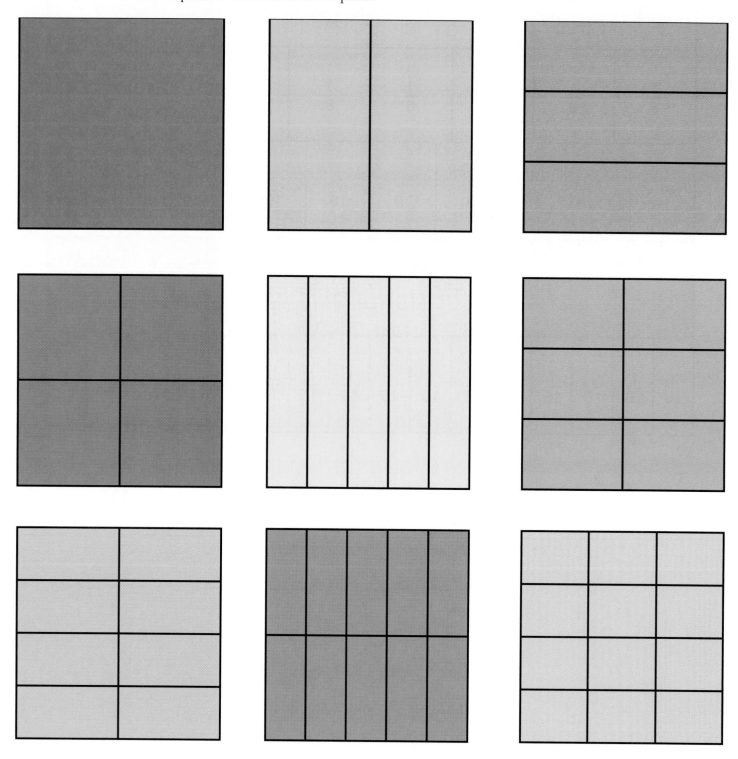

Pattern: ***Fraction Circles***
Directions: Copy the pattern on a variety of colored and patterned papers; or make a paper copy, and use it as a pattern to make circles of felt or other heavy material.

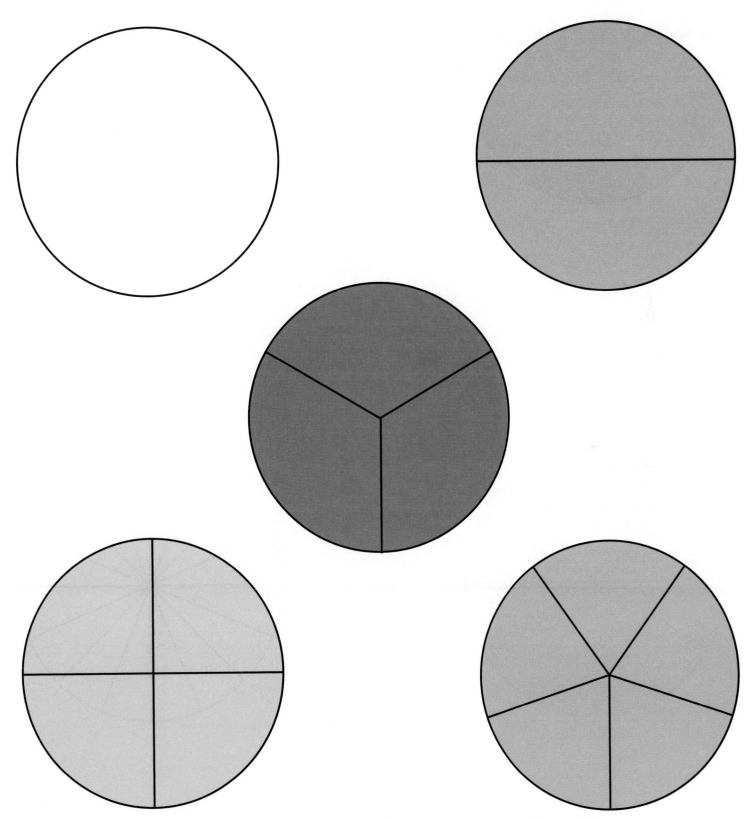

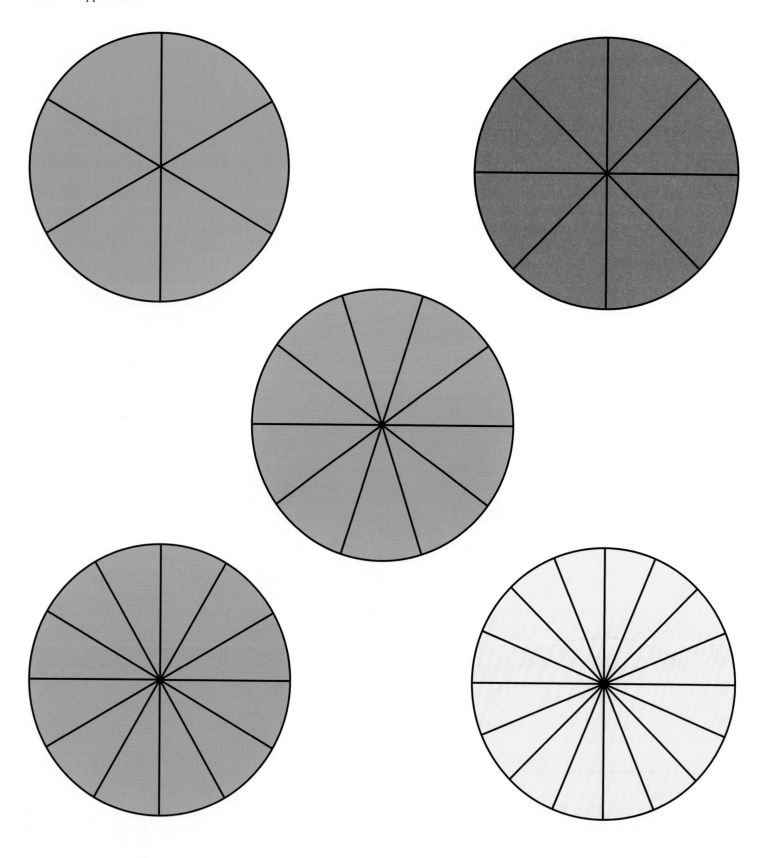

Pattern: ***Pattern Shapes***
Directions: Use pattern to make cut-outs from construction paper. You might use a different color for each shape or several colors for one shape.

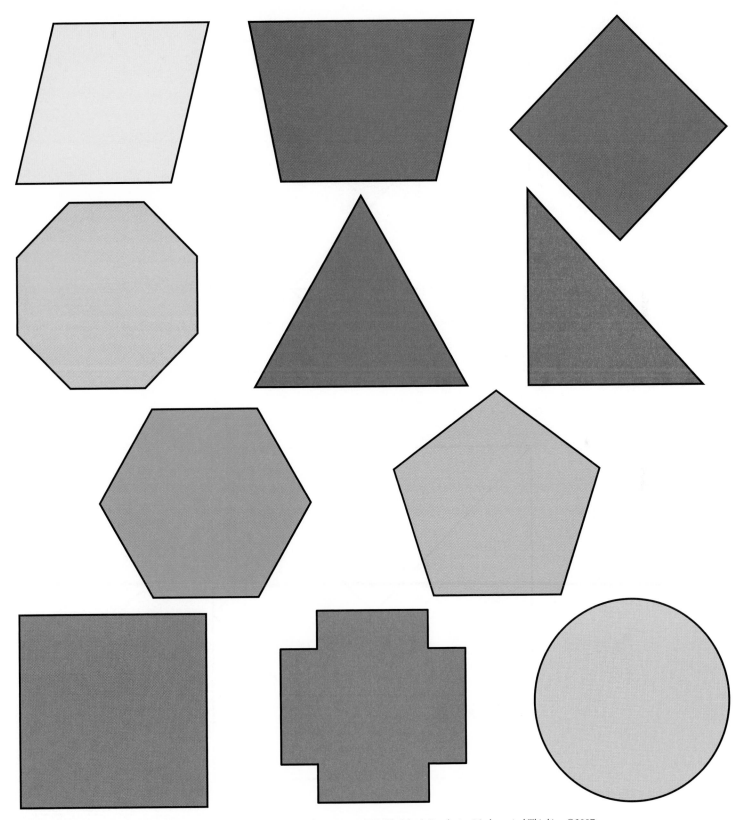

Pattern: **Tangrams**

Directions: Copy the patterns on card stock. Use as patterns to make multiple sets of tangrams with construction paper. Have students cut out two sets of tans, each in a different color. Use the tans to solve attached puzzles and to explore geometric properties of the various shapes.

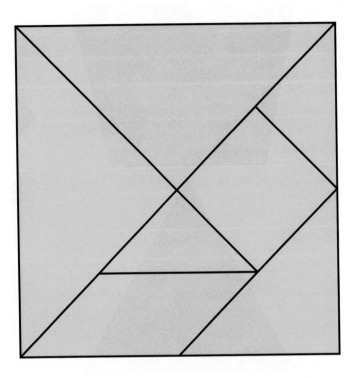

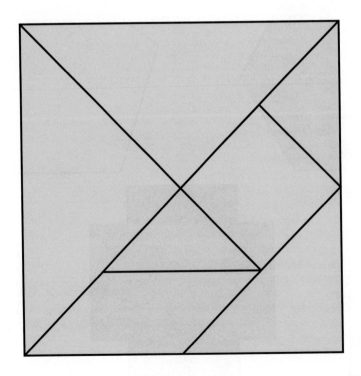

Tangram Puzzles

Tangram Solutions

Pattern: ***Geoboard***
Directions: Copy the pattern on thin paper, such as onionskin. Lay the pattern over a square of bulletin-board-quality cork or other material. Insert a pushpin at each point on the pattern. Tear away the paper. Use rubber bands to create shapes on the board.

Pattern: **Base-10 Blocks**

Directions: Make multiple copies on cardstock or other paper that will hold up with multiple handlings. Cut out the blocks and use them to model base-10 relationships.

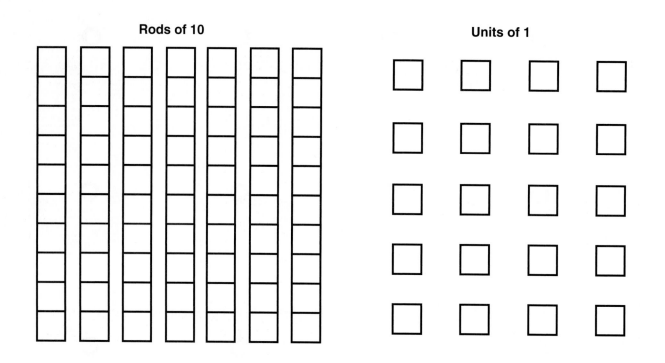

Rods of 10   **Units of 1**

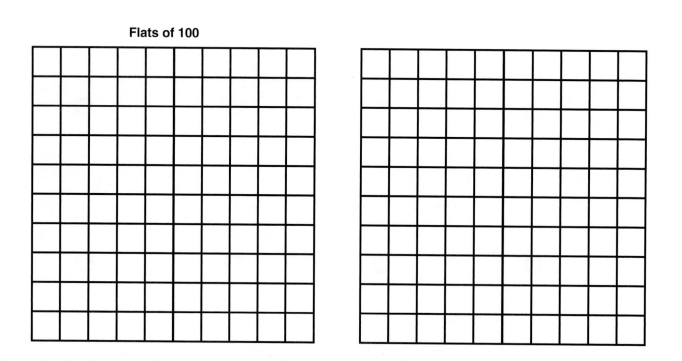

Flats of 100

Note: To make a cube with a volume of 1,000 units, copy six flats and tape them together to form a six-sided box.

Pattern: ***Counters***
Directions: Copy on card stock. Cut and manipulate.

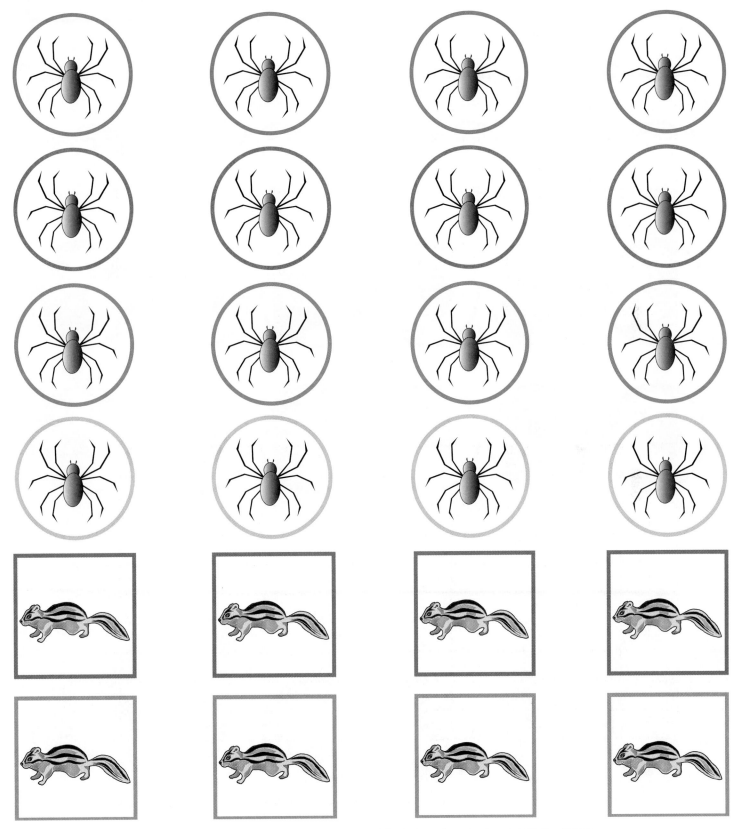

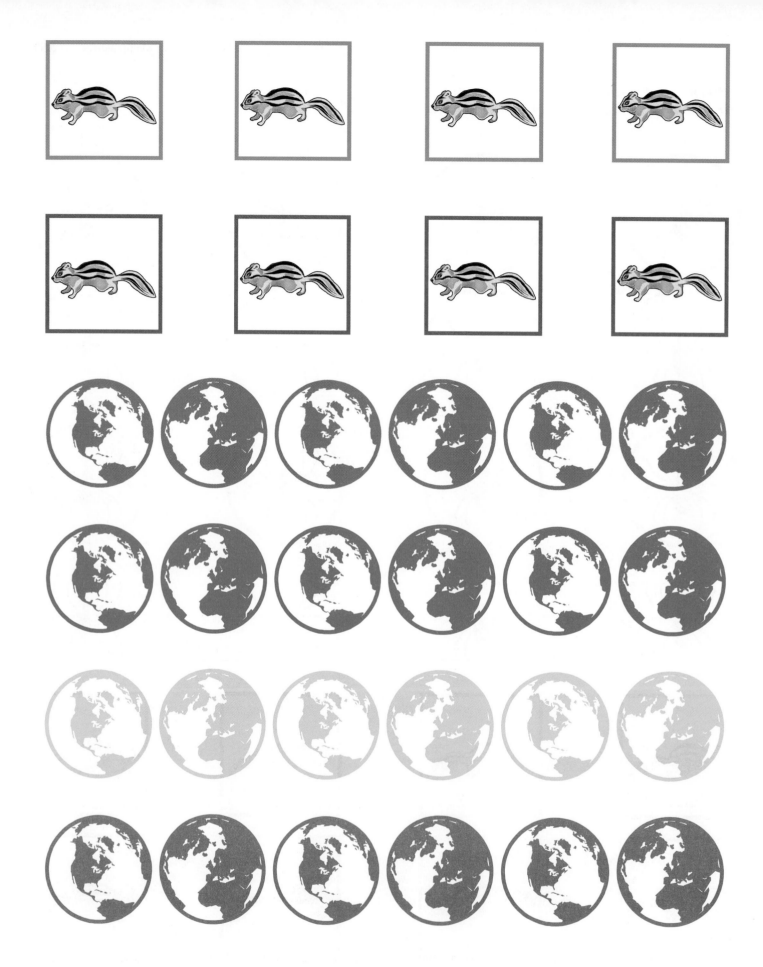

356

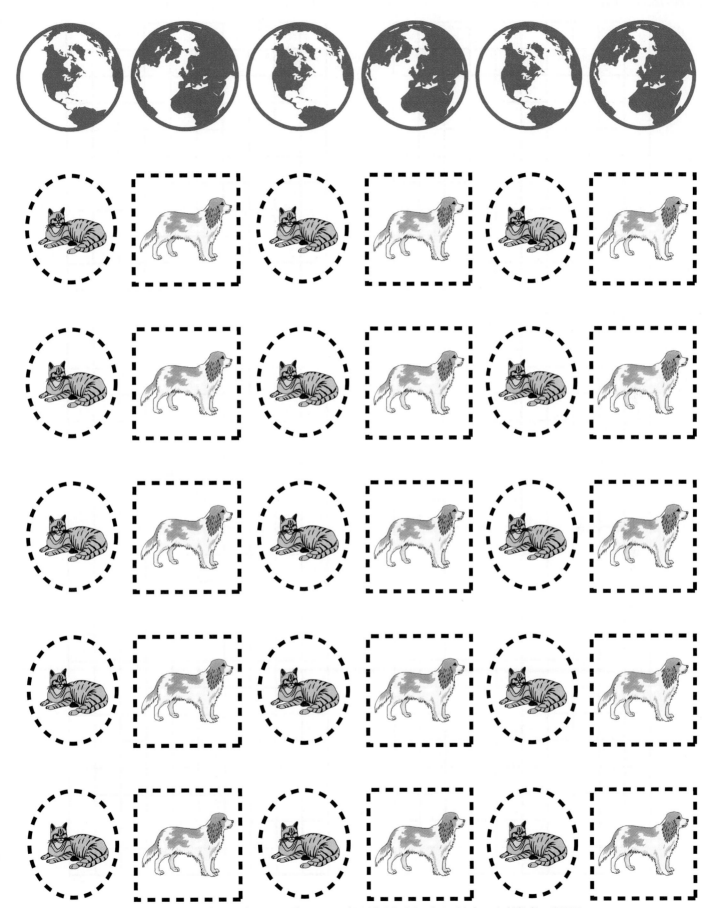

Pattern: *Decimal Squares*
Directions: Copy on worksheets to be used with activities for modeling and comparing decimals.

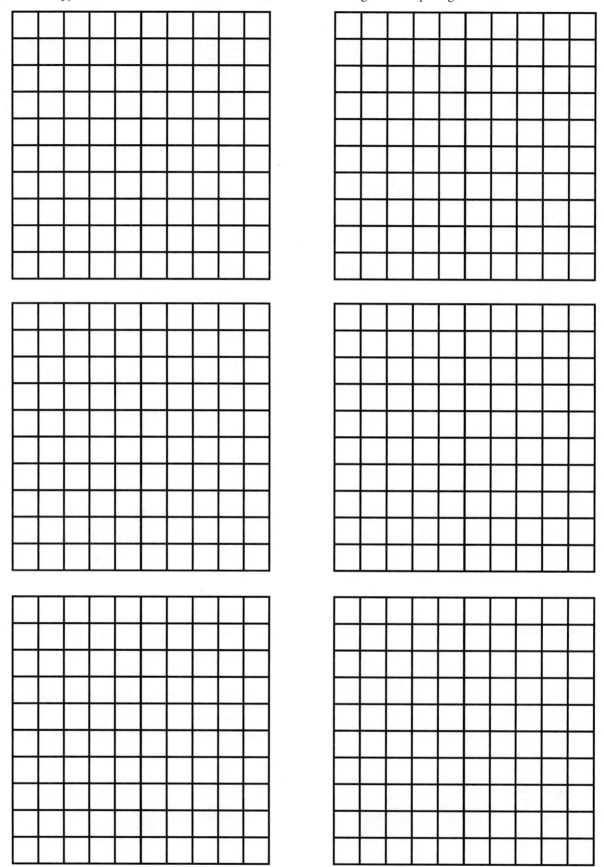

Pattern: **Multiplication Arrays**

Directions: Make a copy of the Multiplication Table and arrays for each student. Have students cut out the arrays. On the back of each one write the multiplication fact it represents. Then position each array at the zero point on the table and fill in the rest of the numbers. Write the number of units in the array on the table square covered by the array's right bottom square. Use the table and arrays to explore multiplication and to introduce the concepts of area and perimeter. (Adapted from a manipulative activity developed by Becca Rainey.)

Build Your Own Multiplication Tools
(using your rectangular arrays)

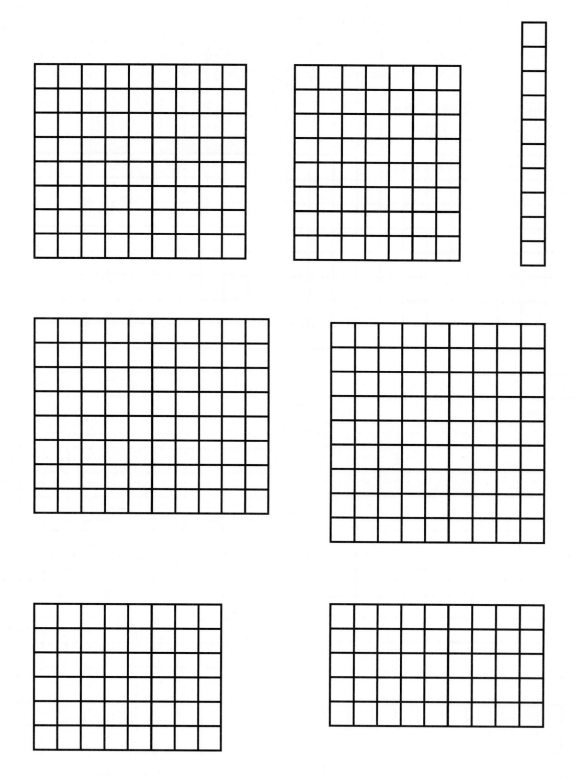

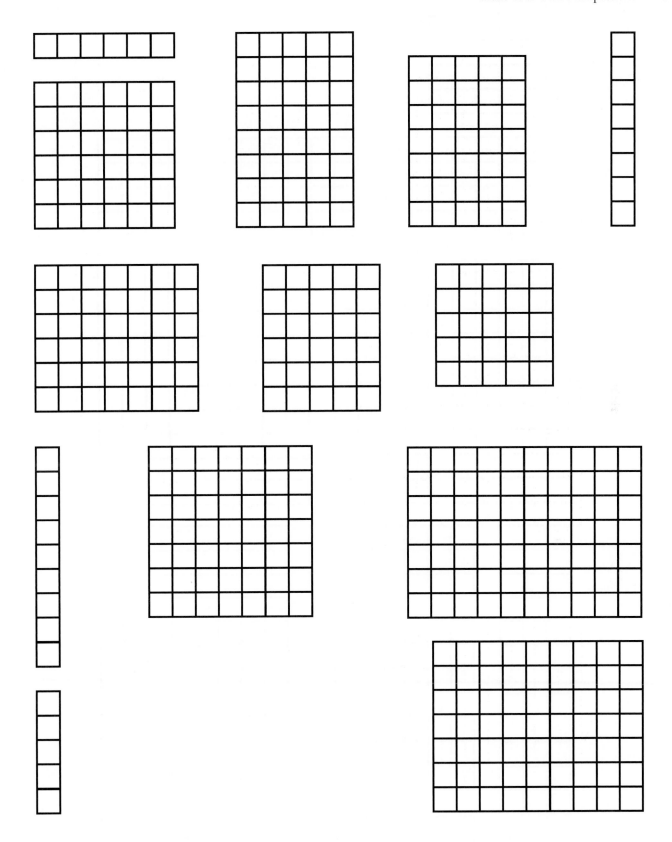

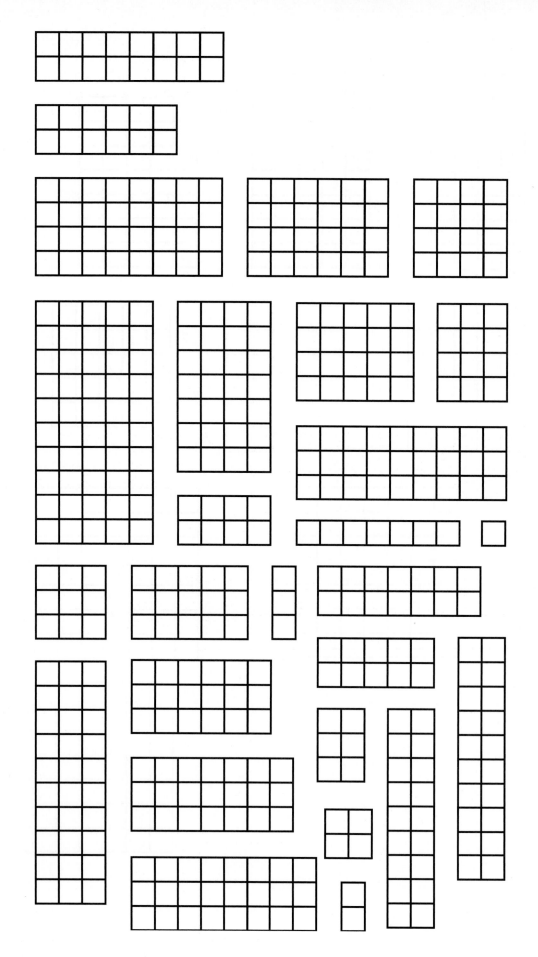

362

Pattern: *Polygon Cutouts*

Directions: Copy the cutouts on card stock or other heavy paper. Make at least 10 copies each of the smaller polygons (triangles through hexagons) and 5 copies of the larger polygons. Use the cutouts to explore the properties of each type of polygon. Have students cut, sort, and order the shapes. Then use the multiple copies to discover which polygons and combinations of polygons will tessellate and why (Adapted from Peterson 2000, 348–57).

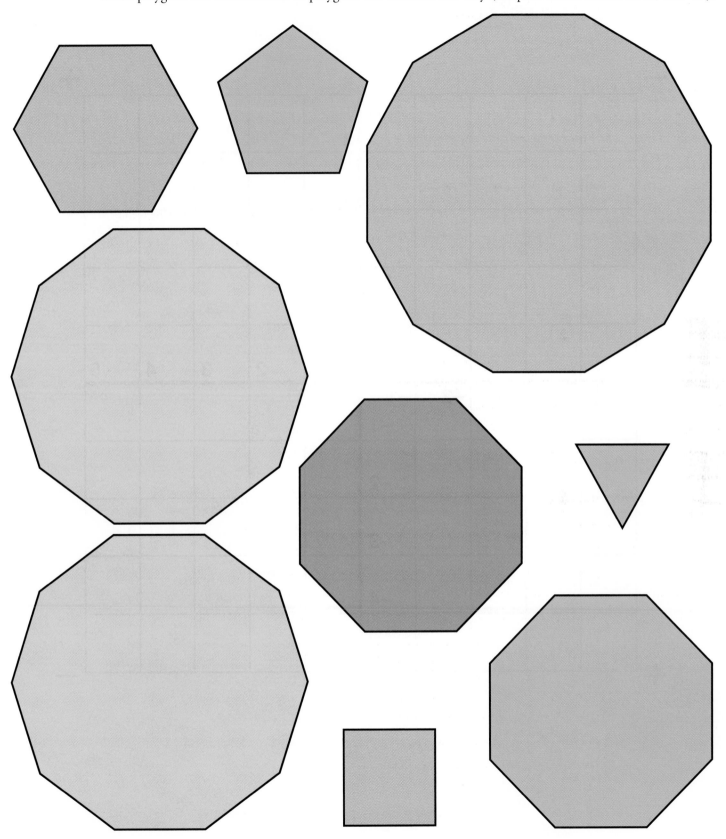

Blackline Masters

Modified Cartesian Coordinate Grid

Geoboard Dot Paper

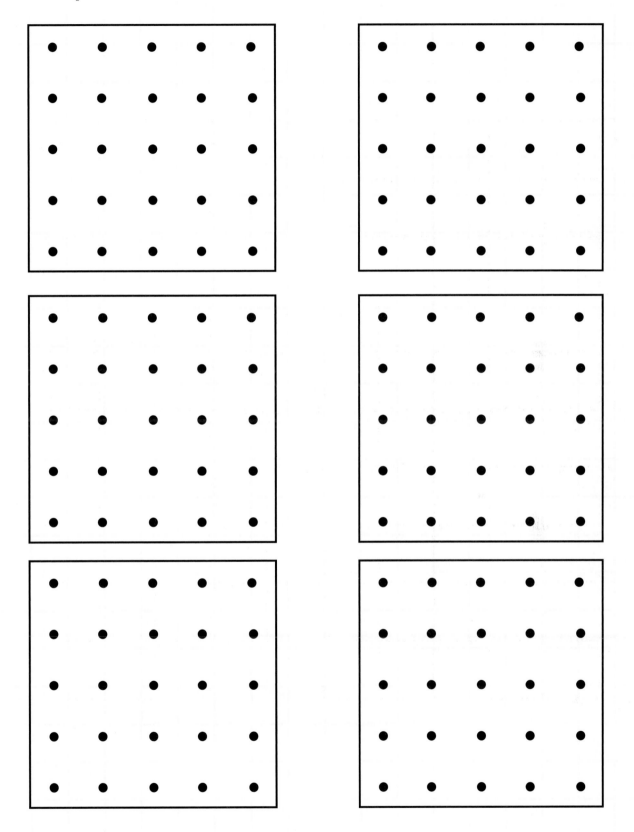

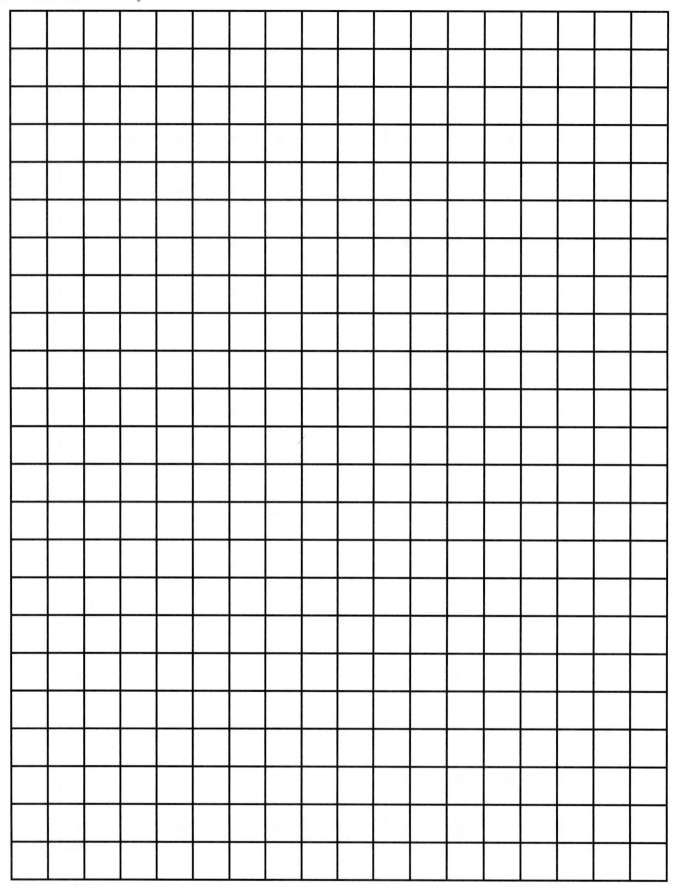

Triangular Grid Paper

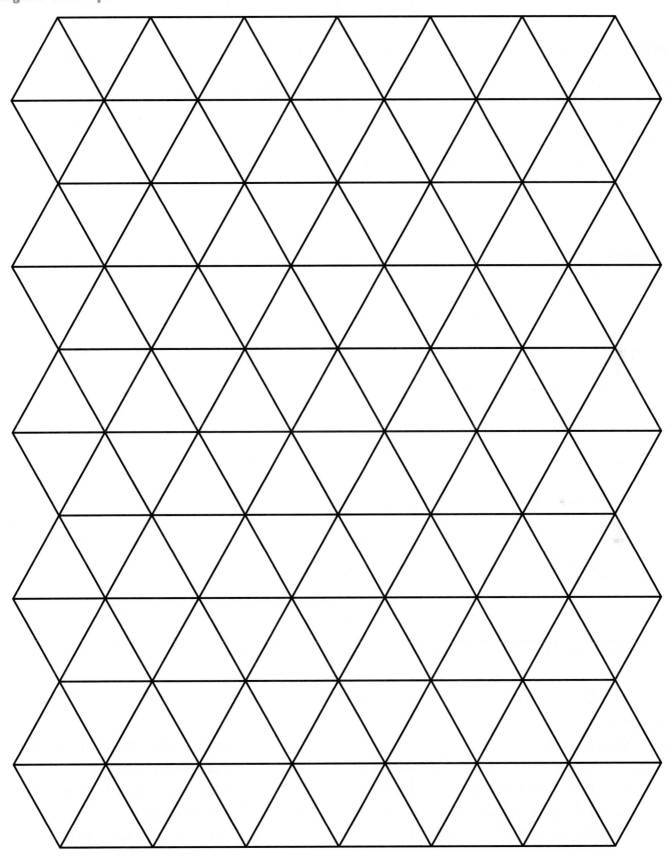

Classroom Observation

Name _____   Class _____

Date _____   Teacher _____

Activity _____

Comments:

Checklist:

_____ stays on task	_____ applies standard algorithms
_____ shows understanding of concepts	when appropriate
_____ represents work appropriately	_____ asks appropriate questions
_____ devises own problem-solving	_____ is engaged
strategies when appropriate	_____ can explain answers

Portfolio Checklist Form (Go to "Teaching Forms" on the CD-ROM to print or complete online.)

Portfolio Checklist

Name _____   Class _____

Assignment	Date	Score	Comments

Learning/Teaching Plan Form (Go to "Teaching Forms" on the CD-ROM to print or complete online.)

Learning/Teaching Plan

Class and/or grade level:

Concepts to be learned:

Learning objectives:

Materials needed:

Procedure:

1. Describe how you will introduce the activity or lesson and how you will motivate students.

2. Explain the teaching method(s) you will use—problem solving, discovery learning manipulatives, ` and so forth.

3. Write out the activities and/or problem-solving situations.

Assessment:

1. How will you assess process?

2. How will you assess product?

Extensions:

1. How can you extend this activity or lesson to the next level—another concept, degree of difficulty, and so forth?

2. How can you connect this activity or lesson to other learning?

Inquiry-Based Lesson Plan Form (Go to "Teaching Forms" on the CD-ROM to print or complete online.)

Inquiry-Based Lesson Plan

Overview

(Describe the activity overall. Explain the purpose and main ideas.)

Grade Levels:

NCTM Standards	
Content	*Process*
☐ Number and Operations	☐ Problem Solving
☐ Algebra	☐ Reasoning and Proof
☐ Geometry	☐ Communication
☐ Measurement	☐ Connections
☐ Data Analysis and Probability	☐ Representation

Activity Lesson Plan

*What ideas or concepts will students **explore?***

(List concepts or objectives individually.)

What materials will you need?

(List materials and/or resources needed for the activity.)

What questions could you ask?

(Compose questions to engage students, initiate activity, prompt problem solving, and promote discovery and mathematical thinking.)

What will you do?   (Describe what you will do to prepare and introduce the activity, including demonstrations and so forth.)

What will students do?   (Describe the procedures.)

What strategies might students   (Describe the kinds of problem-solving activities you expect to see.)
***invent** or construct?*

What insights, connections, or   (Describe specific outcomes of the activity—what you expect sutdents
applications might students   to learn and understand, including assessment criteria.)
discover?

What extensions can you make?   (Describe other activities to continue and extend learning objectives.)

Appendix B

Resources: Mathematics in Literature

Stories Listed by NCTM Content Standards

Note: Because a work of literature can cover more than one mathematical idea or concept, you may find the same reference under different categories.

Numbers and Operations

Number Sense

Alda, Arlene. *Arlene Alda's 1 2 3: What Do You See?* Berkeley, CA: Tricycle, 1998.

Bang, Molly. *Ten, Nine, Eight.* New York: Tupelo Books, 1998.

Banya, Istvan. *Zoom.* New York: Viking, 1995.

Beaton, Clare. *One Moose, Twenty Mice.* Cambridge, MA: Barefoot Books, 1999.

Bruce, Colin. *Conned Again, Watson.* New York: Perseus, 2001.

Burns, Marilyn. *Spaghetti and Meatballs for All.* Illust. Debbie Tilley. New York: Scholastic, 1997.

Cole, Joanna. *The Magic School Bus: Lost in the Solar System.* New York: Scholastic, 1990.

Crews, Donald. *Ten Black Dots.* New York: Greenwillow Books, 1986.

Cuyler, Margery. *100th Day Worries.* New York: Simon & Schuster, 2000.

Demarest, Chris L. *Smokejumpers One to Ten.* Illust. Chris L. Demarest. Hong Kong: McElderry Books, 2002.

Emberley, Barbara. *One Wide River to Cross.* Englewood Cliffs, NJ: Prentice Hall, 1976.

Fleischman, Paul. *Weslandia.* Cambridge, MA: Candlewick, 1999.

Florian, Douglas. *The Pig Is Big.* Illust. Douglas Florian. Greenwillow Books, 2000.

Froman, Robert. *Less Than Nothing Is Really Something.* New York: Crowell, 1973.

Frucht, William. *Imaginary Numbers.* (An anthology of mathematical stories.) Hoboken, NJ: Wiley, 1999.

Giganti, Paul. *How Many Snails.* New York: Greenwillow Books, 1988.

Girnis, Margaret. *1 2 3 for You and Me.* Photos by Shirley Leamon Green. Morton Grove, IL: Whitman, 2001.

Goldstone, Bruce. *Ten Friends.* New York: Holt, 2001.

Griffith, Helen V. *How Many Candles.* New York: Greenwillow Books, 1999.

Harshman, Marc. *Only One.* New York: Cobblehill Books, 1993.

Hoberman, Mary Ann. *One of Each.* New York: Scholastic, 1997.

Hutchins, Pat. *1 Hunter.* New York: Morrow, 1986.

Krahn, Fernando, and Maria de la Luz Krahn. *The Life of Numbers.* New York: Simon & Schuster, 1970.

Lester, Helen. *Score One for the Sloths.* Boston: Houghton Mifflin, 2001.

Losi, Carol A. *The 512 Ants on Sullivan Street.* Illust. Patrick Merrell. New York: Scholastic, 1997.

Mack, Stan. *10 Bears in my Bed.* New York: Pantheon Books, 1974.

McGrath, Barbara Barbieri. *The Baseball Counting Book.* Watertown, MA: Charlesbridge, 1999.

———. *More M&M's Math.* Watertown, MA: Charlesbridge, 1998.

McKissack, Patricia C. *A Million Fish . . . More or Less.* New York: Knopf, 1992.

Merriam, Eve. *12 Ways to Get to 11.* New York: Aladdin Books, 1993.

Moore, Inga. *Six Dinner Sid.* New York: Aladdin Books, 1993.

Murphy, Stuart J. *Missing Mittens.* New York: HarperCollins, 2001.

Nolan, Helen. *How Much, How Many, How Far, How Heavy, How Long, How Tall Is 1000?* Illust. Tracy Walker. Toronto: Kids Can Press, 1995.

Oaks, Bill, and Suse MacDonald. *Puzzlers.* New York: Dial Books, 1989.

Razzell, Arthur G., and K. G. O. Watts. *This Is 4: The Idea of a Number.* Garden City, NY: Doubleday, 1967.

Rocklin, Joanne. *How Much Is That Guinea Pig in the Window?* Illust. Meredith Johnson. New York: Scholastic, 1995.

Saul, Carol. *Barn Cat: A Counting Book.* New York: Little, Brown, 1998.

Schlein, Miriam. *More Than One.* New York: Greenwillow Books, 1996.

Schwartz, David M. *G Is for Googol: A Math Alphabet Book.* Berkeley, CA: Tricycle, 1998.

———. *How Much Is a Million?* New York: Mulberry Books, 1993.

Scieszka, Jon. *The Math Curse.* Illust. Lane Smith. New York: Viking, 1995.

Seuss, Dr. *One Fish, Two Fish, Red Fish, Blue Fish.* Illust. Roy McKie. New York: Random House, 1989.

Sitomer, Mindel, and Harry Sitomer. *How Did Numbers Begin?* New York: Crowell, 1976.

Slate, Joseph. *Miss Bindergarten Celebrates the 100th Day of Kindergarten.* New York: Dutton Books, 1998.

Slater, Terry. *Stay in Line.* New York: Scholastic, 1996.

Smith, Maggie. *Counting Our Way to Maine.* Illust. Maggie Smith. New York: Orchard Books, 1995.

Srivastava, Jane Jonas. *Number Families.* New York: Crowell, 1979.

Swinburne, Stephen R. *What's a Pair? What's a Dozen?* Honesdale, PA: Boyds Mills, 2000.

Tahan, Malba. *The Man Who Counted: A Collection of Mathematical Adventures.* New York: Norton, 1993.

Tang, Greg. *Grapes of Math: Mind-Stretching Math Riddles.* New York: Scholastic, 2001.

Turner, Priscilla. *Among the Odds and Evens: A Tale of Adventure.* New York: Farrar, Straus & Giroux, 1999.

Wyler, Rose, and Mary Elting. *Math Fun with Money Puzzlers.* Illust. Patrick Girouard. New York: Messner, 1992.

Zaslavsky, Claudia. *Zero. Is It Something? Is It Nothing?* New York: Watts, 1987.

Counting

Anno, Mitsumasa. *Anno's Counting Book.* New York: HarperCollins, 1987.

Alda, Arlene. *1 2 3: What Do You See?* Berkeley, CA: Tricycle, 1998.

Berenstain, Stan, and Jan Berenstain. *Trouble with Money.* Illust. Jan Berenstain. New York: Random House, 2001.

Blume, Judy. *Freckle Juice.* Illust. Sonia D. Lisker. New York: Macmillan, 1971.

Bowen, Betsy. *Gathering: A Northwoods Counting Book.* Boston: Houghton Mifflin, 1999.

Burns, Marilyn. *Spaghetti and Meatballs for All.* Illust. Debbie Tilley. New York: Scholastic, 1997.

Carle, Eric. *The Very Hungry Caterpillar.* Illust. Eric Carle. New York: Hamilton Children's Books, 1987.

Carlstrom, Nancy White. *Let's Count It Out, Jesse Bear.* New York: Scholastic, 1996.

Christelow, E. *Five Little Monkeys Jumping.* Boston: Houghton Mifflin, 1989.

Dee, Ruby. *Two Ways to Count to Ten: A Liberian Folktale.* New York: Holt, 1988.

Demarest, Chris L. *Smokejumpers One to Ten.* Illust. Chris L. Demarest. Hong Kong: McElderry Books, 2002.

Dickens, Charles. *The Twelve Days of Christmas.* Illust. Mike Eagle. Racine, WI: Western, 1983.

Durea, Olivier. *Deep Down Underground.* New York: Aladdin Books, 1993.

Edwards, Pamela Duncan. *Roar! A Noisy Counting Book.* New York: HarperCollins, 2000.

———. *Warthogs in the Kitchen: A Sloppy Counting Book.* Hyperion, 1998.

Emberley, Barbara. *One Wide River to Cross.* Englewood Cliffs, NJ: Prentice Hall, 1976.

Everett, Percival. *The One That Got Away.* New York: Clarion Books, 1992.

Falwell, Cathryn. *Turtlesplash: Countdown at the Pond.* New York: Greenwillow Books, 2001.

Feelings, Muriel. *Moja Means One: Swahili Counting Book.* New York: Puffin Books, 1992.

Freyman, Saxton, and Joost Elffers. *One Lonely Sea Horse.* New York: Scholastic, 2000.

Giganti, Paul. *Each Orange Had 8 Slices.* New York: Greenwillow Books, 1992.

———. *How Many Snails.* New York: Greenwillow Books, 1988.

Gollub, Matthew. *Ten Oni Drummers.* New York: Lee & Low Books, 2000.

Greenstein, Elaine. *Dreaming: A Countdown to Sleep.* New York: Levine Books, 2000.

Grossman, Bill. *My Little Sister Ate One Hare.* Illust. Kevin Hawkes. New York: Crown, 1996.

Hamm, Dianne Johnston. *How Many Feet in the Bed?* New York: Simon & Schuster, 1991.

Hewitt, Kathryn. *Two By Two.* New York: Harcourt Brace Jovanovich, 1984.

Howard, Katherine. *I Can Count to 100 . . . Can You?* Illust. Michael J. Smollin. New York: Random House, 1979.

Kaye, Marilyn. *A Day with No Math.* Illust. Tim Bowers. Orlando, FL: Harcourt Brace Jovanovich, 1992.

Krahn, Fernando, and Maria de la Luz Krahn. *The Life of Numbers.* New York: Simon & Schuster, 1970.

LeSieg, Theo. *Ten Apples Up on Top!* New York: Random House, 1961.

Lorimer, Lawrence T., reteller. *Noah's Ark.* New York: Random House, 1978.

Lottridge, Celia Barker. *One Watermelon Seed.* Toronto: Oxford University Press, 1986.

MacDonald, Suse. *Numblers.* New York: Dial Books for Young Readers, 1988.

Mack, Stan. *10 Bears in my Bed.* New York: Pantheon Books, 1974.

Maestro, Betsy, and Giulio Maestro. *Harriet Goes to the Circus.* New York: Crown, 1989.

McCloskey, Robert. *Make Way for Ducklings.* New York: Viking, 1969.

McGrath, Barbara Barbieri. *¡A Contar Cheerios!* Illust. Rob Bolster and Frank Mazzola Jr. New York: Scholastic, 1998.

Mallat, Kathy. *Seven Stars More!* New York: Walker, 1998.

Murphy, Stuart J. *Betcha!* New York: HarperCollins, 1997.

———. *A Four Bear Share.* Illust. John Speirs. New York: HarperCollins, 1998.

Nolan, Helen. *How Much, How Many, How Far, How Heavy, How Long, How Tall Is 1000?* Illust. Tracy Walker. Toronto: Kids Can Press, 1995.

Pallotta, Jerry. *The Icky Bug Counting Book.* Watertown, MA: Charlesbridge, 1992.

———. *Reese's Pieces: Count by Tens.* Illust. Rob Bolster. New York: Scholastic, 2004.

———. *Underwater Counting: Even Numbers.* Watertown, MA: Charlesbridge, 2001.

Riddell, Chris. *The Trouble with Elephants.* Illust. Chris Riddell. New York: HarperCollins, 1998.

Rocklin, Joanne. *How Much Is That Guinea Pig in the Window?* Illust. Meredith Johnson. New York: Scholastic, 1995.

Rockwell, Anne. *100 School Days.* Illust. Lizzy Rockwell. Hong Kong: HarperCollins, 2002.

Schumaker, Ward. *In My Garden: A Counting Book.* San Francisco: Chronicle Books, 2000.

Seuss, Dr. *Ten Apples on Top.* Illust. Roy McKie. New York: Random House, 1961.

Sierra, Judy. *Counting Crocodiles.* Illust. Will Hillenbrand. San Diego, CA: Gulliver Books, 1997.

Smith, Maggie. *Counting Our Way to Maine.* Illust. Maggie Smith. New York: Orchard Books, 1995.

Statson, Caroline. *Mountain Meadow 1 2 3.* Boulder, CO: Roberts Rinehart, 1995.

Wadsworth, Ginger. *One on a Web.* Watertown, MA: Charlesbridge, 1997.

———. *One Tiger Growls: A Counting Book of Animal Sounds.* New York: Charlesbridge, 1999.

Walsh, Ellen Stoll. *Mouse Count.* New York: Voyager Books, 1991.

Wells, Robert E. *Can You Count to a Googol?* Morton Grove, IL: Whitman, 2000.

Wells, Rosemary. *Emily's First 100 Days of School.* New York: Hyperion, 2000.

Wyler, Rose, and Mary Elting. *Math Fun with Money Puzzlers.* Illust. Patrick Girouard. New York: Messner, 1992.

Counting (for children with special needs)

Girnis, Margaret. *1 2 3 for You and Me.* Photos by Shirley Leamon Green. Morton Grove, IL: Whitman, 2001.

Addition

Anno, Mitsumasa. *Anno's Magic Seeds.* New York: Philomel Books, 1995.

Berenstain, Stan, and Jan Berenstain. *The Berenstain Bears' Dollar and Sense.* New York: Random House, 2001.

Demarest, Chris L. *Smokejumpers One to Ten.* Hong Kong: McElderry Books, 2002.

Demi. *One Grain of Rice: A Mathematical Folktale.* Illust. Demi. New York: Scholastic, 1997.

Duke, Kate. *One Guinea Pig Is Not Enough.* New York: Puffin Books, 2001.

Ehlert, Lois. *Fish Eyes: A Book You Can Count On.* San Diego, CA: Harcourt Brace, 1990.

Froman, Robert. *Less Than Nothing Is Really Something.* New York: Crowell, 1973.

Giganti, Paul. *Each Orange Had 8 Slices.* New York: Greenwillow Books, 1992.

Harris, Trudy. *100 Days of School.* Brookfield, CT: Milbrook, 1999.

Hulme, Joy. N. *Sea Sums.* Illust. Carol Swartz. New York: Hyperion, 1996.

Leedy, Loreen. *Mission Addition.* New York: Holiday House, 1997.

Lewin, Betsy. *Cat Count.* New York: Scholastic, 1981.

Long, Lynette. *Domino Addition.* Watertown, MA: Charlesbridge, 1996.

McGrath, Barbara Barbieri. *More M&M's Math.* Watertown, MA: Charlesbridge, 1998.

McKissack, Patricia. *A Million Fish . . . More or Less.* New York: Knopf, 1992.

Mahy, Margaret. *The Seven Chinese Brothers.* Illust. Jean and Mou-Sien Tseng. New York: Scholastic, 1990.

Murphy, Stuart J. *A Four Bear Share.* Illust. John Speirs. New York: HarperCollins, 1998.

———. *The Penny Pot.* Illust. Lynne Cravath. New York: HarperCollins, 1998.

———. *Too Many Kangaroo Things to Do!* Illust. Kevin O'Malley. New York: HarperCollins, 1996.

Nolan, Helen. *How Much, How Many, How Far, How Heavy, How Long, How Tall Is 1000?* Illust. Tracy Walker. Toronto: Kids Can Press, 1995.

Schlein, Miriam. *More Than One.* Illust. Donald Crews. New York: Scholastic, 1996.

Seuss, Dr. *One Fish, Two Fish, Red Fish, Blue Fish.* Illust. Roy McKie. New York: Random House, 1989.

Smith, David Eugene. *Number Stories of Long Ago.* Reston, VA: National Council of Teachers of Mathematics, 1997.

Srivastava, Jane Jonas. *Number Families.* New York: Crowell, 1979.

Sturges, Philemon. *Ten Flashing Fireflies.* New York: North-South Books, 1993.

Viorst, Judith. *Alexander, Who Used to Be Rich Last Sunday.* Illust. Ray Cruz. New York: Aladdin Books, 1978.

Subtraction

Anno, Mitsumasa. *Anno's Magic Seeds.* New York: Philomel Books, 1995.

Berenstain, Stan, and Jan Berenstain. *The Berenstain Bears' Dollar and Sense.* New York: Random House, 2001.

Brisson, Pat. *Benny's Pennies.* New York: Bantam Doubleday Dell Books, 1993.

Froman, Robert. *Less Than Nothing Is Really Something.* New York: Crowell, 1973.

Hulme, Joy. N. *Sea Sums.* Illust. Carol Swartz. New York: Hyperion, 1996.

Leedy, Loreen. *Subtraction Action.* New York: Holiday House, 2000.

McKissack, Patricia. *A Million Fish . . . More or Less.* New York: Knopf, 1992.

Mathews, Louise. *The Great Take-Away.* New York: Dodd, Mead, 1980.

Murphy, Stuart J. *Elevator Magic.* New York: HarperCollins, 1997.

———. *Monster Musical Chairs.* New York: HarperCollins, 2000.

———. *The Penny Pot.* Illust. Lynne Cravath. New York: HarperCollins, 1998.

Srivastava, Jane Jonas. *Number Families.* New York: Crowell, 1979.

Sturges, Philemon. *Ten Flashing Fireflies.* New York: North-South Books, 1995.

Toft, Kim Michelle, and Allan Sheather. *One Less Fish.* New York: Charlesbridge, 1998.

Viorst, Judith. *Alexander, Who Used to Be Rich Last Sunday.* Illust. Ray Cruz. New York: Aladdin Books, 1978.

Multiplication

Anno, Mitsumasa. *Anno's Magic Seeds.* New York: Philomel Books, 1995.

———. *Anno's Mysterious Multiplying Jar.* Illust. Mitsumasa Anno. New York: Putnam, 1983.

Daniels, Teri. *Math Man.* New York: Scholastic, 2001.

Demi. *One Grain of Rice: A Mathematical Folktale.* Illust. Demi. New York: Scholastic, 1997.

Giganti, Paul. *Each Orange Had 8 Slices.* New York: Greenwillow Books, 1992.

Leedy, Loreen. *2 × 2 = Boo! A Set of Spooky Multiplication Stories.* New York: Holiday House, 1995.

Murphy, Stuart J. *Betcha.* Illust. S. D. Schindler. New York: HarperCollins, 1997.

———. *Too Many Kangaroo Things to Do!* Illust. Kevin O'Malley. New York: HarperCollins, 1996.

Neuschwander, Cindy. *Amanda Bean's Amazing Dream.* Illust. Liza Woodruff. Sausalito, CA: Math Solutions, 1998.

Pinczes, Elinor J. *A Remainder of One.* Illust. Bonnie MacKain. New York: Scholastic, 1995.

Smith, David Eugene. *Number Stories of Long Ago.* Reston, VA: National Council of Teachers of Mathematics, 1997.

Srivastava, Jane Jonas. *Number Families.* New York: Crowell, 1979.

Thompson, Lauren. *One Riddle, One Answer.* New York: Scholastic, 2001.

Decimals/Percents

Berenstain, Stan, and Jan Berenstain. *The Berenstain Bears' Trouble with Money.* New York: Random House, 1983.

Daniels, Teri. *Math Man.* New York: Scholastic, 2001.

Froman, Robert. *Less Than Nothing Is Really Something.* New York: Crowell, 1973.

Howe, James. *Harold & Chester in Hot Fudge.* New York: Morrow Junior Books, 1990.

Juster, Norton. *The Phantom Tollbooth.* New York: Random House, 1993.

Rocklin, Joanne. *How Much Is That Guinea Pig in the Window?* Illust. Meredith Johnson. New York: Scholastic, 1995.

Sciezka, Jon, and Lane Smith. *The Math Curse.* New York: Penguin, 1995.

Viorst, Judith. *Alexander, Who Used to Be Rich Last Sunday.* Illust. Ray Cruz. New York: Aladdin Books, 1978.

Division/Fractions

Bridwell, Norman. *Clifford, the Big Red Dog.* New York: Scholastic, 1985.

Connell, David, and Jim Thurman. *Mathnet Casebook #1: The Case of the Unnatural.* New York: Scientific American Books for Young Readers; Freeman, 1993.

Daniels, Teri. *Math Man.* New York: Scholastic, 2001.

Dodds, Dayle Ann. *The Great Divide.* Cambridge, MA: Candlewick, 1999.

Dryk, Marti. *The Fraction Family Heads West.* Manchara, TX: Bookaloppy, 1997.

Ginsburg, Mirra. *Two Greedy Bears.* Illust. Jose Arguego and Ariane Dewey. New York: Aladdin Books, 1998.

Howe, James. *Harold & Chester in Hot Fudge.* New York: Morrow Junior Books, 1990.

Hutchins, Pat. *The Doorbell Rang.* New York: Greenwillow Books, 1986.

Juster, Norton. *The Phantom Tollbooth.* New York: Random House, 1993.

Leedy, Loreen. *Fraction Action.* New York: Holiday House, 1994.

Mahy, Margaret. *17 Kings and 42 Elephants.* New York: Dutton Books, 1987.

McMillan, Bruce. *Eating Fractions.* New York: Scholastic, 1991.

Murphy, Stuart J. *Jump, Kangaroo, Jump!* Illust. Kevin O'Malley. New York: HarperCollins, 1999.

———. *Rabbits Pajama Party.* Illust. Frank Remkiewicz. New York: HarperCollins, 1999.

Pinczes, Elinor. *Inchworm and a Half.* Illust. Randall Enos. Boston: Houghton Mifflin, 2001.

———. *One Hundred Hungry Ants.* Illust. Bonnie MacKain. New York: First Scholastic Printing, 1993.

———. *A Remainder of One.* Illust. Bonnie MacKain. New York: Scholastic, 1995.

Sciezka, Jon, and Lane Smith. *The Math Curse.* New York: Penguin, 1995.

Smith, David Eugene. *Number Stories of Long Ago.* Reston VA: National Council of Teachers of Mathematics, 1997.

Srivastava, Jane Jonas. *Number Families.* New York: Crowell, 1979.

Tahan, Malba. *The Man Who Counted: A Collection of Mathematical Adventures.* New York: Norton, 1993.

Thompson, Lauren. *One Riddle, One Answer.* New York: Scholastic, 2001.

Ziefert, Harriet. *Rabbit and Hare Divide an Apple.* Illust. Emily Bolam. New York: Viking, 1998.

Ratio and/or Proportion

Bridwell, Norman. *Clifford, the Big Red Dog.* New York: Scholastic, 1985.

Ginsburg, Mirra. *Two Greedy Bears.* Illust. Jose Arguego and Ariane Dewey. New York: Aladdin Books, 1998.

Mizumura, Kazue. *The Way of the Ant.* New York: Crowell, 1970.

Nolan, Helen. *How Much, How Many, How Far, How Heavy, How Long, How Tall Is 1000?* Illust. Tracy Walker. Toronto: Kids Can Press, 1995.

Norton, Mary. *The Borrowers.* San Diego, CA: Harcourt Brace, 1989.

Peterson, John. *The Littles.* New York: Scholastic, 1967.

———. *The Littles and the Big Storm.* New York: Scholastic, 1979.

———. *The Littles and the Trash Tinies.* New York: Scholastic, 1977.

———. *The Littles Go Exploring.* New York: Scholastic, 1978.

Schwartz, David M. *If You Hopped Like a Frog.* New York: Scholastic, 1999.

Seuss, Dr. *Horton Hears a Who.* New York: Random House, 1954.

Thomas, Patricia. *"Stand back," Said the Elephant. "I'm going to sneeze!"* New York: Lothrop, 1971.

Place Value

Berenstain, Stan, and Jan Berenstain. *The Berenstain Bears' Dollar and Sense.* New York: Random House, 2001.

———. *Trouble with Money.* Illust. Jan Berenstain. New York: Random House, Inc., 2001.

Friedman, Aileen. *The King's Commissioners.* Illust. Susan Guevara. New York: Scholastic, 1994.

McGrath, Barbara Barbieri. *¡A Contar Cheerios!* Illust. Rob Bolster and Frank Mazzola Jr. New York: Scholastic, 1998.

Murphy, Stuart J. *The Penny Pot.* Illust. Lynne Cravath. New York: HarperCollins, 1998.

Pallotta, Jerry. *Reese's Pieces: Count by Tens.* Illust. Rob Bolster. New York: Scholastic, 2004.

Pilegard, Virginia. *The Warlord's Beads.* Gretna, LA: Pelican, 2001.

Rockwell, Anne. *100 School Days.* Illust. Lizzy Rockwell. Hong Kong: HarperCollins, 2002.

St. John, Glory. *How to Count Like a Martian.* New York: Walck, 1975.

Schwartz, David M. *On Beyond a Million: An Amazing Math Journey.* New York: Random House, 1999.

Thompson, Lauren. *One Riddle, One Answer.* New York: Scholastic, 2001.

Time

Base, Graeme. *The Eleventh Hour.* New York: Abrams, 1988.

Bruchac, Joseph, and Jonathan London. *Thirteen Moons on a Turtle's Back: A Native American Year of Moons.* Illust. Thomas Locker. New York: Philomel, 1992.

Duffy, Trent. *The Clock.* Illust. Tobey Welles. New York: Atheneum, 2000.

Frucht, William, *Imaginary Numbers.* (An anthology of mathematical stories.) Hoboken, NJ: Wiley, 1999.

Hooper, Meredith. *Seven Eggs.* New York: HarperCollins, 2001.

Kaye, Marilyn. *A Day with No Math.* Illust. Tim Bowers. Orlando, FL: Harcourt Brace Jovanovich, 1992.

Kellogg, Steven. *I Was Born about 10,000 Years Ago.* New York: Morrow Junior Books, 1996.

Lobel, Anita. *One Lighthouse, One Moon.* New York: Greenwillow Books, 2000.

McCurdy, Michael. *An Algonquian Year: The Year According to the Full Moon.* Boston: Houghton Mifflin, 2000.

Murphy, Stuart J. *Rabbits Pajama Party.* Illust. Frank Remkiewicz. New York: HarperCollins, 1999.

Money

Adams, Barbara J. *The Go-Around Dollar.* New York: Fourwinds, 1992.

Allen, Nancy K. *Once upon a Dime: A Math Adventure.* New York: Charlesbridge, 1999.

Axelrod, Amy. *Pigs Will Be Pigs: Fun with Math & Money.* San Diego CA: Harcourt Brace, 1994.

Brisson, Pat. *Benny's Pennies.* New York: Bantam Doubleday Dell Books, 1993.

Gill, Shelley, and Deborah Tobola. *The Big Buck Adventure.* Watertown, MA: Charlesbridge, 2000.

Khalsa, Dayal Kaur. *How Pizza Came to Queens.* New York: Scholastic, 1993.

Leedy, Loreen. *Fraction Action.* New York: Holiday House, 1994.

Mathis, Sharon Bell. *The Hundred Penny Box.* New York: Puffin Books, 1986.

McMillan, Bruce. *Jelly Beans for Sale.* New York: Scholastic, 1996.

Murphy, Stuart J. *Lemonade for Sale.* Illust. Tricia Tusa. New York: HarperCollins, 1998.

———. *The Penny Pot.* Illust. Lynne Cravath. New York: HarperCollins, 1998.

Peterson, Esther Allen. *Penelope Gets Wheels.* New York: Crown, 1981.

Rocklin, Joanne. *How Much Is That Guinea Pig in the Window?* Illust. Meredith Johnson. New York: Scholastic, 1995.

Schwartz, David M. *If You Made a Million.* New York: Mulberry Books, 1989.

Slater, Teddy, and Anthony Lewis. *Max's Money.* New York: Scholastic, 1998.

Viorst, Judith. *Alexander, Who Used to Be Rich Last Sunday.* New York: Aladdin Books, 1988.

Wells, Rosemary. *Bunny Money.* New York: Dial Books, 1997.

Wiseman, W. *Morris Goes to School.* New York: HarperCollins, 1970.

Wyler, Rose, and Mary Elting. *Math Fun with Money Puzzlers.* Illust. Patrick Girouard. New York: Messner, 1992.

Classification

Blundell, Tony. *Beware of Boys.* Fairfield, NJ: Greenwillow, 1991.

Carlson, Nancy. *Harriet's Halloween Candy.* Minneapolis, MN: Carolrhoda Books, 1982.

Murphy, Stuart J. *A Four Bear Share.* Illust. John Speirs. New York: HarperCollins, 1998.

Reid, Margarette S. *A String of Beads.* Bergenfield, NJ: Dutton Children's Books, 1997.

Slater, Teddy, and Anthony Lewis. *Max's Money.* New York: Scholastic, 1998.

Order

Carlson, Nancy. *Harriet's Halloween Candy.* Minneapolis, MN: Carolrhoda Books, 1982.

Demi. *One Grain of Rice: A Mathematical Folktale.* Illust. Demi. New York: Scholastic, 1997.

Friedman, Aileen. *The King's Commissioners.* Illust. Susan Guevara. New York: Scholastic, 1994.

Hooper, Meredith. *Seven Eggs.* New York: HarperCollins, 2001.

Wyler, Rose, and Mary Elting. *Math Fun with Money Puzzlers.* Illust. Patrick Girouard. New York: Messner, 1992.

Algebra

Patterns and Symmetry

Adshead, Paul S. *One Odd Old Owl.* New York: Child's Play International, 1993.

Alda, Arlene. *Arlene Alda's 1 2 3: What Do You See?* Berkeley, CA: Tricycle, 1998.

Anno, Mitsumasa. *Anno's Magic Seeds.* New York: Philomel Books, 1995.

Appelt, Kathi. *Bat Jamboree.* New York: Mulberry Books, 1996.

Baker, Keith. *Quack and Count.* San Diego, CA: Harcourt Brace, 1999.

Bankin, James, Elizabeth Bankin, and Carol Bankin. *What Do You Mean by "Average"?* Illust. Joel Schick. New York: Lothrop, Lee and Sheperd, 1978.

Barry, David. *The Rajah's Rice: A Mathematical Folktale from India.* New York: Scientific American Books for Young Readers, 1994.

Base, Graeme. *The Eleventh Hour.* New York: Abrams, 1988.

Birch, David. *The King's Chessboard.* New York: Penguin Books, 1988.

Burns, Marilyn. *Spaghetti and Meatballs for All.* Illust. Debbie Tilley. New York: Scholastic, 1997.

Connell, David, and Jim Thurman. *Mathnet Casebook #1: The Case of the Unnatural.* New York: Scientific American Books for Young Readers; Freeman, 1993.

———. *Mathnet Casebook #3: The Case of the Willing Parrot.* New York: Scientific American Books for Young Readers; Freeman, 1994.

Daniels, Teri. *Math Man.* New York: Scholastic, 2001.

Demi. *One Grain of Rice: A Mathematical Folktale.* Illust. Demi. New York: Scholastic, 1997.

De Regniers, Beatrice S. *So Many Cats.* New York: Clarion Books, 1985.

Dodds, Dayle Ann. *The Great Divide.* Cambridge, MA: Candlewick, 1999.

Friedman, Aileen. *A Cloak for a Dreamer.* Illust. Kim Howard. New York: Scholastic, 1994.

Frucht, William. *Imaginary Numbers.* (An anthology of mathematical stories.) Hoboken, NJ: Wiley, 1999.

Giganti, Jr., Paul. *How Many Snails? A Counting Book.* Illust. Donald Crews. New York: Greenwillow Books, 1998.

Ginsburg, Mirra. *Two Greedy Bears.* Illust. Jose Arguego and Ariane Dewey. New York: Aladdin Books, 1998.

Glass, Julie. *The Fly on the Ceiling.* Illust. Richard Walz. New York: Random House, 1998.

Hoban, Tana. *More, Fewer, Less.* New York: Greenwillow Books, 1998.

Hong, Lily Toy. *Two of Everything: A Chinese Folktale.* Morton Grove, IL: Whitman, 1993.

Hulme, Joy. N. *Sea Squares.* New York: Hyperion, 1991.

———. *Sea Sums.* Illustrated by Carol Swartz. New York: Hyperion, 1996.

Losi, Carol A. *The 512 Ants on Sullivan Street.* Illust. Patrick Merrel. New York: Scholastic, 1997.

Nolan, Helen. *How Much, How Many, How Far, How Heavy, How Long, How Tall Is 1000?* Illustrated by Tracy Walker. Toronto: Kids Can Press, 1995.

Oaks, Bill, and Suse MacDonald. *Puzzlers.* New York: Dial Books, 1989.

Owen, Annie. *Annie's One to Ten.* New York: Knopf, 1988.

Packard, Edward. *Big Numbers: And Pictures That Show Just How Big They Are!* Minneapolis, MN: Millbrook, 2000.

Pappas, Theoni. *Math Talk: Mathematical Ideas in Poems for Two Voices.* San Carlos, CA: Wide World, 1991.

Pittman, Helena Clare. *A Grain of Rice.* New York: Skylark Books, 1992.

Reid, Margarette S. *A String of Beads.* Bergenfield, NJ: Dutton Children's Books, 1997.

Sachar, Louis. *Sideways Arithmetic from Wayside School.* New York: Scholastic, 1989.

Schimmel, Annemarie. *The Mystery of Numbers.* Toronto: Oxford University Press, 1993.

Schwartz, David M. *If You Hopped Like a Frog.* New York: Scholastic, 1999.

Slater, Terry. *Stay in Line.* New York: Scholastic, 1996.

Slobodkina, Esphyr. *Caps for Sale: A Tale of a Peddlar, Some Monkeys, and Their Monkey Business.* New York: HarperCollins, 1987.

Srivastava, Jane Jonas. *Number Families.* New York: Crowell, 1979.

Stevens, Jan. Romero. *Twelve Lizards Leaping: A New Twelve Days of Christmas.* Flagstaff, AZ: Rising Moon, 1999.

Tompert, Amy. *Grandfather Tang's Story: A Tale Told with Tangrams.* Illust. Robert Andrew Parker. New York: Dragonfly Books, 1990.

Geometry

Abbott, Edwin A. *Flatland: A Romance of Many Dimensions.* Illust. Edwin A. Abbott. Reprinted, New York: Barnes & Noble Books, 1983. Harper & Row, 1899.

Allen, Pamela, *Mr. Archimedes' Bath.* Illust. Pamela Allen. Melbourne, Australia: Angus & Robertson, 1992.

Appelt, Kathi. *Bats Around the Clock.* Illust. Melissa Sweet. New York: HarperCollins, 2000.

Base, Graeme. *The Eleventh Hour.* New York: Abrams, 1988.

Briggs, Raymond. *Jim and the Beanstalk.* Illust. Raymond Briggs. New York: Paper Star, 1997.

Bruce, Colin, *Conned Again, Watson.* New York: Perseus, 2001.

Burger, Dionys. *Sphereland: A Fantasy About Curved Spaces and an Expanding Universe.* New York, NY: HarperCollins, 1983.

Burns, Marilyn. *Spaghetti and Meatballs for All.* Illust. Debbie Tilley. New York: Scholastic, 1997.

————. *The Greedy Triangle.* Illust. Gordon Silveria. New York: Scholastic, 1994.

Carle, Eric. *The Grouchy Ladybug.* Illust. Eric Carle. Glenwood, IL: Scott Foresman, 1996.

Clement, Rod. *Counting on Frank.* Milwaukee, WI: Gareth Stevens, Children's Books, 1991.

Connell, David, and Jim Thurman. *Mathnet Casebook #4: The Map with a Gap.* New York: Scientific American Books for Young Readers; Freeman, 1994.

Crews, Donald. *Bicycle Race.* New York: Greenwillow Books, 1985.

Dash, Joan. *The Longitude Prize.* Illust. Dusan Petricic. New York: Frances Foster Books, 2000.

de Rubertis, Barbara. *Lulu's Lemonade.* Illust. Billin-Frye Paige. New York: Kane, 2000.

Dodds, Doyle. *The Shape of Things.* Illust. Julie Lacome. Cambridge, MA: Candlewick, 1994.

Duffy, Trent, *The Clock.* Illust. Tobey Welles. New York: Atheneum, 2000.

Ehlert, Lois. *Color Farm.* Illust. Lois Ehlert. New York: HarperCollins, 1992.

————. *Color Zoo.* Illust. Lois Ehlert. New York: HarperCollins, 1989.

————. *Planting a Rainbow.* Illust. Lois Ehlert. New York: Harcourt Brace, 1988.

Emberley, Ed. *The Wing on a Flea: A Book About Shapes.* New York: Little, Brown, 2001.

Florian, Douglas. *The Pig Is Big.* Illust. Douglas Florian. New York: Greenwillow Books, 2000.

Friedman, Aileen. *The Cloak for the Dreamer.* Illust. Kim Howard. New York: Scholastic, 1994.

Frucht, William. *Imaginary Numbers.* (An anthology of mathematical stories.) Hoboken, NJ: Wiley, 1999.

George, Jean Craighead. *Look to the North: A Wolf Pup Diary.* Illust. Lucia Washburn. New York: HarperCollins, 1997.

Giganti, Paul. *How Many Snails? A Counting Book.* Illust. Donald Crews. New York: Greenwillow Books, 1988.

Greene, Rhonda Gowler. *When a Line Bends. . . . A Shape Begins.* Illust. James Kaczman. Boston: Houghton Mifflin, 1997.

Hightower, Susan. *Twelve Snails to One Lizard: A Tale of Mischief and Measurement.* New York: Simon & Schuster, 1997.

Hoban, Tana. *Cubes, Cones, Cylinders, and Spheres.* Illust. Tana Hoban (photographer). New York: Greenwillow Books, 1998.

————. *More, Fewer, Less.* Illust. Tana Hoban (photographer). New York: Greenwillow Books, 1998.

————. *Shapes, Shapes, Shapes.* Illust. Tana Hoban (photographer). New York: Greenwillow Books, 1986.

Hopkinson, Deborah. *Fannie in the Kitchen: The Whole Story from Soup to Nuts of How Fannie Farmer Invented Recipes with Precise Measurements.* Illust. Nancy Carpenter. New York: Atheneum, 2001.

Kaye, Marilyn. *A Day with No Math*. Illust. Tim Bowers. Orlando, FL: Harcourt Brace Jovanovich, 1992.

Lasky, Kathryn. *The Librarian Who Measured the Earth*. New York: Little, Brown, 1994.

Lobel, Anita. *One Lighthouse, One Moon*. Illust. Anita Lobel. New York: Greenwillow Books, 2000.

Maccarone, G. *Three Pigs, One Wolf, and Seven Magic Shapes*. New York: Scholastic, 1997.

Mahy, Margaret. *The Seven Chinese Brothers*. Illust. Jean and Mou-Sien Tseng. New York: Scholastic, 1990.

Mathis, Sharon Bell. *The Hundred Penny Box*. New York: Puffin Books, 1986.

Norton, Mary. *The Borrowers*. San Diego, CA: Harcourt Brace, 1989.

Oaks, Bill, and Suse MacDonald. *Puzzlers*. New York: Dial Books, 1989.

Pappas, Theoni. *Math Talk: Mathematical Ideas in Poems for Two Voices*. San Carlos, CA: Wide World, 1991.

Riddell, Chris. *The Trouble with Elephants*. Illust. Chris Riddell. New York: HarperCollins, 1998.

Rocklin, Joanne, and Marilyn Burns. *The Case of the Backyard Treasure*. Illust. John Speirs. New York: Cartwheel Books, 1998.

Schwartz, David M. *If You Hopped Like a Frog*. New York: Scholastic, 1999.

Stevens, Janet, and Susan S. Crummel. *Cook-a-Doodle-Doo!* Illust. Janet Stevens. New York: Harcourt Brace, 1999.

Tompert, Amy. *Grandfather Tang's Story: A Tale Told with Tangrams*. Illust. Robert Andrew Parker. New York: Dragonfly Books, 1990.

Geometric Progression

Demi. *One Grain of Rice: A Mathematical Folktale*. Illust. Demi. New York: Scholastic, 1997.

Garry, David. *The Rajah's Rice: A Mathematical Folktale from India*. New York: Scientific American Books for Young Readers, 1994.

Tangrams

Maccarone, G. *Three Pigs, One Wolf, and Seven Magic Shapes*. New York: Scholastic, 1997.

Razzell, Arthur G., and K. G. O. Watts. *This Is 4: The Idea of a Number*. Garden City, New York: Doubleday, 1967.

Tompert, Amy. *Grandfather Tang's Story: A Tale Told with Tangrams*. Illust. Robert Andrew Parker. New York: Dragonfly Books, 1990.

Geometric Shapes: Triangles, Rectangles, Rhombuses, Solids, Squares, Circles, Cones, Cylinders

Burns, Marilyn. *The Greedy Triangle*. Illust. Gordon Silveria. New York: Scholastic, 1994.

Emberley, Ed. *The Wing on a Flea: A Book. About Shapes*. New York: Little, Brown, 2001.

Hoban, Tana. *Shapes, Shapes, Shapes*. Illust. Tana Hoban (photographer). Greenwillow Books, 1986.

Kaye, Marilyn. *A Day with No Math*. Illust. Tim Bowers. Orlando, FL: Harcourt Brace Jovanovich, 1992.

Neuschwander, Cindy. *Sir Cumference and the Dragon of Pi: A Math Adventure*. Illust. Wayne Geehan. Watertown, MA: Charlesbridge, 1999.

———. *Sir Cumference and the First Round Table: A Math Adventure*. Illust. Wayne Geehan. Watertown, MA: Charlesbridge, 1997.

———. *Sir Cumference and the Great Knight of Angleland: A Math Adventure*. Illust. Wayne Geehan. Watertown, MA: Charlesbridge, 2001.

Razzell, Arthur G., and K. G. O. Watts. *This Is 4: The Idea of a Number*. Garden City, NY: Doubleday, 1967.

Srivastava, Jane Jonas. *Number Families.* New York: Crowell, 1979.

Tompert, Amy. *Grandfather Tang's Story: A Tale Told with Tangrams.* Illust. Robert Andrew Parker. New York: Dragonfly Books, 1990.

Area

Burns, Marilyn. *Spaghetti and Meatballs for All.* Illust. Debbie Tilley. New York: Scholastic, 1997.

Perimeter

Burns, Marilyn. *Spaghetti and Meatballs for All.* Illust. Debbie Tilley. New York: Scholastic, 1997.

Dimensionality

Abbott, Edwin A. 1899. *Flatland: A Romance of Many Dimensions.* Illust. Edwin A. Abbott. Reprinted, New York: Barnes & Noble Books, 1983. Harper & Row, 1899.

Emberley, Ed. *The Wing on a Flea: A Book About Shapes.* New York: Little, Brown, 2001.

Impey, Rose. *The Flat Men.* New York: Barron's, 1988.

Measurement

Allbright, Viv. *Ten Go Hopping.* London: Faber & Faber, 1985.

Axelrod, Amy. *Pigs in the Pantry: Fun with Math and Cooking.* New York: Simon & Schuster Books for Young Readers, 1997.

Blume, Judy. *Freckle Juice.* Illust. Sonia O. Lisker. New York: Macmillan, 1971.

Blundell, Tony. *Beware of Boys.* New York: Greenwillow Books, 1991.

Briggs, Raymond. *Jim and the Beanstalk.* Illust. Raymond Briggs. New York: Paper Star, 1997.

Bruce, Colin. *Conned Again, Watson.* New York: Perseus, 2001.

Bruchac, Joseph, and Jonathan London. *Thirteen Moons on a Turtle's Back: A Native American Year of Moons.* Illust. Thomas Locker. New York: Philomel, 1992.

Burger, Dionys. *Sphereland: A Fantasy About Curved Spaces and an Expanding Universe.* New York: HarperCollins, 1983.

Burns, Marilyn. *Spaghetti and Meatballs for All.* Illust. Debbie Tilley. New York: Scholastic, 1997.

Carle, Eric. *The Grouchy Ladybug.* Illust. Eric Carle. Glenwood, IL: Scott Foresman, 1996.

Clement, Rod. *Counting on Frank.* Milwaukee, WI: Gareth Stevens Children's Books, 1991.

Crews, Donald. *Bicycle Race.* New York: Greenwillow Books, 1985.

Dash, Joan. *The Longitude Prize.* Illust. Dusan Petricic. New York: Frances Foster Books, 2000.

de Rubertis, Barbara. *Lulu's Lemonade.* Illust. Billin-Frye Paige. New York: Kane, 2000.

Dewdney, A. K. *200% of Nothing: An Eye-Opening Tour through the Twists and Turns of Math Abuse and Innumeracy.* Hoboken, NJ: John Wiley, 1993.

Dodds, Doyle. *The Shape of Things.* Illust. Julie Lacome. Cambridge, MA: Candlewick, 1994.

Duffy, Trent. *The Clock.* Illust. Tobey Welles. New York: Atheneum, 2000.

Edwards, Pamela Duncan. *Warthogs in the Kitchen: A Sloppy Counting Book.* Hyperion, 1998.

Ehlert, Lois. *Color Farm.* Illust. Lois Ehlert. New York: HarperCollins, 1992.

———. *Color Zoo.* Illust. Lois Ehlert. New York: HarperCollins, 1989.

———. *Planting a Rainbow.* Illust. Lois Ehlert. New York: Harcourt Brace, 1988.

Emberley, Ed. *The Wing on a Flea: A Book About Shapes.* New York: Little, Brown, 2001.

Florian, Douglas. *The Pig Is Big.* Illust. Douglas Florian. New York: Greenwillow Books, 2000.

Friedman, Aileen. *The Cloak for the Dreamer.* Illust. Kim Howard. New York: Scholastic, 1994.

Froman, Robert. *Less Than Nothing Is Really Something.* New York: Crowell, 1973.

Frucht, William. *Imaginary Numbers.* (An anthology of mathematical stories.) Hoboken, NJ: Wiley, 1999.

George, Jean Craighead. *Look to the North: A Wolf Pup Diary.* Illust. Lucia Washburn. New York: HarperCollins, 1997.

Giganti, Jr., Paul. *How Many Snails? A Counting Book.* Illust. Donald Crews. New York: Greenwillow Books, 1988.

Gilleo, Alma. *About Meters.* Elgin, IL: Child's World, 1977.

Glass, Julie. *The Fly on the Ceiling.* Illust. Richard Walz. New York: Random House, 1998.

Greene, Rhonda Gowler, *When a Line Bends. . . . A Shape Begins.* Illust. James Kaczman. Boston: Houghton Mifflin, 1997.

Grimm, The Brothers. *The Six Comrades.* New York: Random House, 1986.

Hightower, Susan. *Twelve Snails to One Lizard: A Tale of Mischief and Measurement.* New York: Simon & Schuster Books for Young Readers, 1997.

Hoban, Tana. *Cubes, Cones, Cylinders, and Spheres,* Illust. Tana Hoban (photographer). New York: Greenwillow Books, 2000.

———. *More, Fewer, Less.* Illust. Tana Hoban (photographer). New York: Greenwillow Books, 1986.

Hopkinson, Deborah. *Fannie in the Kitchen: The Whole Story from Soup to Nuts of How Fannie Farmer Invented Recipes with Precise Measurements.* Illust. Nancy Carpenter. New York: Atheneum, 2001.

Johnston, Tony. *Farmer Mack Measures His Pig.* New York: Harper & Row, 1986.

Lasky, Kathryn. *The Librarian Who Measured the Earth.* New York: Little, Brown, 1994.

Lobel, Anita. *One Lighthouse, One Moon.* Illust. Anita Lobel. New York: Greenwillow Books, 2000.

Khalsa, Dayal Kaur. *How Pizza Came to Queens.* New York: Scholastic, 1989.

Kaye, Marilyn. 1992. *A Day with No Math.* Illust. Tim Bowers. Orlando, FL: Harcourt Brace Jovanovich, 1992.

Lionni, Leo. *Inch by Inch.* New York: Astor-Honor, 1960.

Mahy, Margaret. *The Seven Chinese Brothers.* Illust. Jean and Mou-Sien Tseng. New York: Scholastic, 1990.

McCurdy, Michael. *An Algonquian Year: The Year According to the Full Moon.* Boston: Houghton Mifflin, 2000.

Neuschwander, Cindy. *Sir Cumference and the Dragon of Pi: A Math Adventure.* Illust. Wayne Geehan. Watertown, MA: Charlesbridge, 1999.

———. *Sir Cumference and the First Round Table: A Math Adventure.* Illust. Wayne Geehan. Watertown, MA: Charlesbridge, 1997.

———. *Sir Cumference and the Great Knight of Angleland: A Math Adventure.* Illust. Wayne Geehan. Watertown, MA: Charlesbridge, 2001.

Norton, Mary. *The Borrowers.* San Diego, CA: Harcourt Brace, 1989.

Razzell, Arthur G., and K. G. O. Watts. *This Is 4: The Idea of a Number.* Garden City, NY: Doubleday, 1967.

Rocklin, Joanne, and Marilyn Burns. *The Case of the Backyard Treasure.* Illust. John Speirs. New York: Cartwheel Books, 1998.

Sierra, Judy. *Counting Crocodiles.* Illust. Will Hillenbrand. San Diego, CA: Gulliver Books, 1997.

Sitomer, Mindel, and Harry Sitomer. *How Did Numbers Begin?* New York: Crowell, 1976.

Stevens, Janet, and Susan S. Crummel. *Cook-a-Doodle-Doo!* Illust. Janet Stevens. New York: Harcourt Brace, 1999.

Wells, Robert E. *Is a Blue Whale the Biggest Thing There Is?* Morton Grove, IL: Whitman, 1993.

Willard, Nancy. *The High Rise Glorious Skittle Skat Roaring Sky Pie Angel Food Cake.* Illust. Richard Jesse Watson. San Diego, CA: Harcourt Brace, 1990.

Statistics and Data Analysis

Briggs, Raymond. *Jim and the Beanstalk.* Illust. Raymond Briggs. New York: Paper Star, 1997.

Bruce, Colin. *Conned Again, Watson.* New York: Perseus, 2001.

Cushman, Jean. *Do You Wanna Bet? Your Chance to Find Out About Probability.* Illust. Martha Weston. Boston: Houghton, 1991.

Hoban, Tana. *More, Fewer, Less.* Illust. Tana Hoban (photographer). New York: Greenwillow Books, 1998.

James, Elizabeth, and Carol Bankin. *What Do You Mean by "Average"?* Illust. Joel Schick. New York: Lothrop, Lee & Shepard, 1978.

Statistics and Probability

Arthur, Lee, Elizabeth James, and Judith B. Taylor. *Sportsmath.* New York: Lothrop, Lee & Shepard, 1975.

Briggs, Raymond. *Jim and the Beanstalk.* Illust. Raymond Briggs. New York: Paper Star, 1997.

Bruce, Colin. *Conned Again, Watson,* New York: Perseus, 2001.

Demi. *One Grain of Rice: A Mathematical Folktale.* Illust. Demi. New York: Scholastic, 1997.

Frederique and Papy. *Graph Games.* New York: Crowell, 1971.

Frucht, William. *Imaginary Numbers.* (An anthology of mathematical stories.) Hoboken, NJ: Wiley, 1999.

Hoban, Tana. *More, Fewer, Less.* New York: Greenwillow Books, 1998.

Mathis, Sharon Bell. *The Hundred Penny Box.* New York: Puffin Books, 1986.

Murphy, Stuart J. *Seaweed Soup.* New York: HarperCollins, 2001.

Nozaki, Akihiro, and Mitsumasa Anno. *Anno's Hat Tricks.* New York: Philomel Books, 1985.

Pappas, Theoni. *Math Talk: Mathematical Ideas in Poems for Two Voices.* San Carlos, CA: Wide World, 1991.

Shapiro, Irwin. *Twice Upon a Time.* New York: Scribner's, 1973.

Slobodkina, Esphyr. *Caps for Sale: A Tale of a Pedlar, Some Monkeys, and Their Monkey Business.* New York: HarperCollins, 1987.

Spohn, Kate. *Clementine's Winter Wardrobe.* New York: Orchard Books, 1989.

Other Topics

Multicultural

Bruchac, Joseph, and Jonathan London. *Thirteen Moons on a Turtle's Back: A Native American Year of Moons.* Illust. Thomas Locker. New York: Philomel, 1992.

Feelings, Muriel. *Moja Means One: Swahili Counting Book.* Illust. Tom Feelings. New York: Puffin Books, 1992.

Gollub, Matthew. *Ten Oni Drummers.* New York: Lee & Low Books, 2000.

Grossman, Virginia. *Ten Little Rabbits.* San Francisco: Chronicle Books, 1991.

Hong, Lily Toy. *Two of Everything: A Chinese Folktale.* Morton Grove, IL: Whitman, 1993.

McCurdy, Michael. *An Algonquian Year: The Year According to the Full Moon.* Boston: Houghton Mifflin, 2000.

Nikola-Lisa, W. *Can You Top That?* New York: Lee & Low Books, 2000.

Pilegard, Virginia. *The Warlord's Beads.* New York: Pelican, 2001.

Pittman, Helena Clare. *A Grain of Rice.* New York: Skylark Books, 1992.

Stevens, Jan Romero. *Twelve Lizards Leaping: A New Twelve Days of Christmas.* Flagstaff, AZ: Rising Moon, 1999.

Thompson, Lauren. *One Riddle, One Answer.* New York: Scholastic, 2001.

Cartesian Coordinate System

Froman, Robert. *Less Than Nothing Is Really Something.* New York: Crowell, 1973.

Glass, Julie. *The Fly on the Ceiling.* Illust. Richard Walz. New York: Random House, 1998.

Code Breaking: Problem Solving Involving Codes

Connell, David, and Jim Thurman. *Mathnet Casebook #1: The Case of the Unnatural.* New York: Scientific American Books for Young Readers; Freeman, 1993.

Rocklin, Joanne, and Marilyn Burns. *The Case of the Backyard Treasure.* Illust. John Speirs. New York: Cartwheel Books, 1998.

Classic Literature

Carroll, Lewis. *Alice's Adventures in Wonderland.* Chicago: Rand McNally, 1950.

——— . *The Hunting of the Snark.* New York: Simon & Schuster, 1962.

——— . *Through the Looking-Glass and What Alice Found There.* Rutland, VT: Tuttle, 1968.

Grimm, The Brothers. *The Six Comrades.* New York: Random House, 1986.

Verne, Jules. *The Mysterious Island.* New York: Grosset & Dunlap, 1956.

——— . *Twenty Thousand Leagues Under the Sea.* Cleveland, OH: World, 1946.

Geography and Reading Maps

Connell, David, and Jim Thurman. *Mathnet Casebook #4: The Map with a Gap.* New York: Scientific American Books for Young Readers; Freeman, 1994.

Fleming, Denise. *Buster.* Illust. Denise Fleming. New York: Holt, 2003.

Spanish Language

McGrath, Barbara Barbieri. *¡A Contar Cheerios!* Illust. Rob Bolster and Frank Mazzola Jr. New York: Scholastic, 1998.

Prime Numbers

Srivastava, Jane Jonas. *Number Families.* New York: Crowell, 1979.

Multiples/Factors

Anno, Mitsumasa. *Anno's Mysterious Multiplying Jar.* Illust. Mitsumasa Anno. New York: Putnam, 1983.

Srivastava, Jane Jonas. *Number Families.* New York: Crowell, 1979.

Wahl, John, and Stacey Wahl. *I Can Count the Petals of a Flower.* Reston, VA: National Council of Teachers of Mathematics, 1985.

References

Abbott, Edwin A. *Flatland: A Romance of Many Dimensions.* New York: Barnes & Noble, 1983.

Abbott, Edwin A., Dionys Burger, and Isaac Asimov. *Sphereland: A Continuing Speculation on an Expanding Universe.* New York: HarperCollins, 1994.

Abrohms, Alison. *Rainbow Fraction Tiles: Activity Guide.* Vernon Hills, IL: Learning Resources, n.d.

Ahlberg, Ann. *Children's Ways of Handling and Experiencing Numbers.* Göteborg Studies in Educational Sciences 113. Göteborg, Sweden: Acta Universitatis Gothoburgensis, 1997.

Algebra: Tools for a Changing World. Englewood Cliffs, NJ: Prentice Hall, 1997.

Anno, Matsumasa. *Anno's Magic Seeds.* New York: Philomel Books, 1995.

Amend, Bill. *Foxtrot Beyond a Doubt.* Kansas City, MO: Andrews & McNeel, 1997.

———. *Wildly Foxtrot.* Kansas City, MO: Andrews & McNeel, 1995.

American Association for the Advancement of Science. "Benchmarks For Scientific Literacy." *Benchmarks On-Line.* Washington, D.C.: Author, 2000. http://www.project2061.org/tools/benchol.

———. *Science for All Americans: Education for a Changing Future.* Washington, D.C.: Author, 1989. http://www.project2061.org.

Axelrod, Amy. *Pigs Will Be Pigs.* New York: Harcourt Brace, 1994.

Baek, Jae-Heen. "Children's Invented Algorithms for Multidigit Multiplication Problems." In *The Teaching and Learning of Algorithms in School Mathematics,* NCTM 1998 Yearbook, ed. Lorna J. Morrow and Margaret J. Kenney, pp. 151–60. Reston, VA: National Council of Teachers of Mathematics, 1998.

Ball, Deborah Loewenberg, and Hyman Bass. "Making Mathematics Reasonable in School." In *A Research Companion to Principles and Standards for School Mathematics,* ed. Jeremy Kilpatrick, W. Gary Martin, and Deborah Schifter, pp. 27–44. Reston, VA: National Council of Teachers of Mathematics, 2003.

Baroody, Arthur J. "Children's Difficulties in Subtraction: Some Causes and Questions." *Journal for Research in Mathematics Education* 15 (1984): 203–13.

———. "The Development of Children's Informal Addition." In *Proceedings of the Fifth Annual Meeting of the North American Chapter of the International Group for the Psychology of Mathematics Education,* ed. J. C. Bergeron and N. Herscovies, vol. 1, pp. 222–29. Montreal: Université de Montreal, Faculte des Sciences del Education.

———. "The Development of Preschoolers, Counting Skills and Principles." In *Pathways to Number: Children's Developing Numerical Abilities,* ed. Jacqueline Bideaud, C. Mejac, and J.-P. Fischer, pp. 99–126. Hillsdale, NJ: Erlbaum, 1992.

———. "How and When Should Place-Value Concepts and Skills Be Taught?" *Journal for Research in Mathematics Education* 21 (July 1990): 281–86.

———. "Kindergartners' Mental Addition with Single-digit Combinations." *Journal for Research in Mathematics Education* 29 (March 1989): 159–72.

Beaton, Albert E., Ina V. S. Mullis, Michael O. Martin, Eugeno J. Gonzales, Dana L. Kelly, and Teresa A. Smith. *Mathematics Achievement in the Middle School Years: IEA's Third International Mathematics and Science Study (TIMSS).* Chestnut Hill, MA: TIMSS International Study Center, Boston College, 1996.

Berkson, William, and John Wettersten. *Learning from Error: Karl Popper's Psychology of Learning.* La Salle, IL: Open Court, 1984.

Betz, William. "Functional Competencies in Mathematics—Its Meaning and Its Attainment." *Mathematics Teacher* 41 (1948): 195–206.

Biehler, Robert F., and Jack Snowman. *Psychology Applied to Teaching.* 7th ed. Boston: Houghton Mifflin, 1993.

Bransford, John D., Linda Zech, Daniel Schwartz, Brigid Barron, Nancy Vye, and The Cognition and Technology Group at Vanderbilt. "Fostering Mathematical Thinking in Middle School Students: Lessons from Research." In *The Nature of Mathematical Thinking,* ed. Robert J. Sternberg and Talia Ben-Zeev, pp. 203–50. Mahwah, NJ: Erlbaum, 1996.

Briggs, Raymond. *Jim and the Beanstalk.* New York: Putnam & Grosset, 1970.

Brown, Jeff. *Flat Stanley.* New York: Harper Trophy, 1992.

Brownell, William A. "A Critique of the Committee of Seven's Investigation on the Grade Placement of Arithmetic Topics." *Elementary School Journal* (March 1938): 495–508.

Bruner, Jerome S. *The Relevance of Education.* New York: Norton, 1971.

———. *Toward a Theory of Instruction.* New York: Norton, 1966.

Burns, Marilyn. *The Greedy Triangle.* New York: Scholastic, 1994.

———. *Math: Facing an American Phobia.* Sausalito, CA: Math Solutions Publications, 1998.

———. *Spaghetti and Meatballs for All: A Mathematical Story.* New York: Scholastic, 1997.

———. "Teaching for Understanding: A Focus on Multiplication." In *New Directions for Elementary School Mathematics,* NCTM 1989 Yearbook, ed. Paul R. Trafton and Albert P. Shulte, pp. 123–33. Reston, VA: National Council of Teachers of Mathematics, 1989.

Burrill, Gail, and Joan Ferrini-Mundy. "A Framework for Constructing a Vision of Algebra: A Discussion Document." In *The Nature and Role of Algebra in the K–14 Curriculum: Proceedings of a National Symposium,* pp. 145–90. Washington, DC: National Academy Press, 1998.

Cai, Jinfa, and Wei Sun. "Developing Students' Proportional Reasoning: A Chinese Perspective. In *Making Sense of Fractions, Ratios, and Proportions,* NCTM 2002 Yearbook, ed. Bonnie Litwiller and George Bright, pp. 195–205. Reston, VA: National Council of Teachers of Mathematics, 2002.

Campbell, Patricia F., Thomas E. Rowan, and Anna R. Suarez. "What Criteria for Student-Invented Algorithms?" In *The Teaching and Learning of Algorithms in School Mathematics,* NCTM 1998 Yearbook, ed. Lorna J. Morrow and Margaret J. Kenney. pp. 49–55. Reston, VA: National Council of Teachers of Mathematics, 1998.

Card, S., T. P. Moran, and A. Newell. *The Psychology of Human-Computer Interaction.* Hillsdale, NJ: Erlbaum, 1983.

Carpenter, Thomas P., Elizabeth Fennema, Megan Loef France, Linda Levi, and Susan B. Empson. *Children's Mathematics: Cognitively Guided*

Instruction. Reston, VA, and Portsmouth, NH: National Council of Teachers of Mathematics and Heinemann, 1949.

Carpenter, Thomas P., and J. M. Moser. "The Acquisition of Addition and Subtraction Concepts." In *Acquisition of Mathematical Concepts and Processes*, ed. R. Lesh and M. Landau, pp. 7–44. New York: Academic Press, 1983.

———. "The Acquisition of Addition and Subtraction Concepts in Grades One through Three." *Journal for Research in Mathematics Education* 15 (1984): 179–202.

Center for Applied Special Technology. "Teaching Strategies: Envisioning Future Curriculum." Peabody, MA: Author, 1998. http://www.cast.org/strategies/curriculum_future.html.

Chaddock, Gail Russell. "Lots of Students, Not Enough Teachers." Boston: Christian Science Publishing Society, 1998. http://www.csmonitor.com/durable/1998/09/15/fp51s/csm.shtml.

Chambers, Donald L., ed. *Putting Research into Practice in the Elementary Grades: Readings from Journals of the National Council of Teachers of Mathematics.* Reston, VA: National Council of Teachers of Mathematics, 2002.

Charles, Randall, Frank Lester, and Phares O'Daffer. *How to Evaluate Progress in Problem Solving.* Reston, VA: National Council of Teachers of Mathematics, 1987.

Charles, Randall I., and Edward A. Silver, eds. *The Teaching and Assessing of Mathematical Problem Solving.* Hillsdale, NJ: Erlbaum; Reston, VA: National Council of Teachers of Mathematics, 1988.

Clements, Douglas H. "Touching Length Measurement: Research Challenges." *School Science and Mathematics* 99 (January 1999): 5–11.

Clements, Douglas H., and J. S. Meredith. *Turtle Math* [computer program]. Montreal: Logo Computer Systems, 1994.

Clements, Douglas H., and Julie Sarama. "The Earliest Geometry." *Teaching Children Mathematics* 7 (October 2000): 82–86.

Cobb, Paul, Ada Boafi, Kay McClain, and Joy Whitenack. "Reflective Discourse and Collective Reflection." *Journal for Research in Mathematics Education* 28 (May 1997): 258–77.

Colorado Model Content Standards: Mathematics. Denver: Colorado Department of Education, September 2005. http://www.cde.state.co.us/cdeassess/standards/pdf/math.pdf.

Conference Board of the Mathematical Sciences. "Letter of Appreciation to the National Council of Teachers of Mathematics." In *Principles and Standards for School Mathematics.* Reston, VA: National Council of Teachers of Mathematics, 2000.

———. CBMS Mathematical Education of Teachers Project. Washington, DC: Mathematical Association of America, 2000. http//www.maa.org/cbms.

Copeland, Richard W. *How Children Learn Mathematics: Teaching Implications of Piaget's Research.* New York: Macmillan, 1970.

———. *How Children Learn Mathematics: Teaching Implications of Piaget's Research.* 2nd ed. New York: Macmillan, 1974.

———. *How Children Learn Mathematics: Teaching Implications of Piaget's Research.* 4th ed. New York: Macmillan, 1984.

Cowan, R., and M. Renton. "Do They Know What They Are Doing? Children's Use of Economical Addition Strategies and Knowledge of Commutativity." *Educational Psychology* 16 (1996): 409–22.

Coxford, Arthur F., James T. Fey, Christian K. Hirsch, Harold L. Schoen, Gail Burrill, Eric W. Hart, Ann E. Watkins, Mary Jo Messenger, and Beth Ritsema. *Contemporary Mathematics: A Unified Approach.* Chicago: Everyday Learning, 1996.

Cramer, Kathleen, Merlyn J. Behr, Richard Lesh, and Thomas Post. *The Rational Number Project Fraction Lessons: Level 1 and Level 2.* Dubuque, IA: Kendall Hunt, 1997.

Cramer, Kathleen, and Apryl Henry. "Using Manipulative Models to Build Sense for Addition of Fractions." In *Making Sense of Fractions, Ratios, and Proportions*, NCTM 2002 Yearbook, ed. Bonnie Litwiller and George Bright, pp. 41–48. Reston, VA: National Council of Teachers of Mathematics, 2002.

Crary, David. "Gambling Rising Among Youths." *Albuquerque Journal*, 14 July, 2003, A3.

Crowley, Mary L. "The Van Hiele Model of the Development of Geometric Thought." In *Learning and Teaching Geometry, K–12*, NCTM 1987 Yearbook, ed. Mary Montgomery Lindquist and Albert P. Shulte, pp. 1–16. Reston, VA: National Council of Teachers of Mathematics, 1987.

Culotta, E. "The Reform Agenda: Emerging Consensus." *Science* 250 (December 1990): 1328.

Davidenko, Susan. "Building the Concept of Function from Students' Everyday Activities." *Mathematics Teacher* (February 1997). Reprinted in *Algebraic Thinking, Grades K–12: Readings from NCTM's School-Based Journals and Other Publications*, ed. Barbara Moses, pp. 206–12. Reston, VA: National Council of Teachers of Mathematics, 1999.

Davidson & Associates. *Math Blaster, K–5.* Torrance, CA: Author, 1999.

Davis, Brent. *Teaching Mathematics: Toward a Sound Alternative.* New York: Garland, 1996.

Dehaene, S., and L. Cohen. "Towards an Anatomical and Functional Model of Number Processing." *Mathematical Cognition* 1 (1995): 83–120.

Deming, Richard. *Metric Power: Why and How We Are Going Metric.* New York: Nelson, 1974.

Dienes, Z. P. *Building Up Mathematics.* New York: Hutchinson, 1960.

Donlan, Chris. "Basic Numeracy in Children with Specific Language Impairment." *Child Language Teaching and Therapy* 9 (1993): 95–104.

———. "Number Without Language? Studies of Children with Specific Language Impairments." In *The Development of Mathematical Skills*, ed. Chris Donlan, pp. 255–74. Hove, East Sussex, UK: Psychology Press, 1998.

Dowker, Ann. "Individual Differences in Normal Arithmetic Development." In *The Development of Mathematical Skills*, ed. Chris Donlan, pp. 275–302. Hove, East Sussex, UK: Psychology Press, 1998.

Drew, David. E. *Aptitude Revisited: Rethinking Math and Science Education for America's Next Century.* Baltimore: Johns Hopkins University Press, 1996.

Driscoll, Mark. *Fostering Algebraic Thinking: A Guide for Teachers Grades 6–10.* Portsmouth, NH: Heinemann, 1999.

Eisenhower National Clearinghouse for Mathematics and Science Education. *Teacher Change: Improving Mathematics.* Columbus, OH: Author, 1999. http://change.enc.org.

Ekeblad, Eva. *Children Learning Numbers: A Phenomenographic Excursion into First-Grade Children's Arithmetic.* Götenberg Studies in Education Sciences 105. Göteborg, Sweden: Acta Universitatis Gothoburgensis, 1996.

Elya, Susan. *Eight Animals on the Town.* New York: Putnam's, 2000.

Empson, Susan B. "Equal Sharing and Shared Meaning: The Development of Fraction Concepts in a First-Grade Classroom." *Cognition and Instruction* 17 (1999): 283–342.

———. "Equal Sharing and the Roots of Fraction Equivalence." *Teaching Children Mathematics* 7 (March 2001): 421–25.

———. "Organizing Diversity in Early Fraction Thinking." In *Making Sense of Fractions, Ratios, and Proportions*, NCTM 2002 Yearbook, ed. Bonnie Litwiller and George Bright, pp. 29–40. Reston, VA: National Council of Teachers of Mathematics, 2002a.

———. "Using Sharing Situations to Help Children Learn Fractions." In *Putting Research into Practice in the Elementary Grades*, ed. Donald C. Chambers, pp. 122–27. Reston, VA: National Council of Teachers of Mathematics, 2002b.

Enriquez, Alberto. "Class Captures National Award." *Mail Tribune*, 29 April 1997.

Ernest, Paul. *Constructing Mathematical Knowledge: Epistemology and Mathematics Education.* London: Falmer, 1994.

Everyday Learning Corporation. *Everyday Math.* New York: McGraw-Hill, 1999.

Ferrini-Mundy, Joan, Glenda Lappan, and Elizabeth Phillips. "Experiences with Patterning."

Teaching Children Mathematics (February 1997). Reprinted in *Algebraic Thinking, Grades K–12: Readings from NCTM's School-Based Journals and Other Publications,* ed. Barbara Moses, pp. 112–19. Reston, VA: National Council of Teachers of Mathematics, 1999.

Fey, James T., and Richard A. Good. "Rethinking the Sequence and Priorities of High-School Mathematics Curricula." In *The Secondary School Mathematics Curriculum,* ed. Christian Hirsch and Marilyn J. Zweny, pp. 43–52. Reston, VA: National Council of Teachers of Mathematics, 1985.

Fischbein, E., M. Deri, M. S. Nello, and M. S. Marino. "The Role of Implicit Models in Solving Verbal Problems in Multiplication and Division." *Journal for Research in Mathematics Education* 16 (1985): 3–17.

Flores, Alfino. "Profound Understanding of Division of Fractions." In *Making Sense of Fractions, Ratios, and Proportions,* NCTM 2002 Yearbook, ed. Bonnie Litwiller and George Bright, pp. 237–46. Reston, VA: National Council of Teachers of Mathematics, 2002.

Forman, Susan L., and Lynn Arthur Steen. "Beyond Eighth Grade: Functional Mathematics for Life and Work." In *Learning Mathematics for a New Century,* ed. Maurice J. Burke and Francis R. Curcio, pp. 127–57. Reston, VA: National Council of Teachers of Mathematics, 2000.

Friedman, Aileen. *A Cloak for the Dreamer.* Illus. Kim Howard. New York: Scholastic, 1994.

Freudenthal, Hans. *Mathematics as an Educational Task.* Dordrecht, Netherlands: Reidel, 1973.

Frye, D., N. Braisby, J. Lowe, C. Maroudas, and J. Nicholls. "Young Children's Understanding of Counting and Cardinality." *Child Development* 60 (1989): 1158–71.

Fulkner, Karen P., Linda Levi, and Thomas P. Carpenter. "Children's Understanding of Equality: A Foundation for Algebra." *Teaching Children Mathematics* 6 (December 1999): 232–36.

Fuson, Karen C. *Children's Counting and Concepts of Number.* New York: Springer-Verlag, 1988.

———. "Issues in Place-Value Concepts and Multidigit Addition and Subtraction Learning and Teaching." *Journal for Research in Mathematics Education* 21 (July 1990): 272–80.

———. "More Complexities in Subtraction." *Journal for Research in Mathematics Education* 15 (1984): 214–25.

Fuson, Karen C., and D. J. Briars. "Base-Ten Blocks as a First-and Second-Grade Learning/Teaching Setting for Multidigit Addition and Subtraction and Place-Value Concepts." *Journal for Research in Mathematics Education* 21 (1990): 180–206.

Fuson, Karen C., and Adrienne M. Fuson. "Instruction Supporting Children's Counting On for Addition and Counting Up for Subtraction." *Journal for Research in Mathematics Education* 23 (January 1992): 72–78.

Fuson, Karen C., and James W. Hall. "The Acquisition of Early Number Word Meanings: A Conceptual Analysis and Review." In *The Development of Mathematical Thinking,* ed. Herbert P. Ginsburg, pp. 49–107. New York: Academic Press, 1983.

Fuson, Karen C., and Gordon B. Willis. "Subtracting by Counting Up: More Evidence." *Journal for Research in Mathematics Education* 19 (November 1988): 402–20.

Gallistel, C. Randolph, and Rachel Gelman. "Preverbal and Verbal Counting and Computation." *Cognition* 44 (1992): 43–74.

Gelman, Rachel, and C. Randoph Gallistel. *The Child's Understanding of Number.* Cambridge, MA: Harvard University Press, 1978.

Georgia Performance Standards. Atlanta: Georgia Department of Education, 2005. www.georgiastandards.org and www.glc.K12.ga.us.

Germaine-McCarthy, Yvelyne. *Bringing the NCTM Standards to Life: Exemplary Practices for Middle Schools.* Larchmont, NY: Eye on Education, 2001.

Ginsburg, Herbert P. "Toby's Math." In *The Nature of Mathematical Thinking,* ed. Robert J. Sternberg and Talian Ben-Zeev, pp. 175–202. Mahwah, NJ: Erlbaum, 1996.

Glasgow, Robert, Gay Ragan, Wanda M. Fields, Robert Reys, and Deanna Wasman, "The Decimal Dilemma." *Teaching Children Mathematics* 7 (October 2000): 89–93.

Glass, Julie. *The Fly on the Ceiling.* New York: Random House, 1998.

Goals 2000: Educate America Act of 1994. H.R. 1804, 103d Cong., 2d sess. Pub. L. No. 102-227. Washington, DC: U.S. Government Printing Office, 1994.

Gonzales, P., J. C. Guzman, L. Partelow, E. Pablke, L. Jocelyn, O. Kastberg, and T. Williams. *Highlights from the Trends in International Mathematics and Science Study (TIMSS) 2003.* Washington, DC: U.S. Department of Education, National Center for Education Statistics, 2004.

Greenes, Carole, and Carol Findell. "Developing Students' Algebraic Reasoning Abilities." In *Developing Mathematical Reasoning in Grades K–12.* NCTM 1999 Yearbook, ed. Lee V. Stiff and Frances R. Curcio, pp. 127–37. Reston, VA: National Council of Teachers of Mathematics, 1999.

Gullberg, Jan. *Mathematics: From the Birth of Numbers.* New York: Norton, 1997.

Harris, John W., and Horst Stocker. *Handbook of Mathematics and Computational Science.* New York: Springer-Verlag, 1998.

Harvey, Francis A., and Christina W. Charnitski. "Improving Mathematics Instruction Using Technology: A Vygotskian Perspective." ERIC Document ED#423837. 1998. http://www.eric.ed.gov/ERICDocs/data/ericdocs2/content_storage_01/0000000b/80/11/1b/45.pdf.

Hawkins, Evelyn F., Francis B. Stancavage, and John A. Dossey. *School Policies and Practices Affecting Instruction in Mathematics: Findings from the National Assessment of Educational Progress.* Washington, DC: U.S. Department of Education, National Center for Education Statistics, 1998.

Hegarty, Mary, Richard E. Mayer, and Carolyn Green. "Comprehension of Arithmetic Word Problems: Evidence from Students' Eye Fixations." *Journal of Educational Psychology* 84 (March 1992): 76–84.

Hegarty, Mary, Richard E. Mayer, and Christopher A. Monk. "Comprehension of Arithmetic Word Problems: A Comparison of Successful and Unsuccessful Problem Solvers." *Journal of Educational Psychology* 87 (March 1995): 18–32.

Herrera, Teresa, and Kimberly S. Roempler. "Classroom Resources for Inquiry and Problem Solving." *ENC Focus Features* (retrieved August 2005) http://www.enc.org/features/focus/archive.

Hirsch, Christian. "Functions and Relations: A Unifying Theme for School Algebra in Grades 9–12." In *The Nature and Role of Algebra in the K–14 Curriculum: Proceedings of a National Symposium,* ed. Susan Williams and David Molina, pp. 61–65. Washington, DC: National Academy Press, 1988.

Hodges, Margaret. *Gulliver in Lilliput.* New York: Holiday House, 1995.

Hogben, Lancelot. *Mathematics for the Millions: How to Master the Magic of Numbers.* New York: Norton, 1993.

Huff, Darrell. *How to Lie with Statistics.* New York: Norton, 1993.

Huinker, DeAnn. "Examining Dimensions of Fraction Operation Sense." In *Making Sense of Fractions, Ratios, and Proportions,* NCTM 2002 Yearbook, ed. Bonnie Litwiller and George Bright, pp. 72–78. Reston, VA: National Council of Teachers of Mathematics, 2002.

Hutchins, Pat. *The Doorbell Rang.* New York: Mulberry, 1986.

Ifrah, Georges. *The Universal History of Numbers: From Prehistory to the Invention of the Computer.* Trans. David Bellos, E. F. Harding, Sophie Wood, and Ian Monk. New York: Wiley, 2000.

Individuals with Disabilities Education Improvement Act (IDEA). H.R. 1350, 108th Cong. Pub. L. No. 108-446. Washington, DC: U.S. Government Printing Office, 2004. http://www.vesid.nysed.gov/specialed/idea/108-446.pdf.

Jonassen, David H., Kyle L. Peck, and Brent G. Wilson. *Learning with Technology: A Constructivist*

Perspective. Englewood Cliffs, NJ: Prentice Hall, 1999.

Kamii, Constance, and Faye B. Clark. "Measurement of Length: The Need for a Better Approach to Teaching." *School Science and Mathematics* 97 (March 1997): 116–21.

Kamii, Constance, and Mary Ann Worthington. "Teaching Fractions: Fostering Children's Own Reasoning." *In Developing Mathematical Reasoning in Grades K–12,* NCTM 1999 Yearbook, ed. Lee V. Stiff and Frances R. Curcio, pp. 82–92. Reston, VA: National Council of Teachers of Mathematics, 1999.

Kaput, James J. "Transforming Algebra from an Engine of Inequity to an Engine of Mathematical Power by 'Algebrafying' the K–12 Curriculum." In *The Nature and Role of Algebra in the K–14 Curriculum: Proceedings of a National Symposium,* ed. Susan Williams and David Molina, pp. 25–26. Washington, DC: National Academy Press, 1998.

Keller, Fred. "Goodbye, Teacher. . . ." *Journal of Applied Behavior Analysis* 1 (1968): 79–89.

Kent, Laura B., Joyce Arnosky, and Judy Mc-Monagle. "Using Representational Contexts to Support Multiplicative Reasoning." In *Making Sense of Fractions, Ratios, and Proportions,* NCTM 2002 Yearbook, ed. Bonnie Litwiller and George Bright, pp. 145–61. Reston, VA: National Council of Teachers of Mathematics, 2002.

Kieran, Carolyn. "Helping to Make the Transition to Algebra." *Arithmetic Teacher* (March 1991). Reprinted in *Research into Practice in the Elementary Grades: Readings from Journals of the National Council of Teachers of Mathematics,* ed. Donald L. Chambers, pp. 221–24. Reston, VA: National Council of Teachers of Mathematics, 2002.

———. "The Learning and Teaching of School Algebra." In *Handbook of Research on Mathematics Teaching and Learning,* ed. Douglas A. Grouws, pp. 392–419. New York: Macmillan, 1992. Reprinted in *Algebraic Thinking, Grades K–12: Readings from NCTM'S School-Based Journals and Other Publications,* pp. 341–61. Reston, VA: National Council of Teachers of Mathematics, 1999.

Kieren, Thomas E. "Personal Knowledge of Rational Numbers: Its Intuitive and Formal Development." In *Number Concepts and Operations in the Middle Grades,* ed. James Hiebert and Merlyn J. Behr, pp. 162–81. Hillsdale, NJ: Erlbaum, 1988.

Kirkman, Rick, and Jerry Scott. "Baby Blues." *Albuquerque Journal,* 21 May 2001, p.B7.

Koester, Beverly A. "Prisms and Pyramids: Constructing Three-Dimensional Models to Build Understanding." *Teaching Children Mathematics* 9 (April 2003): 436–42.

Kouba, Vicky L. "Children's Solution Strategies for Equivalent Set Multiplication and Division Word Problems." *Journal for Research in Mathematics Education* 20 (March 1989): 147–58.

Lachman, Roy, Janet L. Lachman, and Earl C. Butterfield. *Cognitive Psychology and Information Processing: An Introduction.* Hillsdale, NJ: Erlbaum, 1979.

Lamon, Susan J. "Presenting and Representing: From Fractions to Rational Numbers." In *The Roles of Representation in School Mathematics,* NCTM 2001 Yearbook, ed. Albert Cuoco and Frances R. Curcio, pp. 146–65. Reston, VA: National Council of Teachers of Mathematics, 2001.

Lamon, Susan J. *Teaching Fractions and Ratios for Understanding: Essential Knowledge and Instructional Strategies for Teachers.* Mahwah, NJ: Erlbaum, 1999.

Lampert, Magdalene. "Teaching and Learning Long Division for Understanding in School." In *Analysis of Arithmetic for Mathematics Teaching,* ed. Gaea Leinhardt, Ralph Putnam, and Rosemary A. Hattrup. pp. 221–82. Hillsdale, NJ: Erlbaum, 1992.

Lanius, Cynthia S., and Susan E. Williams. "Proportionality: A Unifying Theme for the Middle Grades." *Mathematics Teaching in the Middle School* 8 (April 2003): 392–96.

Lasky, Kathryn. *The Librarian Who Measured the Earth.* Boston: Little, Brown, 1994.

Lawson, Anton E., and John W. Renner. "Piagetian Theory and Biology Teaching." *American Biology Teacher* 37 (September 1975): 336–43.

Leedham, John, and Derick Unwin. *Programmed Learning in the Schools.* London: Longman, 1965.

Lein, Amy. "Jazz and Math: Rhythmic Innovations." Washington, DC: Public Broadcasting Service. http://www.pbs.org/jazz/classroom/chythmicinnovations.htm.

Leitze, Annette Ricks, and Sue Tinsley May. "Assessing Problem-Solving Thought." *Mathematics Teaching in the Middle School* 4 (February 1999): 305–31.

Lemke, M. A., E. Pahlke, L. Partelow, D. Miller, T. Williams, Dr. Kastberg, and L. Jocelyn. *International Outcomes of Learning in Mathematics Literacy and Problem Solving: PISA 2003 Results from the U.S. Perspective.* Washington, DC: U.S. Department of Education, National Center for Education Statistics, 2004.

Leo, John. "That So-called Pythagoras." *U.S. News & World Report,* 26 May 1997, 14.

Lieberthal, E. M. *Complete Book of Fingermath.* New York: McGraw-Hill, 1979.

Lindquist, M. M. *Results from the Fourth Mathematics Assessment of the National Assessment of Educational Progress.* Reston, VA: National Council of Teachers of Mathematics, 1989.

Litwiller, Bonnie, and George Bright, eds. *Making Sense of Fractions, Ratios, and Proportions,* NCTM 2002 Yearbook. Reston, VA: National Council of Teachers of Mathematics, 2002.

Long, Lynette. *Painless Algebra.* New York: Barron's Educational Series, 1998.

Macaruso, Paul, and Scott M. Sokol. "Cognitive Neuropsychology and Developmental Dyscalculia." In *The Development of Mathematical Skills,* ed. Chris Donlan, pp. 201–25. Hove, East Sussex, UK: Psychology Press, 1998.

MacCarone, Grace. *The Silly Story of Goldie Locks and the Three Squares.* New York: Scholastic, 1996.

Mack, Nancy K. "Learning Fractions with Understanding: Building on Informal Knowledge." *Journal for Research in Mathematics Education* 21 (January 1990): 16–32.

———. "Making Connections to Understand Fractions." In *Putting Research into Practice in the Elementary Grades,* ed. Donald L. Chambers, pp. 137–40. Reston, VA: National Council of Teachers of Mathematics, 2002.

Malloy, Carol E., and Susan N. Friel. "Perimeter and Area Through the Van Hiele Model." *Mathematics Teaching in the Middle School* 5 (October 1999): 87–91.

Martinez, Joseph G. R. "Building Conceptual Bridges from Arithmetic to Algebra." *Mathematics Teaching in the Middle School* 7 (February 2002): 326–31.

———. "Exploring, Inventing, Discovering Mathematics: A Pedagogical Response to TIMSS." *Mathematics Teaching in the Middle School* 7 (October 2001): 114–19.

———. "Helping Students Understand Factors and Terms." *Mathematics Teacher* 81 (December 1988): 747–51.

———. "Preventing Math Anxiety: A Prescription." *Academic Therapy* 23 (November 1987): 119.

———. "Thinking and Writing Mathematically: 'Achilles and the Tortoise' as an Algebraic Word Problem." *Mathematics Teacher* 94 (April 2001): 248–52.

Martinez, Joseph G. R., and Nancy C. Martinez. "Approaching Geometry Through Literature." *ENC Focus,* in press.

———. "Chinese Stick Math: Engaging Students in Place Value and Base-10 Concepts." *ENC Focus* (September 2004). www.enc.org/features/focus/archivemathroots2.

———. *Math without Fear: A Guide for Preventing Math Anxiety in Children.* Boston: Allyn & Bacon, 1996.

———. "Raising Middle School Math Standards Without Raising Anxiety." *Middle School Journal* 34 (March 2003): 27–35.

———. *Reading and Writing to Learn Mathematics*. Needham Heights, MA: Allyn & Bacon, 2001.

———. "Teaching Math with Stories." *Teaching K–8* 30 (January 2000): 55.

Marton, F., and Shirley Booth. *Learning and Awareness*. Mahwah, NJ: Erlbaum, 1997.

Mathematical Association of America. "New Teacher Preparation Standards Emphasize Performance." Washington, DC: Author, 2000. http://www.maa.org/news/ncate.html.

Mathematically Correct. "2 plus 2." 29 May 1997. http://ourworld.compuserve.com//homepages/mathman.

Maurer, Stephen B. "What Is an Algorithm? What Is an Answer?" In *The Teaching and Learning of Algorithms in School Mathematics*, NCTM 1998 Yearbook, ed. Lorna J. Morrow and Margaret J. Kenney. pp. 21–31. Reston, VA: National Council of Teachers of Mathematics, 1998.

Mayer, Richard E. *Thinking, Problem Solving, Cognition*. 2nd ed. New York: Freeman, 1992.

Mayer, Richard E., and Mary Hegarty. "The Process of Understanding Mathematical Problems." In *The Nature of Mathematical Thinking*, ed. Robert J. Sternberg and Talia Ben-Zeev, pp. 29–53. Mahwah, NJ: Erlbaum, 1996.

McLeish, John. *The Story of Numbers: How Mathematics Has Shaped Civilization*. New York: Fawcett Columbine, 1991.

McLeod, Douglas B., and Verna M. Adams, eds. *Affect and Mathematical Problem Solving: A New Perspective*. New York: Springer-Verlag, 1989.

Midobuche, Eva. "Building Cultural Bridges between Home and the Mathematics Classroom." *Teaching Children Mathematics* 7 (May 2001): 500–2.

Mitchell, J. H., E. F. Hawkins, F. G. Stancavage, and J. A. Dossey. *Estimation Skills, Mathematics-in-Context, and Advanced Skills in Mathematics*. Washington, DC: U.S. Department of Education, Office of Educational Research and Improvement, National Center for Education Statistics, 1999a.

———. *Student Work and Teacher Practices in Mathematics*. Washington, DC: Office of Educational Research and Improvement, National Center for Education Statistics, 1999b.

Moore, Eliakim Hastings. "On the Foundation of Mathematics." *Science* n.s. 17 (March 1903): 401–16.

Moore, Sara Delano, and William P. Bintz. "Teaching Geometry and Measurement through Literature." *Mathematics Teaching in the Middle School* 8 (October 2002): 78–83.

Moses, Barbara, ed. *Algebraic Thinking, Grades K–12: Readings from NCTM's School-Based Journals and Other Publications*. Reston, VA: National Council of Teachers of Mathematics, 1999.

Moyer, Patricia S. "Using Representations to Explore Perimeter and Area." *Teaching Children Mathematics* 8 (September 2001): 52–59.

Muschla, Judith A., and Gary Robert Muschla. *The Math Teacher's Book of Lists*. Englewood Cliffs, NJ: Prentice Hall, 1995.

National Center for Education Statistics. *The Condition of Education*. Washington, DC: U.S. Department of Education, Office of Educational Research and Improvement, 1996, 1997, 1998, 1999.

———. *National Assessment of Educational Progress (NAEP): Mathematics Assessment*. Washington, DC: Author, 1991, 1996, 2003, 2004, 2005.

———. *Trends in International Mathematics and Science Study (TIMSS)*. Washington, DC: Author, 2003. http://nces.ed.gov/timss/Results03.

National Council of Supervisors of Mathematics. "National Council of Supervisors of Mathematics Position Paper on Basic Skills." *Arithmetic Teacher* 25 (October 1977): 18–22.

———. "Essential Mathematics for the Twenty-first Century: The Position of the National Council of Supervisors of Mathematics." *Arithmetic Teacher* 27 (September 1989): 44–46.

National Council of Teachers of Mathematics. *An Agenda for Action: Recommendations for School Mathematics of the 1980s*. Reston, VA: Author, 1980.

———. *Assessment Standards for School Mathematics*. Reston, VA: Author, 1995.

———. *Curriculum and Evaluation Standards for School Mathematics*. Reston, VA: Author, 1989.

———. *Principles and Standards for School Mathematics*. Reston, VA: Author, 2000.

———. *Principles and Standards for School Mathematics: Discussion Draft*. Reston, VA: Author, 1998.

———. *Professional Standards for Teaching Mathematics*. Reston, VA: Author, 1991.

National Education Goals Panel. *The National Education Goals Report: Building a Nation of Learners*. Washington, DC: Author, 1995.

Neuman, Dagmar. *The Origin of Arithmetic Skills: A Phenomenographic Approach*. Göteborg, Sweden: Acta Universitatis Gothoburgensis, 1987.

Neuschwander, Cindy. *Sir Cumference and the Dragon of Pi*. Illus. Wayne Geehan. Watertown, MA: Charlesbridge, 1999.

———. *Sir Cumference and the First Round Table: A Math Adventure*. Illus. Wayne Geehan. Watertown, MA: Charlesbridge, 1997.

———. *Sir Cumference and the Great Knight of Angleland*. Illus. Wayne Geehan. Watertown, MA: Charlesbridge, 2001.

No Child Left Behind Act of 2001. H.R. 1, 107th Cong. Pub. L. 107-110. Washington, DC: U.S. Government Printing Office. http://www.ed.gov/policy/elsec/leg/esea02/107-110.pdf.

Nortman-Wolf, Sherry. *Base 10 Block Activities*. Lincolnshire, IL: Learning Resources, 1990.

Norwood, Karen S., and Glenda Carter. "Journal Writing: An Insight into Students' Understanding." *Teaching Children Mathematics* 1 (November 1994): 146–48.

Nunes, Terezinha, and P. Bryant. *Children Doing Mathematics*. Oxford: Blackwell, 1996.

Nunes, Terezinha, and Constanza Moreno. "Is Hearing Impairment a Cause of Difficulties in Learning Mathematics?" In *The Development of Mathematical Skills*, ed. Chris Donlan, pp. 227–54. Hove, East Sussex, UK: Psychology Press, 1998.

Nunes, Terezinha, A. D. Schliemann, and D. W. Carraher. *Street Mathematics and School Mathematics*. Cambridge, MA: Cambridge University Press, 1993.

Orkwis, Raymond, and Kathleen McLane. *A Curriculum Every Student Can Use: Design Principles for Student Access*. ERIC OSEP Topical Brief. Washington, DC: Office of Special Education Programs, Fall 1998.

Papert, Seymour. *The Children's Machine: Rethinking School in the Age of the Computer*. New York: Basic Books, 1993.

———. *Mindstorms: Children, Computers and Powerful Ideas*. New York: Basic Books, 1982.

Pappas, Theoni. "The Day the Number Line Fell Apart." In *Fractals, Googols, and Other Mathematical Tales*, pp. 38–39, 50. San Carlos, CA: Wide World Publishing/Tetra, 1993.

———. *Fractals, Googols and Other Mathematical Tales*. San Carlos, CA: Wide World Publishing/Tetra, 1993.

PBS TeacherSource. "How Much Do You Weigh in Outer Space?" *Mathline*. Washington DC: Public Broadcasting Service, 2000. www.pbs.org/teachersource/mathline/concepts/space2/activity2.shtm.

———. "Lesson Plan 9: One Potato, Two Potato, Inca Style!" *Mathline*. Washington, DC: Public Broadcasting Service. www.pbs.org/opb/conquistadors/teachers/teachershtm.

———. "Money Counts." *Mathline*. Elementary School Math Project Video. Washington DC: Public Broadcasting Service, 1997.

Peak, L. *Pursuing Excellence*. Washington, DC: U.S. Department of Education, National Center for Education Statistics, 1996.

Perie, Marianne, Wendy S. Grigg, and Gloria S. Dion. *The Nation's Report Card: Mathematics 2005*. NCES 2006-453. U.S. Department of Education, Institute of Education Sciences, National Center for Education Statistics. Washington, DC: U.S. Government Printing Office, 2005.

Perie, Marianne, and Rebecca Moran. *NAEP 2004 Trends in Academic Progress: Three Decades of Student Performance in Reading and Mathematics*.

NCES-2005-464. U.S. Department of Education, Institute of Education Sciences, National Center for Education Statistics. Washington, DC: U.S. Government Printing Office, 2005.

Peterson, Blake E. "From Tessellation to Polyhedra: Big Polyhedra." *Mathematics Teaching in the Middle School* 5 (February 2000): 348–56.

Phillip, Randolph A. "The Many Uses of Algebraic Variables." *Mathematics Teacher* (October 1992). Reprinted in *Algebraic Thinking, Grades K–12: Readings from NCTM's School-Based Journals and Other Publications*, ed. Barbara Moses, pp. 157–62. Reston, VA: National Council of Teachers of Mathematics, 1999.

Phillips, John L., Jr. *Piaget's Theory: A Primer*. San Francisco: Freeman, 1981.

Piaget, Jean. *The Child's Conception of Number*. London: Routledge & Kegan Paul, 1969.

———. *The Origins of Intelligence in Children*. New York: International Universities Press, 1952.

———. *Six Psychological Studies*. New York: Vintage Books, 1967.

Piaget, Jean, and Barbel Inhelder. *The Child's Conception of Space*. New York: Humanities Press, 1963.

———. *Memory and Intelligence*. New York: Basic Books, 1973.

———. *The Psychology of the Child*. New York: Basic Books, 1969.

Piaget, Jean, B. Inhelder, and A. Szeminska. *The Child's Conception of Geometry*. Trans. E. A. Lunzer. London: Routledge & Kegan Paul, 1948, 1960.

Pinczes, Elinor J. *A Remainder of One*. Illus. Bonnie McKain. New York: Scholastic, 1995.

Plisko, Val W. "The Release of the 2003 Trends in International Mathematics and Science Study (TIMSS)." Commissioner's Remarks, 14 December 2004. Washington, DC: U.S. Department of Education, National Center for Education Statistics, 2004. http://nces.ed.gov/commissioner/remarks2004/12_2004.asp.

Polya, George. *How to Solve It: A New Aspect of Mathematical Method*. 2nd ed., Princeton, NJ: Princeton University Press, 1973.

———. *Mathematical Discovery: On Understanding, Learning, and Teaching Problem Solving*. New York: Wiley, 1981.

Post, Thomas, and Kathleen Cramer. "Children's Strategies in Ordering Rational Numbers." In *Putting Research into Practice in the Elementary Grades*, ed. Donald C. Chambers. pp. 141–44. Reston, VA: National Council of Teachers of Mathematics, 2002.

Powell, Carol A., and Robert P. Hunting. "Fractions in the Early-Years Curriculum: More Needed, Not Less." *Teaching Children Mathematics* 10 (September 2003): 6–7.

Price, Glenda. "Quantitative Literacy Across the Curriculum." In *Why Numbers Count: Quantitative Literacy for Tomorrow's America*, ed. Lynn Arthur Steen, pp. 155–60. New York: College Entrance Examination Board, 1997.

Quigley, Winthrop. "Youngsters Beat New York Stock Exchange Index." *Albuquerque Journal*, 15 May 2003. http://www.abqjournal.com.

Rand, Richard E. "Visual Fractions: An On-Line Fraction Tutorial." http://www.visualfractions.com/.

Reece, Charlotte Strange, and Constance Kamii. "The Measurement of Volume: Why Do Young Children Measure Inaccurately?" *School Science and Mathematics* 101 (November 2001): 356–61.

Reese, C. M., K. E. Miller, and John A. Dossey. *NAEP 1996 Mathematics Report Card for the Nation and the States*. Washington, DC: National Center for Education Statistics, 1997.

Reich, Robert B. *The Work of Nations: Preparing Ourselves for Twenty-first Century Capitalism*. New York: Knopf, 1991.

Reinhart, Steven C. "Never Say Anything a Kid Can Say!" *Mathematics Teaching in the Middle School* 5 (2000): 438–42.

Research, Development, and Accountability, Albuquerque Public Schools. *Teacher Instructions: Mary Quite Contrary K–2*. By Christina Fritz. Albuquerque, NM: Author, 2002.

Resnick, Lauren B. "A Developmental Theory of Number Understanding." In *The Development of Mathematical Thinking*, ed. Herbert P. Ginsburg, pp. 109–51. New York: Academic Press, 1983.

Riddle, Margaret, and Bette Rodzwell. "Fractions: What Happens between Kindergarten and the Army?" *Teaching Children Mathematics* 7 (December 2000): 202–6.

Riley, Mary S., Jane G. Greeno, and Joan I. Heller. "Development of Children's Problem-Solving Ability in Arithmetic." In *The Development of Mathematical Thinking*, ed. Herbert P. Ginsburg, pp. 153–92. New York: Academic Press, 1983.

Riley, Richard W. "The State of Mathematics Education: Building a Strong Foundation for the 21st Century." Address to the Joint Mathematics Meeting of the American Mathematical Society and the Mathematical Association of America, January 1998. http://www.ed.gov/inits.html#2.

Rittle-Johnson, Bethany, and Robert S. Siegler. "The Relation between Conceptual and Procedural Knowledge in Learning Mathematics: A Review." In *The Development of Mathematical Skills*, ed. Chris Donlan, pp. 75–110. East Sussex, UK: Psychology Press, 1998.

Russell, Susan Jo. "Mathematical Reasoning in the Elementary Grades." In *Developing Mathemat-ical Reasoning in Grades K–12*, NCTM 1999 Yearbook, ed. Lee V. Stiff and Frances R. Curcio, pp. 1–12. Reston, VA: National Council of Teachers of Mathematics, 1999.

Russell, Susan Jo, and Jan Mokros. "What Do Children Understand about Averages?" In *Putting Research into Practice in the Elementary Grades*, ed. Donald L. Chambers, pp. 226–31. Reston, VA: National Council of Teachers of Mathematics, 2002.

Schoenfeld, Alan H., and Abraham Arcavi. "On the Meaning of Variable." *Mathematics Teacher* (September 1988). Reprinted in *Algebraic Thinking, Grades K–12: Readings from NCTM's School-Based Journals and Other Publications*, ed. Barbara Moses, pp. 150–56. Reston, VA: National Council of Teachers of Mathematics, 1999.

Scieszka, Jon. *Math Curse*. Illus. Lane Smith. New York: Viking, 1995.

Scully, Janet, Barry Scully, and Jack Le Sage. *Algetiles: Algebra Made Easy*. Barrie, Canada: Exclusive Educational Products, 1991.

Secada, Walter G. "Race, Ethnicity, Social Class, Language, and Achievement in Mathematics." In *Handbook of Research on Mathematics Teaching and Learning*, ed. Douglas A. Grouws, pp. 623–60. New York: Macmillan, 1992.

Seymour, Elaine. "The Loss of Women from Science, Mathematics, and Engineering Undergraduate Majors: An Explanatory Account." *Science Education* 79, no. 4 (1995a): 437–73.

———. "Revisiting the 'Problem Iceberg': Science, Mathematics, and Engineering Students Still Chilled Out." *Journal of College Science Teaching* 24, no. 6 (1995b): 392–400.

Sharp, Janet M., Joe Garofalo, and Barbara Adams. "Children's Development of Meaningful Fraction Algorithms: A Kid's Cookies and a Puppy's Pills." In *Making Sense of Fractions, Ratios, and Proportions*, NCTM 2002 Yearbook, ed. Bonnie Litwiller and George Bright, pp. 18–28. Reston, VA: National Council of Teachers of Mathematics, 2002.

Shaughnessy, Catherine A., Jennifer E. Nelson, and Norma A. Norns. *NAEP 1996 Mathematics Cross-State Data Compendium for Grade 4 and Grade 8 Assessment: Findings from the State Assessment in Mathematics of the National Assessment of Educational Progress*. Washington, DC: U.S. Department of Education, National Center for Education Statistics, 1998.

Shaughnessy, J. Michael, and William F. Burger. "Spadework Prior to Deduction in Geometry." *Mathematics Teacher* 78 (September 1985): 419–28.

Shirley, Lawrence. "Using Ethnomathematics to Find Multicultural Mathematical Connections." In *Connecting Mathematics across the Curriculum*, NCTM 1995 Yearbook, ed. Peggy

A. House and Arthur F. Coxford, pp. 34–43. Reston, VA: National Council of Teachers of Mathematics, 1995.

Shulman, Lee S. "Psychology and Mathematics Education." In *Mathematics Education: The Sixty-ninth Yearbook of the National Society for the Study of Education*, ed. Edward G. Begel, pp. 23–71. Chicago: National Society for the Study of Education, 1970.

Siebert, David. "Connecting Informal Thinking and Algorithms: The Case of Division of Fractions." In *Making Sense of Fractions, Ratios, and Proportions*, NCTM 2002 Yearbook, ed. Bonnie Litwiller and George Bright, pp. 247–56. Reston, VA: National Council of Teachers of Mathematics, 2002.

Siegel, L. S. "The Development of Quantity Concepts: Perceptual and Linguistic Factors." In *Children's Logical and Mathematical Cognition: Progress in Cognitive Developmental Research*, ed. C. J. Brainerd. New York: Springer-Veslog, 1982.

Siegler, Robert S., and K. Crowley. "Constraints on Learning in Nonprivileged Domains." *Cognitive Psychology* 27 (1994): 194–226.

Siegler, Robert S., and J. Shrager. "Strategy Choices in Addition: How Do Children Know What to Do?" In *Origins of Cognitive Skills*, ed. C. Sophian, pp. 229–93. Hillsdale, NJ: Erlbaum, 1984.

Silver, Edward A. "Using Conceptual and Procedural Knowledge: A Focus on Relationships." In *Conceptual and Procedural Knowledge: The Case of Mathematics*, ed. James Hiebert, pp. 181–89. Hillsdale, NJ: Erlbaum, 1986.

Silver, Edward A., Lora A. Shapiro, and Adam Deutsch. "Sense Making and the Solution of Division Problems Involving Remainders: An Examination of Middle School Students' Solution Processes and Their Interpretations of Solutions." *Journal for Research in Mathematics Education* 24 (March 1993): 117–35.

Skemp, Richard R. "Relational Understanding and Instrumental Understanding." *Arithmetic Teacher* 26 (November 1978): 9–15.

Skinner, B. F. "Reflections on a Decade of Teaching Machines." *Teachers College Record* (November 1963): 63ff. Rpt. in B. F. Skinner, *Cumulative Record: A Selection of Papers*, 3rd ed., pp. 194–207. New York: Appleton-Century-Crofts, 1972.

Smith, David Eugene. "A General Survey of the Progress of Mathematics in Our High Schools in the Last Twenty-Five Years." In *NCTM First Yearbook*, pp. 1–31. N.P., 1926.

Smith, John P., III. "The Development of Students' Knowledge of Fractions and Ratios." In *Making Sense of Fractions, Ratios, and Proportions*, NCTM 2002 Yearbook, ed. Bonnie Litwiller and George Bright, pp. 3–17. Reston, VA: National Council of Teachers of Mathematics, 2002.

Smith, Michael K. *Humble Pi: The Role Mathematics "Should" Play in American Education.* Amherst, NY: Prometheus Books, 1994.

Sophian, Catherine. "A Developmental Perspective on Children's Counting." In *The Development of Mathematical Skills*, ed. Chris Donlan, pp. 27–46. Hove, East Sussex, UK: Psychology Press, 1998.

Spatz, Chris, and James O. Johnston: *Basic Statistics: Tales of Distribution*, 4th ed. Pacific Grove, CA: Brooks/Cole, 1989.

Steele, D. F., and A. A. Arth. "Math Instruction and Assessment: Preventing Anxiety, Promoting Confidence." *Schools in the Middle* 7, no. 3 (1998): 44–48.

Steencken, Elena P., and Carolyn A. Maher. "Young Children's Growing Understanding of Fraction Ideas." In *Making Sense of Fractions, Ratios, and Proportions*, NCTM 2002 Yearbook, ed. Bonnie Litwiller and George Bright, pp. 49–60. Reston, VA: National Council of Teachers of Mathematics, 2002.

Steffe, Leslie P., and John Olive. "The Problem of Fractions in the Elementary School." In *Putting Research into Practice in the Elementary Grades*, ed. Donald L. Chambers, pp. 128–32. Reston, VA: National Council of Teachers of Mathematics, 2002.

Sternberg, Robert J. "What Is Mathematical Thinking?" In *The Nature of Mathematical Thinking*, ed. Robert J. Sternberg and Talia Ben Zeev, pp. 303–18. Reston, VA: National Council of Teachers of Mathematics, 1996.

Stevens, John H. "Statement on NAEP 2003 Mathematics and Reading Results." Washington, DC: National Assessment Governing Board, National Assessment of Educational Progress, 2003. http://www.nagb.org/release/statement.

Stewart, Ian. *Flatterland: Like Flatland, Only More So.* Cambridge, MA: Perseus, 2001.

Stiff, Lee V. "Preface" In *Developing Mathematical Reasoning in Grades K–12*, NCTM 1999 Yearbook, ed. Lee V. Stiff and Frances R. Curcio, pp. vii–viii. Reston, VA: National Council of Teachers of Mathematics, 1999.

Stiff, Lee V., and Frances R. Curcio, eds. *Developing Mathematical Reasoning in Grades K–12, 1999 Yearbook.* Reston, VA: National Council of Teachers of Mathematics, 1999.

Stiggins, Richard J. *Classroom Assessment for Student Success.* Washington, DC: National Education Association, 1998.

Stigler, Stephen M. *The History of Statistics: The Measurement of Uncertainty Before 1900.* Cambridge, MA: Belknap Press of Harvard University Press, 1986.

Summers, George J. *New Puzzles in Logical Deduction.* New York: Dover, 1968.

Sund, Robert B. *Piaget for Educators: A Multimedia Program.* Columbus, OH: Merrill/Prentice Hall, 1976.

Sweeney, Elizabeth S., and Robert J. Quinn. "Concentration: Connecting Fractions, Decimals, & Percents." *Mathematics Teaching in the Middle School* 5 (January 2000): 324–28.

Swetman, D. L. "Fourth Grade Math: The Beginning of the End?" *Reading Improvement* 3 (1994): 173–76.

Taber, Susan B. "Go Ask Alice about Multiplication of Fractions." In *Making Sense of Fractions, Ratios, and Proportions*, NCTM 2002 Yearbook, ed. Bonnie Litwiller and George Bright, pp. 61–71. Reston, VA: National Council of Teachers of Mathematics, 2002.

Tate, William F., and Howard C. Johnson. "Mathematical Reasoning and Educational Policy." In *Developing Mathematical Reasoning in Grades K–12*, NCTM 1999 Yearbook, ed. Lee V. Stiff, and Frances R. Curcio, pp. 221–33. Reston, VA: National Council of Teachers of Mathematics, 1999.

Taylor, Judith V. "Young Children Deal with Data." *Teaching Children Mathematics* 4 (November 1997): 146–49.

Telese, James A., and Jesse Abete Jr. "Diet, Ratios, Proportions: A Healthy Mix." *Mathematics Teaching in the Middle School* 8 (September 2002): 8–14.

Thatcher, Debra H. "The Tangram Conundrum." *Mathematics Teaching in the Middle School* 6 (March 2001): 394–99.

Thompson, Charles S., and William S. Bush. "Improving Middle School Teachers' Reasoning About Proportional Reasoning." *Mathematics Teaching in the Middle School* 8 (April 2003): 298–403.

Thompson, Denisse R., Richard A. Austin, and Charlene E. Beckmann. "Using Literature as a Vehicle to Explore Proportional Reasoning." In *Making Sense of Fractions, Ratios, and Proportion*, NCTM 2002 Yearbook, ed. Bonnie Litwiller and George Bright, pp. 130–37. Reston, VA: National Council of Teachers of Mathematics, 2002.

Tobias, Sheila. *Overcoming Math Anxiety.* 2nd ed. New York: Norton, 1993.

Tompert, Ann. *Grandfather Tang's Story.* Illus. Robert Andrew Parker. New York: Crown Publishers, 1990.

U.S. Department of Education. "Facts about . . . Math Achievement." Washington, DC: Author, 2004. http://www.ed.gov/print/nclb/methods/math/math.html.

———. Mathematics and Science Initiative. 2004. http://www.ed.gov/print/rschstat/research/progs/mathscience/describe.html.

U.S. Department of Education, Institute for Education Sciences, National Center for Education Statistics. *The Nation's Report Card: Mathematics Highlights 2003*, NCES 2004-451, by J. S. Braswell, M. C. Daane, and

W. S. Grigg. Washington, D.C: U.S. Government Printing Office, 2003.

U.S. Department of Education, National Center for Education Statistics. *Pursuing Excellence.* NCES 97-198, by Lois Peak. Washington, D.C.: U.S. Government Printing Office, 1996.

———. *Pursuing Excellence: Comparisons of International Eighth-Grade Mathematics and Science Achievement from a U.S. Perspective, 1995 and 1999.* NCED 2001-028, by Patrick Gonzales, Christopher Calsyn, Leslie Jocelyn, Kitty Mak, David Kastberg, Sousan Arafeh, Trevor Williams, and Winnie Tsen. Washington, DC: U.S. Government Printing Office, 2000.

———. *Pursuing Excellence: A Study of U.S. Fourth-Grade Mathematics and Science Achievement in International Context.* NCES 97-255. Washington, DC: U.S. Government Printing Office, 1997a.

———. *Pursuing Excellence: A Study of U.S. Twelfth-Grade Mathematics and Science Achievement in International Context.* NCES 98-049. Washington, DC: U.S. Government Printing Office, 1998.

U.S. Department of Education, Office of Educational Research and Improvement. *Attaining Excellence: TIMSS as a Starting Point to Examine Teaching: Moderator's Guide to Eighth-Grade Mathematics Lessons: United States, Japan, and Germany.* Washington, DC: U.S. Government Printing Office, 1997b.

———. *Moderator's Guide to Eighth Grade Mathematics Lessons. United States, Japan, and Germany, Attaining Excellence: TIMSS as a Starting Point to Examine Teaching:* Washington, DC: Author, 1997c.

———. *Student Work and Teacher Practices in Mathematics.* NCES 1999-453, by Julia A. Mitchell, Evelyn F. Hawkins, Pamela M. Jakwerth, Frances B. Stancavage, and John A. Dossey. Washington, DC: U.S. Government Printing Office, 1999.

Vance, James H. "Numbers Operations from an Algebraic Perspective." *Teaching Children Mathematics* 4 (January 1998): 282–85.

Van Hiele, Pierre M. *Structure and Insight: A Theory of Mathematics Education.* Orlando, FL: Academic Press, 1986.

Van Lehn, Kurt. "On the Representation of Procedures in Repair Theory." In *The Development of Mathematical Thinking,* ed. Herbert P. Ginsburg, pp. 197–252. New York: Academic Press, 1983.

von Glasersfeld, Ernst. "A Radical Constructivist View of Basic Mathematical Concepts. In *Constructing Mathematical Knowledge: Epistemology and Mathematics Education,* ed. Paul Ernest, pp. 5–71. London: Farmer, 1994.

Wadsworth, Barry V. *Piaget's Theory of Cognitive and Affective Development: Foundations of Constructivism.* 5th ed. White Plains, NY: Longman, 1996.

Warrington, Mary Ann. "How Children Think about Division with Fractions." In *Putting Research into Practice in the Elementary Grades,* ed. Donald L. Chambers. pp. 140–45. Reston, VA: National Council of Teachers of Mathematics, 2002.

Warrington, Mary Ann, and Constance Kamii. "Multiplication with Fractions: A Piagetian, Constructivist Approach." *Mathematics Teaching in the Middle School* 3 (February 1998): 339–45.

Washburne, Carleton. "Mental Age and the Arithmetic Curriculum: A Summary of the Committee of Seven Grade Placement Investigations to Date." *Journal of Educational Research* 23 (March 1931): 210–31.

Watanabe, Tad. "Let's Eliminate Fractions from Primary Curricula!" *Teaching Children Mathematics* 8 (October 2001): 70–72.

Watterson, Bill. *The Essential Calvin and Hobbes.* Kansas City, MO: Andrews and McMeel, 1988.

———. *The Indispensable Calvin and Hobbes.* Kansas City, MO: Andrews and McMeel, 1992.

Webster's New World Dictionary of the American Language. 2nd college ed. New York: Simon & Schuster, 1980.

Welchman-Tischler, Rosamond. *Start with Manipulatives.* White Plains, NY: Cuisenaire, 1992.

West, John. *In the Mind's Eye: Visual Thinkers, Gifted People with Learning Difficulties, Computer Images, and the Ironies of Creativity.* Buffalo, NY: Prometheus Books, 1991.

Williams, Susan E., and David Molina. "Algebra: What All Students Can Learn." In *The Nature and Role of Algebra in the K–14 Curriculum: Proceedings of a National Symposium,* ed. Susan Williams and David Molinar, pp. 41–44. Washington, DC: National Academy Press, 1998.

Wilson, Guy M. "The Social Utility Theory as Applied to Arithmetic, Its Research Basis, and Some of Its Implications." *Journal of Educational Research* 41 (January 1948): 321–37.

Woodbury, Sonia. "Teaching Toward the Big Ideas of Algebra." *Mathematics Teaching in the Middle School* 6 (December 2000): 226–31.

Wynn, Karen. "Children's Acquisition of the Number Words and the Counting System." *Cognitive Psychology* 24 (1992): 220–51.

———. "Numerical Competence of Infants." In *The Development of Mathematical Skills,* ed. Chris Donlan, pp. 1–25. Hove, East Sussex, UK: Psychology Press, 1998.

Yackel, Erna. "A Foundation for Algebraic Reasoning in the Early Grades." In *Putting Research into Practice in the Elementary Grades,* ed. Donald L. Chambers, pp. 197–201. Reston, VA: National Council of Teachers of Mathematics, 2002.

Yerushalmy, M., and J. C. Schwartz. "Seizing the Opportunity to Make Algebra Mathematically and Pedagogically Interesting." In *Integrating Research on Teaching and Learning Mathematics,* ed. E. Fennema, T. P. Carpenter, and S. L. Lamon, pp. 41–68. Albany: State University of New York Press, 1999.

Young, Sharon L., and Robbin O'Leary. "Creating Numerical Scales for Measuring Tools." *Teaching Children Mathematics* 8 (March 2002): 400–5.

Zilliox, Joseph T., and Shannon G. Lowrey. "Many Faces Have I." *Mathematics Teaching in the Middle School* 3 (November–December. 1997): 180–81.

Zometool. *Manual 2.0.* Denver, CO: Author, 1999.

Subject/Topic Index

abstract, 325
accessibility, 28–29, 77, 82–83, 92, 194–197
accommodation, 37–38
achievement, 324
Achilles and the Tortoise, 339–340
addition, 8, 109, Chapter 6, 127 ff, 275, 278–280,
    307–332, 338
  addend, 163, 308
  alternative algorithm, 149
  commutative principle, 127, 137
  counting-all algorithm (sum procedure), 136
  counting-on algorithm (min procedure),
    136–137
  literature, Appendix B, 376–377
  mental calculations, 140–141
  multi-digit numbers, 127, 142ff
  repeated addition, 161, 282
  single-digit numbers, 127, 134–137
  standard procedure addition, 147
  trading and regrouping, 145–147, 150–152
affective domain, 48, 58, 59, 64, 72
  association, 59
  bridges, 323, 326, 343
  interactions, 60, 61
  journals, 88–89
  repetition, 59
algebra, 9, Chapter 10, 218ff, 321, 336, 337
  algebra for all, 219–220, 240
  algebraic expressions, 332, 336
    equivalent, 336
  algebraic thinking, 10, 218ff
  big ideas, 218, 221ff
    equality, 221, 224–225
    functions, 221, 227–229
    proportion, 221, 231–233
    symbolic representation, 219, 229–231, 238
    variables, 226–227, 240
  conceptual bridges, 233–236, 240
    connections, 234–235
    hands-on activities, 234
    real-life and imaginative contexts, 234, 240
  curriculum, 218, 220, 240
    algebrafying the mathematics curriculum, 221
  Equate, 225
  equations, 219, 221, 225, 226–227, 231,
    237, 240
    linear, 336
  habits of mind, 220–222
  inquiry, 222–223
  language, 220
  literature, Appendix B, 381–382
  patterns, 219, 229, 237, 240
  prealgebra, 220
  solutions, 332
  story problems, 237

algorithm, 154, 279, 285, 324, 325
  alternative algorithms for addition and
    subtraction, 149
  area, 219
  counting-all to add, 136, 145
  counting-all/taking-away to subtract, 137
  counting-down to subtract, 139
  counting-on to add, 136–137, 145
  counting-up to subtract, 138–139
  definition, 159
  division, 165ff, 311
  fractions, 279
    addition, 275
    conventional, 279–280
    formal, 308
    inverting and multiplying (IM), 284–285
  informal, 135–139, 145ff, 159ff, 165ff, 176
  multiplication, 158–164, 310
  questions to assess effectiveness, 175
  standard procedure addition, 147
  standard procedure subtraction, 148
  volume, 216
  whole numbers, 279, 308, 311
alphanumeric puzzle, 332
American Association for the Advancement of
    Science (AAAS), 1, 12, 15, 16, 188
  Benchmarks, 16, 17, 191, 192
American Mathematical Society, 10
arithmetic, 8
art, 80, 174–175, 179, 186–187, 328
assessment, 21, 77, 86–92, 254, 330, 340–341
  classroom observations, 87, Appendix A, 368
  NCTM, 12, 14
  performance outcomes, 89–90
  portfolios, 88, Appendix A, 369
  rubrics, 87
  tests, 89–91
    standardized tests, 91
    teacher-made tests, 90–91
assimilation, 37–38
averages, 259–262, 267, 331

Baby Blues, 98
base-10 blocks, 116–117, 122–123, 142–148,
    170–171, 294, 298, 299, 307, 308,
    Appendix A, 354
base-10 number system, 97, 119–123, 124, 142ff,
    154, 157, 170–171, 297, 312, 341
  Chinese stick math, 150–152
  extended notation, 146
  face value, 119–120, 154
  Incan quipus, 117
  place value, 119–120, 125, 154, 160, 297
    literature, Appendix B, 380
  three stages in children's understanding, 120–123

    stage 1, counting to combining, 120–121
    stage 2, combining to structuring, 121–122
    stage 3, structuring to formalizing, 122–123
  West African shepherds, 111
base-20 number system, 112, 341–343
  Mayan, 112, 119, 329, 341–343
    architecture, 342
    pyramids, 341–343
  Inuits, 119
behaviorism, 33, 34–36
benchmark, 302, 303
bilingual education, 187–188, 194–196

calculator, 306, 310, 320, 333
  TI-108, 312
Calvin and Hobbes, 79
cardinal numbers, 98, 100, 127, 129–131
  counting, 129, 131
  totaling, 129, 131
Cartesian coordinate system, 303, 304, 334, 335
  Modified Cartesian Coordinate Grid, 363
  x axis, 304
  x plane, 304
  y axis, 304
  y plane, 304
Center for Applied Special Technology (CAST), 42,
    43, 78, 92
child as learning machine, 36
child as thinker, 36
Chinese stick math, 150–152, 330
circle (*see also* geometry, manipulatives, and
    measurement), 17, 266, 271, 302, 308
  colored, 276–277
  fraction, 270
  graphs, 295
  percent, 307
  representations, 286
circumference, 331
classification
  literature, Appendix B, 381
classroom as learning laboratory, 33
classroom dynamics, 33
classroom observation, 88
classroom store, 30
cognition, 33, 218, 265, 332
cognitive domain, 48, 58–59, 64, 72
  interactions, 60, 61
cognitive hunger, 63–64
cognitive learning theory, 37
collaborative learning, 33
Colorado Model Content Standards 2005, 17
comics, 78–79, 331
computers and programmed instruction, 34
concept learning, 30, 37
concept maps, 63, 85

Author/Name Index